Vintage	Red Bordeaux		White			
	Médoc/Graves	Pom/(St-Em)				
2020	7–8					
2019	7–9					
2018	8–9					
2017	6–8					
2016	8–9					
2015	7–9	8				7–9
2014	7–8	6–		8–9		7–8
2013	4–7	4–7	8–9	7–8		8–9
2012	6–8	6–8	5–6	7–9		8–9
2011	7–8	7–8	8–10	7–8		5–7
2010	8–10	7–10	7–8	7–9		8–9
2009	7–10	7–10	8–10	7–9		8–9
2008	6–8	6–9	6–7	7–8		7–8
2007	5–7	6–7	8–9	8–9		6–8
2006	7–8	7–8	7–8	8–9		6–8
2005	9–10	8–9	7–9	8–10		8–9
2004	7–8	7–9	5–7	6–7		6–8
2003	5–9	5–8	7–8	6–7		6–7
2002	6–8	5–8	7–8	7–8		7–8

France, continued

Vintage	Burgundy			Rhône	
	Côte d'Or red	Côte d'Or white	Chablis	North	South
2020	6–8	7–9	6–8	7–8	6–8
2019	7–9	7–10	7–9	8–9	7–9
2018	6–9	7–8	7–9	7–9	6–8
2017	6–9	8–9	8–9	7–9	7–9
2016	7–8	6–8	5–7	7–9	8–9
2015	7–9	6–8	7–8	8–9	8–9
2014	6–8	8–9	7–9	7–8	6–8
2013	5–7	6–7	6–8	7–9	7–8
2012	8–9	7–8	7–8	7 9	7 9
2011	7–8	7–8	7–8	7–8	6–8
2010	8–10	8–10	8–10	8–10	8–9
2009	7–10	7 8	7–8	7–9	7–8
2008	7–9	7–9	7–9	6–7	5–7
2007	7–8	8–9	8–9	6–8	7–8

Beaujolais 20 19 18 17 15 14; crus will keep. **Mâcon-Villages** (w) drink: 20 19 18 17 15. **Loire** (sw Anjou and Touraine) best recent vintages: 20 19 18 15 10 09 07 05 02 97 96 93 90; Bourgueil, Chinon, Saumur-Champigny: 20 19 18 17 15 14 10 09 06 05 04. **Upper Loire** (Sancerre, Pouilly-Fumé): 20 19 18 17 15 14. **Muscadet:** DYA.

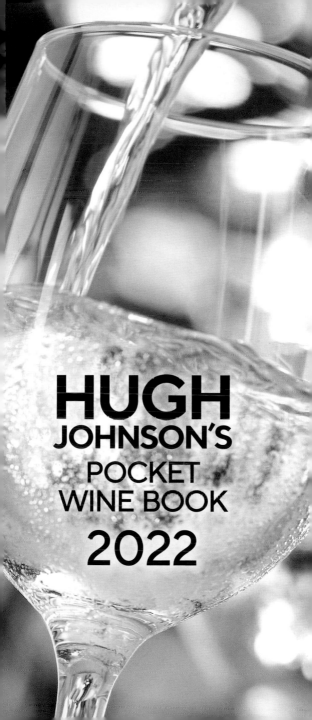

HUGH
JOHNSON'S
POCKET
WINE BOOK
2022

Hugh Johnson's Pocket Wine Book 2022

Edited and designed by Mitchell Beazley,
an imprint of Octopus Publishing Group Limited,
Carmelite House, 50 Victoria Embankment
London EC4Y 0DZ
www.octopusbooks.co.uk

An Hachette UK Company
www.hachette.co.uk

Distributed in the US by Hachette Book Group
1290 Avenue of the Americas
4th and 5th Floors
New York, NY 10020
www.octopusbooksusa.com

ISBN (UK): 978-1-78472-688-1
ISBN (US): 978-1-78472-796-3

General Editor **Margaret Rand**
Commissioning Editor **Hilary Lumsden**
Senior Editor **Pauline Bache**
Proofreader **Jacqui Lewis**
Art Director **Yasia Williams-Leedham**
Designer **Jeremy Tilston**
Picture Researchers **Giulia Hetherington and Jennifer Veall**
Senior Production Manager **Katherine Hockley**

Printed and bound in China

Mitchell Beazley would like to acknowledge and thank the following
for supplying photographs for use in this book:

Alamy Stock Photo Eckhard Supp 336; Iconpix 325. **Cephas Picture Library
Ltd.** © Herbert Lehmann 335; © Jean-Bernard Nadeau 7. **Familia Torres** 331.
iStock dardespot 14; MarkSwallow 1, 321. **Quinta do Crasto** 326. **Rathfinny
Wine Estate/Viv Blakey** 329. **Shutterstock** 5PH 323. **Stockfood** © StockFood/
Eising Studio – Food Photo & Video 332. **Unsplash** David JDT 10; Kelsey
Knight 12; Mauro Lima 6. **Dom Fleming** 8

HUGH
JOHNSON'S
POCKET
WINE BOOK
2022

GENERAL EDITOR
MARGARET RAND

Contributors

To be up-to-date in the vinous affairs of every wine-producing country in the world is impossible for one person, so this book is put together with the invaluable help of a team of knowledgeable contributors.

Key: ❶ Facebook; **❷** Instagram; **❸** Twitter; **❹** website; **❺** book/press; **❻** blog/other media

Helena Baker, Czechia, Slovakia: **❶** helena.baker.73; **❷** bakerwine837; **❸** @HelenaB62554469; **❹** bakerwine.cz

Kristel Balcaen, Belgium: **❷** kristel_balcaen; **❹** wineandwords.be

Amanda Barnes, South America: **❶** @SouthAmericaWineGuide; **❷** @southamericawineguide; **❸** @amanda_tweeter; **❺** *South America Wine Guide*

Lana Bortolot, US SW States, Mexico: **❷** @pourLana; **❺** *Forbes*

Juliet Bruce Jones MW, Midi, Provence, Corsica: **❶** latasque; **❷** domainelatasque; **❹** domainelatasque.com

Jim Budd, Loire, Savoie: **❶** jim.budd.94; **❸** @jymbudd; **❹** les5duvin.wordpress.com; **❻** jimsloire-blog.blogspot.com, investdrinks-blog.blogspot.com

Ch'ng Poh Tiong, Asia: **❶**+**❷** Chngpohtiong, 100TopChineseRestaurants, wineguru.com.sg; **❹** chngpohtiong.com, wineguru.com.sg, 100chineserestaurants.com; **❺** *International Congress of Chinese Cuisine & Wine*

Michael Cooper, NZ: **❶** MichaelCooperNZWine **❹** michaelcooper.co.nz **❺** *New Zealand Wines: Michael Cooper's Buyer's Guide, Wine Atlas of New Zealand*

Ian D'Agata, Italy: **❷** iandagata_vino; **❹** iandagata.com, terroirsense.com/en; **❺** *Inside Barolo Crus People Places, Italy's Native Wine Grape Terroirs, Native Wine Grapes of Italy*

Michael Edwards, Champagne, Alsace: **❶** Michael's Bulles de Champagne; **❷** edwardsmichaelfrank; **❸** @michaelfrankedw; **❺** *Finest Wines of Champagne*

Sarah Jane Evans MW, Spain: **❶** Sarah Jane Evans MW; **❷** sjevansmw; **❸** @SJEvansMW; **❹** sarahjaneevans.com; **❺** *The Wines of Northern Spain*

Caroline Gilby MW, E Europe, Cyprus: **❶** Caroline Gilby MW; **❷** Caroline Gilby; **❸** @CarolineGilbyMW; **❹** carolinegilby.wordpress.com; **❺** *The Wines of Bulgaria, Romania and Moldova*

Anthony Gismondi, Canada: **❶**+**❷** @gismondiwine; **❸** @thespitter; **❹** Gismondiwine.com; **❺** *The Vancouver Sun*; **❻** BC Food & Wine Radio Podcast

Susan H Gordon MFA, US E States: **❷** @susanhillaryg; **❺** *ForbesLife, Gastronomica*

Paul Gregutt, Oregon: **❶**+**❷**+**❸** @paulgwine; **❺** *Washington Wines & Wineries, Wine Enthusiast*

Michael Karam, Lebanon: **❺** *Wines of Lebanon, Arak and Mezze, Tears of Bacchus, Lebanese Wine: A Complete Guide*

Anne Krebiehl MW, Austria: **❷**+**❸** @anneinvino; **❺** *The Wines of Germany*

James Lawther, B'x: **❺** *The Finest Wines of Bordeaux, The Heart of Bordeaux, On Bordeaux*

Konstantinos Lazarakis MW, Greece: **❶** Konstantinos Lazarakis II; **❷** Konstantinos Lazarakis MW; **❸** @Lazarakis; **❹** wspc.gr; **❺** *The Wines of Greece*

John Livingstone-Learmonth, Rhône: **❸** @drinkrhone; **❹** www.drinkrhone.com; **❺** *The Wines of the Northern Rhône*

Michele Longo, Italy: **❷** @michele_nebbiolo; **❹** iandagata.com; **❺** *Inside Barolo Crus People Places; Barolo&Co*

Campbell Mattinson, Australia: **❷** @Campbell Mattinson; **❹** winefront.com.au; **❺** *The Wine Hunter: Maurice O'Shea, The Man Who Changed Australian Wine*

Adam Sebag Montefiore, Israel, Turkey, N Africa: **❹** adammontefiore.com, wines-israel.com; **❺** *Jerusalem Post, The Wine Route of Israel, Wines of Israel*

Jasper Morris MW, Burgundy, Jura: **❷** jaspermorris_insideburgundy; **❸** @justjasper; **❹** insideburgundy.com; **❺** *Inside Burgundy*

Marcel Orford Williams, SW France: buyer, The Wine Society; **❸** @owmarcel

Margaret Rand, General Editor: *see book's back flap*; **❹** margaretrand.com

André Ribeirinho, Portugal: **❶**+**❷**+**❸** @andrerib; **❹** andrerib.co

Ulrich Sautter, Germany, Switzerland, Luxembourg: **❺** falstaff.com, weinverstand.de

Eleonora Scholes, Black Sea & Caucasus: **❷** @spaziovino; **❹** spaziovino.com

Sean P Sullivan, Washington State & Idaho: **❶**+**❷** wawinereport; **❸** @wawinereport; **❹** wawinereport.com; **❺** *Wine Enthusiast*

Tim Teichgraeber, California: **❷** @timskyscraper; **❻** modernwine.blogspot.com

Philip van Zyl, S Africa: **❺** *Platter's South African Wine Guide*

Contents

How to use this book	6
Margaret Rand's Agenda 2022	8
Hugh Johnson replies	9
Vintage report 2020	10
Ten wines to try in 2022	12
Grape varieties	14
Wine & food	25
France	38
Châteaux of Bordeaux	100
Italy	122
Germany	154
Luxembourg & Belgium	173
Spain	174
Portugal	191
Switzerland	204
Austria	209
England	216
Central & Southeast Europe	218
Hungary, Bulgaria, Slovenia, Croatia,	
Bosnia & Herzegovina, Kosovo, North Macedonia,	
Serbia, Montenegro, Czechia, Slovakia, Romania, Malta	
Greece	234
Eastern Mediterranean & North Africa	237
Cyprus, Israel, Lebanon, Turkey, North Africa	
Asia & Black Sea & Caucasus	241
United States	243
Mexico	272
Canada	273
South America	275
Chile, Argentina, Brazil, Uruguay, Other SA Wines	
Australia	284
New Zealand	298
South Africa	308
Supplement – The ten best things about wine right now	321
Front endpaper: Quick-reference vintage charts	
Back endpaper: A little learning/The right temperature	

The top line of most entries consists of the following information:

1. Aglianico del Vulture Bas

2. ★★★

3. 12' 13 14 15 16' 17 (18)

1. Aglianico del Vulture Bas

Wine name and region. Abbreviations of regions are listed in each section.

2. ★★★

Indication of quality – a necessarily rough-and-ready guide:

★	plain, everyday quality
★★	above average
★★★	excellent
★★★★	outstanding, compelling
★ etc.	Stars are coloured for any wine that, in our experience, is usually especially good within its price range. There are good everyday wines as well as good luxury wines. This system helps you find them.

We try to be objective, but no wine rating can ever be wholly objective.

3. 12' 13 14 15 16' 17 (18)

Vintage information: those recent vintages that are outstanding, and of these, which are ready to drink this year, and which will probably improve with keeping. Your choice for current drinking should be one of the vintage years printed in **bold** type.

Buy light-type years for further maturing.

17 etc.	recommended years that may be currently available
16' etc.	vintage regarded as particularly successful for the property in question
13 etc.	years in bold should be ready for drinking (those not in bold will benefit from keeping)
15 etc.	vintages in colour are those recommended as first choice for drinking in 2022. (*See also* Bordeaux introduction, p.100)
(18) etc.	provisional rating

The German vintages work on a different principle again: *see* p.171.

Abbreviations

Style references appear in brackets where required:

r	red
w	white
dr	dry
sw	sweet
s/sw	semi-sweet
sp	sparkling

DYA	drink the youngest available
NV	Non Vintage; in Champagne this means a blend of several vintages for continuity
CHABLIS	properties, areas or terms cross-referred within the section; all grapes cross-ref to Grape Varieties chapter on pp.14–24
Foradori	entries styled this way indicate wine especially enjoyed by Margaret Rand and/or the author of that section (mid-2020–21)

For help in sourcing wines in this book we recommend winesearcher.com

If you have any feedback, please contact us on pocketwine@octopusbooks.co.uk

This year, it's hail and farewell – or, as Hugh would undoubtedly say, *ave atque vale*. Hugh is handing over his baby to me after 44 editions; a generous act, and a trusting one. I shall try not to drop it.

It is Hugh who taught all of us – not just to write, but to write about wine. Wine has its facts, its laboratory analyses, its lists of soil types and wind directions. It has its marketing guff about emotion and vision and uniqueness. There is the investor's focus on points and price growth. And between these three poles there is another story, about the resonance of wine in human life, how it evolves by reacting to economic, political and climate change, and above all, how it has, for the last 50 years, got better and better and better. Hugh has traced this story in many ways and in many places. This is the most abbreviated of them. It aims to tell readers which wines are most worthy of their attention, and why. It aims to do something that the internet cannot do, and that wine magazines cannot do: it is a mini-encyclopedia that blends facts with opinions. Glance at it in search of recommendations and you will find just that. Look further for the understanding and experience behind those recommendations and you will find that too. And in every issue you will find a supplement, different every year, which sheds more light on a particular aspect of wine.

We will be celebrating our contributors more from now on. Most live in the regions they report on and are immersed in their wines. They write for the Pocket Book because they share our view of what wine should be: balanced, fresh, alive, sometimes idiosyncratic. We have never followed fashion into the further reaches of power, extraction and oak (from which it has now mercifully returned), and we are sceptical of what marketing departments tell us. Sometimes we get it wrong. We change things and people don't like it. But we want to hear, and so on page 7 you'll find an email address you can use for feedback. Tick us off if you want to. We can take it.

Most people, this past year, have had to take more than they thought possible. There have been forest fires on a horrendous scale, as well as coronavirus and all the economic and social damage of that. For most consumers, good wine – perhaps better wine than we drank before – has been a daily pleasure in a difficult year. And we cannot say too strongly that by paying a bit more, you get much, much more.

I always recall a certain British wine merchant who said one day, "always assume your customers know more than you do, but at the same time, try to surprise them." If you swap "readers" for "customers", the sentiment sums up the attitude of this book.

I couldn't have kept this little book going every year for 44 years without a little help from my friends, or in the past 15 years or so without a lot of help from one very good friend.

Gradually it has become more Margaret Rand's book than mine, and I'm delighted, thrilled (and relieved) that she has now taken it on as her own responsibility. It keeps my branding because, after all, a brand is a brand, and there will be no sudden change either of format or philosophy. Margaret is known to many readers, largely for her magazine columns, very often in-depth interviews, that probe as deeply into the wine world as any I know. She can go deep but remain easy, clear and accessible, not an easy trick. She knows the key people worldwide (or at least knows who they are), and she gets them to 'fess up.

After so many years working together we share the same values; above all curiosity and the passion for good honest characterful wine, wherever in the world it comes from. Listing wines is one thing, valuing them is another – and this book is also a guide to value. In the past decades the world has become more and more judgmental, and nowhere more than the world of wine. It is the current fashionable illusion (or pretence) that the quality of wines can be measured in points as precisely as its temperature in degrees. The wine "thermometer" goes up to 100. When you think about it the idea is absurd: there is no precise calibration of something as objective as wine appreciation. Wine by wine, bottle by bottle scores measure someone's appreciation, their pleasure as well as their expertise. Even if it's my own personal pleasure I wouldn't know how to put a precise number on it. 96? 97? 98? Is it my last wine of the day, or my first?

Scoring on a modest scale, say points out of five, is feasible and credible. Out of 20, the way the wine trade often does it, seems to work pretty well – though with fine wines there is often serious bunching around the 16.5 mark. In the 1998 edition of this book I floated a hedonist's alternative, with the lowest score one sniff, the next one sip... and so on up to acquiring the vineyard. In this book I deliberately didn't attempt the impossible. I rely on the consensus of drinkers over time, hence reputation, just as (eg.) the brokers of Bordeaux did when they classified the châteaux in 1855. They used prices over a period of 100 years. We don't have that privilege with new wines, though you can argue that prices over time remain as good a gauge of quality (or rather desirability) as you are going to get. Thanks to our network of correspondents we have tried to keep up with what's fermenting, from Vermont to Uruguay – even if the focus remains on the regions that created the original fine wines. I thank them all, as I do the readers who have kept this boat afloat for 44 (or is it 45?) vintage years.

Hugh replies

Vintage report 2020

2020 was in the end, a good-enough to good year for wine, but easy it was not.

The southern hemisphere was the first to have to work out exactly how to pick grapes and make wine while keeping everybody socially distanced (one-way routes in wineries, no sociable lunches and a great many crossed fingers were part of it) but only S Africa had to deal with government edicts forbidding the sale of wine either at home or abroad. Other countries had a collapse in wine-drinking tourist numbers, and European wineries suffered from US tariffs. It was a toxic combination.

And yet, in the end, the wines turned out well. Not always in **California**, where lots of top Napa reds won't be released because of smoke taint from wildfires; some vineyards and wineries were destroyed by flames. But unaffected wines have good concentration, and some regions – Lodi, Sierra Foothills – reported lower-than-usual sugar levels for the same levels of ripeness. Santa Barbara suffered from smoke, as well as Napa, but whites generally are looking good.

Up in **Oregon**, wildfires near Portland and in the Cascade Mountains sent smoke into the Willamette Valley – enough to lower daytime temperatures, but not enough, mostly, to kill flavours. Lower fruit set at the start of the season meant good ripeness at the end. On the other side of the country, **New York**'s Finger Lakes had a warm and dry summer and made wines of good balance; **Virginia** had problems including late frosts and patchy hail, so quantities are a bit down.

In **Australia**, smoke taint took its toll: Clonakilla's entire vintage near Canberra was wiped out by smoke; Henschke suffered from actual flames, but in McLaren Vale, Steve Pannell reported no smoke taint and nicely late ripening fruit. Geelong, Yarra and Clare are happy too. Disaster, in both Australia and California, has been local; a great many wines emerged untouched, though usually lower in quantity.

Even in **S Africa** – where some grapes were only picked because the government allowed an exception to lockdown rules – Stellenbosch and Swartland had a generous harvest. Chenin Blanc and Chardonnay seem to have done particularly well.

In Europe, **Italy** reports aromatic Sangiovese in Tuscany: August was hot, but nights were relatively cool. Both Barbera and Nebbiolo seem to have flourished in Piedmont; coronavirus restrictions seem to have meant more vineyard owners spending more time in their vines, to the probable benefit of both.

The weather at least had the grace not to throw extra problems their way: there are no reports of storms or hail in either region, though Valpolicella had hideous vineyard damage from a storm, and extremes of weather cut the crop in Franciacorta.

Spain was hit, come summer, by a dispute over falling grape prices, exacerbated by an imbalance of supply and demand in wine: there weren't enough tourists to help drink it, US tariffs reduced exports and domestic consumption is down. Lower limits were set for the amount that could be made in Rueda, Rioja and Cava; in addition, there was mildew in Catalonia and Rioja and oidium in Rueda. Finding pickers was another problem: pickers from abroad often couldn't get in, and locals were either nervous, or didn't want to lose their furlough payments. Quality? Patchy. Some will be very good, some will be okay. Some won't be either.

The **Port** quintas of the Douro abandoned foot-treading and relied on the robots in their lagares. Summer heat was ferocious in the Douro: the average July temperature at Quinta do Vesuvio hit a 40-year record. Dehydration cut the crop, with Touriga Nacional and Tinta Cão grapes showing the best quality at harvest.

Over to supposedly cooler countries: **Germany**, warmer than usual, picked early and with lower acidity: here the revival of vineyards that used to be too cold to be viable is a tool in combating warmer summers. **Austria** looked to be in for a classic coolish year until August changed everything. The Wachau had a big hailstorm on 22 August; the damage was enormous, and rot followed hail. Domäne Wachau says that the rotten bits of every single bunch had to be picked out by hand. Having done that, the quality is good: cool, light wines, tight and fresh. Just not that much of them.

France suffered from US tariffs too: exports fell dramatically. Bordeaux reports a good vintage in spite of an extremely hot year and mildew in places. On the Right Bank they thanked September heat for their reprieve from uneven ripening; on the Left Bank, they were grateful for August rain that broke a drought. Overall Merlot seems to have done better than the Cabernets.

Burgundy had a torrid July and an early vintage, but not a great one. There was a lot of dehydration: pick your producer with care. Champagne had a spat about officially lowered yields because of lower consumption, but the wines look good: fresh Chardonnays, aromatic Pinots.

The Loire had no late frost, for once, and Vouvray is particularly good; the Rhône made great whites, with lovely freshness, and excellent reds; Alsace had perfect conditions and ideally healthy grapes. Sales, however, do not reflect this: the usual story of fewer tourists, and US tariffs.

Lordy lordy. What a year.

Grape varieties

In the past two decades a radical change has come about in all except the most long-established wine countries: the names of a handful of grape varieties have become the ready-reference to wine. In senior wine countries, above all France and Italy, more complex traditions prevail. All wine of old prestige is known by its origin, more or less narrowly defined – not just by the particular fruit juice that fermented. For the present the two notions are in rivalry. Eventually the primacy of place over fruit will become obvious, at least for wines of quality. But for now, for most people, grape tastes are the easy reference point – despite the fact that they are often confused by the added taste of oak. If grape flavours were really all that mattered, this would be a very short book. But of course they *do* matter, and a knowledge of them both guides you to flavours you enjoy and helps comparisons between regions. Hence the originally Californian term "varietal wine", meaning, in principle, made from one grape variety. At least seven varieties – Cabernet Sauvignon, Pinot Noir, Riesling, Sauvignon Blanc, Chardonnay, Gewurztraminer and Muscat – taste and smell distinct and memorable enough to form international wine categories. To these add Merlot, Malbec, Syrah, Sémillon, Chenin Blanc, Pinots Blanc and Gris, Sylvaner, Viognier, Nebbiolo, Sangiovese, Tempranillo. The following are the best and/or most popular wine grapes.

All grapes and synonyms are cross-referenced in SMALL CAPITALS throughout every section of this book.

Grapes for red wine

Agiorgitiko Greek; the grape of Nemea, now planted all over Greece. Versatile and delicious, from soft and charming to dense and age-worthy. A must-try.

Aglianico S Italy's best red, the grape of Taurasi; dark, deep and fashionable.

Alicante Bouschet Used to be shunned, now stylish in Alentejo, Chile, esp old vines.

Aragonez See TEMPRANILLO.

Auxerrois See MALBEC, if red. White Auxerrois has its own entry in White Grapes.

Băbească Neagră Traditional "black grandmother grape" of Moldova; light body and ruby-red colour.

Babić Dark grape from Dalmatia, grown in stony seaside vyds round Šibenik. Exceptional quality potential.

Baga Portugal. Bairrada grape. Dark, tannic, fashionable. Needs a gd grower.

Barbera Widely grown in Italy, best in Piedmont: high acidity, low tannin, cherry fruit. Ranges from serious, age-worthy to semi-sweet and frothy. Fashionable in California and Australia; promising in Argentina.

Blauburger Austrian cross of BLAUER PORTUGIESER, BLAUFRÄNKISCH. Simple wines.

Blauburgunder See PINOT N.

Blauer Portugieser Central European, esp Germany (Rheinhessen, Pfalz, mostly for rosé), Austria, Hungary. Light, fruity reds: drink young, slightly chilled.

Blaufränkisch (Kékfrankos, Lemberger, Modra Frankinja) Widely planted in Austria's Mittelburgenland: medium-bodied, peppery acidity, fresh, berry aromas, eucalyptus. Can be top quality; Austria's star red. Often blended with CAB SAUV or ZWEIGELT. Lemberger in Germany (esp Württemberg), Kékfrankos in Hungary, Modra Frankinja in Slovenia.

Bobal Spain. Can be rustic; best at high altitude. Gd acidity.

Boğaskere Tannic and Turkish. Produces full-bodied wines.

Bonarda Ambiguous name. In Oltrepò Pavese, an alias for Croatina, soft fresh *frizzante* and still red. In Lombardy and Emilia-Romagna an alias for Uva Rara. Different in Piedmont. Argentina's Bonarda can be any of these, or something else. None are great.

Bouchet St-Émilion alias for CAB FR.

Brunello SANGIOVESE, splendid at Montalcino.

Cabernet Franc [Cab Fr] In B'x: more important than CAB SAUV in St-Émilion. Outperforms Cab Sauv in Loire (Chinon, Saumur-Champigny, rosé), in Hungary (depth and complexity in Villány and Szekszárd) and often in Italy. Much of NE Italy's Cab Fr turned out to be CARMENÈRE. Used in B'x blends of Cab Sauv/MERLOT across the world.

Cabernet Sauvignon [Cab Sauv] Characterful: slow-ripening, spicy, herby, tannic, with blackcurrant aroma. Main grape of the Médoc; also makes some of the best California, S American, E European reds. Vies with SHIRAZ in Australia. Grown almost everywhere, but few places make great varietal Cab Sauv: usually benefits from blending with eg. MERLOT, CAB FR, SYRAH, TEMPRANILLO, SANGIOVESE, etc. Makes aromatic rosé. Top wines need ageing.

Cannonau GRENACHE in its Sardinian manifestation; can be v. fine, potent.

Carignan (Carignane, Carignano, Cariñena) Low-yielding old vines now fashionable everywhere from S France to Chile, via S Africa. Lots of depth, vibrancy, but must never be overcropped. Common in N Africa, Spain (as Cariñena), California.

Carignano See CARIGNAN.

Cariñena See CARIGNAN.

Carmenère An old B'x variety now a star, rich and deep, in Chile (pronounced "carmeneary"). B'x is looking at it again.

Castelão See PERIQUITA.

Cencibel See TEMPRANILLO.

Chiavennasca *See* NEBBIOLO.

Cinsault (Cinsaut) A staple of S France, v.gd if low-yielding, hopeless if not. Makes gd rosé. One of parents of PINOTAGE.

Cornalin du Valais Swiss speciality with high potential, esp in Valais.

Corvina Dark and spicy; one of best grapes in Valpolicella blend. Corvinone, even darker, is a separate variety.

Côt *See* MALBEC.

Dolcetto Source of soft, seductive dry red in Piedmont. Now high fashion.

Dornfelder Gives deliciously light reds, straightforward, often rustic, and well-coloured in Germany, parts of the US, even England.

Duras Spicy, peppery, structured; exclusive to Gaillac, parts of Tarn V, SW France.

Fer Servadou Exclusive to SW France, aka Mansois in Marcillac, Braucol in Gaillac and Pinenc in St-Mont. Redolent of red summer fruits and spice.

Fetească Neagră Romania: "black maiden grape" with potential as showpiece variety; can give deep, full-bodied wines with character.

Frühburgunder An ancient German mutation of PINOT N, mostly in Ahr but also in Franken and Württemberg, where it is confusingly known as Clevner. Lower acidity than Pinot N.

Gamay The Beaujolais grape: light, fragrant wines, best young, except in Beaujolais crus (*see* France) where quality can be high, wines for 2–10 yrs. Grown in Loire Valley, Central France, Switzerland, Savoie, Canada. California's Napa Gamay is Valdiguié.

Gamza *See* KADARKA.

Garnacha (Cannonau, Garnatxa, Grenache) Important pale, potent grape for warm climates, fashionable with *terroiristes* because it expresses its site. Can be beefy (Priorat) or delicate (Gredos), but usually quite high alc. The base of Châteauneuf-du-Pape. Also gd for rosé and *vin doux naturel* – esp in S France, Spain, California. Old-vine versions prized in S Australia. Usually blended with other varieties. Cannonau in Sardinia, Grenache in France.

Garnatxa *See* GARNACHA.

Graciano Spanish; part of Rioja blend. Aroma of violets, tannic, lean structure, a bit like PETIT VERDOT. Difficult to grow but increasingly fashionable.

Grenache *See* GARNACHA.

Grignolino Italy: gd everyday table wine in Piedmont.

Kadarka (Gamza) Makes spicy, light reds in E Europe. In Hungary revived, esp for Bikavér.

Kalecik Karasi Turkish: sour-cherry fruit, fresh, supple. Bit like GAMAY. Drink young.

Kékfrankos Hungarian BLAUFRÄNKISCH.

Lagrein N Italian, dark, bitter finish, rich, plummy. DOC in Alto Adige (*see* Italy).

Lambrusco Productive grape of lower Po Valley; cheerful, sweet, fizzy, can be v.gd.

Lefkada Rediscovered Cypriot variety, higher quality than MAVRO. Usually blended as tannins can be aggressive.

Lemberger *See* BLAUFRÄNKISCH.

Malbec (Auxerrois, Côt) Minor in B'x, major in Cahors (alias Auxerrois) and the star in Argentina. Dark, dense, tannic but fleshy wine capable of real quality. High-altitude versions in Argentina best. Bringing Cahors back into fashion.

Maratheftiko Deep-coloured Cypriot grape with quality potential.

Marselan CAB SAUV x GRENACHE, 1961. Gd colour, structure, supple tannins, ages well. A success in China.

Mataro *See* MOURVÈDRE.

Mavro Most planted black grape of Cyprus but only moderate quality. Best for rosé.

Mavrodaphne Greek; means "black laurel". Sweet fortifieds, speciality of Patras, also in Cephalonia. Dry versions too, great promise.

Mavrotragano Greek, almost extinct; now revived; found on Santorini. Top quality.

Mavrud Probably Bulgaria's best. Spicy, dark, plummy late-ripener native to Thrace. Ages well.

Melnik Bulgarian; from the region of the same name. Dark colour and a nice dense, tart-cherry character. Ages well.

Mencía Making waves in Bierzo, N Spain. Aromatic with steely tannins and lots of acidity.

Merlot The grape behind the great fragrant and plummy wines of Pomerol and (with CAB FR) St-Émilion, a vital element in the Médoc, soft and strong in California, Washington, Chile, Australia. Lighter, often gd in N Italy (can be world-class in Tuscany), Italian Switzerland, Slovenia, Argentina, S Africa, NZ, etc. Perhaps too adaptable for own gd: can be v. dull; less than ripe it tastes green. Much planted in E Europe, esp Romania.

Modra Frankinja *See* BLAUFRÄNKISCH.

Modri Pinot *See* PINOT N.

Monastrell *See* MOURVÈDRE.

Mondeuse In Savoie; the skier's red; deep-coloured, gd acidity. Related to SYRAH.

Montepulciano Deep-coloured, dominant in Italy's Abruzzo and important along Adriatic coast from Marches to S Puglia. Also name of a Tuscan town, unrelated.

Morellino SANGIOVESE in Maremma, S Tuscany. Esp Scansano.

Mourvèdre (Mataro, Monastrell) A star of S France (eg. Bandol, growing influence Châteauneuf-du-Pape), Australia (aka Mataro) and Spain (aka Monastrell). Excellent dark, aromatic and tannic, gd for blending. Also in S Australia, California, S Africa.

Napa Gamay Identical to Valdiguié (S France). Nothing to get excited about.

Nebbiolo (Chiavennasca, Spanna) One of Italy's best red grapes; makes Barolo, Barbaresco, Gattinara and Valtellina. Intense, nobly fruity, perfumed wine; tannins now better managed, still improves for yrs.

Negroamaro Puglian "black bitter" red grape with potential for either high quality or high volume.

Nerello Mascalese Sicilian red grape, esp Etna; characterful, best v. elegant, fine.

Nero d'Avola Dark-red grape of Sicily, quality levels from sublime to industrial.

Nielluccio Corsican; plenty of acidity and tannin. Gd for rosé.

Öküzgözü Soft, fruity Turkish grape, usually blended with BOĞASKERE, rather as MERLOT in B'x is blended with CAB SAUV.

País Pioneer Spanish grape in Americas. Rustic; some producers now trying harder.

Pamid Bulgarian: light, soft, everyday red.

Periquita (Castelão) Common in Portugal, esp round Setúbal. Originally nicknamed Periquita after Fonseca's popular (trademarked) brand. Firm-flavoured, raspberryish reds develop a figgish, tar-like quality.

Petite Sirah Nothing to do with SYRAH; gives rustic, tannic, dark wine. Brilliant blended with ZIN in California; also found in S America, Mexico, Australia.

Petit Verdot Excellent but awkward Médoc grape, now increasingly planted in CAB areas worldwide for extra fragrance. Mostly blended but some gd varietals, esp in Virginia.

Pinotage Singular S African cross (PINOT N X CINSAULT). Has had a rocky ride, getting better from top producers. Gd rosé too. "Coffee Pinotage" is espresso-flavoured, sweetish, aimed at youth.

Pinot Crni *See* PINOT N.

Pinot Meunier (Schwarzriesling) [Pinot M] The 3rd grape of Champagne, better known as Meunier, great for blending but can be fine in its own right; a bridge between PINOT N and CHARD. Best on chalky sites (Damery, Leuvigny and Festigny) nr Épernay.

Pinot Noir (Blauburgunder, Modri Pinot, Pinot Crni, Spätburgunder) [Pinot N]
Glory of Burgundy's Côte d'Or; fine in Alsace, Germany; v.gd in Austria, esp in Kamptal, Burgenland, Thermenregion. Light in Hungary; mainstream, light to weightier in Switzerland (aka Clevner). Splendid in Sonoma, Carneros, Central Coast, also Oregon, Ontario, Yarra Valley, Adelaide Hills, Tasmania, NZ's Central Otago, S Africa's Walker Bay. Some v. pretty Chileans. New French clones promise improvement in Romania. Modri Pinot in Slovenia; probably country's best red. In Italy, best in ne, gets worse as you go s. PINOTS BL and GR mutations of Pinot N.

Plavac Mali (Crljenak) Croatian, and related to ZIN, like so much round there. Lots of quality potential, can age well, though can also be alcoholic and dull.

Primitivo S Italian grape, originally from Croatia, making big, dark, rustic wines, now fashionable because genetically identical to ZIN. Early ripening, hence the name. The original name for both seems to be Tribidrag.

Refosco (Refošk) Various DOCs in Italy, esp Colli Orientali. Deep, flavoursome and age-worthy wines, particularly in warmer climates. Dark, high acidity. Refošk in Slovenia and points e, genetically different, tastes similar.

Refošk See REFOSCO.

Roter Veltliner Austrian; unrelated to GRÜNER V. There is also a Frühroter and a Brauner Veltliner.

Rubin Bulgarian cross, NEBBIOLO X SYRAH. Peppery, full-bodied.

Sagrantino Italian grape grown in Umbria for powerful, cherry-flavoured wines.

St-Laurent Dark, smooth, full-flavoured Austrian speciality. Can be light and juicy or deep and structured. Also in Pfalz.

Sangiovese (Brunello, Morellino, Sangioveto) Principal red grape of Tuscany and central Italy. Its characteristic astringency is hard to get right, but sublime and long-lasting when it is. Dominant in Chianti, Vino Nobile, Brunello di Montalcino, Morellino di Scansano and various fine IGT offerings. Also in Umbria (eg. Montefalco and Torgiano) and across the Apennines in Romagna and Marches. Not so clever in the warmer, lower-altitude vyds of the Tuscan coast, nor in other parts of Italy despite its nr-ubiquity. Interesting in Australia.

Sangioveto See SANGIOVESE.

Saperavi The main red of Georgia, Ukraine, etc. Blends well with CAB SAUV (eg. in Moldova). Huge potential, seldom gd winemaking.

Schiava See TROLLINGER.

Schioppettino NE Italian, high acidity, high quality. Elegant, refined, can age.

Schwarzriesling PINOT M in Württemberg.

Sciacarello Corsican, herby and peppery. Not v. tannic.

Shiraz See SYRAH.

Spanna See NEBBIOLO.

Spätburgunder German for PINOT N.

Syrah (Shiraz) The great Rhône red grape: tannic, purple, peppery, matures superbly. Important as Shiraz in Australia, increasingly gd under either name in Chile, S Africa and terrific in NZ (esp Hawke's Bay). Widely grown and a gd traveller.

Tannat Raspberry-perfumed, highly tannic force behind Madiran, Tursan and other firm reds from SW France. Also rosé. The star of Uruguay.

Tempranillo (Aragonez, Cecibel, Tinto Fino, Tinta del País, Tinta Roriz, Ull de Llebre) Aromatic, fine Rioja grape, called Ull de Llebre in Catalonia, Cencibel in La Mancha, Tinto Fino in Ribera del Duero, Tinta Roriz in Douro, Tinta del País in Castile, Aragonez in S Portugal. Now Australia too. V. fashionable; elegant in cool climates, beefy in warm. Early ripening, long maturing.

Teran (Terrano) Close cousin of REFOSCO, esp on limestone (karst) in Slovenia.

Teroldego Rotaliano Trentino's best indigenous variety; serious, full-flavoured, esp on the flat Campo Rotaliano.

Tinta Amarela See TRINCADEIRA.

Tinta del País See TEMPRANILLO.

Tinta Negra (Negramoll) Until recently called Tinta Negra Mole. Easily Madeira's most planted grape and the mainstay of cheaper Madeira. Now coming into its own in Colheita wines (*see* Portugal).

Tinta Roriz See TEMPRANILLO.

Tinto Fino See TEMPRANILLO.

Touriga Nacional [Touriga N] The top Port grape, now widely used in the Douro for floral, stylish table wines. Australian Touriga is usually this; California's Touriga can be either this or Touriga Franca.

Trincadeira (Tinta Amarela) Portuguese; v.gd in Alentejo for spicy wines. Tinta Amarela in the Douro.

Trollinger (Schiava, Vernatsch) Popular pale red in Württemberg; aka Vernatsch and Schiava. Covers group of vines, not necessarily related. In Italy, snappy, brisk.

Ull de Llebre See TEMPRANILLO.

Vernatsch See TROLLINGER.

Xinomavro Greece's answer to NEBBIOLO. "Sharp-black"; the basis for Naoussa, Rapsani, Goumenissa, Amindeo. Some rosé, still or sparkling. Top quality, can age for decades. Being tried in China.

Zinfandel [Zin] Fruity, adaptable grape of California with blackberry-like, and sometimes metallic, flavour. Can be structured and gloriously lush, ageing for decades, but also makes "blush" pink, usually sweet, jammy. Genetically the same as S Italian PRIMITIVO.

Zweigelt (Blauer Zweigelt) BLAUFRÄNKISCH X ST-LAURENT, popular in Austria for aromatic, dark, supple, velvety wines. Also found in Hungary, Germany.

Grapes for white wine

Airén Bland workhorse of La Mancha, Spain: fresh if made well.

Albariño (Alvarinho) Fashionable, expensive in Spain: apricot-scented, gd acidity. Superb in Rías Baixas; shaping up elsewhere, but not all live up to the hype. Alvarinho in Portugal just as gd: aromatic Vinho Verde, esp in Monção, Melgaço.

Aligoté Burgundy's 2nd-rank white grape, now trendy. Sharp wine for young drinking, perfect for mixing with cassis to make Kir, or more serious. Widely planted in E Europe, Russia.

Alvarinho See ALBARIÑO.

Amigne One of Switzerland's speciality grapes, traditional in Valais, esp Vétroz. Full-bodied, tasty, often sweet but also bone-dry.

Ansonica See INSOLIA.

Arinto Portuguese, rather gd; mainstay of aromatic, citrus Bucelas; also adds welcome zip to blends, esp in Alentejo.

Arneis Fine, aromatic, appley-peachy, high-priced NW Italian grape, DOCG in Roero, DOC in Langhe, Piedmont.

Arvine Rare but excellent Swiss *spécialité*, from Valais. Also Petite Arvine. Dry or sweet, fresh, long-lasting wines with salty finish.

Assyrtiko From Santorini; one of the best grapes of the Mediterranean, balancing power, minerality, extract and high acid. Built to age. Could conquer the world...

Auxerrois Red Auxerrois is a synonym for MALBEC, but white Auxerrois is like a fatter, spicier PINOT BL. Found in Alsace and much used in Crémant; also Germany.

Bacchus German-bred crossing, early ripening so grown in England, v. aromatic, can be coarse.

Beli Pinot See PINOT BL.

Blanc Fumé See SAUV BL.

Boal See BUAL.

Bourboulenc This and the rare Rolle make some of the Midi's best wines.

Bouvier Indigenous aromatic Austrian grape, esp gd for Beerenauslese and Trockenbeerenauslese, rarely for dry wines.

Bual (Boal) Makes top-quality sweet Madeira wines, not quite so rich as MALMSEY.

Carricante Italian. Principal grape of Etna Bianco, regaining ground.

Catarratto Prolific white grape found all over Sicily, esp in w in DOC Alcamo.

Cerceal See SERCIAL.

Chardonnay (Morillon) [Chard] The white grape of Burgundy and Champagne, now ubiquitous worldwide, partly because it is one of the easiest to grow and vinify. Reflects terroir but also the winemaker's intentions: often a fashion victim. Can be steely or fat. Also the name of a Mâcon-Villages commune. Morillon in Styria, Austria.

Chasselas (Fendant, Gutedel) Swiss (originated in Vaud). Neutral flavour, can be elegant (Geneva); refined, full (Vaud); exotic, racy (Valais). Fendant in Valais. Makes almost 3rd of Swiss wines but giving way, esp to red. Gutedel in Germany; grown esp in S Baden. Elsewhere usually a table grape.

Chenin Blanc [Chenin Bl] Wonderful white grape of the middle Loire (Vouvray, Layon, etc). Wine can be dry or sweet (or v. sweet), but with plenty of acidity. Superb old-vine versions in S Africa, esp Swartland.

Cirfandl See ZIERFANDLER.

Clairette Important Midi grape, low-acid, part of many blends. Improved winemaking helps.

Colombard Slightly fruity, nicely sharp grape, makes everyday wine in S Africa, California and SW France. Often blended.

Dimiat Perfumed Bulgarian grape, made dry or off-dry, or distilled. Far more synonyms than any grape needs.

Encruzado Portuguese, serious; fresh, versatile, ages well. Esp gd in Dão.

Ermitage Swiss for MARSANNE.

Ezerjó Hungarian, with sharp acidity. Name means "thousand blessings".

Falanghina Italian: ancient grape of Campanian hills. Gd dense, aromatic dry whites.

Fendant See CHASSELAS.

Fernão Pires See MARIA GOMES.

Fetească Albă / Regală Romania has two Fetească grapes, both with slight MUSCAT aroma. F. Regală is a cross of F. Albă and Frâncușă; more finesse, gd for late-harvest wines. F. NEAGRĂ is dark-skinned.

Fiano High quality, giving peachy, spicy wine in Campania, S Italy.

Folle Blanche (Gros Plant) High acid/little flavour make this ideal for brandy. Gros Plant in Brittany, Picpoul in Armagnac, but unrelated to true PICPOUL. Also respectable in California.

Friulano (Sauvignonasse, Sauvignon Vert) N Italian: fresh, pungent, subtly floral. Used to be called Tocai Friulano. Best in Collio, Isonzo, Colli Orientali. Found in nearby Slovenia as Sauvignonasse; also in Chile, where it was long confused with SAUV BL. Ex-Tocai in Veneto now known as Tai.

Fumé Blanc See SAUV BL.

Furmint (Šipon) Superb, characterful. The trademark of Hungary, both as principal grape in Tokaji and as vivid, vigorous dry wine, sometimes mineral, sometimes apricot-flavoured, sometimes both. Šipon in Slovenia. Some grown in Rust, Austria for sweet and dry.

Garganega Best grape in Soave blend; also in Gambellara. Top, esp sweet, age well.

Garnacha Blanca (Grenache Blanc) The white version of GARNACHA/Grenache, much used in Spain and S France. Low acidity. Can be innocuous, or surprisingly gd.

Gewurztraminer (Traminac, Traminec, Traminer, Tramini) [Gewurz] One of the most pungent grapes, spicy with aromas of rose petals, face cream, lychees, grapefruit. Often rich and soft, even when fully dry. Best in Alsace; also gd in Germany (Baden, Pfalz, Sachsen), E Europe, Australia, California, Pacific Northwest and NZ. Can be relatively unaromatic if just labelled Traminer (or variants). Italy uses the name Traminer Aromatico for its (dry) "Gewurz" versions. (The name takes an Umlaut in German.) Identical to SAVAGNIN.

Glera Uncharismatic new name for Prosecco vine: Prosecco is now wine only in the EU, but still a grape name in Australia.

Godello Top quality (intense, mineral) in nw Spain. Called Verdelho in Dão, Portugal, but unrelated to true VERDELHO.

Grasă (Kövérszőlő) Romanian; name means "fat". Prone to botrytis; important in Cotnari, potentially superb sweet wines. Kövérszőlő in Hungary's Tokaj region.

Graševina See WELSCHRIESLING.

Grauburgunder See PINOT GR.

Grechetto Ancient grape of central and S Italy noted for the vitality and stylishness of its wine. Blended, or used solo in Orvieto.

Greco S Italian: there are various Grecos, probably unrelated, perhaps of Greek origin. Brisk, peachy flavour, most famous as Greco di Tufo. Greco di Bianco is from semi-dried grapes. Greco Nero is a black version.

Grenache Blanc See GARNACHA BLANCA.

Grillo Italy: main grape of Marsala. Also v.gd full-bodied dry table wine.

Gros Plant See FOLLE BLANCHE.

Grüner Veltliner [Grüner V] Austria's fashionable flagship white. V. diverse: from simple, peppery, everyday, to great complexity, ageing potential. Useful because gd at all levels. Found elsewhere in Central Europe and outside.

Gutedel See CHASSELAS.

Hárslevelű Other main grape of Tokaji, but softer, peachier than FURMINT. Name means "linden-leaved". Gd in Somló, Eger as well.

Heida Swiss for SAVAGNIN.

Humagne Swiss speciality, older than CHASSELAS. Fresh, plump, not v. aromatic. Humagne Rouge is not related but increasingly popular: same as Cornalin du Aosta. Cornalin du Valais is different. (Keep up at the back, there.)

Insolia (Ansonica, Inzolia) Sicilian; Ansonica on Tuscan coast. Fresh, racy wine at best. May be semi-dried for sweet wine.

Irsai Olivér Hungarian cross; aromatic, MUSCAT-like wine for drinking young.

Johannisberg Swiss for SILVANER.

Kéknyelű Low-yielding, flavourful grape giving one of Hungary's best whites. Has the potential for fieriness and spice. To be watched.

Kerner Quite successful German cross. Early ripening, flowery (but often too blatant) wine with gd acidity.

Királyleányka Hungarian; gentle, fresh wines (eg. in Eger).

Koshu More-or-less indigenous Japanese table-turned-wine grape, much hyped. Fresh, tannic. Orange versions gd.

Kövérszőlő See GRASĂ.

Laški Rizling See WELSCHRIESLING.

Leányka Hungarian. Soft, floral wines.

Listán See PALOMINO.

Longyan (Dragon Eye) Chinese original; gd substantial, aromatic wine.

Loureiro Best Vinho Verde grape after ALVARINHO: delicate, floral. Also in Spain.

Macabeo See VIURA.

Maccabeu See VIURA.

Malagousia Rediscovered Greek grape for gloriously perfumed wines.

Malmsey *See* MALVASIA. The sweetest style of Madeira.

Malvasia (Malmsey, Malvazija, Malvoisie, Marastina) Italy, France and Iberia. Not a single variety but a whole stable, not necessarily related or even alike. Can be white or red, sparkling or still, strong or mild, sweet or dry, aromatic or neutral. Slovenia's and Croatia's version is Malvazija Istarka, crisp and light, or rich, oak-aged. Sometimes called Marastina in Croatia. "Malmsey" (as in the sweetest style of Madeira) is a corruption of Malvasia.

Malvoisie *See* MALVASIA. A name used for several varieties in France, incl BOURBOULENC, Torbato, VERMENTINO. Also PINOT GR in Switzerland's Valais.

Manseng, Gros / Petit Gloriously spicy, floral whites from SW France. The key to Jurançon. Superb late-harvest and sweet wines too.

Maria Gomes (Fernão Pires) Portuguese; aromatic, ripe-flavoured, slightly spicy whites in Barraida and Tejo.

Marsanne (Ermitage) Principal white grape (with ROUSSANNE) of the N Rhône (Hermitage, St-Joseph, St-Péray). Also gd in Australia, California and (as Ermitage Blanc) the Valais. Soft, full wines that age v. well.

Melon de Bourgogne *See* MUSCADET.

Misket Bulgarian. Mildly aromatic; the basis of most country whites.

Morillon CHARD in parts of Austria.

Moscatel *See* MUSCAT.

Moscato *See* MUSCAT.

Moschofilero Pink-skinned, rose-scented, high-quality, high-acid, low-alcohol Greek grape. Makes white, some pink, some sparkling.

Müller-Thurgau [Müller-T] Aromatic wines to drink young. Makes gd sweet wines but usually dull, often coarse, dry ones. In Germany, most common in Pfalz, Rheinhessen, Nahe, Baden, Franken. Has some merit in Italy's Trentino-Alto Adige, Friuli. Sometimes called RIES x SYLVANER (incorrectly) in Switzerland.

Muscadelle Adds aroma to white B'x, esp Sauternes. In Victoria used (with MUSCAT, to which it is unrelated) for Rutherglen Muscat.

Muscadet (Melon de Bourgogne) Light, refreshing, dry wines with seaside tang to complex ones around Nantes. Also found (as Melon) in parts of Burgundy.

Muscat (Moscatel, Moscato, Muskateller) Many varieties; the best is Muscat Blanc à Petits Grains (alias Gelber Muskateller, Rumeni Muškat, Sarga Muskotály, Yellow Muscat). Widely grown, easily recognized, pungent grapes, mostly made into perfumed sweet wines, often fortified, as in France's *vin doux naturel*. Superb, dark and sweet in Australia. Sweet, sometimes v.gd in Spain. Most Hungarian Muskotály is Muscat Ottonel except in Tokaj, where Sarga Muskotály rules, adding perfume (in small amounts) to blends. Occasionally (eg. Alsace, Austria, parts of S Germany) made dry. Sweet Cap Corse Muscats often superb. Light Moscato fizz in N Italy.

Muskateller *See* MUSCAT.

Narince Turkish; fresh and fruity wines.

Neuburger Austrian, rather neglected; mainly in the Wachau (elegant, flowery), Thermenregion (mellow, ample-bodied) and n Burgenland (strong, full).

Olaszrizling *See* WELSCHRIESLING.

Païen *See* SAVAGNIN.

Palomino (Listán) Great grape of Sherry; little intrinsic character, but gains all from production method. Now table wine too. As Listán, makes dry white in Canaries.

Pansa Blanca *See* XAREL·LO.

Pecorino Italian: not a cheese but alluring dry white from a revived variety.

Pedro Ximénez [PX] Makes sweet brown Sherry under its own name, and used in Montilla and Málaga. Also grown in Argentina, the Canaries, Australia, California and S Africa.

Picpoul (Piquepoul) Southern French, best known in Picpoul de Pinet. Should have high acidity. Picpoul Noir is black-skinned.

Pinela Local to Slovenia. Subtle, lowish acidity; drink young.

Pinot Bianco *See* PINOT BL.

Pinot Blanc (Beli Pinot, Pinot Bianco, Weißburgunder) [Pinot Bl] Mutation of PINOT N, similar to but milder than CHARD. Light, fresh, fruity, not aromatic, to drink young. Gd for Italian *spumante*, and potentially excellent in the ne, esp high sites in Alto Adige. Widely grown. Weißburgunder in Germany and best in s: often racier than Chard.

Pinot Gris (Pinot Grigio, Grauburgunder, Ruländer, Sivi Pinot, Szürkebarát) [Pinot Gr] Popular as Pinot Grigio in N Italy, even for rosé, but top, characterful versions can be excellent (from Alto Adige, Friuli). Cheap versions are just that. Terrific in Alsace for full-bodied, spicy whites. Once important in Champagne. In Germany can be alias Ruländer (sw) or Grauburgunder (dr): best in Baden (esp Kaiserstuhl) and S Pfalz. Szürkebarát in Hungary, Sivi P in Slovenia (characterful, aromatic).

Pošip Croatian; mostly on Korčula. Quite characterful and citrus; high-yielding.

Prosecco Old name for grape that makes Prosecco. Now you have to call it GLERA.

Renski Rizling Rhine RIES.

Rèze Super-rare ancestral Valais grape used for *vin de glacier*.

Ribolla Gialla / Rebula Acidic but characterful. In Italy, best in Collio. In Slovenia, traditional in Brda. Can be v.gd. Favourite of amphora users.

Rieslaner German cross (SILVANER x RIES); low yields, difficult ripening, now v. rare. Makes fine Auslesen in Franken and Pfalz.

Riesling Italico *See* WELSCHRIESLING.

Riesling (Renski Rizling, Rhine Riesling) [Ries] The greatest, most versatile white grape, diametrically opposite in style to CHARD. From steely to voluptuous, always positively perfumed, far more ageing potential than Chard. Great in all styles in Germany; forceful and steely in Austria; lime cordial and toast fruit in S Australia; rich and spicy in Alsace; Germanic and promising in NZ, NY State, Pacific Northwest; has potential in Ontario, S Africa.

Rkatsiteli Found widely in E Europe, Russia, Georgia. Can stand cold winters and has high acidity; protects to a degree from poor winemaking. Also in NE US.

Robola In Greece (Cephalonia) a top-quality, floral grape, unrelated to RIBOLLA GIALLA.

Roditis Pink grape, all over Greece, usually making whites. Gd when yields low.

Roter Veltliner Austrian; unrelated to GRÜNER V. There is also a Frühroter and an (unrelated) Brauner Veltliner.

Rotgipfler Austrian; indigenous to Thermenregion. With ZIERFANDLER, makes lively, lush, aromatic blend.

Roussanne Rhône grape of real finesse, now popping up in California and Australia. Can age many yrs.

Ruländer *See* PINOT GR.

Sauvignonasse *See* FRIULANO.

Sauvignon Blanc [Sauv Bl] Distinctive aromatic, grassy-to-tropical wines, pungent in NZ, often mineral in Sancerre, riper in Australia. V.gd in Rueda, Austria, N Italy (Isonzo, Piedmont, Alto Adige), Chile's Casablanca Valley and S Africa. Blended with SÉM in B'x. Can be austere or buxom (or indeed nauseating). Sauv Gris is a pink-skinned, less aromatic version of Sauv Bl with untapped potential.

Sauvignon Vert *See* FRIULANO.

Savagnin (Heida, Païen) Grape for *vin jaune* from Jura: aromatic form is GEWURZ. In Switzerland known as Heida, Païen or Traminer. Full-bodied, high acidity.

Scheurebe (Sämling) Grapefruit-scented German RIES x SILVANER (possibly), v. successful in Pfalz, esp for Auslese and up. Can be weedy: must be v. ripe to be gd.

Sémillon [Sém] Contributes lusciousness to Sauternes but decreasingly important for Graves and other dry white B'x. Grassy if not fully ripe, but can make soft dry wine of great ageing potential. Superb in Australia; NZ and S Africa promising.

Sercial (Cerceal) Portuguese: makes the driest Madeira. Cerceal, also Portuguese, seems to be this plus any of several others.

Seyval Blanc [Seyval Bl] French-made hybrid of French and American vines; v. hardy, attractively fruity. Popular and reasonably successful in E US, England.

Silvaner (Johannisberg, Sylvaner) Can be excellent in Germany's Rheinhessen, Pfalz, esp Franken, with plant/earth flavours and mineral notes. V.gd (and powerful) as Johannisberg in Valais, Switzerland. Lightest of Alsace grapes.

Šipon See FURMINT.

Sivi Pinot See PINOT GR.

Spätrot See ZIERFANDLER.

Sylvaner See SILVANER.

Tămâioasă Românească Romanian "frankincense" grape, with exotic aroma and taste. Belongs to MUSCAT family.

Torrontés Name given to a number of grapes, mostly with an aromatic, floral character, sometimes soapy. A speciality of Argentina; also in Spain. DYA.

Traminac Or Traminec. See GEWURZ.

Traminer Or Tramini (Hungary). See GEWURZ.

Trebbiano (Ugni Blanc) Principal white grape of Tuscany, found all over Italy in many different guises. Rarely rises above the plebeian except in Tuscany's Vin Santo. Some gd dry whites under DOCs Romagna or Abruzzo. Trebbiano di Soave, aka VERDICCHIO, only distantly related. T di Lugana now called Turbiana. Grown in southern France as Ugni Blanc, and Cognac as St-Émilion. Mostly thin, bland wine; needs blending (and more careful growing).

Ugni Blanc [Ugni Bl] See TREBBIANO.

Verdejo The grape of Rueda in Castile, potentially fine and long-lived.

Verdelho Great quality in Australia (pungent, full-bodied); rare but gd (and medium-sweet) in Madeira.

Verdicchio Potentially gd, muscular, dry; central-E Italy. Wine of same name.

Vermentino Italian; sprightly; satisfying texture and ageing capacity. Potential here.

Vernaccia Name given to many unrelated grapes in Italy. Vernaccia di San Gimignano is crisp, lively; Vernaccia di Oristano is Sherry-like.

Vidal French hybrid much grown in Canada for Icewine.

Vidiano Most Cretan producers love this. Powerful, stylish. Lime/apricot, gd acidity.

Viognier Ultra-fashionable Rhône grape, finest in Condrieu, less fine but still aromatic in the Midi. Gd examples from California, Virginia, Uruguay, Australia.

Viura (Macabeo, Maccabéo, Maccabeu) Workhorse white grape of N Spain, widespread in Rioja and Catalan Cava country. Also found over border in SW France. Gd quality potential.

Weißburgunder PINOT BL in Germany.

Welschriesling (Graševina, Laški Rizling, Olaszrizling, Riesling Italico) Not related to RIES. Light and fresh to sweet and rich in Austria; ubiquitous in Central Europe, where it can be remarkably gd for dry and sweet wines.

Xarel·lo (Pansa Blanca) Traditional Catalan grape, used for Cava (with Parellada, MACABEO). Tannic, can age, can be top quality. Lime cordial character in Alella, as Pansa Blanca.

Xynisteri Cyprus's most planted white grape. Can be simple and is usually DYA, but when grown at altitude makes appealing, minerally whites.

Zéta Hungarian; BOUVIER x FURMINT used by some in Tokaji Aszú production.

Zierfandler (Spätrot, Cirfandl) Found in Austria's Thermenregion; often blended with ROTGIPFLER for aromatic, orange-peel-scented, weighty wines.

Wine & food

You can be too detailed about all this. Choosing a wine that goes well with what you're eating enhances both – if you don't believe me, try drinking almost any wine with watercress, and tell me if either benefits – but that doesn't mean that the suggestions here are prescriptive. Choices are always limited by what is available, either at home or on a restaurant wine list. So use this as a guide to the sort of flavours and weight of wine that will work; and then have fun.

On p.37 you'll find a box of can't-go-wrong favourites with food; the entries below give lots of specific matches enjoyed over the years.

Before the meal – apéritifs

This is about mood and the raising of expectations, so don't stint. If it's Champagne, make it decent Champagne. If it's English fizz or good Franciacorta, celebrate it. And don't be afraid to experiment: offer an orange wine, or rosé from magnum, or a glorious Ries, or Fino. Have something on hand for the person (there's always one) who says, "Got any red?", but otherwise, focus on quality, not choice.

First courses

Aïoli More about mood than matching. Cold Provence rosé, PECORINO, ALIGOTÉ. Beer, marc or grappa... you'll hardly notice.

Antipasti / tapas / mezze You can be in Italy, Spain, Greece or Edinburgh: a selection of savoury, salty, meaty, cheesy, fishy, veggie bits and pieces works perfectly with Fino Sherry, XYNISTERI, orange wines. Roasted peppers, aubergines suit fruity reds: CAB FR, KADARKA. Gd Prosecco in emergencies.

Burrata Forget mozzarella; this is the crème de la crème. So a top Italian white, FIANO or Cusumano's GRILLO. I'll try Sauternes one day.

Carpaccio, beef or fish Beef version works well with most wines, incl reds. Tuscan is appropriate, but fine CHARDS are gd. So are pink and Vintage Champagnes. Give Amontillado a try. **Salmon** Chard or Champagne. **Tuna** VIOGNIER, California Chard, Marlborough SAUV BL. Or sake.

Charcuterie / prosciutto / salami High-acid, unoaked red works better than white. Simple Beaujolais, Valpolicella, REFOSCO, SCHIOPPETTINO, TEROLDEGO, BARBERA. If you must have white, it needs acidity. Chorizo makes wines taste metallic. Prosciutto with melon or figs needs full dry or medium white: CHENIN BL, FIANO, MUSCAT, VIOGNIER.

Dim sum Classically, China tea. PINOT GR or classic German dry RIES; light PINOT N. For reds, soft tannins are key. Bardolino, Rioja; Côtes du Rhône. Also NV Champagne or English fizz.

Eggs *See also* SOUFFLÉS. Not easy: eggs have a way of coating your palate. Omelettes: follow the other ingredients; mushrooms suggest red; Côtes du Rhone is a safe bet. With a truffle omelette, Vintage Champagne. As a last resort I can bring myself to drink Champagne with scrambled eggs or eggs Benedict. Florentine, with spinach, is not a winey dish.

 quails' eggs Blanc de Blancs Champagne; VIOGNIER.

 gulls' eggs Push the luxury: mature white burgundy or Vintage Champagne.

 oeufs en meurette Burgundian genius: eggs in red wine with a glass of the same.

Mozzarella with tomatoes, basil Fresh Italian white, eg. Soave, Alto Adige. VERMENTINO from Liguria or Rolle from the Midi. *See also* VEGETABLE/AVOCADO.

Oysters , raw NV Champagne, Chablis, MUSCADET, white Graves, Sancerre, English Bacchus, or Guinness. Experiment with Sauternes. Manzanilla is gd. Flat oysters worth gd wine; Pacific ones drown it in brine.

stewed, grilled or otherwise cooked Puligny-Montrachet or gd NZ CHARD. Champagne is gd with either.

Pasta Red or white according to the sauce:

cream sauce (eg. carbonara) Orvieto, GRECO di Tufo. Young SANGIOVESE.

meat sauce MONTEPULCIANO d'Abruzzo, Salice Salentino, MALBEC.

pesto (basil) sauce BARBERA, VERMENTINO, NZ SAUV BL, Hungarian FURMINT.

seafood sauce (eg. vongole) VERDICCHIO, Lugana, Soave, GRILLO, unoaked CHARD.

tomato sauce Chianti, Barbera, Sicilian red, ZIN, S Australian GRENACHE.

Risotto Follow the flavour:

with vegetables (eg. Primavera) PINOT GR from Friuli, Gavi, youngish SÉM, DOLCETTO or BARBERA d'Alba.

with fungi porcini Finest mature Barolo or Barbaresco.

seafood A favourite dry white.

Nero A rich dry white: VIOGNIER or even Corton-Charlemagne.

Soufflés As show dishes these deserve ★★★ wines:

with cheese Mature red burgundy or B'x, CAB SAUV (not Chilean or Australian), etc. Or fine mature white burgundy.

with fish (esp smoked haddock with chive cream sauce) Dry white: ★★★ burgundy, B'x, Alsace, CHARD, etc.

with spinach (tough on wine) Mâcon-Villages, St-Véran or Valpolicella. Champagne (esp Vintage) can also spark things with the texture of a soufflé.

Fish

Abalone Dry or medium white: SAUV BL, unoaked CHARD. A touch of oak works with soy sauce, oyster sauce, etc. In Hong Kong: Dom Pérignon (at least).

Anchovies Fino, obviously. Franciacorta or Cava.

salade Niçoise Provence rosé.

Bocquerones VERDEJO, unoaked SÉM.

Bacalão Salt cod needs acidity: young Portuguese red or white. Or Italian ditto. Cider or cold beer work well.

Bass, sea Fine white, eg. Clare RIES, Chablis, white Châteauneuf, VERMENTINO from Sardinia, WEISSBURGUNDER from Baden or Pfalz. Rev the wine up for more seasoning, eg. ginger, spring onions; more powerful Ries, not necessarily dry.

Beurre blanc, fish with Deserves gd unoaked white with maturity: Hunter SEM, Premier Cru Chablis, CHENIN BL, RIES, Swartland white blend. Applies to most veg with beurre blanc too.

Caviar Iced vodka (and) full-bodied Champagne (eg. Bollinger, Krug). Don't (ever) add raw onion.

Ceviche Can be applied to anything now, but here, it's fish. Australian RIES or VERDELHO, Chilean SAUV BL, TORRONTÉS. Manzanilla.

Crab (esp Dungeness) and RIES together are part of the Creator's plan. But He also created Champagne.

Chinese, with ginger & onion German RIES Kabinett or Spätlese Halbtrocken. Tokaji FURMINT, GEWURZ.

cioppino SAUV BL; but West Coast friends say ZIN. Also California sparkling.

cold, dressed Top Mosel Ries, dry Alsace or Australian Ries or Assyrtiko.

crab cakes Any of the above.

softshell Unoaked CHARD, ALBARIÑO or top-quality German Ries Spätlese.

Cured fish Salmon can have a whisky cure, a beetroot cure; all have sweetness and pungency. With gravadlax, sweet mustard sauce is a complication. SERCIAL

Madeira (eg. 10-yr-old Henriques), Amontillado, Tokaji Szamarodni, orange wine. Or NV Champagne.

Curry S African CHENIN BL, Alsace PINOT BL, Franciacorta, fruity rosé, not too pale and anodyne; look at other flavours. Prawn and mango need more sweetness, tomato needs acidity. Fino can handle heat. So can IPA or Pilsner.

Fish pie (with creamy sauce) ALBARIÑO, Soave Classico, RIES Erstes Gewächs, Mâcon Blanc, Spanish GODELLO.

Grilled, roast or fried fish Also applies to **fish & chips, tempura, fritto misto, baked…**
cod, haddock CHARD, PINOT BL, MALVAZIJA; **plaice, flounder** Light, fresh whites.
Dover sole Perfect with fine wines: white burgundy or equivalent.
halibut, turbot, brill Best rich, dry white; top Chard, mature RIES Spätlese.
monkfish Meaty but neutral; full-flavoured white or red, according to sauce.
mullet, grey VERDICCHIO, unoaked Chard, rosé.
oily fish like **herrings, mackerel, sardines** More acidity, weight: ASSYRTIKO, VERDELHO, FURMINT, rosé.
perch, sandre Top white burgundy, Mosel, Grand Cru Alsace, mature top fizz.
red fish like **salmon, red mullet** PINOT N. For salmon, also best Chard, Grand Cru Chablis, top Ries.
skate, ray Delicate, but brown butter, capers need oomph: Alsace, ROUSSANNE, CHENIN BL.
swordfish Full-bodied dry white (or why not red?) of the country. Nothing grand.
trout Gd Chard, Furmint, Ries, Malvazija, Pinot N.
tuna Best served rare (or raw) with light red: young Loire CAB FR or red burgundy. Young Rioja is a possibility.
whitebait Crisp dry whites, eg. Furmint, Greek, Touraine SAUV BL, Verdicchio, white Dão, Fino Sherry, rosé. Or beer.

Ikan bakar This classic Indonesian/Malay grilled fish works well with GRÜNER V.

Kedgeree Full white, still or sparkling: Mâcon-Villages, S African CHARD, GRÜNER V, German Grosses Gewächs or (at breakfast) Champagne.

Lobster with a rich sauce Eg. Thermidor: Vintage Champagne, fine white burgundy, Cru Classé Graves, Roussanne, top Australian CHARD. Alternatively, for its inherent sweetness, Sauternes, Pfalz Spätlese, even Auslese.
plain grilled, or cold with mayonnaise NV Champagne, Alsace RIES, Premier Cru Chablis, Condrieu, Mosel Spätlese, GRÜNER V, Hunter SEM, or local fizz.

Mussels Marinière MUSCADET *sur lie*, Premier Cru Chablis, unoaked CHARD.
curried Alsace RIES or PINOT BL.

Paella, shellfish Full-bodied white or rosé, unoaked CHARD, ALBARIÑO, or GODELLO. Or local Spanish red.

Prawns, crayfish with garlic Keep the wine light, white, or rosé, and dry.
with mayonnaise Menetou-Salon or Reuilly.
with spices Up to and incl chilli, go for a bit more body, but not oak: dry RIES or Italian, eg. FIANO, Grillo. *See also* CURRY.

Sardines in saor Try top Prosecco, and I mean top.

Sashimi Koshu comes into its own here, either as orange or white, and can deal with wasabi and soy, within reason. Otherwise try white with body (Chablis Premier Cru, Alsace RIES) with white fish, PINOT N with red. Both need acidity. Simple Chablis can be too thin. If soy is involved, then low-tannin red (again, Pinot). Remember sake (or Fino).

Scallops An inherently slightly sweet dish, best with medium-dry whites.
in cream sauces German Spätlese, Montrachets or top Australian CHARD.
grilled or seared Hermitage Blanc, GRÜNER V, Pessac-Léognan Blanc, Vintage Champagne or PINOT N.
with Asian seasoning NZ Chard, CHENIN BL, GODELLO, Grüner V, GEWURZ.

Scandi fish dishes Scandinavian dishes often have flavours of dill, caraway, cardamom and combine sweet and sharp flavours. Go for acidity and some weight: FALANGHINA, GODELLO, VERDELHO, Australian, Alsace or Austrian RIES.

Shellfish Dry white with plain boiled shellfish, richer wines with richer sauces. RIES is the grape.

    plateaux de fruits de mer Chablis, MUSCADET de Sèvre et Maine, PICPOUL de Pinet, Alto Adige PINOT BL.

Smoked fish All need freshness and some pungency; Fino Sherry works with all.

    eel Often with beetroot, crème fraiche: Fino again, or Mosel RIES.

    haddock Gd Chablis, MARSANNE, GRÜNER V. *See also* SOUFFLÉS.

    kippers Try Oloroso Sherry or Speyside malt.

    mackerel Not wine-friendly. Try Fino.

    salmon Condrieu, Alsace PINOT GR, Grand Cru Chablis, German Ries Spätlese, Vintage Champagne, vodka, schnapps, or akvavit.

    trout More delicate: Mosel Ries.

Squid / octopus Fresh white: ALBARIÑO, MUSCADET, sparkling, esp with salt and pepper squid. Squid ink (risotto, pasta) needs Soave.

Sushi Hot wasabi is usually hidden in every piece. Koshu is 1st choice. Failing that, German QbA Trocken, simple Chablis, ALVARINHO or NV Brut Champagne or KOSHU. Obvious fruit doesn't work. Or, of course, sake or beer.

Tagine N African flavours need substantial whites to balance – Austrian, Rhône – or crisp, neutral whites that won't compete. Go easy on the oak. VIOGNIER or ALBARIÑO can work well.

Taramasalata A Med white with personality, Greek if possible. Fino Sherry works well. Try Rhône MARSANNE.

Teriyaki A way of cooking, and a sauce, used for meat as well as fish. Germans favour off-dry RIES with weight: Kabinett can be too light.

Meat / poultry / game

Barbecues The local wine: Australian, S African, Chilean, Argentine are right in spirit. Reds need tannin and vigour. Or the freshness of cru Beaujolais.

Beef (*see also* **Steak**) **boiled** Red: B'x (eg. Fronsac), Roussillon, Gevrey-Chambertin or Côte-Rôtie. Medium-ranking white burgundy is gd, eg. Auxey-Duresses. In Austria you may be offered skin-fermented TRAMINER. Mustard softens tannic reds, horseradish kills your taste; can be worth the sacrifice.

    roast An ideal partner for fine red of any kind. Even Amarone. *See* above for mustard. The silkier the texture of the beef (wagyu, Galician, eg.), the silkier the wine. Wagyu, remember, is about texture; has v. delicate flavour.

    stew, daube Sturdy red: Pomerol or St-Émilion, Hermitage, Cornas, BARBERA, SHIRAZ, Napa CAB SAUV, Ribera del Duero, or Douro red.

    stroganoff Dramatic red: Barolo, Valpolicella Amarone, Priorat, Hermitage, late-harvest ZIN. Georgian SAPERAVI or Moldovan Negru de Purkar.

Boudin blanc Loire CHENIN BL, esp when served with apples: dry Vouvray, Saumur, Savennières; mature red Côte de Beaune if without.

Boudin noir/morcilla Local SAUV BL or CHENIN BL (esp in Loire). Or Beaujolais cru, esp Morgon. Or light TEMPRANILLO. Or Fino.

Brazilian dishes Pungent flavours that blend several culinary traditions. Rhônish grapes work for red, or white with weight: VERDICCHIO, Californian CHARD. Or a Caipirinha (better not have two).

Cajun food Gutsy reds, preferably New World: ZIN, CARMENÈRE, SHIRAZ. Fish or white meat: off-dry RIES, MARSANNE, ROUSSANNE. Or, of course, cold beer.

Cassoulet Red from SW France (Gaillac, Minervois, Corbières, St-Chinian or Fitou) or SHIRAZ. But best of all Fronton, Beaujolais cru or young TEMPRANILLO.

Chicken / turkey / guinea fowl, roast Virtually any wine, incl v. best bottles of dry to medium white and finest old reds (esp burgundy). Sauces can make it match almost any fine wine (eg. coq au vin; the burgundy can be red or white, or *vin jaune* for that matter).

    chicken Kiev Alsace RIES, Collio, CHARD, Bergerac rouge.

    fried Sparkling works well.

Chilli con carne Young red: Beaujolais, TEMPRANILLO, ZIN, Argentine MALBEC, Chilean CARMENÈRE. Or beer.

Chinese dishes Food in China is regional – like Italian, only more confusing. It's easiest to have both white and red; no one wine goes with all. Peking duck is pretty forgiving. Champagne becomes a thirst quencher. Beer too.

    Cantonese Big, slightly sweet flavours work with slightly oaky CHARD, PINOT N, off-dry RIES. GEWURZ is often suggested but rarely works; GRÜNER V is a better bet. You need wine with acidity. Dry sparkling (csp Cava) works with textures.

    Shanghai Richer and oilier than Cantonese, not one of wine's natural partners. Shanghai tends to be low on chilli but high on vinegar of various sorts. German and Alsace whites can be a bit sweeter than for Cantonese. For reds, try MERLOT – goes with the salt. Or mature Pinot N, but a bit of a waste.

    Szechuan VERDICCHIO, Alsace PINOT BL, or v. cold beer. Mature Pinot N can also work; but *see* above. The Creator intended tea.

    Taiwanese LAMBRUSCO works with traditional Taiwan dishes if you're tired of beer.

Choucroute garni Alsace PINOT BL, PINOT GR, RIES, or lager.

Cold roast meat Generally better with full-flavoured white than red. Mosel Spätlese or Hochheimer and Côte Chalonnaise are v.gd, as is Beaujolais. Leftover Champagne too.

Confit d'oie / de canard Young, tannic red B'x, California CAB SAUV and MERLOT, Priorat cuts richness. Alsace PINOT GR or GEWURZ match it.

Coq au vin Red burgundy. Ideal: one bottle of Chambertin in the dish, two on the table. *See also* CHICKEN.

Dirty (Creole) rice Rich, supple red: N7 PINOT N, GRENACHE MA, BARRADA, MALBEC.

Duck / goose PINOT N is tops. Or rich white, esp for goose: Pfalz Spätlese or off-dry Grand Cru Alsace. With oranges or peaches, the Sauternais propose drinking Sauternes, others Monbazillac or RIES Auslese. Mature and weighty Vintage Champagne handles accompanying red cabbage surprisingly well. So does decent Chianti.

    Peking *See* CHINESE DISHES.

    roast breast & confit leg with Puy lentils Madiran (best), St-Émilion, Fronsac.

    wild duck Worth opening gd Pinot N. Austrian or Tuscan red (easy on the oak) is also gd.

    with olives Top-notch Chianti or other Tuscans.

Filipino dishes Spanish-influenced flavours, lots of garlic, bell peppers, adobo, not necessarily super-spicy. Fashionable in San Francisco and soon nr you. Straightforward unoaked white with acidity (adobo can have a burst of vinegar) or fizz, Côtes de Gascogne, Rueda, RIES, rosé, even light red.

Foie gras Sweet white: Sauternes, Tokaji Aszú 5 Puttonyos, late-harvest PINOT GR or RIES, Vouvray, Montlouis, Jurançon *moelleux*, GEWURZ. Old dry Amontillado can be sublime.

    hot Mature Vintage Champagne. But never CHARD, SAUV BL, or (shudder) red.

Game birds, young, roast The best red wine you can afford, but not too heavy. Partridge is more delicate than pheasant, which is more delicate than grouse. Up the weight of wine accordingly, starting with youngish PINOT N, BLAUFRANKISCH, SYRAH, GARNACHA, and moving up.

    cold game Best German RIES or mature Vintage Champagne.

older birds in casseroles Gevrey-Chambertin, Pommard, Châteauneuf, Dão, or Grand Cru Classé St-Émilion, Rhône.

well-hung game Vega Sicilia, great red Rhône, Ch Musar.

Game pie, hot Red: Oregon PINOT N, St-Émilion Grand Cru Classé.

cold Gd-quality white burgundy or German Erstes Gewächs, cru Beaujolais, or Champagne.

Goat (Hopefully kid). As for lamb.

Jamaican curry goat *See* INDIAN DISHES.

Goulash Flavoursome young red: Hungarian Kékoportó, ZIN, Uruguayan TANNAT, Douro red, MENCÍA, young Australian SHIRAZ, SAPERAVI. Or dry Tokaj Szamarodni.

Haggis Fruity red, eg. young claret, young Portuguese red, New World CAB SAUV or MALBEC or Châteauneuf. Or, of course, malt whisky.

Ham, cooked Softer red burgundies: Volnay, Savigny, Beaune; Chinon or Bourgueil; sweetish German white (RIES Spätlese); lightish CAB SAUV (eg. Chilean), or New World PINOT N. And don't forget the heaven-made match of ham and Sherry.

Hare Jugged hare calls for flavourful red: not-too-old burgundy or B'x, Rhône (eg. Gigondas), Bandol, Barbaresco, Ribera del Duero, Rioja Res. The same for saddle or for hare sauce with pappardelle.

Indian dishes Various options: dry Sherry is brilliant. Choose a fairly weighty Fino with fish, and Palo Cortado, Amontillado, or Oloroso with meat, according to weight of dish; heat's not a problem. The texture works too. Otherwise, medium-sweet white, v. cold, no oak: Orvieto *abboccato*, S African CHENIN BL, Alsace PINOT BL, TORRONTÉS, Indian sparkling, Cava or NV Champagne. Rosé is gd all-rounder. For tannic impact Barolo or Barbaresco, or deep-flavoured reds, ie. Châteauneuf, Cornas, Australian GRENACHE or MOURVÈDRE, or Valpolicella Amarone – will emphasize the heat. Hot-and-sour flavours need acidity.

Sri Lankan More extreme flavours, coconut. Sherry, rich red, rosé, mild white.

Japanese dishes A different set of senses come into play. Texture and balance are key; flavours are subtle. Gd mature fizz works well, as does mature dry RIES; you need acidity, a bit of body, and complexity. Dry FURMINT can work well. Umami-filled meat dishes favour light, supple, bright reds: Beaujolais perhaps, or mature PINOT N. Full-flavoured *yakitori* needs lively, fruity, younger versions of the same reds. KOSHU with raw fish – but why not sake? Orange Koshu with wagyu beef. *See also* SASHIMI, SUSHI, TERIYAKI.

Korean dishes Fruit-forward wines seem to work best with strong, pungent Korean flavours. PINOT N, Beaujolais, Valpolicella can all work: acidity is needed. Non-aromatic whites: GRÜNER V, SILVANER, VERNACCIA. Beer too.

Lamb, roast One of the traditional and best partners for v.gd red B'x, or its CAB SAUV equivalents from the New World. In Spain, finest old Rioja and Ribera del Duero Res or Priorat, in Italy ditto SANGIOVESE. Fresh mint is gd, but mint sauce should be banned.

milk-fed This is delicate and deserves top, delicate B'x, burgundy, or top (delicate) Spanish.

slow-cooked roast Flatters top reds, but needs less tannin than pink lamb. *See also* TAGINES.

Liver Young red: Beaujolais-Villages, St-Joseph, Médoc, Italian MERLOT, Breganze CAB SAUV, ZIN, Priorat, Bairrada.

calf's Red Rioja Crianza, Fleurie. Or a big Pfalz RIES Spätlese.

Mexican food Californians favour RIES: Calavera restaurant in Oakland lists 33 RIES, mostly German. Or beer.

Moussaka Red or rosé: Naoussa, SANGIOVESE, Corbières, Côtes de Provence, Ajaccio, young ZIN, TEMPRANILLO.

Mutton A stronger flavour than lamb, and not usually served pink. Needs a strong sauce. Robust red; top-notch, mature CAB SAUV, SYRAH. Sweetness of fruit (eg. Barossa) suits it.

'Nduja Calabria's spicy, fiery spreadable salumi needs a big, juicy red: young Rioja, Valpol, CAB FR, AGLIANICO, CARIGNAN, NERELLO MASCALESE.

Osso bucco Low-tannin, supple red such as DOLCETTO d'Alba or PINOT N. Or dry Italian white such as Soave.

Ox cheek, braised Superbly tender and flavoursome, this flatters the best reds: Vega Sicilia, St-Émilion. Best with substantial wines.

Oxtail Rather rich red: St-Émilion, Pomerol, Pommard, Nuits-St-Georges, Barolo, or Rioja Rcs, Priorat or Ribera del Duero, California or Coonawarra CAB SAUV, Châteauneuf, mid-weight SHIRAZ, Amarone.

Paella Young Spanish wines: red, dry white, or rosé: Penedès, Somontano, Navarra, or Rioja.

Pastrami Alsace RIES, young SANGIOVESE, or St-Émilion.

Pâté Chicken liver calls for pungent white (Alsace PINOT GR or MARSANNE), a smooth red eg. light Pomerol, Volnay, or NZ PINOT N. More strongly flavoured (duck, etc.) needs Gigondas, Moulin-à-Vent, Chianti Classico, or gd white Graves. Amontillado can be marvellous match.

Pigeon or squab PINOT N perfect; young Rhône, Argentine MALBEC, young SANGIOVESE. Try Franken SILVANER Spätlese. With luxurious squab, top quite tannic red.
  pastilla Depends on sweetness of dish. As above, or if authentically sweet, try RIES Spätlese, Alsace PINOT GR with some sweetness.

Pork A perfect rich background to a fairly light red or rich white.
  belly Slow-cooked and meltingly tender, needs red with some tannin or acidity. Italian would be gd: Barolo, DOLCETTO, or BARBERA. Or Loire red, or lightish Argentine MALBEC. With Chinese spices, VIOGNIER, CHENIN BL.
  Mangalica pork Fashionable, fatty. KÉKFRANKOS, or other brisk red.
  pulled Often with spicy sauce: juicy New World reds.
  roast Deserves ★★★ treatment: Médoc is fine. Portugal's suckling pig is eaten with Bairrada; S America's with CARIGNAN; Chinese is gd with PINOT N.
  with prunes or apricots Something sweeter. eg. Vouvray.

Pot au feu, bollito misto, cocido Rustic red wines from region of origin; SANGIOVESE di Romagna, Chusclan, Lirac, Rasteau, Portuguese Alentejo or Spain's Yecla or Jumilla.

Quail Succulent little chick deserves tasty red or white. Rioja Res, mature claret, PINOT N. Or mellow white: Vouvray, St-Péray.

Quiche Egg and bacon are not great wine matches, but one must drink something. Alsace RIES or PINOT GR, even GEWURZ, is classical. Beaujolais could be gd too.

Rabbit Lively, medium-bodied young Italian red, eg. AGLIANICO del Vulture, REFOSCO; Chiroubles, Chinon, Saumur-Champigny or Rhône rosé.
  as ragu Medium-bodied red with acidity: Aglianico, NEBBIOLO.
  with mustard Cahors.
  with prunes Bigger, richer, fruitier red.

Satay McLaren Vale SHIRAZ, Alsace or NZ GEWURZ. Peanut sauce: problem for wine.

Sauerkraut (German) German RIES, lager or Pils. (But see also CHOUCROUTE GARNI.)

Singaporean dishes Part Indian, part Malay and part Chinese, Singaporean food has big, bold flavours that don't match easily with wine – not that that bothers the country's many wine-lovers. Off-dry RIES is as gd as anything. With meat dishes, ripe and supple reds: Valpolicella, PINOT N, DORNFELDER, unoaked MERLOT, or CARMENÈRE.

Steak Rare steak needs brisker, more tannic reds; well-done needs juicy, fruity reds, eg. young Argentine MALBEC. Fattier cuts need acidity, tannin.
  au poivre A fairly young Rhône red or CAB SAUV. Nothing too sweetly fruity.

fillet Silky red: Pomerol or PINOT N.

Fiorentina (bistecca) Chianti Classico Riserva or BRUNELLO.

from older cattle Has deep, rich savouriness. Top Italian, Spanish red.

Korean *yuk whe* (world's best steak tartare) Sake.

ribeye, tomahawk, tournedos Big, pungent red: Barolo, Cahors, SHIRAZ, Rioja.

sirloin Suits most gd reds. B'x blends, Tuscans.

tartare Vodka or light young red: Beaujolais, Bergerac, Valpolicella. Aussies drink GAMAY with kangaroo tartare, charred plums, Szechuan pepper.

T-bone Reds of similar bone structure: Barolo, Hermitage, Australian CAB SAUV or Shiraz, Chilean SYRAH, Douro.

Wagyu Delicate, silky red, or orange wine.

Steak-&-kidney pie or pudding Red Rioja Res or mature B'x. Pudding (with suet) wants vigorous young wine. Madiran with its tannin is gd.

Stews & casseroles Burgundy such as Nuits-St-Georges or Pommard if fairly simple; otherwise lusty, full-flavoured red, eg. young Côtes du Rhône, BLAUFRÄNKISCH, Corbières, BARBERA, SHIRAZ, ZIN, etc.

Sweetbreads A rich dish, so grand white wine: Rheingau RIES or Franken SILVANER Spätlese, Grand Cru Alsace PINOT GR, or Condrieu, depending on sauce.

Tagines Depends on what's under the lid, but fruity young reds are a gd bet: Beaujolais, TEMPRANILLO, SANGIOVESE, MERLOT, SHIRAZ. Amontillado is great. Amarone is fashionable.

chicken with preserved lemon, olives VIOGNIER.

Tandoori chicken RIES or SAUV BL, young red B'x or light n Italian red served cool. Also Cava and NV Champagne, or, of course, Palo Cortado or Amontillado Sherry.

Thai dishes Ginger and lemon grass call for pungent SAUV BL (Loire, Australia, NZ, S Africa) or RIES (Spätlese or Australian). Most curries suit aromatic whites with a touch of sweetness: GEWURZ also gd.

Tongue Gd for any red or white of abundant character. Alsace PINOT GR or GEWURZ, gd GRÜNER V. Also Beaujolais, Loire reds, BLAUFRÄNKISCH, TEMPRANILLO and full, dry rosés.

Veal A friend of fine wine. Rioja Res, CAB blends, PINOT N, NEBBIOLO, German or Austrian RIES, Vouvray, Alsace PINOT GR, Italian GRECO di Tufo.

Venison Big-scale reds, incl MOURVÈDRE, solo as in Bandol or in blends. Rhône, Languedoc, B'x, NZ Gimblett Gravels or California CAB SAUV of a mature vintage; or rather rich white (Pfalz Spätlese or Alsace PINOT GR).

with sweet & sharp berry sauce Try a German Grosses Gewächs RIES, or Chilean CARMENÈRE, or SYRAH.

Vietnamese food RIES, dry or up to Spätlese, German, Austrian, NZ, also GRÜNER V, SÉM. For reds, PINOT N, CAB FR, BLAUFRÄNKISCH.

Vitello tonnato Full-bodied whites: CHARD. Light reds (eg. Valpolicella) served cool. Or a southern rosé.

Wild boar Serious red: top Tuscan or Priorat. NZ SYRAH. I've even drunk Port; Amarone would be a compromise.

Vegetable dishes
With few tannins to help or hinder, matching wine to veg is about sweetness, acidity, weight and texture. *See also* FIRST COURSES.

Agrodolce Italian sweet-and-sour, with pine kernels, sultanas, capers and vinegar, and perhaps anchovies. This points to fresh white: VERDICCHIO, unoaked CHARD. Or orange.

Artichokes Not great for wine. Incisive dry white: NZ SAUV BL; Côtes de Gascogne or Greek (precisely, 4-yr-old MALAGOUSIA, but easy on the vinaigrette); VERMENTINO.

Orange wine, yes; red no, unless you absolutely have to, in which case go for acidity: LAGREIN, DOLCETTO.

Asparagus is lightly bitter, and needs acidity, if it needs wine at all, which is debatable. RIES is classic; SAUV BL (or English Bacchus) echoes the flavour. Unoaked young SÉM or CHARD, esp Australian; Chard gd with melted butter, hollandaise. Dry MUSCAT, or Jurançon Sec. Argument for trying a really sweet wine too, maybe not Yquem.

Aubergine Comes in a multitude of guises, usually pungent. Sturdy reds with acidity are a gd bet: SHIRAZ, Greek, Lebanese, Bulgarian, Hungarian, Turkish. Structured white, eg. VERDICCHIO, or go further and have orange wine.

Avocado Not a wine natural. Dry to slightly sweet RIES Kabinett will suit the dressing. Otherwise, light and fresh: ALIGOTÉ, TREBBIANO, PINOT GRIGIO.

Beetroot Mimics a flavour found in red burgundy. You could return the compliment. New-wave (ie. light) GRENACHE/GARNACHA is gd, as well, as is Gamay.

Cauliflower roast, etc. Go by the other (usually bold) flavours. Try Austrian GRÜNER V, Valpolicella, NZ PINOT N.

    cauliflower cheese Crisp, aromatic white: Sancerre, RIES Spätlese, MUSCAT, ALBARIÑO, GODELLO. CHARD too, and Beaujolais-Villages.

    with caviar – yes, really. Vintage Champagne.

Celeriac, slow-roast or puréed Won't interfere with rest of dish. Acidity works well, so classic CAB blends, Beaujolais, PINOT N, according to dish.

    remoulade with smoked ham Needs bright red: DOLCETTO, simple GAMAY, Valpolicella. Or white GRÜNER V.

Chestnuts In a slow-cooked daube or as purée, look for earthy, rich red: Tuscan or S Rhône.

Chickpeas Look at other flavours. Casserole works with TEMPRANILLO, S French reds.

    hummus Any simple red, pink or white, or, of course, Fino.

Chilli Some like it hot, but not with your best bottles. Tannic wines become more tannic; if you like that, go for it. Light, fruity reds and whites are refreshing: TEMPRANILLO, Chilean MERLOT, NZ SAUV BL. Same for harissa. *See also* MEAT/CHILLI CON CARNE, CHINESE DISHES, INDIAN DISHES.

Couscous with vegetables Young red with a bite: SHIRAZ, Corbières, Minervois; rosé; orange wine; Italian REFOSCO or SCHIOPPETTINO.

Dhal Comes with many variations, but all share aromatic earthiness. Simple, warm-climate reds work best: CARMENÈRE, Dão, s Italian.

Fennel-based dishes SAUV BL: Pouilly-Fumé or NZ; SYLVANER or English SEYVAL BL; or young TEMPRANILLO. Deeply flavoured braised fennel is gd with light GAMAY, PINOT N.

Fermented foods *See also* SAUERKRAUT, CHOUCROUTE GARNI, KOREAN DISHES. *Kimchi* and *miso* are being worked into many dishes. Fruit and acidity are generally needed. If in sweetish veg dishes, try Alsace.

Grilled Mediterranean vegetables Italian whites, or for reds Brouilly, BARBERA, TEMPRANILLO or SHIRAZ.

Lentil dishes Sturdy reds such as Corbières, ZIN or SHIRAZ. *See also* DHAL.

Macaroni cheese As for CAULIFLOWER CHEESE.

Mushrooms (in most contexts) A boon to most reds and some whites. Context matters as much as species. Pomerol, California MERLOT, Rioja Res, top burgundy or Vega Sicilia.

    button or Paris with cream Fine whites, even Vintage Champagne.

    ceps / porcini Ribera del Duero, Barolo, Chianti Rúfina, Pauillac or St-Estèphe, NZ Gimblett Gravels.

    on toast Best claret, even Port.

Onion / leek tart / flamiche Fruity, off-dry or dry white: Alsace PINOT GR or GEWURZ is classic; Canadian, Australian or NZ RIES; Jurançon. Or Loire CAB FR.

Peppers, cooked Mid-weight Rhône grapes, CARMENÈRE, Rioja; or ripe SAUV BL (esp with green Hungarian wax peppers).

    stuffed Full-flavoured red, white, or pink: Languedoc, Greek, Spanish. Or orange.

Pickled foods & vinegar Vinegar and wine don't go, it's true, but pickled foods are everywhere. Try Alsace, German RIES with CHOUCROUTE/SAUERKRAUT. With pickled veg as part of a dish, just downgrade the wine a bit (no point in opening best bottles) and make sure it has some acidity. (Or have beer.) In dressings, experiment with vinegars: Sherry vinegar can work with Amontillado, etc., big reds; Austrian apricot vinegar is delicate; balsamic can work with rich Italian reds. Wine just has to work harder than it used to.

Pumpkin / squash ravioli or risotto Full-bodied, fruity dry or off-dry white: VIOGNIER or MARSANNE, demi-sec Vouvray, Gavi or S African CHENIN. For red: MERLOT, ZIN.

Radicchio , in a salad Eg. with cold game, points towards brisk, acid reds: NEBBIOLO, LAGREIN, or white VERMENTINO.

    roast This is easier: Valpolicella, SANGIOVESE, BLAÜFRANKISCH.

Ratatouille (or Piperade) Vigorous young red: Chianti, NZ CAB SAUV, MERLOT, MALBEC, TEMPRANILLO, Languedoc. Or gd rosé.

Roasted root veg Sweet potatoes, carrots, etc., often mixed with eg. beetroot, cabbage, garlic, onions and others have plenty of sweetness. Rosé, esp with some weight, or orange wine. Pesto will tilt it towards white.

Saffron Found in sweet and savoury dishes, and wine-friendly. Rich white: ROUSSANNE, VIOGNIER, PINOT GR. Orange wines can be gd too. With desserts, Sauternes or Tokaji. *See also* MEAT/TAGINES.

Salsa verde Whatever it's with, it points to more acidity, less lushness in the wine.

Seaweed (Nori) Depends on the context. *See also* SUSHI. Iodine notes go well with Austrian GRÜNER V, RIES.

Sweetcorn fritters Often served with a hot, spicy sauce. Rosé, orange or neutral white all safe.

Tahini Doesn't really affect wine choice. Go by rest of dish.

Tapenade Manzanilla or Fino Sherry, or any sharpish dry white or rosé. Definitely not Champagne.

Truffles Black truffles are a match for finest Right Bank B'x, but even better with mature white Hermitage or Châteauneuf. White truffles call for best Barolo or Barbaresco of their native Piedmont. With buttery pasta, Lugana. Or at breakfast, on fried eggs, BARBERA.

Watercress, raw Makes every wine on earth taste revolting.

Wild garlic leaves, wilted Tricky: a fairly neutral white with acidity will cope best.

Desserts

Apple pie, strudel, or tarts Sweet German, Austrian or Loire white, Tokaji Aszú, or Canadian Icewine.

Apples Cox's Orange Pippins with Cheddar cheese Vintage Port.

    Russets with Caerphilly Old Tawny, or Amontillado.

Bread-&-butter pudding Fine 10-yr-old Barsac, Tokaji Aszú, Australian botrytized SEM.

Cakes *See also* CHOCOLATE, COFFEE, RUM. BUAL or MALMSEY Madeira, Oloroso or Cream Sherry. Asti, sweet Prosecco.

Cheesecake Sweet white: Vouvray, Anjou, or Vin Santo – nothing too special.

Chocolate Don't try to be too clever. Texture matters. BUAL, California Orange MUSCAT, Tokaji Aszú, Australian Liqueur Muscat, 10-yr-old Tawny or even young Vintage Port; Asti for light, fluffy mousses. Or VDN Banyuls, Maury or Rivesaltes. Some like Médoc with bitter black chocolate, though it's a bit of a waste of both. A trial of Syrah with bitter chocolate showed that you shouldn't, ever. Armagnac, or a tot of gd rum.

Christmas pudding, mince pies Tawny Port, Cream Sherry or that liquid Christmas pudding itself, PEDRO XIMÉNEZ Sherry. Tokaji Aszú. Asti, or Banyuls.

Coffee desserts Sweet MUSCAT, Australia Liqueur Muscats, or Tokaji Aszú.

Creams, custards, fools, syllabubs See also CHOCOLATE, COFFEE, RUM. Sauternes, Loupiac, Ste-Croix-du-Mont or Monbazillac.

Crème brûlée Sauternes or Rhine Beerenauslese, best Madeira, or Tokaji Aszú.

Ice cream and sorbets Give wine a break.

Lemon flavours For dishes like tarte au citron, try sweet RIES from Germany or Austria or Tokaji Aszú; v. sweet if lemon is v. tart.

Meringues (eg. Eton Mess) Recioto di Soave, Asti or sweet Vintage Champagne.

Nuts (incl praliné) Finest Oloroso Sherry, Madeira, Vintage or Tawny Port (nature's match for walnuts), Tokaji Aszú, Vin Santo, or Setúbal MOSCATEL. Cashews and Champagne. Pistachios with Fino. **Salted nut parfait** Tokaji Aszú, Vin Santo.

Orange flavours Experiment with old Sauternes, Tokaji Aszú, or California Orange MUSCAT.

Panettone Vinsanto. Jurançon *moelleux*, late-harvest RIES, Barsac, Tokaji Aszú.

Pears in red wine Rivesaltes, Banyuls, or RIES Beerenauslese.

Pecan pie Orange MUSCAT or Liqueur Muscat.

Raspberries (no cream, little sugar) Excellent with fine reds that themselves taste of raspberries: young Juliénas, Regnié. Even better with cream and something in the Sauternes spectrum.

Rum flavours (baba, mousses) MUSCAT – from Asti to Australian Liqueur, according to weight of dish.

Strawberries, wild no cream With red B'x (most exquisitely Margaux) poured over. **with cream** Sauternes or similar sweet B'x, Vouvray *moelleux*, or Vendange Tardive Jurançon.

Summer pudding Fairly young Sauternes of a gd vintage.

Sweet soufflés Sauternes or Vouvray *moelleux*. Sweet (or rich) Champagne.

Tiramisú Vin Santo, young Tawny Port, MUSCAT de Beaumes-de-Venise, Sauternes, or Australian Liqueur Muscat. Better idea: skip the wine.

Trifle Should be sufficiently vibrant with its internal Sherry (Oloroso for choice).

Zabaglione Light-gold Marsala or Australian botrytized SEM, or Asti.

Wine & cheese

Counter-intuitively, white is a safer option than red. Fine red wines are slaughtered by strong cheeses. Principles to remember (despite exceptions): first, the harder the cheese, the more tannin the wine can have; second, the creamier the cheese, the more acidity is needed in the wine – and don't be shy of sweetness. Cheese is classified by its texture and the nature of its rind, so its appearance is a guide to the type of wine to match it.

Bloomy-rind soft cheeses: Brie, Camembert, Chaource Full, dry white burgundy or Rhône.

Blue cheeses The extreme saltiness of Roquefort or most blue cheeses needs sweetness: Sauternes, Tokaji, youngish Vintage or Tawny Port, esp with Stilton. Intensely flavoured old Oloroso, Amontillado, Madeira, Marsala and other fortifieds go with most blues. Dry red does not. Trust me.

Cooked cheese dishes fondue Trendy again. Light, fresh white as above.

    frico Traditional in Friuli. Cheese baked or fried with potatoes or onions; high-acid local REFOSCO (r), or RIBOLLA GIALLA (w).

    macaroni or cauliflower cheese See VEGETABLE DISHES/CAULIFLOWER.

    Mont d'Or Delicious baked, and served with potatoes. Fairly neutral white with freshness: GRÜNER V, Savoie.

Fresh cream cheese, fromage frais, mozzarella Light crisp white: Chablis, Bergerac, Entre-Deux-Mers; juicy rosé can work too.

Hard cheeses – Gruyère, Manchego, Parmesan, Cantal, Comté, old Gouda, Cheddar Hard to generalize, relatively easy to match. Gouda, Gruyère, some Spanish, and a few English cheeses complement fine claret or CAB SAUV and great SHIRAZ/SYRAH. But strong cheeses need less refined wines, preferably local ones. Granular old Dutch red Mimolette, Comté or Beaufort gd for finest mature B'x. Also for Tokaji Aszú. But try tasty whites too.

Natural rind (mostly goats' cheese) – St-Marcellin Sancerre, light SAUV BL, Jurançon, Savoie, Soave, Italian CHARD; or young Vintage Port.

Semi-soft cheeses – Livarot, Pont l'Evêque, Reblochon, Tomme de Savoie, St-Nectaire Powerful white B'x, even Sauternes, CHARD, Alsace PINOT GR, dryish RIES, S Italian and Sicilian whites, aged white Rioja, dry Oloroso Sherry. The strongest of these cheeses kill almost any wines. Try marc or Calvados.

Washed-rind soft cheeses – Langres, mature Époisses, Maroilles, Carré de l'Est, Milleens, Münster Local reds, esp for Burgundian cheeses; vigorous Languedoc, Cahors, Côtes du Frontonnais, Corsican, S Italian, Sicilian, Bairrada. Also powerful whites, esp Alsace GEWURZ, MUSCAT. Gewurz with Munster, always.

Food & your finest wines

With v. special bottles, the wine guides the choice of food rather than vice versa. The following is based largely on gastronomic conventions, some bold experiments and much diligent and ongoing research.

Red wines

Amarone Classically, in Verona, risotto all'Amarone or pastissada. But if your butcher doesn't run to horse, then shin of beef, slow-cooked in more Amarone.

Barolo, Barbaresco Risotto with white truffles; pasta with game sauce (eg. pappardelle alla lepre); porcini mushrooms; Parmesan.

Great Syrahs: Hermitage, Côte-Rôtie, Grange; Vega Sicilia Beef, venison, well-hung game; bone marrow on toast; English cheese (Lincolnshire Poacher) but also hard goats' milk and ewes' milk cheeses such as England's Lord of the Hundreds. I treat Côte-Rôtie like top red burgundy.

Great Vintage Port or Madeira Walnuts or pecans. A Cox's Orange Pippin and a digestive biscuit is a classic English accompaniment.

Red Bordeaux v. old, light, delicate wines, (eg. pre-59) Leg or rack of young lamb, roast with a hint of herbs (not garlic); entrecôte; simply roasted (and not too well-hung) partridge; roast chicken never fails.

    fully mature great vintages (eg. 59 61 82 85) Shoulder or saddle of lamb, roast with a touch of garlic; roast ribs or grilled rump of beef.

    mature but still vigorous (eg. 89 90) Shoulder or saddle of lamb (incl kidneys) with rich sauce. Fillet of beef marchand de vin (with wine and bone marrow). Grouse. Avoid beef Wellington: pastry dulls the palate.

Merlot-based Beef (fillet is richest) or well-hung venison. In St-Émilion, lampreys.

Red burgundy Consider the weight and texture, which grow lighter and more velvety with age. Also the character of the wine: Nuits is earthy, Musigny flowery, great Romanées can be exotic, Pommard is renowned for its four-squareness. Roast chicken or (better) capon is a safe standard with red burgundy; guinea fowl for slightly stronger wines, then partridge, grouse, or woodcock for those progressively more rich and pungent. Hare and venison (chevreuil) are alternatives.

    great old burgundy The Burgundian formula is cheese: Époisses (unfermented); a fine cheese but a terrible waste of fine old wines. *See* above.

vigorous younger burgundy Duck or goose roasted to minimize fat. Or faisinjan (pheasant cooked in pomegranate juice). Coq au vin, or lightly smoked gammon.

Rioja Gran Reserva, Top Duero reds Richly flavoured roasts: wild boar, mutton, saddle of hare, whole suckling pig.

White wines

Beerenauslese / Trockenbeerenauslese Biscuits, peaches, greengages. But TBAs don't need or want food.

Condrieu, Château-Grillet, Hermitage Blanc Pasta, v. light, scented with herbs, tiny peas or broad beans. Or v. mild tender ham. Old white Hermitage loves truffles.

Grand Cru Alsace Gewurz Cheese soufflé (Münster cheese).

> **Pinot Gr** Roast or grilled veal. Or truffle sandwich (slice a whole truffle, make a sandwich with salted butter and gd country bread – not sourdough or rye – wrap and refrigerate overnight. Then toast it in the oven. Thanks, Dom Weinbach).
>
> **Ries** Truite au bleu, smoked salmon, or choucroute garni.
>
> **Vendange Tardive** Foie gras or tarte tatin.

Old Vintage Champagne (not Blanc de Blancs) As an apéritif, or with cold partridge, grouse, woodcock. The evolved flavours of old Champagne make it far easier to match with food than the tightness of young wine. Hot foie gras can be sensational. Don't be afraid of garlic or even Indian spices, but omit the chilli.

> **late-disgorged old wines** have extra freshness plus tertiary flavours. Try with truffles, lobster, scallops, crab, sweetbreads, pork belly, roast veal, chicken. Saffron is flattering to old Champagne.
>
> **old Vintage Rosé** Pigeon, veal.

Sauternes Simple crisp buttery biscuits (eg. langues de chat), white peaches, nectarines, strawberries (without cream). Not tropical fruit. Pan-seared foie gras. Lobster or chicken with Sauternes sauce. Ch d'Yquem recommends oysters (and indeed lobster). Experiment with blue cheeses. Rocquefort is classic, but needs one of the big Sauternes.

Tokaji Aszú (5–6 puttonyos) Foie gras recommended. Fruit desserts, cream desserts, even chocolate can be wonderful. Roquefort. It even works with some Chinese, though not with chilli – the spice has to be adjusted to meet the sweetness. Szechuan pepper is gd. Havana cigars are splendid. So is the naked sip.

Top Chablis White fish simply grilled or *meunière*. Dover sole, turbot, halibut are best; brill, drenched in butter, can be excellent. (Sea bass is too delicate; salmon passes but does little for the finest wine.)

Top white burgundy, top Graves, top aged Ries Roast veal, farm chicken stuffed with truffles under the skin, or sweetbreads; richly sauced white fish (turbot for choice) or scallops, white fish as above. Lobster, wild salmon.

Vouvray moelleux, etc. Buttery biscuits, apples, apple tart.

Fail-safe face-savers

Some wines are more useful than others – more versatile, more forgiving. If you're choosing restaurant wine to please several people, or just stocking the cellar with basics, these are the wines: **Red** Alentejo, BARBERA d'Asti/d'Alba, BLAUFRÄNKISCH, Beaujolais, Chianti, GRENACHE/ GARNACHA if not overextracted/overoaked, young MALBEC (easy on the oak), PINOT N, SYRAH (more versatile than Shiraz), Valpolicella. **White** Alsace PINOT BL, ASSYRTIKO, cool-climate CHARD, CHENIN BL from the Loire or S Africa, Fino Sherry, GRÜNER V, dry RIES, Sancerre, gd Soave, VERDICCHIO. Always go for the best producer you can afford, and don't get too hung up on appellations or even vintages, within reason. If you can't afford gd Chablis, buy Assyrtiko, not cheap Chablis.

France

More heavily shaded areas are
the wine-growing regions.

Abbreviations used in the text:

Al	Alsace
Beauj	Beaujolais
Burg	Burgundy
B'x	Bordeaux
Cas	Castillon-Côtes de Bordeaux
Chab	Chablis
Champ	Champagne
Cors	Corsica
C d'O	Côte d'Or
Fron	Fronsac
L'doc	Languedoc
Lo	Loire
Mass C	Massif Central
Prov	Provence
N/S Rh	Northern/Southern Rhône
Rouss	Roussillon
Sav	Savoie
SW	Southwest
AC	appellation contrôlée
ch, chx	château(x)
dom, doms	domaine(s)

Reading this book, it's obvious that nobody needs to buy French wine. What does France make, these days, that other countries can't do as well? There is great Chardonnay from New Zealand and California; great Syrah from South Africa: fabulous Garnacha/Grenache from Spain or Australia; great sparkling from England, Spain and many others; Bordeaux blends from many, many places. France has more competition at all levels than it has ever had before. The excitement, you could argue, has moved elsewhere.

Yet the classic regions of France, for most consumers, remain the touchstone. Pinot is judged by how closely it approaches the precision and detail of great red burgundy; Chardonnay ditto for white. Refer to a wine as a "Bordeaux blend", as we do, and you are making its allegiance clear; the same goes for "Rhône blends". The lawyers of Champagne have removed all reference to that region in any description of the technique of making any other sparkling wine, but the model is clear as soon as you taste.

But France is not above following other countries' fashions. Bordeaux obediently became bigger and richer, sometimes too much so, in the race

France entries also cross-reference to Châteaux of Bordeaux

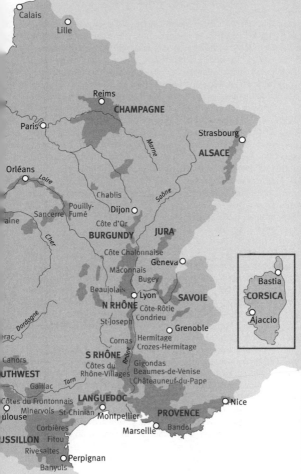

to please an American critic; now it has returned to what it does best. Some Rhône wines can be similarly afflicted. Burgundy has a different problem: in hot summers, when ripeness moves up several notches, the wines can taste like something from further south. Crowd-pleasing, but disturbing to lovers of a cooler style. In these years, if you want a really stony Chablis style, you might need to look at the Jura. France has some tricks up its sleeve yet, but we might have to look for them.

Recent vintages of the French classics

Red Bordeaux

Médoc / Red Graves For many wines, bottle-age is optional: for these it is indispensable. Minor chx from light vintages may need only 1 or 2 yrs these days, but even modest wines of gd yrs can improve for 10 or so, and the great chx of these yrs can profit from double that time.

2020 Cab Sauv rich, dark, expressive. High alc but elegance prevails. Merlot, Petit Verdot gd too. Low yields due to small berries (hot, dry summer).

2019 Great balance; concentration but freshness as well. A high percentage of Cab Sauv in blends. Potential to age.

2018 Pure, aromatically intense Cab Sauv. Rich, powerful (alcs high) but balance there. Long-term potential, but yields uneven due to mildew, hail.

2017 Attractive wines: gd balance, fairly early drinking. Volumes often small.

2016 Cab Sauv with colour, depth, structure. Vintage to look forward to.

2015 Excellent Cab Sauv yr, but not structure of 05 10. Some variation. Keep.

2014 Cab Sauv bright, resonant. Gd to v.gd; classic style, beginning to open.

2013 Worst since 92. Patchy at Classed Growth level. For early drinking.

2012 Difficulties ripening Cab Sauv but early drinking charm. Don't reject.

2011 Mixed quality, better than its reputation. Classic freshness, moderate alc. After an awkward phase, opening up.

2010 Outstanding. Magnificent Cab Sauv, deep-coloured, concentrated, firm. Keep for yrs.

Fine vintages: 09 08 06 05 00 98 96 95 90 89 88 86 85 82 75 70 66 62 61 59 55 53 49 48 47 45 29 28.

St-Émilion / Pomerol

2020 Merlot rich and gourmand. Cabs Fr/Sauv also v.gd. Great potential.

2019 Drought. Merlot excellent on limestone, clay soils. Suffered on sandier reaches.

2018 Powerful but pure. Best from limestone, clay soils. Yields affected by mildew.

2017 Gd balance, classic fruit-cake flavours. Will be quite early drinking.

2016 Conditions as Méd. Some young vines suffered in drought but overall excellent.

2015 Great yr for Merlot. Perfect conditions. Colour, concentration, balance.

2014 More rain than the Méd so Merlot variable. V.gd Cab Fr. Drinking now.

2013 Difficult flowering (so tiny crop), rot in Merlot. Modest yr, early drinking.

2012 Conditions as Méd. Merlot marginally more successful. Drinking now.

2011 Complicated, as Méd. Gd Cab Fr. Pomerol best overall? Don't shun it.

2010 Outstanding. Powerful wines, high alc. Concentrated. Time in hand.

Fine vintages: 09 05 01 00 98 95 90 89 88 85 82 71 70 67 66 64 61 59 53 52 49 47 45.

Red Burgundy

Côte d'Or Côte de Beaune reds generally mature sooner than grander wines of Côte de Nuits. Earliest drinking dates are for lighter commune wines, eg. Volnay, Beaune; latest for GCs, eg. Chambertin, Musigny. Even the best burgundies are more attractive young than equivalent red B'x. It can seem magical when they really blossom yrs later.

2020 V. small crop of concentrated wines – remains to be seen about their balance.

2019 Lush, luxurious with many great wines, a few are too high octane. Best will age effortlessly.

2018 Set to be a legend but watch out for some overripe or flawed wines – those apart, many brilliant sumptuous reds, should drink well young or old.

2017 Survived frosts! Big crop, attractive wines, mostly ripe enough, stylish lighter wines, slight preference for Côte de Nuits.

2016 Short, frosted crop but some spectacular reds with great energy, fresh acidity. Keep them locked away though.

2015 Dense, concentrated wines, as 05, but with the additional juiciness of 10. Earning stellar reputation; don't miss. Lesser appellations attractive now.

2014 Beaune, Volnay, Pommard hailed once again. Attractive fresh reds, some wines lack depth. Take a look soon.

2013 Destined to be overlooked after succession of fine vintages to follow. Côte de Beaune tricky after hail but some stars in Côte de Nuits, esp GCs. Lesser wines ready.

2012 Côte de Beaune gd where not hail damaged. Fine quality if small crop in Côte de Nuits, exuberant yet classy. Has been overlooked – time to dig these out of storage.

2011 Some parallels with 07. Early harvest, lighter wines, now accessible. Gd to go now.

2010 Turning into great classic: pure, fine-boned yet also with impressive density. Village wines and some PCs open for business.

Fine vintages: (drink or keep) 09 05 02 99 96 93 (mature) 90 89 85 78 76 71 69 66 64 62 59.

White Burgundy

Côte d'Or White wines are now rarely made for ageing as long as they were in the past, but top wines should still improve for 10 yrs or more. Most Mâconnais and Chalonnais (St-Véran, Mâcon-Villages, Montagny) usually best drunk early (2–3 yrs).

2020 Better crop than reds in volume, quality. Looks thrilling if acidity holds up.

2019 Great vintage if you are comfortable with richer style, as most have retained balance. Structure is great, aromatics riper.

2018 Saved by size of crop in a hot yr. More potential than first thought. Delicious from start yet with power to age.

2017 Modern classic, now becoming v. interesting. Ripe, balanced, consistent wines with enough acidity. Save best appellations, enjoy rest.

2016 Small, frosted crops, inconsistent results. Approach with caution.

2015 Rich, concentrated; warm, dry summer. Most picked early have done well, later wines may be too heavy. Similar to 09 but more successes.

2014 Finest, most consistent vintage for generation. White fruit flavours, elegant, balanced. Start drinking, but make sure to keep best for later.

2013 Rot affected, should be drunk up.

2012 Clean, classic; crisp finish. Holding up nicely but mostly approachable.

2011 Gd wines from conscientious producers, some flesh, gd balance. Attractive early, start drinking up.

Fine vintages (all ready): 10 09 08 07 05 02 99 96 93 92 85 79 73 59.

Chablis GC Chab of vintages with both strength and acidity really need at least 5 yrs, can age superbly for 15 or more; PCs proportionately less, but give them 3 yrs at least. Then, for the full effect, serve them at cellar temperature, not iced, and decant them. Yes, really.

2020 May have been too hot and too dry for some vyds. Fingers crossed.

2019 Small crop of concentrated wine: typical marine Chab, with exotic notes.

2018 Vintage of century for volume: attractive quality, will be ready soon. But 17 even better.

2017 Despite frost again, classical style, much more exciting than 16. Gaining in stature, keep if you can.

2016 Hail, frost, more hail, hardly any wine, often unbalanced. Move along.

2015 Hot, dry summer; rich, ripe wines with concentrated core. Keep GCs.

Fine vintages: 12 10 08 02 00.

Beaujolais

20 Frighteningly early harvest but v. promising quality. 19 Hot dry summer after early frost, should be gd. 18 Hot summer, but some exciting and well-balanced wines. 17 Large crop but hideous hail in Fleurie, Moulin-à-Vent. 16 Large crop of juicy wines, unless hailed (Fleurie). 15 Massive wines, best outstanding, others alc monsters.

SW France

2020 Summer heatwave, drought. A little uneven maybe, but in general, a gd and occasionally exceptional yr.

2019 Spring storms brought havoc, esp Bergerac. Heatwave summer rescued what was left. Small crop, fine quality.

2018 Big yr. Dry white mostly ready 2020. Most reds (esp oaked) and sweet whites 2021 on. Heftier styles will need longer.

2017 Subtler yr than most. Excellent drinking 2021. Madiran, Cahors will keep.

2016 Satisfactory rather than brilliant; won't last much longer except big reds.

2015 Marvellous full, fruity yr. Sweet whites, big reds will keep for many yrs.

Languedoc-Roussillon

2020 Summer not too hot, lovely balanced wines with gd acidity, freshness. Rouss small vintage, gd quality.

2019 Hot dry summer; some sunburn. Gd to v.gd, but small vintage.

2018 Mildew, but best are vibrant (r/w). Pic St-Loup: powerful, rich, v.gd reds.

2017 Small, spring frost, v.gd: Rouss possibly better than 15; Cabardes (r) balanced, will age, (w) acidity, fruit.

2016 Generally excellent. Reds balanced, will age; whites fresh, fruity.

Northern Rhône

Depending on site and style, can be as long-lived as burgundies. White Hermitage can age as red. Hard to generalize, but don't be in a hurry (r or w).

2020 Best: v.gd; another v. hot, dry summer. Côte-Rôtie convincing, Hermitage gd, Cornas gd fruit. Top whites, esp if Marsanne-based, v.gd.

2019 Tremendous reds, highish degrees, flair at Côte-Rôtie; tannins well absorbed, like 16 with more stuffing, acidity slightly better than 18. Whites concentrated, sunswept, NB Hermitage, St-Joseph.

2018 V.gd; scaled up reds; yr for top terroirs, which beat climate. V. rich Hermitage (r), similar Côte-Rôtie. Crozes variable. Whites v. successful: depth, surprising freshness. NB Condrieu, Hermitage, St-Péray.

2017 V.gd, esp Côte-Rôtie. Full reds, deeper than 16, show sunshine, packed-in, firm tannins, so need time. Whites for hearty food, Condrieu variable.

2016 Gd–v.gd, reds harmonious, tinkling, classic at Côte-Rôtie. NB Cornas, Crozes-Hermitage reds. Marvellous Hermitage whites, other whites gd, clean.

2015 Excellent, v. concentrated reds everywhere, lots of tannin, wonderful, v. long-lived Hermitage, Côte-Rôtie. Time essential. Full whites, can be heady.

2014 Juicy reds, have gained depth over time. Excellent whites: content, style, freshness.

2013 V.gd reds, with tight body, crisp tannin, freshness. Best still closed in 2021. 20–25 yrs life. Exceptional whites (Hermitage, St-Joseph, St-Péray).

2012 V.gd Hermitage, open-book Côte-Rôtie. Fresh reds come together well, will last 15 yrs+. Whites have style, freshness.

2011 Gd Hermitage, Cornas. Côte-Rôtie more body recently. Whites satisfactory.

Southern Rhône

2020 Gd but variable, needs selection. Best (esp gd terroirs): rich, full, gd
    acidity, shrugged off drought. Whites tricky from less gd zones, so stick
    to main names, places.

2019 V.gd across board. Deep Grenache, savoury fullness, embedded tannins.
    Châteauneuf back on form, Gigondas excellent. Top names will demand
    patience. Whites v.gd, full-bodied.

2018 Mixed, can be gd: cherry-pick. Shocking crop loss in Châteauneuf, esp
    organic. Note, Valréas, Visan, Vinsobres: higher, later vyds. Also Lirac,
    Rasteau. V. full whites.

2017 V.gd, but can be variable. Full, bold reds, but tannins can be chewy from
    drought. Most strict top doms did best. Gd Rasteau, Visan. Full whites.

2016 Wonder yr, excellent for all (Châteauneuf, old-vines Grenache triumph).
    Sensuous reds: fruit bonanza, masses of life. Sun-filled whites; keep
    some to mature.

2015 V.gd: rich, dark, lots of body, firm tannins, often enticing flair. Quality
    high across board (Gigondas). V.gd, full whites.

2014 Gd in places, aromatic finesse returns to Châteauneuf. Stick to best
    names. NB Gigondas, Rasteau, Cairanne. Fresh whites.

2013 Tiny crop. Sparky, vibrant, slow-burn reds, v. low Grenache yields: atypical
    wines. Châteauneuf best from old vines. V.gd, long-lived whites.

2012 Dashing reds, lively, gd tannins. Open-book vintage. Food-friendly whites.

2011 Sunny, supple, can be fat, drink quite soon. Alc issue. Decent whites.

Champagne

2020 Warm summer; mid-August harvest, large crop. 18 19 20 make
    miraculous trio. Top doms in Côte des Blancs waited until start of Sept
    for full maturity, phenolic ripeness.

2019 Small crop, v.gd quality. Fresher wines, pure fruit, tension, better acidity
    than much-lauded 18.

2018 Huge crop. Best in Pinot GCs of N Montagne. Chard more mixed: heat
    stress, some lowish acidity.

2017 Rain: Chard on Côte des Blancs the saviour. Athletic wines of grace, energy.

2016 Underrated. Gently expressive Pinot Ns give much pleasure.

2015 Hot yr. Some wines are sweaty with blurred aromas; others are little
    triumphs, eg. new mid-priced Bollinger based on 15.

2014 Suzuki fruit fly plagued black grapes. Gd ripe yr for rich Chard.

2013 Picked Oct; more complex flavours. Excellent Chard, Salon back on form.
    NB Deutz 13 Blanc de Blancs.

Fine vintages: 12 10 09 08 07 06 04 02 00 98 96 95 92 90.

The Loire

2020 Incredible 7th successive v.gd yr. Early vintage – gd quality, quantity.

2019 Well-balanced wines but volume down, esp Muscadet, Anjou – April frost.

2018 Exceptional quality, esp reds. Gd sweet, less enthusiasm for dry whites.
    Some comparing with 47.

2017 Gd quality, April frosts again. Bourgueil, Menetou-Salon, Sancerre spared.

2016 Low quantity (April frosts), but quality gd for those who still had a crop.
    Sancerre spared.

Alsace

2020 May be most refined, elegant, scented across board, as growers master
    climate change.

2019 Hot; e-facing hills, esp GCs, may be v.gd, ripe, dry (Ries, Pinot Gr, Gewurz). Wines from plains could be a problem.

2018 Warm, but fresh wines. Gewurz, Pinot Gr, Ries tops in high altitude GCs.

2017 One of best since World War Two, but small crop. Recalls 71 08.

2016 Poised, finely balanced vintage and plenty of it, unlike 13 14 15.

2015 Rich vintage, one of driest ever. Great Pinot Gr; little volume but ripe, still fresh Sylvaner.

2014 Gewurz, Pinot Gr attacked by Suzuki fruit fly. Ries, Sylvaner winners.

Fine vintages: 12 10 08 07 04 02 96 95 92 90.

Abelé, Henri Champ ★★★ New name for Abel Lepitre, oldest house, now focusing on exports. Best CUVÉE Sourire de Reims **12 15**, new Sourire Rosé 15 voluptuous, from Les Riceys (AUBE), expansive burgundian style. Gd value.

Abymes Sav ★→★★ Limestone zone, S Chambéry, steep slopes, by APREMONT. DYA Vin de SAV AC cru. Jacquère grape (80% min) Try: A et M Quenard, des Anges, Labbé, Perrier, R Berlioz, Ravier.

AC or AOC (Appellation Contrôlée) / AOP Government control of origin and production (but not quality) of most top French wines; around 45% of total. Now being converted to AOP (Appellation d'Origine Protegée – which is much nearer the truth than Contrôlée).

Agenais SW Fr ★ DYA IGP of Lot-et-Garonne. Beautiful country, best for Vieille Prune spirit. Simple wines from wide choice of SW grape varieties. A few DOMS (eg. Boiron, Campet, Lou Gaillot).

Agrapart Champ ★★★★ Pascal A makes fine-drawn CHAMP from scrupulously tended vyds. Real focus on terroir. Fine top Avizoise 10 **17'**.

Allemand, Thierry N Rh ★★★★ 90' 91' 95' 99' 01' 05' 06' 07' 08' 09' 10' 12' 13' 15' 16' 17' 18' 19' 20 Offbeat, talented owner, compelling CORNAS from organic 5-ha DOM, low sulphur. Two v. deep, rocky wines, v. high prices. Top is Reynard (profound, complex; 20 yrs+), Chaillot (bursting fruit, floral) drinks earlier.

Alliet, Philippe Lo ★★★ 14' 15' 16 17' 18' **19'** 20' Excellent CHINON. Tradition, VIEILLES VIGNES and two steep s-facing vyds e of Chinon: Coteau de Noiré (top CUVÉE), L'Huisserie. Tiny amount Chinon white.

Aloxe-Corton Burg ★★→★★★ 05' 09' 10' 12' 15' **17** 18' 19' 20' N end of CÔTE DE BEAUNE, famous for GC CORTON, CORTON-CHARLEMAGNE, but less interesting at village or PC level. Reds attractive if not overextracted. Recent warm vintages have softened tannins. Best DOMS: Follin-Arbelet, Rapet, Senard, TOLLOT-BEAUT.

Alsace ★★→★★★★ Sheltered e slope of Vosges and 1800 sun hrs make France's Rhine wines: aromatic, fruity, full, drier styles back in vogue. More emphasis on rich diversity of terroirs, esp in wines for ageing, eg. RIES up to 20 yrs (esp 10' **17' 18** 19). Most sold by variety. *See* VT, SGN.

Alsace Grand Cru Al ★★★→★★★★ 08' 10' 12 13 14 (esp RIES) **15 17'** 18 '19 20' Restricted to 51 of best-named vyds (approx 1600 ha, 800 in production) and four noble grapes (PINOT GR, Ries, GEWURZ, MUSCAT). GC rules require greater min ripeness. Local management specifies extra rules for each cru. Plan afoot for PC in gd sites. Great houses (eg. LÉON BEYER, TRIMBACH) now embrace GC status.

Amirault, Yannick Lo ★★★→★★★★ 15' 16' 17' 18' 19' (20) Yannick and son Benoît. Organic. Top BOURGUEIL/ST NICOLAS DE BOURGUEIL. Best: La Mine (St Nicolas), La Petite CAVE, Le Grand Clos, Les Quartiers (Bourgueil). Small parcel of CHENIN BL

Angerville, Marquis d' C d'O ★★★★ Bio superstar in VOLNAY, not just classy but classical too, esp legendary CLOS des Ducs (MONOPOLE). Enjoy Champans, Taillepieds as well. *See also* DOM DU PÉLICAN for Jura interests.

Anjou Lo ★→★★★★ Region and AC: ANJOU, SAUMUR. mainly CHENIN BL dry whites, juicy reds, incl GAMAY; fruity CAB FR-based Anjou Rouge; robust tannic ANJOU-VILLAGES,

CAB FR/CAB SAUV. Mainly dry SAVENNIÈRES; lightly sweet to rich COTEAUX DU LAYON Chenin Bl; rosé (dr and s/sw), esp CABERNET D'ANJOU, sparkling mainly CRÉMANT. Big natural wine movement often VDF.

Anjou Blanc Lo ★→★★★★ 17' 18' 19' 20' Increasingly important, exciting AOP for dry white; 20% CHARD and/or SAUV BL can used with CHENIN BL, but best pure Chenin. From quaffers to complex, v.gd, long-lived (esp sites in Layon, even QUARTS DE CHAUME): sweet difficult to sell. Future crus/Anjou Villages Blanc? Best: Bablut, Baudouin, BELARGUS, Bergerie, CADY, Delesvaux, Forges, Juchepie, Leroy (VDF), Ogereau, Passavant, PIERRE-BISE, Plaisance, Terra Vita Vinum.

Anjou-Coteaux de la Loire Lo ★★→★★★ 17 18' Tiny (15 producers) AOP: sweet CHENIN BL of Angers; esp CH de Putille, Delaunay, Fresche, Musset-Roullier.

Anjou-Villages Lo ★→★★★ 14' 15' 16' 17' 18' 19' (20') Structured red AC (CAB FR/ CAB SAUV, a few pure Cab Sauv). Can be tannic; needs ageing. Best: Bergerie, Branchereau, Brizé, CADY, CH PIERRE-BISE, CLOS de Coulaine, Delesvaux, Ogereau, Sauveroy, Soucherie. Sub-AC Anjou-Villages-Brissac same zone as COTEAUX DE L'AUBANCE; look for Bablut, CH de Varière, Fontaines, Haute Perche, Montigilet, Princé, Richou – now Terra Vita Vinum.

Aphillanthes, Dom Les S Rh ★★→★★★ 16' 17 18' 19' Organic, bio DOM in PLAN DE DIEU, punchy, terroir wines, value. Two CUVÉES: des Galets, VIEILLES VIGNES (50S GRENACHE). RASTEAU 1921; CÔTES DU RH-VILLAGES 3 CÉPAGES (r); CÔTES DU RH (r).

Apremont Sav ★★ Largest cru of SAV, just s of Chambéry. Crisp Jacquère whites on limestone. Keep up to 5 yrs. Try: 13 Lunes, Cavagna, Dacquin, Dupaz, Masson, Perrier, Ravier, Richel, Viallet.

Arbin Sav ★★ SAV cru. Dark, spicy MONDEUSE. Drink to 8 yrs+. Try: *l'Idylle*, Magnin, *Mérande, P Grisard*, Quenard, Trosset.

Arbois Jura ★★→★★★ 10' 12 14' 15' 16 18' 19 AC of n Jura, great spot for wine, cheese, walking and Louis Pasteur museum. CHARD, and/or SAVAGNIN whites, VIN JAUNE, reds from Poulsard, Trousseau or PINOT N. Try terroir-true Stephane TISSOT, fresh *ouillé* styles from DOM DU PÉLICAN, oxidative (*typés*) whites from Overnoy/Houillon, plus all-rounders AVIET, Pinte, Renardières, Rolet.

Ardèche S Rh ★→★★ 17' 18 19' IGP Rocky granite hills w of Rh, fewer wines, growers preferring looser VDF status. Quality up, often gd value. Fresh, clear reds, some oaked (pity): VIOGNIER (eg. CHAPOUTIER, Mas de Libian), MARSANNE. Best from SYRAH, also GAMAY (often old vines), CAB SAUV (Serret). Restrained, burgundy-style Ardèche CHARD by LOUIS LATOUR (Grand Ardèche too oaky). CH de la Selve; DOMS de Vigier, du Grangeon, Flacher, JF Jacouton; Mas d'Intras (organic).

Arjolle, Dom de l' L'doc ★★★ Large Côtes de Thongue family-run estate. Range incl Equilibre, Equinoxe, Paradoxe, varietals and blends, and two original VDF: Z for ZIN, K for CARMENÈRE.

Arlaud C d'O ★★★→★★★★ Leading MOREY-ST-DENIS estate energized by Cyprien A and siblings. Beautifully poised, modern wines with depth, class from exceptional BOURGOGNE Roncevie up to GCS. Fine range of Morey PCS, esp Ruchots.

Arlay, Ch d' Jura ★★★ Historic producer with imposing CH, 25 ha vyds, best wine VIN JAUNE.

Arlot, Dom de l' C d'O ★★→★★★ AXA-owned estate; stylish, fragrant wines across the range from HAUTES-CÔTES to GC ROMANÉE-ST-VIVANT. Star buy is NUITS CLOS des Forêts St-Georges.

Armand, Comte C d'O ★★★★ Graceful POMMARD? Try MONOPOLE CLOS des Epeneaux for ageless wine. Gd value from AUXEY, VOLNAY too.

Arnoux-Lachaux C d'O ★★★★ New star in VOSNE-ROMANEE. All change under Charles Lachaux, viticulture, vinification, quality, price. Ethereal wines of v. highest order.

Aube CHAMP's S vyds, aka Côte des Bar – v.gd PINOT N by great Reims houses eg. KRUG, VEUVE CLICQUOT. Aube 11' excels.

Aubert et Matthieu L'doc ★★★ New, go-ahead NÉGOCIANT started by two friends. From best L'DOC terroirs eg. LA LIVINIÈRE, TERRASSES DU LARZAC. Hors Piste IGP. CHARD, PINOT N from cooler areas. Sustainable, eco-packaging, striking labels.

Aupilhac, Dom d' L'doc ★★★ Sylvain Fadat, pioneer of MONTPEYROUX, cultivates s-facing old-vine MOURVÈDRE, old-vine CARIGNAN as well as n-facing, higher-altitude SYRAH and whites on Mt Baudile for Les Cocalières.

Auxey-Duresses C d'O ★★→★★★ (r) 15' 16 17 18' 19' 20' (w) 14' 15' 17' 18 19' 20' CÔTE DE BEAUNE village in valley behind MEURSAULT, enjoying global warming. Similar *whites offer value*, reds now ripen properly. Best: (r) COCHE-DURY, COMTE ARMAND, d'Auvenay (Les Boutonniers), Gras, Paquet, Prunier; (w) Diconne, Lafouge, LEROUX, Paquet, Vincent.

Aveyron SW Fr ★ IGP DYA. Quaffing wines from Roquefort country. Try DOMS Bertau, Bias.

Aviet, Lucien Jura ★★ Fine ARBOIS grower, nicknamed Bacchus – not after the grape, presumably. Gd value, eg. attractive light Poulsard and tangy SAVAGNIN.

Avize Champ ★★★★ Côte des Blancs GC CHARD, home to finest growers AGRAPART, Bonville, SELOSSE, Thienot. Huge co-op Union CHAMP provides base wines to biggest houses. Its *Pierre Vaudon* brand is worth seeking out.

Aÿ Champ Revered PINOT N village, home of BOLLINGER, DEUTZ. Mix of merchants and growers' wines, some in barrel (eg. Claude Giraud, master of Argonne oak), some in tanks. *Gosset-Brabant* Noirs d'Aÿ excels. Aÿ Rouge (AC COTEAUX CHAMPENOIS) now excellent in ripe yrs (esp 15' 18'). Wines typically have weight, power, even rare CHARDS.

Ayala Champ Reborn AŸ house, owned by BOLLINGER. Fine BRUT Zéro, BLANC DE BLANCS; ace Perlé d'Ayala 08' 12' 15' 16 17'. Precision, purity. Energy under Caroline Latrive, chef de CAVE: her debut the 160th Anniversary Collection 07' from seven GCS, majority CHARD (67%), low dosage.

Bachelet Burg ★★→★★★★ Widespread family name in S c D'O. Look out for: B-Monnot (esp BÂTARD-MONTRACHET, PULIGNY), Bernard B (Maranges), Jean-Claude B (CHASSAGNE, ST-AUBIN, etc.). No relation to Denis B (great GEVREY-CHAMBERTIN).

Bandol Prov ★★★ Top reds of Prov, for ageing. MOURVÈDRE, plus GRENACHE, CINSAULT. Real personality; different styles from limestone or clay soil. Rosé now main production; can be v. pale, Prov-style, or gutsier from Mourvèdre. Some white: CLAIRETTE, UGNI BL, occasionally SAUV BL. Tops: DOMS de la Bégude, du Gros'Noré, La Bastide Blanche, Lafran Veyrolles, La Suffrène, Mas de la Rouvière, *Pibarnon*, Pradeaux, *Tempier*, Terrebrune, Vannières.

Banyuls Rouss ★★→★★★ Undervalued (magic word) VDN, oxidized or not, from GRENACHE of all colours. Young, fresh style is *rimage*, but stars are RANCIOS, long-aged, pungent, intense. Try with chocolate. Best: DOMS du Mas Blanc, la Rectorie, la Tour Vieille, Madeloc, Vial Magnères; Coume del Mas, Les Clos de Paulilles. *See also* MAURY.

Barbier, Christopher L'doc ★★★ Aka M. BOURBOULENC: shows what this underrated grape can do, in maritime vyds nr LA CLAPE. DOM de Simonet IGP, unoaked, gd value. Les Terres Salées, oaked, keep 5 yrs for full glory. Terres Salées red succeeds with MERLOT where most L'DOC growers struggle. Competent La Clape under CH Bouïsset label.

Baronne, La L'doc ★★★ Innovative Lignières family own large CORBIÈRES estate. Bio, min intervention, amphorae, concrete eggs; presses all the buttons. Alaric, Les Chemins, Les Lanes and (CARIGNAN planted 1892) Pièce de Roche. IGP Hauterive. Sulphur-free Les Chemins de Traverse, and excellent VDF Grenache Gr.

Barrique A B'X (and Cognac) term for oak barrel holding 225 litres. Fashion now dictates more subtle oak, used more subtly. Average price €750/barrel.

Barsac Saut ★★→★★★★ 05 09' 11' 13 14 15' 16' 18 19 (20) Neighbour of SAUT with v. similar botrytized wines from lower-lying limestone soil; fresher, less powerful. Top: *Climens*, COUTET, DOISY-DAËNE, *Doisy-Védrines*. Value: Cantegril, La Clotte Cazalis, Liot.

Barthod, Ghislaine C d'O ★★★→★★★★ A reason to fall in love with CHAMBOLLE-MUSIGNY, if you haven't already. Wines of perfume, delicacy yet depth, concentration. Unbeatable range of 11 different PCS, incl Charmes, Cras, Fuées, Les Baudes. Son Clément now in charge, expect continuity.

Bâtard-Montrachet C d'O ★★★★ 08′ 09′ 10 12 14′ 15 17′ 18 19′ 20′ 12-ha GC downslope from LE MONTRACHET. Grand, hefty wines that should need time; more power than neighbours BIENVENUES-B-M and CRIOTS B-M. Seek out: BACHELET-Monnot, BOILLOT (both H and JM), CARILLON, FAIVELEY, GAGNARD, LATOUR, LEFLAIVE, LEROUX, MOREY, OLIVIER LEFLAIVE, PERNOT, Ramonet, SAUZET, VOUGERAIE.

Baudry, Dom Bernard Lo ★★→★★★ 16′ 17′ 18′ 19′ 20′ Mixed soils: sand, gravel and limestone. V.gd CHINONS, from CAB FR (r/rosé), CHENIN BL too; drink Les Granges early; CLOS Guillot, Croix Boissée, Les Grézeaux. Organic. Mathieu B in charge. Ageable.

Baudry-Dutour Lo ★★→★★★ 18′ 19′ 20′ CHINON's largest producer. Run by J-M Dutour and Christophe Baudry. Big, reliable range: light to age-worthy (r/w). CHX de la Grille, de la Perrière, de St Louans (r/w), du Roncée; l'ainsi fait, 3 Coteaux (w) IGP SAUV BL.

Baumard, Dom des Lo ★★ ˙★★★ 17′ 18′ 19′ 20′ ANJOU DOM, best known for CHENIN BL, incl CLOS Ste Catherine, Quarts de Chaume, SAVENNIÈRES (Clos du Papillon, Clos St Yves).

Baux-de-Provence, Les Prov ★★→★★★ Stunning, touristy village, centre of AC, almost all organic/bio. White: CLAIRETTE, GRENACHE BL, Rolle, ROUSSANNE. Red: CAB SAUV, SYRAH, GRENACHE. TRÉVALLON best, prefers IGP Alpilles. Others: Dalmeran, d'Estoublon, DOM Hauvette, Gourgonnier, Lauzieres, Mas de Carita, Mas de la Dame, Mas Ste Berthe, Romanin, Terres Blanches, Valdition, atypical Milan.

Béarn SW Fr AOP (r) ★→★★ 18 19 (20) (w/rosé) DYA. Reds from ★ JURANÇON co-op, DOMS Lapeyre Guilhémas. Same grapes as MADIRAN and Jurançon. Rarities such as Ruffiat de Moncade grape worth looking up.

Beaucastel, Ch de S Rh ★★★★ 90′ 95′ 99′ 05′ 06′ 07′ 09′ 10′ 12′ 13′ 15′ 16′ 17′ 18 19′ 20 Large, organic CHÂTEAUNEUF estate, classic galet stone soils: old MOURVÈDRE, 100-yr-old ROUSSANNE. Dark-fruited, recently more polished wines, overt elegance, drink at 2 yrs or from ′7–8. Intense, top-quality 60% Mourvèdre Hommage à Jacques Perrin (r). Wonderful, complex old-vine Roussanne: enjoy over 5–25 yrs. Genuine, stylish, deep own-vines CÔTES DU RH Coudoulet de Beaucastel (r), lives 10 yrs i. Famille Perrin GIGONDAS (v.gd), RASTEAU, VINSOBRES (best) all gd, authentic. Note organic Perrin Nature Côtes du Rh (r/w). Growing N Rh merchant venture, Maison Les Alexandrins (elegant). (*See also* Tablas Creek, California.)

Beaujolais ★ DYA. Basic appellation of huge Beauj region. A love-or-hate wine: love for its simple fresh fruit, best from growers in hills. Dislike overcropped industrial examples. Can now be sold as COTEAUX BOURGUIGNONS.

Beaujolais Primeur / Nouveau Beauj More of an event than a drink. The BEAUJ of the new vintage, hurriedly made for release at midnight on the 3rd Wednesday in Nov. Enjoy juicy fruit but don't let it put you off real thing.

Beaujolais-Villages Beauj ★★ 15′ 17 18′ 19′ 20′ Challenger vyds to the ten named crus, eg. MOULIN-À-VENT. May specify best village, eg. Lantigné. Try CH de Basty, Ch des Vergers, F Berne, F Forest, JM BURGAUD, N Chemarin. Some do B-V Nouveau too.

Beaumes-de-Venise S Rh ★★ (r) 09′ 10′ 12′ 13′ 15′ 16′ 17′ 18 19′ (MUSCAT) DYA. Village nr GIGONDAS, mix high and plain vyds, noted for VDN Muscat apéritif/dessert. Serve v. cold: grapey, honeyed, eg. DOMS Beaumalric, Bernardins (complex, traditional), Coyeux, Durban (rich, long life), Fenouillet (brisk), JABOULET, Perséphone (stylish), Pigeade (fresh, v.gd), VIDAL-FLEURY, co-op Rhonéa. Also robust, smoky, grainy reds. CH Redortier, Doms Cassan, Durban, de Fenouillet, la Ferme St-Martin (organic), les Baies Gouts, Mathiflo, St-Amant (gd w). Leave for 2–3 yrs. Simple whites (some dry Muscat, VIOGNIER).

Beaumont des Crayères Champ ★★★ Bijou co-op nr Épernay for top MEUNIER; now international brand. Fleur de Prestige top value 18' 19' 20'; CHARD-led CUVÉE Nostalgie 10. New Fleur de Meunier BRUT Nature 12' 15 18' 20'.

Beaune C d'O ★★★ 05' 09' 10' 11 12 14 15' 16 17 18' 19' 20 Centre of Burgundy wine trade, classic merchants: BOUCHARD, CHANSON, DROUHIN, JADOT, LATOUR; and more recent contenders Bernstein, Lemoine, LEROUX, Pacalet. Top DOMS: Bellène, Besancenot, Croix, DE MONTILLE, Dominique LAFON, plus iconic HOSPICES DE BEAUNE. Graceful, perfumed PC reds offer value, eg. Bressandes, Cras, VIGNES Franches; more power from Grèves. Try Aigrots, CLOS St-Landry and esp *Clos des Mouches (Drouhin)* for whites.

Beauregard, Ch de Burg ★★→★★★ Exceptional range of unmissable POUILLY-FUISSÉ from Frédéric Burrier. Try Les Reisses, Ménétrières, Vers Cras. Fine BEAUJ too: FLEURIE, MOULIN-À-VENT.

Becker, Caves J Al ★★★ Stylish wines, incl poised, taut GC Froehn in Zellenberg, prime RIES country. Exceptional 17'; contrast with Ries GC Mandelberg 18'. Ripe *Sylvaner* 18 20'. Bio precepts of extra freshness defend wines against acute climate change.

Bee, Dom of the Rouss ★★★ Justin Howard-Sneyd MW farms "4 ha of nectar" nr MAURY. Bee-side GRENACHE gd value. Les Genoux single-vyd, 100-yr-old vines the bee's knees.

Belargus, Dom Lo ★★★→★★★★ 18' 19 (20) High-quality, exciting bio DOM owned by Ivan Massonnat, incl Pithon-Paillé ANJOU, QUARTS DE CHAUME, SAVENNIÈRES. Mainly dry CHENIN from single vyds, esp steep, iconic Clos des Treilles.

Bellet Prov ★★ Diminutive (70 ha) AC within city of Nice. Gd Rolle white, age-worthy. Red from Folle Noire (DYA), Braquet for rosé. CH de Bellet best; also Ch de Cremat, Collet de Bovis; DOMS de la Source, de Toasc, Via Julia Augusta. CLOS St-Vincent v. highly regarded.

Bellivière, Dom de Lo ★★→★★★★ 18' 19' 20' COTEAUX DU LOIR, JASNIÈRES, Pineau d'Aunis (r) from Eric, Christine, son Clément. Les Arches de Bellivière (NÉGOCIANT).

Bergerac SW Fr ★→★★★★ 15' 17 18 19 (20) AOP. More continental climate produces fuller-bodied wines. Côtes de Bergerac for sweet whites or fuller reds from lower yields. Huge variations in styles, quality. Best from ★★★ *Tour des Gendres*, DOM de l'Ancienne Cure, ★★ CH de la Jaubertie, Moulin Caresse, Thénac, Tirecul La Gravière. *See* sub-AOPs MONBAZILLAC, MONTRAVEL, PÉCHARMANT, ROSETTE, SAUSSIGNAC.

Berthet-Bondet, Jean Jura ★★ Biggest producer (still small) of CH-CHALON VIN JAUNE but reliably covers all bases for Jura red, white and CRÉMANT. COTES DU JURA tradition v.gd value.

Bertrand, Gérard L'doc ★★→★★★★ Ex-rugby player grower-NÉGOCIANT, covering most of L'DOC at all prices. Lots of bio. Flagship: CH l'Hospitalet (LA CLAPE) with top Hospitalis. Aspirational, expensive CLOS d'Ora (MINERVOIS-LA LIVINIÈRE). Also zero-sulphur Prima Nature, Villemajou (CORBIÈRES cru Boutenac), l'Aigle (LIMOUX), v.gd Sauvageonne rosé TERRASSES DU LARZAC, Cabrières (ultra-premium CLOS du Temple rosé), Ch de la Soujeole (Malepère). IGP Dom Cigalus and numerous brands eg. Code Rouge fizz, Hampton Water Rosé celebrity hook-up with Jon Bon Jovi.

Besserat de Bellefon Champ ★★ Épernay house specializing in gently sparkling CHAMP (old CRÉMANT style). Part of LANSON-BCC group. Respectable quality, gd value, esp 13 14 17' (tiny but excellent). Opulent flavours in trio 18 19 20.

Beyer, Léon Al ★★★★ Top family house, arch-traditionalists delivering intense, dry gastronomic wines listed by many Michelin-starred restaurants. Best, and calling card, is lovely RIES Comtes d'Eguisheim 17', a true great for long life. With climate change, PINOT N better and better; succulent 18', finesse in 20'.

Bichot, Maison Albert Burg ★★→★★★★ Major BEAUNE merchant/grower with BIO DOMS in BEAUJOLAIS (Rochegrès), CHABLIS (LONG-DEPAQUIT), MERCUREY (Adélie), NUITS (CLOS Frantin), POMMARD (Pavillon); v. sound source with increasing flair.

Bienvenues-Bâtard-Montrachet C d'O ★★★→★★★★ 04 07 08 09 10 12 14' 15 17' 18 19' 20' Fractionally lighter version of BÂTARD, more initial grace, super-succulence. Best: BACHELET, CARILLON, FAIVELEY, LEFLAIVE, PERNOT, Ramonet, VOUGERAIE.

Billaud Chab ★★★→★★★★ Difficult CHAB choice between DOM Billaud-Simon back on form under FAIVELEY ownership and Samuel B's sensational wine under his own label. Both brilliant.

Billecart-Salmon Champ ★★★★ Revered family house with 7th-generation head and gifted young chef de CAVE ensure on-going top quality. New innovative long lees-aged Billecart No.1, 100% MEUNIER extra BRUT, pure, generous, tense. CUVÉE Louis BLANC DE BLANCS 07 ready, will keep. Superb CLOS St-Hilaire 98, ace 02'. NF Billecart, summit of range, perhaps greatest 02; excellent underrated 07'. Elisabeth Salmon Rosé 08 great value.

Bize, Simon C d'O ★★★ Chisa B makes sensational BIO whole-bunch-style reds at all levels from BOURGOGNE to gd cru LATRICIERES-CHAMBERTIN. Look out for SAVIGNY Grands Liards, Guettes Vergelesses and tasty whites too.

Blagny C d'O ★★→★★★★ 05' 09' 10' 12 14 15' 16' 17 18' 19' 20' Hamlet on hillside above MEURSAULT and PULIGNY. Own AC for austere yet fragrant reds, diminishing volumes. Whites sold as Meursault-Blagny PC. Best vyds: La Jeunelotte, Pièce Sous le Bois, Sous le Dos d'Ane. Best growers: (r) Lamy-Pillot, LEROUX, Matrot; (w) de Cherisey, JOBARD, LATOUR, LEFLAIVE, Matrot.

Blanc de Blancs Any white wine made from white grapes only, esp CHAMP. Description of style, not quality.

Blanc de Noirs White (or slightly pink or "blush", or "gris") wine from red grapes, esp CHAMP: can be solid in style, but many now more refined; better PINOT N and new techniques.

Blanck, Paul & Fils Al ★★★→★★★★ Old family of growers at Kientzheim. Now among best in Haut-Rhin. Finest from 6-ha GC Furstentum (RIES, GEWURZ, PINOT GR), sumptuous GC SCHLOSSBERG (great Ries 17' 18'). Excellent Classique generics: tiptop, great value. Lovely MUSCAT 18, chemical free, terroir driven.

Blanquette de Limoux L'doc ★★ Crisp, appley fizz, pretty, fun; 90% Mauzac plus CHARD, CHENIN BL. AC CRÉMANT de LIMOUX, more classic with Chard, Chenin Bl, PINOT N, and less Mauzac. Gd rosé too. Sieur d'Arques co-op is biggest, gd enough. Also **Antech**, Delmas, **Laurens**, RIVES-BLANQUES, Robert; several newcomers – DOMS Jo Riu, La Coume-Lumet, Les Hautes Terres, Monsieur S.

Blaye B'x ★→★★★ 14 15 16 17 19 (20) Designation for better reds (lower yields, higher vyd density, longer maturation) from AC BLAYE-CÔTES DE B'X.

Blaye-Côtes de Bordeaux B'x ★→★★ 14 15 16' 17 19 (20) Mainly MERLOT-led red AC on right bank of Gironde. A little dry white (mainly SAUV BL). Best CHX: Bel Air la Royère, Cantinot, des Tourtes, Gigault (CUVÉE Viva), Haut-Bertinerie, Haut-Grelot, Jonqueyres, Magdeleine Bouhou, Monconseil-Gazin, Mondésir-Gazin, Montfollet, Peybonhomme Les Tours, Roland la Garde, Ste-Luce Bellevue. Also go ahead VIGNERONS de Tutiac co-op for whites and reds.

Boeckel, Dom Al ★★★ VIGNERONS since 1600s; DOM started 1853, 23 ha, organic. RIES Wibbelsberg, CLOS Eugenie is rich, rounded 15; may be better still in 18. Zotzenberg unique GC for top *Sylvaner*, Ries truly great in 17', so elegant in 19, 20 to come. V.gd CRÉMANT.

Boillot C d'O Leading Burgundy family. Look for ★★★ Jean-Marc (POMMARD), esp fine, long-lived whites; ★★→★★★★ Henri (MEURSAULT), potent, stylish (r/w); ★★★ Louis (CHAMBOLLE) for great reds from both Côtes, and his brother Pierre (DOM Lucien B) ★★→★★★ (GEVREY). Marthe Henry B (Meursault) no close relation makes interesting post-modern wines.

Boisset, Jean-Claude Burg Ultra-successful merchant/grower group created over last 50 yrs. Boisset label from amazing new winery in NUITS and esp own vyds *Dom de la Vougeraie* excellent. Recent additions to empire: (Burg) brands Alex Gambal, VINCENT GIRARDIN. Also projects in California (Gallo connection), Canada, Chile, Uruguay.

Boizel Champ ★★★ Exceptional value, rigorous quality, family run. Well-aged BLANC DE BLANCS NV, esp on base of 13' 17'. CUVÉE Sous Bois purity without overwoodiness. Prestige Cuvée Joyau de France, esp Rosé 12 will drink sublimely 2021–22.

Bollinger Champ ★★★★ Great classic house, ever better, more tension. BRUT Special NV singing since 2012; RD 04; Grande Année 08 12'. PINOT N-led, innovative Vintage Rosé 06 powerful, with high 30% of Côte aux Enfants rouge (14). New special small CUVÉES showing new faces of Pinot N villages; fine PN VZ 15 fairly priced. *See also* LANGLOIS-CH.

Bonneau du Martray, Dom C d'O (r) ★★★ (w) ★★★★ Reference producer for CORTON-CHARLEMAGNE, bought 2016 by Stanley Kroenke, owner of Screaming Eagle (California) and Arsenal FC (UK). Intense wines designed for long (c.10 yrs) ageing, glorious mix of intense fruit, underlying minerals. Small amount of fine red CORTON.

Top trend in white burg: Aligoté in every way, shape or form.

Bonnes-Mares C d'O ★★★★ 90' 93 96' 99' 02' 05' 09' 10' 12' 15' 16' 18 19 20 GC between CHAMBOLLE-MUSIGNY and MOREY-ST-DENIS with some of latter's wilder character. Sturdy, long-lived wines, less fragrant than MUSIGNY. Best: ARLAUD, Bart, Bernstein, BRUNO CLAIR, DE VOGÜÉ, Drouhin-Laroze, DUJAC, Groffier, H BOILLOT, JADOT, MORTET, ROUMIER, VOUGERAIE.

Bonnezeaux Lo ★★★→★★★★ 16 17 18' 19 20 80 Long-lived sweet CHENIN BL, three sw-facing slopes (schist) in COTEAUX DU LAYON. Best: CHX de Fesles, la Varière (Les Melleresses); DOMS Fontaines, les Grandes VIGNES, Mihoudy, Petit Val, Petite Croix. Potentially GC.

Bordeaux ★→★★ 18 19 (20) Catch-all AC for generic B'x (represents nearly half region's production). Most brands (*Dourthe*, Michel Lynch, MOUTON CADET, *Sichel*) are in this category. Co-ops a big source. *See* CHX Bauduc, Beauregard-Ducourt, BONNET, Joinin, La Freynelle (Cabernet Sauvignon), Lamothe-Vincent, Reignac.

Bordeaux Supérieur B'x ★→★★ 15 16 17 18 19 (20) Higher min alc, lower yield, longer ageing than the last. Mainly bottled at property. Consistent CHX: Camarsac, Fleur Haut Gaussens, Grand Village, Grée-Laroque, Jean Faux, Landereau, Le Pin Beausoleil, Malromé, *Parenchère* (CUVÉE Raphaël), Penin, *Pey la Tour* (Rés), Reignac, *Thieuley*, Turcaud.

Borie-Manoux B'x Admirable B'x shipper, CH-owner: BATAILLEY, LA CROIX DU CASSE, DOM DE L'EGLISE, LYNCH-MOUSSAS, TROTTEVIEILLE. Also owns NÉGOCIANT Mähler-Besse.

Bouchard Père & Fils Burg ★★→★★★★ Dynamic BEAUNE merchant, all-round, robust style, age-worthy. Whites best in MEURSAULT and GC, esp CHEVALIER-MONTRACHET. Flagship reds: Beaune VIGNE de L'Enfant Jésus, CORTON, *Volnay Caillerets Ancienne Cuvée Carnot*. *See also* WILLIAM FÈVRE (CHAB).

Bouches-du-Rhône Prov ★ IGP from Marseille environs. Simple, hopefully fruity, reds from s varieties, plus CAB SAUV, GRENACHE, MERLOT, SYRAH.

Bourgeois, Famille Lo ★★→★★★★ 17' 18' 19' 20' Dynamic leading SANCERRE grower-merchant. Wines from all Central Lo AOPS and Petit Bourgeois (IGP). Best: Etienne Henri, Jadis, La Bourgeoise (r/w), Le Graveron (r Monts Damnés), Les

Ruchons (w Silex), MD de Bourgeois, Sancerre d'Antan. Top wines v. age-worthy. Also v.gd CLOS HENRI in Marlborough, NZ.

Bourgogne Burg ★→★★ (r) 15′ 17 18′ 19′ 20′ (w) 14′ 17′ 18 19′ 20′ Ground-floor AC for burg, ranging from mass-produced to bargain beauties. Sometimes comes with subregion attached, eg. CÔTE CHALONNAISE, HAUTES-CÔTES and now, C D'O. Whites from CHARD unless B ALIGOTÉ. Reds from PINOT N unless declassified BEAUJ crus (sold as B GAMAY) or B Passetoutgrains (Pinot/Gamay mix, must have 30%+ of former).

Bourgueil Lo ★★→★★★ 15′ 16 17′ 18′ 19′ (20′) Full-bodied, gd-value TOURAINE (r/rosé), mainly CAB FR. Gd vintages age 50 yrs+. *Amirault*, Ansodelles, Audebert, Chevalerie, Courant, de la Butte, Gambier, Lamé Delisle Boucard, Ménard, Minière, Nau Frères, Omasson, Revillot, Rochouard.

Bouscassé, Dom SW Fr ★★★ 15′ 17 18 19 (20) MADIRAN Palace. BRUMONT's Napa Valley style home. Reds a shade quicker to mature than oaky flagship Montus. VIEILLES VIGNES, 100% TANNAT, is star.

Bouvet-Ladubay Lo ★★→★★★ SAUMUR sparkling CRÉMANT DE LO. Big range: Saphir, Trésor (w/rosé), Taille Princesse Blanc de Gérard Depardieu SAUMUR-CHAMPIGNY Les Nonpareils best.

Bouzereau C D'O ★★→★★★★ The B family infest MEURSAULT, in a gd way. DOM Michel B is leader but try also Jean-Marie B, Philippe B (CH de Citeaux), Vincent B or B-Gruère & Filles for gd-value whites.

Bouzeron Burg ★★ 17′ 18 19 20′ CÔTE CHALONNAISE village with unique AC for ALIGOTÉ, esp golden version. Stricter rules and greater potential than straight BOURGOGNE Aligoté. Chanzy and esp A & P de Villaine outstanding. Same village makes gd CHARD, PINOT N as Bourgogne Côte Chalonnaise.

Bouzy Rouge Champ ★★★ 09 12 15′ 18′ Still red of famous PINOT N village. Formerly like v. light burg, now with more intensity (climate change, better viticulture), also refinement. VEUVE CLICQUOT, Colin and Paul Bara best producers.

Boxler, Albert Al ★★★★ Compact DOM, classic AL, as complex as great burgundy. Artisan precepts, brilliant RIES GC Sommerberg 14 and PINOT GR Res 10. Exceptional quality/price ratio PINOT BL 18.

Brocard, J-M Chab ★★→★★★ Successful quality grower-merchant. Sustainable mix of volume/value CHAB lines and high-class individual bottlings. Look for Chab Ste Claire. Son Julien B has bio range under 7 Lieux label.

Brochet, Emmanuel Champ ★★★ Bijou producer, exceptional CHAMP from steep Mont Bernard. Extra BRUT pure, exhilarating, winemaking slow and patient, in barrel 9 mths. Certified organic, no fining or filtration. Excelled in sumptuous 18′.

Brouilly Beauj ★★ 17 18′ 19′ 20′ Largest of ten BEAUJ crus: solid, rounded wines with some depth of fruit, approachable early but can age 3–5 yrs. Top growers: CHX de la Chaize (new owners), Thivin; DOMS Chermette, JC Lapalu, L&R Dufaitre, Piron.

Brumont, Alain SW Fr ★★★★ MADIRAN's pioneer and living icon, creator of BOUSCASSÉ, La Tyre, MONTUS, but also quaffing Gascogne ★ Torus and range of quaffable IGPS. ★★★ PACHERENCS (dr/sw) outstanding.

Brut Champ Term for dry classic wines of CHAMP. Most houses/growers have reduced dosage (adjustment of sweetness) in recent yrs. But great Champ can still be made at 8–9g residual sugar.

Brut Ultra / Zéro Term for bone-dry wines (no dosage) in CHAMP (also known as Brut NATURE); fashionable, esp with sommeliers, quality better with warmer summers: needs ripe yr, old vines, max care, eg. *Pol Roger Pure*, ROEDERER Brut Nature Philippe Starck 12′, Veuve Fourny Nature.

Bugey Sav ★→★★ AC. Light, fresh sparkling, *pétillant*, still. Three sectors, n–s: Belley, Cerdon, Montagnieu. Eight Bugey ACs. Whites mainly CHARD; ALIGOTÉ, Jacquère,

Roussette. Red/rosé: GAMAY, MONDEUSE, PINOT N. Try: Angelot, Carrel, Lingot-Martin, Monin, Peillot, Pellerin, Renardat-Fache, Rondeau-Guinet, Trichon.

Burgaud Beauj ★★★ Jean-Marc from MORGON, top bottlings of Charmes, Côte du Py, Grands Cras, etc., with fine ageing potential, but juicily attractive from day one. Nephew Alexandre promising too.

Buxy, Caves de Burg ★→★★ Leading CÔTE CHALONNAISE co-op for decent CHARD, PINOT N, source of many merchants' own-label ranges. Easily largest supplier of AC MONTAGNY.

Buzet SW Fr ★★ 18 19 (20) AOP. Plummy cousin of B'X. Dominated by exemplary co-op, incl CHX de Guèyze, Padère. Ch Pierron is worthy indie producer.

Cabernet d'Anjou Lo ★→★★ DYA. ANJOU's largest AOP, lightly sweet rosé: CAB FR/CAB SAUV. Try: Bablut, Bergerie, CH PIERRE-BISE, Chauvin, Clau de Nell, de Sauveroy, Grandes VIGNES, Montgilet, Ogereau, Plessis-Duval.

Cabidos SW Fr ★★★ 15 16 17 Proper CH in BÉARN, but outside JURANÇON. Similar wines. ★★ Gaston Phoebus is dry PETIT MANSENG. ★★★ St Clément is gorgeous golden sweet version. L'Or de Cabidos would rival many top-rated sweets.

Cadillac-Côtes de Bordeaux B'x ★★→★★★ 15 16 18 19 (20) Long, narrow, hilly zone on right bank of Garonne. Mainly MERLOT with CABS SAUV/FR. Medium-bodied, fresh reds; quality v. varied. Best: Alios de Ste-Marie, Biac, *Carsin*, CH Carignan, CLOS Chaumont, Clos Ste-Anne, de Ricaud, Grand-Mouëys, Lamothe de Haux, Laroche, Le Doyenné, Mont-Pérat, Plaisance, Réaut (Carat), *Reynon*, Suau.

Cady, Dom Lo ★★→★★★ 17' 18' 19' 20 V.gd organic family estate in ANJOU with accent on CHENIN, incl Cheninsolite (dr), COTEAUX DU LAYON, esp Chaume.

Cahors SW Fr ★★★ 15' 16 18' 19 (20) Historical AOP on River Lot. Devasted by 1956 frosts but now wrestling back its MALBEC birthright. All red (some IGP W). Styles continue to change with, mercifully, less extraction. Easy-drinking ★★ CH de Hauterive, CLOS Coutale. More substance from ★★★ *Clos Triguedina*, Clos Troteligotte, Clos d'Un Jour, CH DU CÈDRE, de la Bérengeraie, DOM Cosse-Maisonneuve, Haut-Monplaisir; ★★ Chx Gaudou, Hautes-Serres, La Coustarelle, Les Croisille, Lamartine, Mas La Périé, Ponzac, Vincens.

Cailloux, Les S Rh ★★★ 78' 81' 90' 98' 03' 05' 09' 10' 16' 18 19' 21-ha CHÂTEAUNEUF DOM; elegant, profound, spiced, handmade reds, fab value. Special wine Centenaire, oldest GRENACHE 1889 noble, dear, max elegant 16' 19'. Also DOM André Brunel (esp gd-value CÔTES DU RH red Est-Ouest).

Cairanne S Rh ★★→★★★ 10' 15' 16' 17' 18 19' Many options from *garrigue* soils, wines of character, dark fruits, mixed herbs, refinement, texture, esp CLOS Romane, DOMS Alary (style, organic), Amadieu (pure, bio), Boisson (punchy), Brusset (deep), Clos des Mourres (organic), Cros de Romet, Escaravailles (flair), Grosset, Hautes Cances (true, traditional until 19), Jubain, *Oratoire St Martin* (detail, classy, bio), Rabasse-Charavin (punchy), Richaud (size, great fruit), Roche. Food-friendly, gd whites.

Calmel & Joseph L'doc ★★→★★★ Skilled NÉGOCIANT. Villa Blanche IGPS from international and local varietals gd value. Terroir range from various ACS. ST-CHINIAN, TERRASSES DU LARZAC stand out. Gets better every yr.

Canard-Duchêne Champ House owned by ALAIN THIÉNOT. Now run by next generation. ★★★ CUVÉE Léonie. Improved Authentique Cuvée (organic) 12' 13 15 17' 18' 20. Single-vyd Avize Gamin 12 13 17'19' 20'.

Canon-Fronsac B'x ★★→★★★ 14 15 16 18 19' (20) Small enclave within FRON, otherwise same wines. Environmental action. Best: rich, full and finely structured. Try: Barrabaque, Canon Pécresse, Cassagne Haut-Canon la Truffière, GABY, Grand-Renouil, La Fleur Cailleau, MOULIN PEY-LABRIE, Pavillon, Vrai Canon Bouché.

Caraguilhes, Ch de L'doc ★★→★★★ Organic CORBIÈRES estate with consistent, accessible range on Boutenac terroir. La Font Blanche (w) unoaked, floral, gd value. Classique (r) fruity, peppery bomb. L'Echappé Belle shows how gd CARIGNAN can be. Solus top wine, ages well.

Carillon C d'O ★★★ Contrasting PULIGNY brothers: Jacques unchangingly classical; try PC Referts. François for exciting modern approach. Try Combettes, Folatières. Village Puligny great from both.

Carrel, Jeff L'doc, Rouss ★★→★★★ NÉGOCIANT, winemaker, eclectic range of L'DOC, ROUSS. Many AC, IGP, a lot bio. Les Darons GRENACHE gd value; Morillon sumptuous botrytis CHARD. Imaginative, on the up.

Cassis Prov ★★ DYA. From hills round port/resort e of Marseille; pricey because, well, it's Prov. Whites develop richness with age; savoury, saline. Based on BOURBOULENC, CLAIRETTE, MARSANNE, UGNI BL. Look for: CH Barbanau, *Clos Ste-Magdeleine*, DOM de la Ferme Blanche, Fontcreuse, Paternel.

Castelmaure L'doc ★★→★★★ Excellent co-op in wilds of CORBIÈRES. Lots of CARIGNAN. Easy-drinking La Pompadour; Grand CUVÉE screams terroir: dark fruit, wild herbs, hot stone. N°3 flagship, brooding, big. Keep 5 yrs.

Castelnau, De Champ ★★★ Rising co-op. Cellarmaster Elisabeth Sarcelet insists on longer lees-ageing in excellent BLANC DE BLANCS and vintage 02. Innovative Prestige Collection Hors d'Age blended from best wines, different each yr: current release CCF2067 led by fine MEUNIER.

Castigno, Ch L'doc ★★ Belgian-owned ST-CHINIAN estate turning sleepy village of Assignan into tourist spot with restaurants, hotel, sustainable, cork-clad, bottle-shaped winery. Secrets des Dieux oaky, aged SYRAH/CARIGNAN/GRENACHE. Stylish Grace des Anges ROUSSANNE-based white.

Castillon-Côtes de Bordeaux B'x ★★→★★★ 14 15 16 18 19 (20) Appealing e neighbour of ST-ÉM with improved quality; similar wines, usually less plump. 230 growers; 25% organic. Top: Alcée, Ampélia, Cap de FAUGÈRES, CLOS Les Lunelles, Clos Louie, *Clos Puy Arnaud*, Côte Montpezat, *d'Aiguilhe, de l'A*, de Pitray, Joanin Bécot, *La Clarière-Laithwaite*, l'Aurage, Le Rey, *l'Hêtre*, Montlandrie, Poupille, Roquevieille, Veyry.

Cathiard, Dom Sylvain C d'O ★★★★ Sébastien C makes wines of astonishing quality from VOSNE-ROMANÉE, esp Malconsorts, Orveaux, Reignots, plus NUITS-ST-GEORGES Aux Thorey, Murgers. Seductive young, will mature to splendour.

Cave Cellar, or any wine establishment.

Cave coopérative Growers' co-op winery; over half of all French production. Wines often well-priced, probably not most exciting. Many co-ops closing down.

Cazes, Dom Rouss ★★★ Big, bio, impressive. VDN eg. RIVESALTES Ambré, Tuilé, Grenat and sensational aged Aimé Cazes. MAURY SEC. Ambre (sw w GRENACHE BL), Le Canon du Maréchal GRENACHE/SYRAH; Top red Crédo CÔTES DU ROUSS-VILLAGES with Ego, Alter. CLOS de Paulilles BANYULS, COLLIOURE.

Cébène, Dom de L'doc ★★★★ Brigitte Chevalier makes thrilling FAUGÈRES from

---

Chablis

There is no better expression of the all-conquering CHARD than the full but tense, limpid but stony wines it makes on the rolling limestone hills of CHAB. Most use little or no new oak to mask the precision of their terroirs. Investigate. **Top:** BILLAUD, Droin, LAROCHE, Michel (L), MOREAU (C), Pinson, RAVENEAU, V DAUVISSAT, W FÈVRE. **Challengers:** Bernard Defaix, Bessin, CHABLISIENNE, Collet, Dampt (family), Davenne, Droin, DROUHIN-Vaudon, Duplessis, Grossot, J-M BROCARD, LAROCHE, LONG-DEPAQUIT, Malandes, MOREAU-Naudet, N&G Fèvre, Picq, Piuze, Pommier, Oudin, Tribut. **Up-and-coming:** A&C Gautheron, d'Henri, E&E Vocoret, J & Fils Dauvissat, Lavantureux, Vrignaud. **Organic/natural:** CH de Béru, de Moor, Goulley, Julien Brocard, Pattes Loup.

high-altitude, organic vyds. Flagship Felgaria, mostly MOURVÈDRE, is elegance, power. Ages well. Les Bancels SYRAH et al earlier drinking, no less fine. Belle Lurette shows what CARIGNAN can do.

Cédre, Ch du SW Fr ★★→★★★ 15' 16 17 18 19 (20) Verhaeghe brothers make best-known modern-style CAHORS. Choice of styles, prices. Delicious ★★ MALBEC IGP for everyday drinking.

Cendrillon, Dom de la L'doc ★★★ Joyeux family make polished, terroir-driven wines nr Narbonne. Organic. Nuance, creamy, oaky blend of eight varieties, incl PETIT MANSENG/GRENACHES BL/Gr/ALBARIÑO. Inédite (r) classy CORBIÈRES.

Cépage Grape variety. *See* pp.14–24 for all.

Cérons B'x ★★ 14 15' 16 18 19 Smallest AC in B'X. Sweet wines next to SAUT but less intense. Best: CHX de Cérons, DE CHANTEGRIVE, CLOS Bourgelat, du Seuil, Grand Enclos.

Chablis ★★→★★★ 14' 15 17' 18' 19' 20 Such an evocative name; such beautiful wines when they stay true to their marine mineral origins. CHARD grape with crushed oyster shells.

Chablis Grand Cru Chab ★★★→★★★★ 10' 12' 14' 15 17' 18' 19' 20 Contiguous s-facing block overlooking River Serein, most concentrated CHAB, needs 5–15 yrs to show detail. Seven vyds: Blanchots (floral), Bougros (incl Côte Bouguerots), CLOS (usually best), Grenouilles (spicy), Preuses (cashmere), Valmur (structure), Vaudésir (plus brand La Moutonne). Many gd growers.

Chablisienne, La Chab ★★→★★★ Exemplary CO-OP responsible for huge slice of CHAB production, esp supermarket own-labels. Trade up to bio CUVÉES of PETIT-CHAB and Chab. Top wine is GC CH Grenouilles.

Chablis Premier Cru Chab ★★★ 14' 15 17' 18' 19' 20 Well worth premium over straight CHAB: better sites on rolling hillsides. Mineral favourites: Montmains, Vaillons, Vaucoupin, softer style Côte de Léchet, Fourchaume; greater opulence from Mont de Milieu, *Montée de Tonnerre*, Vaulorent.

Chambertin C d'O ★★★★ 90' 93 96' 99' 02' 05' 09' 10' 12' 14 15' 16 17 18' 19' 20' Called the King of Burg, but in touch with its feminine side. Imperious wine; amazingly dense, sumptuous, long-lived, expensive. Producers who match potential incl Bernstein, BOUCHARD PÈRE & FILS, Charlopin, Damoy, DOM LEROY, DUGAT-Py, DROUHIN, MORTET, ROSSIGNOL-TRAPET, ROUSSEAU, TRAPET.

Chambertin-Clos de Bèze C d'O ★★★★ 90' 93 96' 99' 02' 03 05' 09' 10' 12' 14 15' 16 17 18' 19' 20' Splendid neighbour to CHAMBERTIN, slightly more accessible in youth, velvet texture, deeply graceful. Best: Bart, B CLAIR, Damoy, D Laurent, DROUHIN, Drouhin-Laroze, Duroché, FAIVELEY, Groffier, JADOT, Prieuré-Roch, ROUSSEAU.

Chambolle-Musigny C d'O ★★★→★★★★ 93 99' 02' 05' 09' 10' 12' 15' 16 17 19' 20 Silky, velvety wines from CÔTE DE NUITS: Charmes, Combe d'Orveau for substance, more chiselled from Cras, Fuées, seduction from Amoureuses, plus GCS BONNES MARES, MUSIGNY. Superstars: BARTHOD, MUGNIER, ROUMIER, VOGÜÉ. Try Amiot-Servelle, DROUHIN, Felettig, Groffier, HUDELOT-Baillet, Pousse d'Or, RION, Sigaut.

Champagne Sparkling wines of PINOTS N/M and CHARD: 33,805 ha, heartland c.145 km

---

A trio of Champagne growers to watch

Brice, Bouzy: top-flight grower with model 8 ha for rich PINOT N and original CÔTEAUX CHAMPENOIS BOUZY ROUGE. Gifted Christophe Constant (ex-JL Vergnon, LE MESNIL) new chef de CAVES. **J-B Geoffroy**, Cumières and AY: admired grower/winemaker. Deft hand with MEUNIER as much as with PINOT N. **Roger-Constant Le Maire**, Hautvillers/Villers-sous-Châtillon: specialist in long-aged, atypical CHAMP, super-fresh CUVÉES – no malolactic, no fining or filtration, min lees-ageing 4–5 yrs.

(90 miles) e of Paris. Sales 300 million bottles+/yr. Some PINOT BL in AUBE adds freshness. Other sparkling wines, however ace, cannot be called Champ.

Champagne le Mesnil Champ ★★★ Top-flight CO-OP in greatest GC CHARD village. Exceptional CUVÉE Sublime 08' 09 13 15 17' 19 from finest sites. Majestic Cuvée Prestige 05 triumphs against odds. Real value.

Chandon de Briailles, Dom C d'O ★★★ DOM defined by bio farming, min sulphur, whole bunches, no new oak. Brilliantly pure perfumed reds reaching new heights, esp CORTON-Bressandes, Île de Vergelesses, PERNAND-VERGELESSES.

Chanson Père & Fils Burg ★→★★★ Resurgent BEAUNE merchant, quality whites (CLOS DES MOUCHES, CORTON-Vergennes) and stylish idiosyncratic reds (whole-cluster aromatics), esp CLOS des Fèves.

Chapelle-Chambertin C d'O ★★★ 99' 02' 05' 09' 10' 12' 14 15' 16 18' 19' 20' Lighter neighbour of CHAMBERTIN; thin soil does better in cooler, damper yrs. Fine-boned wine, less meaty. Top: Damoy, DROUHIN-Laroze, JADOT, PONSOT, ROSSIGNOL-TRAPET, TRAPET, Tremblay.

Chapoutier N Rh ★★→★★★★ Talkative grower-merchant at HERMITAGE. Broadly stylish reds via low-yield, plot-specific, expensive CUVÉES. Intense GRENACHE CHÂTEAUNEUF – Barbe Rac, Croix de Bois (r); CÔTE-RÔTIE La Mordorée; Hermitage – L'Ermite (outstanding r/w), Le Pavillon (granite, deep r), Cuvée de l'Orée (w), Le Méal (w). Also ST-JOSEPH Les Granits (r/w). *Hermitage whites* outstanding, all old-vine MARSANNE. Gd-value Meysonniers Crozes. Also vyds in COTEAUX D'AIX-EN-PROV, CÔTES DU ROUSS-VILLAGES (gd DOM Bila-Haut), RIVESALTES. Also own Ferraton at Hermitage, BEAUJ house Trenel, CH des Ferrages (Prov), has AL vyds and Australian joint ventures, esp Doms Tournon and Terlato & Chapoutier (fragrant); also Portuguese Lisboa project, Douro too, hotel, wine bar in Tain.

Charbonnière, Dom de la S Rh ★★★ 05' 09' 10' 16' 17 18 19' 17-ha CHÂTEAUNEUF estate run by sisters. Consistent Tradition (r), deep, special: VIEILLES VIGNES (vigour, best), authentic Mourre des Perdrix, also Hautes Brusquières. V. elegant, pure white. Also sound, peppery VACQUEYRAS red.

Chardonnay As well as a white wine grape, also the name of a MÂCON-VILLAGES commune, hence Mâcon-Chardonnay.

Charlemagne C d'O ★★★★ 14' 15' 17' 18 19' 20' Almost extinct sister appellation to CORTON-C, revived by DOM DE LA VOUGERAIE from 2013. Same rules as sibling.

Charlopin C d'O ★★→★★★ Philippe C makes impressive range of reds from GEVREY base. BOURGOGNE C D'O, MARSANNAY for value, gd range GC for top of line. Son Yann C, DOM C-Tissier also exciting.

Charmes-Chambertin C d'O ★★★★ 99' 02' 03 05' 09' 10' 12' 15' 16 17 18' 19' 20' GEVREY GC, 31 ha, incl neighbour MAZOYÈRES-CHAMBERTIN. Raspberries and cream plus dark-cherry fruit, sumptuous texture, fragrant finish. So many gd names: ARLAUD, BACHELET, Castagnier, Coquard-Loison-Fleurot, DUGAT, DUJAC, Duroché, LEROY, MORTET, Perrot-Minot, Roty, ROUSSEAU, Taupenot-Merme, VOUGERAIE.

Chartogne-Taillet Champ A disciple of SELOSSE, Alexandre Chartogne is a star. Ideal BRUT Ste Anne NV and single-vyds Le Chemin de Reims and Les Barres; striking energy. High hopes for magic trio 18 19 20.

Charvin, Dom S Rh ★★★ 01' 06' 07' 09' 10' 12' 15' 16' 17' 18' 19' Real terroir truth at 8-ha CHÂTEAUNEUF estate, 85% GRENACHE, no oak, only one handmade CUVÉE. Spiced, mineral, high-energy red, vintage accuracy. Recent gd white. Top-value, genuine, mineral, long-lived CÔTES DU RH (r).

Chassagne-Montrachet C d'O ★★→★★★★ (w) 02' 04 05' 08' 09' 12' 14' 15 17' 18' 19' 20' Large village at s end of CÔTE DE BEAUNE. Great white vyds Blanchot, Cailleret, Romanee, Ruchottes GCS. Try: Coffinet, COLIN, GAGNARD, MOREY, Pillot families plus DOMS Heitz-Lochardet, MOREAU, Niellon, Ramonet. Time for a red revival? Best red vyds: Boudriotte, Clos St-Jean, Morgeot

> **Châteauneuf: kings of the castle**
> Top names in this enormous and varied (soils, blends, styles) appellation:
> CHX DE BEAUCASTEL, Fortia, Gardine (also w), Mont-Redon, Nalys, Nerthe,
> RAYAS, Sixtine, Vaudieu; DOMS Barroche, Beaurenard (bio), Bois de Boursan,
> Bosquet des Papes, Chante Cigale, Chante Perdrix, CHARBONNIÈRE, CHARVIN,
> CLOS DES PAPES, CLOS du Caillou, Clos du Mont-Olivet, Clos St-Jean, Cristia,
> de la Biscarelle, de la Janasse, de la Vieille Julienne (bio), du Banneret,
> Fontavin, Font-de-Michelle, Grand Tinel, Grand Veneur, Henri Bonneau,
> LES CAILLOUX (value), Marcoux, Mas du Boislauzon, Pegaü, Pierre André
> (bio), Porte Rouge, P Usseglio, R Usseglio (bio), Roger Sabon, St-Préfert,
> Sénéchaux, Vieux Donjon, VIEUX TÉLÉGRAPHE.

Château (Ch) Means an estate, big or small, gd or indifferent, particularly in B'X (*see* pp.100–121). Means, literally, castle or great house. In Burg, DOM is usual term.

Château-Chalon Jura ★★★★ 96 99' 00 05' 09 10' 12 Not a CH but AC and village, the summit of VIN JAUNE style from SAVAGNIN grape. An unfortified, winey version of Sherry. Min 6 yrs barrel-age, not cheap but gd value. Ready to drink (or cook a chicken in) when bottled, but gains with further age. Fervent admirers search out BERTHET-BONDET, MACLE, TISSOT or Bourdy for old vintages.

Château-Grillet N Rh ★★★★ 01' 04' 07' 09' 10' 12' 14' 15' 16' 17' 18 19' 20' France's smallest AC. 3.7-ha, picturesque amphitheatre s of CONDRIEU, sandy-granite terraces, much gd vyd care. Bought by F Pinault of CH LATOUR in 2011, prices way up, wine *en finesse*, less rich these days. Can be great at 20 yrs. Scented, oily, precise VIOGNIER: drink at cellar temperature, decanted, with refined dishes.

Châteaumeillant Lo ★→★★ 19' 20' Dynamic but isolated AC s Bourges. Mostly light red GAMAY, PINOT N, plus VIN GRIS with 10% PINOT GR allowed. BOURGEOIS, Chaillot, Gabrielle, Goyer, Joffre, Joseph MELLOT, Lecomte, Nairaud-Suberville, Roux, Rouzé, Siret-Courtaud.

Châteauneuf-du-Pape S Rh ★★★→★★★★ 01' 07' 09' 10' 12 16' 17 19' Nr Avignon, large, 3200 ha+. About 50 gd DOMS (remaining 85 fair, uneven to poor). Up to 13 grapes (r/w), led by GRENACHE, also SYRAH, MOURVÈDRE (increasing), Counoise. Warm, spiced, textured, long-lived; should be fine, pure, magical, but until mid-2010s too many heavy, sip-only Parker-esque wines. Small, traditional names often gd value. Prestige old-vine wines (v.gd Grenache 16', 19'). To avoid: late-harvest, new oak, 16% alc, too pricey. Grand whites: fresh, fruity, or replete, smooth, best can age 15 yrs+. For top names, *see* box, above.

Chave, Dom Jean-Louis N Rh ★★★★ 00 01' 03' 04 05' 07' 09' 10' 11' 12' 13' 15' 16' 17' 18' 19' 20 Excellent family DOM at heart of HERMITAGE, gd mix of soils, so blending artful. Classy, silken, long-lived reds, incl v. occasional Cathelin. V.gd, stylish, complex white (mainly MARSANNE); occasional VIN DE PAILLE. ST-JOSEPH reds dark, great fruit, plot-specific CLOS Florentin (since 2015) v. stylish; also lively J-L Chave brand St-Joseph Offerus, jolly CÔTES DU RH Mon Coeur, sound value merchant Hermitage Farconnet (r), Blanche (w).

Chavignol Lo SANCERRE village. Steep vyds Cul de Beaujeu/Les Monts Damnés dominate picturesque vibrant village. Clay-limestone soil gives excellent full-bodied, mineral whites, reds ageing 15 yrs+. V. fine young producers: *Vincent Delaporte*, Pierre Martin, *Alphonse Mellot*, *Boulay*, *Bourgeois*, Cotat, Dagueneau, Paul Thomas, Thomas Laballe.

Chénas Beauj ★★★ 15' 16 18' 19' 20' Smallest BEAUJ cru, between MOULIN-À-VENT and JULIÉNAS, gd value, meaty, age-worthy, merits more interest. Thillardon is reference DOM, but try also Janodet, LAPIERRE, Pacalet, Piron, Trichard, co-op.

Chevalier-Montrachet C d'O ★★★★ 04 08 09' 10 12 14' 15 17' 18' 19' 20' Just above MONTRACHET on hill, just below in quality; brilliant crystalline wines, dancing

FRANCE

white fruit and flowers. Long-lived but can be accessible early. Top grower is LEFLAIVE, special CUVÉES Les Demoiselles from JADOT, LOUIS LATOUR and La Cabotte from BOUCHARD. Also: Chartron, COLIN (P), Dancer, DE MONTILLE, Niellon, VOUGERAIE.

Cheverny Lo ★→★★ 19′ 20′ AC in S Blois. White from SAUV BL (majority)/CHARD blend. Light reds mainly GAMAY, PINOT N (also CAB FR, CÔT). *Cour-Cheverny* 100% Romorantin: ages v. well, best up to ★★★. Try: Cazin, Clos Tue-Boeuf (also VDF), de Montcy, de Veilloux, du Moulin, H Villemade, *Huards* (bio), Tessier. Much low-lying: v. frost-prone.

Chevillon, R C d'O ★★★ With GOUGES, the reference DOM for NUITS-ST-GEORGES PCS: Bousselots, Chaignots, Pruliers more accessible; Cailles, Les St-Georges, Vaucrains for long term.

Chevrot C d'O ★★ Pablo and Vincent C great source for juicy MARANGES, esp Sur les Chênes, PC Croix Moines. Decent whites, esp ALIGOTÉ Tilleul, Maranges Fussière. CRÉMANT too. Lively wines, fair prices.

Chidaine, François Lo ★★★ 17′ 18′ 19′ 20′ V.gd MONTLOUIS single vyds, bio. His VOUVRAY, incl CLOS Baudoin, stupidly has to be VDF, TOURAINE (Cher Valley). Accent on precise SEC, DEMI-SEC that age well. Also Le Chenin d'Ailleurs (LIMOUX) to compensate for LO frosts. Project in Spain too.

Chignin Sav ★→★★ AC: GAMAY, Jacquère, MONDEUSE, PINOT N. Chignin-Bergeron is ROUSSANNE. Try: Gonnet, Partage.

Chinon Lo ★★→★★★ 15′ 16′ 17′ 18′ 19′ (20′) Light to rich top TOURAINE CAB FR from sand, gravel, limestone. Best age 30 yrs+. A little dry CHENIN BL. Best: *Alliet*, *Baudry*, BAUDRY-DUTOUR, Coulaine, Couly-Dutheil, Grosbois, JM Raffault, Jourdan-Pichard, Landry, L'R, Moulin à Tan, *Noblaie*, P&B Couly, Pain, Petit Thouars, Pierre Sourdais, Saut au Loup; now extensive frost protection.

Chiroubles Beauj ★★ 15′ 18′ 19′ 20′ BEAUJ cru in hills above FLEURIE: fresh, fruity, savoury wines. Growers: Berne, CH de Javernand, Cheysson, Lafarge-Vial, Métrat, Passot, Raousset, or merchants DUBOEUF, Trenel.

Chorey-lès-Beaune C d'O ★★ 09′ 10′ 12 15′ 17 18 19′ 20 Village just s of BEAUNE. TOLLOT-BEAUT remains reference for this affordable, uncomplicated AC, DOM Gay promising. Try also Arnoux, DROUHIN, Guyon, JADOT, Rapet, ROUGET.

Chusclan S Rh ★→★★ 16′ 18 19′ CÔTES DU RH-VILLAGES with gd-quality Maison Sinnae (ex-Laudun-Chusclan co-op), incl fresh whites, often MARSANNE, ROUSSANNE, VIOGNIER. Soft reds, cool, elegant rosés. Best co-op labels (r) Chusclan DOM de l'Olivette, Excellence, CÔTES DU RH Femme de Gicon (r), Éléments Terra (w), LIRAC Dom St-Nicolas. Also full CH Signac (best Chusclan, can age), Dom La Romance (fresh, organic), special CUVÉES from André Roux.

Clair, Bruno C d'O ★★★→★★★★ Top-class CÔTE DE NUITS estate for supple, subtle, savoury wines. Gd-value MARSANNAY, old-vine SAVIGNY La Dominode, GEVREY-CHAMBERTIN (CLOS ST-JACQUES, Cazetiers), standout CHAMBERTIN-CLOS DE BÈZE. Best whites from CORTON-CHARLEMAGNE, MOREY-ST-DENIS.

Clairet B'x Between rosé/red. B'x Clairet is AC. Try CHX Fontenille, THIEULEY, Turcaud.

Clairette de Die N Rh ★★ NV Rh/low Alpine bubbly: flinty or (better) MUSCAT sparkling (s/sw). Much underrated, muskily fruited, gd value, low degree; or dry CLAIRETTE, can age 3 yrs. NB: Achard-Vincent, Carod, David Bautin (organic), Jaillance (value), J-C Raspail (organic, IGP SYRAH), Poulet et Fils (terroir, Chatillon-en-Diois s). Must try.

Clape, Dom Pierre, Olivier N Rh ★★★→★★★★ 01′ 03′ 05′ 06′ 07′ 09′ 10′ 12′ 14′ 15′ 16′ 17′ 18′ 19′ 20 Les rois de CORNAS. Top location SYRAH vyds, many old vines, gd granite soil work. Profound, complex reds, vintage accuracy, need 6 yrs+, live 25+. Bright fruit in youngish-vines label Renaissance. Superior CÔTES DU RH, VDF (r), ST-PÉRAY (gd style, improved).

Clape, La L'doc ★★★→★★★★ Limestone massif on Med nr Narbonne. MOURVÈDRE hotspot with SYRAH, GRENACHE for characterful herb-scented reds plus salty, herbal whites from BOURBOULENC, will age. CHX Anglès, Camplazens, La Combe St Paul, LA NÉGLY, Laquirou, l'Hospitalet, Mire l'Etang, Pech-Céleyran, Pech-Redon, Ricardelle, ROUQUETTE-SUR-MER, Sarrat de Goundy.

Climat Burg Individual named vyd at any level, esp in C D'O, eg. MEURSAULT Tesson, MAZOYÈRES-CHAMBERTIN. UNESCO World Heritage status.

Clos Distinct (walled) vyd, often in one ownership (esp AL, Burg, CHAMP). Often prestigious.

Clos Canarelli Cors ★★★ Revered bio estate in S. AC Corse Figari. Reviving indigenous grapes plus more mainstream NIELLUCCIO, SCIACARELLO. Core range aged in and named after amphorae, worth seeking out. Excellent Tarra di Sognu (r/w) top.

Clos Cibonne Prov ★★★ Small estate nr Toulon, making red/rosé from rare, local Tibouren as AOP CÔTES DU PROV. Wonderful traditional labels, gastronomic, ethereal wines. Tentations range is fruitier, early drinking.

Clos de la Roche C d'O ★★★★ 90' 93' 96' 99' 02' 05' 08 09' 10' 15' 16' 17 18' 19' 20' Underrated though not underpriced: maybe finest GC of MOREY-ST-DENIS, as much grace as power, more savoury than sumptuous, blueberries. Needs time. DUJAC, H LIGNIER, PONSOT references but try Amiot, ARLAUD, Bernstein, Castagnier, Coquard, LEROY, LIGNIER-Michelot, Pousse d'Or, Remy, ROUSSEAU.

Clos des Fées Rouss ★★ Organic philosophy, wines with character from range of terroirs. Les Sorcières (r/w) consistently gd CÔTES DU ROUSS. Les CLOS des Fées Herve Bizeul (r) top-notch. Gd IGP COTES DE CATALANES (w old-vine GRENACHE BL).

Clos des Lambrays C d'O ★★★ 05' 09' 10' 15' 16' 18' 19' 20' All-but-MONOPOLE GC vyd at MOREY-ST-DENIS, now belongs to LVMH. Big investment and new winemaker from 2019 to bring leap in quality. Previously attractive, early picked, spicy, stemmy style.

Clos des Mouches C d'O ★★★ (w) 02 05' 09' 10' 14' 15 17' 18 19' 20' PC vyd in several Burg ACS. Mostly reds (PINOT N), but most famous for glorious Beaune white. Mouches = honeybees; see label of DROUHIN's iconic BEAUNE bottling. Also BICHOT, CHANSON (Beaune); plus CLAIR, MOREAU, Muzard (SANTENAY); Germain (MEURSAULT).

Clos des Papes S Rh ★★★★ 01' 03' 04' 05' 07' 09' 10' 12' 13' 14' 15' 16' 17' 18' 19' 20 Always high-class CHÂTEAUNEUF DOM of Avril family, v. small yields, burg elegance; v. stylish, provocative red (mainly GRENACHE, MOURVÈDRE, drink at 2–3 yrs or from 8+); top white (six varieties, intricate, allow time, merits noble cuisine; 2–3 yrs, then 10–20).

Clos de Tart C d'O ★★★★ 02' 05' 08' 10' 13' 14 15' 16' 17 18' 19' 20' Expensive MOREY-ST-DENIS GC. Now part of Pinault/Artemis empire (CHX GRILLET, LATOUR, etc.) with new winemaker. Picking earlier than before, but will style lighten and freshen?

Clos de Vougeot C d'O ★★★→★★★★ 90' 99' 02' 03' 05' 09' 10' 12' 13' 15' 16 17 18' 19' 20' CÔTE DE NUITS GC with many owners. Occasionally sublime, needs 10 yrs+ to show real class. Loving recent warm vintages. Style, quality depend on producer's philosophy, technique, position. Top: ARNOUX-LACHAUX, BOUCHARD, Castagnier, CH de la Tour, Coquard-Loison-Fleurot, DROUHIN, EUGÉNIE, *Faiveley*, Forey, GRIVOT, *Gros*, HUDELOT-Noëllat, JADOT, LEROY, LIGER-BELAIR (both), MÉO-CAMUZET, MONTILLE, MORTET, MUGNERET-Gibourg, PONSOT, *Vougeraie*, Y Clerget.

Clos du Gravillas L'doc ★★★ Franco-American couple, traditional L'DOC grapes on chalky white soils, NE MINERVOIS. Eclectic: characterful PIQUEPOUL/Terret (w), L'Inattendu oakier GRENACHE BL/Gr. St Jean de Minervois elegant VDN. Splendid Lo Vielh CARIGNAN from 100-yr-old vines.

Clos du Mesnil Champ ★★★★ KRUG's famous walled vyd in GC LE MESNIL. Long-lived, pure CHARD vintage, great mature yrs like 95 *à point* till 2023+; 02 and remarkable 03 08' 13' will be classics, as will 17' 19'.

Clos du Roi C d'O ★★→★★★ Frequent Burg vyd name. The king usually chose well. Best vyd in GC CORTON (DE MONTILLE, Pousse d'Or, VOUGERAIE); top PC vyd in MERCUREY, future PC (still waiting) in MARSANNAY. Less classy in BEAUNE.

Clos Rougeard Lo ★★★★ 09 10 11 12 14 Iconic small DOM, bought by M and O Bouygues (CH MONTROSE). Finesse, long-lived: SAUMUR Blanc, SAUMUR-CHAMPIGNY. Quality yes, but now pricey trophy wines.

Clos St-Denis C d'O ★★★ 90' 93' 96' 99' 02' 05' 09' 10' 12' 15' 16' 17 18' 19' 20' GC at MOREY-ST-DENIS. Sumptuous in youth, silky with age. Outstanding from DUJAC, PONSOT (Laurent P from 2016). Try also Amiot-Servelle, ARLAUD, Bertagna, Castagnier, Coquard-Loison-Fleurot, Heresztyn-Mazzini, JADOT, Jouan, LEROUX.

Clos Ste-Hune Al ★★★★ Legendary TRIMBACH single site from GC ROSACKER. Greatest RIES in AL? Super 10 13 16 17' 18' 20. Austere, needs a decade ageing; complex wine for gastronomy. GC SCHLOSSBERG more luxuriant, floral.

Clos St-Jacques C d'O ★★★★ 90' 93 96' 99' 02' 05' 09' 10' 12' 15' 16 17 18' 19' 20' Hillside PC in GEVREY-CHAMBERTIN with perfect se exposure. Shared by five excellent producers: CLAIR, ESMONIN, FOURRIER, JADOT, ROUSSEAU; powerful, age-worthy, velvety reds ranked (and often priced) above many GCs.

Clos St-Landelin Al ★★ →★★★★ Great name, esp fine, full-bodied GC *Vorbourg Ries* and PINOT GR 17' 18 20. *Pinot N Cuvée "V"* 15 18' ripe, wine rich, is region's best, exceptional in 15'. Only surpassed by 18'.

Clusel-Roch, Dom N Rh ★★★ 01 05' 09' 10' 11 12' 13' 14 15' 16' 17' 18' 19' 20 Organic CÔTE-RÔTIE DOM (rare), gd range vyds, mostly Serine (pre-clone SYRAH). Tight wines, patience rewarded. Les Schistes gd entry point, high-quality plot wines La Viallière, Les Grandes Places (schist, iron). Son Guillaume C makes v. drinkable CÔTEAUX DU LYONNAIS (r/w).

Only Rh appellation n of Vienne is Seyssuel, 6 km (4 miles) away, pure schist.

Coche-Dury C d'O ★★★★ Top MEURSAULT DOM led by Raphaël C in succession to legend Jean-François. Exceptional whites from ALIGOTÉ to CORTON-CHARLEMAGNE; v. pretty reds too. Stratospheric prices. Gd-value cousin Coche-Bizouard (eg. Meursault Goutte d'Or) sound, but not same style.

Colin C d'O ★★★ →★★★★ Leading CHASSAGNE and ST-AUBIN family; current generation turning heads with brilliant whites, esp Pierre-Yves C-MOREY, DOM Marc C, Joseph C (from 2017) and cousins Philippe C, Bruno C. Next generation, Simon C in wings.

Colin-Morey Burg ★★★ Pierre-Yves C-M has made his name with vibrant tingling whites, esp from *St-Aubin* and CHASSAGNE PC, with their characteristic gun-flint bouquets. Great wines in youth and for ageing.

Collin, Ulysse Champ Cerebral grower on Côteaux du Petit Morin, sw of Vertus. Single-vyd wines only, all subtly oaked, low but not zero dosage. ★★★ Les Pierrières BLANC DE BLANCS, base of 15.

Collines Rhodaniennes N Rh ★★ IGP major value, character, quality, incl v.gd Seyssuel (v. nr Vienne, schist, steep), crisp granite hillside, plateau reds, often from top estates. ("Rhodanienne" = "of the Rhône".) Mostly SYRAH (best), plus MERLOT, GAMAY, mini-CONDRIEU VIOGNIER (best). Reds: A Paret, A PERRET, Bonnefond, CLOS de la Bonnette (organic), E Barou, Hameau Touche Boeuf, *Jamet*, Jasmin, J-M Gérin, L Chèze, Monier-Pérreol (bio), N Champagneux, S Ogier, S Pichat, ROSTAING. Whites: Alexandrins, A Perret (v.gd), Barou, F Merlin, *G Vernay*, P Marthouret, X Gérard, Y Cuilleron.

Collioure Rouss ★★ Same vyds as BANYULS, stunning views from steep terraces overlooking Med. Mainly GRENACHE of all colours. Rosé can be serious. Top: DOMS Augustin, Bila-Haut, de la Rectorie, du Mas Blanc, du Traginer, La Tour Vieille, Madeloc, Vial-Magnères; Coume del Mas, Les CLOS de Paulilles. Co-ops Cellier des Templiers, l'Étoile.

Combe Blanche, Dom L'doc ★★→★★★ Eclectic mix of of fine, long-lived LA LIVINIÈRE (Chandelière, La Galine), PINOT N, TEMPRANILLO from n-facing slopes. AC MINERVOIS and CINSAULT Misunderstood gd value. CLOS du Causses gd, fragrant GRENACHE.

Comté Tolosan SW Fr ★ Usually DYA. Catch-all IGP covering most of SW. Kaleidoscope of styles, mostly entry level; ★★ DOM de Ribonnet stands out among a host of mostly moderate wines. *See* PYRÉNÉES-ATLANTIQUES.

Condrieu N Rh ★★★→★★★★ 16' 18' 19 20' Ancient home of VIOGNIER; floral, perfumed airs, pear, apricot flavours from sandy granite slopes. Best: pure, precise (18 over 19); but beware excess oak, sweetness, alc. Growers adapting to v. hot yrs; 80 growers, not all gd. Rare white *ami* for asparagus. Best: A Paret, *A Perret* (all three wines gd), Boissonnet, CHAPOUTIER, CLOS de la Bonnette (organic), C Pichon, DELAS, Faury (esp La Berne), F Merlin, F Villard (lighter recently), Gangloff, GUIGAL, *G Vernay* (fine, incl excellent Coteau de Vernon), Monteillet, Niéro, ROSTAING, St Cosme, X Gérard (value), Y Cuilleron.

Corbières L'doc ★→★★★ Characterful red, plenty of CARIGNAN, particularly Boutenac. Some v.gd white; styles reflect contrasts of terroir from coastal lagoons to dry foothills of Pyrénées. Try: CHX Aiguilloux, Aussières, Borde-Rouge, CARAGUILHES, Grand Moulin, LA BARONNE, Lastours, la Voulte Gasparets, Les Clos Perdus, Les Palais, *Ollieux Romanis*, Pech-Latt; DOMS de Fontsainte, DE LA CENDRILLON, de Villemajou, du Grand Crès, du Vieux Parc, Trillol; Clos de l'Anhel, Grand Arc, Sainte-Croix, Serres Mazard. *Castelmaure* co-op.

Cornas N Rh ★★★ 01' 05' 09' 10' 12' 15' 16' 17' 18' 19' 20' Top-quality N Rh SYRAH, v. fashionable. Dark, strongly fruited, always mineral-lined. Some made for overt early fruit, really need 5 yrs+. Stunning 10 15. Top: *Allemand* (top two), Balthazar (traditional), M Bourg, *Clape* (benchmark), Colombo (oak), Courbis (modern), Delas, Dom du Tunnel, Dumien Serrette, G Gilles (style), J&E Durand (racy fruit), Lemenicier, Lionnet (organic), M Barret (bio), P&V Jaboulet, Tardieu-Laurent (full, oak), Voge (swish, oak), V Paris.

Corsica / Corse ★→★★★ Should be wonderful, with that scenery; often is. Plenty of variety; altitude, sea winds give freshness. Reds elegant, spicy from SCIACARELLO, structured from rarer NIELLUCCIO aka SANGIOVESE. *Gd rosés.* Tangy, herbal VERMENTINO whites. Also VDN sweet MUSCATS. Local varieties enjoying revival. Nine ACS incl crus Patrimonio in n, Ajaccio to w. AC Corse plus villages Calvi, Coteaux du Cap Corse, Sartène. IGP for whole island: Île de Beauté. Top: Abbatucci, Alzipratu, CLOS CANARELLI, Capitoro, Columbo, d'Alzeto, Fiumicicoli, *Nicrosi*, *Peraldi*, PIERETTI, Poggiale, Saperale, *Torraccia*, YVES LECCIA, Vaccelli, Venturi.

Corton C d'O ★★★→★★★★ 90' 99' 02' 03' 05' 09' 10' 12' 15' 17 18' 19' 20' Largely overpromoted GC, but can be underrated from best vyds CLOS DU ROI, Bressandes, Renardes, Rognet. Wines can be fine, elegant, not all blockbusters. References: BOUCHARD, CHANDON DE BRIAILLES, DRC, Dubreuil-Fontaine, FAIVELEY (CLOS des Cortons), Follin-Arbelet, MÉO-CAMUZET, Rapet, TOLLOT-BEAUT. Under the radar and can be gd value: Bichot, Camille Giroud, Capitain-Gagnerot, Clavelier, DOM des Croix, H&G Buisson, Mallard, Pousse d'Or, Terregelesses. Best whites from Vergennes vyd. eg. CH de MEURSAULT, CHANSON, HOSPICES DE BEAUNE.

Corton-Charlemagne C d'O ★★★→★★★★ 04 05' 09' 10' 14' 15' 17' 18 19' 20' Potentially scintillating GC, invites mineral descriptors, should age well; sw- and w-facing limestone slopes, plus band round top of hill. Top: BIZE, *Bonneau du Martray*, BOUCHARD, CLAIR, *Coche-Dury*, FAIVELEY, HOSPICES DE BEAUNE, JADOT, Javillier, LATOUR, Mallard, MONTILLE, Rapet, Rollin. DRC 1st vintage 19. *See also* CHARLEMAGNE.

Costières de Nîmes S Rh ★→★★★ North of Rhône delta, sw of CHÂTEAUNEUF, comparable v. stony soils, Mistral-blown. Gd quality, value. Red (GRENACHE, SYRAH) full, spiced, up to 10 yrs. Best: CHX de Grande Cassagne, de Valcombe, d'Or et des Gueules (full), L'Ermitage, Mas Carlot (gd fruit), Mas des Bressades (top fruit),

Mas Neuf, Montfrin (organic), Mourgues-du-Grès (organic), Nages, Roubaud, Tour de Béraud, Vessière (w); DOMS de la Patience (organic), du Vieux Relais, Galus, M Gassier, M KREYDENWEISS (bio), Petit Romain, Terres des Chardons (bio). Gd, lively, table-friendly rosés; some stylish whites (gd ROUSSANNE).

Côte Chalonnaise Burg ★★ Region immediately s of C D'O; always threatening to be rediscovered. Lighter wines, lower prices. BOUZERON for ALIGOTÉ, **Rully** for accessible, juicy wines in both colours; **Mercurey** and GIVRY have more structure and can age; MONTAGNY for leaner CHARD.

Côte d'Or Burg Département name applied to central and principal Burg vyd slopes: CÔTE DE BEAUNE and CÔTE DE NUITS. Not used on labels except for BOURGOGNE C d'O AC, finally introduced for 17 vintage.

Côte de Beaune C d'O ★★→★★★★ C D'O's s half. Also a little-seen AC in its own right applying to top of hill above BEAUNE itself. Try from DROUHIN: largely declassified Beaune PC. Also VOUGERAIE.

Côte de Beaune-Villages C d'O ★★ 15' 17 18' 19' 20' Reds from lesser villages of s half of C D'O. Nowadays usually NÉGOCIANT blends.

Côte de Brouilly Beauj ★★ 15' 17 18' 19' 20' Variety of styles as soils vary on different flanks of Mont Brouilly. Merits a premium over straight BROUILLY. Reference is CH THIVIN, but try also Blain, Brun, Dufaitre, LAFARGE-Vial, Pacalet.

Côte de Nuits C d'O ★★→★★★★ C D'O's n half. Nearly all red, from CHAMBOLLE-MUSIGNY, MARSANNAY, FIXIN, GEVREY-CHAMBERTIN, MOREY-ST DENIS, NUITS-ST GEORGES, VOSNE-ROMANÉE, VOUGEOT.

Correct spelling of "Pinot" only agreed in 1896, to distinguish from Pineau d'Aunis.

Côte de Nuits-Villages C d'O ★★ 05' 09' 10' 12' 15' 16 17 18' 19' 20' Junior AC for extreme n/s ends of CÔTE DE NUITS; can be bargains. Chopin, Gachot-Monot, Jourdan specialists. Top single-vyds CLOS du Chapeau (Arlot), Croix Violette (FOURNIER), Faulques (Millot), Leurey (JJ Confuron), Meix Fringuet (TRAPET), Montagne (many), Robignotte (Jourdan), Vaucrains (JADOT). Some fun whites too.

Côte Roannaise Lo ★★ 19' 20' AC on lower slopes of granite hills w of Roanne, V.gd GAMAY. Try: Bonneton, Désormière, Fontenay, Giraudon, Paroisse, Plasse, Pothiers, Sérol, Vial; v. interesting white IGP Urfé: ALIGOTÉ, CHARD, CHENIN BL, ROUSSANNE, VIOGNIER.

Côte-Rôtie N Rh ★★★→★★★★ 01' 05' 09' 10' 12' 15' 16' 17' 18' 19' 20' Most refined Rh red, mainly SYRAH, some VIOGNIER, granite, schist soils, style links to Burg. Violet aromas, pure (esp 16 19), complex, v. fine with age (5–10 yrs+). Exceptional, v. long-lived 10 15, racy 19. Top: *Barge* (traditional), B Chambeyron, Billon, Bonnefond (oak), Bonserine (esp La Garde), Burgaud, CHAPOUTIER, **Clusel-Roch** (organic), DELAS, DOM de Rosiers, Duclaux, Gaillard (oak), Garon, GUIGAL (long oaking), *Jamet*, Jasmin, Jean-Luc Jamet, J-M Gérin, J-M Stéphan (organic), Lafoy, Levet (traditional), *Rostaing* (fine), S Ogier (oak), Semaska, VIDAL-FLEURY (La Chatillonne), Xavier Gérard.

Coteaux Bourguignons Burg ★ DYA. Mostly reds, GAMAY, PINOT N. New AC since 2011 to replace BOURGOGNE Grand Ordinaire and to sex up basic BEAUJ. Market accepting the change. Rare whites ALIGOTÉ, CHARD, MELON, PINOTS BL/GR.

Coteaux Champenois Champ ★★★ (w) DYA. AC for still wines of CHAMP, eg. BOUZY. Vintages as for Champ. Better reds with climate change (12'). Impressive range of Coteaux Champenois Grands Blancs based on 17' by CHARLES HEIDSIECK, as gd as fine white burg.

Coteaux d'Aix-en-Provence Prov ★★ Lots of styles from big AC centred on Aix: CAB SAUV in cooler n: Pigoudet, Revelette, Vignelaure. Med grapes often more interesting in warmer spots. Chx Beaupré, Calissanne, La Realtière, Les Bastides, Les Béates; DOM d'Eole (on Alpilles), du CH Bas; Villa Baulieu. See also LES BAUX-EN-PROV, PALETTE.

Coteaux d'Ancenis Lo ★→★★ 19 20' AOP, slopes, both sides of Loire e of Nantes. Age-worthy sweet *Malvoisie* (PINOT GR); light red, rosé GAMAY, (CAB FR, 10% max), esp Guindon, Landron-Chartier, Merceron-Martin, Paonnerie (natural), Pléiade, Quarteron.

Coteaux de l'Aubance Lo ★★→★★★ 15' 16 17 18' 19 20 Small AC nr Angers, less steep than COTEAUX DU LAYON. Age-worthy sweet CHENIN BL. Nervier, usually less rich than COTEAUX DU LAYON. Esp *Bablut*, CH Princé, Haute-Perche, *Montgilet*, Rochelles, Ste-Anne, Terra Vita Vinum, Varière.

Coteaux de Saumur Lo ★★→★★★ 15' 16 17 18' 20 Age-worthy late-harvest CHENIN BL – delicate, citrus, honeyed, esp CH de Bréze, Champs Fleuris, GRATIEN & MEYER, Nerleux, Robert et Marcel, Targé, Vatan.

Coteaux des Baronnies S Rh ★→★★ DYA. Rh IGP in lonely hills e of VINSOBRES, nr Nyons. SYRAH (best), CAB SAUV, MERLOT, CHARD (gd value), also GRENACHE, CINSAULT, etc. Genuine, fresh country wines: improving mild reds, clear VIOGNIER. NB: DOMS du Rieu-Frais, Le Mas Sylvia, Rosière (bio).

Coteaux du Giennois Lo ★→★★ 18' 19' 20' Small AC, scattered vyds. Bright, citric SAUV BL like lighter SANCERRE; can be v.gd, gd value. Light reds blend GAMAY/ PINOT N. Best: *Berthier*, *Bourgeois*, Langlois, Charrier, Émile Balland, Paulat, Treuillet, *Villargeau*.

Coteaux du Layon Lo ★★→★★★★ 16 17 18' 19 20' Heart of ANJOU: top long-lived sweet CHENIN BL. Seven villages can add name to AC. Chaume now Layon PC. Top ACs: BONNEZEAUX, QUARTS DE CHAUME. Growers: Baudouin, Bellevue, Breuil, *Ch Pierre-Bise*, Chauvin, *Delesvaux*, Fesles, Forges, Guegniard, Juchepie, *Ogereau*, Soucherie. Great wine, sadly difficult to sell.

Coteaux du Loir Lo ★→★★★ 18' 19' 20' AOP Le Loir a n tributary of La Loire: exciting dynamic region incl *Jasnières*. Steely, fine, precise, long-lived CHENIN BL, reds: GAMAY, peppery Pineau d'Aunis – also fizz, plus Grolleau (rosé), CAB, CÔT. Best: Ange Vin, Breton, *Dom de Bellivière* (v.gd), Fresneau, Gigou, Janvier, Le Briseau, Les Maisons Rouges, Roche Bleue.

Coteaux du Lyonnais Beauj ★ DYA. Jnr BEAUJ. Best en PRIMEUR. Guillaume Clusel.

Coteaux du Quercy SW Fr ★ 15' 16 (18) (20) AOP between CAHORS and GAILLAC. Hearty country wines based on CAB FR plus TANNAT or MALBEC. Active co-op challenged by independents: ★★ DOMS du Guillau, Lacoste, Revel.

Coteaux du Vendômois Lo ★→★★ 19' 20' AC in Le Loir valley. Gd VIN GRIS from Pineau d'Aunis and peppery reds, also blends of CAB FR, GAMAY, PINOT N. Whites: CHARD, CHENIN BL. Best: Brazilier, Cave du Vendômois, Four à Chaux, J Martellière, Montrieux, Patrice Colin.

Coteaux Varois-en-Provence Prov ★→★★ Higher, inland "Provence Vert" is cooler. Home of "Hollywood corner": Miraval by Brad Pitt and Angelina Jolie, and neighbouring Margui by George Lucas. Otherwise, SYRAH and VIOGNIER in cooler n, interesting IGP Coteaux du Verdon. Try CHX Duvivier, Trians; DOMS des Aspras, du Deffends, du Loou, Les Terres Promises, Routas, St Mitre. Correns is 1st all-organic commune in France.

Côtes Catalanes Rouss ★★★ Wines so much better than IGP status suggests. From fruity gd value from big Vignerons de Perpignan co-op to serious age-worthy wines from some of ROUSS's finest growers. GAUBY, CH DE L'OU among others use it for top wines.

Côtes d'Auvergne Lo, Mass C ★★ 19' 20' Exciting, dynamic AC nr Clermont-Ferrand. GAMAY, PINOT N, CHARD. Villages: Boudes, Chanturgue, Châteaugay, Corent (gd rosé), Madargues (r). Producers: Cave St-Verny, *Les Chemins de l'Arkose*, Maupertuis (VDF), Miolanne, *Montel*, Pelissier, *Sauvat*. Also IGP Puy de Dôme (incl SYRAH).

Côtes de Bordeaux B'x ★ AC launched in 2008 for reds. Embraces and permits cross-blending between CAS, FRANCS, BLAYE, CADILLAC and Ste-Foy. Growers who want to maintain *the identity of a single terroir* have stiffer controls (NB) but can put Cas, Cadillac, etc. before Côtes de B'x. BLAYE-CÔTES DE B'X, FRANCS-CÔTES DE B'X and Ste-Foy-Côtes de B'x also produce a little dry white. 950 growers in group; represents 10% B'x production (65 million bottles/yr). Try CHX Dudon, Lamothe de Haux, Malagar.

Côtes de Bourg B'x ★→★★ 15 16 18 19 (20) Solid, savoury reds, a little white from e bank of Gironde. Mainly MERLOT but 10% MALBEC (80% pre-phylloxera). Top CHX: Brûlesécaille, Bujan, *Falfas*, Fougas-Maldoror, Grand-Maison, Grave (Nectar VIEILLES VIGNES), Haut-Guiraud, Haut-Macô, Haut-Mondésir, Macay, Mercier, Nodoz, *Roc de Cambes*, Rousset, Sociondo, Tour des Graves.

Côtes de Duras SW Fr ★→★★ 15 17' 18' 19 (20) Affordable AOP s of BERGERAC; Bergerac lookalike. Best known for crisp white. Berticot co-op is sound. ★★ DOMS de Laulan, Grand Mayne.

Côtes de Gascogne SW Fr ★→★★ DYA IGP. Mostly in Gers; largest producer of IGP white in France. Largely contiguous with Armagnac. Grassa family of ★★ DOM TARIQUET and La Hitaire helped introduce countless grape varieties. Typically, clean, aromatic, light. ★★ Doms JOY, Ménard, Miselle, Pellehaut; Combebelle from ever-impressive PLAIMONT co-op a well known brand.

Côtes de Millau SW Fr IGP ★ DYA. From nearby Gorges du Tarn. Foster's Millau viaduct celebrated in wines from popular co-op. ★ DOMS du Vieux Noyer, La Tour-St-Martin best of independents.

Parts of France with the most indigenous vine varieties are SW and Sav.

Côtes de Provence Prov ★→★★★ DYA. Prov rosè paradigm has conquered the world: pale, paler, palest, maybe at expense of flavour, but it's the colour of money. Whites (increasingly 100% Rolle) and reds (SYRAH and GRENACHE with MOURVÈDRE nearer coast) can be more interesting. Fréjus, La Londe, Pierrefeu, STE-VICTOIRE, Notre Dame des Anges are subzones. Leaders: CLOS CIBONNE (primarily Tibouren), Gavoty (superb); CHX D'ESCLANS, de Selle (Ott), Gasqui (bio), La Gordonne, La Mascaronne; Estandon VIGNERONS, Mirabeau, Rimauresq. See BANDOL, COTEAUX D'AIX, COTEAUX VAROIS.

Côtes de Toul Al ★ DYA. V. light wines from Lorraine; mainly VIN GRIS.

Côtes du Brulhois SW Fr ★ 16 17 18 19 (20) Small AOP nr Agen producing a softer version of TANNAT (obligatory) with CAB SAUV, MERLOT, MALBEC in support. Local co-op unusually supportive of a few independents.

Côtes du Forez Lo ★→★★ 19' 20' Most s Lo AC, level with CÔTE-RÔTIE; v.gd GAMAY (r/rosé) a must-try. Try Bonnefoy, CLOS de Chozieux, Guillot, Mondon & Demeure, Real, Verdier/Logel. Exciting IGP (w): CHARD, CHENIN BL, PINOT GR, RIES, ROUSSANNE, VIOGNIER.

Côtes du Jura Jura ★★→★★★ 10 12 14 15' 16 18' 19' 20' Revitalized region, big on natural wines; trendy with sommeliers, so pricey. Light perfumey reds from PINOT N, Poulsard, Trousseau. Try whites from fresh, fruity CHARD to deliberately oxidative SAVAGNIN or blends. Great food wines. See: AVIET, BERTHET-BONDET, *Ch d'Arlay*, GANEVAT, LABET, MACLE, MAIRE, *Pélican*, *Tissot*. Try also: *Bourdy*, J-M Petit, Pignier, Pinte. *See also* ARBOIS, CH CHALON, L'ÉTOILE ACS.

Côtes du Marmandais SW Fr ★→★★ (r) 15' 16 18 19 (20) AOP. Neighbour of B'x, but increasingly eccentric in style thanks to local Abouriou grape and SYRAH. ★★★ Cult winemaker Elian da Ros, CH Beaulieu (ages v. well); ★★ Doms Beyssac, Bonnet, Cavenac and Ch Lassolle blend it with usual B'x grapes. ★★ Ch de Beaulieu Syrah-based. Co-ops (95% total production) still dull.

Côtes du Rhône S Rh ★→★★ 19' The base of S Rh, 170 communes, incl gd SYRAH of Brézème, St-Julien-en-St-Alban (N Rh). Ranges between enjoyable, handmade,

> **Village life: the best of Côtes du Rhône-Villages**
> For best of this gd-value appellation, try: Gadagne, MASSIF D'UCHAUX,
> PUYMÉRAS, SIGNARGUES, VISAN. CHX Fontségune, Signac; DOMS Aure,
> Bastide, Bastide St Dominique, *Biscarelle*, Bois St Jean, Cabotte (bio),
> Coulange, Coste Chaude (organic), Crève Coeur (bio), Echevin (gd w),
> Florane (bio), Grand Veneur, Grands Bois (organic), Gravennes,
> Janasse, Jérome, *Les Aphillanthes* (bio), Mas de Libian (bio), Montbayon,
> Montmartel (organic), Mourchon, Pasquiers (organic), Pique-Basse
> (organic, gd w), *Rabasse-Charavin*, Réméjeanne, Renjarde, Romarins,
> Saladin (organic), St-Siffrein, Ste-Anne, Valériane, Viret; CAVE de RASTEAU,
> Les VIGNERONS d'Estézargues.

high quality (esp CHÂTEAUNEUF estates, numbers rising, gd value) and dull, mass
produced. Lively fruit now common. Mainly GRENACHE, also SYRAH, CARIGNAN.
Most best drunk young. Vaucluse top, then GARD (Syrah). Whites improving
fast, value.

Côtes du Rhône-Villages S Rh ★→★★★ 16' 17' 19' Filled, spiced reds from 7700
ha, incl 22 named S Rh villages (Nyons new in 2020), numbers up and up,
some obscure. Best are generous, lively, gd value. Red heart is GRENACHE, plus
SYRAH, MOURVÈDRE. Improving whites, often incl VIOGNIER, ROUSSANNE added to rich
base CLAIRETTE, GRENACHE BL – gd with food. *See* CHUSCLAN, LAUDUN, PLAN DE DIEU
(gd choice), SABLET, ST-GERVAIS, SÉGURET (quality), VALRÉAS, VISAN (improving, many
organic). (*See* box, above, for best growers.)

Côtes du Roussillon-Villages Rouss ★→★★★ Varied styles, often v.gd: lots of
CARIGNAN, also old-vine GRENACHE BL and Gris for whites; 32 villages: Caramany,
Latour de France, Les Aspres, Lesquerde, Tautavel singled out on label. Gd Brial
co-op plus v.gd individual estates: Boucabeille, CAZES, Charles Perez, CLOS DES FÉES,
Clot de l'Oum, des Chênes, GAUBY, Les VIGNES de Bila-Haut from CHAPOUTIER, Mas
Becha, Mas Crémat, Modat, Piquemal, Rancy, Roc des Anges, Thunevin-Calvet.
See also CÔTES CATALANES.

Côtes du Vivarais S Rh ★ 19' Mostly DYA. Across hilly, isolated ARDÈCHE country w
of Montélimar. Much improved: cool fruit, easy-drinking, based on GRENACHE,
SYRAH; some more deep, oak-aged reds. NB: Gallety (best, full, lives well), Mas de
Bagnols, VIGNERONS de Ruoms (v.gd value).

Coulée de Serrant Lo ★★ 12 13 14 15 16 18 (20) Historic, remarkable CHENIN BL AOP
7-ha site overlooking Lo in heart of SAVENNIÈRES. Nicolas Joly bio-pope, daughter
Virginie in charge. Frost-prone. Disappointingly variable wines that really ought
to be better.

Courcel, Dom de C d'O ★★★ Idiosyncratic POMMARD estate, late-picking specialist of
whole-bunch techniques; fine floral wines when it works. Top: age-worthy PCS
Rugiens and Épenots, plus interesting Croix Noires.

Crémant AC for quality classic-method sparkling from AL, B'X, BOURGOGNE, Die, Jura,
LIMOUX, Lo, Luxembourg, SAV. Many gd examples.

Crémant de Loire Lo ★★→★★★ AOP. Sparkling from ANJOU-SAUMUR, TOURAINE, CHEVERNY.
Grapes: CAB FR, CAB SAUV, CHARD, CHENIN BL, Grolleau, Orbois, Pineau d'Aunis,
PINOT N. Around 16.5 million bottles p.a. Best: Ackerman, Arnaud Lambert,
Aulée, Bouvet-Ladubay, De Chanceny, LANGLOIS-CHATEAU, Michaud, Nerleux.

Crépy Sav ★★ AC on s side Lake Geneva. Light white from Altesse, CHARD, CHASSELAS.
Try: Fichard, La Tour de Marignan, Mercier, Ripalle.

Criots-Bâtard-Montrachet C d'O ★★★ 09 10 12 14' 15 17' 18 19' Tiny and much
morsellated MONTRACHET satellite, 1.57 ha. Anybody had a great one, apart from
d'Auvenay if you're v. rich? Maybe from Blain- or Fontaine-GAGNARD, LAMY. Now
also Caroline MOREY.

FRANCE (side tab)

Cros Parantoux Burg ★★★★ Cult PC in VOSNE-ROMANÉE made famous by the late Henri Jayer. Now made to great acclaim and greater price by DOMS ROUGET and MÉO-CAMUZET. But Brûlées better in cool vintages?

Cros, Pierre L'doc ★★★ Maverick producer; mainstream wines incl MINERVOIS VIEILLES VIGNES CARIGNAN; Les Aspres, 100% SYRAH, butch and brilliant. Age-worthy. Mal Amiès light and fruity from forgotten L'DOC varieties. NEBBIOLO and TOURIGA N here too.

Crozes-Hermitage N Rh ★★→★★★ 15' 16' 17' 18 19' 20 SYRAH from mostly flat, alluvial vyds nr River Isère, hot summer challenges: dark-berry, licorice, tar; most early drinking (2–5 yrs). Reserved, complex, cooler from granite hills nr HERMITAGE: fine, red-fruited, take time. Best (simple CUVÉES) ideal for grills, parties. Some oaked, older-vine wines cost more, can age. Top: *A Graillot*, Aléofane (r/w), Belle (organic), Chapoutier, *Dard & Ribo* (organic), Delas (Le CLOS v.gd, DOM des Grands Chemins), E Darnaud, G Robin; Doms Combier (organic), de Thalabert of JABOULET, des Entrefaux, des Hauts-Châssis, des Lises (fine), *du Colombier* (*Gaby* great), Dumaine (organic), *Fayolle Fils & Fille* (v. stylish), Habrard (organic), Les Bruyères (bio, big fruit), Machon, Martinelles, Melody, Michelas St Jemms, Mucyn (fine), Remizières (oak), Rousset, Ville Rouge, Vins de Vienne, Y Chave. Drink *white* (MARSANNE) early, v.gd vintages recently. Value.

Cuve close Quicker method of making sparkling in tank. Bubbles die away in glass much quicker than with *méthode traditionnelle*.

Cuvée Usually indicates a particular blend. In CHAMP, means 1st and best wines off the press.

Dagueneau, Didier Lo ★★★→★★★★ 12' 13 14' 15' 16' 17 18' (19) (20) SAUV BL benchmark. Pouilly-Fumé but VDF from 2017 due to legal dispute; stunningly precise, age-worthy. Louis-Benjamin (winemaker) and sister Charlotte Dagueneau. Try esp: Buisson Renard, Pur Sang, Silex. Also SANCERRE (Le Mont Damné, CHAVIGNOL), Les Jardins de Babylone (JURANÇON).

Dauvissat, Vincent Chab ★★★★ Imperturbable bio producer of CHAB using old barrels and local 132-litre *feuillettes*. Grand, age-worthy wines similar to RAVENEAU cousins. Best: La Forest, Les CLOS, Preuses, Séchet. Try also DOM Jean D & Fils (no relation).

Deiss, Dom Marcel Al ★★★ Bio grower at Bergheim. Favours blends from vyds with different varieties co-planted; mixed success, variable. Best wine RIES Schoenenbourg 13' 17' outstanding; 20 will be super-refined.

Delamotte Champ Fine, small, CHARD-dominated house. Managed with SALON by LAURENT-PERRIER. BRUT, BLANC DE BLANCS, brilliant 07' 08 13 ★★★; great trio 18 19 20. Most regrettably Dominique Demarville, widely respected chef de CAVE (ex-VEUVE CLICQUOT) appointed at LAURENT-PERRIER Jan 2020, felt it necessary to leave abruptly within 4 mths. Watch this space.

Delas Frères N Rh ★★★ Vyd owner/merchant in N Rh, with CONDRIEU, CROZES-HERMITAGE, CÔTE-RÔTIE, HERMITAGE vyds. Quality high, chic new cellars. Best: Côte-Rôtie Landonne, Hermitage DOM des Tourettes (r/w), *Les Bessards* (r, granite terroir, v. fine, smoky), ST-JOSEPH Ste-Épine (r, tight, interesting); S Rh: esp CÔTES DU RH St-Esprit (r), Grignan-les-Adhémar (r, value). Whites lighter recently. Owned by ROEDERER.

Delaunay, Edouard C d'O ★★→★★★ Old Burg name revived in NUITS and l'Étang-Vergy by Laurent D. Gd range NÉGOCIANT CUVÉES all price points. Off to gd (re-)start.

Demi-sec Half-dry: but in practice more like half-sweet (eg. CHAMP typically 45g/l dosage).

Derenoncourt, Stéphane B'x Leading international consultant; self-taught, focused on terroir. Environmental audit. Own property, *Dom de l'A* in CAS.

Deutz Champ One of top small CHAMP houses, ROEDERER family-owned; gets better and better. Straight Brut 12' lovely, harmonious. Top-flight CHARD CUVÉE Amour de Deutz 06, Amour de Deutz Rosé 06. *Superb Cuvée William Deutz* 95 08' 09' exquisite. New Parcelles d'AŸ 10 12'. BLANC DE BLANCS 13 brilliant value.

Dirler-Cadé, Dom Al Marriage (2000) of Jean Dirler/Ludivine Cadé meant 23 ha in warm sandstone soils. Substance and finesse. Some certified bio. Marvellous old-vines MUSCAT GC Saering 16 17' 18' 19 20. Excellent Saering RIES, rich yet finely sketched 10 14' 16' 17' 18 19 20.

Domaine (Dom) Property, except next entry. *See* under name, eg. TEMPIER, DOM.

Dom Pérignon Champ Vincent Chaperon, now chef de CAVE, brings own style to this luxury CUVÉE of MOËT & CHANDON. Ultra-*consistent quality in incredible quantities*; maintained with creamy allure, esp with 10–15 yrs bottle-age. Plénitude releases have long bottle-age, recent disgorgement, huge price, at 7, 16, 30 yrs+ (P1, P2, P3); superb P2 98; still vibrant P3 70. More PINOT N focus in DP since 2000, esp underrated exquisite 06 in both Blanc and Rosé. Made a 2010, only one of great Champ cuvées to do so: small quantity, fierce selection of rot-affected Pinot N. Jury still out.

Dopff au Moulin Al ★★★→★★★★ Eminent family producer, esp GEWURZ GCS Brand, Sporen 09 16 18' 20'; lovely RIES SCHOENENBOURG 13 exceptional come 2020; *Sylvaner de Riquewihr 14.* Pioneer of AL CRÉMANT; v.gd CUVÉES: Bartholdi, Julien, Bio. Specialist in classic dry wines.

Doué, Didier Champ ★★★ Probably best producer of fine, sculptured CHARD on high sunny hill of Montgueux above Troyes. Avoids oak, wants finesse, elegance. Great in 18'.

Dourthe B'x Sizeable merchant/grower with nine properties; quality emphasis; incl CHX BELGRAVE, LA GARDE, LE BOSCQ, Grand Barrail Lamarzelle Figeac, PEY LA TOUR, RAHOUL, REYSSON. *Dourthe No 1* (esp w) well-made generic B'X.

Drappier, Michel Champ Great family-run AUBE house, characterful CHAMP. DOM of fine PINOT N, 60 ha+, certified bio; *Pinot-led NV*, BRUT ZÉRO, Brut *sans souffre*, Millésime d'Exception 12; ace Prestige CUVÉE Grande Sendrée 12 18' 20. Cuvée Quatuor (four CÉPAGES). Superb 95' 82 (magnums). Constant research into early C17 vines resistant to climate change. More use of large oak *foudres*.

DRC (Dom de la Romanée-Conti) C d'O ★★★★ Grandest estate in Burg (or world). This emperor is definitely wearing clothes. MONOPOLES ROMANÉE-CONTI and LA TÂCHE, major parts of ÉCHÉZEAUX, GRANDS-ÉCHÉZEAUX, RICHEBOURG, ROMANÉE-ST-VIVANT and a tiny part of MONTRACHET. Also CORTON from 2009, CORTON-CHARLEMAGNE from 2019. Crown-jewel prices. Keep top vintages for decades.

Drouhin, Joseph & Cie Burg ★★★→★★★★ Fine family-owned grower/NÉGOCIANT in BEAUNE; vyds (all bio) incl (w) Beaune *Clos des Mouches*, MONTRACHET (Marquis de LAGUICHE) and large CHAB holdings. Stylish, fragrant reds from pretty CHOREY-LÈS-BEAUNE through great ranges in Beaune, CHAMBOLLE, VOSNE (NB Petits Monts) and now GEVREY. Also Dom Drouhin Oregon (*see* US).

Duboeuf, Georges Beauj ★★→★★★ From hero – saviour of BEAUJ – to less so (too much BEAUJ NOUVEAU), always major player and still v. sound source for multiple Beauj crus and MÂCON bottlings. Georges D RIP 2020; son Franck has been in charge for some yrs.

Dubosc, André SW Fra Pioneering grower/agronomist; man behind PLAIMONT, AOP SAINT MONT and renaissance of Arrufiac, Manseng Noir, TANNAT vines. Host of ancient varieties uncovered, now subject of study. Heart and soul of Gascony.

Dugat C d'O ★★★ Cousins Claude and Bernard (Dugat-Py) made excellent, deep-coloured GEVREY-CHAMBERTIN, respective labels. Both flourishing with new generation. Tiny volumes, esp GCS, huge prices, esp Dugat-Py. Collector territory. But try village Gevrey from either for a (just) affordable thrill.

Dujac, Dom C d'O ★★★→★★★★ MOREY-ST-DENIS grower originally noted for sensual, smoky reds, from unbeatable village Morey to outstanding GCS, esp CLOS DE LA ROCHE, CLOS ST-DENIS, ÉCHÉZEAUX. Slightly more mainstream these days. Gd *whites* from Morey and PULIGNY. Lighter merchant wines as D Fils & Père and DOM Triennes in COTEAUX VAROIS.

Dureuil-Janthial Burg ★★ Top DOM in RULLY in capable hands of Vincent D-J, with *fresh, punchy whites* and cheerful, juicy reds. Try Maizières (r/w) or PC Meix Cadot (w).

Duval-Leroy Champ Family-owned house, 200 ha of mainly fine CHARD crus, focus on DOM wines. V.gd Fleur de CHAMP NV. Top Blanc de Prestige *Femme 13* ★★★★ one of Champ's top prestige CUVÉES. Also great in 18' 19.

Échézeaux C d'O ★★★ 99' 02' 05' 09' 10' 12' 15' 16 17 18' 19' 20' A GC next to CLOS DE VOUGEOT, but totally different style: lacy, ethereal, scintillating. Can vary depending on exact location. Best: ARNOUX-LACHAUX, Berthaut-Gerbet, Bizot, Coquard-Loison-Fleurot, DRC, DUJAC, EUGÉNIE, G NÖELLAT, GRIVOT, GROS, Guyon, Lamarche, LIGER-BELAIR, MÉO-CAMUZET, Millot, MUGNERET, Mugneret-Gibourg, Naudin-Ferrand, ROUGET, Tardy, Tremblay.

Ecu, Dom de l' Lo ★★★ 19' 20' Big range of wines; many livid labels. Bio. MUSCADET SÈVRE ET MAINE, GROS PLANT, VDF. Gd CAB FR, PINOT N. New winery, many amphorae.

Edelzwicker Al ★ DYA. Blended light white. CH d'Ittenwiller, HUGEL Gentil gd.

Eguisheim, Cave Vinicole d' Al ★★ Model co-op. Excellent value: fine GCS Hatschbourg, HENGST, Ollwiller, Spiegel. Owns Willm. Top label: WOLFBERGER. Best: Armorié, Grande Rés 10, Sigillé. Gd CRÉMANT, PINOT N, esp 15' 18.

Eminades, Les L'doc ★★→★★★★ Luc Bettoni makes elegant, textured wines at small ST-CHINIAN bio estate. Montmajou GRENACHE BL/MARSANNE, Sortilège SYRAH triumphs.

Entraygues et du Fel and Estaing SW Fr ★→★★ DYA. Two tiny AOP neighbours in almost vertical terraces above Lot Valley. Bone-dry CHENIN BL for whites, esp ★★ DOMS Laurent Mousset (gd reds, esp La Pauca, excellent rosé), Méjanassère. ★★ Nicolas Carmarans making wines in and out of AOP.

Entre-Deux-Mers B'x ★→★★ DYA. Often gd-value dry white B'x (drink *entre deux huitres*) from between the Rivers Garonne and Dordogne. Best: CHX Beauregard Ducourt, BONNET, Fontenille, Haut-Rian, Landereau, *Le Coin* (for Sauv Gr), Les Arromans, Lestrille, Marjosse, Martinon, Nardique-la-Gravière, Sainte-Marie, *Tour de Mirambeau*, Turcaud, Vignol.

Esclans, Ch d' ★★★ Sacha Lichine founder of canny Prov estate marketing rosé as lifestyle choice for export. Part owned by LVMH. Garrus GRENACHE, ROLLE, oaked is top-notch, expensive, will age. Rock Angel gd quality, value. Whispering Angel hugely successful NÉGOCIANT brand.

Esmonin, Dom Sylvie C d'O ★★★ Rich, dark wines from fully ripe grapes, whole-bunch vinification and new oak. Best: GEVREY-CHAMBERTIN VIEILLES VIGNES, CLOS ST-JACQUES. Fairly priced for top burg.

Etoile, L' Jura ★★ AC of Jura best known for elegant CHARD grown on limestone and marl. VIN JAUNE and VIN DE PAILLE also allowed but not reds. DOM de Montbourgeau is reference, esp En Banode. Also try: Cartaux-Bougaud, Philippe Vandelle.

Eugénie, Dom C d'O ★★★→★★★★ Artemis Estates' 1st foray into burg. Intense, dark wines now hitting stride. CLOS VOUGEOT, GRANDS-ÉCHÉZEAUX best, but try village CLOS d'Eugenie.

Faiveley, Dom Burg ★★→★★★★ More grower than merchant, revitalized by Erwan F since 2005, incl major overhaul of facilities. Now making high-class reds and sound whites. Leading light in CÔTE CHALONNAISE, but save up for top wines from CHAMBERTIN-CLOS DE BÈZE, CHAMBOLLE-MUSIGNY, CORTON *Clos des Cortons*, NUITS. Also own classy DOM Billaud-Simon (CHAB).

Faller, Théo / Weinbach, Dom Al ★★★→★★★★ Probably finest vyds in AL, wines of great **character and elegance**. Drier gastronomic style, supremely expressed in GC SCHLOSSBERG **10 13 17'**. Also RIES L'Inedit: mineral complexity. SGN GEWURZ as gd as it gets.

Faugères L'doc ★★→★★★ Rare instance of single-soil AC: schist on s-facing foothills of Cevennes; signature style is freshness to balance rich fruit. Will age. Elegant whites from GRENACHE BL, MARSANNE, ROUSSANNE, VERMENTINO. Drink CH DE LA LIQUIÈRE; DOMS Ancienne Mercerie, Bardi-Alquier, CÉBÈNE, Chenaie, des Trinités, Grézan, Léon Barral, Mas d'Alezon, Méteore, Ollier-Taillefer, St Antonin, Sarabande.

60% of Faugères producers are organic/bio. Only 60%?

Fèvre, William Chab ★★★→★★★★ Biggest owner of CHAB GCS; Bougros Côte Bougerots and Les CLOS outstanding. Small yields, no expense spared, priced accordingly, top source for rich, age-worthy wines and some more humble. Cousins N&G Fèvre also sound.

Fiefs Vendéens Lo ★→★★★ 18' 19' 20' AC from the Vendée nr Sables d'Olonne, some serious producers. CHARD, CHENIN BL, MELON, SAUV BL (W), CAB FR, CAB SAUV, GAMAY, Grolleau Gris, Négrette, PINOT N (r/rosé). Try: Coirier, Dom St-Nicolas (excellent), Mourat (organic), Prieuré-la-Chaume (bio).

Fitou L'doc ★★→★★★ Mostly CARIGNAN, so expect rugged richness, spice. Wines that taste of the sun. Two parts: schist on inland hills s of Narbonne; and chalk, limestone nr coast. Seek out: CHX de Nouvelles, Grand Guilhem, Champs des Soeurs; DOMS Bertrand-Bergé, JONES, Lérys.

Fixin C d'O ★★★ 05' 09' 10' 12' 14 15' 16 17 18' 19' 20' Worthy, undervalued n neighbour of GEVREY-CHAMBERTIN. Sturdy, sometimes splendid reds, can be rustic but enjoying warmer vintages. Best vyds: Arvelets, CLOS de la Perrière, Clos du Chapitre, Clos Napoléon. Top locals: Berthaut-Gerbet, Gelin, Joliet, Naddef. Try also Bart, CLAIR, FAIVELEY, MORTET.

Fleurie Beauj ★★★ 15' 18' 19' 20' Top BEAUJ cru for perfumed, strawberry fruit, silky texture. Racier from La Madone hillside, richer below. Classic: CHX BEAUREGARD, Chatelard, de Poncié; DOMS Brun, Chignard; CLOS de la Roilette, Depardon, DUBOEUF, Métrat, co-op. Naturalists: Balagny, Dutraive, Métras, Pacalet, Sunier. Newcomers: Chapel, Clos de Mez, Dom de Fa, Hoppenot, Lafarge-Vial.

Foncalieu L'doc ★→★★ Well run group of co-ops, focus on IGP and AC between Carcassonne and Beziers. Behind many gd value brands, incl Le Versant varietal red/white. Also DOM Haut Gléon, CORBIÈRES.

Fourrier, Dom C d'O ★★★★ Jean-Marie F has taken a sound GEVREY-CHAMBERTIN DOM to new levels, with cult prices to match. Sensual vibrant reds at all levels. Best: CLOS ST-JACQUES, Combe aux Moines, GRIOTTE-CHAMBERTIN. *See also* Bass Phillip (Australia).

Francs-Côtes de Bordeaux B'x ★★ 14 15 16 18 19 (20) Tiny B'x AC next to CAS. Fief of Thienpont (PAVIE-MACQUIN) family. Mainly red; MERLOT led (60%). Some gd white (eg. Charmes-Godard); 50% of growers organic. Top CHX: Clos Fontaine, Cru Godard, Francs, La Prade, Marsau, Puyfromage, *Puygueraud*.

Fronsac B'x ★★→★★★★ 14 15 16 18 19' (20) Great-value, hilly AC w of ST-ÉM. MERLOT-led on clay-limestone; some ageing potential. Top CHX: Arnauton, DALEM, Fontenil, *La Dauphine*, La Rivière, La Rousselle, LA VIEILLE CURE, LES TROIS CROIX, Haut-Carles, Mayne-Vieil (CUVÉE Alienor), *Moulin-Haut-Laroque*, Puy Guilhem, Tour du Moulin, Villars. *See also* CANON-FRON.

Fronton SW Fr ★★ 16 18 19 (20) AOP n of Toulouse. Must be based on rare (sometimes unblended) Négrette grape (flavours of violets, cherries, licorice). Often blended with SYRAH. ★★★ CHX Baudare, Bouissel, Caze, du Roc, Laurou, Plaisance; ★★ *Ch Bellevue-la-Forêt* best known. Also ★ Boujac, Clamens, La Colombière, Viguerie de Belaygues. No AOP for whites as yet.

Fuissé, Ch Burg ★★→★★★ Smart operation in POUILLY-FUISSÉ with long track record. Concentrated oaky whites. Top terroirs Le CLOS, Combettes. Also BEAUJ crus, eg. JULIÉNAS.

Gagnard C d'O ★★→★★★ Respected clan in CHASSAGNE. Long-lasting wines, esp Caillerets, BÂTARD from Jean-Noël G; while Blain-G, Fontaine-G have full range incl rare CRIOTS-BÂTARD, MONTRACHET itself. Gd value offered by all Gagnards. Decent Chassagne reds all round.

Gaillac SW Fr ★→★★ 18' 19' (20) Widely scattered vyd ne of Toulouse. Cornucopia of grapes incl Braucol (Fer), Duras, SYRAH (r), Len de l'El, Mauzac (w). Prunelard is gaining ground for red, while Ondenc (w) has legendary status at PLAGEOLES. Quality depressingly variable but look for ★★★ DOMS Brin, Causse-Marines, d'Escausses, La Ramaye, La Vignereuse, Le Champ d'Orphée, L'Enclos des Roses, Peyres-Roses, Plageoles, Rotier. Perlé is refreshing, summery white with slight prickle; can be delicious. Co-ops do it well and cheaply.

Ganevat Jura ★★★→★★★★ CÔTES DU JURA superstar. Single-vyd CHARD (eg. Chalasses, Grand Teppes). Also innovative reds. Beware cult pricing.

Gauby, Dom Gérard Rouss ★★★ Pioneer nr village of Calce. Bio, increasingly natural; lots of innovation; son taking over. High-altitude vyds up to 550m (1804ft), chalk for fresh acidity. Try: Les Calcinaires VIEILLES VIGNES (r/w), Muntada. Dessert wine Le Pain du Sucre. Associated with DOM Le Soula.

Gayda, Dom L'doc, Rouss ★→★★★ S African/Anglo owners; Burgundian winemaker at modern winery; restaurant nr LIMOUX. Grapes sourced locally and from MINERVOIS La LIVINIÈRE, ROUSS for top Villa Mon Rêve. Modern, stylish wines, gd value. Figure Libre CAB FR v.gd.

Gevrey-Chambertin C d'O ★★★ 05' 09' 10' 12' 15' 16 17 18' 19' 20' Major AC for fine savoury reds at all levels up to great CHAMBERTIN and GC cousins. Top PCS Cazetiers, Combe aux Moines, Combottes, CLOS ST-JACQUES. Value from single-vyd village wines (En Champs, La Justice) and VIEILLES VIGNES bottlings. Top: BACHELET, BOILLOT, Burguet, Damoy, Drouhin-Laroze, DUGAT, Dugat-Py, Duroché, ESMONIN, FAIVELEY, FOURRIER, Harmand-Geoffroy, Heresztyn-Mazzini, LEROY, Magnien (H), Marchand-Grillot, MORTET, ROSSIGNOL-TRAPET, Roty, ROUSSEAU, Roy, SÉRAFIN, TRAPET, and all gd merchants. Rebourseau is returning to life too.

Gigondas S Rh ★★→★★★ 01' 05' 06' 09' 10' 12' 13' 15' 16' 17' 18 19' Top S Rh red. V. pretty vyds on stony clay-sand *garrigue* plain rise to alpine limestone hills e of Avignon; GRENACHE, plus SYRAH, MOURVÈDRE. Full, clear, menthol-fresh wines; best give fine dark-red fruit. Top 10 15 16 19. More oak recently, higher prices, but genuine local feel in many. Try: Boissan, Bosquets (gd modern), Bouïssière (flair, punchy), Cayron (gd traditional), CH de Montmirail, CH DE ST COSME (flair), *Clos des Cazaux* (value), CLOS du Joncuas (organic, traditional), DOM *Famille Perrin*, Goubert, Gour de Chaulé (fine), Grapillon d'Or, Les Pallières, Longue Toque, Moulin de la Gardette (stylish), Notre Dame des Pallières, P Amadieu (v. consistent), Pesquier (genuine), Pourra (robust, character), *Raspail-Ay*, Roubine, *St Gayan* (long-lived), Santa Duc (now stylish), Semelles de Vent, Teyssonières. Heady rosés.

22 Rh Villages, a lot, some obscure. Rousset, St-Pantaléon, anyone? Thought not.

Gimonnet, Pierre Champ ★★★→★★★★ On n Côte des Blancs, 28 ha of GCS and PCS making beautifully consistent CHARD. Ace CUVÉE Gastronome for seafood 13 15. Not a fan of single-vyd CHAMP. Cuvées Fleuron, Club unmatched complex expression of great Chard 13 17' 19 20 for long ageing due to intricate assembly of diverse vyds.

Ginglinger, Dom Paul Al Michel, 13th-generation, makes pure, terroir-expressive racy RIES, PINOT BL. Excellent CRÉMANT.

Girardin, Vincent C d'O ★★→★★★ White-specialist MEURSAULT-based NÉGOCIANT, part of BOISSET group. Pierre-Vincent G, son of the original, is installed afresh in Meursault, showing promise.

Givry Burg ★★ 15' 17 18' 19' 20' Top tip in CÔTE CHALONNAISE for tasty reds that can age. Better value than MERCUREY. Rare whites nutty in style. Best (r): CELLIER AUX MOINES, CLOS Salomon, *Faiveley*, F Lumpp, JOBLOT, Masse, Thénard.

Goisot Burg ★★★ Guilhem & J-H G, outstanding bio producers of single-vyd bottlings of ST-BRIS (SAUV BL) and Côtes d'Auxerre for CHARD, PINOT N. Nobody else comes close.

Gonon, Dom N Rh ★★★ 09' 10' 11 12 13' 14 15' 16' 17 18' 19' 20' Top estate at ST-JOSEPH, in high demand; bros Pierre and Jean work organically, hand-graft cuttings on 10 ha prime old vyds. Mainly whole-bunch, old 600-litre casks, aromatic, peppered, iron-fused red, most savoury, textured, compelling *Les Oliviers* (w), both live 20 yrs.

Gosset Champ Oldest house, based in AŸ, owned by Cointreau. Chef de CAVE Odilon de Varine is passionate about terroir. Grand Blanc de MEUNIER a 1st for house; mainly 07, elegant, aged on CHARD lees. Prestige Celebris Extra BRUT one of best, a classic in 04. Sublime double-aged Gosset Célébrissime 95' In same spirit; new long-aged Gosset 12 Ans de Cave a Minima.

Gosset-Brabant Champ AŸ grower, great PINOT N vyds. Noirs d'Aÿ 12 15 18' 19 20' cathedral of top Pinot flavours.

Gouges, Henri C d'O ★★★ Reference point over several generations for meaty, long-lasting NUITS-ST-GEORGES with Grégory G now at helm. Great range of PC vyds, eg. CLOS des Porrets, Vaucrains and esp Les St-Georges. Also rare, excellent *white Nuits*, from PINOT BL.

Graillot, Dom Alain N Rh ★★★ 13' 15' 16' 17 18' 19' 20 Alain revitalized CROZES-HERMITAGE in 1985; 20 ha organic vyds, whole-bunch ferments. Dashing CROZES (r): La Guiraude special selection, serious, long life. Crozes (w), ST-JOSEPH (r). Son Maxime: Crozes DOM des Lises, gd merchant range Equis.

Gramenon, Dom S Rh ★★→★★★ 18' 19' 20 Organic since decades, bio since 2007, at height in lower Drôme. Fruit purity, v. low sulphur, gd range. CÔTES DU RH: La Papesse (Grenache), La Sagesse, Poignée des Raisins (fun), Sierra du Sud (SYRAH).

GC (Grand Cru) Official term meaning different things in different areas. One of top Burg vyds with its own AC. In AL, one of 51 top vyds, each now with its own rules. In ST-ÉM, 60% of production is St-Ém GC, often run of the mill. In MÉD: five tiers of GC CLASSÉS. In CHAMP top 17 villages are GCs. Since 2011 in Lo for QUARTS DE CHAUME, and emerging system in L'DOC. Take with pinch of salt in Prov.

Grande Rue, La C d'O ★★★ 05' 06 09' 10' 12' 15' 16 18' 19' 20' MONOPOLE of DOM Lamarche, GC between LA TÂCHE, ROMANÉE-CONTI. Quality, consistency improved under Nicole L. Fascinating blood-orange hallmark across vintages.

Grands-Échézeaux C d'O ★★★★ 90' 93 96' 99' 02' 05' 09' 10' 12' 15' 17 18' 19' 20' Superlative GC next to CLOS DE VOUGEOT, but with a MUSIGNY silkiness. More weight than most ÉCHÉZEAUX. Top: BICHOT (CLOS Frantin), Coquard-Loison-Fleurot, DRC, DROUHIN, EUGÉNIE, G NOËLLAT, Lamarche, Millot.

Grange des Pères, Dom de la L'doc ★★★ Next door to MAS DE DAUMAS GASSAC, and IGP. Red from CAB SAUV, SYRAH, MOURVÈDRE; white 80% ROUSSANNE, plus CHARD, MARSANNE. Difficult to get hold of but pretty special if you can.

Gratien, Alfred and Gratien & Meyer Champ ★★★ BRUT 93 12 13 15' 18' Small but beautiful CHAMP house, owned by Henkell Freixenet. Brut NV. CHARD-led Prestige CUVÉE Paradis Brut, Rosé (MV). Fine, v. dry, lasting, oak-fermented wines incl *The Wine Society's house Champagne*. Careful buyer of top crus, esp CHARD from favourite growers. Also Gratien & Meyer in SAUMUR.

Graves B'x ★→★★ 15 16 18 19 (20) Gravel soils provide name. Appetizing grainy reds from MERLOT, CAB SAUV, fresh SAUV/SÉM (dr w). Graves Superieures denotes *moelleux*. Some of best values in B'X today. Top CHX: ARCHAMBEAU, Brondelle, CHANTEGRIVE, CLOS Bourgelat, *Clos Floridène*, CRABITEY, de Cérons, Ferrande, Fougères, Grand Enclos du Ch de Cérons, Haura, Magneau, Pont de Brion, RAHOUL, *Respide Medeville*, Roquetaillade La Grange, Saint-Robert (CUVÉE Poncet Deville), Seuil, *Vieux Ch Gaubert*, Villa Bel Air.

Graves de Vayres B'x ★ DYA. Tiny AC within E-2-M zone. Red, white, *moelleux*.

Grignan-les-Adhémar S Rh ★ ›★★ 19' Mid-Rh AC; best reds medium weight, spiced, herbal. Leaders: Baron d'Escalin, DELAS (value), La Suzienne (value); CHX Bizard, La Décelle (incl CÔTES DU RH w); DOMS de Bonetto-Fabrol, de Montine (stylish r, gd w/rosé, also Côtes du Rh r), Grangeneuve best (esp VIEILLES VIGNES), St-Luc.

Griotte-Chambertin C d'O ★★★★ 90' 96' 99' 02' 05' 09' 10' 12' 15' 16 17 18' 19' 20' Small GC next to CHAMBERTIN; nobody has much volume. Brisk red fruit, with depth, ageing potential, from DROUHIN, DUGAT, Duroché, FOURRIER, *Ponsot (Laurent)*.

Gripa, Dom N Rh ★★★ 10' 13' 15' 16' 17' 18' 19' 20' Top ST-JOSEPH, ST-PÉRAY DOM, elegant whites a speciality. St-Joseph Le Berceau (w) 100% 60-yr+ MARSANNE; *St-Péray Les Figuiers*, mainly ROUSSANNE. Both St-Joseph reds gd, top Le Berceau tracks vintage: deep 15, pure-fruit 16, dense 17, bold 18, rich 19.

Grivot, Jean C d'O ★★★›★★★★ VOSNE-ROMANÉE DOM that keeps on improving, likely to continue as Mathilde G starts to take over. Superb range of PCS (NB Beaux Monts and NUITS Boudots) topped by GCS CLOS DE VOUGEOT, ÉCHÉZEAUX, RICHEBOURG. Higher prices these days.

A yr in Burg: 51 wks of complaints about prices, 1 wk when new vintage sells out.

Gros, Doms C d'O ★★★›★★★★ Family of VIGNERONS in VOSNE-ROMANÉE with stylish wines from Anne (sumptuous RICHEBOURG), succulent reds from Michel (CLOS de Réas), Anne-Françoise (now in BEAUNE) and Gros Frère & Soeur (CLOS VOUGEOT En Musigni). Not just GCS; try value HAUTES-CÔTES DE NUITS. Also Anne's DOM Gros-Tollot in MINERVOIS. Change of generation at all four doms, but no changes in style evident yet.

Gros Plant du Pays Nantais Lo ★›★★ AC DYA. Gros Plant (FOLLE BLANCHE); much better than reputation. Racy, saline, married to oysters. Best: Basse Ville, ECU, Haut-Bourg, Luneau-Papin, Poiron-Dabin, Preuille. Sparkling: pure or blended.

Guigal, Ets N Rh ★★›★★★★ Justly famous, always-expanding grower-merchant: CÔTE-RÔTIE mainly, plus CONDRIEU, CROZES-HERMITAGE, HERMITAGE, ST-JOSEPH, 52-ha CHÂTEAUNEUF CH de Nalys, plus two lots of 7-ha and 18-ha vyds there. Merchant: Condrieu, Côte-Rôtie, Crozes-Hermitage, Hermitage, S Rh. Owns DOM de Bonserine (ripe, oaked Côte-Rôtie), VIDAL FLEURY (fruit, quality on up) Top, v. expensive Côte-Rôties La Mouline, La Landonne, La Turque (ultra rich, 42 mths new oak, so atypical), also v.gd Hermitage, St-Joseph VIGNES de l'Hospice; all reds dense. Standard wines: gd, esp *brilliant-value Côtes du Rh* (r/w/rosé). Best whites: Condrieu, Condrieu La Doriane (oaky), Hermitage.

Hautes-Côtes de Beaune C d'O ★★ (r) 15' 18' 19' 20' (w) 17' 18 19' 20' Generic BOURGOGNE AC for villages in hills behind CÔTE DE BEAUNE. Attractive lighter reds, whites for early drinking, both putting on weight in warmer times. Best whites: Devevey, Rollin, Thevenot-le-Brun. Top reds: Carré, Champy (Boris), CHEVROT, Duband, Jacob, Magnien (Sebastien), Naudin (Claire), Parigot, Vantey.

Hautes Côtes de Nuits C d'O ★★ (r) 15' 18' 19' 20' Generic BOURGOGNE AC for villages in hills behind CÔTE DE NUITS. Sweet spots are villages of Arcenant, Concoeur and plateau above NUITS and VOSNE. Doing well in these warmer times. Best whites: MÉO-CAMUZET, Thevenot-le-Brun. Top reds: Faure, GROS, Hoffmann-Jayer, LIGER-BELAIR, Naudin (Claire), Verdet.

Haut-Médoc B'x ★★›★★★★ 14 15 16' 18 19' (20) Prime source of dry, digestible CAB/

MERLOT reds. Usually gd value. Plenty of CRUS BOURGEOIS. Wines usually sturdier in n; finer in s. Five Classed Growths (BELGRAVE, CAMENSAC, *Cantemerle*, *La Lagune*, LA TOUR-CARNET). Other top CHX: Arnauld, BELLE-VUE, CAMBON LA PELOUSE, Charmail, CISSAC, CITRAN, COUFRAN, D'AGASSAC, *de Lamarque*, Lamothe-Bergeron, LANESSAN, Larose Perganson, *Malescasse*, Malleret, REYSSON, SÉNÉJAC, *Sociando-Mallet*, Taillan.

Haut-Poitou Lo ★→★★ 18' 19' Isolated AC for CAB SAUV, CAB Fr, CHARD, GAMAY, PINOT N, SAUV BL. Dynamic Ampelidae (IGP) dominates. Also La Tour Beaumont, Lacheteau (Ohh Poitou!), Morgeau La Tour.

Heidsieck, Charles Champ ★★★★ Iconic CHAMP house, small but beautiful, wines as brilliant as ever. *NV Brut* all purity and subtle ripe complexity. Peerless Blanc des Millénaires 04'. Exceptional Vintage 12' lovely now, also a keeper to 2030; older Collection greats in fine maturity, esp 83 81; CHAMP Charlie Prestige CUVÉE could be reintroduced from 2023. New BLANC DE BLANCS NV, nicely priced, delicious fruit, added tension.

Heidsieck Monopole Champ Once-great CHAMP house. Fair-quality, gd-price Gold Top 09 12 15. Part of VRANKEN group.

Hengst Al A GC for powerful wines: top GEWURZ from JOSMEYER, ZIND-HUMBRECHT; also AUXERROIS, CHASSELAS, PINOT N.

Henriot Champ A v. fine family CHAMP house. Ace BLANC DE BLANCS de CHARD NV; Brut 98' 02' 08; Brut Rosé 09. Exceptional new prestige CUVÉE Hemera 05 06 – catch stocks at auction of long-lived former prestige cuvée Les Enchanteleurs big, powerful 88'. Talented Alice Tétienne, ex-Krug, new chef de CAVE. Also owns BOUCHARD PÈRE & FILS, FÈVRE.

Hermitage N Rh ★★★→★★★★ 01' 05' 06' 07' 09' 10' 11' 12' 13' 15' 16' 17' 18' 19' 20' (10 15 brilliant.) Part granite hill on e Rhône bank with grandest, deepest, majestic SYRAH and complex, nutty/white-fruited, fascinating, v.-long-lived white (MARSANNE, some ROUSSANNE) best left for 6–7 yrs+. Best: Alexandrins, Belle (organic), *Chapoutier (bio, magic w)*, Colombier, DELAS, Faurie (pure), GUIGAL, Habrard (w), *J-L Chave* (rich, elegant), M Sorrel (mighty Le Gréal r, retired 2018), Paul Jaboulet Aîné (refined), Philippe & Vincent Jaboulet (r/w), Tardieu-Laurent (oak). TAIN co-op gd (esp Gambert de Loche r, VIN DE PAILLE W).

Horizon, Dom de l' Rouss ★★★ Pure expression of rugged ROUSS terroir under IGP CÔTES CATALANES from old vines nr Calce. Mar y Muntanya gd value SYRAH. Gd gastronomic rosé.

Hortus, Dom de l' L'doc ★★★ Dynamic, family-run PIC ST-LOUP estate. Fine SYRAH-based reds: elegant Bergerie and oak-aged Grande CUVÉE (r). Intriguing Bergerie IGP Val de Montferrand (w) with seven grapes. Also CLOS du Prieur (r) in cooler TERRASSES DU LARZAC.

Hospices de Beaune C d'O Spectacular medieval foundation with grand charity auction of CUVÉES from its 61 ha for Beaune's hospital, 3rd Sunday in Nov, run by Christie's. Individuals can buy as well as trade. Winemaker Ludivine Griveau making consistently fine wines. Try BEAUNE cuvées, VOLNAYS or expensive GCS, (r) CORTON, ÉCHÉZEAUX, MAZIS-CHAMBERTIN, (w) BÂTARD-MONTRACHET. Quality high; bargains unlikely; charity is the point.

Hudelot C d'O ★★★ VIGNERON family in CÔTE DE NUITS. H-NOËLLAT (VOUGEOT) is top class, esp GCS ROMANÉE-ST-VIVANT, RICHEBOURG, while H-Baillet (CHAMBOLLE) is challenging with punchy reds.

Huet Lo ★★★★ 16' 17 18' 19' 20' Renowned VOUVRAY DOM. Anthony Hwang also owns Királyudvar in Tokaji, Hungary. CHENIN BL reference. Bio since 1990. Single-vyds: CLOS du Bourg and Le Mont on Première Côte, Le Haut Lieu nearby. V. age-worthy, esp sweet: from 1919... 03 05 06 07 08 10 11 15. Also *pétillant*.

Hugel & Fils Al ★★→★★★★ Revered AL house at Riquewihr, led by 12th-generation Jean-Philippe Hugel, no longer opposed to GC designation. Estate famed for

FRANCE

late-harvest, esp RIES, GEWURZ VT, SGN. Superb Ries Schoelhammer 07 10 13 17 from GC site.

IGP (Indication Géographique Protegée) Potentially most dynamic category in France (150+ regions), scope for experimentation. Replacing VdP, but new terminology still not accepted by every area. Zonal names most individual: eg. CÔTES DE GASCOGNE, Côtes de Thongue, Pays des Cévennes, Haute Vallée de l'Orb, among others. Enormous variety in taste, quality, but never ceases to surprise.

Irancy Burg ★★ 15' 16 17 18' 19 Structured red made nr CHAB from PINOT N and more rustic local César. Elbows-on-table stuff, beware hot vintages. Best vyds: Mazelots, Palotte. Best: Cantin, Ferrari, GOISOT, Renaud, Richoux.

Irouléguy SW Fr ★→★★★ 15' 16 18' 19 (20) From lusciously green hillsides in the Basque country. Reds based on TANNAT, Axéria (CAB FR). Look out for rediscovered vines like Arrouya (Manseng Noir), Erremaxaoua. Best from ★★★ Arretxea, Bordaxuria, Brana, Ilarria. Fruity white based on Petit Courbu and both MANSENGS; ★★★ Brana, also for fruit-based spirits, gin.

Jaboulet Aîné, Paul N Rh Grower-merchant at Tain. Organic vyds, well worked, across HERMITAGE, CONDRIEU, CORNAS, CROZES-HERMITAGE, CÔTE-RÔTIE, ST-JOSEPH. Wines polished, sleek, would love more soul. Once-leading producer of HERMITAGE, esp ★★★★ La Chapelle (legendary 61 78 90), quality varied since 90s, some revival since 2010 on reds. Also CORNAS St-Pierre, Crozes Thalabert (can be stylish), Roure (sound). Merchant of other Rh, notably VACQUEYRAS, VENTOUX (r, quality/ value). Whites lack true Rh body, drink most young, range incl new v. expensive La Chapelle (w, not every yr).

Jacquart Champ ★★★ Simplified range from co-op-turned-brand, concentrating on what it does best: PC Côte des Blancs CHARD from member growers. Fine range of Vintage BLANC DE BLANCS 13 17 19' 20'. V.gd Vintage Rosé 12.

Jacquart, André Champ ★★★ Marie Doyard has 24 ha incl 18 ha in GC LE MESNIL. Flagship Mesnil Experience. Ace Vintage trio 18' 19' 20'; BLANC DE BLANCS specialist.

Jacquesson Champ ★★★★ Ace Dizy house for precise, v. dry wines. Outstanding single vyd Avize CHAMP Caïn 12'. Corne Bautray, all CHARD. Dizy 10 13' innovative *numbered NV cuvées* 730' 731 732 733 734 735 738 739 739 740 741 742 743. Focus on intrinsic character of each base-wine harvest rather than notional consistency yr on yr.

Jadot, Louis Burg ★★→★★★★ Dynamic BEAUNE merchant making powerful whites (DIAM corks) and well-constructed age-worthy reds with significant vyd holdings in BEAUJ, C D'O, MÂCON; esp POUILLY-FUISSÉ (DOM Ferret), MOULIN-À-VENT (CH des Jacques, *Clos du Grand Carquelin*). On v. gd form at moment.

Jamet, Dom N Rh ★★★★ 05' 09' 10' 12 13' 14 15' 16' 17' 18' 19' 20' Top, illustrious CÔTE-RÔTIE, v.-long-lived, complex *vins de terroir* from many sites, mostly schist. Classic red intricate, dashing fruit, top Côte Brune (r) is mighty, smoky, mysterious. Also high-grade CÔTES DU RH (r/w), COLLINES RHODANIENNES (r).

Jasnières Lo ★★→★★★ 18' 19' 20' Dynamic AOP. Long-lived CHENIN BL, dry to sweet, s-facing slopes Loir Valley. Try: Breton, *Bellivière*, Gigou, Janvier, J-B Métais, L'Ange Vin (also VDF), Le Briseau, Les Maisons Rouges, *Roche Bleue*, Ryke. Climate change double-edged – warmer summers, more April frosts.

Jobard C d'O ★★★ VIGNERON family in MEURSAULT. Antoine J for esp long-lived Poruzots, Genevrières, CHARMES plus reds from former DOM Mussy (POMMARD) from 2019. Rémi J for immediately classy Meursaults, esp Poruzots.

Joblot Burg ★★ Jean-Marc J was reference producer for GIVRY. Now retired; daughter Juliette in charge.

Jones, Dom Rouss ★★→★★★ Englishwoman Katie J; consistently gd FITOU, Côtes du ROUSS. Terroir wines with modern twist. Lively social media: join her on live vyd rambles, learn a thing or two over morning coffee.

Josmeyer Al ★★→★★★★ Exceptional family AL house, pioneer of bio viticulture, centred on RIES GC Hengst 13 14 16 17' 18' 19 20. Intriguing single-vyd Pinot AUXERROIS. Untimely death of Jean Meyer and departure of his son-in-law, a fine winemaker; now steadied by Jean's daughters Isabelle (oenologist) and Celine (MD).

Juliénas Beauj ★★★ 15' 16 17 18' 19' 20' Deserves to be better known for deep-fruited BEAUJ, esp for CLIMATS Beauvernay, etc. DOM Perrachon leads the way, try also Audras (Clos de Haute Combe), Aufranc, Besson, Burrier, CH BEAUREGARD, CH FUISSÉ, Chignard, Dom Granit Doré, Trenel.

Jurançon SW Fr ★→★★★ (sw) 15' 16' 18 19 (20) (dr) 16 17' 18' 19 (20) Separate AOPS for sweet and dry whites. Balance of richness, acidity the key to quality. ★★★ DOMS *Cauhapé*, Guirardel, Lapeyre, Larrédya, Larrouyat. ★★ CH Jolys; Doms Bellegarde, Bordenave, Castéra, du Ciinquau; CLOS Benguères, Nigri, Uroulat. ★ Gan co-op gd value. *See also* CABIDOS.

Kaefferkopf Al ★★★ The 51st GC of AL at Ammerschwihr. Permitted to make blends as well as varietal wines, possibly not top-drawer.

Kientzler, Andre Al ★★→★★★★ Family DOM, 5th generation. Lush sensual GEWURZ GC Kirchberg 16 17'18' 19 20; VT dessert wines. Exemplary care in vyds.

Kreydenweiss, Marc Al ★★→★★★★ Bio for decades. Rich diversity of soils: GC Moenchberg on limestone for PINOT GR and majestic RIES Kastelberg on black schist, ages for up to 20 yrs 10 17'★★★★ 18' 19 20. Also in COSTIÈRES DE NÎMES.

Krug Champ Supremely prestigious de luxe house. ★★★★ Grande CUVÉE, esp 160th Edition based on 04; 167th Edition (11 base) v. graceful despite questionable reputation of base yr. Vintage 98 02 04; Rosé; CLOS DU MESNIL 02 98; CLOS D'AMBONNAY 95'98' 00; Krug Collection 69 76'81 85. Rich, nutty wines, oak-fermented; highest quality, ditto price. Shame they never released even a bit of 12, truly great yr.

Kuentz-Bas Al ★★→★★★ Among highest AL vyds, organic/bio, serious yet accessible wines: drier RIES 13 17' 20. Fine PINOT GR, GEWURZ VT 09 12 17.

Labet, Dom Jura ★★★ Key CÔTES DU JURA estate in s part of region (Rotalier). Best-known for range of single-vyd CHARD whites, eg. En Billat, En Chalasse, La Bardette; gd PINOT N, VIN JAUNE.

Ladoix C d'O ★★ (r) 09' 10' 12 15' 17 18' 19' 20' (w) 14' 15 17' 18 19' 20' Fresh, exuberant whites, eg. Grechons, and juicy reds, esp Les Joyeuses. Key producers: (w) Chevalier, FAIVELEY, Loichet; (r) Capitain-Gagnerot, CH DE MEURSAULT, Mallard, Naudin-Ferrand, Ravaut. Those with more cash try Le Clou from Prieuré-Roch.

Lafarge, Michel C d'O ★★★★ RIP Michel L, 1928–2020. Outstanding bio, VOLNAY estate run by Frédéric L, Unbeatable PCS *Clos des Chênes*, CLOS du CH des Ducs. Also fine BEAUNE, esp Grèves (r) and Clos des Aigrots (w). Plus FLEURIE project, Lafarge-Vial.

Lafon, Dom des Comtes Burg ★★★★ Fabulous bio MEURSAULT DOM, with long-lasting red VOLNAY *Santenots* equally outstanding. Value from excellent Mâconnais wines: Héritiers L label. Dominique L makes own CÔTE DE BEAUNE wines separately.

Laguiche, Marquis de C d'O ★★★★ Largest owner of Le MONTRACHET and a fine PC CHASSAGNE, both excellently made by DROUHIN.

Lalande de Pomerol B'x ★★→★★★ 10' 14 15 16 18 19 (20) Progressing satellite neighbour of POM. Largely MERLOT. Varied terroir: clay, gravel, sand. Top CHX: Ame de Musset, Belles-Graves, Chambrun, Enclos de Viaud, Garraud, Grand Ormeau, Haut-Chaigneau, Jean de Gué, La Chenade, LA FLEUR DE BOÜARD, La Sergue, Les Cruzelles, *Les Hauts Conseillants*, Pavillon Beauregard, Sabines, Samion, Siaurac, *Tournefeuille*.

Lallier Champ Artisan CHAMP from GC parcels AŸ PINOT N. New Black Label R series 12 and 13 base ace expression of each yr. Lovely Oger CHARD too. New top cellarmaster: to watch.

FRANCE

Lamy C d'O ★★★ DOM Hubert L is go-to address for ST-AUBIN. Breathtakingly fresh, concentrated whites, often from higher-density plantings. Reds now worthy of note. Also DOMS L-Caillat (intense w), more traditional L-Pillot in CHASSAGNE.

Landes SW Fr DYA IGP area in far sw, similar to CÔTES DE GASCOGNE. Better known for sand dunes. DOM de Lamballe is decent enough: try its Sables Fauves. Coteaux de Chalosse is separate IGP: lots of weird vines. Try TURSAN co-op.

Landron, Doms Lo ★★→★★★ 19' 20' Flamboyant Jo L. V.gd bio MUSCADET SÈVRE ET MAINE: incl Amphibolite, Fief du Breil.

Langlois-Chateau Lo ★★→★★★ SAUMUR, SANCERRE (Fontaine-Audon/Thauvenay). BOLLINGER-owned. Gd selection CRÉMANT DE LO. Range of still Loires, incl v.gd Saumur Blanc VIEILLES VIGNES 16' 17', CHINON, POUILLY-FUMÉ, SAUMUR-CHAMPIGNY.

Languedoc Region and sprawling AC from Nîmes to Spanish border, inland to Carcassonne and LIMOUX. Theoretically bottom of the pyramid of L'doc ACs with other levels more specific, based on region and terroir. eg. FAUGÈRES, MINERVOIS, ST-CHINIAN. Subregions incl Cabrières, Grès de Montpellier, PÉZENAS, Quatourze, St-Saturnin, St-Georges d'Orques. Clairette du L'doc tiny AC for white CLAIRETTE. Top of hierarchy: crus incl CORBIÈRES-Boutenac, LA LIVINIÈRE, PIC ST LOUP, LA CLAPE, TERRASSES DU LARZAC. Usual L'doc grapes: (r) CARIGNAN, CINSAULT, GRENACHE, MOURVÈDRE, SYRAH; (w) GRENACHE BL, ROUSSANNE, VERMENTINO, but many others. IGP d'Oc covers whole region, regional IGPs too. Phew!

Most relaxing way to explore L'doc vyds: cruise Canal du Midi, an engineering miracle c.1694.

Lanson Champ ★★★ Major house, owned by PAILLARD. Black Label NV; Rosé NV; Vintage BRUT on a roll, esp 02 08 12 15 18'. Ace prestige NV Noble CUVÉE BLANC DE BLANCS, rosé and vintage. Brut vintage single-vyd CLOS Lanson 12 Extra Age multi-vintage, Blanc de Blancs esp gd. Experienced new winemaker Hervé Dantan (since 15) allows some malo for a rounder style.

Lapierre, Marcel Beauj ★★★ Mathieu and Camille L continue cult DOM making sulphur-free MORGON. Range of styles and CUVÉES on offer.

Laplace, Dom SW Fr Oldest and at one time only producer of MADIRAN. Still at top. Top wine ★★★ CH d'Aydie, needs time. Odie d'Aydie less so. Beautifully polished, less extracted than before; ★★ Les Deux Vaches; ★ Aramis excellent intros to TANNAT – lighter, rounder. Excellent ★★★ PACHERENCS (dr sw). Sweet fortified Maydie (think BANYULS) gd with chocolate.

Laroche Chab ★★ Major player in CHAB with quality St Martin blend, Vieille Voye special CUVÉE, exceptional GC *Res de l'Obediencerie* named for historic HQ (worth a visit). Winemaker Gregory Viennois involved in NÉGOCIANT IRANCY project. Also Mas La Chevalière in L'DOC.

Latour, Louis Burg ★★→★★★★ Famous traditional family grower-merchant making full-bodied whites from C D'O vyds (esp CORTON-CHARLEMAGNE), Mâconnais, Ardèche (all CHARD), while reds are looking classier – CORTON, ROMANÉE-ST-VIVANT. Also owns Henry Fessy in BEAUJ.

Latricières-Chambertin C d'O ★★★★ 96' 99' 05' 09' 10' 12' 15' 16 17 18' 19' 20' GC next to CHAMBERTIN. Deep soil and cooler site gives rich earthy wines in warm dry yrs. Best: ARNOUX-LACHAUX, BIZE, Drouhin-Laroze, Duband, Duroché, FAIVELEY, LEROY, Remy, ROSSIGNOL-TRAPET, TRAPET.

Laudun S Rh ★→★★ 18' 19' Sound CÔTES DU RH-VILLAGE, on w bank. Clear, peppy whites. Red-fruit, peppery reds (much SYRAH), lively rosés. Immediate flavours from Maison Sinnae (old name Laudun-CHUSCLAN) co-op. Dom Pelaquié best, esp fresh white. Also CHX Courac, de Bord, Juliette; DOMS Duseigneur (bio), Carmélisa, Maravilhas (bio, character, r/w), Olibrius.

Laurent-Perrier Champ Important house; family presence less obvious. BRUT NV

(CHARD-led) perfect apéritif; v.gd skin-contact Rosé. Fine vintages: 08 12'. Grand Siècle CUVÉE multi-vintage on form, peerless Grand Siècle Alexandra Rosé 12 ★★★★. Question mark over future direction after abrupt departure of eminent cellarmaster Dominique Demarville, mid-2020.

Lavantureux Chab ★★ Specialist source for PETIT CHAB, CHAB, esp single-vyd Vauprin. BOURGOGNE Epineuil reds from 2019.

Leccia, Yves Cors ★★★ Small bio DOM nr Bastia. Intense, precise fruit rather than oak. AC Patrimonio El Croce, IGP Île de Beauté YL. Worth seeking out.

Leflaive, Dom Burg ★★★★ Reference PULIGNY-MONTRACHET DOM restored to top quality and prices. Total revamp with new director and winemaker since 2016. Outstanding GC, incl LE MONTRACHET, CHEVALIER and *fabulous PCs*: Pucelles, Combettes, Folatières, etc. Value from developing s Burg range, eg. MÂCON Verzé.

Leflaive, Olivier C d'O ★★→★★★ White specialist NÉGOCIANT at PULIGNY-MONTRACHET. Smart wines of late, spot on with BOURGOGNE Les Sétilles as with own GC vyds. Reds work in progress. Also La Maison d'Olivier, hotel, restaurant, tasting room.

Leroux, Benjamin C d'O ★★★ BEAUNE-based NÉGOCIANT equally at home in red or white. C D'O only, strengths (w) in MEURSAULT with increasing DOM and (r) BLAGNY, GEVREY, VOLNAY. Smart wines in every sense.

Leroy, Dom C d'O ★★★★ Lalou Bize L, BIO pioneer, delivers extraordinary quality from tiny yields in VOSNE-ROMANÉE and from DOM d'Auvenay. Both fiendishly expensive even ex-dom. As is amazing treasure trove of mature wines from family NÉGOCIANT Maison L.

Liger-Belair, Comte C d'O ★★★★ Comte Louis-Michel L-B makes brilliantly ethereal wines in VOSNE-ROMANÉE, an ever-increasing stable headed by LA ROMANÉE. Try also village La Colombière, PC Reignots and NUITS-ST-GEORGES crus. In Oregon, Chile.

Liger-Belair, Thibault C d'O ★★★→★★★★ New winery in NUITS-ST-GEORGES, for succulent bio burg from generics up to Les St-Georges and GC RICHEBOURG. Some NÉGOCIANT whites. Also range of stellar old-vine single-vyd MOULIN-À-VENT.

Lignier C d'O ★★★ Family in MOREY-ST-DENIS. Whole range from Laurent L (DOM Hubert L) brilliant, esp CLOS DE LA ROCHE. V.gd PCS from Virgile L-Michelot, esp Faconnières, but Dom Georges L divides opinion.

Lilbert Champ Bijou DOM, highest standards. Young CHARDS hard as diamond, but age gracefully for 30 yrs. Entry-level Perlé GC NV a gd intro.

Limoux L'doc ★★→★★★ Bustling market town best known for sparkling BLANQUETTE and CREMANT de Limoux. Gd value. AC Limoux for stylish still white from CHARD, CHENIN, Mauzac; barrel aged. Red AC: MERLOT, plus SYRAH, GRENACHE, CABS. PINOT N in CRÉMANT and for IGP Haute Vallée de l'Aude. Growers: CH de Gaure; DOMS de Baronarques, Begude, de Fourn, de l'Aigle, Mouscaillo, RIVES-BLANQUES; Cathare, Jean-Louis Denois.

Liquière, Ch de la L'doc ★★ Unpretentious fruity AC FAUGÈRES, family estate. Les Amandières (r/w/rosé) terrific value. Cistus old vines (r/w). Malpas top SYRAH.

Montpellier satellites

Near France's 7th largest city are revived and est terroirs, names appended to AC L'DOC. Some compelling wines. Grès de Montpellier is biggest, surrounding city. CHX Haut Blanville, St Martin de Garrigue (smart PICPOUL too); DOMS Haut Blanville, L'Engarran, Roquemale, Saumarez; Mas de Novi, all top-notch. Historic St-Georges d'Orques in sw appreciated by Thomas Jefferson. Doms de la Marfée, Henry stars here. CH PUECH-HAUT kingpin of St-Drézéry to nw; 40 mins drive is Cabrières, fast emerging as rosé hotspot, thanks to GÉRARD BERTRAND's Clos du Temple. MUSCATS de Mireval and Frontignan by the Med and Lunel in e, sweet fragrant delights, often v.gd value.

Lirac S Rh ★★→★★★ 10' 15' 16' 17' 18 19' Four villages nr TAVEL, stony, quality soils. Spiced red (life 5 yrs+), gd impetus from CHÂTEAUNEUF owners via clearer fruit, more brio. Reds best, esp DOMS Carabiniers (bio), *de la Mordorée* (organic, best, r/w), Duseigneur (bio) Giraud, Joncier (bio, character), Lafond Roc-Epine (organic), La Lôyane, La Rocalière (organic, gd fruit), Maby (Fermade, gd w), Maravilhas (bio), Marcoux (stylish), Plateau des Chênes; CHX Boucarut (organic, revived), de Bouchassy (gd w), de Manissy (organic), de Montfaucon (v.gd w, incl CÔTES DU RH), Mont-Redon, St-Roch; Mas Isabelle (handmade), P Usseglio, Rocca Maura (esp w), R Sabon. Whites on the up, convey freshness, body, go 5 yrs.

Listrac-Médoc H-Méd ★★→★★★ 14 15 16' 18 19 (20) Much-improved AC for savoury red B'X; now more fruit, depth and MERLOT due to clay soils; 65 growers (of which 31 attached to Grand Listrac co-op). Best CHX: Cap Léon Veyrin, CLARKE, FONRÉAUD, Fourcas-Borie, FOURCAS-DUPRÉ, FOURCAS-HOSTEN, l'Ermitage, LESTAGE, Liouner, MAYNE-LALANDE, Reverdi, SARANSOT-DUPRÉ.

Livinière, La L'doc ★★★ AC from 2020; former cru of MINERVOIS. Stricter selection, lower yield, longer ageing. SYRAH with GRENACHE, CARIGNAN, MOURVÈDRE. Vyds up to 400m (1312ft): fresh acidity. Try: CHX Faiteau, L'Ostal, Oustal-Blanc, Maris, Mignan; CAS Centeilles, Clos des Roques, Clos l'Ora; DOMS Ancely, COMBE BLANCHE, Fauzon, Piccinini.

Londe, La Prov ★★ Maritime vyds. Chanel has moved in here and bought DOM de l'Ille; LVMH owns Galoupet. Others: CLOS Mireille, Dom Perzinsky, Léoube, St Marguerite. Coastal schist subzone of CÔTES DE PROV, incl island of Porqueyrolle (three vyds).

Long-Depaquit Chab ★★★ BICHOT owned CHAB DOM with famous flagship brand, GC La Moutonne.

Lorentz, Gustave Al ★★→★★★ Grower-merchant at Bergheim. RIES is strength in GCS Altenburg de Bergheim, Kanzlerberg, age-worthy 12 13 14 16 18 19. Young volume wines (esp *Gewurz*) well made. Fine new organic Evidence GEWURZ 16 17.

Lot SW Fr ★→★★ DYA IGP of Lot département increasingly useful to CAHORS growers for rosés and whites not allowed in AOP (eg. CLOS de Gamot, CH DU CÈDRE). Look beyond AOP for ★★ DOMS Belmont, Sully, Tour de Belfort.

Loupiac B'x ★★ 14 15 16 18 19 (20) Minor SÉM-dominant *liquoreux*. Lighter, fresher than SAUT across River Garonne. Top CHX: CLOS Jean, Dauphiné-Rondillon, *de Ricaud*, du Cros, Les Roques, *Loupiac-Gaudiet*, Noble.

Luberon S Rh ★→★★ 16' 18 19' Hilly annex to S Rh, fashionable for tourists; terroir is v. dry, can be no more than okay. Excess of technical wines. SYRAH plays lead role. Whites improving. Bright star: CH de la Canorgue (organic). Also gd: Chx Clapier, Edem, Fontvert (bio, gd w), Puy des Arts (w), Ravoire, St-Estève de Neri (improver), Tardieu-Laurent (rich, oak); DOMS de la Citadelle (organic), Fontenille (organic), La Cavale (swish), Le Novi (terroir), Marrenon, Maslauris (organic), Val-Joanis; Laura Aillaud; gd-value La Vieille Ferme (w/rosé, can be VDF).

Lussac-St-Émilion B'x ★★ 15 16 18 19 (20) Most n of ST-ÉM satellites; lightest in style. Top CHX: Barbe Blanche, Bel-Air, Bellevue, Courlat, Croix de Rambeau, DE LUSSAC, La Rose-Perrière, Le Rival, LYONNAT, Mayne-Blanc.

Macle, Dom Jura ★★★ Legendary producer of CH-CHALON VIN JAUNE for long ageing. Best drunk 10 yrs after bottling. Also CÔTES DU JURA.

Mâcon Burg ★ DYA. Simple, juicy GAMAY reds and most basic rendition of Mâconnais whites from CHARD.

Mâcon-Villages Burg ★★ 14' 17' 18 19' 20' Chief appellation for Mâconnais whites. Individual villages may also use their own names eg. Mâcon-Lugny. Co-ops at Lugny, Terres Secretes, Viré for quality-price ratio, plus *brilliant grower wines* from Guffens-Heynen, Guillot, Guillot-Broux, LAFON, LEFLAIVE, Maillet, Merlin. Also major NÉGOCIANTS, DROUHIN, LATOUR, etc.

Macvin Jura From France, not Scotland. Grape juice is fortified by local marc to make a sweet apéritif between 16–22% alc. Most Jura producers make one. Usually white, can be red.

Madiran SW Fr ★★→★★★ oo' o5' 10 12 15' 16 18 19 (20) Gascon AOP. France's home of TANNAT grape. Lighter styles gaining ground over traditional dark heavy-weights: ★★★ CHX BOUSCASSÉ, MONTUS (owner BRUMONT: 15% entire AOP), Laffitte-Teston, *Laplace*. Wide ranges from ★★★ Chx Arricaud-Bordès, de Gayon; DOMS Berthoumieu, Capmartin, Damiens, Dou Bernés, Labranche-Laffont, Laffont, Pichard; CLOS Basté. Doms ★★ Barréjat, ★★ Crampilh, Maouries not far behind.

Madura, Dom La L'doc ★★★ Ex-*régisseur* of B'X CH FIEUZAL created own estate in ST-CHINIAN. Stylish Classique, Grand Vin. White an original blend of SAUV BL/PICPOUL.

Maillard, Nicolas Champ ★★★ Uses stainless steel, a little oak. PC Platine 12 15 18 19 ageing beautifully, esp in magnums.

Mailly Grand Cru Champ Top co-op, all GC grapes. Prestige CUVÉE des *Echansons* 08 12' for long ageing. Sumptuous Echansons Rosé 12; refined, classy L'Intemporelle 15 18 19'. Sébastien Moncuit, cellarmaster since 14, a real talent.

Maire, Henri Jura ★ Former legend, creator of Vin Fou, still a huge producer, mostly from own vyds, sometimes using DOM names eg. Sobief, Bregand, or supermarket brand Auguste Pirou. Part of BOISSET empire.

Mann, Albert Al ★★→★★★★ Distinguished grower at Wettolsheim; irreproachable excellence. Deft winemaking in stainless steel, larger casks, barriques. V.gd AUXERROIS, ace range of GCS: HENGST, SCHLOSSBERG (esp 17'). Great red PINOT N Les Stes Claires in 15 18' 19. Immaculate bio vyds.

Maranges C d'O ★★ 15' 17 18' 19' 20' Name to watch. Robust well-priced reds from s end of CÔTE DE BEAUNE. Try PCS Boutière, Croix Moines, Fussière. Best: BACHELET-Monnot, Chevrot, Giroud, Rouges Queues.

Best intro to cooking of the SW: *Goose Fat & Garlic* (J Strang). Hugely enjoyable.

Marcillac SW Fr ★★ 15' 18 19 (20) AVEYRON AOP based on Mansois (aka FER SERVADOU). Fruity, curranty/raspberry food wines you either love or hate. Best at 3 yrs. Try with strawberries as well as charcuterie or sausages. ★★ DOM du Cros largest independent grower (gd w IGPS too), also Doms des Boissières, Laurens. Excellent co-op. Recent heatwave vintages outstanding.

Margaux H-Méd ★★→★★★★★ 08 09' 10' 15 16' 18 19' (20) Most s MÉD communal AC. Famous for elegance, fragrance; reality is more diverse. Top CHX: BOYD-CANTENAC, BRANE-CANTENAC, DAUZAC, DU TERTRE, FERRIÈRE, GISCOURS, ISSAN, KIRWAN, LASCOMBES, MALESCOT-ST-EXUPÉRY, MARGAUX, PALMER, RAUZAN-SÉGLA. Gd-value Chx: ANGLUDET, Arsac, Deyrem Valentin, LABÉGORCE, LA TOUR DE MONS, Paveil de Luze, SIRAN.

Marionnet, Henry Lo ★★→★★★ 19' 20' TOURAINE DOM famous for ungrafted vyds (sandy soil), rare vines, esp Romorantin; made famous by Henry M, now run by son Jean-Sebastién. SAUV BL (top CUVÉE L'Origine), GAMAY, *Provignage* (150-yr-old+ Romorantin vines), La Pucelle de Romorantin, Renaissance. Managing historic vyd at CH de Chambord, incl Menu Pineau, Romorantin.

Marsannay C d'O ★★→★★★ (r) 15' 17 18' 19' 20 Most n AOC of CÔTE DE NUITS, *still* hoping to get PCS (eg. Champ Salomon, CLOS du Roy, Longeroies); 1st step has gained new village-level vyds from 2019, eg. Chapitre and Montre-cul. Accessible, crunchy, fruit-laden reds, from energetic producers: Audoin, Bart, Bouvier, Charlopin, CLAIR, Derey, Fournier, *Pataille*. V.gd unfashionable *rosé* needs 1–2 yrs; whites less exciting.

Mas Amiel Rouss ★★★ Leading MAURY, Côtes du ROUSS, IGP. Look for Altaïr (w), Origine, Vers le Nord, Vol de Nuit from v.old CARIGNAN/GRENACHE, others. Plus excellent VDN from young, fruity *grenat*, to venerable RANCIO 20- to 40-yr-old Maury aged in 60-litre glass demijohns, intensely sweet and savoury.

Mas Bruguière L'doc ★★★ Family estate, 7th-generation, in PIC ST-LOUP. L'Arbouse, La Grenadière and Les Mûriers.

Mas de Daumas Gassac L'doc ★★★→★★★★ Star since 80s; now run by 2nd generation Samuel Guibert, who uses horses in vyd. CAB-based age-worthy reds from apparently unique soil. Perfumed white from CHENIN blend; super-CUVÉE Émile Peynaud (r); Rosé Frizant. V.gd sweet Vin de Laurence (MUSCAT/SERCIAL).

Mas de l'Ecriture L'doc ★★→★★★ Father-daughter team; exquisite reds; small organic TERRASSES DU LARZAC estate.

Mas, Doms Paul L'doc ★★ Jean-Claude Mas directs huge empire from Grès de Montpellier to ROUSS. Mainly IGP. Working on organics, bio and low sulphur. Wine tourism, restaurant. Arrogant Frog range; also Côté Mas, La Forge, Les Tannes, Les VIGNES de Nicole and DOMS Ferrandière, Crès Ricards in TERRASSES DU LARZAC, Martinolles in LIMOUX; CHX Lauriga in ROUSS, Villegly in MINERVOIS.

Mas Jullien L'doc ★★★★ TERRASSES DU LARZAC star: typical Larzac freshness. MOURVÈDRE, CARIGNAN red: Autour de Jonquières, Carlan, États d'Âme, Lous Rougeos from L'DOC varieties. Carignan Bl and Gr, CHENIN BL for white.

Massif d'Uchaux S Rh ★★ 16′ 18′ 19′ Gd Rh village, clearly fruited, fresh, spiced reds, not easy to sell, but best genuine, stylish. NB: CH St-Estève (incl gd old vine VIOGNIER), DOMS *Cros de la Mûre* (character, gd value), de la Guicharde, La Cabotte (bio, on top form), Renjarde (sleek fruit).

Maury Rouss ★★→★★★ Sweet VDN from GRENACHES Noir/BL/Gr on island of schist. Ambré, tuilé and RANCIO styles; try old rancio with chocolate. Now characterful dry red, AC Maury SEC prompted by recent improvements, led by *Mas Amiel*. Also Doms de Lavail, Lafage, Pouderoux and Maury Co-op.

Mazel, Le S Rh ★★ 18′ 19′ Mother lode for Rh Vin Nature, no sulphur, S ARDÈCHE. Gérald Oustric 1st vinified in 1997, carbonic maceration, vats only (no wood), low alc CARIGNAN, GRENACHE; whites CHARD, VIOGNIER notably. All VDF.

Mazis- (or Mazy-) Chambertin C d'O ★★★★ 90′ 93 96′ 99′ 05′ 09′ 10′ 12′ 15′ 16′ 17 18′ 19′ 20′ GC of GEVREY-CHAMBERTIN, top class in upper part; intense, *heavenly wines*. Best: Bernstein, DUGAT-PY, FAIVELEY, HOSPICES DE BEAUNE, LEROY, MORTET, ROUSSEAU, Tawse (ex-Maume).

Mazoyères-Chambertin C d'O ★★★★ Can be sold as CHARMES-CHAMBERTIN, but more growers now labelling M as such. Style is different: less succulence, more stony structure. Try DUGAT-PY, MORTET, Perrot-Minot, Taupenot-Merme, Tawse.

Médoc B'x ★★ 15 16 18 19 (20) AC for reds in low-lying n part of Méd peninsula (aka Bas-Méd). Often more guts than grace. Can be gd value but be selective. Top CHX: CLOS Manou, d'Escurac, Fleur La Mothe, *Goulée*, GREYSAC, *La Tour-de-By*, Laujac, LES ORMES-SORBET, LOUDENNE (Le Ch), Lousteauneuf, *Patache d'Aux*, POITEVIN, *Potensac*, PREUILLAC, Ramafort, *Rollan-de-By* (HAUT-CONDISSAS), TOUR HAUT-CAUSSAN, TOUR ST-BONNET, Vieux Robin.

Meffre, Gabriel S Rh ★★→★★★ Consistent S Rh merchant, owns gd GIGONDAS DOM Longue Toque (top is Hommage GM). Fruit quality up, less oak. Makes CHÂTEAUNEUF (gd St-Théodoric, also small doms), VACQUEYRAS St-Barthélemy too. Reliable to gd S/N Rh Laurus (oak) range, esp CONDRIEU, HERMITAGE (w) and ST-JOSEPH.

Mellot, Alphonse Lo ★★→★★★★ 17′ 18′ 19′ 20′ Top SANCERRE, bio, all handpicked (r, a revelation/w), incl La Moussière (r/w), *Cuvée Edmond*, *Génération XIX* (r/w); gd single-vyds: *Satellite* (from CHAVIGNOL) – Demoiselle, *En Champs*; Les Pénitents (Côtes de la Charité IGP) CHARD, PINOT N. Cellars under centre of Sancerre.

Menetou-Salon Lo ★★→★★★ 18′ 19′ 20′ AOP nr SANCERRE; SAUV BL. Reds (PINOT N) can be v.gd. Best: BOURGEOIS, Clement (Chatenoy), *Gilbert* (bio), *Henry Pellé*, Jacolin, Jean-Max Roger, Joseph Mellot, Teiller, Tour St-Martin.

Méo-Camuzet C d'O ★★★★ Noted DOM in VOSNE-ROMANÉE; icons Brûlées, CROS

PARANTOUX, RICHEBOURG. Value from M-C Frère et Soeur (NÉGOCIANT branch) and plenty of choice in between. Sturdy, oaky wines that age well.

Merande, Ch de Sav ★★ Owned by DOM Genoux, bio. Gd value, esp APREMONT, ARBIN.

Mercurey Burg ★★→★★★ 15′ 16 17 18′ 19′ 20′ Leading village of CÔTE CHALONNAISE, firmly muscled reds, aromatic whites. Try BICHOT, Champs de l'Abbaye, CH *de Chamirey*, CH de Santenay, DOM de Suremain, FAIVELEY, *Juillot-Theulot*, Lorenzon, M Juillot, Raquillet.

Merlin Burg ★★→★★★ Olivier and Corinne M put MÂCON La Roche Vineuse on map. Splendid Les Cras bottling. V.gd MOULIN-À-VENT and increasing POUILLY-FUISSÉ range now with their sons on board. Co-owners CH des Quarts with Dominique Lafon.

Mesnil-sur-Oger, Le Champ Top Côte des Blancs village, v. long-lived CHARD. Best: André Jacquart, JL Vergnon (until 17), KRUG CLOS du Mesnil, PIERRE PÉTERS. Needs 10 yrs+ ageing.

Méthode Champenoise Champ Traditional method of putting bubbles into CHAMP by re-fermenting wine in its bottle. Outside Champ region, makers must use terms "classic method" or *méthode traditionnelle*.

Meursault C d'O ★★★→★★★★ 09′ 10′ 12 14′ 15 17′ 18 19′ 20′ Potentially great full-bodied whites from PCS: Charmes, Genevrières, Perrières, more nervy from hillside vyds *Narvaux*, Tesson, *Tillets*. Producers: Ballot-Millot, BOILLOT, Boisson-Vadot, BOUZEREAU, Boyer-Matenot, *Ch de Meursault*, COCHE-DURY, *de Montille*, Ente, Fichet, Girardin, *Javillier*, JOBARD, *Lafon*, Latour, LEROUX, Matrot, Mikulski, *P Morey*, Potinet-Ampeau, PRIEUR, Rougeot, *Roulot*. Try de Cherisey for Meursault-BLAGNY.

Burg and Jura creep 1–2cm (0.4–0.8in) closer every 100 yrs; 15-min journey, in 100 million yrs′ time.

Meursault, Ch de C d'O ★★★ Huge strides lately at this newly bio 61-ha estate of big-biz Halley family: improving reds from BEAUNE, POMMARD, VOLNAY. Some stunning whites, esp MEURSAULT, also v.gd BOURGOGNE Blanc, PULIGNY PC.

Minervois L'doc ★★→★★★ Lots to choose from in this undulating region ne of Carcassonne. Characterful, herbal reds, esp CHX Coupe-Roses, d'Agel, de Gourgazaud, de Homs, La Grave, La Tour Boisée, Oupia, St-Jacques d'Albas, Ste Eulalie, Senat, Villerambert-Julien; DOMS CLOS Centeilles, COMBE BLANCHE, l'Ostal Cazes; Abbaye de Tholomiès, Borie-de-Maurel, PIERRE CROS, Pierre Fil, Laville-Bertrou, Maris. Gros and Tollot (from Burg) raising bar. LA LIVINIÈRE newly elevated cru. St Jean de Minervois is delicious fresh MUSCAT VDN: Barroubio, CLOS DU GRAVILLAS best.

Miquel, Laurent L'doc ★★→★★★ Innovative producer with vyds in CORBIÈRES, ST-CHINIAN. Renowned for aromatic whites IGP, VIOGNIER, ALBARIÑO. Powerful, elegant CAB FR. Also NÉGOCIANT, with Nord Sud, Solas, VENDANGES Nocturnes.

Mis en bouteille au château / domaine Bottled at CH, property, or estate. NB: *dans nos CAVES* (in our cellars) or *dans la région de production* (in the area of production) often used but mean little.

Moët & Chandon Champ By far largest CHAMP house, impressive quality for such a giant. Fresher, drier BRUT Imperial NV. New rare prestige CUVÉE MCIII "solera" concept aimed at rich oenophiles, daunting complexity at sky-high price. Better value in Grand Vintages Collection, long lees-aged; new sumptuous, elegant 09 08 a little severe. Ace 12′ ★★★★. Impressive winery in AUBE making v.gd PINOT N in volume. Outposts across Europe, New World. *See also* DOM PÉRIGNON.

Monbazillac SW Fr ★★→★★★ 15′ 17 18 19 BERGERAC sub-AOP: ★★★★ *Tirecul-la-Gravière* up there with best SAUTERNES. ★★★ CLOS des Verdots, L'Ancienne Cure, Les Hauts de Caillavel, co-op's *Ch de Monbazillac*. ★★ CHX de Belingard-Chayne, Grande Maison, Kalian, Le Faget, Monestier la Tour, Pech La Calevie, Pécoula.

Monopole A vyd under single ownership.

Montagne-St-Émilion B'x ★★ 10' 15 16 18 19 (20) Largest satellite of ST-ÉM. Solid reputation. Top CHX: Beauséjour, CLOS de Boüard, Corbin, Croix Beauséjour, Faizeau, La Couronne, Maison Blanche, Roc de Calon, Roudier, Teyssier, Tour Bayard, Vieux Bonneau, Vieux Ch Palon, *Vieux Ch St-André*.

Montagny Burg ★★ 14' 15 17 18 19' 20' CÔTE CHALONNAISE village with crisp whites, mostly in hands of CAVES DE BUXY but gd NÉGOCIANTS too, incl LOUIS LATOUR, O LEFLAIVE. Reference local grower is *S Aladame*, but try also Berthenet, Cognard, *Feuillat-Juillot*, Lorenzon.

Monthélie C d'O ★★→★★★ 15' 16 17 18' 19' 20' Pretty reds, grown uphill from VOLNAY, but a touch more rustic. Les Duresses best PC. Try BOUCHARD PÈRE & FILS, *Ch de Monthélie* (Suremain), *Coche-Dury*, Darviot-Perrin, LAFON. Whites mostly neutral.

Montille, de C d'O ★★★ Dense, spicy, whole-bunch reds from BEAUNE, VOLNAY (esp Taillepieds), POMMARD (Rugiens), CÔTE DE NUITS (Malconsorts) and exceptional whites from MEURSAULT, plus outstanding PULIGNY-MONTRACHET Caillerets. Since 2017 CH de Puligny wines are incl under de Montille. New projects in Sta Rita Hills (California) and Hokkaido (Japan).

Montlouis sur Loire Lo ★★→★★★★ 17' 18 19' 20' Sister AC to VOUVRAY in Lo. Top CHENIN BL; sparkling incl *Pétillant Originel*. Dry white: cooler vintages often best. Top: Berger, Chanson, *Chidaine*, Delecheneau, Jousset, Merias, Pierres Ecrites, Saumon, *Taille-aux-Loups*, Vallée Moray, *Weisskopf.*

Montpeyroux L'doc ★★★ Lively village at foot of Mt Baudile with growing number of gd growers. Aspiring to cru status. Try: Chabanon, DOM d'AUPILHAC, Jasse-Castel, Villa Dondona; Divern. Newcomers: Joncas, Mas d'Amile. Serious co-op.

Montrachet (or Le Montrachet) C d'O ★★★★ 02' 04 05 08 09' 10 12 14' 15 17 18 19' 20' The GC vyd that lent name to both PULIGNY and CHASSAGNE. Should be greatest white burg for intensity, richness of fruit and perfumed persistence. Top: BOUCHARD, COLIN, DRC, LAFON, LAGUICHE (DROUHIN), LEFLAIVE, Ramonet.

Montravel SW Fr ★★ (r) 15' 18' 19 20 (w/rosé) DYA. Sub-AOP of BERGERAC. Modern-style reds must be oak-aged. ★★★ DOMS de Bloy, de Krevel. ★★ CHX Jonc Blanc, Masburel, Masmontet, Moulin-Caresse. ★★ Dry white from same and many other growers. .

Montus, Ch SW Fr ★★★★ 00' 05 09 10 12' 14 15' 16 17 18 19 (20) Alain BRUMONT's flagship property, famous for long-extracted oak-aged wines. Long-lived all-TANNAT reds, much prized by lovers of old-fashioned MADIRAN. Classy sweet and dry white barrel-raised PACHERENC-DU-VIC-BILH. La Tyre, Prestige equal to Classed Growths.

Mordorée, Dom de la S Rh ★★★ 15' 16' 17' 18' 19' 20 Top estate at TAVEL, organic, rosés with flair, drive; also LIRAC, La Reine des Bois (r/w). Gd CHÂTEAUNEUF La Reine des Bois (incl 1929 GRENACHE), La Dame Voyageuse (r). Nifty VDF La Remise (r/w/rosé).

Moreau Chab ★★→★★★★ Widespread family in CHAB, esp *Dom Christian M*, noted for PC Vaillons Cuvée Guy M and GC Les CLOS des Hospices. Louis M has more commercial range; DOM M-Naudet makes concentrated wines for longer keeping. .

Moreau C d'O ★★→★★★★ At s end of C d'O. Outstanding CHASSAGNE PCS from DOM Bernard M; fine La Cardeuse (r). Tidy range of SANTENAY, MARANGES from David M. Neither related to CHAB dynasty.

Morey, Doms C d'O ★★★ VIGNERON family in CHASSAGNE. Current generation incl Caroline M and husband Pierre-Yves COLIN-M, Sylvain, Thomas (v. fine pure whites), Vincent (plumper style), Thibault M-Coffinet (LA ROMANÉE). Also Pierre M in MEURSAULT for Perrières and BÂTARD.

Morey-St-Denis C d'O ★★★→★★★★ 99' 02' 05' 09' 10' 12' 15' 16' 17 18' 19' 20' Terrific source of top-grade red burg, to rival neighbours GEVREY-CHAMBERTIN,

CHAMBOLLE-MUSIGNY. GCS CLOS DE LA ROCHE, CLOS DE LAMBRAYS, CLOS DE TART, CLOS ST-DENIS. Many gd producers: Amiot, ARLAUD, Castagnier, Coquard-Loison-Fleurot, CLOS DE TART, *Clos des Lambrays*, *Dujac*, H LIGNIER, LIGNIER-Michelot, Magnien, Perrot-Minot, PONSOT, Remy, *Roumier*, Taupenot-Merme, Tremblay. Interesting whites too, esp PC Monts Luisants.

Morgon Beauj ★★★ 14 15′ 17 18′ 19′ 20′ Powerful BEAUJ cru; volcanic slate of Côte du Py makes meaty, age-worthy wine, clay of Les Charmes for earlier, smoother drinking. Grands Cras, Javernières of interest too. *Burgaud*, CH de Pizay, Ch des Lumières (JADOT), *Desvignes*, Foillard, Gaget, Godard, *Lapierre*, Piron, Sunier.

Mortet, Denis C d'O ★★★→★★★★ Arnaud M on song with powerful yet refined reds from BOURGOGNE Rouge to CHAMBERTIN. Key wines GEVREY-CHAMBERTIN Mes Cinq Terroirs, PCS Champeaux, Lavaut St-Jacques. From 2016 separate Arnaud M label, equally brilliant, incl CHARMES- and MAZOYÈRES-CHAMBERTIN.

Moueix, J-P et Cie B'x Libourne-based NÉGOCIANT and proprietor named after founder Jean-Pierre. Son Christian runs company with his son Edouard. CHX: BELAIR-MONANGE, CLOS La Madeleine, HOSANNA, LA FLEUR-PÉTRUS, *La Grave à Pomerol*, LATOUR-À-POMEROL, *Trotanoy*. In California, Dominus Estate.

Moulin-à-Vent Beauj ★★★ 09′ 11′ 14 15′ 18′ 19′ 20′ Grandest BEAUJ cru, transcending GAMAY grape. Weight, spiciness of Rh but matures towards rich, gamey PINOT flavours. Increasing interest in single-vyd bottlings from eg. *Ch des Jacques*, *Ch du Moulin-à-Vent*, DOM Labruyère, JADOT's Janin, Janodet, *Merlin* (La Rochelle), Rottiers. More and more interest from C D'O producers eg. BICHOT (Rochegres), L BOILLOT (Brussellions), T LIGER-BELAIR (Les Rouchaux).

Moulis H-Méd ★★→★★★ 14 15 16 18 19 (20) Tiny inland AC w of MARGAUX. Honest, gd-value wines. Best offer fruit and charm. Top CHX: Anthonic, Biston-Brillette, BRANAS GRAND POUJEAUX, BRILLETTE, Caroline, *Chasse-Spleen*, Dutruch Grand Poujeaux, *Gressier Grand Poujeaux*, MAUCAILLOU, *Mauvesin Barton*, *Poujeaux*.

Mourgues du Grès, Ch S Rh ★★→★★★ 16′ 17 18′ 19′ 20 Front rank COSTIÈRES DE NÎMES estate, organic, v.gd range for early drinking, incl racy rosé (Dorés, Galets Rouges, Rosés). Firmer Capitelles: Terre d'Argence (mostly SYRAH), Terre de Feu (mainly GRENACHE).

Moutard Champ Original champion of local Arbanne grape. Also eaux de vie. Greatly improved quality, esp CHARD Persin 14 and CUVÉE des 6 CÉPAGES 11 15′ 18 19′.

Mugneret C d'O ★★★→★★★★ VIGNERON family in VOSNE-ROMANÉE. Sublime, stylish wines from Georges M-Gibourg (esp ÉCHÉZEAUX), now matched by transformed DOM Gérard M. Also DOM Mongeard-M.

Mugnier, J-F C d'O ★★★★ Outstanding grower of CHAMBOLLE-MUSIGNY *Les Amoureuses*, *Musigny*. Do not miss PC Fuées. Finesse, not muscle. Equally at home with MONOPOLE NUITS-ST-GEORGES CLOS de la Maréchale. No longer sells young vintages of MUSIGNY to avoid infanticide.

Mumm, GH & Cie Champ Powerful house owned by Pernod Ricard. New chef de CAVE, v. talented Laurent Fresnet (ex-HENRIOT) since 2019, a new renaissance? Mumm de Verzenay BLANC DE NOIRS 08, ★★★ RSVR BLANC DE BLANCS 12′. Mumm de Cramant, renamed Blanc de Blancs, elegantly subtle. Cordon Rouge much improved. New 6 Ans extra lees-aged release. Also in Napa Valley, California.

Muscadet Lo ★→★★★ 18′ 19′ 20′ Popular, bone-dry white from nr Nantes. Made for fish, seafood. Often great value. Best SUR LIE. Choose zonal ACS: *see* following entries; v.gd age-worthy MUSCADET CRUS COMMUNAUX; 10% CHARD allowed in generic Muscadet.

Muscadet-Coteaux de la Loire Lo ★→★★ 19′ 20′ Small AC. Esp Carroget, Guindon, Landron-Chartier, Merceron-Martin, Pléiade, Quarteron, VIGNERONS de la Noëlle.

Muscadet Côtes de Grand Lieu Lo ★→★★★ 18′ 19′ 20′ MUSCADET zonal AOP by Atlantic. Best: *Eric Chevalier*, *Haut-Bourg*, *Herbauges*, Malidain.

FRANCE

Muscadet Crus Communaux Lo ★★→★★★ MUSCADET's exciting top level. Long lees-ageing from specified soil sites – due to legal quirk can't be labelled SUR LIE. Complex wines, great value. Seven crus: Clisson, Gorges, Goulaine, La Haye Fouassière, Le Pallet, Monnières-St Fiacre, Mouzillon-Tillières. Champtoceaux, Côtes de Grandlieu, Vallet in progress.

Muscadet Sèvre et Maine Lo ★→★★★ 18' 19' 20' Largest and best MUSCADET zone. Increasingly gd, v.gd value. Top incl: *Bonnet-Huteau*, Brégeon, Briacé, *Caillé*, Chereau Carré, Cormerais, Delhommeau, Douillard, Gadais, *Grand Mouton*, Gunther-Chereau, Haute Fevrie, Huchet, L'ECU, *Landron*, *Lieubeau*, *Luneau-Papin*, Olivier, *Pèpière*, Sauvion. Can age decade+. Try the seven CRUS COMMUNAUX.

Musigny C d'O ★★★★ 93 96' 99' 02' 05' 09' 10' 12' 15' 17 18 19' 20' Most beautiful red burg. GC lent its name to CHAMBOLLE-MUSIGNY. Hauntingly fragrant but with sinuous power beneath. Best: DE VOGÜÉ, DROUHIN, FAIVELEY, JADOT, LEROY, *Mugnier*, PRIEUR, ROUMIER, VOUGERAIE.

Nature Unsweetened, esp for CHAMP: no dosage. Fine if v. ripe grapes, raw otherwise.

Negly, Ch la L'doc ★★★★ Dynamic LA CLAPE estate, impressive range from salty Brise Marine (w) La Côte (r), and La Falaise (r) for everyday to icon La Porte du Ciel (SYRAH), MOURVÈDRE-based L'Ancely and CLOS des Truffiers from oldest Syrah vyd in L'DOC, nr PÉZENAS.

Négociant-éleveur Merchant who "brings up" (ie. matures) the wine.

Noëllat C d'O ★★★ Noted VOSNE-ROMANÉE family. Georges N transformed by arrival of Maxime Cheurlin in 2010: try NUITS Boudots, Vosne Petits-Monts and GC ÉCHÉZEAUX, also some gd-value lesser appellations. Cousins at Michel N starting to cause a stir. *See also* v. stylish HUDELOT-N in VOUGEOT.

The entire Jura vyd is about the size of three villages in Burg.

Nuits-St-Georges C d'O ★★→★★★★ 99' 02' **05' 09'** 10' 12' 15' 16 17 18' 19 20' Three parts to this major AC: Premeaux vyds for elegance (various CLOS: de la Maréchale, des Corvées, des Forêts, St-Marc), centre for dense dark plummy wines (Cailles, Les St-Georges, Vaucrains) and n side for the headiest (Boudots, Cras, Murgers, Richemone). Many fine growers: Ambroise, ARLOT, ARNOUX-LACHAUX, CATHIARD, Chauvenet, CHEVILLON, Confuron, *Faiveley*, Gavignet, GOUGES, GRIVOT, Lechéneaut, LEROY, *Liger-Belair*, Machard de Gramont, Michelot, Millot, *Mugnier*, *Rion*.

Oratoire St Martin, Dom de l' S Rh ★★★ 12' 13' 15' 16' 17' 18' 19' 20 At CAIRANNE, 28 ha choice vyds. Top-grade bio reds, with much purity, Les Douyes (1905 GRENACHE, MOURVÈDRE), Haut Coustias (vines c.70 yrs). Gd table white (esp Rés Seigneurs, CLAIRETTE).

Orchidées Lo ★→★★★ Formerly Ackerman. NÉGOCIANT/estates incl ckerman, Celliers du Prieuré, Donatien-Bahuaud, Drouet Frères (Pays Nantais), Hardières (Layon), Monmousseau (TOURAINE), Perruche (SAUMUR), Rémy-Pannier, Varière (ANJOU), CH de SANCERRE.

Orléans Lo ★ DYA. Important in C19; minor AC now. Mostly CHARD, VIN GRIS, rosé, reds (PINOT N, esp PINOT M). Also **Orléans-Clery** tiny AOP (r) ★ DYA CAB FR: Chant d'Oiseaux, CLOS St-Fiacre, Deneufbourg.

Osmin, Lionel SW Fr Well-respected NÉGOCIANT, offering full range of SW wines in all styles.

Ostertag, Dom Al ★★★ Ace bio grower, more interested in terroir than varietal expression. Great RIES, esp Muenchberg 10 14 18', barrique-fermented, intense Muenchberg PINOT GR 15. Lovely PINOT N Fronholtz 12 15 18'; 19 small, but all fresh, classic.

Ou, Ch de l' Rouss ★★★→★★★★ Go-ahead organic estate. Beautifully crafted, all colours, styles. Secrets de Schist elegance, power. Rhapsody GRENACHE icon wine. Sublime MAURY VDN from old vintages.

> **Jura jewels**
> What other region has so many styles? They seem to like confusing
> customers – sommeliers love the game. **Dry whites** from CHARD, many
> single-vyd versions now. Also tangy blends with SAVAGNIN. Fresh or
> deliberately **oxidative** pure Savagnin exciting too; many made in natural
> style can be pretty gamey. *See* ARBOIS, CÔTES DU JURA, L'ETOILE. *Vin typé* on
> labels means heading towards Sherry. *Vin ouillé* means "ullaged": the
> barrel has been topped up to avoid oxidation. **Light reds** from PINOT N,
> Poulsard, Trousseau, or blends. Some more rosé than red. Côtes du
> Jura, Arbois. Aged **sherrified whites** known as VIN JAUNE. *See* CH-CHALON.
> Intensely sweet **vin de paille** made fom red and white grapes. Fortified
> **Macvin**, local version of ratafia. Classic producers: BOURDY, MACLE,
> Overnoy. Avant garde: A&M TISSOT, GANEVAT, PÉLICAN, Pignier. Volume/
> value: co-ops (known here as CAVES Fruitières), Boilley, HENRI MAIRE,
> J Tissot, LABET.

Pacherenc du Vic-Bilh SW Fr ★★→★★★ White AOP contiguous with MADIRAN. Gros,
Petit MANSENG, sometimes Petit Courbu and local Aruffiac produce dry and sweet
styles. Made by most Madiran growers but note too ★★ CH de Mascaaras. Dry
DYA, but sweet, esp if oaked, can be matured.

Paillard, Bruno Champ ★★★→★★★★ Newish grande marque has built empire.
Top-quality BRUT Première CUVÉE NV, Rosé Première Cuvée; refined style, esp
in long-aged BLANC DE BLANCS 04, NPU 04 02'. Brut NATURE has clever use of
PINOT N. Bruno P heads LANSON-BCC group of mainly family houses; daughter
Alice taking over at Paillard.

Palette Prov ★★★ Characterful reds, tiny AC nr Aix. MOURVÈDRE, GRENACHE; fragrant
rosés, intriguing forest-scented whites; also oddities like FURMINT. Traditional,
serious *Ch Simone*, Crémade, Henri Bonnaud.

Partagé, Dom Sav ★★ Tiny bio DOM in CHIGNIN, v.gd. Previously Gilles Berlioz.
Altesse, JACQUÈRE, MONDEUSE, ROUSSANNE. Fun wines: El-hem, La Deuse, Le Jaja,
Les Christine, Les Filles, Les Fripons, Princesse.

Pauillac H-Méd ★★★→★★★★ 00' 05' 09' 10' 15 16' 18' 19' (20) Communal AC in n
MÉD with 18 Classed Growths, incl LAFITE, LATOUR, MOUTON. Famous for long-lived
wines, the acme of CAB SAUV. Other top CHX: CLERC MILON, DUHART-MILON, GRAND-PUY-
LACOSTE, LYNCH-BAGES, PICHON-BARON, PICHON-LALANDE, PONTET-CANET. Gd-value Chx:
FONBADET, La Fleur Peyrabon, PIBRAN.

Pays d'Oc, IGP L'doc ★→★★★ Largest IGP, covering whole of L'DOC-ROUSS. Extremes
of quality from simple, quaffing varietals to innovative, exciting; 58 different
grapes allowed. CARIGNAN, esp old vines, increasingly popular. Big players incl:
Bruno Andreu, DOM PAUL MAS, GÉRARD BERTRAND, Jeanjean and co-op FONCALIEU.

Pécharmant SW Fr ★★ 15' 17 18 19 (20) BERGERAC inner AOP on edge of town. Iron
and manganese in soil generate biggest, longest-living wines of area. Veteran
★★★ CH deTiregand, DOM du Haut-Pécharmant, l'Ancienne Cure; ★★ Chx
Beauportail, Champarel, Corbiac, du Rooy, Terre Vieille; Dom des Bertranoux.

Peira, La L'doc ★★★★ Superlative TERRASSES DU LARZAC DOM making intense and
complex reds. La Peira (SYRAH/GRENACHE), Las Flors de la Peira (Syrah/Grenache/
MOURVÈDRE), Obriers de la Peira (CARIGNAN/CINSAULT).

Pélican, Dom du Jura ★★★ VOLNAY'S MARQUIS D'ANGERVILLE venture in Jura, starting
with legend Jacques Puffeney's vyds made in fresh styles. Still developing ideas.

Pennautier, Ch de L'doc Dubbed "Versailles of Languedoc", owned by Lorgeril
family who have vyds and buy fruit. Signature AC Cabardès, CAB SAUV/MERLOT/
GRENACHE/SYRAH. L'DOC richness, B'X restraint.

Pernand-Vergelesses C d'O ★★★ (r) 05' 09' 10' 12 15' 17 18' 19' 20' (w) 14' 15' 17' 18'

FRANCE

19' 20' Village hosting w-facing part of CORTON-CHARLEMAGNE. Now less austere, different vyds thrive in each colour. (r) Île des Vergelesses; (w) Combottes, Sous Frétille. Local DOMS CHANDON DE BRIAILLES, Dubreuil-Fontaine, Rapet, Rollin lead way but try also Berthelemot, JADOT.

Perret, André N Rh ★★★ 10' 12 15' 16' 17 18' 19' 20' CONDRIEU DOM, 1st class. Three wines, classic, stylish CLOS Chanson, rich, lingering Chéry. Also ST-JOSEPH (r/w), bright-fruit classic red, serious, flowing old-vine Les Grisières (r). Gd COLLINES RHODANIENNES (r/w) also.

Perrier, Joseph Champ ★★★→★★★★ Fine family-run CHAMP house with v.gd PINOTS N/M vyds, esp in own Cumières DOM. Ace Prestige CUVÉE Joséphine 12'; BRUT Royale NV as generous as ever but more precise with less dosage. Distinctive, tangy BLANC DE BLANCS 08 13' 17' 19 20. Now drier, finer CUVÉE Royale Brut NV; older BLANC DE BLANCS vintages age well esp 95. Owner Jean-Claude Fourmon, one of Champ's great characters, easing reins to son.

Perrier-Jouët Champ 1st (in C19) to make dry CHAMP for UK market; strong in GC CHARD, best for gd vintage and de luxe Belle Epoque 04 12' ★★★★ in painted bottle. BRUT NV; Blason de France NV; Blason de France Rosé NV; Belle Epoque Rosé 06. Fine new BLANC DE BLANCS. New chef de CAVE, Séverine Fresrin.

Pessac-Léognan B'x ★★★→★★★★ 05' 09' 10' 15 16 18 19' (20) AC created in 1987 for best part of n GRAV, incl all Crus Classés (1959): DOM DE CHEVALIER, HAUT-BAILLY, HAUT-BRION, LA MISSION-HAUT-BRION, PAPE-CLÉMENT, SMITH HAUT LAFITTE, etc. Aspiring unclassified: LES CARMES HAUT-BRION. Firm, full-bodied, earthy reds; B'x's finest dry whites. Value from Baulos-Charmes, Brown, Le Sartre.

Péters, Pierre Champ ★★★★ Tiptop Côte des Blancs estate. Les Chétillons probably longest-lived in CHAMP: 05 07 13 14 17'. No wood; pristine. Linking with Prov's CH Mireval to make rosé Champ.

Petit Chablis Chab ★ DYA. Thirst-quenching mini-CHAB from outlying vyds mostly not on kimmeridgian clay. Best wines from BILLAUD, BROCARD, DAUVISSAT, Defaix, LAVANTUREUX, Pommier, RAVENEAU and co-op LA CHABLISIENNE.

Pézenas L'doc Charming medieval town, birthplace Molière. AC L'DOC, diverse soils, fun to explore. Big gun PAUL MAS and smaller estates Mas Gabriel. DOMS Allegria, La Croix Gratiot, Magellan, Prieuré St Jean de Bebian, TURNER-PAGEOT; Villa Tempora.

Pfersigberg Al GC in two parcels; v. aromatic wines. GEWURZ does v. well. RIES from BRUNO SORG, DOM PAUL GINGLINGER, LÉON BEYER (Comtes d'Eguisheim).

Philipponnat Champ ★★→★★★★ Small house, intense, esp in pure Mareuil-sur-AŸ CUVÉE under careful oak 18. Now owned by LANSON-BCC group. NV, Rosé NV, BRUT, Cuvée 1522 04. Famous for majestic single vyd *Clos des Goisses* 04, CHARD-led 08; exceptional late-disgorged vintage 09.

Picpoul de Pinet L'doc ★→★★ DYA. AC for PICPOUL around Pinet, darling of sommeliers as different but oh-so-likeable. Vyds overlooking oyster farms by Med; wines have salty tang, lemony freshness. Perfect with seafood. Best not oaked. Co-ops Pinet, Pomérols do gd job, also DOMS *Félines-Jourdan*, La Croix Gratiot, Petit Roubié, St Martin de la Garrigue.

Pic St-Loup L'doc ★★→★★★★ AC n of Montpellier with dramatic scenery; some high vyds. Cooler, more rain gives elegance to wines; 50% min SYRAH plus GRENACHE, MOURVÈDRE. Reds for ageing; white potential considerable but still AC L'DOC or IGP Val de Montferrand. Growers: Bergerie du Capucin, Cazeneuve, CH PUECH-HAUT, CLOS de la Matane, Clos Marie, de Lancyre, DOM DE L'HORTUS, Gourdou, Lascaux, MAS BRUGUIÈRE, Mas Peyrolle, Valflaunès. Tiny co-op Hommes et Terres du Sud v.gd.

Pierre-Bise, Ch Lo ★★→★★★★ 16 17 18' 19' 20' V.gd DOM in COTEAUX DU LAYON, incl Chaume, *Quarts de Chaume*, SAVENNIÈRES (incl ROCHE-AUX-MOINES). ANJOU-GAMAY, ANJOU-VILLAGES, ANJOU BLANC: Haut de la Garde. Inspirational Claude Papin, architect of QUARTS DE CHAUME GC, now semi-retired, son René in charge. Excellent single-vyd sweet.

Pilgrims SW Fr History of SW dominated by Pilgrims' Way to Compostela. For 1000 yrs, pilgrims have been passing through, taking refreshment from the progenitors of today's AOP's: BERGERAC; CAHORS; IROULEGUY; MARCILLAC; SAINT MONT and so on, and carrying ideas and grape varieties with them. You can't understand the SW without taking pilgrims into account.

Pillot C d'O ★★★ Talented family in CHASSAGNE, known for whites. Look for F&L P, Jean-Marc P (CLOS St-Marc), esp DOM Paul P for sublime PCS Grandes Ruchottes, LA ROMANÉE, etc.

Pinon, François Lo ★★★ 15' 16 17 18' 19' 20' From Cousse Valley, Vernou, VOUVRAY. Reputation made by François (died Jan 2021), son Julien in charge; v.gd.

Piper-Heidsieck Champ ★★★ On surging wave of quality. Dynamic Brut Essentiel with more age, less sugar, floral yet vigorous; great with sushi, sashimi. Prestige Rare, now made as separate brand in-house, is a jewel, precise, pure, refined texture 08 12' 18' 19' 20'. Exceptional Rare Rosé 12'.

Plageoles, Dom SW Fr Defenders and rebels guarding true GAILLAC style. Rare local grapes rediscovered incl Ondenc (base of ace sweet ★★★ Vin d'Autan), ★★ Prunelard (r, deep fruity), Verdanel (dr w, oak-aged) and countless sub-varieties of Mauzac. More reds from Braucol (FER SERVADOU), Duras.

Plan de Dieu S Rh ★→★★ 16' 17' 18 19' Village nr CAIRANNE with stony, vast, windswept *garrigue* plain. Heady, full throttle, peppery, mainly GRENACHE wines; drink with game, casseroles. Wide choice. Best: CH la Couranҫonne, CLOS St Antonin, Le Plaisir, DOMS APHILLANTHES (bio, character), Arnesque, Durieu (full), Espigouette, Favards (organic), La Bastide St Vincent, Longue Toque, Martin (traditional), Pasquiers (organic), St-Pierre.

Inhabitants of Épernay known as Sparnacians, from Roman name of town.

Pol Roger Champ ★★★★ Family-owned Épernay house. BRUT Rés NV excels, dosage lowered since 2012; Brut 04 06 08', lovely 09 12'; Rosé 09; BLANC DE BLANCS 09. Fine *Pure* (no dosage). Sumptuous CUVÉE Sir Winston Churchill 02, seductive 09; a blue-chip choice for judicious ageing, best value of prestige cuvées.

Pomerol B'x ★★★→★★★★ 01' 05' 09' 10' 15 16' 18' 19' (20) Tiny, pricey AC w of ST-ÉM; MERLOT-led, plummy to voluptuous styles, but long life. Top CHX on clay, gravel plateau: CLINET, HOSANNA, L'ÉGLISE-CLINET, L'ÉVANGILE, LA CONSEILLANTE, LAFLEUR, LA FLEUR-PÉTRUS, LE PIN, PETRUS, TROTANOY, *Vieux-Ch-Certan*. Occasional value (BOURGNEUF, FEYTIT-CLINET, LA POINTE).

Pommard C d'O ★★★→★) 90' 96' 99' 03 05' 09' 10' 12 15' 16' 17 18' 19' 20' Stand by for revolution as Pommard thrives in recent warmer conditions Best vyds: Rugiens for power, Epenots for grace. Classics: BICHOT (DOM du Pavillon), BOILLOT, CH de Pommard, COMTE ARMAND, DE COURCEL, DE MONTILLE, HOSPICES DE BEAUNE, Parent. To watch: Clerget, Commaraine, Launay-Horiot, Lejeune, Rebourgeon-Mure, Violot-Guillemard.

Pommery Champ ★★ Historic house with spectacular cellars; brand now owned by VRANKEN. BRUT NV steady bet, no fireworks; Rosé NV; Brut 04 08 09 12'. Once outstanding CUVÉE Louise 02 04 less striking recently. Planting in England.

Ponsot, Dom C d'O ★★→★★★★ Idiosyncratic, top-quality MOREY-ST-DENIS DOM. Rose-Marie P now in charge. Key wines: *Clos de la Roche*, PC Monts Luisants (ALIGOTÉ). No significant changes in style.

Ponsot, Laurent C d'O ★★→★★★★ The man who made the DOM PONSOT wines for 30 yrs left the family business to create his own haute couture label nearby in 2016. Kept the sharecropping contracts, incl amazing GRIOTTE-CHAMBERTIN, CLOS ST-DENIS, and has added fine range in both colours. Buying vines too. Watch these spaces.

FRANCE

Pouilly-Fuissé Burg ★★→★★★ 14' 15 17 18 19' 20' Top AC of MÂCON; potent, rounded but intense whites from around Fuissé, more mineral style in Vergisson. Enjoy young or with age. PC classification finally in place for 2020 vintage; hurrah! Top: Barraud, Bret, CH de Beauregard, CH DE FUISSÉ, Ch des Quarts, Ch des Rontets, Cordier, Cornin, Drouin, Ferret, Forest, Merlin, Paquet, Robert-Denogent, Rollet, Saumaize, Saumaize-Michelin, VERGET, Vessigaud.

Pouilly-Fumé Lo ★★→★★★★ 18' 19' 20' SANCERRE's e-bank neighbour. SAUV BL. Benefits from 2–3 yrs in bottle. Best: Bain, Belair, Bouchié-Chatellier, Bourgeois, Cailbourdin, CH de Favray, Ch de Tracy, Chatelain, *Didier Dagueneau* (VDF from 2017), E&A Figeat, Landrat-Guyollot, Jean Pabiot, *Jonathan Pabiot*, Jolivet, Joseph Mellot, Ladoucette, *Masson-Blondelet*, *Redde*, Saget, Serge Dagueneau & Filles, Tabordet, Treuillet.

Pouilly-Loché Burg ★★ 14' 15 17 18 19' 20' Least known of Mâconnais' Pouilly family. Reference: CLOS des Rocs. Try also Bret Bros, Tripoz and local CAVE des GCS Blancs.

Pouilly-sur-Loire Lo ★★ DYA. Now historical curiosity. In C19 Pouilly supplied Paris with CHASSELAS table grapes. Same area POUILLY-FUMÉ. Just 27 ha remain – still made by Gitton, Jonathan Pabiot, Landrat-Guyollot, Masson-Blondelet, Redde, Serge Dagueneau & Filles.

Pouilly-Vinzelles Burg ★★ 14' 15 17 18 19' 20' Between POUILLY-LOCHÉ and POUILLY-FUISSÉ geographically and in quality. Outstanding vyd: Les Quarts. Best: Bret Bros, CH de V, DROUHIN, Valette. Volume from CAVE des GRANDS CRUS Blancs.

PC (Premier Cru) First Growth in B'X; 2nd rank of vyds (after GC) in Burg, 2nd rank in LO: one so far, COTEAUX DU LAYON Chaume.

Premières Côtes de Bordeaux B'X ★→★★ 16 18 19 (20) Same zone as CADILLAC-CÔTES DE B'X but for sweet whites only. SÉM-dominated *moelleux*. Generally early drinking. Best CH DE Crabitan-Bellevue, du Juge, Fayau, *Suau*.

Prieur, Dom Jacques C d'O ★★★ Major MEURSAULT estate with range of underplayed GCS from MONTRACHET to MUSIGNY. Style aims at weight from late-picking and oak more than finesse. New project Labruyère-Prieur in Burg. Owners Famille Labruyère also have CHAMP and MOULIN-À-VENT projects plus CH ROUGET (B'X).

Primeur "Early" wine for refreshment and uplift; esp from BEAUJ; VDP too. Wine sold en primeur is still in barrel, for delivery when bottled.

Producteurs Plaimont SW Fr France's most dynamic co-op, bestriding SAINT MONT, MADIRAN and CÔTES DE GASCOGNE like the colossus it is. Has abandoned B'X varieties for grapes traditional to SW, incl some pre-phylloxera discoveries. All colours, styles, mostly ★★, all tastes, purses. *See* ANDRÉ DUBOSC.

Propriétaire récoltant Champ Owner-operator, literally owner-harvester.

Puech-Haut CH L'doc ★★★ AC L'DOC St Drézéry. Powerful Prestige (r/w), Tête de Belier (r/w/rosé) swish wine, packaging. IGP Argali rosé gd value. Owns ★★★ PIC ST-LOUP Lavabre.

Puisseguin St-Émilion B'X ★★ 10' 15 16 18 19 (20) Most e of four ST-ÉM satellites; MERLOT-led; meaty but firm. Top CHX: Beauséjour, Branda, Clarisse, DES LAURETS, Durand-Laplagne, Fongaban, Guibot la Fourvieille, Haut-Bernat, l'Anglais, La Mauriane, Le Bernat, Soleil.

Puligny-Montrachet C d'O ★★★→★★★★ 09' 10' 12 14' 15 17' 18 19' 20' Floral, fine-boned, tingling white burg. Decent at village level, Enseignières vyd exceptional, outstanding PCS, esp: Caillerets, Champ Canet, Combettes, Folatières, Pucelles, plus amazing MONTRACHET GCS. Producers: *Carillon*, Chartron, CH de Puligny, Chavy, *Dom Leflaive*, *Drouhin*, Ente, *J-M Boillot*, *O Leflaive*, Pernot, *Sauzet*, Thomas-Collardot.

Puyméras S Rh ★ 18 19' Sound, secluded Rh village, high vyds, mild plum-fruited reds based on GRENACHE, fair whites, decent co-op. Limited choice. Note CAVE la Comtadine, DOM du Faucon Doré (bio), Puy du Maupas.

> **Rosé all year round**
> Rosé is no longer just a summer wine: so here are some to see you through the winter too. Clos du Temple, GÉRARD BERTRAND, top quality and price. CH D'ESCLANS Rock Angel, cool Prov; CH La Coste, bio finesse, gd value; CH PUECH-HAUT, swish bottle and wine. DOM La Tasque Aurelia, CARIGNAN richness and freshness (maker: Juliet Bruce-Jones of this parish); Dom Lafage Miraflors, strawberries; Dom Pieretti, Corsica's finest rosé; DOM TEMPIER, best of BANDOL, try in magnum; Dom Turner-Pageot 48 Heures, deep colour, rich, gastronomic.

Pyrénées-Atlantiques SW Fr Mostly DYA. IGP in far sw for wines outside local AOPs. ★★★ CABIDOS in middle of nowhere (superb dr and sw PETIT MANSENG w varietals that will age), ★★ DOM Moncaut (JURANÇON in all but name nr Pau).

Quarts de Chaume Lo ★★★→★★★★ 07′ 10′ 11′ 14′ 15′ 16 17 18′ 20′ Remarkable site in Layon, CHENIN BL. Best richly textured. Top: Baudouin, Belargus, Bellerive, Branchereau, *Ch Pierre-Bise*, FL, *Guegniard*, *Ogereau*, Suronde. Cryoextraction now banned. Sadly difficult to sell this nectar.

Quincy Lo ★★ 18′ 19′ 20′ Revived AOP, SAUV BL on low-lying sand/gravel banks. Try: *Ballandors*, l'Epine, Mardon, Portier, Rouzé, *Siret-Courtaud*, *Tremblay*, Villalin.

Rancio Rouss Describes complex, evolved aromas from extended, oxidative ageing. Reminiscent of Tawny Port, or old Oloroso Sherry. Associated specifically with BANYULS, MAURY, RASTEAU, RIVESALTES. Can be a grand experience; don't miss.

Rangen Al Most s GC of AL at Thann; v. steep (average 90%) slopes, volcanic soils. Top: majestic RIES ZIND-HUMBRECHT (CLOS St Urbain 08′ 10′ 17′), SCHOFFIT (St-Théobald 15′ 17′). Fascinating contrast with Z-H St-Théo: supreme finesse, no oak.

Rasteau S Rh ★★ 12′ 15′ 16′ 17′ 18 19′ 20 Full-on, some suave reds from mainly clay soils, mostly GRENACHE. Best in hot yrs, consistent quality. NB: Beaurenard (bio, serious, age well), Cave Ortas/Rhonéa, CH La Gardine, Ch du Trignon, Famille Perrin; DOMS Beau Mistral, Collière (stylish), Combe Julière (punchy), Coteaux des Travers (bio), Didier Charavin, Elodie Balme (soft), Escaravailles (style), Girasols, Gourt de Mautens (talented, IGP from 2010), Gramiller (organic), Grand Nicolet (depth, character), Grange Blanche, Rabasse-Charavin (full), M Boutin, Soumade (polished), *St Gayan*, Trapadis (bio). Grenache dessert VDN: quality on the up (Doms Banquettes, Combe Julière, Coteaux des Travers, Escaravailles, Trapadis). Rasteau doms also gd source CÔTES DU RH (r).

Raveneau Chab ★★★★ Topmost CHAB producers, using classic methods for *extraordinary long-lived wines*. A little more modern while still growing in stature of late. Excellent value (except in 2ndary market). Look for PC Butteaux, Chapelot, Vaillons and GC Blanchots, Les CLOS.

Rayas, Ch S Rh ★★★★ 05′ 06′ 07′ 09′ 10′ 11′ 15′ 16′ 17′ 19′ Outstanding, lost-in-time, one-off 13-ha CHÂTEAUNEUF estate, tiny yields, sandy soils. Sensuous reds (100% GRENACHE) whisper quality, offer delight, age superbly. White Rayas (CLAIRETTE, GRENACHE BL) v.gd over 20 yrs+. Stylish second label, Pignan, empties your wallet. Supreme CH Fonsalette CÔTES DU RH, incl marvellous long-lived SYRAH. Decant all; each is an occasion. No 18 (mildew); gd Ch des Tours VACQUEYRAS (peppery), VDP.

Regnié Beauj ★★ 15′ 17 18′ 19 20′ Most recent BEAUJ cru, lighter wines on sandy soil, meatier nr MORGON. Starting to get good gd growers now. Try: A Sunier, Burgaud, Chemarin, de la Plaigne, Dupré, J Sunier, Rochette.

Reuilly Lo ★→★★★ 18′ 19′ 20′ Revived AC just w of QUINCY. SAUV BL, rosés and *Vin Gris* PINOT N and/or *Pinot Gr*. Some fine PINOT N reds. Best: *Claude Lafond* (run by daughter Natalie), *Jamain*, Mardon/Tabordet, Renaudat, Rouze, Sorbe.

Riceys, Les Champ DYA. Key AC in AUBE for notable PINOT N rosé. Producers: *A Bonnet*, Brice, Jacques Defrance, Morize. Great 09′; ace 15′.

FRANCE

Richebourg C d'O ★★★★ 90' 93' **96'** 99' 02' 05' 09' **10'** 12' 15' 16 17 18' 19' 20' VOSNE-ROMANÉE GC. Supreme burg with great depth of flavour, vastly expensive. Growers: DRC, GRIVOT, GROS, HUDELOT-NOËLLAT, LEROY, LIGER-BELAIR, MÉO-CAMUZET.

Rion C d'O ★★→★★★ Related DOMS in NUITS-ST-GEORGES, VOSNE-ROMANÉE. Patrice R for excellent Nuits CLOS St-Marc, Clos des Argillières and CHAMBOLLE-MUSIGNY. Daniel R for Nuits and Vosne PCS; Bernard R more Vosne-based. All fairly priced.

Rivesaltes Rouss ★★ Underappreciated VDN with styles Ambré, Tuilé, Rosé, RANCIO/ Hors d'Age. Muscat de Rivesaltes AC fragrant, youthful. Look for: Boucabeille, des Chênes, des Schistes, DOM CAZES, Puig-Parahy, Rancy, Roc des Anges, Sarda-Malet, Valmy, Vaquer. You won't be disappointed.

Rives-Blanques, Ch L'doc ★★★ LIMOUX. Irish-Dutch couple with son Jean Ailbe make BLANQUETTE and CRÉMANT. Limoux white (and rosé), incl unusual 100% MAUZAC, Occitania, blend Trilogie and age-worthy CHENIN BL Dédicace.

Roederer, Louis Champ ★★★★ Peerless family-owned house/DOM. Enviable vyds, much organic/bio. BRUT Premier NV all finesse, flavour; Brut **12'** BLANC DE BLANCS 12 13 15 17' 19' 20'. Brut Saignée Rosé shines; magnificent *Cristal* bio (since 2012) 08. Superb Cristal Vinothèque Blanc, Rosé 95; Brut NATURE Philippe Starck (all Cumières 09 12 18' 20'.) Also owns CH PICHON-LALANDE, DEUTZ. *See also* California.

Rolland, Michel B'x Veteran French consultant winemaker and MERLOT specialist (B'x and worldwide). Owner of FONTENIL in FRON. *See* Argentina (Clos de los Siete).

Rolly Gassmann Al ★★★ Revered DOM, esp Moenchreben vyd. Off-dry, rich, sensuous GEWURZ CUVÉE Yves 08 09 12 16 17' 18 19. Now into bio, more finesse. Mineral zesty RIES 13 16 17' 18 19'. Fine PINOT N 15 intense, gentle tannins.

Romanée, La C d'O ★★★★ 09' 10' **12'** 15' 16' 17 18' 19' 20. Tiniest GC in VOSNE-ROMANÉE, MONOPOLE of COMTE LIGER-BELAIR. Exceptionally fine, perfumed, intense: now on peak form and understandably expensive.

Romanée-Conti, La C d'O ★★★★ 90' 93' **96'** 99' 00 02' 05' 09' 10' 12' 14' 15' 16' 17 18' 19' 20' GC in VOSNE-ROMANÉE, MONOPOLE of DRC. Most celebrated GC in Burg, gold dust. On fabulous form these days. Patience required, for 10–20 yrs. But beware geeks bringing fake gifts.

Romanée-St-Vivant C d'O ★★★★ 90' 99' 02' 05' 09' **10'** 12' 15' 16' 17 18' 19' 20' GC in VOSNE-ROMANÉE. Downslope from LA ROMANÉE-CONTI, haunting perfume, delicate but intense. Ready a little earlier than famous neighbours. Growers: if you can't afford ARNOUX-LACHAUX, DRC or LEROY, or indeed CATHIARD or HUDELOT-NÖELLAT now, try ARLOT, Follin-Arbelet, JJ Confuron, LATOUR, Poisot. Nobody letting side down.

Rosacker Al GC at Hunawihr. Limestone/clay makes some of longest-lived RIES in AL (CLOS STE-HUNE).

Rosé d'Anjou Lo ★→★★ DYA. Rosé – off-dry to sweet (largely Grolleau). Big AOP. Popular, increasingly well made. Look for: Bergerie, Bougrier, Clau de Nell, Fontaines, Grandes VIGNES, Mark Angeli (VDF).

Rosé de Loire Lo ★→★★ Dry rosé mainly from ANJOU. Grapes: Grolleau Gris/Noir, CAB FR, CAB SAUV, GAMAY; PINOT N. AC. Best: Bablut, Bois Brinçon, Branchereau, CADY, CAVE de SAUMUR, Fontaines, Ogereau, Passavant, PIERRE-BISE, Soucherie.

Rosette SW Fr ★★ Tiny AOP DYA. Birthplace of BERGERAC, now reviving traditional off-dry apéritif whites. Also gd with foie gras or mushrooms. Avoid oaked versions that deny the style. CLOS Romain; CHX Combrillac, de Peyrel, Monplaisir, Puypezat-Rosette, Spingulèbre; DOMS de Coutancie, de la Cardinolle, du Grand-Jaure.

Rossignol-Trapet C d'O ★★★ Equally bio cousins of DOM TRAPET, with healthy holdings of GC vyds, esp CHAMBERTIN. Gd value across range from GEVREY VIEILLES VIGNES up. Also some BEAUNE vyds from Rossignol side.

Rostaing, Dom N Rh ★★★ 01' 05' **09'** 10' **12'** 13' 15' 16' 17' 18' 19' 20' High-quality CÔTE-RÔTIE DOM: five tightly knit wines from top sites, all v. fine, pure, clear, discreet oak, wait 6 yrs+, decant. Complex, enticing, top-class Côte Blonde

(5% VIOGNIER), Côte Brune (iron), also La Landonne (dark fruits, 20–25 yrs). Mineral, firm Condrieu, also IGP COLLINES RHODANIENNES (r/w), L'DOC Puech Noble (r/w).

Rouget, Dom C d'O ★★★★ Renamed as DOM R rather than Emmanuel R with new generation refreshing dom famed for Henri Jayer connection and CROS PARANTOUX vyd. Fine NUITS-ST-GEORGES, VOSNE-ROMANÉE, as well as GCS.

Roulot, Dom C d'O ★★★→★★★★ Jean-Marc R leads outstanding MEURSAULT DOM, now cult status so beware secondary-market prices. Great PCS, esp CLOS des Bouchères, Perrières; value from top village sites Luchets, Meix Chavaux, esp Clos du Haut Tesson. Catch his next movie too.

Roumier, Georges C d'O ★★★★ Reference DOM for BONNES-MARES and other *brilliant Chambolle* wines (incl Amoureuses, Cras) from Christophe R. Long-lived wines but still attractive early. Cult status means hard to find now at sensible prices. Best value is MOREY CLOS de la Bussière.

Rouquette-sur-Mer, Ch L'DOC ★★★★ Impressive LA CLAPE estate, vyds and *garrigue* right by Med. Arpège (w), crisp, herby, terrific value. CLOS de la Tour oaky MOURVÈDRE/SYRAH, also l'Absolu, both excellent.

Rousseau, Dom Armand C d'O ★★★★ Unmatchable GEVREY-CHAMBERTIN DOM thrilling with balanced, fragrant, refined, age-worthy wines from village to GC, esp CLOS ST-JACQUES. No changes expected anytime soon.

Roussette de Savoie Sav ★★ Regional AOC, same area as AOC SAVOIE – 10% of its wines; 100% ROUSSETTE. Try: Carrel, Curtet, de la Mar, *Grisard*, *Mérande*, Quénard, Ravier, Vuillen.

Roussillon Often linked with L'DOC, and incl in AC L'DOC but has distinct identity. Exciting region with different soils and topography, innovative producers. Lots of old vines. GRENACHE key variety. Largest AC Côtes du Rouss. Gd-value spicy reds. Original, traditional VDN (eg. BANYULS, MAURY, RIVESALTES). Also serious age-worthy table wines (r/w). *See* COLLIOURE, CÔTES CATALANES, CÔTES DU ROUSS-VILLAGES, MAURY (Sec) and box below.

Ruchottes-Chambertin C d'O ★★★★ 99' 02' 05' 09' 10' 12' 15' 16 17' 18' 19' 20' Tiny GC neighbour of CHAMBERTIN. Less weighty but ethereal, intricate, lasting, great finesse. Top growers: MUGNERET-Gibourg, ROUMIER, ROUSSEAU. Try also CH de MARSANNAY, H Magnien, Marchand-Grillot, Pacalet.

Ruinart Champ ★★★★ Oldest CHAMP house? (1729). High standards going higher still. Rich, elegant. R de Ruinart BRUT NV; Ruinart Rosé NV; R de Ruinart Brut **08**. Prestige CUVÉE *Dom Ruinart* one of two best vintage BLANC DE BLANCS in Champ (viz 90' esp in magnum, 02 04' 07'). DR Rosé also v. special **06** 04'. NV Blanc de Blancs much improved. High hopes for 13', classic cool lateish vintage. Winemaker Fred Panaiotis top of his game.

Rully Burg ★★ (r) 15' 17 18' 19' 20' (w) 17' 18 19' 20' CÔTE CHALONNAISE village. *Light, fresh, tasty, gd-value whites.* Reds all about the fruit, not structure. Try Champs

---

Roussillon – the quiet revolution

The majestic, craggy scenery and sleepy villages of the Agly, Têt and Tech Valleys are a hotbed of innovation, driven by small producers who like to experiment. Growers make most of varied terroirs, altitude and old low-yielding vines, esp GRENACHE (r/w) and CARIGNAN for depth, complexity: brooding fruit, notes of minerality/hot stones. Age well too. CÔTES DU ROUSS-VILLAGES or lowly IGP CÔTES DU CATALANES on label but as usual it's grower that counts. DOMS Casenove, DE L'OU, GÉRARD GAUBY, JONES, L'Enfants, L'HORIZON, La Préceptorie Centernach, Le Soula, Mas Llossanes, Matassa, OF THE BEE, Olivier Pithon, Padié, Roc des Anges, Soulanes, TRELOAR, Vaquer. Don't forget often sublime VDN from BANYULS, MAURY, RIVESALTES.

l'Abbaye, Devevey, DROUHIN, **Dureuil-Janthial**, FAIVELEY, Jacqueson, Jaeger-Defaix, Jobard (C), Ninot, **Olivier Leflaive**, Rodet.

Sablet S Rh ★★ 18' 19' CÔTES DU RH-VILLAGE on plain nr GIGONDAS. Easy wines, some deeper. Sandy soils, neat red-berry reds, esp CAVE CO-OP Gravillas, CH Cohola (organic), du Trignon; DOMS de Boissan (organic, full), Les Goubert (r/w), Pasquiers (organic, full), Piaugier (r/w). Gd full whites for apéritifs, food: Boissan, SAINT GAYAN.

St-Amour Beauj ★★ 18' 19' 20' Most n BEAUJ cru: mixed soils, so variable character, but signs of revival. Try: Cheveau, DOM de Fa, Patissier, **Pirolette**, Revillon.

St-Aubin C d'O ★★★ (w) 14' 15 17 18' 19' 20' Fine source for **lively, refreshing whites**, challenging PULIGNY, CHASSAGNE, esp on price. Also pretty reds mostly for early drinking. Best vyds: Chatenière, **En Remilly**, Murgers Dents de Chien. Best growers: BACHELET (JC), COLIN (Joseph, Marc), COLIN-MOREY, **Lamy**. Value Prudhon

St-Bris Burg ★ DYA. Unique AC for SAUV BL in n Burg. Fresh, lively, but also worth keeping from GOISOT or de Moor. Try also Bersan, Davenne, Simonnet-Febvre.

St-Chinian L'doc ★→★★★ Large hilly area nr Béziers with schist in nw, clay and limestone in se. Sound reputation. Incl CRUS Berlou (mostly CARIGNAN) Roquebrun (mostly SYRAH) on schist. Warm, spicy reds, based on SYRAH, GRENACHE, CARIGNAN, MOURVÈDRE. Whites from ROUSSANNE, MARSANNE, VERMENTINO, GRENACHE BL. Gd co-op Roquebrun; CH CASTIGNO, Viranel; DOMS Borie la Vitarèle, des Jougla, La Dournie, LA MADURA, LES EMINADES, Navarre, Rimbert; CLOS Bagatelle, Mas Champart, Mas de Cynanques, Terre des Dames.

St Cosme, Ch de S Rh ★★★ 06' 09' 10' 11' 12' 13' 14' 15' 16' 17' 18' 19' At GIGONDAS, 15 ha bio estate; wine with flair, drive, oak. Plot-specific CÔTES DU RH Les Deux Albion (r), Gigondas Le Poste. Owner CH de Rouanne, VINSOBRES (2018). Gd N Rh merchant range, esp CONDRIEU, CÔTE-RÔTIE.

Ste-Croix-du-Mont B'x ★★ 13 15 16 18 19 (20) AC making sweet, white **liquoreux**. Soils consist of fossilized oysters. Best: rich, creamy, can age. Top CHX: Crabitan-Bellevue, du Mont, La Caussade, La Rame, **Loubens**.

St-Émilion B'x ★★→★★★★★ 05' 09' 10' 15' 16 18 19' (20) Big MERLOT-led district on B'x's Right Bank, currently on a roll. CAB FR also strong. UNESCO World Heritage site. ACS St-Ém and (lots of) St-Ém GC (geographically same area). Top designation St-Ém PREMIER GRAND CRU CLASSÉ. Warm, full, rounded style but much diversity due to terroir, winemaking and blend. Best firm, v. long-lived. Top CHX: ANGÉLUS, AUSONE, CANON, CHEVAL BLANC, FIGEAC, PAVIE.

St-Estèphe H-Méd ★★→★★★★ 00' 05' 09' 10' 15 16' 18 19' (20) Most n communal AC in the MÉD. Solid, structured wines for ageing. Lots of new investors. Five Classed Growths: CALON-SÉGUR, COS D'ESTOURNEL, COS-LABORY, LAFON-ROCHET, MONTROSE. Top unclassified estates: CAPBERN, DE PEZ, HAUT-MARBUZET, LE BOSCQ, LE CROCK, LILIAN LADOUYS, MEYNEY, ORMES-DE-PEZ, PHÉLAN-SÉGUR.

Ste-Victoire Prov ★★ Subzone of CÔTES DE PROV, s limestone slopes of Montagne Ste-Victoire: much-needed freshness in hotter vintages. DOMS de St Ser, Gassier benefit from high altitude. Mathilde Chapoutier (rosé), v.gd IGP Dom Richeaume.

St-Gall Champ Brand of Union-CHAMP, top co-op at AVIZE. BRUT NV; Extra Brut NV; Brut BLANC DE BLANCS NV; Brut Rosé NV; Brut Blanc de Blancs 08; CUVÉE Orpale Blanc de Blancs 02' 08' 17'. Fine-value PINOT-led **Pierre Vaudon NV**. Makes top **vins clairs** for some great houses.

Saint Gayan, Dom S Rh ★★★ 01' 05' 06' 07' 10' 15' 16' 17' 18' 19' Top 16-ha GIGONDAS address, v.-consistent, long-lived wines; 80% GRENACHE Origine great value. V.gd, full RASTEAU Ilex (r), charming SABLET L'Oratory (w).

St-Georges-St-Émilion B'x ★★ 10' 15 16 18 19 (20) Tiny ST-ÉM satellite. Sturdy, structured. Best CHX: Calon, CLOS Albertus, Macquin-St-Georges, St-André Corbin, St-Georges, Tour du Pas-St-Georges.

St-Gervais S Rh ★→★★ 18 19' Village on w bank; gd soils but v. limited choice. Co-op low-key; best by far is long-lived (10 yrs+) DOM Ste-Anne red (direct, firm, MOURVÈDRE licorice flavours), gd VIOGNIER. Also Dom Clavel (Regulus r).

St-Joseph N Rh ★★→★★★ 05' 09' 10' 12' 15' 16' 17' 18' 19' 20' Mainly granite vyds, 64 km (40 miles) n–s, some high, along w bank of N Rh. SYRAH reds. Best, oldest vyds nr Tournon: stylish, red-fruited wines; further n darker, peppery, younger oak. More complete, interesting than CROZES-HERMITAGE, esp CHAPOUTIER (Les Granits), **Gonon** (top class), **Gripa**, GUIGAL (VIGNES de l'Hospice), **J-L Chave**; also Alexandrins, Amphores (bio), A PERRET (Grisières), Boissonnet, Chèze, Courbis (modern), Coursodon (racy, modern), Cuilleron, E Darnaud, Delas, J&E Durand, Faury, Ferraton, F Villard, Gaillard, P Marthouret, Monier-Perréol (bio), P-J Villa, S Blachon, Vallet, Vins de Vienne. Gd food-friendly *white (mainly Marsanne)*, esp A PERRET, Barge, *Chapoutier* (Les Granits), Cuilleron, Curtat, Dom Faury, Gonon, Gouye, **Gripa**, GUIGAL, J Pilon, Vallet.

St-Julien H-Méd ★★★→★★★★★ 00 05' 09' 10' 15 16' 18 19' (20) Super consistent mid-MÉD communal AC; 11 classified (1855) estates own most of vyd area; incl BEYCHEVELLE, BRANAIRE-DUCRU, DUCRU-BEAUCAILLOU, GRUAUD-LAROSE, LAGRANGE, LÉOVILLES (x3), TALBOT. Epitome of harmonious, fragrant, savoury red.

Saint Mont SW Fr ★★ (r) 15' 16 17 18 19 (20) AOP from Gascon heartlands. Similar to Madiran but often softer, less intense. PRODUCTEURS PLAIMONT'S ANDRÉ DUBOSC largely responsible for creating this AOP, PP makes most of the wine. Try ★★★ CH de Sabazan. White is dry, PACHERENC-like, less intense and terrific value.

Most profitable wine regions, pre-coronavirus: Champ, then Prov. Least: L'doc, Lo.

St Nicolas de Bourgueil Lo ★→★★★ 16' 17' 18' 19' 20' Almost identical to BOURGUEIL: CAB FR. Light wines from sand/gravel; fuller-bodied from limestone slopes. Try: David, Delanoue, *Frédéric Mabileau*, Jamet, Laurent Mabileau, Mabileau-Rezé, Ménard, Mortier, Taluau-Foltzenlogel, Vallée, *Yannick Amirault*, Xavier Amirault.

St-Péray N Rh ★★ 18' 19' 20' Stylish white (MARSANNE/ROUSSANNE) from hilly granite, some lime vyds opposite Valence, lots of fast new planting. Once *famous for fizz*; classic-method bubbles well worth trying. (A Voge, J-L Thiers, R Nodin, TAIN co-op). Still white should have grip: smoky, flinty. Best: CHAPOUTIER, Clape (pure), Colombo (stylish), Cuilleron, *du Tunnel* (v. elegant), Gripa (v.gd), J&E Durand, J-L Thiers, L&C Fayolle, R Nodin, TAIN co-op, Vins de Vienne, Voge (oak).

St-Pourçain Lo, Mass C ★→★★ AOC 19' 20' Increasingly gd red/rosé (GAMAY, PINOT N), 100% Pinot N banned, white from local Tressalier and/or CHARD, SAUV BL. Growers: *Bérioles*, Bellevue, Clos de Breuilly, Grosbot-Barbara, Les Terres d'Ocre, Nebout, Pétillat, Ray, VIGNERONS de St-Pourçain (majority of production).

St-Romain C d'O ★★ (w) 15 17' 18' 19' 20' *Crisp whites* from side valley of CÔTE DE BEAUNE. Excellent value by Burg standards. Best vyds Combe Bazin, Sous la Roche, Sous le CH. Specialists Alain Gras, de Chassorney, and outstanding H&G Buisson, but most NÉGOCIANTS have a gd one. Some fresh reds too. Watch this space.

St-Véran Burg ★★ 17 18' 19 20' Southern AOC either side of POUILLY-FUISSÉ. Try CH de Beauregard, Chagnoleau, Corsin, Deux Roches, Litaud, Merlin; most gd POUILLY-FUISSÉ growers for single vyds. Gd-value DUBOEUF, Poncetys, Terres Secretes co-op.

Salon Champ ★★★★ Original BLANC DE BLANCS, from LE MESNIL in Côte des Blancs. Tiny quantities. Awesome reputation for long-lived luxury-priced wines: in truth, inconsistent. On song recently, viz 83' 90 97', but 99 disappoints. *See also* DELAMOTTE. Both owned by LAURENT-PERRIER, whose widely respected chef de CAVE, Dominique Demarville, abruptly left. Watch future developments.

Sancerre Lo ★→★★★★ 16' 17' 18' 19' 20' Reference for SAUV BL, some v.gd PINOT N. Best producers meticulous. Move to single vyds. Best: *Alphonse Mellot, Boulay, Bourgeois, Claude Riffault*, Cotat, Dezat, D Roger, *François Crochet*, Fleuriet,

Fouassier, Jean-Max Roger, Jolivet, Joseph Mellot, L Crochet, Natter, Neveu, P&N Reverdy, Paul Prieur, Pierre Martin, *Pinard*, Raimbault, Roblin, Thomas, Thomas Laballe, *Vacheron*, Vatan, Vattan, *Vincent Delaporte*.

Sang des Cailloux, Dom Le S Rh ★★★ 10' 12' 13' 15' 16' 17' 18' 19' Best VACQUEYRAS DOM, 17 ha, bio, *garrigue* thrust. Classic red rotates name every 3 yrs, Azalaïs (18), Floureto (19), Doucinello (20). Top Lopy red ages well. Solid Un Sang Blanc (w).

Santenay C d'O ★★→★★★ 05' 09' 12 14 15' 16 17 18' 19' 20' The s end of CÔTE DE BEAUNE, potential for fine reds; don't overlook. Best vyds: CLOS de Tavannes, Clos Rousseau, Gravières (r/w). Some gd whites too, eg, Charmes. Local producers: Bachey-Legros, Chevrot, J Girardin, MOREAU, Muzard, Vincent. Try also Giroud, JADOT (now incl DOM Prieur-Brunet), LAMY.

Saumur Lo ★→★★★★ 17 18' 19' (20') Big AOP. Whites, light to age-worthy; often easy reds except SAUMUR-CHAMPIGNY; Saumur Rosé (Cabs). CRÉMANT most important, Saumur MOUSSEUX. Saumur-Le-Puy Notre-Dame AOP for CAB FR (mainly). Best: *Antoine Foucault*, *Arnaud Lambert*, BOUVET-LADUBAY, CH de Brézé, CLOS Mélaric, *Clos Rougeard*, Ditterie, Guiberteau, Nerleux, Paleine, Parnay, René-Hugues Gay, Robert et Marcel, Rocheville, Targé, *Villeneuve*, Yvonne.

Saumur-Champigny Lo ★★→★★★★ 16' 17' 18' 19' (20') Can be top CAB FR from nine-commune AC, gd vintages age 15–20 yrs+. Best: *Antoine Sanzay*, *Arnaud Lambert*, *Bonnelière (value)*, Bruno Dubois, Champs Fleuris, historic CLOS Cristal (now co-op-run), *Clos Rougeard* (cult), Cune, Ditterie, Filliatreau, Hureau, Nerleux, Petit St-Vincent, Robert et Marcel (co-op), Roches Neuves, Rocheville, St-Vincent, Seigneurie, Targé, Vadé, Val Brun, *Villeneuve*, Yvonne.

Saussignac SW Fr ★★ 16' 17 18' 19 (20) BERGERAC sub-AOP, adjoining MONBAZILLAC, producing similar sweet wines perhaps with shade more acidity. Best: ★★★ DOMS de Richard, La Maurigne, Les Miaudoux, Lestevénie; ★★ CHX Le Chabrier, Le Payral, Le Tap.

Sauternes B'x ★★→★★★★ 05 09' 11' 13 14 15' 16' 18 19 (20) AC making France's best *liquoreux* from "noble rotted" grapes. Luscious, golden and age-worthy. Classified (1855) CHX: D'YQUEM, GUIRAUD, *Lafaurie-Peyraguey*, LA TOUR BLANCHE, RIEUSSEC, SIGALAS-RABAUD, SUDUIRAUT. Aspiring unclassified: *Fargues*, *Raymond-Lafon*. Value from DOM de l'Alliance, HAUT-BERGERON, Les Justices.

Sauzet, Etienne C d'O ★★★ Leading DOM in PULIGNY with superb range of PCS (Combettes, Champ Canet best) and GC BÂTARD-M. Concentrated, lively wines. Certified bio, once again capable of ageing.

Savennières Lo ★★→★★★★ 16 18' 19' 20' Small ANJOU AC, high reputation, variable style and quality; v. long-lived dry whites (CHENIN BL) with marked acidity – a few DEMI-SEC. Baudouin, BAUMARD, *Belurgus*, *Bergerie*, Boudignon, Closel, DOM FL, Epiré, *Laureau*, Mahé, Mathieu-Tijou, *Morgat*, *Ogereau*, Pierre-Bise, Soucherie. Top sites: CLOS Picot, COULÉE DE SERRANT, ROCHE-AUX-MOINES.

Savennières Roche-aux-Moines Lo ★★ →★★★ 16 18' 19 20' SAVENNIÈRES 33-ha cru. Top CHENIN BL. Best: Baraut, *Dom FL*, Forges, *Laureau*, Moines, Pierre-Bise. Ages well.

Savigny-lès-Beaune C d'O ★★★ 05' 09' 10' 15' 18' 19' 20' Important village next to BEAUNE; similar mid-weight wines, savoury touch (but can be rustic). Top vyds: Dominode, Guettes, Lavières, Vergelesses. Local growers: *Bize*, Camus-Bruchon, *Chandon de Briailles*, Chenu, Girard, Guillemot (w), Guyon, Pavelot, Rapet, *Tollot-Beaut*. Plus exceptional CUVÉES from CLAIR, DROUHIN, LEROY.

Savoie ★★→★★★ Alpine wines. AC incl three other ACs, 20 crus, incl APRÉMONT, CHIGNIN, CRÉPY, Jongieux, Ripaille. Regional ACs: CRÉMANT de Sav, ROUSSETTE DE SAV (Altesse), SEYSSEL; 25 grapes (r) mainly GAMAY, MONDEUSE, (w) Altesse, CHARD, CHASSELAS, Jacquère, Mondeuse Bl, ROUSSANNE.

Schlossberg Al GC at Kientzheim famed since C15. Glorious compelling RIES from FALLER 10 and new TRIMBACH; 15 is great Ries yr here.

Schlumberger, Doms Al ★★→★★★★ Vast, top-quality AL DOM owning c.1% of all Al vyds; rich wines from S Al; GCS Kitterlé and racy Saering show rare breed 08, exceptional 17' 18 19 20. Rare RIES, signature CUVÉE Ernest and now GC Kessler GEWURZ lovely in underrated 16. Great PINOT GR in recent sunny yrs are v. special. Serious alternative to white burg.

Schoenenbourg Al A v. rich, successful Riquewihr GC: PINOT GR, RIES, v. fine VT, SGN, esp DOPFF AU MOULIN. Also v.gd MUSCAT. HUGEL Schoelhammer from here.

Schoffit, Dom Al ★★★★ Exceptional Colmar grower, superb late-harvest GEWURZ, PINOT GR VT GC RANGEN CLOS St-Théobald 10' 17' 18' 20' on volcanic soil. Contrast with RIES GC Sonnenberg 13 15 16 17' on limestone. Delicious Harth CHASSELAS. No oak = super-elegance, esp drier styles.

Sec Literally means dry, though CHAMP so called is medium-sweet (and can be welcome at breakfast, teatime, weddings).

Séguret S Rh ★★ 16' 17' 18 19' Striking hillside village nr GIGONDAS in Rh-Villages top three. Vyds on both warm plain and cool heights. Mainly GRENACHE, peppery, quite deep reds, some full-on; bright-fruited table whites. Esp CH la Courançonne (gd w), DOMS Amandine, Crève Coeur (bio), de Cabasse, de l'Amauve (fine, gd w), Fontaine des Fées (organic), Garancière, J David (organic), Maison Plantevin (organic), Malmont, Mourchon, Pourra (intense, time), Soleil Romain.

SGN (Sélection des Grains Nobles) Al Term coined by HUGEL for AL equivalent to German Beerenauslese, subject to ever-stricter rules. *Grains nobles* are grapes with "noble rot" for v. sweet wines.

Selosse, Anselme Champ ★★★★ Leading grower, an icon for many. Vinous, oxidative style, oak-fermented. Son Guillaume adding finesse: Version Originale still vibrant after 7 yrs on lees. Top probably MESNIL Les Carelles: saline, complex, akin to MEURSAULT Perrières with bubbles. 99 v. stylish; 02 a baby, worth waiting for.

There is 300m (984ft) of chalk in Champ: took 35 million yrs to lay down.

Sérafin, Dom C d'O ★★★ Now niece Frédérique in charge, continuing Christian S recipe: deep colour, intense flavours, new wood: Look for back vintages as wines need to age. Try Cazetiers, CHARMES-CHAMBERTIN, GEVREY-CHAMBERTIN VIEILLES VIGNES.

Seyssel Sav ★★ Small regional AC. Light wines (w/sp). Grapes: Altesse, CHASSELAS (sp only), Molette. Try: de la Brune, G Lambert (organic, Royal Seyssel), Mollex.

Sichel & Co B'x Respected B'X merchant est in 1883 (Sirius a top brand). Family run, 7th generation at helm. Interests in CHX ANGLUDET, Argadens, PALMER and in CORBIÈRES (Ch Trillol).

Signargues S Rh ★→★★ 16' 17' 18 19' Modest CÔTES DU RH village, v. dry *garrigue* soils between Avignon and Nîmes (w bank). Spicy, sizeable reds to drink within 4–5 yrs, can be heady. NB: Bellevue, CAVE Estézargues (gd range), CH Terre Forte (bio), CLOS d'Alzan, Haut-Musiel, La Font du Vent; DOMS des Romarins, Valériane.

Simone, Ch Prov ★★★ Historic estate outside Aix, where Churchill painted Mont STE-VICTOIRE. Rougier family for c.200 yrs. Virtually synonymous with AC PALETTE; n-facing slopes on limestone with clay, gravel give freshness. Many vines over 100 yrs old. Age-worthy whites well worth seeking out; characterful rosé, elegant reds from GRENACHE, MOURVÈDRE, with rare grape varieties Castet, Manosquin (r).

Sipp, Louis Al ★★→★★★ Trades in big volumes of young wines, but also two GCS: fine RIES GC Kirchberg 13 16. luscious GEWURZ GC Osterberg VT 09 15 16 18 19. Gd classic dry wines too.

Sipp-Mack Al ★★→★★★ Fine traditional DOM in Hunawihr, great village for peerless dry mineral wines (CLOS STE-HUNE). Similar quality here but cheaper. Also RIES GC ROSACKER and expansive PINOT GR. Charming holiday lets.

Sorg, Bruno Al ★★★ Small grower at Eguisheim, GCS Florimont (RIES 13 14 16' great 17') and PFERSIGBERG (MUSCAT) 18'. Immaculate eco-friendly vyds.

FRANCE

Sur lie "On the lees". Most MUSCADET is bottled straight from the vat, for max zest, body, character.

Tâche, La C d'O ★★★★ 90' 93' 96' 99' 02' 03 05' 09' 10' 12' 15' 16' 17 18' 19' 20' GC of VOSNE-ROMANÉE, MONOPOLE of DRC. Firm in its youth, but how glorious with age. More tannic than stablemates but becomes headily perfumed, luxurious.

Taille-aux-Loups, Dom de la Lo ★★★→★★★★ 17 18' (r) 19' 20' Jacky Blot, meticulous top producer, with wife Joëlle, son Jean-Philippe. Barrel-fermented MONTLOUIS, VDF (aka VOUVRAY) mainly dry esp single-vyds: CLOS Mosny, **Michet** (Montlouis), **Venise** (Vouvray); **Triple Zéro** Montlouis pétillant (w/rosé); v.gd BOURGUEIL DOM de la Butte; v. age-worthy.

Tain, Cave de N Rh ★★→★★★ Top N Rh co-op, many mature vyds, incl 25% of HERMITAGE. Steady to v.gd red Hermitage, esp Epsilon (oak), Gambert de Loche (best), bountiful white Hermitage Au Coeur des Siècles, give value. Gd ST-JOSEPH (r/w), ST-PÉRAY (two wines), interesting Bio (organic) range (St-Joseph), others modern, mainstream. Gd recent plot-specific CROZES reds, eg. Saviaux. Distinguished, genuine VIN DE PAILLE.

Taittinger Champ ★★★★ Family-run Reims house, exquisite elegant wines. BRUT NV, Rosé NV, Brut Vintage Collection Brut 89 95'. Epitome of apéritif style, inimitable weightlessness. Ace luxury **Comtes de Champagne** 95', classic 08. Comtes Rosé also shines 12'. New cellarmaster fills Loec Dupont's big shoes. New English bubbly project in Kent, DOM Evremond. See Dom Carneros (California).

Tavel S Rh ★★ DYA. Historic GRENACHE rosé, aided by white grapes for texture, should be bright red, full, herbal, for vivid Med dishes. Now some lighter, Prov-style, often for apéritif: a shame. Top: CHX Aquéria, de Manissy (organic), La Genestière (organic), Ségriès, **Trinquevedel** (organic); DOM de l'Anglore (no sulphur), **Dom de la Mordorée** (organic), Carabiniers (bio), Corne-Loup, GUIGAL, Lafond Roc-Epine (organic), Maby, Moulin-la-Viguerie, Prieuré de Montézargues (organic), Rocalière (organic, v. fine), Tardieu-Laurent, VIDAL-FLEURY.

Tempier, Dom Prov ★★★★ Iconic BANDOL: where Lucien and Lulu Peyraud revived AC in 30s. Tops for elegance, concentration, longevity. Single-vyds La Tourtine, Cabassaou pure expressions MOURVÈDRE. Smart rosé.

Terrasses du Larzac L'doc ★★★ Great terroir. High AC on limestone with cold nights makes fresh, stylish reds. Attracts innovative growers who assemble small plots of vines; 50%+ organic/bio. Try: Cal Demoura, Combarela, Jonquières, LA PEIRA, Mas Conscience, MAS DE L'ÉCRITURE, MAS JULLIEN, Malavielle, Montcalmès, Pas de l'Escalette. Neighbouring AC L'DOC St-Saturnin: DOMS Archimbaud, Virgile Joly.

Thénard, Dom Burg ★★→★★★★ Historic producer with large holding of MONTRACHET, mostly sold on to NÉGOCIANTS. Should be better known for v.gd reds from home base in GIVRY.

Thévenet, Jean Burg ★★★ Top MÂCONNAIS purveyor of rich, some semi-botrytized CHARD, eg. CUVÉE Levroutée at **Dom de la Bongran**. Also DOMS de Roally and Emilian Gillet.

Thézac-Perricard SW Fr ★★ 16 18' 19 IGP. Lighter version of adjoining CAHORS (reds from MALBEC, MERLOT). Sandrine Annibal's ★★ DOM de Lancement the one independent. Lively co-op nearly as gd.

Thiénot, Alain Champ Young house, new generation Stan and Garance now in charge. Ever-improving quality; fairly priced ★★★ BRUT NV; Rosé NV Brut; vintage Stanislas 02 04 06 08' 09 12' 13 15. Voluminous VIGNE aux Gamins (single-vyd AVIZE 02 04 06). CUVÉE Garance CHARD 07 sings, classic 08 for long haul. Also owns CANARD-DUCHÊNE, JOSEPH PERRIER and CH Ricaud in LOUPIAC.

Thivin, Ch Beauj ★★→★★★ Eight generations of Geoffray family make great Côte de Brouilly. Single-vyd bottlings cover soil types. Sept VIGNES blend also a winner.

Thomas, André & fils Al ★★★ Bijou DOM, 6 ha in Ammerschwihr. PINOT BL from

50-yr-old vines. Excellent RIES Kaefferkopf 10 13 16 17' 19 20. Superb GEWURZ VIEILLES VIGNES 05 09 15 17' 18. Organic precepts.

Tissot Jura Dominant family around ARBOIS. ★★ Jacques T offers volume, value. ★★★ Stephane T (also as André & Mireille Tissot), cult pioneer of single-vyd CHARD, VIN JAUNE using bio/natural methods; top CRÉMANT du Jura, Indigène.

Tollot-Beaut C d'O ★★★ Consistent CÔTE DE BEAUNE grower with 20 ha in BEAUNE (Grèves, CLOS du Roi), CORTON (Bressandes), SAVIGNY (esp MONOPOLE PC Champ Chevrey) and at CHOREY-LÈS-BEAUNE base (NB: Pièce du Chapitre). Easy-to-love fruit-and-oak combo. Gd CORTON-CHARLEMAGNE too.

Touraine Lo ★→★★★ 19' 20' Big region, many AOPS (eg. BOURGUEIL, CHINON, VOUVRAY) plus umbrella AC with fruity reds (CAB FR, CÔT, GAMAY, PINOT N), whites (SAUV BL), rosés, fizz. Touraine Village ACs: AZAY-LE-RIDEAU, Chenonceaux, MESLAND, NOBLE-JOUÉ, Oisly. Best: Biet, Bois-Vaudons, Cellier de Beaujardin, Corbillières, Desroches-Manois, Echardières, Fontenay, Garrelière, *Gosseaume*, Joël Delaunay, *La Chapinière*, Lacour, Mandard, *Marionnet*, Morantin, Presle, Prieuré, Ricard, *Roussely*, Sauvète, Tue-Boeuf, Villebois.

Touraine-Amboise Lo ★→★★★ 18' 19' 20' Village AOP. François Ier entry blend (GAMAY/CÔT/CAB FR); but Côt top red; CHENIN BL top white. Best: Bessons, Closerie de Chanteloup, *Frissant*, Gabillière, *Grange Tiphaine*, Mesliard, Montdomaine, Plou. Amboise cru (Chenin Bl, Côt) ongoing.

Touraine-Azay-le-Rideau Lo ★★ 19 20' Small TOURAINE sub-AC. Mostly rosé (Grolleau 60% min); white, dry and off-dry CHENIN BL. Best: Aulée, Bourse, *Grosbois*, Paget, *Roche*. Frost-prone.

Touraine-Mesland Lo ★→★★★ 19' 20' Minor TOURAINE villages AC (nine producers), mainly red, rosé. Try: Grandes Espérances, Terres Noires.

Touraine-Noble Joué Lo ★→★★ DYA. AOP; v.gd rosé from PINOTS (N/M/GR). Best: Astraly, Blondeau, Cosson, Dupuy, *Rousseau*. Also gd MALVOISIE (VDF).

Trapet C d'O ★★★ Long-est GEVREY-CHAMBERTIN DOM making sensual bio wines from eye-catching COTEAUX BOURGUIGNONS up to GC CHAMBERTIN plus AL whites by marriage. Next generation pushing boundaries. *See* cousins ROSSIGNOL-TRAPET.

Treloar, Dom Rouss ★★★ Anglo-NZ owners. Old vines, traditional varieties, organic. Terre Promise IGP COTES CATALANES wild ferment in barrel; MACABEU/Grenache Gr/ Carignan Bl (w) and One Block GRENACHE of special interest. New: skin-contact MUSCAT d'Alexandrie.

Trévallon, Dom de Prov ★★★ Famous DOM at LES BAUX, created by Eloi Dürrbach; joined by daughter Ostiane. No GRENACHE, so must be IGP Alpilles. Huge reputation fully justified: meticulous viticulture, age-worthy wines. Intense CAB SAUV/SYRAH. Barrique-aged MARSANNE/ROUSSANNE, drop of CHARD and now GRENACHE BL.

Trimbach, FE Al ★★★★ Matchless grower of RIES on limestone soils at Ribeauvillé, esp austere CLOS STE-HUNE: 71 89 still great; 13 17' 18 19 20' classically cool; almost-as-gd (much cheaper) *Frédéric Emile* 10 12 13 14 16 17'. Dry, elegant wines for great cuisine. Look out for 1st GC label: from vyds of Couvent de Ribeauville.

Tursan SW Fr ★★ Mostly DYA. AOP in LANDES. Super-chef Michel Guérard makes ★★★ lovely wines in chapel-like cellar at CH de Bachen, but not traditional Tursan. Real thing from ★★ DOM de Perchade. Lovely dry white from ★★ Dom de Cazalet (two MANSENGS plus rare local Baroque). Worthy co-op rather outclassed.

Vacqueyras S Rh ★★ 07' 09' 10' 15' 16' 17' 18 19' Hearty, spicy, GRENACHE-fuelled neighbour of GIGONDAS, hot, flat vyds; for game, big flavours. Lives 10 yrs+. NB: CHX de Montmirail, *des Tours* (v. fine); *Clos des Cazaux* (gd value); DOMS Amouriers (organic), Archimbaud-Vache, Charbonnière, CLOS de Caveau (organic), Couroulu (v.gd), Famille Perrin, Font de Papier (organic), Fourmone, Garrigue, Grapillon d'Or, Monardière (organic), Montirius (bio), Montvac (organic), Roucas Toumba (organic), SANG DES CAILLOUX (organic, esp Lopy),

Semelles de Vent, Verde; JABOULET. Whites substantial, table wines (Ch des Roques, Clos des Cazaux, SANG DES CAILLOUX).

Val de Loire Lo Mainly DYA. One of France's four regional IGPs, formerly Jardin de la France.

Valençay Lo ★→★★ 19' 20' Small AOP, TOURAINE; SAUV BL, (CHARD); reds CÔT, GAMAY, PINOT N. Try: Delorme, Garnier, Jourdain, Lafond, *Preys*, Sinson, Vaillant, VIGNERONS de Valençay.

Valréas S Rh ★★ 16' 17' 18' 19' CÔTES DU RH-VILLAGE in windy N Vaucluse truffle area, quality rising; large co-op. Spicy, sometimes heady, red-fruited mostly GRENACHE red, improving white. Esp CH la Décelle, CLOS Bellane, Mas de Ste-Croix; DOMS des Grands Devers, du Séminaire (organic), du Val des Rois (organic), *Gramenon* (bio), Prévosse (organic).

Vendange Harvest. **VT (Vendange Tardive)** Late-harvest; AL equivalent to German Auslese but usually higher alc.

Venoge, de Champ ★★★ Venerable house, precise, more elegant under LANSON-BCC ownership. Gd niche blends: Cordon Bleu Extra-BRUT, Vintage BLANC DE BLANCS 00 04 06 08 12 13 14 16 17. Excellent Vintage Rosé 09 CUVÉE 20 Ans, Prestige Cuvée Louis XV 10-yr-old BLANC DE NOIRS.

90% Côtes de Prov is AC rosé. Red/white worth exploring though.

Ventoux S Rh ★★ 18 19' Widespread AC circles around much of Mont Ventoux between Rh and Prov. A few front-running DOMS v.gd value rcds. Tangy red (GRENACHE/SYRAH), café-style to fuller, peppery, rising quality), rosé, gd white (more oak). Best: CH Unang (organic, gd w), Ch Valcombe, CLOS des Patris (organic), Gonnet, La Ferme St Pierre (w/rosé, organic), La Vieille Ferme (r, can be VDF), St-Marc, Terra Ventoux, VIGNERONS Mont Ventoux; DOMS Allois (organic), Anges, Berane, Brusset, Cascavel, Champ-Long, Croix de Pins (gd w), du Tix, Fondrèche (organic), Grand Jacquet, Martinelle (organic), Murmurium, Olivier B (organic), PAUL JABOULET, Pesquié, Pigeade, St-Jean du Barroux (organic), Terres de Solence, Verrière, VIDAL-FLEURY, Vieux Lazaret, Vignobles Brunier and co-op Bédoin.

Vernay, Dom Georges N Rh ★★★★ 16' 17' 18' 19' 20' Top CONDRIEU name; three wines, balance, stylish; Terrasses de l'Empire *apéritif de luxe*; Chaillées d'Enfer, richness; Coteau de Vernon, mysterious, intricate, supreme style, lives 20 yrs+. CÔTE-RÔTIE, ST-JOSEPH (r) clear fruit, restrained. V.gd IGP COLLINES RHODANIENNES (r/w).

Vervesin, Laurent Champ Young grower rejoins family Oger DOM. Organic principles in Original BLANC DE BLANCS GC 13, 15% oak, clear, precise. Aubeline GC, fuller, liked in Scandinavia.

Veuve Clicquot Champ ★★★★ Historic house. Singing Yellow Label NV, a soupçon of 5% oak. Best DEMI-SEC NV, CUVÉE Extra BRUT Extra Age based on reserve wines, 2010–1990. Vintage Rés 04 06 08 12' a magical wonder of perfect maturity, elegant acidity: best yr for PINOT N since 1952? Luxe La Grande Dame (GD) 12' is 92% Pinot N yet so graceful. Older vintages of GD stay course effortlessly in 04 (110 02, deemed too butch for GD) gloriously in 89, firmly in 71. GD Rosé 06 delicious, ready. Didier Mariotti new cellarmaster from 2020.

Veuve Devaux Champ ★★ Premium brand of powerful Union Auboise co-op. Excellent aged Grande Rés NV, and Œil de Perdrix Rosé, Prestige CUVÉE D 08, BRUT Vintage 09 12 15' 17 18 19.

Vézelay Burg ★→★★ Age 1–2 yrs. Lovely location (with abbey) in NW Burg. Promoted to full AC for tasty whites from CHARD. Also try revived MELON (COTEAUX BOURGUIGNON) and light PINOT (generic BOURGOGNE). Best: DOM de la Cadette, des Faverelles, Elise Villiers, La Croix Montjoie.

Vidal-Fleury N Rh ★★→★★★ GUIGAL-owned merchant/grower of CÔTE-RÔTIE. Top-quality, intricate, v. stylish *La Chatillonne* (from Blonde, 12% VIOGNIER, oak, wait

min 7 yrs). Wide range, improving. Gd CAIRANNE, CHÂTEAUNEUF (r/
rosé), MUSCAT DE BEAUMES-DE-VENISE, ST-JOSEPH (r/w), TAVEL, VENTOUX.

Vieille Ferme, La S Rh ★→★★ Reliable v.gd-value brand from Famille Perrin of CH
DE BEAUCASTEL; much now labelled VDF, with VENTOUX (r), LUBÉRON (w/rosé) in some
countries (France, Japan). Back on form recently, incl rosé, red.

Vieilles Vignes Old vines, which can give particular depth and complexity. Eg. DE
VOGÜÉ, MUSIGNY, Vieilles Vignes. But no rules about age and can be a tourist trap.
Can a vine be old if it's younger than you are?

Vieux Télégraphe, Dom du S Rh ★★★ 01' 05' 07' 09' 10' 12' 14' 15' 16' 17' 18' 19' High-
quality estate; classic big-stone plateau soils, tight, slow burn red CHÂTEAUNEUF;
top two wines La Crau (crunchy, packed), Pied Long et Pignan (sandy, v.
pure, elegant, no 18). Also rich, *garrigue* white *La Crau* (v.gd 15 16 18 19), CLOS
La Roquète (refined, great with food, 15 16 18 19). Owns fine, slow-to-evolve,
complex GIGONDAS DOM Les Pallières with US importer Kermit Lynch.

Vignelaure, Ch de Prov ★★★ Well est, now Swedish owned estate, AC COTEAUX D'AIX
EN PROVENCE. CAB SAUV, SYRAH at 300m (984ft) give red of depth, freshness. Will
age 10 yrs. Gd rosé. Intriguing ROUSSANNE, Rolle, SEM.

Vigne or vignoble Vineyard (vyd), vineyards (vyds).

Vigneron Vine-grower.

Villeneuve, Ch de Lo ★★★→★★★★ 10' 14' 15' 16' 17' 18' 19' (20') Top estate: balance
is key; age brilliantly. SAUMUR Bl (age-worthy Les Cormiers, 20 yrs+), SAUMUR-
CHAMPIGNY (esp VIEILLES VIGNES, Grand CLOS). Organic.

VdF (Vin de France) Replaces Vin de Table, but with mention of grape variety, vintage.
Often blends of regions with brand name. Can be source of unexpected delights
if talented winemaker uses this category to avoid bureaucractic hassle; eg. DIDIER
DAGUENEAU, Yves Cuilleron VIOGNIER (N Rh); S ARDÈCHE, ANJOU hotbeds of VdF.

VdP (Vin de Pays) *See* IGP.

Vin de paille Wine from grapes dried on straw mats, so v. sweet, like Italian passito.
Esp in the Jura. *See also* CHAVE, VIN PAILLÉ DE CORRÈZE.

VDN (Vin Doux Naturel) Sweet wine fortified with wine alc, so sweetness natural,
not strength. Speciality of ROUSS based on GRENACHES BL/Gr/N. Top, esp aged
RANCIOS, can finish a meal on a sublime note. Gd MUSCAT from BEAUMES DE VENISE,
Frontignan, Lunel, RIVESALTES, ROUSS, St Jean de Minervois.

Vin gris "Grey" wine is v. pale pink, made of red grapes pressed before fermentation
begins – unlike rosé, which ferments briefly before pressing. Or from eg.
PINOT GR, not-quite-white grapes. "Œil de Perdrix" means much the same; so
does "blush".

Vin jaune Jura ★★★ Speciality of Jura; inimitable yellow wine. SAVAGNIN, 6 yrs+ in
barrel without topping up, develops flor, like Sherry but no added alc. Expensive
to make. Separate AC for top spot, CH-CHALON. Sold in unique 62cl Clavelin
bottles. S TISSOT specializes in single-vyd bottlings, Baudy in old vintages.

Vin paillé de Corrèze SW Fr 25 small growers and a tiny co-op once more making a
wine once recommended to breast-feeding mothers. Not-too-ripe grapes laid on
straw to make pungent wine for brave. Try ★ Christian Tronche.

Vinsobres S Rhs ★★ 16' 17' 18' 19' Low-profile AC notable for quality SYRAH, mix
hillside, high-plateau vyds. Best reds give smooth depth, to drink with red meats,
age 10 yrs. New DOMS emerging. Leaders: CAVE la Vinsobraise, CH Rouanne, Clos
Volabis (organic); DOMS Chaume-Arnaud (bio), Constant-Duquesnoy, Famille
Perrin (*Hauts de Julien* top class, Cornuds value), Jaume (modern), Moulin (gd
r/w), Péquélette (bio), Peysson (organic), Serre Besson, Vallot (bio).

Viré-Clessé Burg ★★ 14' 17' 18 19' 20' AC based around two of best white villages
of MÂCON. Known for exuberant rich style, sometimes late-harvest. Specialists
Bonhomme, Chaland, DOM de la Verpaille, Gandines, Gondard-Perrin,

Guillemot-Michel, J-P Michel, *Thévenet*. Try also Bret Bros, LAFON, and all gd Mâconnais NÉGOCIANTS.

Visan S Rh ★★ 16' 17' 18' 19' Progressive RH VILLAGE, now top three: peppery mainly GRENACHE reds, sound depth, clear fruit; some softer, plenty organic. Whites okay. Best: DOMS Bastide, Coste Chaude (organic), Dieulefit (bio, low sulphur), Florane (bio), Fourmente (bio esp Nature), Guintrandy (organic), Montmartel (organic), Philippe Plantevin, Roche-Audran (organic), VIGNOBLE Art Mas (organic).

Vogüé, Comte Georges de C d'O ★★★★ Aristo CHAMBOLLE estate with lion's share of LE MUSIGNY. Great from barrel, but takes many yrs in bottle to reveal glories. Unique white Musigny.

Volnay C d'O ★★★→★★★★ 90' 99' 05' 09' 10' 15' 16 17' 18 19 20 Top CÔTE DE BEAUNE reds, except when it hails or gets too hot. Can be structured, should be silky, astonishing with age. Best vyds: Caillerets, Champans, CLOS des Chênes, Santenots (more clay), Taillepieds and MONOPOLES Clos de la Bousse d'Or, Clos de la Chapelle, Clos des Ducs, Clos du CH des Ducs. Reference growers: D'ANGERVILLE, *de Montille*, *Lafarge*, Pousse d'Or. V.gd too from Bitouzet-Prieur, Bouley, Buffet, *Clerget*, H BOILLOT, Glantenay, HOSPICES DE BEAUNE, LAFON, N Rossignol.

Vosne-Romanée C d'O ★★★→★★★★ 90' 93' 96' 99' 02' 05' 09' 10' 12 15' 16' 17 18' 19' 20' Village with Burg's grandest crus (eg. ROMANÉE-CONTI, LA TÂCHE) and outstanding PCS Beaumonts, Brûlées, Malconsorts, etc. There are (or should be) no common wines in Vosne. Just question of price... Top names: ARNOUX-LACHAUX, Bizot, CATHIARD, Coquard-Loison-Fleurot, DRC, EUGÉNIE, GRIVOT, GROS, Lamarche, LEROY, LIGER-BELAIR, MÉO-CAMUZET, MUGNERET, NOËLLAT, ROUGET. I really like Clavelier, Forey, Guyon, Tardy too.

Vougeot C d'O ★★★ 99' 02' 05' 09' 10' 12' 15' 16 17 18' 19' 20 Mostly GC as CLOS DE VOUGEOT but also village and PC, Cras, Petits Vougeots, and outstanding white MONOPOLE *Clos Blanc de V.* Best: Clerget, Fourrier, HUDELOT-NOËLLAT, LEROUX, *Vougeraie*.

Vougeraie, Dom de la C d'O ★★★→★★★★ Bio DOM uniting all BOISSET's vyd holdings. Fine-boned, perfumed wines, most noted for sensual GCs, esp BONNES-MARES, CHARMES-CHAMBERTIN, MUSIGNY. Fine whites too, with unique *Clos Blanc de Vougeot* and four GCs incl unique CHARLEMAGNE.

Vouvray Lo ★→★★★★ (dr) 16 17 18' 19' 20' (sw) 08 09' 10 11 15' 16 18' AC. Limestone bluffs on n bank of Loire can produce top dry/sweet white. DEMI-SEC is classic style, but in best yrs *moelleux*, rich but balanced by acidity, is almost immortal. Fizz: *pétillant*, fine local speciality. Best: *Aubuisières*, *Autran*, Bonneau, Brunet, *Carême*, Champalou, Clos Baudoin (VDF), *F&J Pinon*, Florent Cosme, Fontainerie, *Foreau*, Gaudrelle, *Huet*, Mathieu Cosme, Meslerie (Hahn), Perrault-Jadaud, Rouvre, *Taille-aux-Loups* (VdF), Vigneau-Chevreau. Old vintages can be amazing.

Zind Humbrecht, Dom Al ★★★★ One of the greats. Vyds incl GC Brand, HENGST and volcanic RANGEN at Thann; 18' outstanding, CSP PINOT GR. All expensive. For easier prices, MUSCAT GC Goldert from ancient vyd, dry, floral, structured and great with asparagus 16.

Good breeding

Artaban, Floréal, Vidoc, Voltis – new hybrid grapes, bred in France for disease resistance. Reduces spraying by 90%, so organic farming easier, cheaper. Crossing US/European vines is not new and started in C19, but in France outlawed since 50s for all but VDF as quality iffy. These fab four hybrids are allowed for some IGP, not AC (yet). What are the wines like? First on the market, FONCALIEU (L'DOC), is fruity, lively Artaban (r). Time will tell. VOLNAY Vidoc, anyone?

Châteaux of Bordeaux

Abbreviations used in the text:

B'x	Bordeaux
Bar	Barsac
Cas	Castillon-Côtes de Bordeaux
E-2-M	Entre-Deux-Mers
Fron	Fronsac
Grav	Graves
H-Méd	Haut-Médoc
L de P	Lalande de Pomerol
List	Listrac
Marg	Margaux
Méd	Médoc
Mou	Moulis
Pau	Pauillac
Pe-Lé	Pessac-Léognan
Pom	Pomerol
Saut	Sauternes
St-Ém	St-Émilion
St-Est	St-Estèphe
St-Jul	St-Julien

AC	appellation contrôlée
ch(x)	château(x)
dom(s)	domaine(s)

How much does terroir matter in Bordeaux? Obviously it matters. The gravel of parts of the Médoc, the clay of St-Estèphe, the clay and the pure limestone of the Right Bank – all these respond differently to the sort of extreme weather that we see year after year. Gravel will drain faster, and then dry out in a drought, giving stressed, uncomfortable vines. Clay will hold water better: St-Estèphe often survives droughts better than other parts of the Haut-Médoc. The limestone of St-Émilion both drains and maintains a steady water table, so if you want even maturity in an extreme summer, that's the place to look for it. In addition, rain coming from the west tends to fall on the

Châteaux of Bordeaux entries also cross-reference to France.

Médoc more than on the Right Bank, and differing rainfall patterns can make or break a vintage. In 2020 the vintage was saved for some on the Left Bank by August rain, but for the Right Bank, by September heat.

But if you want real expression of every nuance of terroir, the traditional place to look has always been Burgundy. Bordeaux is about brands, and winemaking, as much as it is about terroir. Yes, every château is focusing on precision now, on fermenting smaller parcels separately, and on the sort of viticulture that cares for the soil and its micro inhabitants. Terroir matters in Bordeaux. But it matters rather as it matters in Champagne; as a component of the whole, rather than as the whole in itself. Vintage 2020 followed a similar pattern to 19 – a wet winter then a hot, very dry summer. An early harvest started with the latter conditions, then finished in the rain. A similarity with 18 was also seen with a severe attack of mildew in the spring. This, localized hail, and tiny berrries resulting from the hot, dry summer, mean yields are generally low. Quality, though, is there (despite high alcohols) with colour, concentration and fine tannins – another vintage for the cellar. Luckily, there are still plenty of vintages for drinking. The luscious 09s are tempting at whatever level. The 08s have come into their own. The 10s are just opening (as are the "classic" 14s), although the Grands Crus need longer. For early drinking try the often-charming 12s or underrated 11s, which have improved with bottle-age. Mature vintages to look for are 96 (best Médoc), 98 (particularly Right Bank), 00 01 (Right Bank again), 04 and 06. Some of the splendid 05s are also opening, although patience is still a virtue here. Dry white Bordeaux remains consistent in quality and value with another good vintage in 20. Remember that fine white Graves can age as well as white burgundy – sometimes better. And Sauternes continues to offer an array of remarkable years, 20 small in quantity but with a qualitative *tri* in October. The problem here is being spoilt for choice. Even moderate years like 06 and 08 offer approachability and a fresher touch while the great years (09 11 15) have the concentration and hedonistic charm that makes them indestructible.

A, Dom de L' Cas ★★ 10' 11 12 14 15 16 18 19 Leading Ste-Colombe-based property owned by STÉPHANE DERENONCOURT and wife. Consistent quality.

Agassac, D' H-Méd ★★ 10' 11 14 15 16' 18 19 Newly promoted (2020) CRU BOURGEOIS EXCEPTIONNEL. Consistent CH in s H-MÉD. Modern, accessible style.

Aiguilhe, D' Cas ★★ 10' 11 12 14 15 16 18 19 Von Neipperg-owned estate. Same stable as CANON-LA-GAFFELIÈRE, LA MONDOTTE. MERLOT-led *power and finesse*. Also Le Blanc d'Aiguilhe.

Andron-Blanquet St-Est ★★ 10' 11 14 15 16' 18 Sister to COS-LABORY. Can be value.

Angélus St-Ém ★★★★ 00' 01 04 05 06 07 09 10' 15' 16' 17 18' 19' 20 PREMIER GRAND CRU CLASSÉ (A) since 2012 so prices high. Pioneer of modern ST-ÉM; dark, rich, sumptuous. More finesse in 19. Lots of CAB FR (min 40%). Organic conversion. 18 bottle engraved with red phoenix. Second label: Carillon d'Angélus (new, high-tech cellar from 2019). Also No 3 d'Angélus.

Angludet Marg ★★ 09' 10' 11 14 15' 16' 18' 19 Sixth-generation SICHEL-owned property. CAB SAUV, MERLOT, 13% PETIT VERDOT. Fragrant, stylish. Often gd value.

Archambeau Grav ★★ (r) 15 16 18 (19) (w) 17 18 19 Illats-based property owned by Dubourdieu family for generations. Gd *fruity dry white*; fragrant MERLOT/CAB (50/50) reds. Also rosé.

Arche, D' Saut ★★ 07 09' 10' 11 14 15 16 17' 18 (19) Second Growth steadily being overhauled. New cellar (2019). Can be value.

Armailhac, D' Pau ★★★ 05' 08 09' 10' 12 14 15' 16' 17 18 19 20 Substantial Fifth Growth. (MOUTON) ROTHSCHILD-owned. New cellar (2021). On top form, fair value.

Aurelius St-Ém ★★ 15 16 18 (19) Top CUVÉE from go-ahead ST-ÉM CO-OP; 16,000 bottles annually. Modern, MERLOT-led, new oak, concentrated.

Ausone St-Ém ★★★★ 00' 01' 03' 04 05' 06' 07 08 09' 10' 11 12 13 14 15' 16' 17 18' 19' 20 Tiny, illustrious PREMIER GRAND CRU CLASSÉ (A) owned by Vauthier family. Only c.1500 cases; vyds s- and se-facing, sheltered from winds; lots of CAB FR (65% in 19). Long-lived wines with volume, texture, finesse. At a price. Second label: Chapelle d'Ausone (500 cases). *La Clotte*, FONBEL, MOULIN-ST-GEORGES, Simard sister estates.

75% of bulk B'x sells for less than €1000/tonneau (900l).

Balestard la Tonnelle St-Ém ★★ 10 11 14 15 16 17 18 (19) 20 Historic property on limestone plateau, owned by Capdemourlin family. Modern, MERLOT-led.

Barde-Haut St-Ém ★★→★★★ 05' 06 07 08 09 10 11 14 15' 16 18 19' Merlot-led GRAND CRU CLASSÉ. Sister property of CLOS L'ÉGLISE, HAUT-BERGEY.

Bastor-Lamontagne Saut ★★ 10 11 13 14 15 16 17 18 19 Large SÉM-led Preignac estate. Owned by Grands Chais de France. Earlier-drinking style. Second label: Les Remparts de Bastor. Also dry white B de B-L.

Batailley Pau ★★★ 05' 06 08 09' 10' 11 12 14 15 16 17 18 19 20 Gd-value, BORIE-MANOUX-owned Fifth Growth. Second label: Lions de Batailley.

Beaumont H-Méd ★★ 05' 08 09' 10' 12 14 15 16 18 19 Large CRU BOURGEOIS Supérieur (2020). Sister to BEYCHEVELLE; early maturing, easily enjoyable wines.

Beauregard Pom ★★★ 04 05' 08 09' 10' 12 14 15' 16' 19' Much improved POM. Owned by SMITH HAUT LAFITTE and Galeries Lafayette families. Organic certification. Second label: Benjamin de Beauregard. Also Pavillon Beauregard in L DE P. B&B accommodation.

Beau-Séjour-Bécot St-Ém ★★★ 00' 05 06 08 09' 10' 11 12 14 15 16 18 19 20 Distinguished PREMIER GRAND CRU CLASSÉ (B) owned by Bécot family. Limestone plateau location. Old quarried cellars for bottle storage. Lighter touch these days but still gd ageing potential.

Beauséjour-Duffau St-Ém ★★★ 01 05' 08 09' 10' 11 12 14 15 16 17 18' 19' Tiny PREMIER GRAND CRU CLASSÉ (B) owned by Duffau-Lagarrosse family since 1847; managed by Nicolas Thienpont (PUYGUERAUD). Rich, cellar-worthy.

Beau-Site St-Est ★★ 08 09 10 11 12 15 16 18 19 Gd-value ST-EST cru owned by BORIE-MANOUX; C18 cellar. Supple, fresh, accessible.

Bélair-Monange St-Ém ★★★ 05' 06 08 09' 10' 11 12 13 14 15 16' 17 18 19 20 PREMIER GRAND CRU CLASSÉ (B) on limestone plateau and côtes. Owned by J-P MOUEIX since 2008. Huge investment in vyd and new cellar. Refined style with more intensity and precision these days. Second label: Annonce de Bélair-Monange.

Belgrave H-Méd ★★ 05' 08 09' 10' 11 12 14 15 16 17 18 19 Consistent n H-MÉD Fifth Growth. Environmental certification. Modern-classic in style. Can be value. Second label: Diane de Belgrave.

Bellefont-Belcier St-Ém ★★ 05' 06 08' 09' 10' 12 14 15' 16 17 18 19' 20 GRAND CRU CLASSÉ on s côtes, owned by Vignobles K. Quality on the up (esp 19).

Belle-Vue H-Méd ★★ 09 10 11 12 14 15' 16 17 18 19 Newly promoted (2020) CRU BOURGEOIS Exceptionnel. Dark, dense but firm; 15–25% PETIT VERDOT in blend.

Berliquet St-Ém ★★ 05' 08 09 10 11 14 15' 16' 17 18 19' 20 Tiny GRAND CRU CLASSÉ on plateau and côtes. Same ownership/management as CANON (since 2017). Powerful but gaining in precision.

Bernadotte H-Méd ★★ 09' 10' 11 14 15' 16' 17 CRU BOURGEOIS Supérieur (2020). Owned by a Hong Kong-based group. Hubert de Boüard (ANGÉLUS) consults. Environmental certification. Savoury style.

Beychevelle St-Jul ★★★ 05' 06 08 09' 10' 11 12 13 14 15' 16' 17 18 19' Sizeable Fourth Growth owned by Castel and Suntory. Wines of consistent *elegance* rather than power. Glass-walled winery. Second label: Amiral de Beychevelle.

Biston-Brillette Mou ★★ 09 10' 11 12 14 15 16' 18 (19) Family-owned CRU BOURGEOIS Supérieur (2020). Gd-value, attractive, early drinking wines.

Bonalgue Pom ★★ 08 09 10 11 12 14 15 16 18 19 Accessible MERLOT-led POM from sand, gravel, clay soils. Gd value for AC. Owned by Libourne NÉGOCIANT JB Audy. Sisters CLOS du Clocher; CH du Courlat in LUSSAC-ST-ÉM.

Bonnet B'x ★★ (r) 15 16 18 19 (w) DYA. Forged by André Lurton; now run by son Jacques. Big producer of some of best E-2-M and red (Rés) B'X. LA LOUVIÈRE, *Couhins-Lurton*, ROCHEMORIN and Cruzeau in PE-LÉ same stable.

Bon Pasteur, Le Pom ★★★ 05' 06 08 09' 10' 11 12 14 15' 16 17 18 19 Tiny cru on ST-ÉM border. Hong Kong-based owner. MICHEL ROLLAND makes the wine. Ripe, opulent, seductive. Second label: L'Etoile de Bon Pasteur.

Boscq, Le St-Est ★★ 08 09' 10 11 12 14 15' 16' 17 18 19' Newly promoted (2020) CRU BOURGEOIS Exceptionnel. Consistently great value.

Bourgneuf Pom ★★ 05' 06 08 09 10 11 12 14 15' 16' 17 18 19' 20 Owned by Vayron family. MERLOT-led (80%). Subtle, savoury wine. As gd-value as it gets.

Bouscaut Pe-Lé ★★★ (r) 05 06 08 09 10' 11 12 14 15 16' 18 19 (w) 11 12 13 14 15 16 17 19 GRAV Classed Growth. MERLOT-based reds with CAB SAUV and a little MALBEC. Sappy, age-worthy SAUV BL/SÉM *whites*.

Boyd-Cantenac Marg ★★★ 05' 06 08 09' 10' 11 12 14 15 16 18 (19) Tiny Cantenac-based Third Growth. Owned and run by Lucien Guillemet. CAB SAUV-dominated. Gd value. POUGET same stable. Second label: Jacques Boyd.

Branaire-Ducru St-Jul ★★★ 05' 06 08 09' 10' 11 12 13 14 15 16' 17 18' 19 Consistent Fourth Growth; regularly gd value; ageing potential. François-Xavier Maroteaux at helm. Second label: *Duluc*.

Branas Grand Poujeaux Mou ★★ 05' 06 08 09 10 12 14 15' 16' 18 19' Neighbour of CHASSE-SPLEEN, POUJEAUX. Expanded vyd in 2020. Investment. Rich, modern style. Sister to Villemaurine in ST-ÉM. Second label: Les Eclats de Branas.

Brane-Cantenac Marg ★★★→★★★★ 00' 01 05' 06 08 09' 10' 11 12 13 14 15' 16' 18 19' CAB SAUV-led Second Growth. Sometimes CARMENÈRE. Classic, fragrant MARG with structure to age. Second label: *Buron de Brane*, value, consistency.

Brillette Mou ★★ 08 09 10 11 12 14 15 16' 18 19 Reputable DOM on gravelly soils. Owned by Flageul family. Gd depth. Second label: Haut Brillette.

Cabanne, La Pom r ★★ 00' 05 06 09 10 12 14 15' 16' 18 19 MERLOT-dominant (94%) on deep clay soils. Firm when young; needs bottle-age. Owned by Estager family.

Caillou Saut ★★ 05 06 07 08 09' 10' 11' 13 15' 16 18 (19) Second Growth BAR for pure *liquoreux*. 90% SÉM. Second label: Les Erables. Also dry white Le Blanc Sec.

Calon-Ségur St-Est ★★★★ 00' 01 04 05' 06 07 08 09' 10' 11 12 14 15' 16' 17 18' 19' 20 Third Growth on flying form; more CAB SAUV these days. Firm but fine, complex. Eric Boissenot consults. Second label: Le Marquis de Calon.

Cambon la Pelouse H-Méd ★★ 09 10' 11 12 14 15 16' 18 19 Big, reliable CRU BOURGEOIS Exceptionnel (2020). Owned by Aussie group TWE.

Rolland retreat

Veteran winemaking consultant MICHEL ROLLAND is easing back on the throttle. He has reduced the number of clients he personally oversees and handed over majority ownership of his oenology business to his long-time colleagues Julien Viaud, Jean-Philippe Fort and Mikael Laizet. The remaining shares will be relinquished over the next 5 yrs. The legendary Rolland nose is not yet down and out but sniffing gently towards retirement.

Camensac, De H-Méd ★★ 08 09 10' 11 12 14 15 16 18' 19 Fifth Growth in n H-MÉD. Owned by Merlaut family (GRUAUD-LAROSE, CHASSE-SPLEEN). Steady improvement; recent vintages clearly better. Second label: La Closerie de Camensac.

Canon St-Ém ★★★★ 04 05' 06 07 08' 09' 10' 11 12 13 14 15' 16' 17 18' 19' 20 Esteemed PREMIER GRAND CRU CLASSÉ (B) with vyd on limestone plateau. Wertheimer-owned, like BERLIQUET, RAUZAN-SÉGLA, ST-SUPÉRY and DOM de l'Ile in Provence. Now flying; elegant, complex wines for long ageing. Second label: Croix Canon.

Canon-la-Gaffelière St-Ém ★★★ 00' 04 05' 06 08 09' 10' 11 12 13 14 15' 16 18 19' 20 PREMIER GRAND CRU CLASSÉ (B) on s foot slope. Same stable as CLOS DE L'ORATOIRE, D'AIGUILHE, LA MONDOTTE. Lots of CABS FR (40%) and SAUV (10%). Ageing in 50% new oak barrels. Stylish, impressive.

Cantemerle H-Méd ★★★ 05' 06 08' 09' 10' 11 12 14 15 16 18 19' Large Fifth Growth in s H-MÉD owned by an insurance company. Renovated and replanted over last 40 yrs. CAB SAUV-led. On gd form and gd value too.

Cantenac-Brown Marg ★★★ 04 05' 06 08 09' 10' 11 12 14 15 16' 18 19' 20 Third Growth owned by Le Lous family since 2019. Vyd expanded 2020; 65% CAB SAUV. New eco winery due 2023. More voluptuous, refined these days. Second label: BriO de Cantenac-Brown.

Capbern St-Est ★★ 08' 09' 10' 11 12 13 14 15' 16' 18 19 20 Capbern-Gasqueton until 2013. Same team as CALON-SÉGUR. Eric Boissenot consults. Gd form and value.

Cap de Mourlin St-Ém ★★ 05 08 09 10 11 12 14 15 16 18 19 20 GRAND CRU CLASSÉ on n slopes. Limestone-clay and sandy soils. Named after owning Capdemourlin family. MERLOT-led (65%). Firm, tannic wines.

Carbonnieux Pe-Lé ★★★ 05' 06 08 09' 10' 11 12 15' 16' 18 19' GRAV Classed Growth owned by Perrin family since 1956. Sterling red/white; large volumes of both. Fresh *whites*, 65% SAUV BL, eg. 17 18 19. Red can age. Second label: La Croix de Carbonnieux. Also CH Tour Léognan.

Carles, De B'x ★★ 05' 08 09 10 11 12 14 15 16 18 19 FRON property. Haut-Carles is prestige CUVÉE; 90% MERLOT. Opulent, modern style.

Carmes Haut-Brion, Les Pe-Lé ★★★ 05' 06 08 09' 10' 11 12' 14 15 16' 17 18' 19' Tiny walled-in vyd in heart of B'x city. CABS FR (40%+) and SAUV-led wines: flying form; structured but suave. Ageing in barrels, *foudres* and amphorae. Philippe Starck-designed winery. Second label: Le C des Carmes Haut-Brion.

Caronne-Ste-Gemme H-Méd ★★ 08 09' 10' 11 12 14 15 16 18 (19) Sizeable n H-MÉD estate. CAB SAUV-led (60%) wines; fresh, structured. Can be gd value.

Carruades de Lafite Pau ★★★ Second label of CH LAFITE. 20,000 cases/yr. Second Growth prices. Refined, smooth, savoury. Accessible but can age.

Carteau Côtes-Daugay St-Ém ★★ 09 10' 11 14 15 16' 18 19 Gd-value ST-ÉM GRAND CRU; full-flavoured, supple wines from 70% MERLOT.

Certan-de-May Pom ★★★ 05' 06 08 09' 10' 11 12' 14 15' 16' 17 18 19' 20 Tiny vyd on POM plateau. Elegant, complex, long-ageing.

Chantegrive, De Grav ★★→★★★ 09' 10' 11 12 14 15 16 18 19 Leading GRAV estate.

Youthful Bordeaux

BORDEAUX has the reputation of being a wine you don't touch for yrs. That's no longer the case. Riper fruit, selection, modern technology, softer extraction – all have helped to produce more approachable wines with less aggressive tannins. Try some of the supple 17s, richer 18s or refreshing 19s when they appear on the shelf. Go-to ACS with some suggestions incl: B'X SUPÉRIEUR (Parenchère, Turcaud), BLAYE-CÔTES DE B'X (Haut-Bertinerie, Monconseil-Gazin), CADILLAC-CÔTES DE B'X (Carignan, REYNON), CÔTES DE BOURG (Fougas-Maldoror), GRAV (Brondelle, CHANTEGRIVE), LUSSAC-ST-ÉM (DE LUSSAC, La Rose-Perrière), MÉD (Fleur La Mothe, Rollan de By).

Sizeable volume. V.gd quality, value. Hubert de Boüard (ANGÉLUS) consults. CUVÉE Caroline is top, *fragrant white* 17 18 19.

Chasse-Spleen Mou ★★★ 05' 06 08 09' 10' 12 14 15 16' 17 18 19' Big (100 ha), well-known MOU estate. Often outstanding, long-maturing wine; classical structure, fragrance. Second label: L'Oratoire de Chasse-Spleen. B&B, modern art collection.

Chauvin St-Ém ★★ 09 10' 11 12 14 15 16' 18' 19' GRAND CRU CLASSÉ owned by Sylvie Cazes. MERLOT-led; constant progression. Second label: Folie de Chauvin.

65% of E-2-M (w) sold in bottle, but only 19% exported.

Cheval Blanc St-Ém ★★★★ 01' 05' 06 07' 08 09' 10' 11 12 13 14 15' 16' 17 18' 19' PREMIER GRAND CRU CLASSÉ (A) superstar of ST-ÉM, easier to love than buy. Located in nw corner of AC. High CAB FR (60%). Firm, fragrant wines verging on POM. Delicious young; lasts a generation. Second label: Le Petit Cheval (small production). Also 100% SAUV BL Le Petit Cheval Blanc.

Chevalier, Dom de Pe-Lé ★★★★ 00 01' 02 04 05' 06 07 08 09' 10' 11 12 13 14 15' 16' 17 18' 19' 20 Reliable GRAV Classed Growth. Pure, dense, finely textured red. Impressive, complex, long-ageing white has remarkable consistency; wait for rich flavours 14 15' 16' 17' 18 19' 20. DOM de la Solitude, Lespault-Martillac same stable. Second label (r/w): l'Esprit de Chevalier.

Cissac H-Méd ★★ 05 08 09 10 11 12 14 15 16' 17 18 (19) CRU BOURGEOIS Supérieur (2020). Classic CAB SAUV-led wines; used to be austere, now purer fruit. Second label: Reflets du CH Cissac.

Citran H-Méd ★★ 09 10' 14 15 16 18 (19) Sizeable S H-MÉD estate owned by Merlaut family. Medium-weight, ageing up to 10 yrs.

Clarence de Haut-Brion, Le Pe-Lé ★★★ 05 06 07 08 09' 10' 11 12 14 15 16' 17 18 19' Second label of CH HAUT-BRION, previously known as Bahans Haut-Brion. Blend varies with each vintage (usually MERLOT-led), same suave texture, elegance as *grand vin*. More approachable but can age.

Clarke List ★★→★★★ 09' 10' 11 12 14 15 16' 17 18 19 Leading LIST owned by Edmond de Rothschild Heritage. V.gd MERLOT-based (70%) red. Eric Boissenot consults from 2016; style change; more length and precision these days. Also dry white: Le Merle Blanc du CH Clarke.

Clauzet St-Est ★★ 09 10 11 12 14 15 16' 17 Previously gd-value ST-EST. CAB SAUV-led, consistent quality. Property sold 2018; vines acquired by CH LILIAN LADOUYS, brand and buildings by CH La Haye.

Clerc Milon Pau ★★★ 00 04 05' 06 07 08 09 10' 11 12 13 14 15 16' 17 18' 19' 20 Vyd tripled in size since (MOUTON) ROTHSCHILD purchased in 1970. Consistent quality but prices up. New winemaker (2020): Caroline Artaud (ex-FOURCAS-HOSTEN).

Climens Saut ★★★★ 01' 02 03' 04 05 06 07 08 09' 10' 11' 12' 13' 14 15 16' (19) BAR Classed Growth owned by Bérénice Lurton. Concentrated wines with vibrant acidity; ageing potential guaranteed. Certified bio. No 2017 (frost). Second label: Les Cyprès (gd value). Dry white Asphodèle from 2018 (100% SÉM).

Clinet Pom ★★★ 05' 06 07 08 09' 10' 11 12 14 15' 16' 17 18 19 Owned by the Laborde family since 1999. Well located on POM plateau. 80% MERLOT, 20% CAB SAUV. Sumptuous, modern style.

Clos de l'Oratoire St-Ém ★★ 05' 06 08 09 10' 11 12 14 15 16' 18 19 Supple GRAND CRU CLASSÉ, ne slopes ST-ÉM. 80% MERLOT on sand, clay soils.

Clos des Jacobins St-Ém ★★→★★★ 05' 06 08 09 10' 11 12 14 15' 16' 18 19 Côtes GRAND CRU CLASSÉ at top of game. Renovated, modernized, great consistency; powerful, modern style. Hubert de Boüard (ANGÉLUS) consults.

Clos du Marquis St-Jul ★★→★★★ 04 05' 06 08 09' 10' 11 12 13 14 15' 16' 17 18' 19' 20 Owned by Jean-Hubert Delon (same as lofty stablemate LÉOVILLE LAS CAS). Gd ST-JUL character. Second label: La Petite Marquise.

Clos Floridène Grav ★★ (r) 10' 11 12 14 15' 16 18 19 (w) 12 13 14 15 16 17' 18 19 Dubourdieu family-owned/run DOM. SAUV BL/SÉM from limestone provides *fine modern white* GRAV; much-improved, CAB SAUV-led red. CHX DOISY-DAËNE, Haura, REYNON in same stable. Second label (r/w) Drapeaux de Floridène.

Clos Fourtet St-Ém ★★★ 04 05' 06 07 08 09' 10' 11 12 14 15' 16' 17 18 19 PREMIER GRAND CRU CLASSÉ (B) on limestone plateau owned by Cuvelier family. Organic and bio persuasion. Classic, stylish ST-ÉM. Consistently gd form. CH Les Grandes Murailles same stable. Second label: La Closerie de Fourtet.

Clos Haut-Peyraguey Saut ★★★ 05' 06 07 08 09' 10' 11' 12 13 14 15 16 17 18 19 First Growth SAUTERNES located in Bommes. Owned by magnate Bernard Magrez (FOMBRAUGE, PAPE-CLÉMENT same stable). Elegant, SÉM-led (95%), harmonious wines. Second label: Symphonie.

Clos l'Église Pom ★★★ 00 02 04 05' 06 07 08 09' 10 11 12 13 14 15' 16 18 19 Top-flight, consistent POM on edge of plateau. 80% MERLOT, 20% CAB FR on clay-gravel soils. Elegant wine, will age. Second label: Esprit de l'Église.

Clos Puy Arnaud Cas ★★ 08 09' 10 11 12 13 14 15 16' 17 18 19' Leading CAS estate run with passion by Thierry Valette. Certified bio. Wines of depth, bright acidity. Les Acacias is 100% CAB FR.

Clos René Pom ★★ 05' 06 08 09 10 11 12 14 15' 16 18 (19) Family-owned for generations. MERLOT-led with a little spicy MALBEC; planted on sand and gravel soils. Less sensuous than top POM, but gd-value for AC.

Clotte, La St-Ém ★★→★★★ 05 08 09' 10' 11 12 15' 16' 17 18 19' 20 On an upward curve under AUSONE ownership. Second label: L de La Clotte.

Conseillante, La Pom ★★★★ 01 04 05' 06' 07 08 09' 10' 11 12 13 14 15' 16' 17 18 19' 150th anniversary of Nicolas family ownership in 2021; vyd surface area same since this time. Some of noblest, most fragrant POM with structure to age. Second label: Duo de Conseillante.

Corbin St-Ém ★★ 05 08 09 10' 11 12 14 15' 16' 18 19 Consistent, gd-value GRAND CRU CLASSÉ. Gourmand, approachable. Second label: Divin de Corbin.

Cos d'Estournel St-Est ★★★★ 00 01 04 05' 06 07 08 09' 10' 11 12 13 14 15' 16' 17 18 19' 20 Big Second Growth. Refined, suave, high-scoring. Cutting-edge cellars. Too-pricey SAUV BL-dominated white; now more refined. CH La Mascaronne in Provence same ownership (2020). Second label (r/w): Les Pagodes de Cos.

Cos-Labory St-Est ★★→★★★ 00 04 05 06 07 08 09' 10' 11 12 14 15 16' 17 18 19 Small Fifth-Growth neighbour of COS D'ESTOURNEL admirably run by Bernard Audoy; gd value, consistent. Second label: Charme de Cos Labory.

Coufran H-Méd ★★ 08 09' 10 11 12 14 15' 16' 17 18 19 Atypical n HAUT-MÉD estate with 85% MERLOT. Environmental certification. Supple wine with some ageing potential. Second label: N°2 de Coufran.

Couhins-Lurton Pe-Lé ★★→★★★ (r) 08 09 10' 11 12 14 15 16 17 18 19 (w) 05 06 08'

Cru Bourgeois hierarchy 2020
A three-tier classification for CRUS BOURGEOIS was reintroduced in 2020 with a total of 249 chx classified. It sees the return of three quality levels: Cru Bourgeois (179), Cru Bourgeois Supérieur (56) and Cru Bourgeois Exceptionnel (14). Classification was based on a quality assessment conducted by an independent organization, with technical and environmental factors considered. It will be renewable every 5 yrs and initially covers vintages 2018–22. Chx that made CB Exceptionnel status were Arnauld, BELLE-VUE, CAMBON LA PELOUSE, Charmail, D'AGASSAC, d'Arsac, de Malleret, du Taillan, LE BOSCQ, LE CROCK, LESTAGE, LILIAN LADOUYS, MALESCASSE, Paveil de Luze. None of the nine CB Exceptionnel from the annulled 2003 version were in the lineup.

09 10 12 13 14 15' 16 17 18 19 *Fine,* tense, long-lived Classed Growth *white* from SAUV BL (100%). Polished, MERLOT-led (up to 85%) red.

Couspaude, La St-Ém ★★★ 05 06 08 09' 10' 11 12 14 15 16 17 18 19 20 GRAND CRU CLASSÉ owned by Aubert family. Rich, creamy, MERLOT-led, lashings of spicy oak.

Coutet Saut ★★★ 01' 04 05 07 09' 10' 11' 12 13 14' 16 17' 18 19 Baly family owned; technical and commercial assistance from MOUTON-ROTHSCHILD. Consistently v. fine. CUVÉE Madame: v. rich, old-vine selection 01 03 09. Second label: La Chartreuse de Coutet. V.gd dry white, Opalie.

Merlot accounts for 66% of red plantings in B'x.

Couvent des Jacobins St-Ém ★★ 05 06 08 09 10 12 14 15 16' 18 19' GRAND CRU CLASSÉ vinified within walls of town. Organic certification. MERLOT-led with CAB FR, PETIT VERDOT. Ample but fresh.

Crabitey Grav ★★ (r) 09 10 11 12 14 15 16 17 18 19 (w) 15 16 17 18 19 Portets estate with vyd replanted in 80s. Owner Arnaud de Butler makes harmonious CAB SAUV-led reds; small volume of lively SAUV BL (70%), SÉM.

Crock, Le St-Est ★★ 05 06 08 09' 10 11 14 15 16' 18 19' Newly promoted CRU BOURGEOIS Exceptionnel (2020). Same stable as LÉOVILLE-POYFERRÉ. Solid, can age.

Croix, La Pom ★★ 08 09 10 11 12 14 15 16 18 (19) Owned by NÉGOCIANT Janoueix since 1960. Rich, MERLOT-led wine. Also La Croix St-Georges, HAUT-SARPE.

Croix-de-Gay, La Pom ★★★ 05 08 09' 10' 12 14 15 16 17 18 19 Tiny MERLOT-dominant (95%) vyd owned by Chantal Lebreton. La Fleur-de-Gay from separate parcels.

Croix du Casse, La Pom ★★ 08 09 10 11 12 14 15' 16 18 19 Supple, earlier-drinking POM. MERLOT-based (90%+), sandy/gravel soils. Gd value. Owned by BORIE-MANOUX.

Croizet-Bages Pau ★★ 05 06 08 09 10' 11 12 14 15 16' 17 18 19 20 Striving, CAB SAUV-led Fifth Growth. More consistency since 2015 but can improve further. Same owner as RAUZAN-GASSIES.

Cru Bourgeois Méd New three-tier classification in 2020; runs for vintages 2018–2022. 249 CHX all told.

Cruzelles, Les L de P ★★ 09 10 11 12 14 15' 16' 17 18 19' 20 Consistent, gd-value, MERLOT-led (90%) wine. Ageing potential in top yrs. Part of Denis Durantou stable (L'ÉGLISE-CLINET, Montlandrie).

Dalem Fron ★★ 06 08 09' 10' 11 12 14 15 16 17 18' 19 MERLOT-dominated (90%) property. Smooth, ripe, fresh. New cellar 2019.

Dassault St-Ém ★★ 05' 06 08 09' 10 11 12 14 15 16 18' 19 20 Consistent, modern GRAND CRU CLASSÉ. 70% MERLOT, 30% CABS FR/SAUV; 70% new oak barrels. CHX La Fleur, Trimoulet, Faurie de Souchard same stable. Second label: D de Dassault.

Dauphine, De la Fron ★★→★★★ 06' 08 09' 10' 11 12 14 15 16 17 18' 19 Leading FRON estate. Sweeping change over last 20 yrs: renovation, additional land acquired, organic. Now more substance, finesse. Second label: Delphis. Tiny quantity of Le Blanc de La Dauphine (80% SAUV BL, 20% SÉM).

Dauzac Marg ★★→★★★ 00' 05 08' 09' 10' 11 12 14 15 16' 18' 19 Fifth Growth at Labarde. Owned by the Roulleau family since 2019. Eric Boissenot consults. Dense, rich, dark wines. Second label: La Bastide Dauzac. Also fruity Aurore de Dauzac. D de Dauzac is vegan.

Desmirail Marg ★★→★★★ 05 06 09' 10' 11 15 16' 17 18 19 Discreet Third Growth. CAB SAUV-led. Fine, delicate style. Second label: Initial de Desmirail.

Destieux St-Ém ★★ 05' 06 08 09' 10 11 12 14 15 16 18 19 GRAND CRU CLASSÉ; St-Hippolyte. Powerful, modern with plenty of new oak. Cellars recently renovated.

Doisy-Daëne Bar ★★★ 01 04 05' 06 07 08 09 10' 11' 12 13' 14 15' 17' 18' 19 Part of Dubourdieu family stable (CLOS FLORIDÈNE). Produces *fine, sweet Barsac*. L'Extravagant 16 17' 18' 19' intensely rich, expensive, 100% SAUV BL CUVÉE. Also dry white Doisy-Daëne SEC.

Doisy-Védrines Saut ★★★ 01' 03' 04 05' 09 10' 11' 13 14 15' 16' 18' (19) BAR estate named after former owners, Chevaliers de Védrines. *Long-term fave*; delicious, gd value. Second label: Petit Védrines.

Dôme, Le St-Ém ★★★ 05 08 09 10' 11 12 14 15 16 17 18 19 Micro-wine; rich, modern, powerful. Two-thirds old-vine CAB FR, 80% new oak. New winery in 2021 designed by Norman Foster. CH Teyssier (value) same stable.

Dominique, La St-Ém ★★★ 00' 05' 08 09' 10' 11 12 14 15 16' 17 18' 19 20 GRAND CRU CLASSÉ owned by the Fayat family since 1969. Rich, juicy. MERLOT-led (81%). New winemaker in 2019 (ex-HAUT-BAILLY). Rooftop restaurant (La Terrasse Rouge), shop. Second label: Relais de la Dominique.

Value of 1 ha of Pau in late 80s was FF500,000; today it's €2.3 million.

Ducru-Beaucaillou St-Jul ★★★★ 01 02 04 05' 06 07 08 09' 10' 11 12 13 14 15' 16 17 18' 19' Outstanding Second Growth owned by Bruno Borie. Majors in CAB SAUV (85%+). Excellent form; classic cedar-scented claret for long ageing. Le Petit Ducru (formerly Lalande-Borie) and La Croix de Beaucaillou same stable.

Duhart-Milon Rothschild Pau ★★★ 00' 01 03 05' 06 07 08 09' 10' 11 12 14 15 16' 17 18' 19' 20 Fourth Growth by LAFITE ROTHSCHILD. Later-ripening terroir. CAB SAUV-dominated (70%). V. fine quality, esp last 10 yrs.

Durfort-Vivens Marg ★★★ 00 04 05 06 08 09' 10' 11 13 14 15' 16' 17 18 19' 20 Much-improved MARG Second Growth; 16, 19 excellent. CAB SAUV-dominated (90%). Organic, bio certification. Amphorae for vinification. Second labels: Vivens, Relais de Durfort-Vivens.

Eglise, Dom de l' Pom ★★ 00 04 05' 06 08 09 10' 11 12 14 15 16 17 18 19 Oldest vyd in POM (1589). Owned by BORIE-MANOUX. Clay/gravel soils of plateau. Consistent, fleshy of late. CROIX DU CASSE same stable.

Église-Clinet, L' Pom ★★★★ 00' 01' 04 05' 06 07 08 09' 10' 11' 12 13 14 15' 16' 17 18 19' 20 RIP Denis Durantou; put this tiny estate on map. Great consistency; full, concentrated, fleshy, but expensive. Second label: La Petite Église.

Evangile, L' Pom ★★★★ 01' 05 06 07 08 09' 10' 11 12 13 14 15' 16' 17 18' 19' 20 Rothschild (LAFITE)-owned property since 1990: investment. New winemaking team 2020. MERLOT-dominated (80%) with CAB FR. Consistently rich, opulent. Second label: Blason de L'Evangile.

Fargues, De Saut ★★★ 01 02 03' 04 05' 06 07 08 09' 10' 11' 13 14 15' 16' 17' 18 19 Unclassified but top-quality (and price) SAUT owned by Lur-Saluces. Classic Saut: rich, unctuous but refined. Age-worthy.

Faugères St-Ém ★★→★★★ 00' 05 06 08 09' 10' 11 12 14 15 16' 18 19' Sizeable ST-ÉM GRAND CRU CLASSÉ. Rich, bold, modern wines. Sister CHX Péby Faugères (also classified), Cap de Faugères (CAS).

Ferrand, De St-Ém ★★→★★★ 00 01 05 06 08 09 10' 12 14 15 16 18 19 Big St-Hippolyte GRAND CRU CLASSÉ owned by Pauline Bich Chandon-Moët. MERLOT-led (75%); fresh, firm, expressive. Environmental certification.

Ferrande Grav ★★ 09 10 11 12 14 15 16' 17 18 (19) Substantial GRAV property owned by NÉGOCIANT Castel. Much-improved; enjoyable red; fresh white.

Ferrière Marg ★★★ 00' 05 06 08 09 10' 12 14 15 16' 17 18 19 20 Confidential Third Growth in MARG village. Organic, bio certification. Dark, firm, perfumed wines.

Feytit-Clinet Pom ★★→★★★ 00 01 05' 06 08 09' 10' 11 12 13 14 15 16' 18 19' Tiny 6-ha property on w of POM plateau. 90% MERLOT on clay-gravel soils. Top, consistent form; rich, seductive. Relatively gd value.

Fieuzal Pe-Lé ★★★ (r) 01 06 07 08 09' 10' 11 12 14 15 16' 18' 19' (w) 12 13 14 15 16 18 19 Classified PE-LÉ estate owned by Irish Quinn family. Rich, ageable white; generous red. Greater consistency now. Second label (r/w): L'Abeille de Fieuzal.

Figeac St-Ém ★★★★ 00' 01' 02 04 05' 06 07 08 09' 10' 14 15' 16' 17' 18' 19' 20 Large

PREMIER GRAND CRU CLASSÉ (B) currently on roll (magnificent 19 18 16). Classical CH, gravelly vyd with unusual 70% CABS FR/SAUV. Now richer but always elegant wines; need long ageing. Major new winery complex completed in 2021. Second label: Petit-Figeac.

Filhot Saut ★★ 03' 04 05 07 09' 10' 11' 12 13 **14** 15 16 17' 18 Second Growth owned by de Vaucelles family; 60% SÉM, 36% SAUV BL, 4% MUSCADELLE. Richer, purer style from 09.

Fleur Cardinale St-Ém ★★ 05' 06 07 08 09' 10' 11 12 **14 15** 16' 18 19' GRAND CRU CLASSÉ; in overdrive for last 15 yrs. Ripe, unctuous, modern style. Second label: Intuition (from 2019). White from 2021.

Fleur de Boüard, La B'x ★★ →★★★ 05 08 09 10 11 12 13 **14 15** 16' 17 18 19 20 Leading estate in L DE P. Owned by de Boüard family (ANGÉLUS). Dark, dense, modern. Special CUVÉE, Le Plus: 100% MERLOT; more extreme. Visitor-friendly. B&B accommodation. Second label: Le Lion.

Fleur-Pétrus, La Pom ★★★★ 00' 01 04 05' 06 08 **09' 10' 11 12** 13 **14** 15 16 17' 18 19' 20 Top-of-range J-P MOUEIX property on POM plateau. Sizeable: 18.7 ha. 91% MERLOT, 6% CAB FR, 3% PETIT VERDOT. Finer style than PETRUS or TROTANOY.

Fombrauge St-Ém ★★ →★★★ 01 04 05 06' 08 09 10 11 **14** 15 16' 18 19 Substantial (58.6 ha) GRAND CRU CLASSÉ estate. Rich, dark, creamy, opulent. Magrez-Fombrauge is special red CUVÉE; also name for dry white B'X. MICHEL ROLLAND consults.

Fonbadet Pau ★★ 05' 06 08 09' **10'** 12 14 **15** 16' 17 18 19' Small non-classified estate. CAB SAUV led (60%). Less long-lived but reliable. Vintages from 15 a step up.

Fonbel, De St-Ém ★★ 09 10 11 12 14 15 **16** 18 19 20 Consistent source of juicy, fresh, gd-value ST-ÉM. MERLOT-led; incl CARMENÈRE. Same stable as AUSONE.

Fonplégade St-Ém ★★ 04 05 06 08 09' 10 12 **14** 15 16' 18' 19 American-owned GRAND CRU CLASSÉ. Previously concentrated, modern; now more fruit, balance. Bio certification (2019). Second label: Fleur de Fonplégade.

Fonréaud List ★★ 00' 04 05 06 08 09' 10' 11 12 14 **15** 16' 17 18 19 One of bigger, better LIST for satisfying, savoury wines. Now a CRU BOURGEOIS Supérieur (2020). Some ageing potential. Small volume v.gd dry white: Le Cygne.

Fonroque St-Ém ★★★ 05 06 08 09' 10' **12 14 15** 16 18 19 Côtes GRAND CRU CLASSÉ nw of ST-ÉM town. Owned by Guillard family. Firm but fresh and juicy.

Fontenil Fron ★★ 09' 10' 11 12 14 15' 16 17 18' 19 Leading FRON, owned by MICHEL ROLLAND. 100% MERLOT. Ripe, opulent, balanced.

Forts de Latour, Les Pau ★★★★ 00' 01 04' 05' 06 07 08 09 10 11 12 13 14 15 16' 17 18 19' Second label of CH LATOUR (c.40% production); authentic flavour in slightly lighter format; high price. No more en PRIMEUR sales; only released when deemed ready to drink (14 in 2020) but another 10 yrs often pays off.

Fourcas-Dupré List ★★ 05 06 08 09 10' 11 12 15' 16' **17** 18 19 Well-run property, fairly consistent. Acquired by Gérard Jicquel in 2019. Also a dry white.

Fourcas-Hosten List ★★ →★★★ 08 09 10' 11 12 14 15 **16** 17 18 19 Large LIST estate. Organic certification. Finesse and precision these days. New winemaker in 2020 (ex FONPLÉGADE). Also SAUV BL-led dry white.

Vyds are looking like attractive investments, apparently: average return of 2% p.a. Beats the bank.

France, De Pe-Lé ★★ (r) 05 06 08 09 10 11 12 14 **16'** 18 19 (w) 12 13 14 15 16 17 18 19 Unclassified neighbour of FIEUZAL; environmental certification. Ripe, modern reds. White fresh, balanced. Value.

Franc-Mayne St-Ém ★★ 01 05 08 09 **10'** 11 12 **14 15** 16 18 19' Tiny GRAND CRU CLASSÉ on côtes. New ownership and winemaker from 2018. Fresh, structured.

Gaby Fron ★★ 05 06 08 09 10 12 **14 15** 16 17 18 19' Well-sited CANON-FRON estate. MERLOT-dominated. Can age. Special CUVÉE Gaby more intense.

Gaffelière, La St-Ém ★★★ 00' 01 04 05' 06 08 09 10' 11 12 13 14 15 16' 18 19' First Growth owned by the de Malet-Roquefort family. Investment, improvement; part of vyd replanted. Elegant, long-ageing wines. Second label: CLOS la Gaffelière. Puy-Blanquet same stable.

Garde, La Pe-Lé ★★ (r) 05 08 09' 10' 11 12 14 15 16' 18 19 (w) 13 14 16 17 18 19 Unclassified PE-LÉ in Martillac; supple, CAB SAUV/MERLOT reds. Tiny production of SAUV BL (90%), SÉM white. Second label: La Terrasse de La Garde.

Gay, Le Pom ★★★ 05 06 08 09' 10' 11 12 14 15 16 17 18' 19' Neighbour of LAFLEUR. MICHEL ROLLAND consults. Rich, suave with ageing potential. CH Montviel, La Violette same stable. Second label: Manoir de Gay.

In 1855 Lascombes was 17 ha; today it's 120 ha.

Gazin Pom ★★★ 00' 01 04 05 08 09 10' 12 14 15' 16' 17 18' 19' Owned by 5th generation de Bailliencourt family. On v.gd form; generous, long ageing. Second label: L'Hospitalet de Gazin.

Gilette Saut ★★★ 86 88 89 90 96 97 99 Extraordinary small Preignac CH. Family-owned since C18. Vintages back to 1953. Stores its sumptuous wines in concrete vats for 16–20 yrs. Ch Les Justices (SAUT) is sister estate.

Giscours Marg ★★★ 00' 04 05 06 08 09 10' 11 12 14 15 16' 17 18' 19' 20 Substantial Third Growth. CAB SAUV-led (60%). Full-bodied, long-ageing MARG; recent vintages on song. Dutch-owned since 1995; start of renaissance. Second label: La Sirène de Giscours. Little B'X rosé. Tertre is sister CH.

Glana, Du St-Jul ★★ 05 06 08 09 15 16' 17 18 19 Big, unclassified estate. Undemanding; robust; value. Owned by Meffre family since 1961. Second label: Pavillon du Glana.

Gloria St-Jul ★★→★★★ 05 06 07 08 09' 10' 11 12 14 15 16' 17 18 19' Creation of Henri Martin in 70s. CAB SAUV-dominant (65%). Unclassified but sells at Fourth Growth prices. Same stable as ST-PIERRE. Superb form recently.

Grand Corbin-Despagne St-Ém ★★→★★★ 01 05 06 08 09' 10' 11 12 13 14 15 16' 18' 19' Gd-value GRAND CRU CLASSÉ owned by Despagne family; 7th generation at helm. Aromatic wines now with riper, fuller edge. Environmental certification. Le Chemin (POM) sister estate. Second label: Petit Corbin-Despagne.

Grand Cru Classé St-Ém 2012: 64 classified; reviewed every 10 yrs.

Grand-Mayne St-Ém ★★★ 04 05 06 08 09' 10' 11 12 14 15 16' 17 18 19' 20 Impressive GRAND CRU CLASSÉ (75% MERLOT), owned by Nony family. Consistent, full-bodied, structured wines. Second label: Filia de Grand Mayne.

Grand-Puy-Ducasse Pau ★★★ 04 05' 06 07 08 09' 10' 11 12 14 15' 16' 17 18 19' 20 Fifth Growth, steady rise in quality (2019 best yet). 60% CAB SAUV, 40% MERLOT. Reasonable value. Sister to MEYNEY. Second label: Prélude à Grand-Puy-Ducasse.

Grand-Puy-Lacoste Pau ★★★ 00' 04 05' 06 07 08 09' 10' 11 12 13 14 15' 16' 17 18' 19' 20 Fifth Growth famous for CAB SAUV-driven (75%+) PAU to lay down. History dates from C16. Vyd in one block around CH. Second label: Lacoste-Borie.

Grave à Pomerol, La Pom ★★★ 05 06 08 09' 10 11 12 13 14 15 16' 17 18 19' 20 Small J-P MOUEIX property acquired in 1971. Mainly gravel soils. MERLOT-dominant (85%). Gd value. Refined; can age.

Greysac Méd ★★ 09 10' 11 12 14 15 16' 17 18 19 CRU BOURGEOIS Supérieur (2020). Environmental certification. MERLOT-led (65%), fine, fresh, consistent quality.

Gruaud-Larose St-Jul ★★★★ 00' 01 04 05' 06 08 09' 10' 11 12 14 15' 16' 17 18' (19) 20 One of biggest, best-loved Second Growths. Created in 1725; only four owning families since (Merlaut today). Vigorous claret to age. Second label: *Sarget de Gruaud-Larose*.

Guadet St-Ém ★★ 05 06 08 09 10 11 12 14 15 16' 18 (19) Tiny MERLOT-led (80%) GRAND CRU CLASSÉ. Better form recently. DERENONCOURT consults. Bio certification.

Guiraud Saut ★★★ 02 04 05' 06 07 08 09 10' 11' 13 14 15' 16' 17' 19 Classed Growth SAUT; organic certification. Unusual 35% SAUV BL. Restaurant La Chapelle. Visitor-friendly. Dry white G de Guiraud. Second label: Petit Guiraud.

Gurgue, La Marg ★★ 05' 08 09' 10 11 12 14 15 16' 18 19 20 Same ownership as FERRIÈRE. Organic, bio certification. Accessible earlier. Gd value.

Hanteillan H-Méd ★★ 09' 10 12 14 15 16 18 (19) Large CRU BOURGEOIS (2020) at Cissac. Reliable; early drinking. DERENONCOURT consults. Second label: CH Laborde.

Haut-Bages-Libéral Pau ★★★ 00 04 05' 06 08 09' 10' 11 12 14 15' 16 17 19' 20 Medium-bodied Fifth Growth (next to LATOUR). CAB SAUV-led (70%). Organic certification (2019). Reasonable value. Second label: Le Pauillac de Haut-Bages-Libéral.

Haut-Bailly Pe-Lé ★★★★ 00' 01 04 05' 06 07 08' 09' 10' 11 12 14 15' 16' 17 18' 19' 20 Top-quality PE-LÉ Classed Growth. Refined, elegant, CAB SAUV-led red (parcel of v.-old, 100-yr+ vines). New winery in 2021. Second label: Haut-Bailly II from 2018 (previously La Parde de H-B). CH Le Pape (Pe-Lé) same stable.

Haut-Batailley Pau ★★★ 00 04 05 06 07 08 09' 10' 11 12 13 14 15 16' 17 18' 19' Fifth Growth owned by Cazes family (LYNCH-BAGES) since 2017. Reliable; PAU with elegant edge. Second label: Verso (from 2017).

Haut-Beauséjour St-Est ★★ 08 09 10 11 14 15 16 17 (19) Property created, improved by CHAMPAGNE ROEDERER; sold in 2017 to Laffitte Carcasset. MERLOT-led (60%+).

Haut-Bergeron Saut ★★ 05 06 07 09 10 11 13 14 15' 16 17' 18 (19) Consistent non-classified SAUT owned and run by Lamothe family. Vines in SAUT, BAR. Mainly SÉM (90%). Rich, opulent, gd value.

Haut-Bergey Pe-Lé ★★→★★★ (r) 06 09 10 11 12 15 16' 18' 19 (w) 16 18 19 Non-classified property with Classed Growth pretensions. Rich, bold red (from all five B'x varieties). Fresh, SAUV BL-led dry white. Organic, bio certification.

Haut-Brion Pe-Lé ★★★★ 00' 01 03 04 05 06 07 08 09' 10' 11' 12 13 14 15' 16' 17' 18' 19' Only non-MÉD First Growth in list of 1855, owned by American Dillon family since 1935. Documented evidence of wine from 1521. Cellarmaster and vyd manager with over 30 yrs experience. Deeply harmonious, wonderful texture, for many no.1 or 2 choice of all clarets. Constant renovation: next project the *cuvier*. A little *sumptuous dry white* (SAUV BL/SÉM) for tycoons: 15' 16' 17 18 19. Also new La Clarté (w) from both H-B and LA MISSION HAUT-BRION. *See also* La Mission H-B, LE CLARENCE DE HAUT-BRION.

Haut Condissas Méd ★★★ 09' 10' 11 12 14 15 16 17 18 19' Top wine from Jean Guyon stable (*see also* GREYSAC). 5000 cases annually. Sister to CH Rollan-de-By. Rich, exuberant, modern. MERLOT-LED plus 20% PETIT VERDOT.

Haut-Marbuzet St-Est ★★→★★★ 04 05' 06 08' 09 10' 11 15 12 16' 18 19' Started in 1952 with 7 ha; now 70; owned by Duboscq family. Easy to love, but unclassified; 60%+ sold directly by CH. Scented, unctuous wines matured in new oak barriques. CAB SAUV-led WITH MERLOT, CAB FR, PETIT VERDOT. Second label: MacCarthy.

Haut-Sarpe St-Ém ★★ 05 06 08 09 10 11 12 14 15' 16' 18 19 GRAND CRU CLASSÉ owned by Janoueix family since 1930. Organic conversion. Ripe, modern style.

A study at Guiraud (Sauternes) revealed 635 species of insect in the vyd.

Hosanna Pom ★★★★ 00 01 05' 06 08 09 10' 11 12 14 15 16' 17 18 19' 20 Tiny vyd in heart of POM plateau. PÉTRUS a neighbour. MERLOT (70%), CAB FR (30%). Created by J-P MOUEIX in 1999. Power, purity, balance and needs time.

Issan, D' Marg ★★★ 00 04' 05' 06 07 08 09' 10' 11 12 13 14 15' 16' 18' 19' 20 Third Growth with fine moated CH. Fragrant, CAB SAUV-led (60%) wines that age; at top of game. Owned by Cruse and Lorenzetti families. Second label: Blason d'Issan.

Jean Faure St-Ém ★★ 08 09 10' 11 12 14 15 16 18' 19' GRAND CRU CLASSÉ on clay, sand, gravel soils. C18 origins. Organic certification, bio methods. Horses for ploughing. CAB FR-led with a touch of MALBEC; gives fresh, elegant style.

Kirwan Marg ★★★ 00′ 01 04 05′ 06 07 08 09 10′ 11 12 14 15′ 16′ 17 18′ 19′ Third Growth. CAB SAUV-dominant (60%). Modern winery. Dense, fleshy in 90s; now less forced, more finesse. Second label: Charmes de Kirwan.

Labégorce Marg ★★→★★★ 05′ 08 09 10′ 11 12 14 15 16′ 18′ 19 Substantial unclassified MARG owned by Perrodo family. Considerable investment, progression. More muscular style of Marg. CH Marquis-d'Alesme same stable.

Lafaurie-Peyraguey Saut ★★★ 01′ 03′ 04 05′ 06 07 09′ 10′ 11 13 14 15′ 16′ 17′ 18 19 Leading Classed Growth owned by Lalique crystal-owner Silvio Denz (*see* FAUGÈRES). Rich, harmonious, sweet 90% SÉM. Michelin-starred restaurant. Second label: La Chapelle de Lafaurie-Peyraguey. Also SÉM-led dry white B'X.

Lafite-Rothschild Pau ★★★★ 01′ 02 05′ 06 07 08′ 09′ 10′ 11′ 12 13 14′ 15′ 16′ 17 18′ 19′ 20 Big (112 ha) First Growth of famously elusive perfume and style, never great weight, although more dense, sleek these days. Great vintages need keeping for decades. 2018 marks 150th anniversary of acquisition by Baron James de Rothschild. Transition to organics. Second label: CARRUADES DE LAFITE. Also owns CHX DUHART-MILON, L'EVANGILE, RIEUSSEC.

Lafleur Pom ★★★★ 01′ 02 04′ 05′ 06 07 08 09′ 10′ 11 12 13 14 15′ 16′ 17′ 18′ 19′ 20 Superb but tiny family-owned/managed property. Elegant, intense wine for maturing. Expensive. Second label: *Pensées de Lafleur*. Also v.gd Les Champs Libres 100% SAUV BL and Les Perrières (r).

Lafleur-Gazin Pom ★★ 08 09 10 11 12 14 15 16′ 18′ 19 20 Small, gd-value J-P MOUEIX estate. 85% MERLOT, 15% CAB FR. Fine, fragrant, accessible.

Lafon-Rochet St-Est ★★★ 00′ 01 04 05′ 06 07 08 09′ 10′ 11 12 13 14 15′ 16′ 17 18′ 19 Fourth Growth neighbour of COS LABORY. In Tesseron family hands since 1960; Basile now at helm. On gd form. Former PETRUS winemaker consults. Eye-catching canary-yellow buildings and label. Second label: Les Pélerins de Lafon-Rochet.

Lagrange St-Jul ★★★ 01 04 05′ 06′ 08′ 09′ 10′ 11 12 13 14 15′ 16′ 17 18 19′ Substantial (118 ha) Third Growth owned since 1983 by Suntory. Much investment in vyd, cellars. Consistent, fresh. V.gd 19 (80% CAB SAUV). Dry white Les Arums de Lagrange. Second label: Les Fiefs de Lagrange (gd value).

Lagrange Pom ★★ 05 06 09 10 14 15′ 16′ 17 18 19 20 Tiny POM vyd on n edge of plateau. Owned by J-P MOUEIX (1953). 95% MERLOT. Supple, accessible early.

Lagune, La H-Méd ★★★ 04 05′ 08 09′ 10′ 11 12 14 15′ 16′ 17 19 Third Growth in v. s of MÉD. Dipped in 90s; now on form. Fine-edged with more structure and depth. Owner Caroline Frey also winemaker. Bio certification (2021). Second label: Moulin de La Lagune.

Lamarque, De H-Méd ★★ 05′ 06 08 09′ 10′ 11 12 14 15 16 17 18 19′ Medium-sized H-MÉD estate with medieval fortress. Competent, mid-term wines, charm, value. Lots of PETIT VERDOT. Second label: D de Lamarque.

Lanessan H-Méd ★★ 09 10′ 12 11 12 14 15′ 16′ 18 19′ Gd-value classic claret. Property located just s of ST-JUL. Eric Boissenot consults. Environmental certification.

Langoa-Barton St-Jul ★★★ 01 02 04′ 05′ 06 07′ 08′ 09′ 10′ 11 12 13 14 15′ 16′ 17 18′ 19′ Small Third-Growth sister CH to LÉOVILLE BARTON. CAB SAUV-led (57%); charm, elegance. Lilian Barton with son and daughter at helm.

Larcis Ducasse St-Ém ★★★ 04 05′ 06 08 09′ 10 11 12 13 14 15′ 16′ 17 18 19′ PREMIER

Hot air at Lafite
To mark the 150th anniversary of Baron James de Rothschild's acquisition of LAFITE, a tiny hot-air balloon has been added to the 18 label, to give the two women in the foreground of the lithograph something to stare at. The letters CL (150 in roman numerals) are also inscribed on the shoulder of the bottle. One wonders what the other suggestions were.

GRAND CRU CLASSÉ on top form. Managed by Nicolas Thienpont and David Suire; s-facing terraced vyd; 80% MERLOT. Second label: Murmure de Larcis Ducasse.

Larmande St-Ém ★★ 05 06 08 09' 10 12 14 15 16 18' 19' 20 GRAND CRU CLASSÉ in same stable as SOUTARD. Vyd planted to MERLOT (65%), CAB FR (30%), CAB SAUV (5%). Sound but lighter weight.

Laroque St-Ém ★★→★★★ 05 06 08 09' 10' 11 12 14 15 16 17 18' 19' Large GRAND CRU CLASSÉ. Terroir-driven wines. Managed by David Suire (LARCIS DUCASSE).

Latour 1st mentioned in records in 1331, as La Tour de St Maubert.

Larose-Trintaudon H-Méd ★★ 09' 10 11 12 14 15 16 18 19' CRU BOURGEOIS Supérieur (2020). Largest vyd in MÉD (165 ha). 75,000 cases/yr. Sustainable viticulture. Generally for early drinking. Second label: Les Hauts de Trintaudon.

Laroze St-Ém ★★ 05 08 09' 10' 12 14 15 16' 18' 19' GRAND CRU CLASSÉ owned by Guy Meslin. MERLOT-led (70%). Environmental certification. Lighter-framed wines; more depth of late. Second label: La Fleur Laroze.

Larrivet-Haut-Brion Pe-Lé ★★★ (r) 05' 06 08 09 10' 12 14 16' 18' 19 Unclassified PE-LÉ property owned by Gervoson family since 1987; vyd expanded from 17 to 75 ha. Visitor-friendly (decorated concrete egg tanks). Rich, modern red. Voluptuous, aromatic *white* 17 18 19. Second label (r/w): Les Demoiselles.

Lascombes Marg ★★★ 04 05' 06 07 08 09 10' 11 12 14 15' 16 17 18 19 Large (120-ha) Second Growth with chequered history. Wines rich, dark, concentrated, modern with touch of MARG perfume. Lots of MERLOT (50%!). MICHEL ROLLAND consults. Second label: Chevalier de Lascombes.

Latour Pau ★★★★ 00' 01 02 04 05' 06 07 08 09' 10' 11 12 14 15' 16' 17 18' 19' First Growth considered grandest statement of B'X. Profound, intense, almost immortal wines in great yrs; even weaker vintages have unique taste and run for many yrs. Hélène Genin is winemaker. Organic certification. Ceased en PRIMEUR sales in 2012; wines now only released when considered ready to drink (09 and 12 in 20: still too soon). New cellars for more storage. Owned by Pinault family; vines also in Burgundy, Rhône, Napa. Second label: LES FORTS DE LATOUR; *third label: Pauillac*; even this can age 20 yrs.

Latour-à-Pomerol Pom ★★★ 04 05' 06 08 09' 10' 11 12 14 15' 16' 17 18 19' 20 Mix of clay-gravel and loamy soils. Extremely consistent, well-structured wines that age. Relatively gd value.

Latour-Martillac Pe-Lé ★★→★★★ (r) 04 05' 06 08 09' 10' 11 12 14 15' 16 17 18' 19 GRAV Cru Classé owned by Kressmann family. Environmental certification. Regular quality; gd value; (w) 17 18 **19**. Second label (r/w): Lagrave-Martillac.

Laurets, Des St-Ém ★★ 10 12 14 15 16 18 19 Substantial property owned by Edmond de Rothschild Heritage. MERLOT-led. Sélection Parcellaire from old-vine plots.

Laville Saut ★★ 09' 10 11' 13 14 15 16 18 (19) Non-classified Preignac estate run by Jean-Christophe Barbe; also lectures at Bordeaux University. SÉM-dominated (85%) with a little SAUV BL, MUSCADELLE. Lush, gd-value, botrytized wine.

Léoville Barton St-Jul ★★★★ 00' 01 04 05' 06 07 08 09' 10' 11 12 13 14' 15' 16' 17 18' 19' Second Growth with longest-standing family ownership; in Anglo-Irish hands of Bartons since 1826. Harmonious, classic claret; CAB SAUV-dominant (74%). Ongoing renovation/extension of cellars incl new gravity-flow *cuverie*. Second label: La Rés de Léoville Barton.

Léoville Las Cases St-Jul ★★★★ 00' 01 02 04' 05' 06 08 09' 10' 11' 12 13 14 15' 16' 17' 18' 19' 20 Largest Léoville and original "Super Second" owned by Jean-Hubert Delon. CAB SAUV dominant but also CAB FR. Elegant, complex wines built for long ageing. Second label: Le Petit Lion. CLOS DU MARQUIS, POTENSAC same stable.

Léoville-Poyferré St-Jul ★★★★ 01 02 04 05' 06 07 08 09' 10' 11' 12 13 14 15' 16' 18' 19' The 100th anniversary of Cuvelier family ownership in 2020. Sara Lecompte

> **Birds and bees in Margaux**
> AC MARG has joined the environmental fray by launching a programme
> to plant hedges and trees, protect green corridors and delay the mowing
> of fields and pastures. A reduction in the use of chemicals is not yet
> part of the scheme but 80% of the producers no longer use herbicides
> and insecticides and the same % are already engaged in some sort
> of environmental action (organics, HVE certification, etc.). Here's to
> wholesome Marg.

Cuvelier now at helm. "Super Second" level; dark, rich, spicy, long-ageing wines. *Ch Moulin-Riche* a separate 21-ha parcel. LE CROCK same stable.

Lestage List ★★ 08 09 10 11 12 14 15 16' 18 19' Recently (2020) promoted CRU BOURGEOIS Exceptionnel. Same stable as FONRÉAUD. Firm, slightly austere. Also dry white La Mouette.

Lilian Ladouys St-Est ★★ 08 09' 10' 11 12 14 15 16' 17 18' 19' Sizeable (80 ha) CRU BOURGEOIS Exceptionnel (2020). Owned by Lorenzetti family. Environmental certification. More finesse in recent vintages. Second label: La Devise de Lilian.

Liversan H-Méd ★★ 10 14 15 16' 18 19 CRU BOURGEOIS (2020) in n H-MÉD; vyd in single block; owned by Advini group. Round, savoury, early drinking.

Loudenne Méd ★★ 09 10 14 15 16 18 19' Large MÉD estate, now Chinese-owned and labelled Loudenne Le CH. Landmark C17 pink-washed *chartreuse* by river. Visitor-friendly. 50/50 MERLOT/CAB SAUV reds. SAUV BL-led white.

Louvière, La Pe-Lé ★★★ (r) 04 05' 06 07 08 09' 10' 11 12 14 15 16' 18 (w) 16 17 18 Vignobles André Lurton property. Excellent white (100% SAUV BL), red of Classed Growth standard (60/40 CAB SAUV/MERLOT). *See also* COUHINS-LURTON, ROCHEMORIN.

Lussac, De St-Ém ★★ 10 14 15 16 18 (19) Top estate in LUSSAC-ST-ÉM. Plenty of investment. Supple red, rosé. Second label: Le Libertin.

Lynch-Bages Pau ★★★★ 01 02 04' 05' 06 07 08 09' 10' 11 12 13 14 15 16' 17 18 19' 20 Always popular, now a star, far higher than its Fifth Growth rank. Rich, dense CAB SAUV-led wine. Owned by Cazes family (Jean-Charles at helm). Second label: Echo de Lynch-Bages. Gd white, *Blanc de Lynch-Bages*. New winery in 2020. HAUT-BATAILLEY, ORMES-DE-PEZ same stable.

Lynch-Moussas Pau ★★ 05' 08 09 10' 11 12 14 15 16 17 18 19' 20 Fifth Growth; 100th anniversary of Castéja ownership in 2019. Lighter PAU (75% CAB SAUV), but much improved.

Lyonnat St-Ém ★★ 10 14 15 16 18 (19) Leading LUSSAC-ST-ÉM owned by Milhade family. MERLOT-led; more precision lately. Also special CUVÉE Emotion.

Malartic-Lagravière Pe-Lé ★★★ (r) 09 10 14 15' 16' 18 19' (w) 17 18 19 GRAV Classed Growth. Loads of investment. Eric Boissenot consults from 2019. Visitor-friendly. Rich, modern, CAB SAUV-led red; a little lush *white* (majority SAUV BL). CH Gazin Rocquencourt (PE-LÉ) same stable.

Malescasse H-Méd ★★ 08 09 10 11 12 14 15' 16' 17 18 19 Newly promoted CRU BOURGEOIS Exceptionnel (2020). Investment, upgrade. Ripe, fleshy, polished.

Malescot-St-Exupéry Marg ★★★ 05' 07 08 09' 10' 11 12 14 15' 16' 17 18' 19 MARG Third Growth owned by Jean-Luc Zuger. Ripe, fragrant, finely structured wines. Second label: Dame de Malescot.

Malle, De Saut ★★★ (w sw) 01' 03' 05 06 09 10' 11' 13 14 15' 16' 17' 18 19 Second Growth, vyds in Preignac, Fargues. Fine, medium-bodied SAUT. Second label: Les Fleurs de Malle.

Margaux, Ch Marg ★★★★ 01' 02 04' 05' 06' 07 08 09' 10' 11 12 13 14 15 16' 17 18' 19' 20 First Growth; most seductive, fabulously perfumed, consistent wines. Owned by Mentzelopoulos family (1977). CAB SAUV-dominated (as much as 90%). The *grand vin* represents around 37% of total production. Second label: Pavillon Rouge

09 10' 16' 18' 20. Third label: Margaux du CH Margaux from 2009. *Pavillon Blanc* (100% SAUV BL): best white of MÉD, recent vintages fresher 17 18' 19' 20.

Marojallia Marg ★★★ 05' 06 08 09' 10 11 12 15 16 17 18' 19' Micro-CH looking for big prices for big, rich, un-MARG-like wines. CAB SAUV-led (70%). CLOS Margalaine from young vines.

Marquis-de-Terme Marg ★★→★★★ 04 05' 06 08 09' 10' 11 12 14 15 16' 17 18' 19' Fourth Growth with vyd dispersed around MARG. Investment, progression in recent yrs. Second label: La Couronne. Restaurant with chef Grégory Coutenceau from 2021.

Maucaillou Mou ★★ 08 09 10 11 12 14 15' 16' 18 19' Large, consistent MOU estate. Dourthe family owners. Clean, value wines. Second label: N°2 de Maucaillou.

Mayne Lalande List ★★ 09 10 11 12 14 15 16 17 18 19 Leading LIST estate. Hubert de Boüard consults. Full, finely textured. B&B accomodation too.

Mazeyres Pom ★★ 09 10 14 15 16' 18 19' Lighter but consistent POM. Earlier-drinking, MERLOT-led. Organic, bio certification. Same owner as FONROQUE.

Meyney St-Est ★★→★★★ 00 03 04 05' 06 08 09' 10' 11' 12 14 15' 16' 17 18' 19' Big river-slope vyd, superb site next to MONTROSE. Structured, age-worthy; CAB SAUV-led (60%) but lots of PETIT VERDOT as well (16% in 2019). Gd value at this level. Second label: Prieur de Meyney.

Mission Haut-Brion, La Pe-Lé ★★★★ 00' 01 02 04 05' 06 07 08 09' 10' 11 12 13 14 15' 16' 17' 18' 19' Acquired by Dillon family of neighbouring HAUT-BRION in 1983. Considerable investment since. Consistently grand-scale, full-bodied, long-maturing wine. Second label: La Chapelle de la Mission. Magnificent SÉM-dominated white: previously Laville Haut-Brion; renamed La Mission Haut-Brion Blanc 17' 18 19'. Second label: La Clarté (fruit from both H-Bs).

Monbousquet St-Ém ★★★ 05' 08 09' 10' 11 12 14 15 16' 18 19 20 GRAND CRU CLASSÉ on Dordogne plain. Transformed by Gérard Perse (*see* PAVIE). Concentrated, oaky, voluptuous. Rare *v.gd Sauv Bl/Sauv Gr* (AC B'x). Second label: Angélique de Monbousquet.

Monbrison Marg ★★→★★★ 05' 06 08 09' 10' 11 12 14 15' 16 18 19 Tiny property owned by Vonderheyden family. CAB SAUV-led (60%). Delicate, fragrant MARG.

Mondotte, La St-Ém ★★★→★★★★ 04 05' 06 07 08 09' 10' 11 12 13 14 15' 16 17 18 19' Tiny (4.5 ha) PREMIER GRAND CRU CLASSÉ on limestone-clay plateau; 75% MERLOT, 25% CAB FR; intense, firm, virile wines. Organic certification. Same von Neipperg stable as CANON-LA-GAFFELIÈRE.

Montrose St-Est ★★★★ 00' 02 04 05' 06 07 08 09' 10' 11 12 13 14 15' 16' 17 18' 19' 20 Second Growth with riverside vyd. Famed for forceful, long-ageing claret. Vintages 1979–85 were lighter. Bouygues brothers owners. Massive environmental programme: biodiversity, recuperation of carbon dioxide, compost. Second label: *La Dame de Montrose* (new roses label from 2019).

Moulin du Cadet St-Ém ★★ 05 08 09 10' 11 12 14 15' 16 17 18' 19' 20 Tiny GRAND CRU CLASSÉ on ST-ÉM plateau; 100% MERLOT. Same owner as SANSONNET. Formerly robust, now more finesse.

There are 29 wine co-ops in B'x.

Moulinet Pom ★★ 08 09 10 11 12 15 18 19 Large CH for POM: 25 ha. MERLOT-led. Lighter style. DERENONCOURT consults.

Moulin-Haut-Laroque Fron ★★ 09' 10' 11 12 14 15' 16 17 18' 19' Leading FRON property owned by Hervé family. Consistent, structured, can age.

Moulin Pey-Labrie Fron ★★ 08 09' 10' 12 15 16 17 18 (19) MERLOT-led CANON-FRON owned by Hubau family. Sturdy, well-structured wines that can age.

Moulin-St-Georges St-Ém ★★★ 08 09' 10' 11 12 14 15' 16' 17 18' 19' 20 Lively, fresh, well-constituted. Gd value at this level. Same stable as AUSONE, FONBEL.

> **All change at Mouton**
>
> A new management and winemaking team has been put in place at MOUTON-ROTHSCHILD and the other CHX owned by Baron Philippe de Rothschild SA. As of July 2020 Ariane Khaida, formerly of NÉGOCIANT Duclot, replaces Philippe Dhalluin (now retired) as executive director while Jean-Emmanuel Danjoy takes on the technical responsibilty for Mouton, D'ARMAILHAC and CLERC MILON where he was previously technical director. Former technical director of Mouton, Erick Tourbier, remains as an advisor for both the estates and company brands. There's a lot of responsibility to share around.

Mouton Rothschild Pau ★★★★ oo' o1' o2 o4' o5' o6 o7 o8' o9' 1o' 11 12 13 14 15' 16' 17' 18' 19' 20 Rothschild-owned since 1853. Most exotic, voluptuous of PAU First Growths; at top of game. New winemaker in 2020, Jean-Emmanuel Danjoy (ex-CLERC MILON); former winemaker, Philippe Dhalluin (since 2003), retired. White Aile d'Argent (SAUV BL/SÉM) now more graceful. Second label: *Le Petit Mouton*. *See also* D'ARMAILHAC.

Nairac Saut ★★ o5' o6 o7 o9 1o 11 13 15 BAR Second Growth run by brother and sister, Nicolas and Eloïse Tari-Heeter. C17 origins. Rich but fresh. Second label: Esquisse de Nairac.

Nénin Pom ★★★ o4 o5 o6 o8 o9' 1o' 11 12 14 15' 16' 17 18' 19' 20 Large POM estate owned by Jean-Hubert Delon. Plenty of investment; evidently paid off as wines now restrained but generous, precise, built to age. Increase in CAB FR (40%). Gd-value second label: Fugue de Nénin.

Olivier Pe-Lé ★★★ (r) o5' o6 o8 o9' 1o' 12 14 15 16' 17 18 19' (w) 17 18 19' Beautiful GRAV Classed Growth owned by Bethmann family. Structured red (55% CAB SAUV), juicy SAUV BL-led (75%) white. Gd value at this level.

Ormes-de-Pez St-Est ★★ o4 o5 o6 o8' o9' 1o' 11 12 14 15' 16' 17 18 19' Same stable as LYNCH-BAGES (Cazes family). Consistent, full, age-worthy.

Ormes-Sorbet, Les Méd ★★ o9' 1o' 11 12 14 15 16' 17 18 19 Reliably consistent MÉD cru. Boivert family owners. CAB SAUV (65%), MERLOT (30%), PETIT VERDOT (5%). Elegant, gently oaked wines.

Palmer Marg ★★★★ oo o2 o4 o5' o6' o7 o8 o9' 1o' 11 12 13 14 15' 16' 17 18' 19' 20 Third Growth on par with "Super Seconds" (occasionally Firsts). Voluptuous wine of power, complexity and much MERLOT (40%). Dutch (Mähler-Besse) and British (SICHEL) owners. Bio philosophy, certification. Now selling 50% en PRIMEUR and releasing vintage at ten yrs (2010 in 2020). Second label: *Alter Ego de Palmer*.

Pape-Clément Pe-Lé ★★★★ (r) oo' o4 o5 o6 o7 o8 o9' 1o' 11 12 13 14 15' 16' 17 18' 19' (w) 14 15 16 17' 18 19 Historic estate in B'x suburbs. Owned by magnate Bernard Magrez. MICHEL ROLLAND consults. Dense, long-ageing reds. Tiny production of rich, oaky white. Second label (r/w): Clémentin.

Patache d'Aux Méd ★★ o9 1o 11 12 14 15 16' 18 19 Sizeable CRU BOURGEOIS (2020). CAB SAUV-led (50%). DERENONCOURT consults. Part of Advini group.

Pavie St-Ém ★★★★ oo' o1 o2 o5' o6 o7 o8 o9' 1o' 11 12 13 14 15' 16' 17 18 19' 20 PREMIER GRAND CRU CLASSÉ (A) splendidly sited on plateau and s côtes. State-of-the-art winery. Intense, strong wines for ageing; recent vintages less extreme. MERLOT-led but now more CABS FR/SAUV (50% in 19). Second label: Arômes de Pavie.

Pavie-Decesse St-Ém ★★★ o5 o6 o7 o8 o9' 1o' 11 12 14 15' 16 17 18 19' 20 Tiny GRAND CRU CLASSÉ. 90% MERLOT. As powerful, muscular as sister PAVIE.

Pavie-Macquin St-Ém ★★★ oo' o1 o4 o5' o6 o7 o8 o9' 12 15 16' 17 18' 19' PREMIER GRAND CRU CLASSÉ (B); vyd on limestone plateau; 80% MERLOT, 20% CABS FR/SAUV. Winemaker Nicolas Thienpont. DERENONCOURT consults. Sturdy, full-bodied wines need time. Second label: Les Chênes de Macquin.

Pédesclaux Pau ★★ 05 06 09 10' 11 12 13 14' 15 16' 18 19' Underachieving Fifth Growth revolutionized by owner Jacky Lorenzetti. Extensive investment since 2014; gravity-fed cellar (no pumps), more vyds. More fruit/flavour.

Petit-Village Pom ★★★ 04 05 06 07 08 09' 10' 11 12 13 14 15' 16' 17 18' 19 Much-improved estate on POM plateau. New owner from 2020: BEAUREGARD. Same winemaker (Diana Berrouet-Garcia). Suave, dense, increasingly finer tannins.

Petrus Pom ★★★★ 00' 01 02 04 05' 06 07 08 09' 10' 11' 12 13 14 15' 16' 17' 18' 19' 20 (Unofficial) First Growth of POM: MERLOT solo *in excelsis*. 11.5-ha vyd on blue clay gives 2500 cases of massively rich, concentrated wine for long ageing. One of 50 most expensive wines in world. Owner Jean-François Moueix. Winery recently renovated. No second label.

Pey La Tour B'x ★★ 14 15 16 18 19 Large (176 ha) DOURTHE property. Quality-driven B'X SUPÉRIEUR. Three red CUVÉES: Rés du CH (MERLOT-led) top; rosé, dry white.

Peyrabon H-Méd ★★ 05 06 09' 10 11 12 15 16 17 18 (19) Savoury CRU BOURGEOIS Supérieur (2020); NÉGOCIANT Millésima owner. Also La Fleur-Peyrabon in PAU.

Pez, De St-Est ★★★ 05' 06 08 09' 10' 11 12 13 14 15' 16' 17 18' 19' Same stable as PICHON-L COMTESSE. MERLOT/CAB SAUV aged 12–18 mths in oak barrel. Dense, reliable.

Phélan-Ségur St-Est ★★★ 04 05' 06 08 09 10' 11 12 13 14 15' 16' 17 18' 19' Reliable, top-notch, unclassified CH with Irish origins; long, supple style. Véronique Dausse manages for Belgian owner. Second label: Frank Phélan.

Pibran Pau ★★ 05 06 08 09' 10' 11 12 13 14 15 16' 17 18' 19' 20 Earlier-drinking PAU allied to PICHON-BARON. Almost 50/50 MERLOT/CAB SAUV.

Pichon-Baron Pau ★★★★ 01 02 03 04 05' 06 07 08 09' 10' 11 12 13 14 15' 16' 17 18' 19' 20 Owned by AXA; formerly CH Pichon-Longueville (until 2012). Second Growth on flying form. Powerful, long-ageing PAU at a price. Second labels: Les Tourelles de Longueville (approachable: more MERLOT); Les Griffons de Pichon Baron (generally CAB SAUV-dominant).

Pichon-Longueville Comtesse de Lalande (Pichon Lalande) Pau ★★★★ 00 01 02 04 05' 06 07 08 09' 10' 11 12 13 14 15' 16' 17 18' 19' 20 ROEDERER-owned Second Growth, neighbour of LATOUR. Always among top performers; long lived wine of famous breed. MERLOT-marked in 80s, 90s; more CAB SAUV in recent yrs (71% in 19). Modern winery; organic tendence. Second label: *Rés de la Comtesse*.

Pin, Le Pom ★★★★ 00 01' 04 05' 06' 07 08' 09' 10' 11 12 14 15 16' 17 18' 19' 20 The original B'X cult wine owned by Jacques Thienpont. Only 2.8 ha. Tiny modern winery in vyd. 100% MERLOT; almost as rich as its drinkers; prices are out of sight. Ageing potential. L'If (ST-ÉM), L'Hêtre (CAS) are stablemates.

Plince Pom ★★ 05 06 08 09 10 11 12 14 15 16' 18 (19) Vyd in one block, 72% MERLOT. Lighter style of POM on sandy soils.

Pointe, La Pom ★★ 05' 06 08 09' 10 11 12 14 15' 16' 18 19 Large (for POM), well-run estate (Eric Monneret manager); progress in last 15 yrs. Gd value.

One bottle of Mouton-Rothschild 1945 sold for £9920 in 2020: £1653/glass.

Poitevin Méd ★★ 10 11 12 14 15 16 17 18 (19) Recently promoted CRU BOURGEOIS Supérieur (2020). Consistent quality.

Pontet-Canet Pau ★★★★ 00 01 02 04 05' 06' 07 08 09' 10' 11 12 14 15 16' 17 18' 19' 20 Large, bio-certified, Tesseron family-owned Fifth Growth. Radical improvement has seen prices soar. Long-time winemaker (31 yrs), J-M Comme, stepped down 2020. Second label: Les Hauts de Pontet-Canet.

Potensac Méd ★★→★★★ 05' 08 09' 10' 11 12 13 14 15 16' 17 18' 19' 20 Top of range MÉD. Firm, long-ageing wines; gd value. MERLOT-led (45%) but lots of old-vine CAB FR. Second label: Chapelle de Potensac.

Pouget Marg ★★ 05' 06 08 09' 10' 12 14 15' 16 18 (19) Unsung Fourth Growth sister of BOYD-CANTENAC. Blend varies. Sturdy; needs time.

St-Émilion classification – 2012 version

The 2012 classification incl a total of 82 CHX: 18 PREMIERS GRANDS CRUS CLASSÉS and 64 GRANDS CRUS CLASSÉS. The classification, now legally considered an exam rather than a competition, was conducted by a commission of seven, nominated by INAO, none from B'X. CHX ANGÉLUS and PAVIE were upgraded to Premier Grand Cru Classé (A) while added to the rank of Premier Grand Cru Classé (B) were CANON-LA-GAFFELIÈRE, LA MONDOTTE, LARCIS DUCASSE and VALANDRAUD. New to status of Grand Cru Classé were Chx BARDE-HAUT, CLOS de Sarpe, Clos La Madeleine, Côte de Baleau, DE FERRAND, DE PRESSAC, FAUGÈRES, FOMBRAUGE, JEAN FAURE, La Commanderie, La Fleur Morange, Le Chatelet, Péby Faugères, QUINAULT L'ENCLOS, Rochebelle and SANSONNET. The classification is reviewed every 10 yrs, with a new edition due in 2022. The principal amendment to the rules for PGCC status will be that the tasting evaluation will rise from 30% to 50% of the final vote.

Poujeaux Mou ★★ 05 06 08 09 10 11 12 14 15' 16' 17 18 19 Sizeable (70 ha) MOU estate. DERENONCOURT consults. Full, robust wines with ageing potential. Second label: La Salle de Poujeaux.

Premier Grand Cru Classé St-Ém 2012: 18 classified; ranked into A (4) and B (14).

Pressac, De St-Ém ★★ 08 09 10 11 12 14 15' 16' 17 18' 19' GRAND CRU CLASSÉ e of St-Ém town. MERLOT-LED but CABS FR/SAUV, MALBEC, CARMENÈRE. Value.

Preuillac Méd ★★ 09 10 11 12 14 15 16 18 19' Savoury, structured CRU BOURGEOIS Supérieur (2020). MERLOT-led (54%). Second label: Esprit de Preuillac.

Prieuré-Lichine Marg ★★★ 04 05 06 08 09' 10' 11 12 14 15' 16' 17 18' 19' Fourth Growth owned by Ballande group; put on map in 60s by Alexis Lichine. CAB SAUV-led (60%). Parcels in all five MARG communes. Fragrant Marg currently on gd form. Gd SAUV BL/SÉM too.

Puygueraud B'x ★★ 09 10 11 12 14 15' 16' 17 18' 19 Leading CH of this tiny FRANCS-CÔTES DE B'X AC. Owned by Thienpont family since 1946. MERLOT-led. Oak-aged wines of surprising class. Also MALBEC/CAB FR-based cuvée George. A little dry white (SAUV BL/Sauv Gr).

Quinault L'Enclos St-Ém ★★→★★★ 09 10 11 12 14 15 16' 17 18' 19' GRAND CRU CLASSÉ located in Libourne. Same team/owners as CHEVAL BLANC. Plenty of investment. MERLOT-led but 26% CABS SAUV/FR; more freshness, finesse.

Quintus St-Ém ★★★ 11 12 14 15 16' 17 18' 19' Created by Dillons of HAUT-BRION from former Tertre Daugay and L'Arrosée vyds. Gaining in stature; 45% CAB FR in 19. Expensive. Second label: Le Dragon de Quintus.

Rabaud-Promis Saut ★★→★★★ 04 05' 06 07 09' 10 11 12 13 14 15' 16 17' 18 19 First Growth. Quality, gd value. Jean Merlaut (GRUAUD-LAROSE) now major shareholder.

Rahoul Grav ★★ (r) 09' 10 11 12 14 15 16' 17 18 19 Owned by DOURTHE; reliable, MERLOT-led red. SÉM-dominated white 17 18 19'. Gd value.

Ramage-la-Batisse H-Méd ★★ 10 14 15 16 18 (19) Widely distributed CRU BOURGEOIS Supérieur (2020). CAB SAUV-led with MERLOT, PETIT VERDOT, CAB FR.

Rauzan-Gassies Marg ★★★ 05' 06 09 08 09' 10 11 12 15 16' 17 18 19 Second Growth. Same stable as CROIZET-BAGES. Improvement but still lags behind top MARGS. Second label: Gassies.

Rauzan-Ségla Marg ★★★★ 00' 01 02 04' 05' 06 08 09' 10' 11 12 14 15' 16' 17 18' 19' 20 Leading Second Growth long famous for its fragrance; owned by Wertheimers of Chanel. Second label: Ségla (value). BERLIQUET, CANON, ST-SUPÉRY same ownership.

Raymond-Lafon Saut ★★★ 01' 03' 05' 06 07' 09' 10 11' 13 14 15' 17' 18 19 Unclassified SAUT owned by Meslier family producing First Growth quality. Rich, complex wines that age; gd value.

Rayne Vigneau, De Saut ★★★ 01' 03 05' 07 09' 10' 11' 13 14 15' 16' 17 18' 19' Substantial First Growth managed by Vincent Labergère. Suave, age-worthy (74% SÉM). Special CUVÉE Gold. Visitor-friendly. Second label: Madame de Rayne.

Respide Médeville Grav ★★ (r) 10 12 14 15 16 18 19 (w) 16 18 19 Top GRAV property owned by Julie Gonet-Medeville. Elegant red, complex *white*.

Reynon B'x ★★ Leading CADILLAC-CÔTES DE B'X estate. MERLOT-led red 16' 18 19'. B'x white SAUV BL (DYA). Hommage à Denis Dubourdieu 100% PETIT VERDOT.

Reysson H-Méd ★★ 09' 10' 12 14 15 16 18 (19) CRU BOURGEOIS Supérieur (2020). Mainly MERLOT (88%), CAB FR, PETIT VERDOT. Consistent; rich, modern style.

Rieussec Saut ★★★★ 03' 04 05' 06 07 09' 10' 11' 13 14 15' 16' 17 18' 19 First Growth with substantial vyd in Fargues, owned by (LAFITE) Rothschild since 1984. Olivier Trégoat the technical director. Regularly powerful, opulent; a bargain. Second label: Carmes de Rieussec.

Rivière, De la Fron ★★ 09' 10 12 14 15 16' 18 19 Largest (65 ha), most impressive FRON property with C16 CH. MERLOT-led. Chinese-owned. Formerly big, tannic; now more refined. Visitor-friendly; B&B accomodation.

Roc de Cambes B'x ★★ 05 06 07 08 09 10' 12 15' 16' 17 18 19 20 Undisputed leader in CÔTES DE BOURG; savoury, opulent but pricey. Same stable and winemaking as TERTRE-RÔTEBOEUF. Also DOM de Cambes.

Rochemorin, De Pe-Lé ★★ (r) 10' 11 12 14 15 16 18' 19 (w) 16 17 18 19 Large property at Martillac owned by VIGNOBLES André Lurton (Jacques L now at helm). Fleshy, MERLOT-led (55%) red; aromatic white (100% SAUV BL). Fairly consistent quality.

Rol Valentin St-Ém ★★ 09' 10' 11 12 14 15' 16' 17 18 19 Vyd with two separate sites. Rich, modern, MERLOT-led (90%). DERENONCOURT consults.

Rouget Pom ★★ 05' 06 08 09' 10' 11 12 14 15 16' 17 18 19 Sizeable (for POM) go-ahead estate on n edge of plateau. Labruyère family owned; Edouard at helm. MICHEL ROLLAND consults. Rich, unctuous wines. Second label: Le Carillon de Rouget.

St-Georges St-Ém ★★ 06 08 09 10 11 14 15 16 18 (19) Vyd represents 25% of ST-GEORGES AC. MERLOT-led (80%). Gd wine sold direct to public. Second label: Puy St-Georges. Also Trilogie; old vines, 100% MERLOT.

St-Pierre St-Jul ★★★ 04 05' 06 07 08 09' 10' 11 12 14 15' 16' 17 18' 19' Tiny Fourth Growth to follow. CAB SAUV-led (75%). Stylish, consistent, classic. Second label: Esprit de St-Pierre.

Sales, De Pom ★★ 08 09 10' 12 15 16 17 18 19' Biggest vyd of POM (47.6 ha). New impetus since 2017. Ex-PETRUS winemaker consults. Honest, drinkable; can age. Second label: CH Chantalouette.

Sansonnet St-Ém ★★→★★★ 06 08 09' 10' 11 12 14 15 16' 17 18 19' Plateau-based GRAND CRU CLASSÉ. Modern but refreshing. Jean-Luc Thunevin consults. Second label: Envol de Sansonnet.

Saransot-Dupré List ★★ 06 09' 10' 11 12 15 16 18 (19) Recently promoted CRU BOURGEOIS Supérieur (2020). Fleshy, MERLOT-led with 24% CAB SAUV. Dry white B'x.

Sénéjac H-Méd ★★ 05' 06 08 09 10' 12 14 15 16' 18 19' S H-MÉD (Pian) cru. Consistent, well-balanced wines. Drink young or age. TALBOT same stable.

Over 90% of AC St-Jul owned by Classified Growths (1855).

Serre, La St-Ém ★★ 05 06 08 09' 10 12 14 15 16' 17 18' 19' 20 Small GRAND CRU CLASSÉ on plateau. J-P MOUEIX exclusivity. Fresh, stylish wines with fruit.

Sigalas-Rabaud Saut ★★★ 03 04 05 07' 09' 10' 11 13 14 15' 16 17' 18 19' Tiny First Growth. *V. fragrant and lovely*. Second label: Le Lieutenant de Sigalas. La Sémillante dry white. Also Le 5; no sulphur addition.

Siran Marg ★★→★★★ 05 06 08 09' 10' 12 14 15' 16' 17 18' 19' Unclassified MARG estate in Labarde. Owned by Miailhe family. Wines have substance, fragrance. Hubert de Boüard consults. Visitor-friendly. Second label: S de Siran.

Smith Haut Lafitte Pe-Lé ★★★★ (r) 04 05′ 06 07 08 09′ 10′ 11 12 13 14 15′ 16′ 17 18 19′ (w) 17 18 19′ Celebrated Classed Growth with spa hotel (Caudalie), regularly one of PE-LÉ stars. White is full, ripe, sappy; red precise, generous. Second label: Les Hauts de Smith. Also CAB SAUV-based Le Petit Haut Lafitte. Organic certification. New, unnamed vyd in Napa, US (2020).

Sociando-Mallet H-Méd ★★★ 00 04 05 06′ 07 08 09′ 10′ 11 12 14 15′ 16′ 18 19′ Large H-MÉD estate in St-Seurin-de-Cadourne. 2019 last vintage of founder Jean Gautreau (RIP). 54% MERLOT, 46% CABS SAUV/FR. Classed Growth quality. Wines for ageing. Second label: La Demoiselle de Sociando-Mallet.

Sours, De B'x ★★ Valid reputation for popular B'x rosé (DYA). Gd white; acceptable B'x red. Owned by Jack Ma of Alibaba fame.

Soutard St-Ém ★★★ 05 06 08 09 10 11 12 14 15 16′ 17 18′ 19′ 20 *Potentially excellent* GRAND CRU CLASSÉ on limestone plateau. Massive investment, making strides but still room for improvement. MERLOT-led (63%). Visitor-friendly. Second label: Petit Soutard. LARMANDE same stable.

Suduiraut Saut ★★★★ 01′ 02 04 05′ 06 07′ 09′ 10′ 11′ 13 14 15′ 16′ 17′ 18 19′ 20 One of v. best SAUT. SÉM-dominant (90%+); environmental certification. Luscious quality, v. consistent. Second labels: Castelnau de Suduiraut; Lions de Suduiraut (fruitier). Dry wines "S" and entry-level Le Blanc Sec.

Taillefer Pom ★★ 05′ 06 08 09′ 10 11 12 14 15 16 18′ 19 New generation at helm (MOUEIX family branch). MERLOT-led (75%). Sandier soils. Lighter, polished, refined.

Talbot St-Jul ★★★ 00′ 01 02 04 05′ 08 09′ 10′ 11 12 14 15 16 17 18 19 Substantial Fourth Growth in heart of AC ST-JUL. Wine rich, *consummately charming, reliable*. New winemaker from 2018 (ex-LA CONSEILLANTE). Second label: Connétable de Talbot. Approachable SAUV BL-based: Caillou Blanc.

Tertre, Du Marg ★★★ 04 05′ 06 08 09′ 10′ 11 12 14 15′ 16′ 17 18′ 19′ Fifth Growth isolated s of MARG, new owner 2021. Fragrant (20% CAB FR) fresh (5% PETIT VERDOT), fruity but structured wines. Visitor-friendly. Second label: Les Hauts du Tertre. Also Tertre Blanc VDF dry white CHARD/GROS MANSENG/VIOGNIER/SAUV BL.

Tertre-Rôteboeuf St-Ém ★★★★ 00′ 01 02 04 05′ 06′ 07 08 09′ 10′ 11 12 13 14′ 15′ 16′ 17 18 19 20 Tiny, unclassified, ST-ÉM côtes star; concentrated, exotic; can age. Work of François Mitjavile. Frightening prices. V.gd ROC DE CAMBES.

Thieuley B'x ★★ E-2-M supplier of consistent quality AC B'x (r/w); oak-aged CUVÉE Francis Courselle (r/w). Run by sisters Marie and Sylvie Courselle.

Tour-Blanche, La Saut ★★★ 02 04 05′ 06 07′ 08 09′ 10′ 11′ 13 14 15 16′ 17 18′ 19′ Excellent First Growth SAUT; rich, bold, powerful wines on sweeter end of scale. SÉM-dominant (83%). Belvedere with 360° view of AC. Second label: Les Charmilles de La Tour-Blanche.

Tour-Carnet, La H-Méd ★★★ 04 05′ 06 08 09′ 10′ 11 12 14 15 16′ 17 18′ 19′ Large H-MÉD Fourth Growth owned by Bernard Magrez (*see* FOMBRAUGE, PAPE-CLÉMENT). Concentrated, opulent wines. Second label: Les Pensées de La Tour Carnet. Also dry white B'x Blanc de La Tour Carnet. MICHEL ROLLAND consults.

Tour-de-By, La Méd ★★ 05 06 08 09 10 11 12 14 15′ 16′ 17 18 19′ Substantial family-run estate in n MÉD. Popular, sturdy, reliable, CAB SAUV-led (60%) wines; can age. Also rosé and special CUVÉE Héritage Marc Pagès.

Tour de Mons, La Marg ★★ 05′ 06 08 09′ 10 11 12 14 15′ 16′ 18′ 19 Recently promoted CRU BOURGEOIS Supérieur (2020). MERLOT-led (55%). Consistent, gd value.

Tour-du-Haut-Moulin H-Méd ★★ 05′ 06 08 09 10 11 14 15′ 16′ 17 18 (19) CRU BOURGEOIS (2020) in n H-MÉD. Intense, structured wines to age.

Tour-du-Pas-St-Georges St-Ém ★★ 08 09′ 10 11 12 14 15 16 18 (19) ST-GEORGES-ST-ÉM estate run by Delbeck family. Classic style. Second label: Le Sablier.

Tour Figeac, La St-Ém ★★ 05′ 06 08 09′ 10′ 11 12 14 15′ 16′ 17 18′ 19′ 20 GRAND CRU CLASSÉ in "graves" sector of ST-ÉM. Fine, floral. DERENONCOURT consults.

Tour Haut-Caussan Méd ★★ 10' 11 12 14 15 16' 17 18 19 Consistent, Courrian family-run property. 50/50 CAB SAUV/MERLOT. Value.

Tourneufeuille L de P ★★ 08 09 10' 11 12 14 15' 16 18 19 Reliable L DE P on clay and gravel soils. MERLOT-led. Round, fleshy wine.

Tour-St-Bonnet Méd ★★ 10' 12 14 15 16 17 19 MÉD cru at St-Christoly. MERLOT, CABS SAUV/FR, PETIT VERDOT, MALBEC. Reliable. Value.

Trois Croix, Les Fron ★★ 09 10 11 12 14 15 16' 17 18' 19' Léon family-owned property; Bertrand winemaker. Fine, balanced wines from consistent producer. Clay-limestone soils. MERLOT-led. Gd value.

Tronquoy-Lalande St-Est ★★★ 05 06 08 09' 10' 11 12 14 15' 16' 17 18' 19' 20 Same stable as MONTROSE; vyd in one block; much replanting. Consistent, dark, satisfying. Organic leaning. Second label: Tronquoy de Ste-Anne. A little B'X white.

Troplong-Mondot St-Ém ★★★ 05' 06 07 08 09 10 11 12 14 15' 16 17 18' 19' 20 PREMIER GRAND CRU CLASSÉ (B) on limestone plateau. Lots of investment since 2017; new winery, replanting. *Wines of power, depth*; major style change in 2017; more elegance, freshness (earlier picking, less new oak). Second label: Mondot.

Trotanoy Pom ★★★★ 00' 01 04' 05' 06 07 08 09' 10' 11 12 13 14 15' 16' 17 18' 19' 20 One of jewels in J-P MOUEIX crown. 90% MERLOT, 10% CAB FR on clay and gravel soils. Dense, powerful, long ageing.

Trottevieille St-Ém ★★★ 05' 06 07 08' 09' 10' 11 12 14 15 16' 17 18' 19' PREMIER GRAND CRU CLASSÉ (B) owned by BORIE-MANOUX. Greater consistency; wines long, fresh, structured. Lots of CAB FR (50%) incl some pre-phylloxera vines. Second label: La Vieille Dame de Trottevieille.

Valandraud St-Ém r ★★★★ 00' 01' 04 05' 06 08 09' 10 11 12 13 14 15' 16' 17 18 19' PREMIER GRAND CRU CLASSÉ (B) in St-Etienne-de-Lisse. Garage wonder turned First Growth. Formerly super-concentrated; now rich, dense, balanced. Also Virginie de Valandraud and Valandraud Blanc (SAUV BL/Sauv Gr).

Vieille Cure, La Fron ★★ 09' 10' 11 12 13 14 15 16' 17 18' 19' Leading FRON estate; appetizing wines. Value. Jérôme Pignard owner from 2018.

Vieux-Château-Certan Pom ★★★★01' 02 04 05' 06 07 08 09' 10' 11' 12 13 14 15' 16' 17 18' 19' 20 Different in style to neighbour PETRUS; *elegance, harmony, fragrance*. Plenty of old-vine CABS FR/SAUV (30%) one of reasons. Great consistency; long-ageing; a star. Alexandre Thienpont and son Guillaume at helm.

Vieux Ch St-André St-Ém ★★ 09' 10 11 12 14 15' 16' 18 (19) Small MERLOT-based vyd in MONTAGNE-ST-ÉM. Jean-François Berrouet winemaker. *Gd value.*

Villegeorge, De H-Méd ★★ 09' 10 12 14 15 16 18 19 Tiny s H-MÉD owned by Marie-Laure Lurton. CAB SAUV-led (63%). Light but elegant wines.

Vray Croix de Gay Pom ★★★ 05' 06 08 09' 10 11 12 14 15 16' 17 18' (19) Tiny vyd in best part of POM. More finesse of late. Organic certification; bio practices. Owner Suravenir (CALON-SÉGUR). Pénélope Godefroy winemaker.

Yquem Saut ★★★★00 01' 02 03' 04 05' 06' 07 08 09' 10' 11' 13' 14 15' 16' 17' 18' King of sweet, *liquoreux*, wines. Strong, intense, luscious; kept 3 yrs in barrel. Most vintages improve for 15 yrs+, some live 100 yrs+ in transcendent splendour. 100 ha in production (75% SÉM/25% SAUV BL). No Yquem made 51, 52, 64, 72, 74, 92, 2012. Second label "Sauternes" sold uniquely at property. Makes small amount (800 cases/yr) of off-dry, Sauv Bl (75%), Sém (25%) "Y" (pronounced "ygrec").

Baby Yquem

For yrs YQUEM refused the notion of a second label. Now one is available and it's called (drum roll) "SAUTERNES". Employees have been able to buy this earlier drinking CUVÉE since 2014. Each vintage has a number: 2014 is labelled Sauternes 1, 2015 is Sauternes 2, and so on. It's €60/bottle, but only available at the property. Don't forget your shopping bag.

Italy

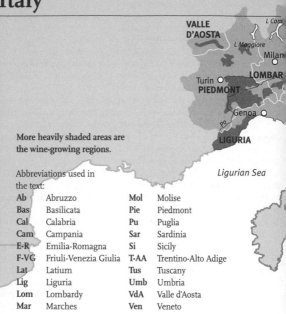

VALLE D'AOSTA

L Com

L Maggiore

Milan

LOMBAR

Turin

PIEDMONT

Genoa

Po

LIGURIA

More heavily shaded areas are the wine-growing regions.

Ligurian Sea

Abbreviations used in the text:

Ab	Abruzzo	**Mol**	Molise
Bas	Basilicata	**Pie**	Piedmont
Cal	Calabria	**Pu**	Puglia
Cam	Campania	**Sar**	Sardinia
E-R	Emilia-Romagna	**Si**	Sicily
F-VG	Friuli-Venezia Giulia	**T-AA**	Trentino-Alto Adige
Lat	Latium	**Tus**	Tuscany
Lig	Liguria	**Umb**	Umbria
Lom	Lombardy	**VdA**	Valle d'Aosta
Mar	Marches	**Ven**	Veneto

In Italy, less is definitely not more. We're talking here not about weight or power – here, it's all about nuance and balance – but about grapes and, yes, confusion. Italy boasts over 550 officially recognized wine grapes. Even Italians get confused. There's a whole slew of similarly named green-, black-, red- and white-monickered varieties all over the country. You can see why: a grape has a bit of a green ("verde") tinge to it? Fine, let's call it Verdello. Or maybe Verduzzo. Or Verduschia, or Verdicchio, or Verdone, or Verdea. Wait a minute, this grape here has a slightly black ("nero") tinge: Okay, let's call it Nerello. That one over there; that will be a Nero. This smaller one looks like a Neretto to me; that other one, a Ner. But wait a minute: my Neretto is different to yours. So my grape is a Neretto di Bairo, yours is a Neretto di San Giorgio. And my Nerello is not yours, because it's from the plain of Mascali and lacks your foliage: so we'll call yours Nerello Cappuccio (from cappuccio, or "cowl", of leaves), and mine will be, logically enough, Nerello Mascalese...

And so it goes. The result is an array of wines of wildly diverse colours, aromas and flavours. Add blends, plus variations from myriad soils, exposures, altitudes, climates, clones and individual winemaking styles – and you realize Italy does exactly the same with wine as it does with its 500 olive cultivars, 400+ cheeses and 100+ (officially codified) pasta shapes. Variety is a way of life here. Be confused, by all means (and use the following pages to be less confused). And enjoy it.

Recent vintages

Amarone, Veneto & Friuli

2020 Veneto: balanced, gd quality, quantity. Friuli: rainy June, uneven, better for whites.

2019 Low quantity. Veneto: gd for Amarone, Soave. Friuli: fair quality.

2018 Optimal weather conditions. Gd for quantity, quality, esp fresh whites.

2017 V. difficult (non-stop rain); weedy Amarones a risk, green reds in general.

2016 V. hot summer; round but low-acid, big reds, chunky whites.

2015 Quantity gd, quality better; v.gd Friuli reds. Fresher than initially thought.

2014 Not memorable for Amarone, better Soave and Friuli whites, Valpolicellas v.gd.

2013 Gd whites. Reds, esp passito, suffered Oct/Nov rain/hail.

Campania & Basilicata

2020 Similar to 19. Classic, balanced but lower quantity. Gd for reds, whites.
2019 Classic, balanced vintage. Best for Aglianico, gd for whites.
2018 Rainy, but whites fresh, lively; sleek reds (Aglianico best).
2017 Low-volume yr of reds plagued by gritty tannins. Whites flat; Greco best.
2016 Cold spring delayed flowering, hot summer allowed catch-up. Fiano best.
2015 Hot, dry early summer = ripe but at times tough reds, broad whites; drink.
2014 Rain; spotty quality. Avoid green Aglianicos, Piedirossos. Whites pretty gd.
2013 Classic perfumed fresh whites, thinner late-picked Aglianicos.

Marches & Abruzzo

2020 Uneven, but quality peaks; rainy June, fresh weather. Gd for late-ripening
      grapes. Lower yield.
2019 Difficult yr. Rainy, cold spring. Low quantity, medium quality.
2018 Patchy spring. More balanced than 17. V. high volume, gd quality (r/w).
2017 Best to forget: hot, droughty. Reds gritty, whites overripe. Low volume.
2016 Rain, cold, lack of sun = difficult yr. Lemony, figgy Pecorino probably best.
2015 Hot summer, whites fresher than expected (esp Trebbiano), reds ripe.
2014 Marches: sleek reds, classic whites. Abruzzo: best for Pecorino.
2013 Whites classically mineral and age-worthy; reds refined, classic, not lean.

Piedmont

2020 Classic. Slightly less balanced than 19, but elegant. Better for Barbera
      than Nebbiolo.
2019 Classic vintage, more balanced than 18. Lower quantity but higher quality.
2018 Despite difficult spring, potentially classic Barolo, Barbaresco.
2017 Among earliest harvests in living memory. Can lack depth.
2016 Potentially top vintage; classic, perfumed, age-worthy Barolo/Barbaresco.
2015 Outstanding Barolo/Barbaresco. Should be long-lived. Barbera, Dolcetto
      gd; Grignolino less so.
2014 Rain: later-picked grapes thrived, early ones (eg. Dolcetto) didn't.
      Barbaresco (not Barolo) best.
2013 Bright, crisp (r/w), improving with time; classic vintage, steely, deep.
Earlier fine vintages: 10 08 06 04 01 00 99 98 97 96 95 90. Vintages to keep:
10 06 01 99 96. Vintages to drink up: 11 09 03 00 97 90 88.

Tuscany

2020 V.gd vintage, but complicated. Less power and alcohol than 19, elegant.
2019 Maybe one of best since 2000. Classic, balanced. Gd quality, quantity.
2018 Reds gd: of steely personality, age-worthiness.
2017 Hot, v. difficult vintage. Better in Chianti Classico than coastal Maremma.
2016 Hot summer, fresh autumn; success across the region. Small crop.
2015 Rich flavourful reds of gd ripeness; some soft.
2014 Quantity up, quality patchy, buyer beware.
2013 Uneven ripening. Not great yr, but some peaks.
Earlier fine vintages: 11 10 08 07 06 04 01 99 97 95 90. Vintages to keep: 10
01 99. Vintages to drink up: 07 06 04 03 00 97 95 90.

Abrigo, Orlando Pie ★★★ Some of most mineral, steely, refined BARBARESCOS. Top:
      Montersino, Meruzzano and new Barbaresco III (100% NEBBIOLO rosé).
Accornero Pie ★★★ Some of Italy's best medium-bodied reds. GRIGNOLINO sings in
      Bricco del Bosco (steel-aged) and Bricco del Bosco Vigne Vecchie (oak-aged).
      Also v.gd BARBERA Cima.

ITALY

Adriano, Marco e Vittorio Pie ★★★ High quality, low prices, BARBARESCO full of early appeal. Top: Basarin, Sanadaive.

Aglianico del Taburno Cam ★→★★★ DOCG Around Benevento. Spicier notes (leather, tobacco) and herbs, higher acidity than other AGLIANICOS. Gd: CANTINA del Taburno, Fontanavecchia, La Rivolta.

Aglianico del Vulture Bas ★→★★★ DOC(G) 11 12 13 15 16 18 (19) DOC after 1 yr, SUPERIORE after 3 yrs, RISERVA after 5. From slopes of extinct volcano Monte Vulture. More floral (violet), dark fruits (plum), smoke, spice than other AGLIANICOS. Top: ELENA FUCCI, GRIFALCO. Also gd: CANTINA di Venosa, CANTINE DEL NOTAIO, D'Angelo, Mastrodomenico, PATERNOSTER, Re Manfredi.

Alba Pie Truffles, hazelnuts and PIE's, if not Italy's, most prestigious wines: BARBERA D'ALBA, BARBARESCO, BAROLO, DOGLIANI (DOLCETTO), LANGHE, NEBBIOLO D'ALBA, ROERO.

Albana di Romagna E-R ★→★★★ DYA. Italy's 1st white DOCG, justified only by sweet PASSITO; dry and sparkling often unremarkable. Best: *Fattori Zerbina Passito*, Giovanna Madonia, PODERE Morini (Cuore Matto PASSITO), Tre Monti.

Alessandria, Fratelli Pie ★★★ Since 1870 top BAROLO producer in VERDUNO. Best crus: Monvigliero, San Lorenzo. V.gd Verduno Speziale.

Allegrini Ven ★★ Popular VALPOLICELLA producer. Elegant AMARONE best. Owner of POGGIO al Tesoro in BOLGHERI, Poggio San Polo in MONTALCINO, TUS.

Almondo, Giovanni Pie ★★★ →★★★★ Top ROERO estate. Best: Roero ARNEIS Bricco delle Ciliegie, Rive del Bricco; outstanding Freisa too; V.gd Roero Bric Valdiana (r).

Alta Langa Pie ★★→★★★ DOCG 1st METODO CLASSICO made in Italy, since mid-C19 in "underground cathedrals". Vintage only, and simply PINOT N, CHARD. Best: COCCHI-BAVA, Contratto, Enrico Serafino, ETTORE GERMANO, Ferdinando Principiano, FONTANAFREDDA, GANCIA, RIZZI.

Altare, Elio Pie ★★★ Now run by Silvia, Elio's daughter. Try BAROLOS: Arborina, Cannubi, Cerretta VIGNA Bricco, Unoperuno (selection from Arborina); also gd LANGHE NEBBIOLO, BARBERA D'ALBA.

Alto Adige (Sudtirol) T-AA DOC Mountainous region with Bolzano its chief city (Austrian until 1919); arguably best Italian whites today but also underrated reds. Germanic vines dominate. GEWURZ, KERNER, SYLVANER, but PINOT GRIGIO too. RIES and GRÜNER V hopelessly overrated; probably world's best PINOT BIANCO. PINOT N often overoaked; *Lagrein* in gd yrs.

Alto Piemonte Pie Cradle of PIE quality in C19 (40,000 ha vyds). Acidic soil, exposure, climate and altitude diversity, ideal for many different NEBBIOLO expressions (here called Spanna). Main DOC(G): BOCA, BRAMATERRA, Colline Novaresi, Coste della Sesia, FARA, GATTINARA, GHEMME, LESSONA, Sizzano, Valli Ossolane. Many outstanding wines. Actually, rarely 100% Nebbiolo: small additions of Croatina, Uva Rara, Vespolina common.

Ama, Castello di Tus ★★★★ If CHIANTI CLASSICO today is well reputed, much credit must go to this top Gaiole estate, among 1st to produce single-vyd Chianti Classico and push for quality in 80s. Gran Selezione VIGNETO Bellavista is best; La Casuccia close second. V.gd San Lorenzo. MERLOT L'Apparita one of Italy's three best.

Amarone della Valpolicella Ven ★★→★★★★ DOCG 10 11' 13 15 16 (17) (18) CLASSICO area (from historic zone), Val d'Illasi, Valpantena (from extended zone) can make unique world-class reds from raisined grapes. Alas, many less than what they should be, despite hype. Choose carefully. (*See also* VALPOLICELLA, and box, p.151.)

Ambra, D' Cam ★★★ On ISCHIA; fosters rare local native grapes. Best: single-vyd Frassitelli (w, 100% Biancolella). V.gd Forastera (w) and reds Dedicato a Mario d'Ambra, La VIGNA dei Mille Anni.

Antinori, Marchesi L&P Tus ★★→★★★★ Since 1385, this family has been protagonist of C20 Italian wine renaissance. Top CHIANTI CLASSICO (TENUTE Marchese Antinori and *Badia a Passignano*), Cervaro (Umb *Castello della Sala*), the two excellent SUPER TUSCANS (TIGNANELLO, SOLAIA) and Prunotto (PIE BAROLO Bussia). Also MONTALCINO (Pian delle Vigne), MONTEPULCIANO (La Braccesca), PUG (Tormaresca), TUS MAREMMA (Fattoria Aldobrandesca).

Antoniolo Pie ★★★ Age-worthy benchmark GATTINARA. Outstanding RISERVAS Osso San, San Francesco, Le Castelle.

Argiano, Castello di Tus ★★★ Distinctive, refined yet flavourful BRUNELLOS from Sesti family estate. Classico Brunello and RISERVA Phenomena equally gd, if different.

Argiolas Sar ★★→★★★ Top producer, native island grapes. Outstanding crus *Turriga* (★★★), Iselis Monica, Iselis Nasco, *Vermentino* di Sardegna (Meri) and top sweet Angialis (mainly local Nasco grape). V.gd Bovale Korem, CANNONAU RISERVA Senes, CARIGNANO DEL SULCIS Is Solinas.

Asti Pie ★→★★ NV Sparkler from MOSCATO Bianco grapes, inferior to MOSCATO D'ASTI, not really worth its DOCG. Try Bera, Cascina Fonda, Caudrina, Vignaioli di Santo Stefano. Now dry version, Asti Secco.

Avignonesi Tus ★★★ Large bio estate. *Italy's best Vin Santo*. Top is VINO NOBILE single-vyd Poggetto di Sopra and Grandi Annate, but MERLOT Desiderio, 50&50 (Merlot/SANGIOVESE), CHARD Il Marzocco creditable internationals.

Azelia Pie ★★★ Distinctive, elegant BAROLOS from Luigi Scavino and son Lorenzo. Some of best crus. Top: Bricco Fiasco, San Rocco and 1st edition of Cerretta.

Azienda agricola / agraria Estate (large or small) making wine from its own grapes.

Badia a Coltibuono Tus ★★★ One of top CHIANTI CLASSICO producers; every wine worth buying: great terroirs spell non-stop success. V.gd SANGIOVETO. Organic certified.

Banfi (Castello or Villa) Tus ★→★★★ Giant of MONTALCINO, at extreme s of zone, but top, limited-production wine POGGIO all'Oro is a great BRUNELLO. V.gd Moscadello.

Barbaresco Pie ★★→★★★★ DOCG 10 11 12 13 14 15 16 18 (19) Often better than BAROLO, Barbaresco's lesser reputation is undeserved. When spot on, the gracefulness, age-worthiness and perfumed intensity is like that of no other wine in Italy – the world, really. Min 26 mths ageing, 9 mths in wood; at 4 yrs becomes RISERVA. (For top crus and producers *see* box, right.)

Barbera d'Alba Pie DOC Unique, luscious, sultry BARBERA, quite different from D'ASTI's more nervy, higher-acid version. AZELIA (Punta), BREZZA, CAVALLOTTO (Cuculo), CONTERNO FANTINO (Vignota), GERMANO ETTORE (della Madre), GIACOMO CONTERNO (Cascina Francia, Ceretta), SOTTIMANO, VIETTI (Scarrone) make benchmarks. COGNO's Pre-Phylloxera is *hors classe*.

Barbera d'Asti Pie Huge DOCG, encompassing v. different soil and climatic characteristics. Wines vary, but characterized by high acidity and fruity notes. SUPERIORE: higher quality (but often overoaked). Nizza (since 2014; previously, Superiore Nizza) is best: 100% BARBERA only from best sites and needs time. Gd: Bava (Pianoalto), BRAIDA, Cascina Castlet, Dacapo, Marchesi di Gresi (Monte Colombo), SCARPA (La Bogliona), Spertino, TENUTA Olim Bauda, *Vietti* (La Crena).

Barbera del Monferrato Superiore Pie DOCG From soils rich in limestone, full-bodied BARBERA with sharpish tannins, gd acidity. Top: Accornero (Bricco Battista and Cima), Castello di Uviglie, Iuli (Barabba, Rossore).

Barberani Umb ★★→★★★ Organic estate on slopes of Lago di Corbara, gd to excellent ORVIETO. Cru Luigi e Giovanna is star, also Polvento, Calcaia (noble rot).

Bardolino Ven DOC(G) DYA Light-bodied fresh red made with VALPOLICELLA's typical grapes; hit with tourists on Lake Garda. Ill-advised plantings of CAB SAUV in order to make bigger wines a tragic idea. Best today are the rosés, called CHIARETTO in this neck of the Italian woods. Look for Cavalchina, *Guerrieri Rizzardi*, Zeni.

Barolo Pie DOCG 06 07 08 09 10' 11 12 13 15 16' 17 (18) "King of wines and wine of kings" 100% NEBBIOLO. 2000 ha zone. Must age 38 mths before release (5 yrs for RISERVA), of which 18 mths in wood. Best are age-worthy, able to join power and elegance, with alluring floral scent and sour red-cherry flavour. Traditionally blend of vyds from different communes, but now most is single-vyd. The concept of "cru" is replaced (in Barolo and Barbaresco at least) by subzones known officially as MGA (Menzioni Geografiche Aggiuntive). Currently Barolo has 11 village mentions and 170(!) additional geographical mentions. Often underrated: Village MGA ("Barolo del Comune di ...") best way to understand different Barolo terroirs. Best: "di Barolo" (Virna), "di Grinzane" (Canonica), "di La Morra" (Ciabot Berton), "di Serralunga" (Ettore Germano, RIVETTO). (For top crus and producers see box, p.128.)

Bartoli, Marco De Si ★★★★ One of best estates in all Italy. Marco spent life promoting "real" MARSALA and his must be tried. Top: 20-yr-old Ventennale, VECCHIO SAMPERI. Delicious table wines (eg. GRILLO Vignaverde and Grappoli del Grillo, ZIBIBBO Pietranera and Pignatello), outstanding sweet Zibibbo di PANTELLERIA **Bukkuram**.

Bastianich F-VG ★★→★★★ FRIULANO Plus one of Italy's 30 best whites; Vespa Bianco not far behind. Reds (Calabrone, REFOSCO del Peduncolo Rosso RISERVA Solo, Vespa Rosso) can be weedy and tough in poor yrs (air-drying unripe grapes is never a gd idea), but in gd vintages can be memorable.

Belisario Mar ★★→★★★ Quality co-op, gd quality/price. Largest producer of VERDICCHIO DI MATELICA. Top: RISERVA Cambrugiano.

Benanti Si ★★★ Benanti family turned world on to ETNA. Bianco SUPERIORE **Pietramarina** one of Italy's best whites. Top: Etna (r) Rovittello Particella 341, Serra della Contessa, "Selezione Contrade" (Rinazzo, Cavaliere, Monte Serra).

Berlucchi, Guido Lom ★★ Makes millions of bottles of METODO CLASSICO fizz. FRANCIACORTA Brut Cuvée Imperiale is flagship. V.gd: Nature Dosaggio Zero 61.

Bersano Pie ★★→★★★ Large volume but gd quality. V.gd: BARBERA D'ASTI, GRIGNOLINO and Ruchè, all inexpensive, delightful.

Bertani Doms Tus ★★→★★★ Long-est producer of VALPOLICELLA, SOAVE. Also owns: Fazi Battaglia (Mar), Puiatti (F-VG), San Leonino (CHIANTI CLASSICO), Trerose (MONTEPULCIANO), Val di Suga (MONTALCINO).

Biondi-Santi Tus ★★★★ Invented BRUNELLO. Top: Brunellos and esp RISERVAS high in acid, tannin requiring decades to develop fully. Recently trying more user-friendly style.

Top Barbaresco by MGA

BARBARESCO has four main communes; four distinct styles – **Barbaresco:** most complete, balanced. Growers incl Asili (BRUNO Giacosa, CA' DEL BAIO, CERETTO, PRODUTTORI DEL BARBARESCO), Martinenga (MARCHESI DI GRESY), Montefico (Produttori del B, ROAGNA), Montestefano (Giordano Luigi, Produttori del B, Rivella Serafino), Ovello (CANTINA DEL PINO, ROCCA ALBINO), Pajè (Roagna), Pora (Ca' del Baio, Produttori del B), Rabaja (Bruno Giacosa, BRUNO ROCCA, CASTELLO DI VERDUNO, GIUSEPPE CORTESE, Produttori del B), Rio Sordo (Cascina Bruciata, Cascina delle Rose, Produttori del B), Roncaglie (PODERI COLLA). **Neive:** most powerful, fleshiest. Albesani (Cantina del Pino, Castello di Neive), Basarin (ADRIANO MARCO E VITTORIO, Giacosa Fratelli, Negro Angelo, PAITIN, SOTTIMANO), Bordini (La Spinetta), Currá (Bruno Rocca, Sottimano), Gallina (Castello di Neive, La Spinetta, Lequio Ugo, ODDERO), Serraboella (Cigliuti), Starderi (La Spinetta). **San Rocco Seno d'Elvio:** readiest to drink, soft. Rocche Massalupo (Lano, TENUTA Barac), Sanadaive (Adriano Marco e Vittorio). **Treiso:** freshest, most refined. Bernardot (Ceretto), Bricco di Treiso (PIO CESARE), Marcarini (Ca' del Baio), Montersino (ORLANDO ABRIGO, ROCCA ALBINO), Nervo (RIZZI), Pajoré (Rizzi, Sottimano), Rombone (Fiorenzo Nada, Luigi Oddero).

Top Barolos by MGA

Here are a few top crus and their best producers: **Bricco Boschis** (Castiglione Falletto) CAVALLOTTO (RISERVA VIGNA San Giuseppe); **Bricco delle Viole** (BAROLO) GD VAJRA; **Bricco Rocche** (Castiglione Falletto) CERETTO; **Briccolina** (Serralunga) RIVETTO; **Brunate** (La Morra, Barolo) Ceretto, GIUSEPPE RINALDI, ODDERO, VIETTI; **Bussia** (Monforte) ALDO CONTERNO (Gran Bussia e Romirasco), FENOCCHIO GIACOMO (Riserva 90 Dì), Oddero (Bussia Vigna Mondoca), PODERI COLLA (Dardi Le Rose); **Cannubi** (Barolo) BREZZA, EINAUDI, FENOCCHIO GIACOMO, LUCIANO SANDRONE, PIRA E FIGLI – CHIARA BOSCHIS, Virna; **Cerequio** (La Morra, Barolo) BOROLI, ROBERTO VOERZIO; **Falletto** (Serralunga) BRUNO GIACOSA (Riserva Vigna Le Rocche); **Francia** (Serralunga) GIACOMO CONTERNO (Barolo Cascina Francia and Monfortino); **Ginestra** (Monforte) CONTERNO FANTINO (Sorì Ginestra and Vigna del Gris), DOMENICO CLERICO (Ciabot Mentin); **Lazzarito** (Serralunga) ETTORE Germano (Riserva), Vietti; **Monprivato** (Castiglione Falletto) GIUSEPPE MASCARELLO (Mauro); **Monvigliero** (VERDUNO) CASTELLO DI VERDUNO, FRATELLI ALESSANDRIA, GB BURLOTTO, PAOLO SCAVINO; **Mosconi** (Monforte) Conterno Fantino, Domenico Clerico, Pira e Figli – Chiara Boschis, PIO CESARE; **Ornato** (Serralunga) Pio Cesare; **Ravera** (Novello) ELVIO COGNO (Bricco Pernice), GD Vajra, Vietti; **Rocche dell'Annunziata** (La Morra) PAOLO SCAVINO (Riserva), RATTI, ROBERTO VOERZIO, Rocche Costamagna, TREDIBERRI; **Rocche di Castiglione** (Castiglione Falletto) BROVIA, Oddero, Vietti; **Vigna Rionda** (Serralunga) Ettore Germano, MASSOLINO VR, Oddero; **Villero** (Castiglione Falletto) Boroli, Brovia, Fenocchio Giacomo, Giuseppe Mascarello. And the Barolo of Bartolo Mascarello blends together Cannubi San Lorenzo, Ruè and Rocche dell'Annunziata. A sommelier's delight.

Bisol Ven ★★★ Owned by FERRARI's Lunelli family; quality leader in PROSECCO. Top: CARTIZZE and Relio Rive di Guia, but Crede Brut is one of Italy's best buys.

Boca Pie DOC *See* ALTO PIEMONTE. Potentially among greatest reds. NEBBIOLO (70–90%), incl up to 30% Uva Rara and/or Vespolina. Volcanic soil. Needs long ageing. Best: *Le Piane*. Gd: Carlone Davide, Castello Conti.

Bolgheri Tus DOC Mid-Maremma, on w coast, cradle of many expensive SUPER TUSCANS, mainly French variety-based. Big name and excellent quality: ALLEGRINI (POGGIO al Tesoro), ANTINORI (Guado al Tasso), GAJA (CÀ MARCANDA), Grattamacco. Le Macchiole, SAN GUIDO (SASSICAIA, the original Super Tuscan) and ORNELLAIA (FRESCOBALDI) are best (incl iconic 100% MERLOT Masseto.)

Bolla Ven ★★ *See* GIV.

Borgo del Tiglio F-VG ★★★→★★★★ Nicola Manferrari is one of Italy's top white winemakers. COLLIO FRIULANO RONCO della Chiesa, MALVASIA Selezione, Rosso della Centa, Studio di Bianco esp impressive.

Borgogno, Virna Pie ★★★ Family estate run by Virna B and sister Ivana. Great value BAROLO from famous crus: Cannubi and Sarmassa. V.gd RISERVA, Barolo Noi.

Boroli Pie ★★★ Achille now runs this winery, totally devoted to BAROLOS. Best: Villero, Brunella (monopole) and Cerequio.

Boscarelli, Poderi Tus ★★★ Small estate with reliably high standard VINO NOBILE DI MONTEPULCIANO. Best: Costa Grande (100% SANGIOVESE single vyd), Nocio dei Boscarelli, RISERVA Sotto Casa.

Bosco, Tenute Si ★★★ Small ETNA estate owned by Sofia B, high quality. Best: ETNA Rosso VIGNA Vico Prephylloxera. V.gd Piano dei Daini (r/w/rosé).

Botte Big barrel, anything from 6–250 hl, usually between 20–50, traditionally of Slavonian but increasingly of French oak. To traditionalists, ideal vessel for ageing wines without adding too much oak smell/taste.

Brachetto d'Acqui / Acqui Pie DYA. Pink version of ASTI made with Brachetto grape; similarly undeserving for most part of its DOCG status.

Braida Pie ★★★ If BARBERA D'ASTI is known today, it's thanks to the Bologna family, world ambassadors for this wine. Top: Bricco dell'Uccellone, Bricco della Bigotta and Ai Suma. V.gd Monella, Montebruna. GRIGNOLINO d'Asti Limonte one of Italy's five best.

Bramaterra Pie DOC *See* ALTO PIEMONTE. Gd: Antoniotti Odilio.

Brezza Pie ★★★ Organic certified. Certainty for those who love traditional BAROLOS. Great value, from famous crus incl Cannubi, Castellero, Sarmassa (esp RISERVA VIGNA Bricco). V.gd BARBERA D'ALBA SUPERIORE, LANGHE NEBBIOLO, Freisa (outstanding).

Brigaldara Ven ★★★ Elegant but powerful benchmark AMARONE from estate of Stefano Cesari.Top: Case Vecie. Try charming Dindarella Rosato, when made.

Brolio, Castello di Tus ★★→★★★ Since 1141 run by RICASOLI family; historic estate is largest and oldest of CHIANTI CLASSICO. Outstanding Gran Selezione Castello di Brolio, Colledilà, Ceniprimo and Roncicone. V.gd also Roncicone (MERLOT).

Brovia Pie ★★★→★★★★ Since 1863, classic BAROLOS in Castiglione Falletto. Organic certified. Top: Ca' Mia, Garblét Sue, Rocche, Villero.

Brunelli, Gianni Tus ★★★ Lovely refined user-friendly BRUNELLOS (top RISERVA) and Rossos from two sites: Le Chiuse di Sotto n of MONTALCINO and Podernovone to s, with views of Monte Amiata.

Brunello di Montalcino Tus 07 09 10' 12 13 15' 16 (17) DOCG World-famous, but quality all over the shop. When gd, memorable and ageless, archetypal SANGIOVESE. Problems derive mostly from greedily enlarged production area (a ridiculous 2000 ha+), much less than ideal for fickle Sangiovese and world class wines. Recent push to turn wine into a blend has been successfully stopped (thus far, at least). (For top producers *see* box, p.130.)

Bucci Mar ★★★→★★★★ Villa Bucci RISERVA one of Italy's 20 best whites. All wines quasi-Burgundian, especially complex VERDICCHIOS, slow to mature but all age splendidly. V.gd red Pongelli.

Burlotto, Commendatore GB Pie ★★★→★★★★ Fabio Alessandria maintains his ancestor Commander GB Burlotto's (among 1st to make/bottle BAROLO in 1880) high quality and focus. BAROLO Monvigliero and superlative Freisa best. Also outstanding: BAROLOS Acclivi and Cannubi, VERDUNO Pelaverga.

Bussola, Tommaso Ven ★★★★ Self-taught maker of some of the great AMARONES, RECIOTOS, RIPASSOS of our time. The great Bepi QUINTARELLI steered him; he steers his two sons. Top TB selection.

Ca' dei Frati Lom ★★★ Foremost quality estate of revitalized DOC LUGANA, I Frati a fine example at entry level; *Brolettino* a superior cru.

Ca' del Baio Pie ★★★ Family estate; best-value producer in BARBARESCO. Outstanding Asili (RISERVA too) and Pora. V.gd Autinbej, LANGHE RIES, Vallegrande.

Ca' del Bosco Lom ★★★★ Arguably Italy's best METODO CLASSICO sparkling, famous FRANCIACORTA estate owned by Zanella family and Santa Margherita Group. Outstanding and unforgettable Dosage Zèro Annamaria Clementi RISERVA (rosé too). Great Dosage Zero and Dosage Zero Noir Vintage Collection practically as gd; also excellent B'x-style Maurizio Zanella (r), PINOT N, CHARD.

Caiarossa Tus ★★★ Dutch-owned (Ch Giscours; *see* B'x) estate, n of BOLGHERI. Excellent Caiarossa Rosso plus reds Aria, Pergolaia.

Calcagno Si ★★★→★★★★ Lilliputian size and Brobdingnagian quality from ETNA family estate. Outstanding mineral NERELLO MASCALESE reds. Top (r) Feudo di Mezzo and Arcurìa. V.gd Ginestra (w), Nireddu (r), Romice delle Sciare (rosé).

Calì, Paolo Si ★★★ Passionate Paolo Calì makes numerous wines highly typical of Vittoria's terroir. Top: CERASUOLO DI VITTORIA Forfice and Frappato. V.gd Manene (r), GRILLO Blues (w) and Mood (rosé/sp).

> **Best of Brunello**
> Any of the below provide a satisfying BRUNELLO DI MONTALCINO, but we
> have put a star next to the ones we think are best: Altesino ★, Baricci ★,
> BIONDI-SANTI ★, Campogiovanni, Canalicchio di Sopra ★, Canalicchio
> di Sotto, Caparzo, Casanova di Neri ★, CASE BASSE ★, Castelgiocondo,
> CASTELLO DI ARGIANO ★, CASTIGLION DEL BOSCO, Ciacci Piccolomini, COL D'ORCIA
> ★, Collemattoni ★, Colombini, Costanti ★, Cupano ★, Donatella Cinelli,
> Eredi, Fossacolle, Franco Pacenti ★, FULIGNI ★, GIANNI BRUNELLI ★, Giodo,
> Il Colle, Il Marroneto ★, Il Paradiso di Manfredi, La Gerla, La Magia, La
> Poderina ★, Le Potazzine ★, Le Ragnaie ★, Le Ripi, LISINI ★, Mastrojanni ★,
> PIAN DELL'ORINO ★, Piancornello, Pieri Agostina, Pieve di Santa Restituta,
> POGGIO ANTICO, POGGIO DI SOTTO ★, San Filippo, Salvioni ★, Sesta di Sopra,
> Silvio Nardi, Siro Pacenti, Stella di Campalto ★, TENUTA IL POGGIONE ★,
> TENUTA di Sesta, Uccelliera, Val di Suga.

Caluso / Erbaluce di Caluso Pie ★→★★★ DOCG Can be still, sparkling (dr) and sweet (Caluso PASSITO). Top: Giacometto, Cieck (Misobolo), Favaro (Le Chiusure), Ferrando (Cariola). V.gd: Orsolani, Salvetti (Brut).

Ca' Marcanda Tus ★★★★ BOLGHERI estate of GAJA. In order of price (high, higher, highest): Promis, Magari, Ca' Marcanda. Grapes mainly international.

Campania Some of Italy's greatest and most age-worthy whites, terroir-driven and full of character. Campania's reds are unfortunately less consistent due to the combination of overripe grapes and too much oak, with some remarkable exceptions. Few international varieties cloud native grapes panorama. FIANO DI AVELLINO may well be Italy's best white zone, TAURASI making better and better reds. Gd producers: BENITO FERRARA, Caggiano, CANTINE Lonardo, COLLI DI LAPIO, D'AMBRA, De Angelis, Fattoria La Rivolta, *Feudi di San Gregorio*, Galardi, Guastaferro, La Sibilla, Luigi Maffini, Luigi Tecce, MARISA CUOMO, *Mastroberardino*, Molettieri, Nicola Mazzella, Perillo, Pierlingeri, Pietracupa, QUINTODECIMO, Reale, Rocca del Principe, Sarno 1860, Terredora, Vadiaperti. MONTEVETRANO makes world-class international mostly CAB wine.

Canalicchio di Sopra Tus ★★★ Top-ten BRUNELLO estate, with pretty B&B nearby. Owner Francesco Ripaccioli keen observer of terroir and MONTALCINO typicity; RISERVA usually spectacular.

Cantina A cellar, winery or even a wine bar.

Capezzana, Tenuta di Tus ★★★ Certified organic production from noble Bonacossi family that made CARMIGNANO's reputation. Now run by founder's children. Excellent Carmignano (Villa di Capezzana and Selezione, Trefiano RISERVA), exceptional VIN SANTO, one of Italy's five best.

Capichera Sar ★★★★ No better VERMENTINO anywhere than that of Ragnedda family, talented enough also to make top reds (Manthenghja CARIGNANO 100%). Top Isola dei Nuraghi Bianco Santigaìni, Vendemmia Tardiva, VIGNA'ngena.

Cappellano Pie ★★★ Now run by Augusto, Teobaldo's son. Highly traditional. Top BAROLOS Gabutti (Piè Franco, from ungrafted NEBBIOLO, and Piè Rupestris). Arguably best Barolo Chinato.

Caprai Umb ★★★→★★★★ MONTEFALCO leader thanks to Marco C. Many outstanding wines eg. 25 Anni and Spinning Beauty (aged 8 yrs). V.gd GRECHETTO Grecante, ROSSO DI MONTEFALCO (smooth, elegant), Valdimaggio and Collepiano (less oak).

Carema Pie ★★→★★★ 07 08 09 10 11 13 15 16' (18) DOC Only 17 ha, n of Turin. Steep terraces and morainic agglomerate soils for light, mineral, intense, outstanding NEBBIOLO. Top: Ferrando (esp Black Label). V.gd Produttori Nebbiolo di Carema (RISERVA).

Carignano del Sulcis Sar ★★→★★★ DOC 09 10 12 13 14 15 (16) From SAR's sw, world-class CARIGNANO that ages gracefully but always boasts early appeal, accessibility. Best: Rocca Rubia and *Terre Brune* from ARGIOLAS, Mesa, SANTADI.

Carmignano Tus ★★★ DOCG 09 10 11 **12** 13 15 16' (17) (18) Fine SANGIOVESE/ B'x-grape blend invented in C20 by late Count Bonacossi of CAPEZZANA. Best: Ambra (Elzana RISERVA), Capezzana (Selezione), Farnete, Le Poggiarelle, Piaggia (Riserva), Pratesi (Il Circo Rosso, Carmione).

Carpineti, Marco Lat ★★★ Phenomenal bio whites from little-known Bellone and GRECO Moro, Greco Giallo varieties. Benchmark Moro and Ludum, one of Italy's best stickies.

Cartizze Ven ★★★→★★★★ DOCG At 107 ha, this PROSECCO super-cru is reportedly 2nd most expensive vyd land in Italy, after BAROLO. V. steep hills in heart of VALDOBBIADENE showcase just how great Prosecco DOCG can be. Usually on sweet side due to fully ripe grapes. Best: BISOL, Bortolomiol, Col Vetoraz, Le Colture, Merotto, NINO FRANCO, Ruggeri.

Case Basse Tus ★★★★ Owner Gianfranco Soldera died 2019: hopefully children will keep up similar lofty level of iconic BRUNELLO. Long oak-aged. Rare, precious.

Castel del Monte Pug ★→★★ (r) **10** 11 13 14 15 16 (w/rosé) DOC DYA. Dry, fresh, increasingly serious, from mid-PUG DOC. Esp *Bocca di Lupo* from Tormaresca (ANTINORI). Il Falcone RISERVA (Rivera) is iconic. V.gd Torrevento (Riserva).

Castel Juval, Unterortl T-AA ★★★ Owned by mountaineer Reinhold Messner. Distinctive, crystalline. Best: WEISSBURGUNDER. V.gd RIES (Windbichel) and PINOT N.

Castellare Tus ★★★ Classy Castellina-in-CHIANTI producer of long standing. 1st-rate SANGIOVESE/MALVASIA Nera I Sodi di San Niccoló and updated CHIANTI CLASSICO, esp RISERVA Il Poggiale. Also POGGIO ai Merli (MERLOT), Coniale (CAB SAUV).

Castell' in Villa Tus ★★★ Individual, traditionalist CHIANTI CLASSICO estate in extreme sw of zone. Wines of class, excellence by self-taught Princess Coralia Pignatelli; v. age-worthy. Top RISERVA.

Castelluccio E-R ★★→★★★ Quality SANGIOVESE from estate run by Fiore family. Top Sangiovese 100% IGT RONCO dei Ciliegi and Ronco delle Ginestre stars.

Castiglion del Bosco Tus ★★★ Ferragamo-owned up-and-coming BRUNELLO producer.

Cataldi Madonna Ab ★★★ Organic certified. Top is PECORINO Frontone, from oldest Pecorino vines in Ab. V.gd: Pecorino Supergiulia, CERASUOLO D'ABRUZZO Piè delle VIGNE, MONTEPULCIANO d'Ab Tonì and Malandrino.

Caudrina Pie ★★★→★★★★ Romano Dogliotti one of best for MOSCATO D'ASTI. Top: La Galeisa and ASTI La Selvatica. V.gd: La Caudrina.

Cavallotto Pie ★★★→★★★★ Organic certified. Solid reference for traditional BAROLO, in Castiglione Falletto. Outstanding RISERVA VIGNA San Giuseppe and Riserva Vignolo, v.gd BARBERA D'ALBA Sup Vigna Cuculo, LANGHE NEBBIOLO. Surprisingly gd GRIGNOLINO, Freisa too.

Cave Mont Blanc VdA ★★★ Quality co-op at foot of Mont Blanc, with ungrafted indigenous 60–100-yr-old Prie Blanc vines. Organic certified. Outstanding sparkling. Top Blanc de Morgex et de la Salle Rayon and Brut MC Extreme; v.gd Cuvée du Prince.

What to drink with *arancini siciliani*? (w) Carricante or (r) Cerasuolo di Vittoria.

Cerasuolo d'Abruzzo Ab ★ DOC DYA ROSATO version of MONTEPULCIANO D'ABRUZZO, don't confuse with red CERASUOLO DI VITTORIA from SI. Can be brilliant; best (by far): CATALDI MADONNA (Pie delle Vigne), EMIDIO PEPE, Praesidium, TIBERIO, VALENTINI. V.gd La Valentina (Spclt), TENUTA Tre Gemme.

Cerasuolo di Vittoria Si ★★ **11** 13 14 15 16 17 18 (19) Blend of Frappato/NERO D'AVOLA. Only SI DOCG, in se, around city of Vittoria, best terroir for Frappato. Try COS, GULFI, OCCHIPINTI ARIANNA, PAOLO CALÌ, PLANETA, Valle dell'Acate (Iri da Iri).

Ceretto Pie ★★★→★★★★ Leading producer of BARBARESCO (Asili, Bernadot), BAROLO

Who makes really good Chianti Classico?
CHIANTI CLASSICO is a large zone with hundreds of producers, so picking out the best is tricky. Top get a ★: AMA ★, ANTINORI, BADIA A COLTIBUONO ★, BROLIO, Capraia, Casaloste, Casa Sola, CASTELLARE, CASTELL' IN VILLA, CASTELLO DI VOLPAIA ★, FELSINA ★, FONTERUTOLI, FONTODI ★, Gagliole, I Fabbri ★, Il Molino di Grace, ISOLE E OLENA ★, Le Boncie, Le Cinciole ★, Le Corti, Le Filigare, Lilliano, Mannucci Droandi, Meleto, MONSANTO ★, Monte Bernardi, Monteraponi ★, NITTARDI, NOZZOLE, Palazzino, Paneretta, Poggerino, POGGIOPIANO, QUERCIABELLA ★, Rampolla, RIECINE, Rocca di Castagnoli, Rocca di Montegrossi ★, RUFFINO, San Fabiano Calcinaia, SAN FELICE, SAN GIUSTO A RENTENNANO ★, Paolina Savignola, Selvole, Tenuta Perano – FRESCOBALDI, Vecchie Terre di Montefili, Verrazzano, Vicchiomaggio, VIGNAMAGGIO, Villa Calcinaia ★, Villa La Rosa ★, Viticcio.

(Bricco Rocche, Brunate, Bussia, Cannubi San Lorenzo, Prapò), plus LANGHE Bianco Blange (ARNEIS). Organic and bio (2015). Wines recently more classic.

Cerruti, Ezio Pie ★★★ Small estate in gd area for MOSCATO: best sweet Sol, naturally dried Moscato. V.gd Fol (dr) and (sp) Ri-Fol. New Mac-Fol (on skins).

Cesanese del Piglio or Piglio Lat ★→★★★ DOCG Medium-bodied red, gd for moderate ageing. Best: Petrucca e Vela, Terre del Cesanese. Cesanese di Affile and Cesanese di Olevano Romano similar.

Chianti Tus ★→★★★ DOCG Its cheerful fiasco was a wine icon many would like to see come back, though quality is all over the place. But when gd: delightfully delicious, easy-going and food-friendly fresh red. Modern-day production zone covers most of TUS; original, historic Chianti production zone between Florence and Siena now called CHIANTI CLASSICO.

Chianti Classico Tus ★★→★★★ DOCG 12 13 15 16' 17 (18') No wine in Italy has improved more over last 20 yrs than Chianti Classico, now often 100% SANGIOVESE. More than 500 producers means inconsistent quality, but best are among Italy's greatest. Made in historic (high, rocky) CHIANTI production zone between Florence and Siena in eight communes. Gran Selezione is new top level, above RISERVA. (See also box, above.)

Chiaretto Ven Pale, light blush-hued rosé (word means "claret"), produced esp around Lake Garda. See BARDOLINO.

Ciabot Berton Pie ★★★ Marco and Paola Oberto, following their father, have turned this La Morra estate into one of best-value producers. V.gd blended BAROLO ("1961" and Barolo di La Morra); crus Roggeri, Rocchettevino have distinctive single-vyd characters. V.gd LANGHE NEBBIOLO 3 Utin.

Cinque Terre Lig ★★ DOC Dry VERMENTINO-based whites from vertiginous LIG coast. Sweet version: Sciacchetrà. Try Arrigoni, Bisson, Buranco, De Battè.

Ciolli, Damiano Lat ★★★ One of most interesting wineries in central Italy. Best is Cirsium, 100% Cesanese d'Affile, 80-yr-old vines. V.gd Silene.

Cirò Cal ★→★★★ DOC Brisk strong red from Cal's main grape, Gaglioppo, or light, fruity white from GRECO (DYA). Best: 'A Vita, Caparra & Siciliani (RISERVA Volvito), IPPOLITO 1845, *Librandi* (Duca San Felice ★★★), San Francesco (Donna Madda, RONCO dei Quattroventi), Santa Venere.

Classico Term for wines from a restricted, usually historic and superior-quality area within limits of a commercially expanded DOC. See CHIANTI CLASSICO, SOAVE, VALPOLICELLA, VERDICCHIO, numerous others.

Clerico, Domenico Pie ★★★ Influential BAROLO innovator, modernist producer of Monforte d'ALBA, esp crus Ginestra (Ciabot Mentin and Pajana) and Mosconi (Percristina only in best vintages, don't miss 10). V.gd Barolo Aeroplanservaj (from Baudana cru).

Cocchi-Bava Pie ★★★ Since 1891 historic producer of vermouth. Now owned by Bava family. Top ALTA LANGA Pas Dosè, Toto Corde, Vermouth RISERVA La Venaria. V.gd BARBERA D'ASTI Stradivario, NIZZA Piano Alto.

Coffele Ven ★★★ Sensitive winemaker, organic certified. Gd SOAVE CLASSICO Castelcerino, crus Ca' Visco and Alzari (100% GARGANEGA), RECIOTO Le Sponde.

Cogno, Elvio Pie ★★★★ Top estate; super-classy, austere, elegant BAROLOS. Best: Bricco Pernice, Ravera, RISERVA VIGNA Elena (NEBBIOLO Rosé clone). V.gd Anas-Cëtta (100% Nascetta), BARBERA D'ALBA Pre-Phylloxera (100-yr-old vines).

Col d'Orcia Tus ★★★ Top-quality MONTALCINO estate (3rd-largest) owned by Francesco Marone Cinzano. Best: BRUNELLO RISERVA POGGIO al Vento, new Brunello Nastagio. Col d'Orcia is valley between Montalcino and Monte Amiata.

Colla, Poderi Pie ★★★→★★★★ Colla family run this winery based on experience of Beppe Colla. Classic, traditional, age-worthy. Top: BARBARESCO Roncaglie, BAROLO Bussia Dardi Le Rose, LANGHE Bricco del Drago. V.gd Pietro Colla Extra Brut and new NEBBIOLO D'ALBA SPUMANTE rosé.

Colli = hills; singular: Colle. **Colline** (singular Collina) = smaller hills. See also COLLIO, POGGIO.

Colli di Catone Lat ★→★★★ Top producer of FRASCATI and IGT. Outstanding aged whites from MALVASIA del Lazio (aka Malvasia Puntinata) and GRECHETTO. Look for Colle Gaio or Casal Pilozzo labels.

Colli di Lapio Cam ★★★ Clelia Romano's estate is Italy's best Fiano producer. Also v.gd GRECO DI TUFO Alèxandros, TAURASI Andrea and the new Fiano Clelia.

Colli di Luni Lig, Tus ★★→★★★ DOC Nr Spezia. VERMENTINO, Albarola whites; SANGIOVESE-based reds easy to drink, charming. Top: Bisson (VIGNA Erta), Giacomelli (Boboli), La Baia del Sole (Oro d'Isèe, Sarticola), Lunae (Numero Chiuso, Etichetta Nera), Ottaviano Lambruschi (Costa Marina).

Collio F-VG ★★→★★★★ DOC Famous white denomination, unfortunately moved steadily to nonsensical Collio Bianco blend rather than highlight terroir differences of its communes, incl coolish San Floriano and Dolegna, warmer Capriva. Happily, Collio boasts glut of talented producers: BORGO DEL TIGLIO, Castello di Spessa, GRAVNER, La Castellada, Livon, MARCO FELLUGA, Podversic, Primosic, Princic, **Radikon**, Renato Keber, RONCO dei Tassi, RUSSIZ SUPERIORE, **Schioppetto**, Venica & Venica, VILLA RUSSIZ.

Colli Piacentini E-R ★→★★ DOC DYA Light gulping wines, often fizzy, from eg. BARBERA, BONARDA (r), MALVASIA di Candia Aromatica, Pignoletto (w).

Colterenzio CS / Schreckbichl T-AA ★★★ Cornaiano-based main player among ALTO ADIGE co-ops. Whites (SAUV BL Lafoa, PINOT BIANCO Berg and new LR) tend to be better than reds. V.gd CAB SAUV Lafoa and PINOT N St Daniel.

Conegliano Valdobbiadene Ven ★→★★ DOCG DYA. Name for top PROSECCO, tricky to say: may be used separately or together.

Conero Mar ★★→★★★ DOCG 15 17 Aka ROSSO CONERO. Small zone making powerful, at times too oaky, MONTEPULCIANO. Try: GAROFOLI (Grosso Agontano), Le Terrazze (Praeludium), Marchetti, Moncaro, Monteschiavo, Moroder (Dorico), UMANI RONCHI (Campo San Giorgio).

Prosecco hills of Conegliano and Valdobbiadene soon to be UNESCO-listed.

Conterno, Aldo Pie ★★★★ Top estate of Monforte d'ALBA, 25 ha for only 80,000 bottles of highest quality. Top BAROLOS Granbussia, Cicala, Colonello and esp Romirasco. V.gd CHARD Bussiador and LANGHE NEBBIOLO Il Favot.

Conterno, Giacomo Pie ★★★★ For many, Monfortino is best wine of Italy. Roberto recently acquired NERVI estate in GATTINARA. Outstanding BARBERAS. Top BAROLO Cascina Francia, Cerretta and now Arione.

Conterno, Paolo Pie ★★→★★★★ Family of NEBBIOLO and BARBERA growers since 1886.

Textbook cru BAROLOS Ginestra and Riva del Bric, plus particularly fine LANGHE *Nebbiolo Bric Ginestra.*

Conterno Fantino Pie ★★★ Organic certified. One of top producers of excellent modern-style BAROLO crus at Monforte: Ginestra (Sorì Ginestra and VIGNA del Gris), Mosconi (Vigna Ped) and Castelletto (Vigna Pressenda). Also gd Ginestrino, NEBBIOLO/BARBERA blend Monprà and CHARD Bastia (one of PIE's best).

Contini Sar ★★★ Benchmark VERNACCIA DI ORISTANO, oxidative-styled whites not unlike v.gd Amontillado or Oloroso. Antico Gregori one of Italy's best whites. Amazing Flor 22 and RISERVA. Gd I Giganti (r).

Conti Zecca Pug ★★→★★★ SALENTO estate. Donna Marzia line of Salento IGT wines is gd value, as is SALICE SALENTINO Cantalupi. Best-known is Nero (NEGROAMARO/CAB SAUV blend).

Cornelissen, Frank ★★★★ Belgian-owned, today one of ETNA's top producers, esp for red. Practically all outstanding, NERELLO MASCALESE Magma usually SI's most expensive wine. V.gd VA and CS (r).

Correggia, Matteo Pie ★★★ Organic certified. Leading producer of ROERO (RISERVA Rochè d'Ampsej, Val dei Preti), Roero ARNEIS, plus BARBERA D'ALBA (Marun) and Roero Arneis Val dei Preti (aged 6 yrs).

Cretes, Les VdA ★★★ Costantino Charrère is father of modern VALLE D'AOSTA viticulture and saved many forgotten varieties. *Outstanding Petite Arvine*, two of Italy's best CHARDS; v.gd Fumin, Torrette and Neige d'Or (w blend).

Cristo di Campobello, Baglio del Si ★★→★★★ Bonetta family estate just e of Agrigento. Top: Grillo La Luci, NERO D'AVOLA Lu Patri.

Crivelli Pie ★★★ Top producer of Ruchè di Castagnole MONFERRATO and of GRIGNOLINO d'Asti. Must-try wines.

CS (Cantina Sociale) Cooperative winery.

Cuomo, Marisa Cam ★★★ Fiorduva is *one of Italy's greatest whites*. V.gd Furore Bianco and Rosso (Costa d'Amalfi).

Custodi delle Vigne dell'Etna, I Si ★★★→★★★★ Family estate run by Mario Paoluzi. Member of the consortium I VIGNERI. Outstanding ETNA Rosso RISERVA Saeculare. V.gd Etna Rosso Aetneus, Etna Bianco Ante.

Cusumano Si ★★→★★★ Producer with 500 ha in various parts of SI. Reds from NERO D'AVOLA, CAB SAUV, SYRAH; whites from CHARD, INSOLIA. Gd quality, value. Best from ETNA (Alta Mora).

Dal Forno Romano Ven ★★★★ VALPOLICELLA, AMARONE, RECIOTO (latter not identified as such any more) v. high quality; vyds outside CLASSICO zone but wines great.

Dei Pie, Tus ★★★ Estate in MONTEPULCIANO, making v.gd VINO NOBILES. Best are: Bossona and cru Madonna della Querce.

Derthona Pie ★→★★★ Wine from Timorasso grapes grown only in COLLI Tortonesi. One of Italy's most *interesting whites*, like v. dry RIES from Rheinhessen. Best: La Colombera (Il Montino), Mariotto, Mutti, Poggio Paolo, Ricci, ROAGNA (Montemarzino), VIGNETI MASSA, VIETTI.

DOC / DOCG Quality wine designation: *see* box, p.153.

Dogliani Pie ★→★★★ DOCG 13 15 16 17 18 Varietal DOLCETTO. Some to drink young, some for moderate ageing. Gd: Chionetti, Clavesana, EINAUDI, Francesco Boschis, Marziano Abbona, Pecchenino, Trediberri.

Donnafugata Si ★★→★★★ Classy range. Reds: ETNA Rosso (Contrada Fragore, Marchesa, Sul Vulcano), Mille e Una Notte, NERO D'AVOLA Sherazade, Tancredi. Whites: Chiaranda, Kebir, Lighea. V. fine MOSCATO PASSITO di PANTELLERIA Ben Ryé.

Duca di Salaparuta Si ★★ Top Duca Enrico and Bianca di Valguarnera. White Kados from GRILLO grapes also gd.

Due Terre, Le F-VG ★★★ Small family-run FRIULI COLLI ORIENTALI estate: Top Sacrisassi Rosso (SCHIOPPETTINO/REFOSCO). V.gd MERLOT, (w) Sacrisassi Bianco.

Einaudi, Luigi Pie ★★★ Founded late C19 by ex-president of Italy, 52-ha estate in DOGLIANI. Solid BAROLOS from Cannubi, Terlo and outstanding Bussia. Top Dogliani (DOLCETTO) from VIGNA Tecc. Waiting for Monvigliero.

Elba Tus ★→★★ DYA. Island's white, TREBBIANO/ANSONICA, can be v. drinkable with fish. Dry reds based on SANGIOVESE. Gd sweet white (MOSCATO) and red (*Aleatico Passito DOCG*). Gd: Acquabona, La Mola, Ripalte, Sapereta.

Enoteca Wine library; also shop or restaurant with ambitious wine list. There is a national enoteca at the fortezza in Siena.

Est! Est!! Est!!! Lat ★ DOC DYA. White from Montefiascone, n of Rome.

Etna Si ★★ →★★★ DOC (r) 12 13 14 15 16 17 (18) One of hottest areas, remarkable development in last decade. 900 ha of vyds on n slopes, high-altitude, volcanic soils. Etna Rosso typically 90/10 blend of NERELLOS MASCALESE/Cappuccio, while Etna Bianco can be pure CARRICANTE or incl CATARATTOS Comune or Lucido. (*See also* box, below.)

Falchini Tus ★★→★★★ Producer of gd DOCG VERNACCIA DI SAN GIMIGNANO.

Falerno del Massico Cam ★★→★★★ DOC ★★ (r) 15 16 18 (19) Falernian wine was Antiquity's most famous wine. Today average only. Best: elegant AGLIANICO reds, fruity dry FALANGHINA whites. Try: Masseria Felicia, Villa Matilde.

Fara Pie *See* ALTO PIEMONTE.

Faro Si ★★★ DOC 13 14 15 16 17 Intense, harmonious red from NERELLO MASCALESE, NERO D'AVOLA and Nocera in hills behind Messina. Top is Bonavita. Palari most famous, but Le Casematte just as gd if not better.

Felline Pug ★★★→★★★★ Gregory Perucci was pioneer in rediscovery of PRIMITIVO and Sussumaniello vines. Top PRIMITIVO DI MANDURIA (Cuvèe Anniversario, Dunico, Giravolta, ZIN). V.gd Sum (Sussumaniello).

Felluga, Livio F-VG ★★★ Consistently fine FRIULI COLLI ORIENTALI, esp blends Terre Alte and Abbazia di Rosazzo; Bianco Illivio, *Pinot Gr*, PICOLIT (Italy's best?), MERLOT/REFOSCO blend Sossó.

Felluga, Marco F-VG *See* RUSSIZ SUPERIORE.

Felsina Tus ★★★ CHIANTI CLASSICO estate of distinction in se corner of zone: classic RISERVA Rancia, IGT Fontalloro (100% SANGIOVESE). V.gd Gran Selezione Colonia.

Fenocchio, Giacomo Pie ★★★→★★★★ Small but outstanding Monforte d'ALBA-based BAROLO cellar. Traditional style. Crus: Bussia (also RISERVA 90Dì), Cannubi, Villero. Outstanding Freisa, one of Italy's 2–3 best.

Ferrara, Benito Cam ★★★ Maybe Italy's best GRECO DI TUFO producer (Terra d'Uva, VIGNA Cicogna). Talent shows in excellent TAURASI (Vigna Quattro Confini) and FIANO (Sequenzha) too.

Summit of Etna

Some of Italy's most exciting wines come from this famous volcano. Vines grow up to 1000m (3281ft) on SI's e coast. *Contrada* is Si's way to express cru: differences in soil, altitude and age of lava flows. Top growers incl: Alberelli di Giodo, BENANTI ★ (r Rovittello, Serra della Contessa, w Pietra Marina), Calabretta, CALCAGNO ★ (r Arcuria, Feudo di Mezzo, w Ginestra), Cottanera (w Calderara, Zottorinoto), Graci (Arcuria, Feudo di Mezzo, w Ginestra), GULFI (Reseca), I CUSTODI DELL'ETNA (r Aetneus, Saeculare, w Ante), I VIGNERI ★ (r Vinupetra, w Aurora), Le Vigne di Eli, PIETRADOLCE ★ (r/w Archineri, Barbagalli, Rampante, Santo Spirito), TASCA D'ALMERITA, (r Rampante, Sciaranuova, w Buonora), TENUTA DI FESSINA ★(r/w Il Musmeci, w A' Puddara), TENUTA DELLE TERRE NERE ★ (r/w Calderα Sottana, Guardiola, San Lorenzo, Santo Spirito), TENUTE BOSCO (VignaVico), Tornatore (Pietrarizzo, Trimarchisa), VINI FRANCHETTI ★ (Guardiola, Rampante, Sciaranuova). Start climbing.

Ferrari – Tenute Lunelli T-AA ★★★→★★★★ Trento maker of one of two best Italian METODO CLASSICOS. Outstanding Giulio Ferrari (RISERVA del Fondatore, Rosé and Selezione); v.gd CHARD-based Brut Riserva Lunelli, Perlè Bianco (gd value), Perlè Zero, PINOT N-based Perlè Nero. TENUTE Lunelli: Castelbuono Umb (Carapace MONTEFALCO), Margon T-AA (Chard Villa Margon and Pinot N Maso Montalto), Podernuovo (TUS – Solenida 100% SANGIOVESE).

Fessina, Tenuta di Si ★★★→★★★★ Silvia Maestrelli has one of youngest and best estates in Rovittello area of ETNA. Elegant wines. Best: EB A'Puddara (w) and Il Musmeci (r/w). V.gd: Erse Moscamento 1911 (r).

Feudi di San Gregorio Cam ★★★ Much-hyped CAM producer, with DOCGS FIANO DI AVELLINO Pietracalda, GRECO DI TUFO Cutizzi and new Goleto, TAURASI Piano di Montevergine. Also gd: Serpico (AGLIANICO); whites ***Campanaro*** (Fiano/Greco), FALANGHINA. Look for new ***Feudi Studi*** line: the most expressive vyds, selected every yr among 700 sites depending on vintage.

Feudo di San Maurizio VdA ★★★★ Outstanding wines from rare native grapes CORNALIN, Mayolet and Vuillermin; last two rank among Italy's greatest reds. V.gd Torrette.

Feudo Montoni Si ★★★★ Exceptional estate in upland e SI. Best: NERO D'AVOLA Lagnusa and Vrucara. V.gd GRILLO della Timpa (w), CATARRATTO del Masso (w), Perricone del Core (r), PASSITO Bianco (sw).

Fiano di Avellino Cam ★★→★★★★ DOCG 12 15 16 18 19 Can be either steely (most typical) or lush. Volcanic soils best. Gd: Ciro Picariello, Colli di Lapio, FEUDI SAN GREGORIO, I Favati (Pietramara), MASTROBERARDINO, Pietracupa, QUINTODECIMO, TENUTA SARNO 1860, Vadiaperti, Villa Diamante.

Fino, Gianfranco Pug ★★★★ Greatest PRIMITIVO, from old, low-yielding bush vines. Outstanding Es among Italy's top 20 reds. V.gd Jo (NEGROAMARO) and Se (Primitivo).

Florio Si ★★→★★★ Historic quality maker of MARSALA. Specialist in Marsala Vergine Secco. Best: RISERVA Donna Franca and Targa. V.gd Baglio Florio.

Folonari Tus ★★→★★★ Folonari family have vyds in TUS and elsewhere. Estates/ wines incl ***Cabreo*** (CHARD and SANGIOVESE/CAB SAUV), La Fuga (BRUNELLO DI MONTALCINO), NOZZOLE (incl top Cab Sauv Pareto).

Fongaro Ven ★★★★ Classic-method fizz Lessini Durello (Durello = grape). High quality, even higher acidity, age-worthy. Top Pas Dosè RISERVA.

Fontanafredda Pie ★★ Since 1858, former royal estates. Large producer of PIE. V.gd BAROLO La Rosa, Alta Langa Brut Nature VIGNA Gatinera.

Fonterutoli Tus ★★★ Historic CHIANTI CLASSICO estate of Mazzei family at Castellina. Notable: CHIANTI CLASSICO Gran Selezione and IGT Mix 36. Also owns TENUTA di Belguardo in MAREMMA and Zisola in SI.

Fontodi Tus ★★★★ One of v. best CHIANTI CLASSICOS. Top Gran Selezione VIGNA del Sorbo and Flaccianello (SANGIOVESE 100%). IGT SYRAH Case Via among best of that variety in TUS.

Foradori T-AA ★★★ Much-loved Elizabetta F is "lady of TRENTINO wine" making outstanding ***Teroldego*** but lovely macerated (too macerated for some), anfora-aged Incrocio Manzoni and Nosiola. Look for TEROLDEGO Morei and Sgarzon (also anfora-aged Cilindrica), plus white Nosiola Fontanasanta. Top remains Teroldego-based Granato.

Franchetti, Vini Si ★★★→★★★★ ETNA estate (former Passopisciaro) run by Franchetti (*see* TENUTA DI TRINORO), contributor to fame of Etna. Outstanding Rosso Franchetti (PETIT VERDOT/Cesanese d'Affile) and NERELLO MASCALESE single-*contrada*. Best: Contrada G, Contrada S and Contrada C. V.gd Contrada R. New Contrada PC (CHARD).

Franciacorta Lom ★★→★★★★ DOCG Italy's zone for top-quality METODO CLASSICO fizz. Best: Barone Pizzini, *Ca' del Bosco*, Cavalleri, MOSNEL, UBERTI, Villa. Also v.gd: Bellavista, Bersi Serlini, Contadi Castaldi, Gatti, Monte Rossa, Ricci Curbastro.

Frascati Lat ★→★★ DOC DYA. Once proud name (Rome's favourite) sadly debased. Large producers continuing to make neutral but mysteriously well-written-about wines leave little hope for change. Buy following small producers only: Borgo del Cedro (SUPERIORE), Castel de Paolis (Superiore), De Sanctis (Abelos Bio), Merumalia (Primo), Villa Simone (RISERVA Filonardi).

Frascole Tus ★★→★★★★ Most n winery of most n CHIANTI RÚFINA zone, small estate run organically by Enrico Lippi, with an eye for typicity. Chianti Rúfina is main driver, but VIN SANTO is to die for.

Frescobaldi Tus ★★→★★★★ Ancient noble family, leading CHIANTI RÚFINA pioneer at NIPOZZANO estate (look for ★★★ *Montesodi*), also BRUNELLO from Castelgiocondo estate, MONTALCINO. Sole owner of LUCE estate (Montalcino), ORNELLAIA (BOLGHERI), TENUTA Perano (top: CHIANTI CLASSICO Gran Selezione Rialzi). Vyds also in COLLIO (Attems), MAREMMA (Ammiraglia), Montespertoli (Castiglioni), Gorgona Island (state prison).

Friuli Colli Orientali F-VG ★★→★★★★ DOC 12 15 16 18 (19) (Was COLLI Orientali del Friuli.) Hilly area of F-VG next to COLLIO. Unlike latter, not just whites, but outstanding reds and v.gd stickies from likes of red Pignolo, SCHIOPPETTINO, Tazzelenghe and white PICOLIT and VERDUZZO Friulano. Top: Aquila del Torre, d'Attimis, Ermacora, Gigante, La Sclusa, LA VIARTE, LE DUE TERRE, LIVIO FELLUGA, MIANI, Meroi, RONCHI DI CIALLA, VIGNA PETRUSSA. Ramandolo DOCG is best sweet Verduzzo (look for Anna Berra). PICOLIT can be Italy's best sweet: Aquila del Torre, Livio Felluga, Marco Sara, Ronchi di Cialla, Vigna Petrussa often amazing.

F-VG's noble Tazzelenghe variety gives mesmerizingly great reds. But only 7 ha left.

Friuli Grave F-VG ★→★★ DOC Previously Grave del Friuli. Largest DOC of F-VG, mostly on plains, often v. rainy, making quality red production tricky. Mostly big volumes, whites best. Look for Borgo Magredo, Di Lenardo, Le Monde, RONCO Cliona, Villa Chiopris.

Friuli Isonzo F-VG ★★★ DOC Used to be just Isonzo. High-alc, luscious, powerful whites from gravel-rich alluvial river plain, a rare flatland high-quality site. Best: LIS NERIS, RONCO DEL GELSO, VIE DI ROMANS. Gd: Borgo Conventi, Pierpaolo Pecorari.

Friuli-Venezia Giulia A ne region hugging Slovenian border, home to Italy's best whites (along with ALTO ADIGE). Hills to ne give best, but alluvial seaside regions (DOC from Annia, Aquileia, Latisana) improving markedly. DOCs Carso, COLLI ORIENTALI, COLLIO, ISONZO best. All have Collio preceded on label by "Friuli".

Frizzante Semi-sparkling, up to 2.5 atmospheres, eg. MOSCATO D'ASTI, much PROSECCO, LAMBRUSCO and the like.

Fucci, Elena Bas ★★★★ AGLIANICO DEL VULTURE Titolo from 55–70-yr-old vines in Mt Vulture's Grand Cru; one of Italy's 20 best. Organic. Outstanding 13 15 17 Anniversary. New Titolo by Amphora (18 months in terracotta amphora).

Fuligni Tus ★★★★ Outstanding producer: BRUNELLO (top RISERVA), ROSSO DI MONTALCINO.

Gaja Pie ★★★★ Old family firm at BARBARESCO led by eloquent Angelo Gaja; daughter Gaia G following. High quality, higher prices. Top: Barbaresco (Costa Russi, Sorì San Lorenzo, Sorì Tildìn), BAROLO (Conteisa, Sperss). Splendid CHARD (Gaia e Rey). Also owns CA' MARCANDA in BOLGHERI, Pieve di Santa Restituta in MONTALCINO. New acquisition on ETNA (with Graci).

Gancia Pie Famous old brand of MUSCAT fizz. Best new Alta Langa (★★★ Cuvée 120, Cuvée 60).

Garda Ven ★→★★ DOC (r) 15 16 (18) (w/rosé) DYA. Divided between Lom and Ven hugging Italy's largest lake, home to easy-going, early drinking, cheap-and-cheerful red, white and rosé. CHIARETTO best. Gd: Cavalchina, Zeni.

Garofoli Mar ★★→★★★ Quality leader in the Mar, specialist in VERDICCHIO (Podium, Serra Fiorese and sparkling Brut RISERVA), CONERO (Grosso Agontano).

Gattinara Pie 11 12 13 15 16 (17) (18) Best-known of a cluster of ALTO PIE DOC(G)s based on NEBBIOLO. Volcanic soil. Suitable for long ageing. Best: ANTONIOLO, CANTINA del Signore, Iarretti Paride, NERVI, Torraccia del Piantavigna, TRAVAGLINI. *See also* ALTO PIEMONTE.

When in Rome: *tonnarelli cacio & pepe* (cheese & pepper) + spicy, fresh Cesanese.

Gavi / Cortese di Gavi Pie ★→★★★ DOCG DYA. Overhyped, but at best subtle dry white of Cortese grapes, though much is dull, simple or sharp. Most comes from commune of Gavi, now known as Gavi del Comune di Gavi. Best: *Bruno Broglia*/La Meirana, Castellari Bergaglio, La Giustiniana, La Scolca, Villa Sparina, Martinetti.

Germano, Ettore Pie ★★★ Small family Serralunga estate run by Sergio and wife Elena. Top BAROLOS: RISERVA Lazzarito, Cerretta and new VIGNA Rionda. V.gd: ALTA LANGA, BARBERA D'ALBA Sup della Madre, LANGHE RIES Herzù. New Alta Langa Riserva BdN (65 mths).

Ghemme Pie ★★→★★★ DOCG NEBBIOLO (at least 85%), incl up to 15% Uva Rara and/or Vespolina. Top: *Antichi Vigneti di Cantalupo* (Collis Braclemae, Collis Carellae), Ioppa (Balsina), Rovellotti (RISERVA). V.gd Torraccia del Piantavigna (VIGNA Pelizzane). *See also* ALTO PIEMONTE.

Ghizzano, Tenuta di Tus ★★★ Historical bio estate on Pisa's hills. Best: (r) Nambrot (B'x blend), Il Ghizzano.

Giacosa, Bruno Pie ★★★★ Italy's greatest winemaker died in 2018, wines still top. Now run by daughter Bruna. Splendid traditional-style BARBARESCOS (Asili, Rabajà), BAROLOS (Falletto, Falletto VIGNA Rocche). Top wines (ie. RISERVAS) get famous red label. Amazing METODO CLASSICO Brut, ROERO ARNEIS (w), Valmaggiore (r).

Girlan, Cantina T-AA ★★→★★★ Quality co-op. Top Le Selezioni line: PINOT N RISERVA (VIGNA Ganger, Trattmann), PINOT BL Flora, VERNATSCH Alte Reben Gschleier. V.gd Pinot Bl Platt & Riegl.

Giuseppe Cortese Pie ★★★ Traditional producer of outstanding BARBARESCO Rabajà (also RISERVA). Also gd LANGHE NEBBIOLO.

Grappa Pungent spirit made from grape pomace (skins, etc., after pressing), can be anything from disgusting to inspirational. What the French call "marc".

Gravner, Josko F-VG ★★★→★★★★ Controversial but talented COLLIO producer (unlike some who copy him), vinifies on skins (r/w) in buried amphorae without temperature control; long ageing, bottling without filtration. Look out for Breg (w blend), RIBOLLA GIALLA (w) and Rosso Breg (Pignolo).

Greco di Tufo Cam DOCG DYA. Tannic, oily whites made with local GRECO variety (different to Cal's also outstanding Greco Bianco). Best: Bambinuto (Picoli), BENITO Ferrara (VIGNA Cicogna), Caggiano (Devon), COLLI di Lapio (Alexandros), Donnachiara, FEUDI DI SAN GREGORIO (Cutizzi), Goleto e FeudiStudi), Macchialupa, *Mastroberardino* (Nova Serra, Vignadangelo), Pietracupa, QUINTODECIMO, Terredora (Loggia della Serra), Vadiaperti (Tornante).

Grifalco Bas ★★★ Small estate in high-quality Ginestra and Maschito subzone. Best: AGLIANICO DEL VULTURE Daginestra, Damaschito (SUPERIORE DOCG from 15). Waiting for Fra (rosé).

Grignolino Pie DYA. Two DOCS: GRIGNOLINO d'Asti and Grignolino del MONFERRATO Casalese. At best, light, perfumed, crisp and high in acidity, tannin. D'Asti: try BRAIDA, Cascina Tavijin, CRIVELLI, Incisa della Rocchetta, Spertino, TENUTA Garetto. Monferrato Casalese: try Accornero (Bricco del Bosco and Bricco del Bosco Vigne Vecchie – vinified like BAROLO), Bricco Mondalino, Castello di Uviglie, PIO CESARE.

Grosjean VdA ★★★ Top quality; best CORNALIN, Premetta. Vigne Rovettaz one of Valle's oldest, largest.

GIV (Gruppo Italiano Vini) Complex of co-ops and wineries, biggest vyd holders in Italy: Bigi, BOLLA, Melini, Negri. Also in S: SI, Bas.

Guardiense, La Cam ★★→★★★ Dynamic co-op, decent-value whites (esp FALANGHINA Senete, FIANO COLLI di Tilio, GRECO Pietralata) and reds (esp I Mille per l'AGLIANICO).

Guerrieri Rizzardi Ven ★★→★★★ Noble family making top-level AMARONE, BARDOLINO. Gd Bardolino CLASSICO Tacchetto, elegant Amarone Villa Rizzardi, but best is Amarone cru Calcarole. V.gd SOAVE Classico Costeggiola.

Gulfi Si ★★★★ Best producer of NERO D'AVOLA in SI; 1st to bottle single-*contrada* (cru) wines. Organic certified. Outstanding: Nerobufaleffj, Nerosanlorè and iconic Nerojbleo; v.gd: CERASUOLO DI VITTORIA CLASSICO, Nerobaronj, Neromaccarj and Carjcanti (w). Interesting Pinò (PINOT N). ETNA Rosso Reseca.

Gutturnio dei Colli Piacentini E-R ★→★★ DOC DYA. BARBERA/BONARDA blend from COLLI PIACENTINI; sometimes frothing.

Haas, Franz T-AA ★★→★★★ Top: PINOT N, LAGREIN (Schweizer), MOSCATO Rosa and IGT blend Manna (w).

Hofstätter T-AA ★★★ Top quality; gd PINOT N. Look for Barthenau VIGNA Sant'Urbano, Vigna Roccolo. Also whites, mainly GEWURZ (esp *Kolbehof*, one of Italy's two best).

IGT (Indicazione Geografica Tipica) Increasingly known as Indicazione Geografica Protetta (IGP). (*See* box, p.153.)

Ippolito 1845 Cal ★→★★ This CIRÒ Marina-based winery claims to be oldest in Cal. Top: Cirò RISERVA COLLI del Mancuso and Ripe del Falco, Pecorello Bianco and GRECO Bianco (Gemma del Sole).

Ischia Cam ★→★★ DOC DYA. Island off Naples, own grape varieties (w: Biancolella, Forastera; r. Piedirosso, also found in Cam). Frassitelli vyd best for Biancolella. Best: Antonio Mazzella (VIGNA del Lume), Cenatiempo (Kalimera), D'AMBRA (Biancolella Frassitelli, Forastera).

Isole e Olena Tus ★★★★ Top CHIANTI CLASSICO estate run by Paolo de Marchi, v. talented winemaker, with superb red IGT Cepparello. Outstanding VIN SANTO, CHIANTI CLASSICO. V.gd CAB SAUV, CHARD, SYRAH. Also owns fantastic PROPRIETÀ SPERINO in LESSONA.

Jermann, Silvio F-VG ★★→★★★ Famous estate with vyds in COLLIO and ISONZO: top white blend Vintage Tunina and Capo Martino. V.gd Vinnae (mainly RIBOLLA GIALLA) and "Where Dreams ..." (CHARD).

Kaltern, Cantina T-AA ★★→★★★ Quality co-op close to the Caldaro lake. Top Quintessenz line: Lago di Caldaro (r), CAB SAUV, SAUV BL.

Köfererhof T-AA ★★★→★★★★ Great whites: KERNER, SYLVANER; MÜLLER-T excellent too.

Lacrima di Morro d'Alba Mar DYA. Curiously named aromatic medium-bodied red from small commune in the Mar, no connection with ALBA or La Morra (PIE). Gd: Mario Lucchetti (Guardengo), Marotti Campi (Orgiolo and Rubico), Stefano Mancinelli and Vicari. For PASSITO: Lucchetti, Stefano Mancinelli (Re Sole).

Count your Grecos: Greco, Greco Bianco, Greco Giallo, Greco Moro, Greco Nero...

Lacryma (or Lacrima) Christi del Vesuvio Cam ★→★★ DOC Vesuvio based on Coda di Volpe (w), Piedirosso (r). Best: De Angelis, Sorrentino; gd Caputo, MASTROBERARDINO, Terredora.

Lageder, Alois T-AA ★★→★★★ Famous ALTO ADIGE producer. Most exciting are single vyd varietals: CAB SAUV Cor Römigberg, CHARD Löwengang, GEWURZ Am Sand, LAGREIN Lindenberg, PINOT N Krafuss, PINOT GR Porer, *Sauv Bl Lehenhof*.

Lagrein Alto Adige T-AA ★★→★★★ DOC 11 12 13 15 16' 18 Alpine red with deep colour, rich palate (plus a bitter hit at back); refreshing pink *Kretzer rosé* made with LAGREIN. Top ALTO ADIGE: CANTINA Bolzano (Taber), Cantina Santa Maddalena, cs Andriano, CS Tramin, Elena Walch, IGNAZ NIEDRIST, LAGEDER, MURI GRIES (Abtei, VIGNA Klosteranger), Putzenhof, TIEFENBRUNNER. From TRENTINO try Francesco Moser's Deamater.

Lambrusco E-R ★→★★★ DYA. 17 different Lambrusco grapes (five mostly planted) make for highly distinct wines, ie. Lambrusco wine does not exist. Plethora of different denominations usually linked to one of five main grapes, so each has its defining characteristcs. When gd, delightful fizzy fresh, lively red that pairs divinely with rich, fatty fare. DOCS: L Grasparossa di Castelvetro, L Salamino di Santa Croce, L di Sorbara. Best: [Sorbara] Cavicchioli (Cristo Secco and Cristo Rose), Cleto Chiarli (Antica Modena Premium), Medici Ermete (Phermento – ancestral method), Paltrinieri. Grasparossa: Cleto Chiarli (Enrico Cialdini), Moretto (Monovitigno and vigna Canova), Pederzana (Canto Libero Semi Secco), Vittorio Graziano (Fontana dei Boschi). Marani: Ermete Medici (Quercioli). Maestri: Ceci (Nero di Lambrusco Otello), Dall'Asta (Mefistofele). Salamino: Cavicchioli (Tre Medaglie Semi Secco), Luciano Saetti (Vigneto Saetti), Medici Ermete (Concerto Granconcerto).

Langhe Pie The hills of central PIE, home of BAROLO, BARBARESCO, etc. DOC name for several Pie varietals plus Bianco and Rosso blends. Those wishing to blend other grapes with NEBBIOLO can at up to 15% as LANGHE NEBBIOLO – a label to follow.

Langhe Nebbiolo Pie ★★→★★★ Like NEBBIOLO D'ALBA (Nebbiolo > 85%) but from a wider area: LANGHE hills. Unlike N d'Alba may be used as a downgrade from BAROLO or BARBARESCO. Gd: ALDO CONTERNO, BURLOTTO, CIABOT BERTON, ETTORE GERMANO, FRATELLI ALESSANDRIA, GIACOMO FENOCCHIO, GIUSEPPE RINALDI, MASSOLINO, PIO CESARE, TREDIBERRI, *Vajra*.

Spaghetti and *bottarga* is perfect with Vernaccia di Oristano or Malvasia di Bosa.

Lessona Pie DOCG See ALTO PIEMONTE. NEBBIOLO (at least 85%). Elegant, age-worthy, fine bouquet, long savoury taste. Best: PROPRIETÀ SPERINO. Gd: Cassina, Colombera & Garella, La Prevostura, TENUTE Sella.

Librandi Cal ★★★ Top producer pioneering research into Cal varieties. V.gd red CIRÒ (*Riserva Duca San Felice* is ★★★), IGT Gravello and Terre Lontane (CAB SAUV/ Gaglioppo blend), Magno Megonio (r) from Magliocco grape, IGT Efeso (w) from Mantonico.

Liguria ★→★★ Narrow ribbon of extreme mtn viticulture produces memorable (w) VERMENTINO, PIGATO, (r) Rossese di Dolceacqua varieties. Look for Giacomelli, La Baia del Sole, Ottaviano Lambruschi (Vermentino); Alessandri, Bio Vio, Bruna, TENUTA di Selvadolce (PIGATO). CINQUE TERRE is beautiful and Sciacchetrà (sw) one of Italy's best stickies; Ormeasco di Pornassio (r) made with Ligurian biotype of DOLCETTO.

Lisini Tus ★★★→★★★★ Historic estate for some of finest, longest-lasting BRUNELLO, esp RISERVA Ugolaia.

Lis Neris F-VG ★★★ Top ISONZO estate for whites. Best: PINOT GR (Gris), SAUV BL (Picol), FRIULANO (Fiore di Campo), Confini and Lis. V.gd Lis Neris Rosso (MERLOT/ CAB SAUV), sweet Tal Luc (VERDUZZO/RIES).

Lo Triolet VdA ★★★ Top PINOT GR producer, v.gd Fumin, Coteau Barrage (SYRAH/ Fumin), MUSCAT and GEWURZ.

Luce Tus ★★★ FRESCOBALDI's estate. Luce (SANGIOVESE/MERLOT blend for oligarchs). Lovely Luce BRUNELLO DI MONTALCINO. Lux Vitis (CAB SAUV/Sangiovese) from 15.

Lugana ★★→★★★ DOC DYA. Much-improved white of s Lake Garda, rivals gd SOAVE next door. Main grape Turbiana (formerly TREBBIANO di Lugana). Best: CA' DEI FRATI (I Frati, esp *Brolettino*), Domini Veneti, Le Morette, Monte del Frà (v.gd also Custoza SUPERIORE Bonomo Sexaginta), Ottella, Roveglia, Tommasi, Zenato (oaked), Zeni (Vigne Alte).

ITALY

Lungarotti Umb ★★→★★★ Leading producer of TORGIANO. Star wines DOC Rubesco, DOCG RISERVA *Monticchio*. Gd Giubilante, MONTEFALCO SAGRANTINO, Sangiorgio (SANGIOVESE/CAB SAUV), VIGNA Il Pino (w blend VERMENTINO/GRECHETTO/TREBBIANO).

Macchiole, Le Tus ★★★★ Organic. One of few native-owned wineries of BOLGHERI; one of 1st to emerge after SASSICAIA, makes *Italy's best Cab Fr* (Paleo Rosso), one of best MERLOTS (Messorio), SYRAHS (Scrio). V.gd Bolgheri Rosso.

Maculan Ven ★★★ Quality pioneer of Ven. Excellent CAB SAUV (Fratta, Palazzotto). Best-known for sweet TORCOLATO (esp RISERVA Acininobili).

Majo Norante, Di Mol ★★→★★★ Best-known of Mol with decent Biferno Rosso Ramitello, Don Luigi Molise Rosso RISERVA, Mol AGLIANICO Contado.

Malvasia delle Lipari Si ★★★ DOC Luscious sweet, from one of many MALVASIA varieties. Best: Capofaro, Caravaglio, Fenech, Lantieri, Marchetta. Gd: Hauner.

Malvirà Pie ★★★→★★★★ Top ROERO producer. Organic certified. Best Roero single-vyd: (r/w) Renesio, Trinità; (w) Saglietto. New ARNEIS RISERVA Saglietto.

Manduria (Primitivo di) Pug ★★→★★★ DOC Manduria is cradle of PRIMITIVO, alias ZIN, so expect wines that are gutsy, alcoholic, sometimes porty. Best: FELLINE, GIANFRANCO FINO, MORELLA. Gd producers, located in Manduria or not: Cantele, Pietraventosa, Polvanera, TENUTE Chiaromonte, Vetrere.

Marchesi di Gresy Pie ★★★ Historical BARBARESCO producer since 1797, from Martinenga cru (monopole). Best: RISERVA Camp Gros and Gajun.

Maremma Tus Once malaria-plagued, S TUS coast area boomed in C20 with easy-going, delicious SANGIOVESE-based reds from DOC(G)s: Monteregio, MORELLINO DI SCANSANO, PARRINA, Pitigliano, Sovana.

Marrone, Agricola Pie ★★★ Small estate, low price but gd-quality BAROLO. Top: Bussia, Pichemej. Gd: ARNEIS, BARBERA D'ALBA SUPERIORE, Favorita.

Marsala Si ★→★★★★ DOC SI's once-famous fortified, created by Woodhouse Bros of Liverpool in 1773. Can be dry to v. sweet; best is bone-dry Marsala Vergine. *See also* DE BARTOLI.

Marzemino Trentino T-AA ★→★★ DOC Pleasant everyday red. Isera and Ziresi are subzones. Best: Eugenio Rosi (Poiema), Grigoletti. Gd: CANTINA d'Isera, Vivallis.

Mascarello Pie ★★★★ Two top producers of BAROLO: the late Bartolo M, of Barolo, whose daughter Maria Teresa continues her father's highly traditional path (v.gd Freisa); and Giuseppe M, of Monchiero, whose son Mauro makes v. fine, traditional-style Barolo from the great *Monprivato* vyd in Castiglione Falletto. Both deservedly iconic.

Masi Ven ★★→★★★ Archetypal yet innovative producer of Verona, led by inspirational Sandro Boscaini. V.gd Rosso Veronese *Campo Fiorin* and Osar (Oseleta). Top AMARONES Costasera, Campolongo di Torbe. Masi Wine Estates: Canevel (VALDOBBIADENE Campofalco, CARTIZZE), Conti Bossi Fedrigotti (Trento Conte Federico, Fojaneghe B'x blend), Serego Alighieri (Amarone Vaio Armaron).

Massa, Vigneti Pie ★★★ Walter Massa brought Timorasso (w) grape back from nr extinction. Top: Coste del Vento, Montecitorio, Sterpi. V.gd: Anarchia Costituzionale (MOSCATO Bianco), Avvelenata (FREISA), BARBERA Monleale.

Massolino Vigna Rionda Pie ★★★ One of finest BAROLO estates, in Serralunga. Excellent Parafada, Margheria have firm structure, fruity drinkability; long-ageing VIGNA Rionda best. V.gd Parussi and LANGHE NEBBIOLO.

Mastroberardino Cam ★★★ Historic top-quality producer of mtn Avellino province in CAM. Top *Taurasi* (Historia Naturalis, Radici, Stilema), also FIANO DI AVELLINO (More Maiorum, Radici, Stilèma), GRECO DI TUFO Nova Serra.

Meroi F-VG ★★★ Dynamic estate. Top FRIULANO, MALVASIA Zittelle Durì, RIBOLLA GIALLA, SAUV BL Zitelle Barchetta.

Metodo classico or tradizionale Italian for "Champagne method".

Miani F-VG ★★★★ Enzo Pontoni is Italy's best white winemaker. Top: FRIULANO

(Buri and Filip), RIBOLLA GIALLA Pettarin, SAUV BL Zitelle. V.gd: Sauv Bl Saurint, CHARD Zitelle, MERLOT, REFOSCO Buri.

Molettieri, Salvatore Cam ★★★ Outstanding: TAURASI, RISERVA VIGNA Cinque Querce. Gd FIANO DI AVELLINO Apianum.

Monaci Pug ★★→★★★ Part of GIV. Characterful NEGROAMARO Kreos (rosé), PRIMITIVO Artas and SALICE SALENTINO Aiace (r).

Monferrato Pie Hills between River Po and Apennines. Main cities: Asti, Canelli and Nizza. Some of Italy's most delicious, fairly priced wines from typical local grapes: BARBERA, Freisa, GRIGNOLINO, MALVASIAS (di Casorzo, di Schierano), Ruché.

Monica di Sardegna Sar ★→★★★ DOC DYA. Delightfully perfumed, medium weight. Best: ARGIOLAS (Iselis), Cantina di Mogoro, CONTINI, Dettori (Chimbanta), Ferruccio Deiana (Karel), Josto Puddu (Torremora), SANTADI (Antigua).

Monsanto Tus ★★★ Esteemed CHIANTI CLASSICO estate. Best: Il POGGIO RISERVA (single vyd). Gd: Chianti Classico (Riserva) and IGT SANGIOVETO.

Montalcino Tus Hilltop town in province of Siena, fashionable and famous for concentrated, expensive BRUNELLO and more approachable, better-value ROSSO DI MONTALCINO, both still 100% SANGIOVESE.

Monte Carrubo Si ★★★ Pioneer Peter Vinding-Diers planted SYRAH on a former volcano s of Etna. Exciting, complex results.

Monte del Frà Ven ★★→★★★ Owned by Bonomo family; v.gd value. Top: AMARONE Lena di Mezzo, Ca' del Magro, Custoza Bonomo Sexaginta.

Montefalco Sagrantino Umb ★★★→★★★★ DOCG Once sweet PASSITO only (still best wine of area), drier version is Italy's most powerfully tannic red that requires optimal growing seasons to show best. Top: Adanti, Antonelli (Chiusa di Pannone and regular), CAPRAI (Collepiano, 25 Anni), Colleallodole, LUNGAROTTI, Pardi (Sacrantino), TENUTA Castelbuono; V.gd Bocale, Perticaia, Ruggeri, Sportoletti, Tabarrini, Villa Mongalli.

Montepulciano d'Abruzzo Ab ★★→★★★ DOC (r) 12 13 14 15 18 Thanks to the new generation of winemakers, Ab's wines (MONTEPULCIANO and TREBBIANO D'ABRUZZO too) have never been better. Reds can be either light, easy-going or structured, rich. Best: Cataldi Madonna (Tonì, Piè delle Vigne), EMIDIO PEPE, Filomusi Guelfi, Praesidium, TIBERIO (Colle Vota and regular), Torre dei Beati (Cocciapazza, Mazzamurello), Valle Reale and of course *Valentini* (best, age-worthy).

Montevertine Tus ★★★★ Organic certified estate in Radda. Outstanding IGT Le Pergole Torte, world-class, pure, long-ageing SANGIOVESE. V.gd Montevertine.

Montevetrano Cam ★★★ Iconic CAM AZIENDA. Superb IGT Montevetrano (AGLIANICO/CAB SAUV/MERLOT). V.gd Core Rosso (Aglianico) and Core Bianco (GRECO, FIANO).

Morella Pug ★★★→★★★★ Gaetano M and wife Lisa Gilbee make outstanding PRIMITIVO (Old Vines, La Signora, new Mondo Nuovo) from c.90-yr-old vines. V.gd: (rosé) Mezzarosa (Primitivo/NEGROAMARO), (w) Mezzogiorno (FIANO).

Morellino di Scansano Tus ★→★★★ DOCG 11 13 15 16' 17 18 MAREMMA's famous SANGIOVESE-based red is best when cheerful and light rather than overoaked and gritty. Best: *Le Pupille* (RISERVA and regular), Moris Farms, PODERE 414, POGGIO ARGENTIERA (Bellamarsilia), Roccapesta (Calestaia), TENUTA Belguardo, Terenzi (Purosangue).

Moris Farms Tus ★★★ One of 1st new-age producers of TUS's MAREMMA; Monteregio and *Morellino di Scansano* DOCS, plus VERMENTINO IGT. Top: iconic IGT Avvoltore (rich SANGIOVESE/CAB SAUV/SYRAH blend) and Morellino di Scansano (basic, RISERVA). But try Vermentino and Rosato Rosamundi.

Moscato d'Asti Pie ★★→★★★ DYA Similar to DOCG ASTI, but usually better grapes; lower alc, lower pressure, sweeter, fruitier, often from small producers. Best DOCG MOSCATO: Ca' d'Gal, Caudrina (La Galeisa), Forteto della Luja, Mongioia,

Saracco, *Vajra*, Vignaioli di Santo Stefano. V.gd: Braida, Cascina Fonda, Il Falchetto, L'Armangia, Perrone, RIZZI.

Mosnel Lom ★★★ Since 1836 Barboglio family has run this organic certified winery in FRANCIACORTA. Top: EBB, Nature, Saten.

Muri Gries T-AA ★★→★★★ Monastery in Bolzano suburb of Gries; traditional and still top producer of LAGREIN ALTO ADIGE DOC. Esp cru Abtei-Muri, Klosteranger.

Nals Margreid T-AA ★★★ Small quality co-op making mtn-fresh whites (esp PINOT BIANCO Sirmian).

Nebbiolo d'Alba Pie ★★→★★★ DOC 11 12 13 14 15 16' 18 (19) (100% NEBBIOLO) Sometimes a worthy replacement for BAROLO/BARBARESCO, though it comes from a distinct area between the two. Best: BREZZA, BRUNO GIACOSA, CERETTO, Hilberg-Pasquero, LUCIANO SANDRONE, ORLANDO ABRIGO, PAITIN, PODERI COLLA.

Nervi Pie ★★★ Historical winery in GATTINARA now owned by Roberto CONTERNO. Best: Molsino, Valferana.

Niedrist, Ignaz T-AA ★★★ LAGREIN Berger Gei RISERVA is reference. So are RIES, WEISSBURGUNDER (Limes), BLAUBURGUNDER Riserva. V.gd SAUV BL Limes and Trias (w blend). Waiting for Mitterberg Rot SYRAH, CHARD vom Kalk.

Nino Franco Ven ★★★→★★★★ Owner Primo Franco makes large volumes of top-notch PROSECCO that age surprisingly well. Among finest: Primo Franco Dry, Riva di San Floriano Brut, Rustico and Grave di Stecca Brut. Excellent CARTIZZE.

Anchovies & salami with bread & butter: typical snack in Pie. Gd with Moscato.

Nipozzano, Castello di Tus ★★★→★★★★ FRESCOBALDI estate in RÚFINA, e of Florence, making excellent CHIANTI Rúfina. Top Nipozzano RISERVA (esp Vecchie Viti) and IGT *Montesodi*. V.gd Mormoreto (B'x blend).

Nittardi Tus ★★→★★★ Reliable source of quality modern CHIANTI CLASSICO. German owned; oenologist Carlo Ferrini.

Nössing, Manni T-AA ★★★★ Outstanding KERNER, MÜLLER-T Sass Rigais, SYLVANER. Benchmark wines.

Notaio, Cantine del Bas ★★→★★★ Organic estate specializing in AGLIANICO (w/rosé/sp/PASSITO). Star is La Firma.

Nozzole Tus ★★→★★★ Famous estate in heart of CHIANTI CLASSICO, n of Greve, owned by FOLONARI. V.gd Chianti Classico RISERVA, excellent CAB SAUV Pareto.

Nuragus di Cagliari Sar ★★ DOC DYA. Lively, uncomplicated, from Nuragus grape, finally gaining visibility. Best: ARGIOLAS (S'Elegas), Mogoro (Ajò), Pala (I Fiori).

Occhio di Pernice Tus "Partridge's eye". A type of VIN SANTO made predominantly from black grapes, mainly SANGIOVESE. *Avignonesi's is definitive*. Also an obscure black variety found in RÚFINA and elsewhere.

Occhipinti, Arianna Sic ★★★ Cult producer, deservedly so. Organic certified. Top: Il Frappato and CERASUOLO DI VITTORIA CLASSICO Grotte Alte. V.gd Bianco SP68, Rosso SP68, NERO D'AVOLA Siccagno.

Oddero Pie ★★★→★★★★ Traditionalist La Morra estate for excellent BAROLO (Brunate, Bussia RISERVA, VIGNA Rionda Riserva, Villero), BARBARESCO (Gallina) crus, plus other serious PIE wines. V.gd value Barolo, RIES. Monvigliero from 2021.

Oltrepò Pavese Lom ★→★★★ Multi-DOC, incl numerous varietals, blends from Pavia province; best is SPUMANTE. Gd growers: Anteo, Barbacarlo, Castello di Cicognola, Conte Vistarino (MC 1865 and PINOT N Bertone), Giorgi, Mazzolino, Travaglino.

Ornellaia Tus ★★★★ 10 11 12 13 15 16 Fashionable, indeed cult, estate nr BOLGHERI now owned by FRESCOBALDI. Top wines of B'x grapes/method: Bolgheri DOC Ornellaia, IGT Masseto (MERLOT), Ornellaia Bianco (SAUV BL/VIOGNIER). Gd: Bolgheri DOC Le Serre Nuove and POGGIO alle Gazze (w).

Orvieto Umb ★→★★★ DOC DYA. One of few areas of Italy where noble rot occurs spontaneously and often. Sweet late-harvest can be memorable though cheap-and-cheerful dry white, v. popular too. Off-dry Amabile less in favour today but delicious. Top: BARBERANI (Luigi e Giovanna) but sweet Calcaia just as gd. Try also: Bigi, Cardeto, *Castello della Sala*, Decugnano dei Barbi, Palazzone; Sergio Mottura (Lat).

Pacenti, Siro Tus ★★★ Modern-style BRUNELLO, ROSSO DI MONTALCINO from small, caring producer.

Paitin Pie ★★→★★★ Pasquero-Elia family have been bottling BARBARESCO since C19. Today back on track making "real" BARBARESCO from cru Serraboella in large barrels. Sorì Paitin Vecchie Vigne is star.

Paltrinieri E-R ★★→★★★ One of top three LAMBRUSCO producers. Among 1st to produce 100% Lambrusco di Sorbara. Best: Leclisse, Secco Radice; v.gd La RISERVA.

Pantelleria Si ★★★ Windswept, black (volcanic) earth SI island off Tunisian coast, famous for superb MOSCATO d'Alessandria stickies. PASSITO versions particularly dense/intense. Try DE BARTOLI (Bukkuram), DONNAFUGATA (Ben Ryé), Ferrandes.

Parrina, La Tus ★★ Popular estate and *agriturismo* on TUS coast dominates DOC Parrina; solid rather than inspired wines.

Passito Tus, Ven One of Italy's most ancient and characteristic styles, from grapes dried briefly under harvest sun (in s) or over a period of weeks or mths in airy attics – a process called *appassimento*. Best-known versions: VIN SANTO (TUS); AMARONE/RECIOTO (Ven), VALPOLICELLA/SOAVE. Try: Loazzolo, MONTEFALCO, ORVIETO, TORCOLATO, VALLONE. Never cheap.

Paternoster Bas ★★★ *See* TOMMASI.

Pepe, Emidio Ab ★★★ Artisanal winery, 15 ha, bio and organic certified. Top MONTEPULCIANO D'ABRUZZO. Gd: TREBBIANO D'ABRUZZO (Old Vines) and PECORINO.

Pie's most planted vine? Not Nebbiolo (3rd); Barbera (1st), Moscato Bianco (2nd).

Petrussa, Vigna F-VG ★★★ Small family estate: high-quality wines. Best: SCHIOPPETTINO di Prepotto (also RISERVA), PICOLIT and Richenza (cuvée of w indigenous grapes, old vines).

Pian dell'Orino Tus ★★★★ Small MONTALCINO estate, committed to bio. BRUNELLO seductive, technically perfect, Rosso nearly as gd. Many epic wines.

Piane, Le Pie ★★★ BOCA DOC resurfaced thanks to Christoph Kunzli. Gd: Maggiorina, Mimmo (NEBBIOLO/Croatina), Piane (Croatina), (w) Bianko (Erbaluce).

Picolit F-VG ★★→★★★ DOCG 12 13 15 16 (18) Potentially Italy's best sweet (most from air-dried grapes; rare late-harvests even better), but plagued by poor versions that don't speak of the grape. Texture ranges from light/sweet (rare) to super-thick (PASSITO). Best: Aquila del Torre, D'Attimis, I Comelli, LIVIO FELLUGA, Marco Sara, Perusini, RONCHI DI CIALLA, Valentino Butussi, VIGNA PETRUSSA. V.gd: Ermacora, Girolamo Dorigo, Paolo Rodaro.

Piedmont / Piemonte In ne, bordering France to the w. Turin is capital. MONFERRATO, LANGHE, ROERO and ALTO PIEMONTE main areas. With TUS, Italy's most important region for quality (10% of all DOC(G) wines). No IGTS allowed. Grapes incl: BARBERA, Brachetto, Cortese, DOLCETTO, Freisa, GRIGNOLINO, MALVASIA di Casorzo, Malvasia di Schierano, MOSCATO, NEBBIOLO, Ruché, Timorasso. *See also* BARBARESCO, BAROLO.

Pieropan Ven ★★★★ Andrea and Dario, Leonildo's son, now run winery. Organic certified. Cru *La Rocca* still ultimate oaked SOAVE; Calvarino best of all. V.gd AMARONE, PASSITO della Rocca.

Pietradolce Si ★★★→★★★★ Faro bros own vyds in key ETNA crus, often pre-phylloxera vines. Top: Etna Rosso Barbagalli, Rampante. V.gd: Archineri (r/w).

Pio Cesare Pie ★★★ Veteran ALBA producer; BAROLO, BARBARESCO in modern (barrique) and traditional (large-cask-aged) versions. Particularly gd NEBBIOLO D'ALBA, *a little Barolo at half the price*. Best: Single-vyd and Classic collections.

Pira e Figli – Chiara Boschis Pie ★★★→★★★★ Organic certified. Must-visit estate. Top: Cannubi, Mosconi, Via Nuova.

Planeta Si ★★★ Leading SI estate with vyds all over island, incl Menfi (Grillo Terebinto), Noto (NERO D'AVOLA Santa Cecilia), Vittoria (CERASUOLO Dorilli), most recently on Etna (Carricante, NERELLO MASCALESE Eruzione 1614). Also: Nocera (r), La Segreta (r/w), Cometa (FIANO).

Podere Tus Small TUS farm, once part of a big estate.

Poggio Tus Means "hill" in TUS dialect. "Poggione" means "big hill".

Poggio Antico Tus ★★★ Paola Gloder looks after 32-ha estate, one of highest in MONTALCINO at c.500m (1640ft). Style is restrained, consistent, at times too herbal.

Poggio Argentiera Tus ★★★ MAREMMA estate owned by TUA RITA. Best: Capatosta (95% SANGIOVESE). V.gd MORELLINO DI SCANSANO and Poggioraso (CAB FR).

Poggio di Sotto ★★★★ Small MONTALCINO estate with a big reputation recently. Has purchased adjacent vyds. Top BRUNELLO, RISERVA and Rosso of traditional character with idiosyncratic twist.

Poggione, Tenuta Il Tus ★★★ MONTALCINO estate, in S; consistently excellent BRUNELLO, ROSSO. Top Brunello RISERVA VIGNA Paganelli. V.gd VIN SANTO.

Poggiopiano Tus ★★ Opulent CHIANTI CLASSICO from Bartoli family. Chiantis are pure SANGIOVESE, but SUPER TUSCAN Rosso di Sera incl up to 15% Colorino. V.gd Colorino Taffe Ta'.

Poggio Scalette Tus ★★ Vittorio Fiore and son Jury run CHIANTI organic estate at Greve. Top: Il Carbonaione (100% SANGIOVESE); needs several yrs bottle-age. Above-average CHIANTI CLASSICO and B'x-blend Capogatto.

Poliziano Tus ★★★ MONTEPULCIANO organic estate of Federico Carletti. Superior if often v. dark, herbal VINO NOBILE (esp cru Asinone and new Le Caggiole); gd IGT Le Stanze (CAB SAUV/MERLOT), Cortona In Violas (Merlot).

Pomino Tus ★★★ DOC (r) 12 13 15 16 17 (18) Appendage of RÚFINA, with fine red and white blends (esp Il Benefizio). Virtually a FRESCOBALDI exclusivity.

Potazzine, Le Tus ★★★★ Organic estate of Gorelli family just S of MONTALCINO. Vyd is quite high. Outstanding BRUNELLOS (also RISERVA) and Rossos, serious and v. drinkable. Try them at family's restaurant in town.

Prà Ven ★★★★ Leading SOAVE CLASSICO producer, esp crus Colle Sant'Antonio, Monte Grande, Staforte v. tasty. Excellent VALPOLICELLA La Morandina, AMARONE (15 top).

Produttori del Barbaresco Pie ★★★ One of Italy's earliest co-ops, perhaps best in the world, makes excellent traditional straight BARBARESCO plus crus Asili, Montefico, Montestefano, Ovello, Pora, Rio Sordo. Super values.

Proprietà Sperino Pie ★★★→★★★★ Top estate of LESSONA. One of best of ALTO PIEMONTE run by Luca De Marchi (*see* ISOLE E OLENA). Outstanding: Lessona; V.gd: L Franc (one of best Italian CAB FR), Rosa del Rosa (NEBBIOLO/Vespolina rosé) and Uvaggio (r).

Prosecco Ven ★→★★ DOC(G) DYA. Prosecco is the wine, GLERA the grape variety. Quality is higher in the VALDOBBIADENE. Look for: Adami, Biancavigna, BISOL, Bortolin, Canevel, Carpenè-Malvolti, Case Bianche, Col Salice, Col Vetoraz, Gregoletto, La Riva dei Frati, Le Colture, Mionetto, NINO FRANCO, Ruggeri, Silvano Follador, Zardetto.

Puglia The "heel" of Italy. Many gd-value reds from likes of Bombino Nero, NEGROAMARO, PRIMITIVO, Susumaniello and Uva di Troia grapes. W Bombino Bianco and aromatic Minutolo most interesting whites, but Verdeca making comeback; by contrast, FIANO is disappointing, best avoided. Dubious winemaking talent and old equipment a real problem. Castel del Monte, Gioia del Colle Primitivo, PRIMITIVO DI MANDURIA, SALICE SALENTINO best denominations.

Quartomoro Sar ★★→★★★ Piero Cella works with old vines, rare local varieties. Best: Memorie di Vite line (Bovale, Monica, Semidano).

Querciabella Tus ★★★ Top CHIANTI CLASSICO estate, bio since 2000. Top IGT Camartina

(CAB SAUV/SANGIOVESE), Batàr (CHARD/PINOT BL) and new single-commune wines (Greve in CHIANTI, Radda in Chianti, Gaiole). V.gd Chianti Classico (and RISERVA).

Quintarelli, Giuseppe Ven ★★★★ Arch-traditionalist artisan producer of sublime VALPOLICELLA, RECIOTO, AMARONE; plus a fine Bianco Secco, a blend of various grapes. Daughter Fiorenza and sons now in charge, altering nothing, incl the ban on spitting when tasting.

Quintodecimo Cam ★★★→★★★★ Oenology professor/winemaker Luigi Moio's beautiful estate. Outstanding: TAURASI VIGNA Grande Cerzito, VIGNA Quintodecimo; great AGLIANICO (Terra d'Eclano), GRECO DI TUFO (Giallo d'Arles).

Ratti, Renato Pie ★★→★★★ Iconic BAROLO estate. Modern wines; short maceration but plenty of substance, esp Barolos Rocche dell'Annunziata and Conca.

Recioto della Valpolicella Ven ★★★→★★★★ DOCG Sweet-wine marketing problems mean this traditional Italian beauty is being made less and less. Shame, esp as always much better than many disappointing overly sweet, overly tannic AMARONES.

Recioto di Soave Ven ★★★→★★★★ DOCG SOAVE from half-dried grapes: sweet, fruity, slightly almondy; sweetness is cut by high acidity. *Drink with cheese.* Best: Anselmi, COFFELE, Gini, PIEROPAN, Tamellini; often v.gd from Ca' Rugate, Pasqua, PRÀ, Suavia, Trabuchi.

Refosco (dal Peduncolo Rosso) F-VG ★★ 12 13 15 16 (18) Most-planted native red grape of region. Best from FRIULI COLLI ORIENTALI DOC. Top: MIANI, VIGNA PETRUSSA, Volpe Pasini. Gd: Ca' Bolani, D'Attimis, La Viarte, LIVIO FELLUGA, MEROI, Valchiarò, Vignai da Duline, Zorzettig (Myò).

Ricasoli Tus Historic Tuscan family. First Italian Prime Minister Bettino R devised the classic CHIANTI blend. Main branch occupies medieval Castello di BROLIO.

Riecine Tus ★★★→★★★★ SANGIOVESE specialist estate at Gaiole since 70s. Riecine di Riecine, La Gioia (100% Sangiovese) potentially outstanding. Gd Tresette (MERLOT).

Rinaldi, Giuseppe Pie ★★★ Beppe R's daughters Marta and Carlotta continue their father's highly traditional path. Outstanding: BARBERA D'ALBA, Brunate, Freisa. Also gd but overrated Tre Tine.

Ripasso Ven *See* VALPOLICELLA RIPASSO.

Riserva Wine aged for a statutory period, usually in casks or barrels.

Rivetti, Giorgio (La Spinetta) Pie ★★★ Fine MOSCATO D'ASTI, excellent BARBERA, series of super-concentrated, oaky BARBARESCOS (Gallina, Starderi, Valeirano). Also owns vyds in BAROLO, CHIANTI COLLI Pisane DOCGS, traditional SPUMANTE house Contratto.

Rivetto Pie ★★★ Bio estate; Enrico R one of most talented young winemakers. Top: BAROLO Briccolina. V.gd Barolo Serralunga, LANGHE NEBBIOLO.

Rizzi Pie ★★★→★★★★ Sub-area of Treiso, commune of BARBARESCO, where Dellapiana family look after 35 ha vyd. Organic. Top crus are Barbaresco Pajore and Rizzi RISERVA Boito. V.gd: ALTA LANGA, Barbaresco (Nervo, Rizzi), MOSCATO D'ASTI.

Roagna Pie ★★★→★★★★ Old vines, massale selection, organic, wild yeast, long maceration and long ageing in large oak casks. Outstanding BARBARESCO Crichet Pajet and BAROLO and BARBARESCO Vecchie Viti ("old vines") line. V.gd also Barolo Pira, Barbaresco Pajè, Timorasso Montemarzino.

Rocca, Albino Pie ★★★→★★★★ A foremost producer of elegant, sophisticated BARBARESCO: top crus Ovello VIGNA Loreto, Ronchi, new Cottà.

Rocca, Bruno Pie ★★★→★★★★ Family estate run by Francesco and Luisa, Bruno's sons. BARBARESCOS with a more traditional style. More elegance than power. Top are BARBARESCOS RISERVA and Maria Adelaide. V.gd: BARBERA D'ASTI, Currà, Rabajà

Rocca delle Macie Tus ★★ Large estate in Castellina-in-CHIANTI run by Sergio Zingarelli. Best: Fizzano, Gran Selezione Sergio Zingarelli.

Roero Pie ★★→★★★★ DOCG 10 11 13 15 16 (18) Wilder, cooler, much sandier soils compared to LANGHE. NEBBIOLO (r) and ARNEIS (w). Best: BRUNO GIACOSA ★, Ca' Rossa,

Cascina Chicco, Cornarea, GIOVANNI ALMONDO, MALVIRÀ ★, MATTEO CORREGGIA ★, Morra, Negro, Rosso, Taliano, Val del Prete, Valfaccenda.

Romagna Sangiovese Mar ★★→★★★ DOC At times too herbal and oaky, but often well-made, even classy SANGIOVESE red. Gd: Ca' di Sopra, Cesari, Condello, Drei Donà, FATTORIA ZERBINA, Nicolucci, Papiano, Paradiso, Tre Monti, Trere, Villa Venti (Primo Segno). Also IGT RONCO delle Ginestre, Ronco dei Ciliegi (CASTELLUCCIO).

Ronchi di Cialla F-VG ★★★→★★★★ Leading F-VG estate, in Cialla subzone of FRIULI COLLI ORIENTALI, run by Rapuzzi family, devoted to local old native grapes. Best: Ciallabianco (blend of RIBOLLA GIALLA/VERDUZZO/PICOLIT), Picolit di Cialla, SCHIOPPETTINO di Cialla. V.gd REFOSCO dal Peduncolo Rosso.

Ronco Term for a hillside vyd in ne Italy, esp F-VG.

Ronco del Gelso F-VG ★★★→★★★★ Tight, pure ISONZO: PINOT GR Sot lis Rivis, FRIULANO Toc Bas and MALVASIA VIGNA della Permuta are regional benchmarks. V.gd Latimis (w blend).

Rosato General Italian name for rosé. Other rosé names incl CHIARETTO from Lake Garda; CERASUOLO from Ab; Kretzer from ALTO ADIGE.

Rossese di Dolceacqua or Dolceacqua Lig ★★→★★★ DOC Interesting reds. Intense, salty, spicy; greater depth of fruit than most. Best: Maccario-Dringenberg (Posaù, Curli), Terre Bianche (Bricco Arcagna). Vgd: Kà Mancinè, Poggi dell'Elmo, TENUTA Anfosso.

Rosso Conero Mar *See* CONERO.

Rosso di Montalcino Tus ★★→★★★ 11 12 13 15 16 18 DOC for earlier maturing wines from BRUNELLO grapes, usually from younger or lesser vyd sites; bargains exist.

Rosso di Montefalco Umb ★★ 12 13 15 16 18 DOC SANGIOVESE/SAGRANTINO blend, often with a splash of softening MERLOT. *See* MONTEFALCO SAGRANTINO.

Rosso di Montepulciano Tus ★ DOC 13 15 16 Junior version of VINO NOBILE DI MONTEPULCIANO, growers similar.

Rosso Piceno / Piceno Mar ★ DOC 13 15 (18) Blend of MONTEPULCIANO (>35%) and SANGIOVESE (>15%). SUPERIORE means it comes only from far s of region. Gd: Boccadigabbia, BUCCI, GAROFOLI, Moncaro, Monte Schiavo, Saladini Pilastri, Santa Barbara, TENUTA di Tavignano, Velenosi.

Ruffino Tus ★→★★★ Venerable CHIANTI firm, at Pontassieve nr Florence, produces reliable wines such as CHIANTI CLASSICO RISERVA Ducale and Ducale Oro.

Rúfina Tus ★★→★★★ Most n subzone of CHIANTI, e of Florence, grows SANGIOVESE at highest altitudes, meaning tight, refined, age-worthy wines. Gd to outstanding:

Old vines, newly modern

You'll be forgiven for never having heard of these grapes, or tasted them. But keep an eye open. **Whites: Albarola** (LIG) citrus, light, saline; **Baratuciat** (PIE) floral, delicately spicy; **Caprettone** (CAM) citrus, v. mineral; **Catalanesca** (Cam) fruity, mineral, low acid; **Durella** (Ven) high-acid, mineral, orchard fruit, v.gd sparkling/late harvest; **Forastera** (Cam) herbal, saline, fleshy; **Nasco** (SAR) herbal, musky, great (dr/sw); **Semidano** (Sar) refined, citrus, mineral, difficult but worth it. **Reds: Avanà** (Pie) garnet-hued, fresh, red berries; **Becuet** (Pie) v. tannic, light, floral; **Cagnulari** (Sar) fresh, fragrant, fruity-floral charm; **Cornalin** (VDA): nobly tannic, delicately smoky-spicy; **Mayolet** (VdA) aromatic, refined, light-bodied, fruity, spicy, one of Italy's best; **Nocera** (SI) rich, fresh herbs, cherries; **Pascale** (Sar) intensely fruity, mineral, medium-bodied; **Susumaniello** (PUG) tannic, dark-cherry, plum; **Tazzelenghe** (F-VG) Italy's best least-known grape, steely, refined, age-worthy; **Uvalino** (Pie) v. tannic, spicy-herbal, blackberry; **Vuillermin** (VdA) semi-aromatic, full-bodied, floral, spicy, v.gd.

Castello del Trebbio, CASTELLO DI NIPOZZANO (FRESCOBALDI), Colognole, Frascole, Grati/Villa di Vetrice, I Veroni, Lavacchio, SELVAPIANA, TENUTA Bossi, Travignoli. Don't confuse with RUFFINO, which has HQ in Pontassieve, Rúfina's main town.

Russiz Superiore F-VG ★★→★★★ LIVIO FELLUGA's brother, Marco, est vyds in various parts of F-VG. Now run by Marco's son Roberto. Wide range; best is PINOT GRIGIO, COLLIO Bianco blend Col Disòre. V.gd PINOT BIANCO RISERVA.

Salento Pug Home to Italy's best rosé from NEGROAMARO (along with Abruzzo's CERASUOLO made from MONTEPULCIANO). But also v.gd Negramaro, with a bit of help from MALVASIA Nera, and now increasingly varietal reds from local Sussumaniello. See also PUG, SALICE SALENTINO.

Highest cellar? Mont Blanc Pavillon Sky Way, 2173m (7129ft). Don't drop your glass.

Salice Salentino Pug ★★→★★★ DOC 11 13 15 16 17 Best-known of Salento's too many NEGROAMARO-based DOCS. RISERVA after 2 yrs. Gd: Cantele, Conti Zecca (Cantalupi), Cosimo Taurino, Leone de Castris (Riserva), Mocavero, Vallone (Vereto Riserva).

Salvioni Tus ★★★★ Aka La Cerbaiola; iconic small, highest-quality MONTALCINO estate run by father and daughter team. BRUNELLO, ROSSO DI MONTALCINO among v. best available and worthy of their high prices.

Sandrone, Luciano Pie ★★★→★★★★ Modern-style ALBA. Deep BAROLOS: Aleste (was Cannubi Boschis), Le Vigne, Vite Talin. Gd NEBBIOLO D'ALBA Valmaggiore.

San Felice Tus ★★★ Important historic TUS grower, owned by Gruppo Allianz, run by Leonardo Bellaccini. Fine CHIANTI CLASSICO and RISERVA POGGIO Rosso from estate in Castelnuovo Berardenga. Gd too: BRUNELLO DI MONTALCINO Campogiovanni; IGT *Vigorello* (1ST SUPER TUSCAN, from 1968).

San Gimignano Tus TUS medieval town known for its towers and dry (w) VERNACCIA DI SAN GIMIGNANO DOCG. Top: Cesani, FALCHINI, Guicciardini Strozza, Il Colombaio, Il Palagione, Montenidoli, Mormoraia, Panizzi, Pietrafitta.

San Giusto a Rentennano Tus ★★★★ Top CHIANTI CLASSICO estate. Organic certified. Outstanding MERLOT (La Ricolma), SANGIOVESE IGT Percarlo, Vin San Giusto (PASSITO); v.gd Chianti Classico, RISERVA Le Baroncole.

San Guido, Tenuta See SASSICAIA.

San Leonardo T-AA ★★★★ Top TRENTINO estate of Marchesi Guerrieri Gonzaga. Main wine is B'x blend, *San Leonardo*, Italy's most claret-like wine; v.gd CARMENÈRE, Villa Gresti (MERLOT/Carmenère).

San Michele Appiano T-AA ★★★ Historic co-op. *Mtn-fresh whites*, brimming with varietal typicity, drinkability, are speciality. Best: The Wine Collection and Appius (selected by Hans Terzer). V.gd PINOT BL Schulthauser and Sanct Valentin line.

Santadi Sar ★★★ SAR's, and one of Italy's, best co-ops, esp for CARIGNANO-based reds *Terre Brune*, Rocca Rubia RISERVA (all DOC CARIGNANO DEL SULCIS). V.gd MONICA DI SARDEGNA Antigua, Shardana and PASSITO Latinia (w).

Santa Maddalena / St-Magdalener T-AA ★→★★★ DOC DYA. Teutonic-style red from SCHIAVA grapes from v. steep slopes behind ALTO ADIGE capital Bolzano. Notable: CS St-Magdalena (Huck am Bach), CS Tramin, Gojer, Rottensteiner, Waldgries.

Sant'Antimo Tus ★★ DOC Lovely Romanesque abbey gives name to catch-all DOC for (almost) everything in MONTALCINO zone that isn't BRUNELLO DOCG or Rosso DOC.

Saracco, Paolo Pie ★★★★ Top MOSCATO D'ASTI. V.gd: CHARD, LANGHE RIES, PINOT N.

Sardinia / Sardegna Italy's 2nd-largest island is home to world-class whites and reds. Look for VERMENTINO DI GALLURA DOCG, VERMENTINO DI SARDEGNA (fruitier, less mineral), Sherry-like VERNACCIA DI ORISTANO, NURAGUS among whites, late-harvest sweet Nasco; forgotten Semidano deserves much better. CANNONAU (GARNACHA) and CARIGNANO most famous reds, but Bovale Sardo and Pascale just as gd.

Sassicaia Tus ★★★★ 04' 05 06 07' 08 09 10 13 15' 16 Italy's sole single-vyd DOC (BOLGHERI), a CAB (SAUV/FR) made on First Growth lines by Marchese Incisa della

Rocchetta at TENUTA SAN GUIDO. More elegant than lush, made for age – and often bought for investment, but hugely influential in giving Italy a top-quality image; 16 extremely elegant, one of best recent yrs.

Satta, Michele Tus ★★★ Virtually only BOLGHERI grower to succeed with 100% SANGIOVESE (Cavaliere). Bolgheri DOC red blends Piastraia, SUPERIORE I Castagni.

Scarpa Pie ★★★ Historic traditional winery in Nizza Monferrato. Top BARBERA D'ASTI La Bogliona, Rouchet (Ruchè) Briccorosa. V.gd BARBARESCO Tettineive, Freisa.

Scavino, Paolo Pie ★★★ Modernist BAROLO producer of Castiglione Falletto, esp crus Rocche dell'Annunziata, Bric del Fiasc, Cannubi, Monvigliero. V.gd new Barolo crus: Ravera and Prapò. Waiting for new Bussia Fantini.

Schiava Alto Adige T-AA ★ DOC DYA. Schiava (VERNATSCH in German) gives practically tannin-free, easy-glugging red from most s territory of German-speaking world. Sadly disappearing from Tyrolean vyds.

Schiopetto, Mario F-VG ★★★ Legendary late COLLIO pioneering estate now owned by Rotolo family. V.gd DOC SAUV BL, *Pinot Bl*, RIBOLLA GIALLA, FRIULANO, IGT blend Blanc des Rosis, etc.

Sella & Mosca Sar ★★★ Major SAR grower and merchant with v. pleasant white Torbato (esp Terre Bianche) and light, fruity VERMENTINO Cala Viola (DYA). Gd Alghero DOC Marchese di Villamarina (CAB SAUV) and Monteluce (Nasco). Also interesting Port-like Anghelu Ruju.

Selvapiana Tus ★★★★ CHIANTI RÚFINA organic estate among Italian greats. Best: RISERVA Bucerchiale, IGT Fornace; but even *basic Chianti Rúfina is a treat*. Also fine red Petrognano, POMINO, Riserva VIGNETO Erchi.

Sforzato / Sfursat Lom ★★★ DOCG Sforzato di VALTELLINA is made AMARONE-like, from air-dried NEBBIOLO grapes. Ages beautifully.

Sicily The Med's largest island, modern source of exciting original wines and value. Native grapes (r Frappato, NERO D'AVOLA, NERELLO MASCALESE; W CATARRATTO, Grecanico, GRILLO, INZOLIA), plus internationals. Vyds on flatlands in w, hills in centre, volcanic altitudes on Mt Etna.

Siddura Sar ★★→★★★ In Gallura area, nw Sar. Best: VERMENTINO di Gallura Superiore Maia and Beru, CANNONAU RISERVA Fòla, Cagnulari Bacco.

Soave Ven ★→★★★ DOC Famous, hitherto underrated, Veronese white. CHARD, GARGANEGA, TREBBIANO di Soave. Wines from volcanic soils of CLASSICO zone can be intense, saline, v. fine, quite long-lived. *See also* RECIOTO.

Solaia Tus ★★★★ 09 10 11 12 13 15 16 CAB SAUV/SANGIOVESE by ANTINORI; needs age.

Sottimano Pie ★★★→★★★★ Family estate. One of most inspired in BARBARESCO (crus: Basarin, Cottà, Currà, Fausoni, Pajorè). V.gd BARBERA D'ALBA, DOLCETTO D'ALBA.

Speri Ven ★★★ VALPOLICELLA family estate. Organic certified. Traditional style. Top: AMARONE Sant'Urbano.

Spumante Sparkling.

Südtirol T-AA German name for ALTO ADIGE.

Superiore Wine with more ageing than normal DOC and 0.5–1% more alc. May indicate a restricted production zone, eg. ROSSO PICENO Superiore.

Almost 28% of world's vine varieties are native to Italy.

Super Tuscan Tus Wines of high quality and price developed in 70s/80s to get round silly laws then prevailing. Now, esp with Gran Selezione on up, scarcely relevant. Wines still generally considered in Super Tuscan category, strictly unofficially: CA' MARCANDA, Flaccianello, Guado al Tasso, Messorio, ORNELLAIA, Redigaffi, SASSICAIA, SOLAIA, TIGNANELLO.

Sylla Sebaste Pie ★★★ Illustrates merits of rare NEBBIOLO Rosé variety: lighter, v. perfumed BAROLO. A beauty.

Tasca d'Almerita Si ★★★ New generation of Tasca d'Almeritas runs historic, still prestigious ETNA estate. High-altitude vyds; balanced IGTS under Regaleali label. Top: NERO D'AVOLA-based *Rosso del Conte* and Etna wines Tascante Sciaranuova and Rampante. V.gd MALVASIA delle Lipari Capofaro, GRILLO Mozia TENUTA Whitaker.

Taurasi Cam ★★★ DOCG 10 11 12 13 15 16 (18) S Italy's 1st DOCG. Best AGLIANICO of CAM: none so potentially *complex, demanding, ultimately rewarding.* 17 communes, four sub-zones (nw, w, Taurasi, s). Top: Contrade di Taurasi (Vigne d'Alto, Coste), Guastaferro (Primum), MASTROBERARDINO (Radici), MOLETTIERI SALVATORE (VIGNA CinqueQuerce), QUINTODECIMO (Vigna Gran Cerzito and Quintodecimo). V.gd: FERRARA BENITO (Vigna Quattro Confini), FEUDI DI SAN GREGORIO (Piano di Montevergine, Rosamilia, Candriano), Perillo.

Tedeschi Ven ★★★ Bevy of v. fine AMARONE, VALPOLICELLA. Amarone Capitel Monte Olmi and RECIOTO Capitel Monte Fontana best.

Cab Fr and Merlot in Veneto since C18, thanks to Napoleon. Sort of thanks...

Tenuta An agricultural holding (*see* under name – eg. SAN GUIDO, TENUTA).

Terlano, Cantina di T-AA ★★★ High-quality co-op, benchmark PINOT BL. Outstanding Rarity special editions of mature white (aged min 10 yrs) and Primo Terlaner I Grande Cuvée (PINOT BL/SAUV BL/CHARD). Vgd: LAGREIN RISERVA Porphyr, Pinot Bl Vorberg, Sauv Bl Quarz.

Teroldego Rotaliano T-AA ★★→★★★ DOC TRENTINO's best local grape makes seriously tasty wine on flat Campo Rotaliano. *Foradori* is tops. Gd: Dorigati, Endrizzi, MEZZACORONA'S RISERVA Nos, Zeni.

Terre Nere, Tenuta delle Si ★★★★ Marc de Grazia shows great wine can be made from NERELLO and CARRICANTE grapes, on coveted n side of Mt Etna. Top: Cuvèe delle Vigne Niche wines, Guardiola and pre-phylloxera La VIGNA di Don Peppino. V.gd Le Vigne di Eli.

Terriccio, Castello del Tus ★★★ Large estate s of Livorno: excellent, v. expensive B'x-style IGT Lupicaia, v.gd IGT Tassinaia and Terriccio (mainly Rhône grapes blend).

Tiberio Ab ★★★★ Outstanding TREBBIANO D'ABRUZZO Fonte Canale (60-yr-old vines) one of Italy's best whites and new MONTEPULCIANO D'ABRUZZO Colle Vota; CERASUOLO D'ABRUZZO, PECORINO also exceptional.

Tiefenbrunner T-AA ★★★→★★★★ Grower-merchant in Teutonic castle (*Turmhof*) in S ALTO ADIGE. Wide range of mtn-fresh white and well-defined red varietals, esp 1000m (3281ft)-high MÜLLER-T *Feldmarschall*, one of Italy's best whites. V.gd CAB SAUV VIGNA Toren, SAUV BL RISERVA Rachtl.

Tignanello Tus ★★★★ 07′ 08 09 10 11 12 13 15 16 SANGIOVESE/CAB SAUV blend, barrique-aged, 1st made 1971 as CHIANTI CLASSICO; with 1975 moved to current blend. Such a large volume of such high quality speaks of ANTINORI family talent.

Tommasi Ven ★★★ The 4th generation now in charge. Top: AMARONE (RISERVA Ca' Florian), VALPOLICELLA Rafael. Other estates in Bas (PATERNOSTER), OLTREPÒ PAVESE (TENUTA Caseo), PUG (Masseria Surani), Ven (Filodora).

Torcolato Ven Sweet white from BREGANZE in Ven; Vespaiolo grapes laid on mats or hung up to dry for mths, as nearby RECIOTO DI SOAVE. Best: CS Beato Bartolomeo da Breganze, MACULAN, Miotti.

Torgiano Umb ★★ DOC and **Torgiano, Rosso Riserva** ★★→★★★ DOCG 09 10 11 12 13 15 16 Gd-to-excellent red from Umb. Top: LUNGAROTTI *Vigna Monticchio* Rubesco RISERVA. Keeps many yrs.

Torrette VdA ★→★★★ DOC Blend based on Petit Rouge and other local varieties. Best: Torrette SUPERIEUR. Gd: Anselmet, D&D, Didier Gerbelle, Elio Ottin, FEUDO DI SAN MAURIZIO, GROSJEAN, LES CRETES.

Tramin, Cantina T-AA ★★★ Quality co-op with benchmark GEWURZ. Outstanding Epokale, Nussbaumer, Terminum. V.gd: PINOT GR Unterebner, CHARD Troy and Le Selezioni line.

Travaglini Pie ★★★ Solid producer of n PIE NEBBIOLO, with v.gd GATTINARA RISERVA, Gattinara Tre VIGNE, pretty-gd MC Nebolè (Nebbiolo) and Coste della Sesia.

Trebbiano d'Abruzzo Ab ★→★★★★ DOC DYA. Generally crisp, simple, but VALENTINI's and Tiberio's Fonte Canale are *two of Italy's greatest* whites. V.gd also EMIDIO PEPE and Valle Reale.

Trediberri Pie ★★★ Dynamic estate, top BAROLO Rocche dell'Annunziata (best value); v.gd BARBERA D'ALBA, LANGHE NEBBIOLO and new DOGLIANI (DOLCETTO).

Trentino T-AA ★→★★★ Varietally named DOC wines; best are perfumed, flavourful, inexpensive. Less successful ones dilute, boring, neutral. Best: GEWURZ, MARZEMINO, MÜLLER-T, Nosiola, SCHIAVA, TEROLDEGO. **Trento DOC** is name of potentially high-quality METODO CLASSICO wines.

Trinoro, Tenuta di Tus ★★★★ Individualist TUS red estate, pioneer in DOC Val d'Orcia between MONTEPULCIANO and MONTALCINO. Heavy accent on B'x grapes in flagship TENUTA di Trinoro, also in Palazzi, Camagi, Tenagli and Magnacosta. *See also* VINI FRANCHETTI (ETNA).

Tua Rita Tus ★★★★ 1st producer, as new BOLGHERI in 90s, of possibly Italy's greatest MERLOT in Redigaffi, also outstanding B'x blend *Giusto di Notri*, SYRAH Per Sempre and Keir (amphora). Also owns POGGIO ARGENTIERA in MAREMMA (best: Capatosta, MORELLINO DI SCANSANO).

Tuscany / Toscana Home of world's top SANGIOVESE. BRUNELLO DI MONTALCINO, CHIANTI CLASSICO, Chianti RÚFINA best, but BOLGHERI just as gd and world-class for international grapes (esp CAB FR, MERLOT), but SASSICAIA (CAB SAUV) is most famous.

Uberti Lom ★★★→★★★★ Historical estate, excellent interpreter of FRANCIACORTA's terroir. Outstanding DeQuinque (blend of 10 yrs) and Comarì del Salem. V.gd Dosaggio Zero Sublimis and Francesco I.

Umani Ronchi Mar ★★→★★★ Leading Mar producer, esp for VERDICCHIO (Casal di Serra, Plenio), CONERO Cumaro, IGTs Le Busche (w), Pelago (r).

Vajra, GD Pie ★★★→★★★★ Leading BAROLO producer in Vergne. Outstanding Bricco delle Viole and LANGHE Freisa Kyè. Gd: Langhe RIES Petracine, Barolos (Albe, Coste di Rose, Ravera), Serralunga's Luigi Baudana Barolos, DOLCETTO Coste & Fossati and BARBERA D'ALBA SUPERIORE.

Val di Cornia Tus ★★→★★★ DOC(G) 10 11 12 13 15 16 Quality zone s of BOLGHERI. MERLOT, MONTEPULCIANO, SYRAH. Look for: Bulichella, Casadei, Gualdo del Re, Terricciola, TUA RITA.

Valentini, Edoardo Ab ★★★★ Collectors seek out his MONTEPULCIANO D'ABRUZZO, TREBBIANO D'ABRUZZO, among Italy's v. best. Traditional, age-worthy.

Valle d'Aosta VdA ★★→★★★ DOC Italy's smallest region makes some of its best reds and whites, though hard to find. DOCs mostly varietal; famous names incl NEBBIOLO-based Arnad Montjovet, Donnas; Torrette (mostly Petit Rouge), Blanc de Morgex, made with Prié (w); Chambave (made with local biotype of white MUSCAT), Nus MALVOISIE (made with PINOT GR), Premetta a lovely light red.

Valle Isarco T-AA ★★ DYA. ALTO ADIGE DOC for seven Germanic varietal whites made

---

Valpolicella: the best

Time to take gd VALPOLICELLA more seriously. AMARONE DELLA VALPOLICELLA and RECIOTO DELLA VALPOLICELLA are now DOCG, while RIPASSO has new rules. Following producers make gd to great wine: ALLEGRINI ★, Begali, Bertani, BOLLA, Boscaini, Brigaldara ★, BRUNELLI, BUSSOLA ★, Ca' la Bianca, Ca' Rugate, Campagnola, CANTINA Valpolicella, Castellani, Corteforte, Corte Sant'Alda, CS Valpantena, DAL FORNO ★, GUERRIERI-RIZZARDI ★, Le Ragose, Le Salette, MASI ★, Mazzi ★, MONTE DEL FRÀ ★, Nicolis, PRÀ, QUINTARELLI ★, Roccolo Grassi ★, Serego Alighieri ★, SPERI ★, Stefano Accordini ★, TEDESCHI ★, TOMMASI ★, Valentina Cubi, Venturini, Viviani ★, ZENATO, Zeni.

along the Isarco (Eisack) River ne of Bolzano. Gd GEWURZ, MÜLLER-T, RIES, SILVANER. Top: Abbazia di Novacella, Eisacktaler, KÖFERERHOF, Kuenhof, MANNI NÖSSING.

Valpolicella Ven ★→★★★★ DOC(G) Light, easy-going red (Valpolicella), medium-bodied to powerfully alc, rich, tannic (AMARONE) super-sweet (RECIOTO). Popular RIPASSO between Valpolicella and Amarone, but few noteworthy. (*See* box, p.151.)

Valpolicella Ripasso Ven ★★→★★★ DOC 10 11 12 13 15 (16) (18) In huge demand, so changes from 2016. Used to be only from VALPOLICELLA SUPERIORE re-fermented (only once) on RECIOTO or AMARONE grapeskins to make a more age-worthy wine. Now can blend 10% Amarone with standard Valpolicella and call it Ripasso. Best: BUSSOLA, Castellani, DAL FORNO, QUINTARELLI, ZENATO.

Valtellina Lom ★→★★★ DOC/DOCG A rare e-w valley, just s of Swiss border. Home of CHIAVENNASCA. Best labelled Valtellina SUPERIORE (five subzones: Grumello, Inferno, Maroggia, Sassella, Valgella), *see* SFORZATO. Top: Fay (Valgella Carteria), AR.PE.PE. (Sassella: RISERVA VIGNA Regina and Riserva Rocce Rosse), Mamete Prevostini (Sassella Sommarovina). For *Sforzato*: Fay (RONCO del Picchio), Mamete Prevostini (Albareda) and Nino Negri (Cinque Stelle).

Vecchio Samperi Si *See* DE BARTOLI.

Verdicchio dei Castelli di Jesi Mar ★★→★★★ DOC DYA. Versatile white from nr Ancona on Adriatic; light and quaffable or sparkling or structured, complex and long-lived (esp RISERVA DOCG, min 2 yrs old). Also CLASSICO. Best: *Bucci* (Riserva), Casalfarneto, Colognola, Coroncino (Gaiospino e Stracacio), GAROFOLI (Podium), Marotti Campi (Salmariano), Sartarelli (Balciana, rare late-harvest, Tralivio), TENUTA di Tavignano (Misco). V.gd Andrea Felici, Fazi Battaglia (Riserva San Sisto), La Staffa, Montecappone, Monte Schiavo, Santa Barbara, UMANI RONCHI.

Verdicchio di Matelica Mar ★★→★★★ DOC DYA. Similar to last, smaller, more inland, higher, so more acidic, so longer-lasting though less easy-drinking young. RISERVA is likewise DOCG. Esp Belisario, Bisci, Borgo Paglianetto, Collestefano, La Monacesca (Mirum).

Verduno Pie ★★★ DOC DYA. Berry and herbal flavours. Top CASTELLO DI VERDUNO (Basadone), Fratelli Alessandria (Speziale), GB BURLOTTO; gd Bel Colle, Reverdito.

Verduno, Castello di Pie ★★★ Husband/wife team, v.gd BARBARESCO Rabaja and Rabajà Bas, BAROLO Monvigliero (also RISERVA) and Massara, VERDUNO Basadone.

Verduzzo F-VG ★★→★★★ DOC (Friuli Colli Orientali) Full-bodied white from local variety. Ramandolo (DOCG) is well-regarded subzone for sweet wine. Top: I Clivi, Marco Sara, Scubla.

Vermentino di Gallura Sar ★★→★★★ DYA. VERMENTINO makes gd light wines in TUS, LIG and all over SAR, but best, most intense in ne corner of island, under this its DOCG name. Try Capichera, CS del Vermentino, CS di Gallura, Depperu, Masone Mannu, Mura, SIDDURA, Zanatta.

Vermentino di Sardegna Lig ★★ DOC DYA. From anywhere on SAR; generally fails to measure up to VERMENTINO DI GALLURA for structure, intensity of flavour. Gd producers: ARGIOLAS, Deiana, Mora e Memo, QUARTOMORO, *Santadi, Sella & Mosca*.

Vernaccia di Oristano Sar ★→★★★★ DOC Flor-affected wine, similar to light Sherry, a touch bitter, full-bodied. Delicious with *bottarga* (dried, salted fish roe). Must try. Top: CONTINI (Antico Gregori ★, RISERVA and Flor 22). Gd: Orro, Serra, Silvio Carta.

Vernaccia di San Gimignano Tus *See* SAN GIMIGNANO.

Viarte, La F-VG ★★→★★★ Organic estate of COLLI ORIENTALI. V.gd: Friulano, SCHIOPPETTINO di Prepotto and Tazzelenghe.

Vie di Romans F-VG ★★★→★★★★ Gianfranco Gallo has built up his father's ISONZO estate to top status. Outstanding Isonzo PINOT GR Dessimis, SAUV BL Piere and Vieris (oaked), Flors di Uis blend and MALVASIA. V.gd Pinot Gr Dessimis.

Vietti Pie ★★★★ Organic estate at Castiglione Falletto owned by Krause Group but still run by Luca Currado and Mario Cordero. Characterful. Textbook BAROLOS: Brunate, Lazzarito, Ravera, Rocche di Castiglione, Villero RISERVA. V.gd BARBARESCO Masseria, BARBERA D'ALBA Scarrone, BARBERA D'ASTI la Crena, new DERTHONA.

Vignamaggio Tus ★★→★★★ Historic, beautiful CHIANTI CLASSICO estate, nr Greve. Leonardo da Vinci painted the *Mona Lisa* here. RISERVA is called – you guessed it.

Vigna (or vigneto) A single vyd, generally indicating superior quality.

Vigneri, I Si ★★★→★★★★ Consortium of growers, also ETNA estate within that consortium, run by Salvo Foti, greatest expert on NERELLO MASCALESE and all Etna varieties. Consortium growers focus on bush-trained vines, native grape varieties and respect for the land. Outstanding estate wines Vinupetra (r). V.gd I Vigneri (r), Aurora (w).

Villa Russiz F-VG ★★★ Historic estate for DOC COLLIO. V.gd SAUV BL and MERLOT (esp de la Tour selections), CHARD, FRIULANO, PINOT BL, PINOT GR.

Vino Nobile di Montepulciano Tus ★★→★★★ 11 12 13 15 16 17 (18') The 1st Italian DOCG (1980). Prugnolo Gentile (SANGIOVESE) based, from TUS town MONTEPULCIANO (distinct from grape). Recent focus on single-vyd wines. Complex, long-lasting Sangiovese expression, often tough with drying tannins. Top: AVIGNONESI, BOSCARELLI, DEI, La Braccesca, POLIZIANO, Salcheto. Also gd: Bindella, Fattoria del Cerro, Fattoria della Talosa, Montemercurio, Valdipiatta. RISERVA after 3 yrs.

Vin Santo / Vinsanto / Vin(o) Santo T-AA, Tus ★★→★★★★ DOC Sweet PASSITO, usually TREBBIANO, MALVASIA and/or SANGIOVESE in TUS (Vin Santo), Nosiola in TRENTINO (Vino Santo). TUS versions extremely variable, anything from off-dry and Sherry-like to sweet and v. rich. May spend 3–10 unracked yrs in small barrels called *caratelli*. *Avignonesi's is legendary*; plus CAPEZZANA, FELSINA, FRASCOLE, ISOLE E OLENA, Rocca di Montegrossi, SAN GIUSTO A RENTENNANO, SELVAPIANA, Villa Sant'Anna, Villa di Vetrice. *See also* OCCHIO DI PERNICE.

Voerzio, Roberto Pic ★★★ BAROLO modernist: concentrated, tannic. More impressive/expensive than delicious. Range incl Brunate, Cerequio, Fossati, La Serra, Rocche dell'Annunziata.

Volpaia, Castello di Tus ★★→★★★ V.gd CHIANTI CLASSICO estate at Radda. Organic certified. Top Chianti Classico RISERVA, Gran Selezione Coltassala (SANGIOVESE/ Mammolo), Balifico (Sangiovese/CAB SAUV).

Zenato Ven ★★★ GARDA wines: v. reliable, sometimes inspired. Also AMARONE, LUGANA, SOAVE, VALPOLICELLA. Look for labels RISERVA Sergio Zenato.

Zerbina, Fattoria E-R ★★★ Leader in Romagna; best sweet ALBANA DOCG (Scacco Matto and AR), v.gd SANGIOVESE (Pietramora); barrique-aged IGT Marzieno.

Zibibbo Si ★★★ Alluring sweet MUSCAT d'Alessandria, most associated with PANTELLERIA and extreme w SI. Dry version exemplified by DE BARTOLI.

Zonin Ven ★→★★ Huge estate owner, based at Gambellara in Ven, but also big in F-VG, TUS, PUG, SI and elsewhere in world (eg. Virginia, US).

What do the initials mean?

DOC (Denominazione di Origine Controllata) Controlled Denomination of Origin, cf. AOC in France.

DOCG (Denominazione di Origine Controllata e Garantita) "G" = "Guaranteed". Italy's highest quality designation. Guarantee? It's still caveat emptor.

IGT (Indicazione Geografica Tipica) "Geographic Indication of Type". Broader and more vague than DOC, cf. Vin de Pays in France.

DOP/IGP (Denominazione di Origine Protetta/Indicazione Geografica Protetta) "P" = "Protected". The EU's DOP/IGP trump Italy's DOC/IGT.

MGA (Menzione Geografica Aggiuntiva) or Additional Geographical Definitions, eg. subzones, cf. crus in France.

Germany

Abbreviations used in the text:

Bad	Baden
Frank	Franken
Hess	Hessische-Bergstrasse
M-M	Mittelmosel
M Rh	Mittelrhein
Mos	Mosel
Na	Nahe
Pfz	Pfalz
Rhg	Rheingau
Rhh	Rheinhessen
Sa-Un	Saale-Unstrut
Sachs	Sachsen
Würt	Württemberg

More heavily shaded areas are the wine-growing regions.

Wine-growing, in Germany, has become a dream job: roughly half the students at Geisenheim – Germany's most important wine university – have no family background in wine. They're drawn to wine by the excitement of it and the touch of rock-star glamour it has acquired, not because of parental pressure. Thirty years ago it was different: students were mainly sons (and occasionally daughters) of growers or merchants. Today, the percentage of female students of oenology varies between 26% and 57%. Because they come to wine from outside, they're committed. They bring in fresh ideas, they know how to communicate, and very often they already possess an astonishing degree of tasting and winemaking experience in their twenties. Be prepared for the next chapter in the success story of German wine: as wines become less acidic – that familiar factor, climate change – so the quality of tannins becomes more important, especially in whites. This is one of the topics the young generation are working on (and some of the veterans too). Ideas include harvesting earlier, macerating or (partly) fermenting on skins, trying spontaneous fermentations, using oak to add structure but not flavour. It's trial and error, of course. But it's done with enormous thoughtfulness, with broad stylistic horizons, and with fine sensibilities. Could there be better prospects?

Recent vintages

Mosel

Mos (incl Saar and Ruwer wines) are so attractive young that their capabilities for developing are not often enough explored. But fine Kabinetts can gain from at least 5 yrs in bottle and often much more: Spätlese from 5–20, and Auslese and BA anything from 10–30 yrs. "Racy" is their watchword. Dry Mos now riper than it has ever been. Saar and Ruwer make leaner wines than Mos, but surpass whole world for elegance and thrilling, steely "breed".

2020 The 3rd yr of drought in row, gd quality, quantity.
2019 Mixed bag, summer too dry, autumn wet. Sound quality, but low quantity (-25%, Ruwer -40%: frost).
2018 Powerful, at times really big wines, but balanced; better acidity than 2003.
2017 Low yield (frost) = high extract. Brilliant Kabinett, Spätlese: steely acidity.
2016 Balanced wines of textbook raciness.
2015 Warm yr, rich Trocken, Spätlesen, Auslesen to keep.
2012 Classic, discreet wines, might turn out to be long-lived.
2011 Brilliant vintage, particularly Saar, Ruwer, sensational TBAs.
2009 Magnificent Spätlesen, Auslesen, gd balance. Keep.
Fine vintages: 08 07 05 04 03 01 99 97 95 94 93 90 89 88 76 71 69 64 59 53 49 45 37 34 21.

Rheinhessen, Nahe, Pfalz, Rheingau, Ahr

Apart from Mos, Rhg wines tend to be longest-lived of all German regions, improving for 15 yrs or more, but best wines from Rhh, Na and Pfz can last as long. Modern dry wines such as Grosses Gewächs (GG) are generally intended for drinking within 2–5 yrs, but the best undoubtedly have the potential to age. The same holds for Ahr Valley reds (and their peers from Bad and other regions of the s): their fruit makes them attractive young, but best wines can develop for 10 yrs and longer. Who will give them a chance?

2020 Early and fast harvest, mid-weight wines, gd fruit, small crop in Ahr.
2019 Complicated yr; drought, heatwaves in July; sunburn (esp Ahr); rain in August, Sept. Classical structured wines with gd acidity. Outstanding Rhg Spätlesen.
2018 Record summer, powerful wines. Growers allowed to acidify.
2017 Roter Hang and Mittelhaardt outstanding: rare combination of freshness and extract.
2016 Quality and quantity mixed, well-balanced Spätburgunder. Lovely Rhg Kabinett.
2015 Hot, dry summer. Rhg excellent, both dry and nobly sweet.
2012 Quantities below average, but v.gd, classical at every level.
2011 Fruity wines, harmonious acidity, now fully mature.
2010 Uneven quality: some v.gd Spätburgunder; dry whites drink now.
2009 Excellent wines, esp dry. Some acidification needed.
Fine vintages: 08 05 03 02 01 99 98 97 96 93 90 83 76 71 69 67 64 59 53 49 45 37 34 21.

Adams, Weingut Rhh ★★→★★★ Simone A proves why in C19 PINOT N from INGELHEIM was among Germany's best.

Adelmann, Weingut Graf Würt ★★→★★★ Old estate (founded 1297), kept young by count Felix A. Excellent LEMBERGER GG (16 17') and white cuvée Die Mauern von Schaubeck.

Ahr ★★→★★★★ Small river valley s of Bonn, elegant, fruit-driven PINOT N from slate. Best: Adeneuer, BERTRAM, Brogsitter, Burggarten, Deutzerhof, Kreuzberg, MEYER-NÄKEL, Nelles, Riske, SCHUMACHER, STODDEN.

Aldinger, Gerhard Würt ★★★→★★★★ Family estate of great versatility. Whites, reds: density, tension. Sensational Brut Nature SEKT (5 yrs lees-ageing) 09' 10 11' 12' 13.

Alte Reben Old vines. But no min age.

Alter Satz Frank Wines from old co-planted (different varieties all mixed up) vyds, esp in FRANK, often more than 100 yrs old and ungrafted. Try (w) Otmar Zang, Scheuring, Scholtens – or Stritzinger (r).

Amtliche Prüfungsnummer (APNr) Official test number, on every label of a quality wine. Useful for discerning different lots of AUSLESE a producer has made from the same vyd.

Assmannshausen Rhg ★★→★★★★ 05' 09 10 13 15' 16 17 18' 19 The only RHG village with almost no RIES – but tradition for *Spätburgunder*. Most famous GROSSE LAGE: Höllenberg (45 ha on slate), but wines from neighbouring plots (Frankenthal, Hinterkirch) can be outstanding too. Growers: Allendorf, BISCHÖFLICHES WEINGUT RÜDESHEIM, CHAT SAUVAGE, K Berg & Sohn, KESSELER, König, KRONE, KÜNSTLER, Schloss Reinhartshausen, SOLVEIGS.

Auslese Wines from selective picking of super-ripe bunches affected by noble rot (*Edelfäule*). Unctuous, but – traditionally – elegant rather than super-concentrated. 99% are sweet, but specialists (JB BECKER, Koehler-Ruprecht) show Auslese TROCKEN can be elegant too.

Ayl Mos ★→★★★ All vyds known since 1971 by name of historically best site: Kupp. Growers: BISCHÖFLICHE WEINGÜTER TRIER, *Lauer*, Vols, ZILLIKEN.

BA (Beerenauslese) Luscious sweet wine from exceptionally ripe, individually selected berries concentrated by noble rot. Rare, expensive.

Bacharach M Rh ★→★★★ Small, idyllic Rhine-side town; centre of M RH RIES. Classified GROSSE LAGE: Hahn, Posten, Wolfshöhle. Growers: Bastian, JOST, Kauer, RATZENBERGER.

Baden Huge sw region and former Grand Duchy, 15,000 ha stretch over 300 km (186 miles), best-known for PINOT N, GRAU- and WEISSBURGUNDER and pockets of RIES, usually dry. Two-thirds of crop goes to co-ops.

Riesling + bubbles

Germany's new SEKT stars are mostly produced on a PINOT basis; the Champagne (*see* France) paradigm prevails. But it is not by chance that king RIES has been, for more than a century, the variety of choice for Sekt producers. Growers to keep the Ries tradition alive incl BASSERMANN-JORDAN, BREUER, BUHL (Suez Vintage), Dr. Kauer (Zero), Frank John, GRIESEL (Rés Dosage Zero), Guntrum, RAUMLAND, Schloss Sommerhausen (avec pläsier), Strauch (ALTE REBEN), WEGELER (Geheimrat J). Single-vyd Sekt from prime sites: Barth (Schützenhaus, Hassel), Biffar (Ungeheuer, Pechstein), DIEL (Goldloch), Gut Hermannsberg (Kupfergrube), HESSISCHE STAATSWEINGÜTER (Baiken, STEINBERG), Schloss Vaux (MARCOBRUNN), Solter (Berg Roseneck), Wegeler (Rothenberg), ZILLIKEN (Rausch). Late Releases: Bamberger (Decade I 09), Bardong (Res 91 01), HEYMANN-LÖWENSTEIN (Fantasie der Schieferterrassen 08), LAUER (Rés 91 92), MOLITOR (Prestige 08).

Bassermann-Jordan Pfz ★★★ Famous historical estate producing powerful RIES from FORST and DEIDESHEIM. Spontaneously fermented, oak-aged and off-dry Ries Ancestrale (from Pechstein vyd) and amphora CAB SAUV.

Battenfeld-Spanier Rhh ★★★ Leading estate with vyds at Hohen-Sülzen, Mölsheim and in neighbouring ZELLERTAL, bio, led by passionate HO Spanier (*see also* KÜHLING-GILLOT). Brilliant Brut Nature 09'.

Becker, Friedrich Pfz ★★→★★★★ Outstanding SPÄTBURGUNDER (Heydenreich, Kammerberg, Sankt Paul, Res) from most s part of PFZ; some vyds actually lie across border in Alsace. Wines need 5–10 yrs cellaring. Gd whites (CHARD, PINOT GR, RIES, WEISSBURGUNDER) too.

Eiswein is endangered species: in 2019, only four producers could harvest one.

Becker, JB Rhg ★★→★★★ 10 11 12 15' 16 17 18' Delightfully old-fashioned, cask-aged (and long-lived) dry RIES, SPÄTBURGUNDER at WALLUF and Martinsthal. Outstanding 15 18, mature vintages (back to 90s) great value.

Bercher Bad ★★★ KAISERSTUHL family estate, v. reliable from ORTSWEIN up to GG, long experience in barrique ageing, best usually Haslen GRAUBURGUNDER and Kesselberg SPÄTBURGUNDER.

Bergdolt Pfz ★★★ Organic estate at Duttweiler, known for food-friendly, age-worthy WEISSBURGUNDER GG Mandelberg. Gd RIES, SPÄTBURGUNDER too. Stunning SEKT (Brut Nature Fluxus).

Bernkastel M-M ★→★★★★ Senior wine town of the M-M, known for timbered houses and flowery, balsamic RIES. GROSSE LAGE: Badstube, DOCTOR, Graben, Johannisbrünnchen, Lay. Top growers: Kerpen, JJ PRÜM, Lauerburg, LOOSEN, MOLITOR, SCHLOSS LIESER, Studert-Prüm, THANISCH (both estates), WEGELER. Kurfürstlay GROSSLAGE name is a deception: avoid.

Bernkasteler Ring Mos One of two MOS growers' associations organizing an auction every yr mid-end Sept. Other is GROSSER RING.

Bertram-Baltes, Weingut Ahr ★★★ Shooting stars in AHR valley. Early picking, moderate use of new oak bring fresh, dense, racy SPÄTBURGUNDER from prime vyds.

Bischöfliches Weingut Rüdesheim Rhg ★★★ 8 ha of best sites in ASSMANNSHAUSEN, JOHANNISBERG, RÜDESHEIM; vault cellar in Hildegard von Bingen's historic monastery. Peter Perabo (ex-KRONE) is *Pinot N specialist*, RIES also v.gd.

Bischöfliche Weingüter Trier Mos ★★ 130 ha of potentially 1st-class historical donations. Not v. reliable; do not buy without prior tasting.

Bocksbeutel Frank Belly-shaped bottle dating back to C18, today only permitted in FRANK and village of Neuweier, BAD. New: modernized, stackable "Bocksbeutel PS" at last.

Bodensee Bad Idyllic district of s BAD and on Bavarian shore of Lake Constance, at altitude: 400–580m (1312–1903ft). Dry MÜLLER-T with elegance, light but delicate SPÄTBURGUNDER. Off-dry TRAMINER can be delicious.

Boppard M Rh ★→★★★ Wine town of M RH with GROSSE LAGE Hamm – an amphitheatre of vines. Growers: Heilig Grab, Lorenz, M Müller, Perll, WEINGART. Unbeatable *value*.

Brauneberg M-M ★★★→★★★★ Top village on M-M; excellent full-flavoured RIES of great raciness. GROSSE LAGE vyds Juffer, Juffer-SONNENUHR. Growers: M Conrad, *F Haag*, KESSELSTATT, MF RICHTER, Paulinshof, Sankt Nikolaus Hospital, SCHLOSS LIESER, THANISCH, *W Haag*.

Bremer Ratskeller Town-hall cellar in n Germany's commercial town of Bremen, founded in 1405, UNESCO World Heritage Site. Oldest wine is a barrel of 1653 RÜDESHEIMER Apostelwein.

Breuer Rhg ★★★→★★★★ Exquisite RIES from RAUENTHAL, RÜDESHEIM and, newly, LORCH. Nonnenberg transforms austerity into age-worthiness, Berg Schlossberg

> **Doctor's secret**
> How is it that BERNKASTEL'S DOCTOR vyd gives RIES of such distinctive
> balsamic spiciness, so different from the wines of its neighbours?
> Some say it's the mesoclimate, the vicinity of Bernkastel's old town. But
> there may be another factor too. Growers speculate that the slope may
> possess an underground water vein linking it to the thermal spring of
> Bad Wildstein, about 1.5 km (1 mile) away as the grape flies. Wildstein's
> thermal water is said to help against rheumatism, gout and circulatory
> disorder. A Doctor a day keeps the doctor away?

90' 96' 97' 08' 12' 13' 14 15' 16 17' 18 has depth at 12% alc, Pfaffenwies (1st
vintage 19') full of floral elegance. Exciting experiments with historic grape
Gelber Orleans.

Buhl, Reichsrat von Pfz ★★★ Historic PFZ estate at DEIDESHEIM. Ex-Bollinger
cellarmaster Mathieu Kauffmann came in 2013, but left in 2019 before the fruit
of his work became clear.

Bürgerspital zum Heiligen Geist Frank ★★★ Ancient charitable estate with great
continuity: only six directors in past 180 yrs. Traditionally made whites (*Silvaner,*
RIES) from best sites in/around WÜRZBURG. SILVANER GG from monopole Stein-
Harfe 15' 16' 17' 18' 19 is a monument.

Bürklin-Wolf, Dr. Pfz ★★→★★★★ 30 ha of best MITTELHAARDT vyds incl important
holdings of FORST's Kirchenstück, Jesuitengarten and Pechstein; bio. Wines
made to age.

Busch, Clemens Mos ★★★→★★★★ Steep Pündericher Marienburg farmed by hand,
bio, for seven GGS from different parcels. Best usually: Felserrasse (mineral,
deep), Raffes (power, balance), Rothenpfad (silky, balsamic). Now also Res line:
2 yrs barrel ageing.

Castell'sches Fürstliches Domänenamt Frank ★★→★★★ Monopoly vyd Schlossberg
will, from 2020 on, exclusively produce SILVANER, and GG will be marketed only
5 yrs after harvest. A great decision by Ferdinand Fürst zu Castell in order to
prove these wines' ageing potential 08 09 11 15' 16 17'.

Chat Sauvage Rhg ★★★ Created out of nothing in 2000, Burgundian approach to
RHG PINOT N. Some CHARD too, and delicate SEKT.

Christmann Pfz ★★★ VDP President Steffen Christmann, MITTELHAARDT bio pioneer,
now joined by daughter Sophie, a PINOT N expert. Promising new Christmann
& Kauffmann SEKT project together with Mathieu Kauffmann (ex-Bollinger,
see France).

Clüsserath, Ansgar Mos ★★★ Tense TRITTENHEIMER Apotheke RIES. KABINETTS delicious.

Corvers-Kauter Rhg ★★★ Organic estate at Mittelheim, 31 ha, making a name for
textbook mineral RÜDESHEIM RIES. Now taken over most of former Langwerth
vyds, incl MARCOBRUNN, RAUENTHAL Baiken.

Crusius, Dr. Na ★★→★★★ Family estate at TRAISEN. Vivid, age-worthy RIES from sun-
baked Bastei and Rotenfels of Traisen and SCHLOSSBÖCKELHEIM. Daughters Judith,
Rebecca bring fresh air.

Deidesheim Pfz ★★→★★★★ Central MITTELHAARDT village and series of GROSSE LAGE
vyds: Grainhübel, Hohenmorgen, Kalkofen, Kieselberg, Langenmorgen. Top
growers: BASSERMANN-JORDAN, Biffar, BUHL, BÜRKLIN-WOLF, CHRISTMANN, Fusser,
MOSBACHER, Seckinger, Siben, Stern, VON WINNING. Gd co-op.

Deinhard, Dr. Pfz ★★→★★★ Since 2008, a brand of the VON WINNING estate, used for
wines with no oak influence.

Diel, Schlossgut Na ★★★→★★★★ Caroline D follows her father: exquisite *GG Ries*
(best usually Burgberg of Dorsheim). Magnificent SPÄTLESEN, serious *Sekt*
(Goldloch RIES and Cuvée Mo).

Doctor M-M Emblematic steep vyd at BERNKASTEL, the place where TBA was invented (1921, THANISCH). Only 3.2 ha, and five owners: both Thanisch estates, WEGELER (1.1 ha), Lauerburg and local Heiligen Geist charity (0.26 ha, leased until 2024 to MARKUS MOLITOR, SCHLOSS LIESER). RIES of extraordinary depth and richness, but pricey – up to a record-breaking 1100€/bottle for Molitor's 18 TROCKEN.

Dönnhoff Na ★★★→★★★★ Cornelius D has found his style: drier and more mineral than father Helmut, but equally delicious. Superb 19s, extract-loaden Felsenberg GG and sensational Hermannshöhle Auslese Einzelpfahl (auction) on top. Tiny quantities of Blanc de Noirs SEKT.

Durbach Bad ★★→★★★ ORTENAU village for full-bodied RIES, locally called Klingelberger. Growers: Alexander Laible, ANDREAS LAIBLE, Graf Metternich, Männle (both), MARKGRAF VON BADEN. Reliable co-op.

Egon Müller zu Scharzhof Mos ★★★★ 59 71 83 90 03 15 16 17 18 19 Legendary SAAR family estate at WILTINGEN with a treasury of old vines. Racy SCHARZHOFBERGER RIES among world's greatest wines: sublime, vibrant, immortal. *Kabinetts* featherlight and long-lived. New (from 18 on): TROCKEN version of Scharzhofberg.

Einzellage Individual vyd site. Never to be confused with GROSSLAGE.

Eiswein Made from frozen grapes with the ice (ie. water content) discarded, thus v. concentrated: of BA ripeness or more. Outstanding Eiswein vintages: 98 02 04 08. Less and less produced in past decade: climate change is Eiswein's enemy.

Eller, Juliane Rhh ★★ Ambitious young grower at Alsheim, known for Juwel series and collaboration with German TV stars Joko und Klaas (*Drei Freunde*).

Emrich-Schönleber Na ★★★ Werner Schönleber and son Frank make precise RIES from Monzingen's classified Frühlingsplätzchen and Halenberg vyds.

Erden M-M ★★★→★★★★ Village on red slate soils; noble AUSLESEN, TROCKEN RIES with rare delicacy. GROSSE LAGE: Prälat and Treppchen. Growers: BREMER RATSKELLER, JJ Christoffel, LOOSEN, MOLITOR, MERKELBACH, Mönchhof, Rebenhof, Schmitges.

Erste Lage Classified vyd, 2nd-from-top level, similar to Burgundy's Premier Cru, only in use with VDP members outside AHR, M RH, MOS, NA, RHH.

Erzeugerabfüllung Bottled by producer. Incl the guarantee that only own grapes have been used. May be used by co-ops also. GUTSABFÜLLUNG is stricter, applies only to estates.

Escherndorf Frank ★★★ Village with steep GROSSE LAGE Lump ("scrap" – as in tiny inherited parcels). Marvellous *Silvaner* and RIES (dr sw). Growers: Fröhlich, H SAUER, R SAUER, Schäffer, zur Schwane.

Feinherb Imprecisely defined traditional term for wines with around 10–25g sugar/litre, not necessarily tasting sweet. More flexible than HALBTROCKEN.

Forst Pfz ★★→★★★★ Outstanding MITTELHAARDT village, a mosaic of individualistic GROSSE LAGE vyds giving RIES of terroir expression, longevity. Most famous: Kirchenstück, Jesuitengarten, Pechstein, but Freundstück, Ungeheuer not far behind. ORTSWEIN usually excellent value. Top growers: Acham-Magin, BASSERMANN-JORDAN, BÜRKLIN-WOLF, H Spindler, Margarethenhof, MOSBACHER, VON BUHL, VON WINNING, WOLF.

Plant that grass!
The iconic Kirchenstück ("church's plot") vyd, considered top PFZ spot since the Royal Bavarian tax commission ranked it 1st in 1828, is immediately behind the church of St Margareta at FORST. The vyd is just 3.5 ha, shared between eight growers – plus the church itself, which owns a small strip of grass there. There'd be room for two rows of RIES on that strip. Why not? Father Bernhard Braun is parish priest. "Maybe the expenses would be too high," he muses. "But sometimes I dream of it." Four-star Communion wine?

> **Grosse Lage / Grosslage: spot the difference**
> *Bereich* means district within an *Anbaugebiet* (region). *Bereich* on a
> label should be treated as a flashing red light; the wine is a blend from
> arbitrary sites within that district. Do not buy. The same holds for wines
> with a GROSSLAGE name, though these are more difficult to identify. Who
> could guess if "Forster Mariengarten" is an EINZELLAGE or a Grosslage?
> (It's Gross.) And it's getting even worse; don't confuse Grosslage with
> GROSSE LAGE: the latter refers to best single vyds, Germany's "Grands
> Crus" according to the classification set up by wine-grower's association
> VDP. But, luckily, this is not the end of the story: chances are that
> Grosslage will disappear in nr future, because it turns out it contradicts
> EU legislation. Growers (who want to get rid of Grosslage as soon as
> possible) and négociants (who want to keep it as long as possible) are
> now fighting for a transition period.

Franken / Franconia Region of distinctive dry wines, esp SILVANER, often bottled in round-bellied flasks (BOCKSBEUTEL). Terrible frost 2020 (-40%).

Fricke, Eva Rhg ★★→★★★ At KIEDRICH and LORCH, 15 ha in conversion to organic. Expressive, taut RIES and excellent, precise PINOT N Rosé SEKT.

Fuder Traditional German cask, sizes 600–1800 litres depending on region, traditionally used for fermentation and (formerly long) ageing.

Fürst, Weingut Frank ★★★→★★★★ *Spätburgunders* 05' 09 10 15' 16 17 18' of great finesse from red sandstone (most dense: Hundsrück, most powerful: Schlossberg, most typical: Centgrafenberg, best value: Bürgstadter Berg). Newly planted Hundsrück parcel, 17,000 vines/ha. FRÜHBURGUNDER and whites equally outstanding.

Gallais, Le Mos EGON MÜLLER ZU SCHARZHOF 2nd estate, with 4-ha-monopoly Braune Kupp at WILTINGEN. Soil is schist with more clay than in SCHARZHOFBERG; AUSLESEN can be exceptional.

Geisenheim Rhg Town primarily known for Germany's university of oenology and viticulture (can be controversial: 3rd-party-funded research, and technocratic winemaking). GROSSE LAGE Rothenberg is underestimated, one of RHG's best.

GG (Grosses Gewächs) "Great/top growth". The top dry wine from a VDP-classified GROSSE LAGE.

Goldkapsel / Gold Capsule Mos, Na, Rhg, Rhh Designation (and bottle seal) mainly for AUSLESE and higher. V. strict selection of grapes, which should add finesse and complexity, not primarily weight and sweetness. Lange Goldkapsel (Long Gold Capsule) is even better. Not a legal term.

Graach M-M ★★★→★★★★ Small village between BERNKASTEL and WEHLEN. GROSSE LAGE vyds: Domprobst, Himmelreich, JOSEPHSHÖFER. Growers: *JJ Prüm*, Kees-Kieren, LOOSEN, MARKUS MOLITOR, SA PRÜM, SCHAEFER, *Selbach-Oster*, Studert-Prüm, WEGELER.

Griesel & Compagnie Hess ★★★ SEKT startup at Bensheim, top Prestige series (Rosé Extra Brut, PINOT Brut Nature). Since 2016, also excellent still wine under Schloss Schönberg label.

Grosse Lage Top level of VDP's classification, but only for VDP members. Dry wine from a Grosse Lage site is called GG. *NB* Not on any account to be confused with GROSSLAGE. Stay awake, there.

Grosser Ring Mos Group of top (VDP) MOS estates, whose annual Sept auction at TRIER sets world record prices.

Grosslage Term destined, maybe even intended, to confuse: a collection of secondary vyds without clear identity. Not on any account to be confused with GROSSE LAGE. New legislation (2020) will abolish the term, but there will be a transition period.

Gunderloch Rhh ★★★→★★★★ Historical NACKENHEIM estate portrayed in Carl Zuckmayer's play *Der fröhliche Weinberg* (1925). Known for nobly sweet RIES and culinary *Kabinett Jean-Baptiste* from prime ROTER HANG sites. Recently increasing emphasis on TROCKEN. Rothenberg GG **15 16 17'** 18' 19'.

Gut Hermannsberg Na ★★★ Former state dom at NIEDERHAUSEN. Some of densest RIES GGS of NA. Kupfergrube from SCHLOSSBÖCKELHEIM is marketed only after 5 yrs. Exquisite SEKT too.

Gutsabfüllung Estate-bottled, and made from own grapes.

Gutswein Wine with no vyd or village designation, but only the producer's name: entry-level category. Ideally, Gutswein should be an ERZEUGERABFÜLLUNG (from own grapes), but is not always the case.

Haag, Fritz Mos ★★★★ BRAUNEBERG's top estate; Oliver H follows footsteps of his late father Wilhelm (died 2020), but wines more modern. *See also* SCHLOSS LIESER.

Haag, Willi Mos ★★→★★★ BRAUNEBERG family estate, led by Marcus H. Old-style RIES, mainly sweet, rich but balanced and inexpensive.

Haart, Julian M-M, Mos ★★→★★★ Talented nephew of Theo H making a name for dense, spontaneously fermented RIES. *See* next entry.

Haart, Reinhold M-M ★★★→★★★★ Best estate in PIESPORT with important holding in famous Goldtröpfchen ("gold droplet") vyd, RIES SPÄTLESEN, AUSLESEN and higher PRÄDIKAT wines are *racy, copybook Mosels* – with great ageing potential.

Haidle Würt ★★★ Family estate now led by young Moritz H, using cool climate of Remstal area for wines of distinctive freshness. Try 19 Pulvermächer RIES Kabinett), outstanding 18 LEMBERGERS Berge and Gehrnhalde.

Halbtrocken Medium-dry with 9–18g unfermented sugar/litre, inconsistently distinguished from FEINHERB (which sounds better).

Hattenheim Rhg ★★→★★★★ Town famous for classic RHG RIES from GROSSE LAGEN Hassel, Nussbrunnen, STEINBERG, Wisselbrunnen. Estates: Barth, HESSISCHE STAATSWEINGÜTER, Kaufmann, Knyphausen, Ress, Schloss Reinhartshausen, SPREITZER. The Brunnen ("well") vyds lie on a rocky basin that collects water, protection against drought.

Heger, Dr. Bad ★★★ KAISERSTUHL estate known for dry parcel selections from volcanic soils in Achkarren and IHRINGEN, esp Vorderer Berg (PINOTS N/GR/BL, RIES) from steepest Winklerberg terraces, and Häusleboden Pinot N from old Clos de Vougeot (*see* France) cuttings planted in 1956. Joachim H now joined by daughter Rebecca.

Heitlinger / Burg Ravensburg Bad ★★→★★★ Two leading estates of KRAICHGAU, under same ownership: Heitlinger more elegant, Burg Ravensburg full-bodied.

Hessische Bergstrasse ★ →★★★ Germany's smallest wine region (only 460 ha), n of Heidelberg. Best: Bergsträsser Winzer co-op, GRIESEL (SEKT), HESSISCHE STAATSWEINGÜTER, Schloss Schönberg, Simon-Bürkle, Stadt Bensheim.

Try nearly extinct Heunisch grape (parent of Chard, 81 others): Breuer, Kloster Pforta.

Hessische Staatsweingüter Hess, Rhg ★★→★★★★ State dom with vinotheque in C12 Cistercian abbey KLOSTER EBERBACH; 238 ha in top sites all along RHG and HESSISCHE BERGSTRASSE. New oenologist Kathrin Puff is giving quality a boost: outstanding Berg Schlossberg PINOT N 18, STEINBERG RIES GG 18, Baiken SPÄTLESE 19.

Heymann-Löwenstein Mos ★★★ Reinhard Löwenstein pioneered terroir-minded viticulture with spontaneously fermented RIES from steep terraces at WINNINGEN nr Koblenz. Now daughter Sarah ready to take over.

Hochheim Rhg ★★→★★★★ Town e of main RHG, on River Main. Rich, earthy RIES from GROSSE LAGE vyds: Domdechaney, Hölle, Kirchenstück, KÖNIGIN VICTORIABERG, Reichestal. Growers: Domdechant Werner, Flick, HESSISCHE STAATSWEINGÜTER, Himmel, KÜNSTLER.

Hock Traditional English term for Rhine wine, derived from HOCHHEIM.

Hövel, Weingut von Mos ★★★ Fine SAAR estate, bio, with vyds at Oberemmel (Hütte is 4.8 ha monopoly), at KANZEM (Hörecker) and in SCHARZHOFBERG.

Huber, Bernhard Bad ★★★→★★★★ Young Julian H has vision of BAD as Germany's Burgundy. Wildenstein SPÄTBURGUNDER is generous, dense, costly; CHARDS ALTE REBEN and Hecklingen Schlossberg tight and demanding. V.gd ORTSWEIN (r/w).

Of all German regions, Ahr has highest proportion of red wine (82.2%).

Ihringen Bad ★→★★★ Village in KAISERSTUHL known for fine SPÄTBURGUNDER, GRAUBURGUNDER (historically also for SILVANER) on steep volcanic Winklerberg. Top growers: DR. HEGER, Konstanzer, Michel, Stigler.

Ingelheim Rhh ★★→★★★ RHH town across Rhine from RHG, with limestone beds under vyds; historic fame for SPÄTBURGUNDER being reinvigorated by ADAMS, Arndt F Werner, Bettenheimer, Dautermann, NEUS, Schloss Westerhaus, Wasem.

Iphofen Frank ★★→★★★ STEIGERWALD village with famous GROSSE LAGE Julius-Echter-Berg. Rich, aromatic, well-ageing SILVANER from gypsum soils. Growers: Arnold, Emmerich, JULIUSSPITAL, Popp, RUCK, Seufert, Vetter, Weigand, WELTNER, *Wirsching*, Zehntkeller.

Jahrgang Year – as in "vintage".

Johannisberg Rhg ★★→★★★★ RHG village. SCHLOSS JOHANNISBERG most famous; other estates incl CHAT SAUVAGE, JOHANNISHOF (ESER), Prinz v. Hessen, Schamari-Mühle. GROSSLAGE (avoid!): Erntebringer.

Johannishof (Eser) Rhg ★★→★★★ Family estate with vyds at JOHANNISBERG, RÜDESHEIM. Johannes Eser makes RIES with perfect balance of ripeness and steely acidity.

Josephshöfer Mos ★★→★★★ GROSSE LAGE vyd at GRAACH, the sole property of KESSELSTATT. Harmonious, berry-flavoured RIES.

Jost, Toni M Rh ★★★ Leading estate in BACHARACH with monopoly Hahn, now led by Cecilia J. Aromatic RIES with nerve, and recently remarkable PINOT N. Family also run estate at WALLUF (RHG).

Jülg Pfz ★★→★★★★ Johannes J produces dense PINOT N and sharply mineral CHARD, SAUV BL from limestone soils at SCHWEIGEN. Family-run wine tavern led by grandmother Erika a gd place to taste hearty cuisine of PALATINATE-Alsace border.

Juliusspital Frank ★★★ Ancient WÜRZBURG charity with top vyds all over FRANK known for *dry Silvaners* that age well. GGS now cellared 1 yr more before sale.

Kabinett See box, p.165. Germany's unique featherweight contribution, increasingly popular, but (or because) climate change makes it ever more difficult to produce.

Kaiserstuhl Bad Extinct volcano nr Rhine in s BAD, notably warm climate, black soil. Altitudes up to 400m (1312ft). SPÄTBURGUNDER, GRAUBURGUNDER of class, renown.

Kanzem Mos ★★★ SAAR village with steep GROSSE LAGE vyd Altenberg (slate, weathered red rock). Growers: BISCHÖFLICHE WEINGÜTER TRIER, VAN VOLXEM, VON OTHEGRAVEN.

Karthäuserhof Mos ★★★★ Outstanding RUWER estate, now led by Richard Grosche (ex-BUHL) and Mathieu Kauffmann (ex-Bollinger). Characteristic neck-only label stands for refreshing dry and sublime sweet wines.

Keller, Franz Bad See SCHWARZER ADLER.

Keller, Klaus Peter Rhh ★★★→★★★★ Star of RHH, cultish for ALTE REBEN RIES G-Max from undisclosed parcel, and GGS Hubacker, Morstein. Also Ries from NIERSTEIN (Hipping, Pettenthal), M-M (PIESPORT Schubertslay). Experimental vyd in Norway.

Kesseler, August Rhg ★★★★ Outstanding estate at ASSMANNSHAUSEN. August K's long-time employees have taken over – and work in same perfectionist manner. Breathtaking 19 RÜDESHEIM Berg Schlossberg RIES, 15 16 Höllenberg PINOT N.

Kesselstatt, Reichsgraf von Mos ★★→★★★★ Annegret Reh-Gartner's successors maintain high levels of quality; 46 ha top vyds on Mosel and both tributaries, incl remarkable stake in SCHARZHOFBERG.

Kiedrich Rhg ★★→★★★★ Top RHG village, almost a monopoly of the WEIL estate, other growers (eg. FRICKE, Knyphausen, PRINZ VON HESSEN) own only small plots. Famous church and choir.

Kloster Eberbach Rhg Atmospheric C12 Cistercian abbey in HATTENHEIM, the place where *The Name of the Rose* was filmed. Domicile of HESSISCHE STAATSWEINGÜTER.

Klumpp, Weingut Bad ★★★ SPÄTBURGUNDER, LEMBERGER of depth, elegance. Markus K is married to Meike Näkel of MEYER-NÄKEL.

Knewitz, Weingut Rhh ★★★ Young brothers Björn and Tobias K needed less than a decade to transform their parents' unknown estate to one of RHH's leading wineries. Masterpiece is Appenheim Hundertgulden RIES 15' 16' 17' 18 19'.

Knipser, Weingut Pfz ★★★→★★★★ Family estate, n PFZ, barrique-aged SPÄTBURGUNDER (iconic RdP 15') straightforward RIES (GG Steinbuckel), Cuvée X (B'x blend). Many specialities, incl historical bone-dry Gelber Orleans.

Königin Viktoriaberg Rhg ★★→★★★ Historic vyd at HOCHHEIM, 4.5 ha along shores of River Main, known for textbook RHG RIES, today run by Flick estate of Wicker. After 1845 visit, Queen Victoria granted owner right to rename vyd as "Queen-Victoria-mountain".

Kraichgau Bad Small district se of Heidelberg. Top growers: HEITLINGER/BURG RAVENSBURG, Hoensbroech, Hummel, KLUMPP.

Kranz, Weingut Pfz ★★★ Top estate at Ilbesheim. Outstanding RIES, SPÄTBURGUNDER, WEISSBURGUNDER from classified Kalmit vyd. Organic.

Krone, Weingut Rhg ★★★ Famous SPÄTBURGUNDER estate with old vyds in ASSMANNSHAUSEN's steep Höllenberg (slate), run by WEGELER.

Kühling-Gillot Rhh ★★★★ Top bio estate, run by Caroline Gillot and husband HO Spanier. Best in already outstanding range of ROTER HANG RIES: GG Rothenberg Wurzelecht from ungrafted, 70 yrs+ vines.

Kühn, Peter Jakob Rhg ★★★ Excellent estate in OESTRICH led by PJ Kühn and son. Obsessive bio vyd management and long macerations shape *nonconformist but exciting* RIES. Res RPJK Unikat aged 4 yrs in cask.

Kuhn, Philipp Pfz ★★★ Reliable; great versatility. RIES (eg. SAUMAGEN, Schwarzer Herrgott), barrel-aged SPÄTBURGUNDER, specialities (FRÜHBURGUNDER, SAUV BL, SEKT).

Künstler Rhg ★★★ Superb dry RIES at HOCHHEIM (Hölle), Kostheim (Weiß Erd), and other side of RHG at RÜDESHEIM (Rottland, Schlossberg).

Kuntz, Sybille Mos ★★★ Progressive organic 12-ha estate at Lieser, esp Niederberg-Helden vyd. MOS TROCKEN pioneer; intense wines, one of each ripeness category, intended for gastronomy, listed in many top restaurants.

Laible, Andreas Bad ★★★ Crystalline dry RIES from DURBACH's Plauelrain vyd (granite). Andreas jnr's younger brother Alexander has an estate of his own.

Landwein Technically "ggA" (*see box, p.172*), meant to label wines with only broadly defined origin. But now popular among ambitious growers to avoid official quality testing (eg. because of spontaneous fermentations, or low sulphur levels). Best known (all from BAD): Brenneisen, Enderle & Moll, Forgeurac, Höfflin, WASENHAUS, ZIEREISEN.

Of all German regions, Mos has highest proportion of white wine (90.6%).

Lauer Mos ★★★ Fine, precise SAAR RIES: tense, poised. Parcel selections from huge Ayler Kupp vyd. Best: Kern, Schonfels, Stirn.

Leitz, Josef Rhg ★★★ RÜDESHEIM-based family estate, outstanding GGS, best usually Berg Schlossberg 10' 11' 12' 13' 15' 16 17 18. Reclaimed some altitude vyds from fallow in Berg Kaisersteinfels. Inexpensive but reliable Eins-Zwei-Dry label.

Liebfrauenstift, Weingut Rhh Owner of best plots of historical LIEBFRAUENSTIFT-KIRCHENSTÜCK vyd. Formerly linked to a merchant house, but now autonomous. Katharina Prüm (of JJ PRÜM) consults. *See* next entry.

Liebfrauenstift-Kirchenstück Rhh Walled vyd in city of Worms; flowery RIES from gravelly soil: Gutzler, Schembs (01' almost youthful in 2017), WEINGUT LIEBFRAUENSTIFT. Don't confuse with Liebfraumilch, a cheap, tasteless imitation.

Loewen, Carl Mos ★★★ RIES of elegance, tension, complexity. Best vyd Longuicher Maximin Herrenberg (planted 1896, ungrafted). Entry-level Ries Varidor excellent *value*.

Loosen, Weingut Dr. M-M ★★→★★★★ Charismatic Ernie L produces fine traditional RIES from old vines in BERNKASTEL, ERDEN, GRAACH, ÜRZIG, WEHLEN. Erdener Prälat AUSLESE cultish for decades, dry Prälat Res (2 yrs cask-ageing, 1st vintage 2011) about to follow. Dr. L Ries, from bought-in grapes, is reliable. *See also* WOLF (PFZ), Ch Ste Michelle (Washington State, US).

Lorch Rhg ★→★★★ Village in extreme w of RHG, conditions more M RH-like than Rhg-like. Sharply crystalline wines, both RIES and PINOT N, now re-discovered. Best: BREUER, CHAT SAUVAGE, FRICKE, KESSELER, SOLVEIGS, von Kanitz.

Löwenstein, Fürst Frank, Rhg ★★★ Princely estate with holdings in RHG, FRANK. Classic RIES from HALLGARTEN, unique SILVANER, Ries from ultra-steep vyd Homburger Kallmuth.

Lützkendorf, Weingut Sa-Un ★★→★★★ Quality leader in SA-UN. Uwe L continuing after his father Udo's death in 2020.

Marcobrunn Rhg Historic 7-ha vyd in Erbach, GROSSE LAGE. Potential for rich, long-lasting RIES. Growers: CORVERS-KAUTER, HESSISCHE STAATSWEINGÜTER, Knyphausen, Schloss Reinhartshausen, von Oetinger.

Markgräflerland Bad Up-and-coming district s of Freiburg, cool climate due to breezes from Black Forest, and limestone soils. Typical GUTEDEL a pleasant companion for local cuisine. Climate change making PINOT varieties successful.

Markgräfler Winzer Bad ★→★★★ Co-op, 940 ha, formerly mediocre, now turned upside-down by ex-LVMH manager. Remarkable new top range DER CHARD, DER SPÄTBURGUNDER.

Markgraf von Baden Bad ★★→★★★ Important noble estate (135 ha) at Salem castle (BODENSEE) and Staufenberg castle (ORTENAU).

Maximin Grünhaus Mos ★★★★ Maximin von Schubert has taken the helm at this supreme RUWER estate; v. traditional winemaking shapes herb-scented, *delicate*, *long-lived Ries*. More than a footnote: creamy WEISSBURGUNDER, elegant PINOT N.

Merkelbach, Weingut M-M ★★→★★★ Tiny estate at ÜRZIG, 2 ha. Brothers Alfred and Rolf (both c.80), inexpensive MOS made not to sip, but to drink. Superb list of old vintages.

Meßmer, Weingut Pfz ★★→★★★ Gregor M left estate, but brother Martin continues to produce consistent quality, best among many specialities Burrweiler Schäwer RIES, from rare schist soil.

Meyer-Näkel Ahr ★★★→★★★★ Meike and Dörte N continue father Werner's work. Fruit-driven, refined SPÄTBURGUNDER from steep terraces at Walporzheimer Kräuterberg 09 12 13' 14 15' 16' 17' and other prime AHR Valley sites. Also in S Africa (Zwalu, with Neil Ellis) and Portugal (Quinta da Carvalhosa).

Mittelhaardt Pfz North-central and best part of PFZ, incl DEIDESHEIM, FORST, RUPPERTSBERG, WACHENHEIM; largely planted with RIES.

Mittelmosel Central and best part of MOS, a RIES Eldorado, incl BERNKASTEL, BRAUNEBERG, GRAACH, PIESPORT, WEHLEN, etc.

Mittelrhein ★★→★★★ Dramatically scenic Rhine area nr tourist-magnet Loreley. Best villages: BACHARACH, BOPPARD, Oberwesel. Delicate yet *steely Ries, underrated* and underpriced. Longtime decline in production now finally halted.

Molitor, Markus M-M, Mos ★★★→★★★★ Growing estate led by perfectionist Markus M. Styles, vyds and vintages in amazing depth. Dry DOCTOR (since 16) fetches €1000+/bottle at auction.

Germany's quality levels

The official range of qualities and styles in ascending order is (take a deep breath):

1 **Wein:** formerly known as Tafelwein. Light wine of no specified character, mostly sweetish.

2 **ggA (geschützte geographische Angabe):** or Protected Geographical Indication, formerly known as LANDWEIN. Dryish Wein with some regional style. Mostly a label to avoid, but some thoughtful estates use the Landwein, or ggA designation to bypass official constraints.

3 **gU (geschützte Urspungsbezeichnung):** or protected Designation of Origin. Replacing QUALITÄTSWEIN. Up to now, only six small-scale appellations in the narrower sense of the word approved by the EU.

4 **Qualitätswein:** dry or sweetish wine with sugar added before fermentation to increase its strength, but tested for quality and with distinct local and grape character. Don't despair.

5 **Kabinett:** dry/dryish natural (unsugared) wine of distinct personality and distinguishing lightness. Can occasionally be sublime – esp with a few yrs' age.

6 **Spätlese:** stronger, sweeter than KABINETT. Full-bodied (but no botrytis). Dry SPÄTLESE (or what could be considered as such) is today mostly sold under Qualitätswein designation (even if not sugared).

7 **Auslese:** sweeter, stronger than Spätlese, often with honey-like flavours, intense and long-lived. Occasionally dry and weighty. The lower the alc (read the label), the sweeter the wine.

8 **Beerenauslese (BA):** v. sweet, dense and intense, but seldom strong in terms of alc. Can be superb.

9 **Eiswein:** from naturally frozen grapes of BA/TBA quality: concentrated, pungent acidity and v. sweet. Should not display botrytis character (but does sometimes).

10 **Trockenbeerenauslese (TBA):** intensely sweet and aromatic; alc is slight. Extraordinary and everlasting.

Mosbacher Pfz ★★★ Some of best GG RIES of FORST: refined rather than massive. Traditional ageing in big oak casks. Excellent SAUV BL too ("Fumé").

Mosel Wine-growing area formerly known as Mosel-Saar-Ruwer, 8740 ha in total, 62% RIES. Conditions on the RUWER and SAAR tributaries are v. different from those along the Mosel (aka Moselle in French).

Moselland Mos, Na, Pfz, Rhh Huge MOS co-op, at BERNKASTEL, after mergers with co-ops in NA, RHH, PFZ; 2000 members, 1900 ha, €81m annual turnover. Little is above average.

Nackenheim Rhh ★→★★★★ NIERSTEIN neighbour with GROSSE LAGE Rothenberg on red shale, famous for *Rhh's richest Ries*, superb TBA. Top growers: **Gunderloch**, KÜHLING-GILLOT.

Nahe Tributary of the Rhine and dynamic region with dozens of lesser-known producers, excellent *value*. Great variety of soils; best RIES from slate has almost MOS-like raciness.

Naturrein "Naturally pure": designation on old labels (pre-1971), indicating as little technical intervention as possible, esp no chaptalizing (sugar added at fermentation).

Neipperg, Graf von Würt ★★★ LEMBERGER and SPÄTBURGUNDER of grace and purity, and v. fine sweet TRAMINER. Count Karl-Eugen von Neipperg's younger brother Stephan makes wine at Canon la Gaffelière in St-Émilion and elsewhere.

Neus Rhh ★★★ Revived historic estate at INGELHEIM, excellent PINOT N (best: Pares).

Niederhausen Na ★★→★★★★ Village of the middle NA Valley. Complex RIES from famous GROSSE LAGE Hermannshöhle and neighbouring steep slopes. Growers: CRUSIUS, **Dönnhoff**, GUT HERMANNSBERG, J Schneider, Mathern.

Nierstein Rhh ★→★★★★ Widely known for banal supermarket wines under GROSSLAGE Gutes Domtal designation (avoid!). Nierstein RIES, which deserves its name, is far from that: rich, tense, complex, eg. GROSSE LAGE vyds Brudersberg, Hipping, Oelberg, Orbel, Pettenthal. Growers: Bunn, Gehring, Gröhl, GUNDERLOCH, Guntrum, Huff (both), KELLER, KÜHLING-GILLOT, Manz, SCHÄTZEL, ST-ANTONY, Strub.

Ockfen Mos ★★→★★★ Village with almost atypical powerful SAAR RIES from GROSSE LAGE vyd Bockstein. Growers: M MOLITOR, OTHEGRAVEN, SANKT URBANS-HOF, VAN VOLXEM, WAGNER, ZILLIKEN.

Odinstal, Weingut Pfz ★★→★★★ Highest vyd of PFZ, 150m (492ft) above WACHENHEIM. Bio farming and low-tech vinification bring pure RIES, SILVANER, GEWÜRZ. Harvest often extends into Nov.

Oechsle Scale for sugar content of grape juice. Until 90s, more Oechsle meant better wine. But global warming has changed game.

Oestrich Rhg ★★→★★★ Exemplary steely RIES, fine AUSLESEN from GROSSE LAGE vyds: Doosberg, Lenchen. Top growers: A Eser, KÜHN, Querbach, SPREITZER, WEGELER.

Ökonomierat-Rebholz Pfz ★★★ Top SÜDLICHE WEINSTRASSE estate: bone-dry, zesty and reliable RIES GGS, best usually Kastanienbusch from red schist 07' 11' 15 16 17 18 19'. Also gd CHARD, SPÄTBURGUNDER.

Oppenheim Rhh ★→★★★ Neighbour of NIERSTEIN, but with different microclimate (no direct Rhine influence) and different soil (limestone rather than red shale). GROSSE LAGE Kreuz, Sackträger. Growers: Guntrum, Kissinger, KÜHLING-GILLOT, Manz. Spectacular C13 church.

Ortenau Bad ★★→★★★ District around and s of city of Baden-Baden. Mainly Klingelberger (RIES) and SPÄTBURGUNDER from granite soils. Top villages: DURBACH, Neuweier, Waldulm.

Ortswein Second rank up in VDP's pyramid of qualities: a village wine, many bargains. See next entry.

Ortswein aus Ersten Lagen Rhh New designation of VDP RHH indicating a village wine grown in classified vyds. Typically a blend of different ERSTE LAGE sites. Funny enough, there are no Erste Lage single-vyd wines in Rhh.

Othegraven, von Mos ★★★ Fine SAAR estate best known for dry and sweet RIES from superb GROSSE LAGE Altenberg at KANZEM. Best known: SPÄTLESE ALTE REBEN. Since 2010 owned by TV star (and von Othegraven family member) Günther Jauch.

Palatinate English for PFALZ.

Pfalz The 2nd-largest German region, 23,680 ha, balmy climate, Lucullian lifestyle. MITTELHAARDT RIES best; S Pfalz (SÜDLICHE WEINSTRASSE) is better suited to PINOT varieties. ZELLERTAL now fashonable: cool climate.

Piesport M-M ★→★★★★ M-M village for rich, aromatic RIES. GROSSE LAGE vyds Domherr, Goldtröpfchen. Growers: Grans-Fassian, Joh Haart, JULIAN HAART, Hain, KESSELSTATT, **Reinhold Haart**, SANKT URBANS-HOF, SCHLOSS LIESER. Avoid GROSSLAGE Michelsberg.

Piwi ★→★★★ Crossings of European and American vines, for fungal resistance ("Pilz-Widerstandsfähigkeit"). Most popular: Regent (r). A new generation of crossings deserves to be followed, eg. Souvignier Gr (w), Satin Noir (r).

Prädikat Legally defined special attributes or qualities. See QMP.

Prinz, Weingut ★★★ Distinctly fresh and elegant RIES from Hallgarten's altitude vyds, organic. KABINETT GOLDKAPSEL in appropriate yrs can be magnificent.

Prinz von Hessen Rhg ★★★ Historic JOHANNISBERG estate, esp gd at SPÄTLESE and above, and mature vintages.

Prüm, JJ Mos ★★★★ 59 71 76 83 90 03 11 15 16 17 18 Legendary WEHLEN estate; also

BERNKASTEL, GRAACH. Delicate but extraordinarily long-lived wines with finesse and distinctive character.

Prüm, SA Mos ★★→★★★ Quality revolution since Saskia A Prüm took over in 2017. Brilliant 19 BERNKASTEL Lay AUSLESE, TROCKEN RIES also much improved.

QbA (Qualitätswein bestimmter Anbaugebiete) "Quality Wine", controlled as to area, grape(s), vintage. May add sugar before fermentation (chaptalization). Intended as middle category, but now VDP obliges its members to label their best dry wines (GGS) as QbA. New EU name gU is scarcely found on labels (*see* box, p.172).

QmP (Qualitätswein mit Prädikat) Top category, meant to replace the NATURREIN designation: no sugaring of must. Six levels according to ripeness of grapes: KABINETT to TBA.

Randersacker Frank ★★→★★★ Village s of WÜRZBURG with GROSSE LAGE Pfülben. One of best FRANKEN villages for RIES. Top growers: Bardorf, BÜRGERSPITAL, JULIUSSPITAL, Schmitt's Kinder, Staatlicher Hofkeller, Störrlein & Krenig.

Ratzenberger M Rh ★★→★★★ Family estate producing racy RIES from BACHARACH and v. fine SEKT.

Rauenthal Rhg ★★→★★★★ *Spicy, austere but complex* RIES from inland slopes. Baiken, Gehrn and Rothenberg vyds contain GROSSE LAGE and ERSTE LAGE parcels, while neighbouring Nonnenberg (monopole of BREUER) is unclassified, despite its equal quality. Top growers: A Eser, Breuer, CORVERS-KAUTER, Diefenhardt, HESSISCHE STAATSWEINGÜTER.

Raumland Rhh ★★★ SEKT expert with deep cellar and full range of fine, balanced cuvées; 1st Sekt-only estate to become VDP member. Best: CHARD Brut Nature (disgorged after 10 yrs), Cuvée Triumvirat, MonRose.

Restsüsse Unfermented grape sugar remaining in (or in cheap wines added to) wine to give it sweetness. Can range from 1g/l in a TROCKEN wine to 300g in a TBA.

Rheingau ★★→★★★★ Birthplace of RIES. Historic s- and sw-facing slopes overlooking Rhine between Wiesbaden and RÜDESHEIM. Classic, substantial Ries, famous for steely backbone, and small amounts of delicate SPÄTBURGUNDER. Also centre of SEKT production.

Rheinhessen ★→★★★★ Germany's largest region by far (26,860 ha and rising), between Mainz and Worms. Much dross, but also treasure trove of well-priced wines from gifted young growers.

Richter, Max Ferd M-M ★★→★★★ Reliable estate, at Mülheim. Esp gd RIES KABINETT, SPÄTLESEN: full and aromatic. Round, pretty Brut (EISWEIN dosage). Thoughtful winemaking.

Riffel Rhh ★★★ Organic family estate with important holdings in Bingen's once-famous Scharlachberg (red soils).

Rings, Weingut Pfz ★★★→★★★★ Brothers Steffen and Andreas R have made a name for dry RIES (esp Kallstadt SAUMAGEN) and precise SPÄTBURGUNDER (Felsenberg im Berntal, Saumagen).

Roter Hang Rhh ★★→★★★★ Leading RIES area of RHH (NACKENHEIM, NIERSTEIN). Name ("red slope") refers to red shale soil.

The next big thing?

Believe it or not, Germany's growers have in all seriousness started to test southern varieties in order to cope with global warming. Among their favourite grapes are (in ascending order of planted surface) PETIT MANSENG, MALBEC, LAGREIN, TEMPRANILLO, VIOGNIER and SYRAH. So far, we're talking about tens of ha, not hundreds. But look at the fate of early ripening grapes that were supposed to deal with the cold: BACCHUS, down 690 ha in 15 yrs, Faberrebe, down 550 ha, Morio-Muskat, down 300 ha.

Ruck, Johann Frank ★★★ Spicy, age-worthy RIES, SCHEUREBE, SILVANER, TRAMINER from IPHOFEN.

Rüdesheim Rhg ★★→★★★★ Most famous RHG RIES on slate, four GROSSE LAGE vyds on so-called Rüdesheimer Berg (Kaisersteinfels, Rosenack, Rottland, Schlossberg). Full-bodied but never clumsy, floral, esp gd in off-yrs. Best: BISCHÖFLICHE WEINGÜT RÜDESHEIM (not to be confused with BISCHÖFLICHE WEINGÜTER TRIER), *Breuer*, CHAT SAUVAGE, CORVERS-KAUTER, HESSISCHE STAATSWEINGÜTER, JOHANNISHOF, *Kesseler*, KÜNSTLER, *Leitz*, Ress.

Ruwer Mos ★★→★★★★ Tributary of MOS nr TRIER, higher in altitude than M-M. Quaffable light dry and intense sweet RIES. Best growers: Beulwitz, Karlsmühle, KARTHÄUSERHOF, KESSELSTATT, MAXIMIN GRÜNHAUS.

Average German household spends a mere 160€/yr on wine.

Saale-Unstrut ★→★★★ A ne region around confluence of these two rivers nr Leipzig. Terraced vyds have Cistercian origins. Quality leaders: Böhme, Born, Gussek, Hey (VDP member), Kloster Pforta, LÜTZKENDORF (VDP), Pawis (VDP).

Saar Mos ★★→★★★★ Tributary of Mosel, bordered by steep slopes. Most austere, steely, *brilliant Ries* of all, consistency favoured by climate change. Villages incl: AYL, KANZEM, OCKFEN, SAARBURG, Serrig, WILTINGEN (SCHARZHOFBERG).

Saarburg Mos Small town in SAAR Valley. Growers: WAGNER and ZILLIKEN. GROSSE LAGE: Rausch.

Sachsen ★→★★★ Region in Elbe Valley around Meissen and Dresden. Characterful dry whites. Best growers: Aust, Drei Herren, Rothes Gut, Schloss Proschwitz, SCHLOSS WACKERBARTH, Schuh, Schwarz, ZIMMERLING.

St-Antony Rhh ★★→★★★★ NIERSTEIN estate with exceptional vyds, known for sturdy ROTER HANG RIES – and reds (BLAUFRÄNKISCH, PINOT N).

Salm, Prinz zu Na, Rhh ★★→★★★ Owner of Schloss Wallhausen in NA and vyds there and at BINGEN (RHH); ex-president of VDP.

Salwey Bad ★★★→★★★★ Leading KAISERSTUHL estate. Konrad S picks early for freshness. Best: GGS Henkenberg and Eichberg GRAUBURGUNDER, Kirchberg SPÄTBURGUNDER and WEISSBURGUNDER.

Sankt Urbans-Hof Mos ★★★ Large family estate led by Nik Weis based in Leiwen, vyds along M-M and SAAR. Limpid RIES, impeccably pure, racy, age well. Also runs a nursery with unique collection of genetically varied Ries.

Sauer, Horst Frank ★★★ Man who put FRANCONIA on sweet wine map. Sensational BA and TBA from ESCHERNDORF's steep Lump vyd; v.gd dry wines too. Now joined by daughter Sandra.

Sauer, Rainer Frank ★★★ Top family estate producing seven different dry SILVANERS from ESCHERNDORF's steep slope Lump. Best: GG am Lumpen, and L 99' 03' 07' 18. Highly recommendable ORTSWEIN and ERSTE LAGE Silvaner.

Saumagen Popular local dish of PFZ: stuffed pig's stomach. Also one of best vyds of region: a calcareous site at Kallstadt producing excellent RIES, PINOT N.

Schaefer, Willi Mos ★★★ Willi S and son Christoph finest in GRAACH (but only 4 ha). MOS RIES at its best: pure, crystalline, feather-light, rewarding at all levels.

Schäfer-Fröhlich Na ★★★→★★★★ NA family estate, 20 ha, known for spontaneously fermented RIES of great intensity, esp incl Bockenau Felseneck and Stromberg, SCHLOSSBÖCKELHEIM Kupfergrube. Brilliant SPÄTLESE, AUSLESE too.

Scharzhofberg Mos ★★→★★★★ Superlative SAAR vyd: a rare coincidence of micro-climate, soil and human intelligence to bring about the perfection of RIES. Top: BISCHÖFLICHE WEINGÜTER TRIER, EGON MÜLLER, KESSELSTATT, VAN VOLXEM, VON HÖVEL.

Schätzel, Weingut Rhh ★★→★★★ 15-ha family estate at NIERSTEIN, Kai S has made a name for brilliant Pettenthal KABINETT, and for dry RIES full of extract (and even tannin) at 11.5% alc. Try 18' Fuchs (= Hipping, but classified LANDWEIN).

Schlossböckelheim Na ★★→★★★★ Village with GROSSE LAGE vyds Felsenberg, Kupfergrube. Firm RIES that needs ageing. Top growers: C Bamberger, CRUSIUS, DÖNNHOFF, GUT HERMANNSBERG, Kauer, SCHÄFER-FRÖHLICH.

Schloss Johannisberg Rhg ★★★ Historic RHG estate and Metternich mansion, 100% RIES, owned by Henkell (Oetker group). Usually v.gd SPÄTLESE Grünlack ("green sealing wax"), reliable GUTSWEIN (Gelblack).

Schloss Lieser M-M ★★★★ Thomas Haag (elder son of FRITZ HAAG estate) produces painstakingly elaborate RIES both dry and sweet from Lieser (Niederberg Helden), BRAUNEBERG, WEHLEN, PIESPORT. Now also small (leased) plot in BERNKASTEL's DOCTOR. Hotel Lieser Castle has no ties to wine estate.

Schloss Proschwitz Sachs ★★→★★★ New team brings notable improvements in Prince zur Lippe's 70 ha estate, Martin Schwarz (estate's 1st cellarmaster in pioneering 90s) consults.

Schloss Vaux Rhg ★★→★★★ Rhg SEKT house best known for single-vyd RIES Sekt (eg. MARCOBRUNN, RÜDESHEIMer SCHLOSSBERG).

Schloss Wackerbarth ★★→★★★ Saxon state dom on outskirts of Dresden, recently on top form, best wines from Radebeul's Goldener Wagen vyd (Protze RIES TROCKEN, ALTE REBEN, TRAMINER SPÄTLESE).

Schnaitmann Würt ★★→★★★★ Excellent barrel-aged reds from Fellbach (nr Stuttgart). Whites (eg. RIES, SAUV BL), SEKT (Evoé!), and wines from lesser grapes (SCHWARZRIESLING, TROLLINGER) tasty too.

Schneider, Markus Pfz ★★ Shooting star in Ellerstadt, PFZ. Full range of soundly produced, trendily labelled wines.

Schoppenwein Café (or bar) wine, ie. wine by the glass.

Schumacher, Paul Ahr ★★★ Perfectionist grower at Marienthal. Age-worthy SPÄTBURGUNDERS (Kräuterberg 09' 11 12 13 15' 16 17' 18).

Schwarzer Adler Bad ★★★→★★★★ Top estate, restaurant(s) at Oberbergen, KAISERSTUHL, led by Fritz Keller (president of German Football Federation DFB) and son Friedrich. PINOTS (r/w) to show that France is nr.

Schwegler, Albrecht Würt ★★★→★★★★ Family estate, 11 ha, led by young Aaron S. Red blends Beryll, Saphir, Granat combine oak influence and ultra pure fruit.

Seeger Bad ★★★ Best producer of the Badische Bergstrasse area s of Heidelberg, known for clever barrel ageing. Reds, whites equally gd.

Sekt ★→★★★★ German sparkling. Avoid cheap offers: bottle fermentation is not mandatory. Serious Sekt producers are making spectacular progress, eg. ALDINGER, Bardong, Barth, RATTENFELD-SPANIER, BERGDOLT, DIEL, GRIESEL, Leiner, Melsheimer, RAUMLAND, Reinecker, Schembs, SCHLOSS VAUX, SCHWARZER ADLER, Solter, S Steinmetz, Strauch, WAGECK, WEGELER, Wilhelmshof, ZILLIKEN. A VDP classification of Sekt vyds is underway.

Selbach-Oster M-M ★★★ Scrupulous ZELTINGEN estate with excellent vyd portfolio, known for classical style and focus on sweet PRÄDIKAT wines.

Sheep are increasingly popular vyd workers: they de-leaf, and keep grass down.

Solveigs Rhg ★★→★★★★ PINOT N specialist with vyds on red slate at ASSMANNSHAUSEN and LORCH, only 2 ha, organic viticulture and minimal winemaking. Best: single-plots Micke 06' 13' 15' 16', Present 95' 99' 03' 04 06 09' 12 13' 15' 16'.

Sonnenuhr M-M Sundial. Name of GROSSE LAGE sites at BRAUNEBERG, WEHLEN, ZELTINGEN.

Spätlese Late harvest. One level riper and potentially sweeter than KABINETT. Gd examples age at least 7 yrs. Spätlese TROCKEN designation almost died out.

Spreitzer Rhg ★★★ Brothers Andreas and Bernd S produce deliciously *racy, harmonious* RIES from vyds in HATTENHEIM, OESTRICH, Mittelheim. Mid-price range ALTE REBEN a bargain. And don't miss SPÄTLESE 303, vintage 19.

Staatsweingut / Staatliche Weinbaudomäne State wine estates or doms exist in BAD (IHRINGEN, Meersburg), MOS (TRIER), PFZ (Neustadt), RHG (HESSISCHE STAATSWEINGÜTER), RHH (OPPENHEIM), SACHS (WACKERBARTH), SA-UN (Kloster Pforta), WÜRT (Weinsberg),.

Steigerwald Frank District in e FRANK. Vyds at considerable altitude. Best: CASTELL, Hillabrand, Roth, RUCK, VETTER, WELTNER, *Wirsching*.

Steinberg Rhg ★★★ Walled-in vyd above HATTENHEIM, est by Cistercian monks 700 yrs ago: a German Clos de Vougeot. Monopoly of HESSISCHE STAATSWEINGÜTER. Classified parcels (14 ha out of 37) have unique soil (clay with fragments of decomposed schist in various colours). Fascinating old vintages (eg. NATURREIN 43, TBA 59). Not to be confused with Stein-Berg GU of WÜRZBURG.

48% of German wine is trocken, 20% halbtrocken, 32% sweet (2019).

Steinwein Frank Wine from WÜRZBURG's best vyd, Stein. Goethe's favourite. Only six producers: BURGERSPITAL, JULIUSSPITAL, L Knoll, Meinzinger, Reiss, Staatlicher Hofkeller. Hugh J once tasted the 1540 vintage.

Stodden Ahr ★★★→★★★★ AHR SPÄTBURGUNDER with a Burgundian touch, delicately extracted, subtle. Best usually ALTE REBEN, Rech Herrenberg. Pricey, but production is tiny.

Südliche Weinstrasse Pfz District known esp for PINOT varieties. Best growers: BECKER, JÜLG, KRANZ, Leiner, Minges, Münzberg, Ö-REBHOLZ, Siegrist, WEHRHEIM.

Taubertal Bad, Frank, Würt ★→★★★ Cool-climate district along River Tauber, divided by Napoleon into BAD, FRANK, WÜRT sections. SILVANER (limestone soils), local red Tauberschwarz. Frost a problem. Hofmann, Schlör, gd co-op at Beckstein.

TBA (Trockenbeerenauslese) Sweetest, most expensive category of German wine, extremely rare, viscous and concentrated with dried-fruit flavours. Made from selected dried-out grapes affected by noble rot (botrytis). Half bottles a gd idea.

Thanisch, Weingut Dr. M-M ★★★ BERNKASTEL estate, founded 1636, famous for its share of the DOCTOR vyd. After family split-up in 1988 two homonymous estates with similar qualities: Erben (heirs) Müller-Burggraef and Erben Thanisch (VDP).

Trier Mos The n capital of ancient Rome, on the Mosel, between RUWER and SAAR. Big charitable estates have cellars here among awesome Roman remains.

Trittenheim M-M ★★→★★★ Racy, textbook M-M RIES if from gd plots within extended GROSSE LAGE vyd Apotheke. Growers: A CLÜSSERATH, Clüsserath-Weiler, E Clüsserath, FJ Eifel, Grans-Fassian, Milz.

Trocken Dry. Defined as max 9g/l unfermented sugar. Today, height of gastronomic fashion. Generally the further s in Germany, the more Trocken wines.

Ürzig M-M ★★★→★★★★ MOS village on red sandstone and red slate, famous for ungrafted old vines and *unique spicy Ries*. GROSSE LAGE vyd: Würzgarten. Growers: Berres, Christoffel, Erbes, *Loosen*, MERKELBACH, *Molitor*, Mönchhof, Rebenhof.

Van Volxem Mos ★★★ Historical SAAR estate revived by obsessive Roman Niewodniczanski. Low yields from top sites (KANZEM Altenberg, OCKFEN Bockstein, SCHARZHOFBERG, WILTINGEN Gottesfuss) bring about monumental (mostly dry) RIES. Spectacular castle-like new cellar building in a Saar loop nr Wiltingen – and capacity to age selected wines 5 yrs+ in tank.

VDP (Verband Deutscher Prädikatsweingüter) Influential association of 200 premium growers setting highest standards. Look for its eagle insignia on wine labels, and for GROSSE LAGE logo on wines from classified vyds. A VDP wine is usually a gd bet. President: Steffen CHRISTMANN.

Wachenheim Pfz ★★★ Celebrated village with, according to VDP, no GROSSE LAGE vyds. See what you think. Top growers: Biffar, BÜRKLIN-WOLF, Karl Schäfer, ODINSTAL, WOLF, Zimmermann (bargain).

Wageck Pfz ★★→★★★ MITTELHAARDT estate for unaffected, brisk CHARD (still/sp), PINOT N of great finesse. Dense, well-ageing Portugieser from vyd planted in 1931.

Wagner, Dr. Mos ★★→★★★ Estate with vyds in OCKFEN and Saarstein led by young Christiane W. SAAR RIES with purity, freshness.

Wagner-Stempel Rhh ★★★ Seriously crafted RHH wines from Siefersheim nr NA border. Best usually RIES GGS Heerkretz (porphyry soil).

Walluf Rhg ★★★ Underrated village, 1st with important vyds as one leaves Wiesbaden going w. GROSSE LAGE vyd: Walkenberg. Growers: *JB Becker, Jost*.

Wasenhaus Mos ★★★ Young Alexander Götze and Christoph Wolber produce burgundy-inspired PINOT N Bellen and PINOT BL Möhlin from limestone sites in MARKGRÄFLERLAND, labelled as LANDWEIN, only 2 ha, all farmed by hand.

Wegeler M-M, Rhg ★★→★★★★ Important family estates in OESTRICH and BERNKASTEL (both in top form) plus a stake in the famous KRONE estate of ASSMANNSHAUSEN. Geheimrat J blend maintains high standards, single-vyd RIES usually outstanding value. Old vintages available ("vintage collection").

Wehlen M-M ★★★→★★★★ Wine village with legendary steep SONNENUHR vyd expressing RIES from slate at v. best: rich, fine, everlasting. Top: JJ PRÜM, Kerpen, KESSELSTATT, LOOSEN, MOLITOR, MF RICHTER, Pauly-Bergweiler, SA PRÜM, Sankt Nikolaus Hospital, SCHLOSS LIESER, SELBACH-OSTER, Studert-Prüm, THANISCH, WEGELER.

Wehrheim, Weingut Dr. Pfz ★★★ Top organic estate of SÜDLICHE WEINSTRASSE. V. dry, culinary style, esp white PINOT varieties.

Weil, Robert Rhg ★★★→★★★★ 17 37 59 90 01 05 09 12 15 16 17 18 19 Outstanding estate in KIEDRICH with GROSSE LAGE vyds Gräfenberg (generous) and Turmberg (austere). Superb sweet KABINETT to TBA (sensational 18 GOLDKAPSEL), dense GG. Now also parcel selection Monte Vacano, available only by subscription (1st yr, 18).

Weingart M Rh ★★★ Outstanding estate at Spay, vyds in BOPPARD (esp Hamm Feuerlay). Refined, taut RIES, low-tech in style, superb value.

Weingut Wine estate.

Weissherbst Pale-pink wine, made from a single variety, often SPÄTBURGUNDER; v. variable quality.

Weltner, Paul Frank ★★★ STEIGERWALD family estate. Densely structured, age-worthy SILVANER from underrated Rödelseer Küchenmeister vyd.

Wiltingen Mos ★★→★★★★ Heartland of the SAAR. SCHARZHOFBERG crowns a series of GROSSE LAGE vyds (Braune Kupp, Braunfels, Gottesfuss, Kupp). Top growers: BISCHÖFLICHE WEINGÜTER TRIER, EGON MÜLLER, KESSELSTATT, LE GALLAIS, SANKT URBANS-HOF, VAN VOLXEM, Vols.

Wind, Katrin Pfz ★★→★★★ Shooting star at Arzheim. Straightforward but nuanced wines, eg. Kalmit FRÜHBURGUNDER, RIES

Winning, von Pfz ★★★→★★★★ DEIDESHEIM estate with prime vyds there and at FORST. *Ries of great purity*, terroir expression, slightly influenced by fermentation in new FUDER casks.

German vintage notation

The vintage notes after entries in the German section are mostly given in a different form from those elsewhere in the book. If the vintages of a single wine are rated, or are for red wine regions, the vintage notation is identical with the one used elsewhere (*see* front jacket flap). But for regions, villages or producers, two styles of vintage are indicated:

Bold type (eg. **16**) indicates classic, ripe vintages with a high proportion of SPÄTLESEN and AUSLESEN; or, in the case of red wines, gd phenolic ripeness and must weights.

Normal type (eg. 17) indicates a successful but not outstanding vintage. Generally, German white wines, esp RIES, can be drunk young for their intense fruitiness, or kept for a decade or even two to develop their potential aromatic subtlety and finesse.

EU terminology
Germany's part in new EU classification involves, firstly, abolishing the term Tafelwein in favour of plain **Wein** – this is, up to now, the only visible change on labels. LANDWEIN is still called Landwein, even if its bureaucratic name would be **geschützte geographische Angabe (ggA)**, or Protected Geographical Indication. Brussels generally allows continued use of est designations. **Geschützte Ursprungsbezeichnung (gU)**, or Protected Designation of Origin, should technically be replacing QUALITÄTSWEIN and QUALITÄTSWEIN MIT PRÄDIKAT, but is, up to now, mainly in place for large geographical units as AHR, BAD, FRANKEN, etc. As it's hard and time-consuming (4–6 yrs) to get recognition for a village- or vyd-specific gU, only six such gUs were in place by end of 2020: Bürgstadter Berg (*see* WEINGUT FÜRST), WINNINGEN Uhlen (parcel-specific Blaufuesser Lay, Laubach, Roth Lay, *see* HEYMANN-LÖWENSTEIN), WÜRZBURGER Stein-Berg, and Monzinger Niederberg (NA). The existing predicates – SPÄTLESE, AUSLESE and so on (*see* box, p.165) – stay in place; the rule for these styles hasn't changed, and isn't going to.

Winningen Mos ★★→★★★ Lower MOS town nr Koblenz; powerful dry RIES. GROSSE LAGE vyds: Röttgen, Uhlen. Top: HEYMANN-LÖWENSTEIN, Knebel, Kröber, R Richter.

Wirsching, Hans Frank ★★★ Renowned estate in IPHOFEN known for classically structured dry RIES, *Silvaner*. Andrea W extends range with spontaneously fermented Ries Sister Act, kosher SILVANER. Occasionally BA, TBA of great purity.

Wittmann Rhh ★★★ Leading bio estate, crystal-pure, zesty dry RIES GGS Brunnenhäuschen, Kirchspiel, and Morstein 05 07' 08 11 12' 15 16 17 18 19'. Top Morstein ALTE REBEN selection La Borne.

Wöhrle Bad ★★★ Organic pioneer (30 yrs), son Markus a PINOT expert, excellent GGS.

Wolf JL Pfz ★★→★★★ WACHENHEIM estate, leased by Ernst LOOSEN of BERNKASTEL. Quality sound and consistent rather than dazzling.

Württemberg Formerly mocked as "TROLLINGER republic", but today dynamic, with many young growers eager to experiment. Best usually LEMBERGER, SPÄTBURGUNDER. Only 30% white varieties. RIES needs altitude vyds.

Würzburg Frank ★★→★★★★ Great baroque city on the Main, famous for its best vyd Stein (STEINWEIN). In 2020, best Stein parcels acknowledged as GU under name of Stein-Berg. Stein-Berg also GROSSE LAGE (as to VDP), as is Stein-Harfe (BÜRGERSPITAL monopoly). Remaining parcels of the Stein vyd are classified ERSTE LAGE.

Zellertal Pfz ★★→★★★★ Area in n PFZ, high, cool, recent gold-rush: BATTENFELD-SPANIER, PHILIPP KUHN, KP KELLER have bought in Zellertal's best vyd Schwarzer Herrgott or neighbouring RHH plot Zellerweg am Schwarzen Herrgott. Gd local estates: Bremer, Janson Bernhard, Schwedhelm, Wick.

Zeltingen M-M ★★→★★★ Top MOS village overshadowed by neighbour WEHLEN despite similiar growing conditions. GROSSE LAGE vyd: SONNENUHR. Top: JJ PRÜM, MOLITOR, SELBACH-OSTER.

Ziereisen Bad ★★→★★★ Outstanding estate in MARKGRÄFLERLAND, advocating LANDWEIN, mainly PINOTS and GUTEDEL. Best are SPÄTBURGUNDERS from small plots: Rhini, Schulen, Talrain. Jaspis = old vine selections.

Zilliken, Forstmeister Geltz Mos ★★★→★★★★ 93 94 95 96 97 99 01 03 04 05 07 08 09 10 11 12 15 16 17 18 19 SAAR family estate: intense racy/savoury *Ries from Saarburg Rausch* and OCKFEN Bockstein, incl superb long-lasting AUSLESE, EISWEIN. V.gd SEKT too (and Ferdinand's gin).

Zimmerling, Klaus Sachs ★★★ Small, perfectionist estate, one of 1st to be est after Berlin wall came down. Best vyd is Königlicher Weinberg (King's v'yd) at Pillnitz nr Dresden. Great 18s (esp RIES, WEISSBURGUNDER).

Luxembourg

Luxembourg vineyards lie upstream of the more famous parts of the Moselle, and the soil is limestone, with more in common with Chablis than Piesport. Only 11% is Riesling. The big ones are Müller-Thurgau (aka Rivaner), Auxerrois and Pinots Blanc/Gris. Crémant fizz is a speciality. Climate change has been kind: 2018 brought the most powerful Pinots of Luxembourg's history, but frost is still a danger (19 17 16). Most whites have strong acidity and some sweetness – labels don't differentiate between dry and off-dry. A common term (but of little significance) is "Premier Grand Cru". More reliable are groups of ambitious winemakers, eg. Domaine et Tradition and Privatwënzer.

Alice Hartmann ★★★→★★★★ Luxembourg's best RIES vyd, Koeppchen (Les Terrasses, 70-yr-old vines, Au Coeur de la Koeppchen, limestone). Also in Burgundy (St-Aubin), Mittelmosel (Trittenheim, and a plot in Scharzhofberg).
Aly Duhr ★★→★★★ Reliable and inexpensive Barrique Blanc (PINOT BL/AUXERROIS), refined Ahn Nussbaum RIES 18'. V.gd Crémant Grande Cuvée.
Bentz, René ★★→★★★ Fresh, elegant, esp Bech-Maacher Gottesgôf RIES.
Bernard-Massard ★→★★★ Big producer, esp Crémant. Top: Ch de Schengen and Clos des Rocher. Sekt in Germany too.
Caves Berna ★★→★★★ Outstanding PINOT N Göllebour, v.gd RIES Vieilles Vignes.
Desom, Dom ★★ →★★★ Wines of power, intensity: Remich Fels CHARD.
Gales ★★→★★★ Reliable. Best: Crémant, Remich Hôpertsbour PINOT GR, Domaine et Tradition labels. Old labyrinth cellar.
Kox, R&L ★→★★★ Foot-trodden Elbling (Rhäifrentsch) from old vines, gd RIES too.
Ruppert, Henri ★★★ RIES TBA-style (see p.165), dense PINOT N Ma Tâche (yes, really).
Pauqué, Château ★★★→★★★★ Passionate Abi Duhr bridges gap between Burgundy and Germany: top RIES (dr/sw). Top barrel-fermented CHARD Clos de la Falaise.
Sunnen-Hoffmann ★★★ Full range of textbook whites, best usually RIES Wintrange Felsberg VV Domaine et Tradition from vyd planted in 1943.
Other good estates: Cep d'Or, Duhr Frères-Clos Mon Vieux Moulin, Fränk Kayl, Häremillen, Kohll-Leuk, Krier Frères, Krier-Welbes, Mathes, Mathis Bastian, Paul Legill, Schlink, Schmit-Fohl, Schumacher-Knepper, Stronck-Pinnel. Doms Vinsmoselle is a union of co-ops.

Belgium

Wedged between northern France and Germany, Belgium's cool climate expresses itself in fresh and food-friendly wines, of which 85% are white or sparkling. Covering 600 ha of vineyards, most estates are small: only c.15 exceed 10 ha. Wine tourism is becoming increasingly popular, in tune with the country's rich gastronomic culture. Many winemakers choose Pinotss Blanc/Gris/Noir, Chardonnay or Auxerrois, while others prefer disease-resistant varieties ie. Johanniter, Regent and Solaris. Noteworthy results also with Riesling, Souvignier Gris, Acolon and the first vintages of Albariño and Grüner Veltliner.

Recommended: Aldeneyck, Bon Baron, Chant d'Eole, Chapitre, Clos d'Opleeuw, Crutzberg, d'Hellekapelle, Driesse, Entre-Deux-Monts, Genoels-Elderen, Gloire de Duras, Hoenshof, Kitsberg, Kluisberg, Lijsternest, Pietershof, Ruffus, Ry d'Argent, Schorpion, Vandeurzen, Vin de Liège, Waes.

Spain

Abbreviations used in the text:

PORTUGAL

Alen	Alentejo
Alg	Algarve
Bair	Bairrada
Bei Int	Beira Interior
Dou	Douro
Lis	Lisboa
Min	Minho
Set	Setúbal
Tej	Tejo
Vin	Vinho Verde

SPAIN

Alel	Alella
Alic	Alicante
Ara	Aragón
Bier	Bierzo
Bul	Bullas
Cád	Cádiz
Can	Canary Islands
C-La M	Castilla-La Mancha
C y L	Castilla y León
Cat	Catalonia
Cos del S	Costers del Segre
Emp	Empordà
Ext	Extremadura
Gal	Galicia
Jum	Jumilla
La M	La Mancha
Mad	Madeira
Mál	Málaga
Mall	Mallorca
Man	Manchuela
Mén	Méntrida
Mont-M	Montilla-Moriles
Mont	Montsant
Mur	Murcia
Nav	Navarra
Pen	Penedès
Pri	Priorat
P Vas	País Vasco
R Bai	Rías Baixas
Rib del D	Ribera del Duero
Rio	Rioja
R Ala	Rioja Alavesa
R Alt	Rioja Alta
R Or	Rioja Oriental
Rue	Rueda
Som	Somontano
U-R	Utiel-Requena
V'cia	Valencia

Vineyard, vineyard, vineyard. This is the theme in Spain. It started in Priorat with the introduction of a Burgundy-style categorization of village wines. That has now been systematized with a top category of Gran Vi de Vinya. Bierzo is moving in a similar direction. Rioja now has its own Viñedo Singular category. Cava is gaining approval for its identification of different zones, which will enable producers to talk about origin for the first time. None of these is perfect, with criticisms both that they go too far, and not far enough. Perhaps, more convincingly, Sherry has joined in. Finally there is a return to naming the vineyard. Pago Macharnudo, Pago Balbaina, Pago Añina… These mystical names have become real again. Sherry is not just made in the bodega; its vineyard origin makes a difference. Another highlight in Spain's viticulture has been a chance to taste the results of the recuperation of ancestral varieties. Miguel Torres Snr was a pioneer in this research. Castilla y León recently revealed the results of a lengthy project looking into rare varieties. One promising discovery is Cenicienta ("Cinderella"), a red that could have commercial value among Rueda's whites. Spain is an ampoelographer's delight: look out for Arcos, Blanco Lexítimo, Forcallà, Gonfaus, Pirene…

Portugal & Spain

SPAIN

Recent Rioja vintages

2020 Rains, mildew in some areas, and hail. Finally, v.gd wines.

2019 Lower yields and overall fine quality, officially *excelente*.

2018 "Good" with lower alc and higher yield.

2017 Dramatic frost led to much-reduced harvest. What was left is v.gd.

2016 Largest harvest since 05, well-balanced wines, plenty to like.

2015 Top wines are as gd as 10, rich and full of character.

2014 After two small vintages, return to quality, quantity.

2013 Cool yr, with rain, later harvest, uneven, with some gd wines.

2012 One of lowest yields for two decades, delivering fine concentration.

2011 Officially *excelente*; not as gd as 10, but powerful with lower acidity.

Aalto Rib del D ★★★→★★★★ Polished, structured wines: Aalto, and flagship PS (from 200 small plots). MARIANO GARCÍA, ex-VEGA SICILIA, builds wines for cellaring. Best with 10 yrs+. Co-owns with Masaveu, owners of Enate (SOM), Fillaboa (R BAI), Murúa (RIO) and v.gd Asturias cider (Valverán).

Abadía de Poblet Pri ★★ Exciting project within Cistercian monastery, burial place of ARA kings. Spain's only winery in a historical monument. SCALA DEI winemaker works with local varieties esp (r) Trepat.

Abadía Retuerta C y L ★★★ Height of luxury: Michelin-starred restaurant, glam hotel, spa – and winery. Just outside RIB DEL D. V.gd white DYA Le Domaine. Serious single-vyd reds, eg. Pago Garduña SYRAH, PV PETIT VERDOT, Pago Valdeballón CAB SAUV. Novartis-owned.

Alberto, Bodegas de Rue ★★★ Exceptional demijohn- and solera-aged oxidative VERDEJO: caramel and walnut, vanilla and raisin. A discovery.

Algueira Rib Sac ★★→★★★ Exceptional producer in RIBEIRA SACRA, expert in its extreme viticulture. Fine selection of elegant wines from local varieties. Outstanding is Merenzao (aka Jura's Trousseau), almost burgundian in style.

Alicante ★→★★★ Take a closer look at Alicante. It's the spiritual home of MONASTRELL, making spicy reds and rare traditional fortified *Fondillón*. But also dry wines from formerly unloved MOSCATEL de Alejandría coming to fore; and local (r) Giró. Top: ARTADI, Enrique Mendoza. Also Finca Collado, Les Freses, Murviedro.

Allende, Finca R Alt ★★→★★★★ Top (in all senses) RIO BODEGA at BRIONES in merchant's house with tower looking over town to vyds, run by irrepressible Miguel Ángel de Gregorio. Single vyds incl mineral Calvario and Mingoritz, grown on limestone. Splendid aromatic Martires (w).

Almacenista Sherry stockholding cellar; ages and provides wines for BODEGAS to increase or refresh stocks. Important in MANZANILLA production. Can be terrific. Few left; many sell direct to consumers, eg. GUTIÉRREZ COLOSÍA, EL MAESTRO SIERRA.

Alonso, Bodegas Man ★★★→★★★★ Part of revival of SANLÚCAR DE BARRAMEDA BODEGAS. Asencio brothers own Dominio de Urogallo (Asturias). Bought exceptional stock of Pedro Romero, incl v. fine SOLERAS of Gaspar Florido. Excellent if super-priced four-bottle collection. More accessibly priced is Velo Flor, 9–10-yr-old MANZANILLA.

Alonso del Yerro Rib del D, Toro ★★→★★★ Stéphane Derenoncourt (B'x consultant) entices elegance from extreme continental climate of RIB DEL D. Transformation since 2016, altogether more delicate. Family business, estate wines. Top wine: María, inky but not overblown. Paydos is its TORO.

Alta Alella Cat ★★→★★★ With toes in the Med and just up the coast from Barcelona. Excellent CAVAS and sweet red Dolç Mataró from MONASTRELL. Organic.

Alvear Mont-M, Ext ★★→★★★★ Historic Alvear has superb array of PX wines in MONT-M. Gd FINO CB and Capataz, lovely sweet SOLERA 1927, unctuous DULCE Viejo. V. fine vintage wines. Also Palacio Quemado BODEGA in Ext. Imaginative appointment of ENVÍNATE team has brought innovative thinking, eg. 3 Miradas series – lower alc wines with FLOR and focus on terroir.

Añada Vintage.

Aragón Former mighty medieval kingdom, stretching s from Pyrénées, home to Calatayud, CAMPO DE BORJA, CARIÑENA, SOM DOS. Once a land of bulk wine from co-ops, now gaining attention for new generation recuperating old vines incl GARNACHA, MACABEO, Moristel (r).

Arizcuren Rio ★★ Javier A trained as architect and designed wineries in RIO, incl his own tiny BODEGA in downtown Logroño (worth a visit). Specializes in GARNACHAS at altitude from R OR, Mazuelo (CARIÑENA) and amphora wine. One to watch.

Arrayán, Bodegas Mén ★★ Winemaker Maite Sánchez is restoring reputation of MÉN with fine GARNACHA and Albillo Real (w).

Artadi Alic, Nav, P Vas, Ala ★★→★★★★ Left RIO DO end 2015, believing it failed to defend quality; now carries Àlava origin. Focus on single vyds: luxuriant La Poza de Ballesteros; dark, stony El Carretil; outstanding El Pisón. Also in ALIC (r El Sequé), NAV (r Artazuri, ROSADO DYA). Izar-Leku TXAKOLÍ (w) from Getaria.

Artuke Rio ★★ Brothers Arturo and Kike de Miguel, transformed family wines. Gloriously elegant wines, subtle use of large oak. Two tiptop single-vyds: El Escolladero, on limestone; La Condenada, on iron-rich sandstone.

Astobiza Ala ★★ Young winery in smallest of TXAKOLÍ DOS, v. fine wines, advised by Ana Martín (*see* CASTILLO DE CUZCURRITA). Mineral Malkoa; also makes gin.

"Atlantic" wines Gal, Rio, P Vas Unofficial collective term for bright, often unoaked style, with firm acidity. Increasingly used to describe crisp, delicate reds, esp in R BAI, or Cantabrian Sea: the TXAKOLIS. Also used to describe cool climatic influences, eg. inland GAL DOS, and specific vintages in R Ala, R Alt.

Ausàs Rib del D ★★ Xavier A, former winemaker at VEGA SICILIA, now consults widely, and has own – young – project: Interpretación.

Baigorri R Ala ★★→★★★ Wines as glamorous as BODEGA's glassy architecture. Gravity-fed, producing bold, modern RIO. Gd restaurant, tasting menus, views.

Barbadillo Man ★→★★★★ Wines from supermarket to superb. Pioneer of MANZANILLA EN RAMA. Top-of-range Reliquía wines unbeatable, esp AMONTILLADO, PALO CORTADO. Sherry guru Armando Guerra advises on adventurous new releases. Bottling tiny quanititics of historical wines, also returning to traditional practices, eg. Mirabras, unfortified PALOMINO. Also Vega Real (RIB DEL D), BODEGA Pirineos (SOM).

Barrio de la Estación Rio The "station quarter" of Haro, from where trains shipped wine to B'x when latter's vines were destroyed by phylloxera. Now home to seven top wineries: BODEGAS Bilbaínas (CODORNÍU), CVNE, GÓMEZ CRUZADO, LA RIOJA ALTA, LÓPEZ DE HEREDIA, MUGA, RODA. Annual open-house day for public, "La Cata del Barrio de la Estación", worth a visit.

Rio with salt: Añana's saltflats based on an ancient inland sea. Striking sight.

Belondrade C y L, Rue ★★→★★★ VERDEJO as it should be but rarely is. Didier B was early (1994) exponent of finesse in RUE, and lees-ageing. Quinta Apollonia (w) and light, summery, Quinta Clarisa TEMPRANILLO (r), both C Y L.

Bentomiz, Bodegas Mál ★★→★★★ Dutch by birth, Spanish by adoption: Clara and André are welcoming hosts in Axarquía, inland from MÁL. Sweet MOSCATEL and MERLOT. Also rare dry Romé (p). Visit restaurant.

Bhilar, Bodegas R Ala ★→★★ David Sampedro is a native of El Villar, and has taken his wines to next level; focus on viticulture, and traditional methods. Bio.

Bierzo ★→★★★★ New flavour of Spanish wine. Aromatic, mid-weight, often crunchily fresh reds from MENCÍA. On slate soils can become perfumed, *Pinot-like.* DO shot to international fame with RAÚL PÉREZ and Ricardo Pérez Palacios (no relation), still names to follow. Take care, quality uneven. Follow the producer. Look for DESCENDIENTES DE J PALACIOS, Raúl Pérez, plus Dominio de Tares, Losada, Luna Berberide, Mengoba, Veronica Ortega. Also fine GODELLO (w).

Bilbao, Ramón Rías, Rib del D, Rio, Rue ★→★★ Major producer making strides in quality, with experimentation. BODEGAS IN RIO, R BAI (Mar de Frades), RUE and RIB DEL D (Cruz de Alba). In R OR delivering fresh GARNACHA at altitude. Latest project, Lalomba winery with two single-vyd wines; Provençal-style ROSADO.

Bodega A cellar; a wine shop; a business making, blending and/or shipping wine.

Butt Sherry 600-litre barrel of long-matured American oak used for Sherry. Filled 5/6 full, allows space for FLOR to grow. Trend for wineries – and whisky distillers – to use former butts for maturation for Sherry influence – eg. CVNE Monopole Clásico, BARBADILLO Mirabras.

Callejuela Sherry, Man ★★→★★★ Blancos have vyds in some of Sherry's most famous PAGOS. Part of the movement to make Sherries with distinct terroir character.

Campo de Borja Ara ★→★★★ Self-proclaimed "Empire of GARNACHA". Heritage of old vines, plus young vyds = 1st choice for gd-value Garnacha, now starting to show serious quality: Alto Moncayo, Aragonesas, Borsao.

Campo Viejo Rio ★→★★ RIO's biggest brand. In addition to value RES, GRAN RES, has varietal GARNACHA, and adds TEMPRANILLO Blanco to white RIO. V.gd top Res Dominio. Part of Pernod Ricard (also owns much-improved YSIOS winery in Rio).

Canary Islands ★→★★★ Seven main islands, nine DOS. TENERIFE has five DOs. One for the vine-hunters: exciting wines from unusual varieties, old vines, distinct microclimates, volcanic soils, unique pruning methods. Dry white LISTÁN (aka PALOMINO) and Marmajuelo, black Listán Negro, Negramoll (TINTA NEGRA), Vijariego. Gd dessert MOSCATELS, MALVASÍAS, esp fortified El Grifo from Lanzarote. Top: Borja Pérez, ENVINATE, SUERTES DEL MARQUÉS. In La Palma, Victoria Pecis Torres. Beware: also plenty of dull wine for tourists.

Cangas ★→★★ Isolated DO in wild Asturias beginning to export. Isolation means unique vines to enjoy: fresh Albarín Blanco, firm reds from Albarín Negro, Verdejo Negro, and most promising, Carrasquín. Producers: Dominio de Urogallo (owned by BODEGAS ALONSO), Monasterio de Corias, VidAs.

Cariñena Ara ★→★★ The one DO that is also the name of a grape variety. Formerly co-op country, offers value. Jorge Navascués, winemaker at RIO'S CONTINO, makes own wines at Navascués Enologia; consults at ARA'S VINO DE PAGO Finca Aylés.

Casa Castillo Jum ★★→★★★★ José María Vicente proves JUM can be tiptop. Family business high up in *altiplano*. V. fine Las Gravas single vyd. Outstanding MONASTRELLS, esp PIE FRANCO (plot escaped fairly recent phylloxera).

Castell d'Encús Cos del S ★★→★★★ Raül Bobet (also of PRI Ferrer-Bobet) has all the cool climates he wants at 1000m (3281ft), for *superbly fresh, original wines*. Ancient meets modern: grapes fermented in C12 granite *lagares*, while winery is up to date. Acusp PINOT, Ekam RIES, Thalarn SYRAH have become classics.

Castilla y León ★→★★★ Spain's largest wine region. Diverse and occasionally confusing but packed with wines to enjoy. DOS: Arlanza, Arribes, BIER, Cigales, RUE, Sierra de Salamanca (one to watch, with r Rufete variety), Tierra de León, Tierra del Vino de Zamora, TORO, Valles de Benavente, Valtiendas. Note catch-all DO Vino de la Tierra de Castilla y León, can be source of fine wines eg. Barco del Corneta, Máquina y Tabla. Top producers: ABADÍA RETUERTA, MARQUÉS DE RISCAL (VERDEJO), Mauro, Ossian, Prieto Pariente. They may be just outside a DO or prefer to escape a DO's regulations or poor reputation.

Castillo de Cuzcurrita R Alt ★★ Lovely walled vyd and castle, top consultant Ana Martín, v. fine RIO.

Castillo Perelada Emp, Nav, Pri ★→★★★ Glamorous estate and tourist destination. Lively CAVAS, esp Gran Claustro; modern red blends. Rare 12-yr-old, SOLERA-aged GARNATXA de l'EMPORDÀ. V. fine Casa Gran del Siurana (PRI). Owns CHIVITE group.

Catalonia Vast DO, covers whole of Cat: seashore, mtn, in-between. Top chefs and top BODEGAS. Yet actual DO is just umbrella, too large to have identity, an excuse for characterless cross-DO blends.

Coming in from the cold

In Spain varieties are either in or out. TEMPRANILLO (and its other forms as Cencibel, Tinta del Pais, Tinto Fino etc) is clearly in; so, to now, is MENCÍA. GARNACHA, derided for being rustic and alcoholic, has been admitted for its finesse. BOBAL and CARIÑENA are knocking at the door. Bobal has the bonus of being easy to pronounce and remember. Yet its origins in the unknown DOS of U-R and MAN make it look like a country cousin. It looks like MUSTIGUILLO's and PONCE's international recognition may push it in, despite the fact that no-one looks keen to plant it anywhere else in the world. Cariñena, RIO'S Mazuelo and France's CARIGNAN, on the other hand, is better known. PRI has woken up to its heritage of centenarian bush-vine Cariñenas on slate soil, and the results are impressive. Seek out MAS DOIX, Mas La Rosa, Terroir al Limit, Trio Infernal, and many more. And in Rio, Miguel Merino and MARQUÉS DE MURRIETA rosado. Cariñena is in.

Cava ★→★★★ Looks like Cava may be getting its house in order. Can Spain's traditional-method sparkling win back customers and reputation? Cava's proposals aim to extend min ageing, organic viticulture, recognition of origin, and more. Producers who lost faith in the DO have formed their own: CLÀSSIC PENEDÈS, Conca del Riu Anoia, CORPINNAT; each with tighter quality regulations. Further, RIO producers, formerly of Cava DO, can use new Rio DO instead.

Cava de Paraje Calificado Cava Launched 2017 by CAVA CONSEJO REGULADOR as top category of single-vyd Cava with stringent rules. Single estate; low or no dosage; min 36 mths age, most exceed that. Currently made by Alta Alella, Can Sala, CODORNÍU, JUVE Y CAMPS, Marqués de la Concordia, Vallformosa.

Cebreros C y L ★→★★ Young (2017) DO illustrating dynamic development of the SIERRA DE GREDOS, with distinct zones identifying themselves. As elsewhere GARNACHA (r) dominates; also Albillo Mayor (w). Look for Daniel Ramos, Ruben Díaz, TELMO RODRÍGUEZ, Rico Nuevo, Soto Manrique.

Celler del Roure V'cia ★→★★ Remarkable BODEGA in s V'CIA. Vast amphorae buried up to neck. V.gd, fresh, elegant; Cullerot, Parotet, Safrà, from local grape varieties.

César Florido Sherry ★→★★★ Master of MOSCATEL, since 1887. Underrated secret of Sherry. Explore gloriously scented, succulent trio: Dorado, Especial, Pasas.

Chacolí *See* TXAKOLI.

Chipiona Sherry Sherry's MOSCATEL grapes come from this sandy coastal zone. Best are floral delicacies, far less dense than PX.

Chivite Nav ★★→★★★ Historic name. Colección 125, incl top CHARD, one of Spain's greatest. Gd late-harvest MOSCATEL. CASTILLO PERELADA providing welcome investment.

Clàssic Penedès Pen Category of DO PEN for traditional-method fizz, more strict rules than Cava. Min 15 mths ageing, organically grown grapes. Members incl Albet i Noya, Colet, LOXAREL, Mas Bertran.

Clos Mogador Pri ★★→★★★ René Jnr's father, René Barbier, was one of PRI's founding quintet and mentor to many. One of 1st wineries to gain a Vi de Finca designation. Lovely Manyetes CARIÑENA.

Codorníu Raventós Cos del S, Pen, Pri, Rio ★→★★★★ Historic art nouveau CAVA winery worth a visit. V. fine single-vyd, single-variety CAVAS DE PARAJE CALIFICADO trio; plus 456, blend of three vyds, most expensive Cava ever. Elsewhere in the group, Legaris in RIB DEL D has v.gd village wines; Raimat in COS DEL S is 100% organic; BODEGA Bilbaínas in RIO has bestseller VIÑA Pomal, back on form. Jewel is outstanding PRI SCALA DEI, which it part owns. Latest project ABADÍA DE POBLET.

Conca de Barberà Cat Small CAT DO once a feeder of fruit to large enterprises, now some excellent wineries, incl ABADÍA DE POBLET, TORRES.

Consejo Regulador Organization that controls a DO – each DO has its own. Quality as inconsistent as wines they represent: some bureaucratic, others enterprising.

Contino R Ala ★★→★★★★ Estate incl one of RIO's great single vyds. Promising developments under winemaker Jorge Navascués. CVNE-owned.

Corpinnat Cat Group of producers of traditional sparkling. More stringent quality. Formed 2018, left CAVA DO 2019. Members: Can Descregut, Can Feixes, GRAMONA, Júlia Bernet, Llopart, Mas Candí, Nadal, RECAREDO, Sabaté i Coca, Torelló.

Corrales, Viña Jer ★★★ Much-awaited 1st release of PETER SISSECK's BODEGA in JEREZ, a FINO from Pago Balbaina, 8–9-yr-old EN RAMA. His intention is to release single-vyd Sherries. Viña La Cruz is AMONTILLADO, from Pago Macharnudo.

Costers del Segre ★→★★★ Geographically divided DO combines mountainous CASTELL D'ENCÙS and lower-lying Castell del Remei, Raimat.

Cota 45 Sherry ★★ From thoughtful, ever-interesting SANLÚCAR winemaker Ramiro Ibáñez. Ube brand is PALOMINO from different famous PAGOS, eg. Carrascal, Miraflores. Saline, appley, unfortified but briefly matured in Sherry BUTTS. Reveals strong terroir differences. *See also* DE LA RIVA, WILLY PÉREZ.

Crianza Declaration of wine age in RIO. Must be min 2 yr old; reds min 1 yr in oak barrels, whites and ROSADOS min 6 mths.

Cusiné, Tomás Cos del S ★★→★★★ Winemaker leading innovative group: wines incl Finca collection, Tomás Cusiné blends. Working in MONT, COS DEL S, CONCA DE BARBERÀ DOS.

CVNE R Ala, R Alt ★★→★★★★ One of RIO's great names, based in Haro's BARRIO DE LA ESTACIÓN, owns 545 ha vyds. Pronounced *"coo-nee"*, Compañia Vinícola del Norte de España, founded 1879. Four Rio wineries: CONTINO, CVNE, Imperial, VIÑA Real. Most impressive at top end. Also wineries in RIB DEL D, VALDEORRAS.

Delgado Zuleta Man ★→★★ Oldest (1744) SANLÚCAR firm. Flagship is 6/7-yr-old *La Goya* MANZANILLA PASADA; also 10-yr-old Goya XL EN RAMA. Impressively aged 40-yr-old Quo Vadis? AMONTILLADO.

Dinastía Vivanco R Alt ★→★★ In Briones, *outstanding wine museum* Vivanco. Makes wide selection of single variety RIO.

DO / DOP (Denominación de Origen / Protegida) Has replaced the former Denominación de Origen (DO) category.

Domecq, Álvaro Sherry, Man ★★→★★★ SOLERAS drawn from former ALMACENISTA Pilar Aranda. Polished wines. Gd FINO La Janda. Excellent 1730 VORS series.

Dulce Sweet. Can be late-harvest, botrytis, or fortifed. Seek out treasures: Alta Alella, BENTOMIZ, GUTIÉRREZ DE LA VEGA, OCHOA, TELMO RODRÍGUEZ, TORRES. Also EMPORDÁ, MÁL, TXAKOLÍ, YECLA.

El Puerto de Santa María One of three towns forming "Sherry Triangle". Production in decline; few BODEGAS remain incl GUTIÉRREZ COLOSÍA, OSBORNE, Terry. Puerto FINOS are prized as less weighty than JEREZ, not as "salty" as SANLÚCAR. Taste Lustau's EN RAMA trio to understand differences of Sherries aged in the three towns.

Empordà Cat ★→★★ One of number of centres of creativity in CAT. Best: CASTILLO PERELADA, Celler Martí Fabra, Pere Guardiola, Vinyes dels Aspres. Quirky, young Espelt grows 17 varieties: try GARNACHA/CARIGNAN Sauló. Sumptuous natural sweet wine from Celler Espolla: SOLERA GRAN RES.

En rama Sherry bottled from butt; v. low filtration, max freshness. Understood to refer to MANZANILLA and FINO, but any Sherry bottled this way is En Rama.

Envinate Quartet of winemakers casting original light on lesser-known regions, Almansa (Albahra), Ext (T. Amarela), RIBEIRA SACRA (Lousas), TENERIFE (Taganan).

Equipo Navazos Sherry, Man ★★★→★★★★ Academic Jesús Barquín and Sherry winemaker Eduardo Ojeda pioneered négociant approach to Sherry, bottling individual BUTTS. Case for ageing MANZANILLA in bottle. Recent releases are fascinating expressions of same SANLÚCAR DE BARRAMEDA Pago Miraflores vyd: outstanding anniversary La Bota no.100, Manzanilla Pasada; elegant no.99 (Palomino 19 without FLOR or fortifification); distinctive I Think Manzanilla.

Escocés Volante, El Gal, Ara ★→★★★ The Scot Norrel Robertson MW was a flying winemaker in Spain, hence the brand. Settled in Calatayud, focuses on old-vine GARNACHA grown at altitude, often blending in local varieties. Individual, characterful wines, part of movement transforming ARA.

Espumoso Means "sparkling", but confusing: incl cheap, injected-bubble wine as well as traditional method, like CAVA.

Fernando de Castilla Sherry ★★→★★★★ Gloriously consistent quality. Seek out Antique Sherries; all qualify as VOS or VORS, but label doesn't say so. Youngest of these, Antique FINO, is fascinating, complex, fortified to historically correct 17% alc. New, v.gd OLOROSO and PX Singular. Also v. fine brandy, vinegar. Favoured supplier to EQUIPO NAVAZOS.

Flor Sherry Spanish for "flower": refers to the layer of *Saccharomyces* yeasts that typically grow and live on top of FINO/MANZANILLA Sherry in a BUTT 5/6 full. Flor consumes oxygen and other compounds ("biological ageing") and protects wine from oxidation. It grows a thicker layer nearer the sea at EL PUERTO and SANLÚCAR, hence finer character of Sherry there. Trend to market unfortified Palomino aged for a short time with flor, a Sherry style with lower alc. Growing interest in creating unfortified wines with flor: Spain, Jura, Argentina, NZ.

Fondillón Alic ★→★★★ Fabled unfortified *rancio* semi-sweet wine from overripe MONASTRELL grapes, made to survive sea voyages. Now matured in oak for min 10 yrs; some SOLERAS of great age. Unfairly fallen out of fashion, production shrinking too fast: Brotons (v. fine 64 70), GUTIÉRREZ DE LA VEGA, Primitivo Quiles. MG Wines with Bodegas Monovár reissuing v. old wines (eg. 50-yr-old).

Freixenet Pen, Cava ★→★★★ Biggest CAVA producer. Best-known for black-bottled Cordón Negro. Casa Sala is CAVA DE PARAJE CALIFICADO. Other Cava brands: Castellblanch, Conde de Caralt, Segura Viudas. Plus: Morlanda (PRI), Solar Viejo (RIO), Valdubón (RIB DEL D), Vionta (R BAI). Also Gloria Ferrer (US), Katnook (Australia), Finca Ferrer (Argentina). Owned by sparkling giant Henkell.

Frontonio Ara Fernando Mora MW making waves seeking out old-vine GARNACHA, GARNACHA BLANCA. Also v.gd MACABEO, from old-vine El Jardín de la Iguales vyd.

Fundador Pedro Domecq Sherry Former Domecq BODEGAS were sliced up through multiple mergers. VORS wines owned by OSBORNE; *Botaina*, *La Ina*, *Rio Viejo*, VIÑA 25 by LUSTAU. Group also incl Terry Centenario brandy, Harvey's, famed for Bristol Cream and v. fine VORS, and Garvey, known for *San Patricio* FINO.

Galicia Isolated nw corner of Spain, destination of pilgrims walking the Camino de Santiago; home to many of Spain's best whites (*see* MONTERREI, R BAI, RIBEIRA SACRA, RIBEIRO, VALDEORRAS) and light, crunchy reds. Isolation ensures rare varieties.

Speciality of Galicia, Basque country: superb tuna, anchovies, shellfish – all in tins.

García, Mariano & Sons Mariano G is a fixture in N and NW Spain. For many yrs his life was VEGA SICILIA, where he was winemaker until 1998. He co-founded AALTO, and launched Mauro (C Y L). He and sons Eduardo and Alberto also run San Román (TORO), Garmón (RIB DEL D), specializing in vyd selection. Arrived in RIO 2020, making 1st vintage in Baños de Ebro.

Genéricos Rio If there's no category shown on the bottle – such as RES – then it's a *genérico*. *Genéricos* need not follow all DO rules on ageing. An unattractive name that gives no guidance, but they can be v.gd or outstanding. A case of needing to know the producer.

Gómez Cruzado R Alt BODEGA tucked in between MUGA and LA RIOJA ALTA in the BARRIO DE LA ESTACIÓN. V.gd Montes Obarenes (w) blend, Pancrudo GARNACHA.

González Byass Sherry, Cád ★→★★★★ Family business (1845). Cellarmaster Antonio Flores is a debonair, poetic, but expert presence. From the *Tío Pepe* SOLERA Flores continues to extract fine EN RAMA and *glorious Palmas series* (latter celebrated 1st decade in 2020). Consistently polished VIÑA AB AMONTILLADO, Matúsalem OLOROSO, Noë PX. Boutique hotel opened 2020 on premises (1st hotel in a working BODEGA in JEREZ). Other wineries: Beronia (RIO), Pazos de Lusco (R BAI), Vilarnau (CAVA), VIÑAS del Vero (SOM); the former O Fournier winery in RIB DEL D; plus (not so gd, but popular) Croft Original Pale Cream Sherry. Finca Moncloa, close to Jerez, produces still reds; also succulent Tintilla de Rota (sweet red fortified).

Gozalo, Ismael Rue ★→★★ Born in heart of VERDEJO country in Nieva, founder of Ossian, Gozalo nows follows natural wine route. Microbio label for remarkable assortment of Verdejos, from pét-nats to amphora-aged, all with no shown origin, and creative labels.

Gramona Cat, Pen ★★→★★★★ Cousins make impressively long-aged traditional-method sparkling, esp Enoteca, *III Lustros*, *Celler Batlle*. Drove founding of CORPINNAT. Inspiring hive of research, incl bio; sweet incl Icewines, experimental wines, table wines. Next generation developing range further. Plenty to watch.

Grandes Pagos Network of mainly family-owned estates across Spain. Don't confuse with VINO DE PAGO. Some are Vinos de Pago but not all. New President Toni Sarrión of MUSTIGUILLO leading promising improvements, recruitment of new members.

Gran Reserva In RIO. red Gran Res ages min 60 mths, of which min 2 yrs in 225-litre barrique, min 2 yrs in bottle. Whites and ROSADOS age min 4 yrs, of which 6 mth in barrel. Seek out superb old Rio vintages, often great value.

Guita, La Man ★→★★★ Classic *Manzanilla* distinctive for sourcing fruit from vyds close to maritime SANLÚCAR. Grupo Estévez-owned (also VALDESPINO).

Gutiérrez Colosía Sherry ★★★★ Rare remaining riverside BODEGA in EL PUERTO. Family business. Former ALMACENISTA. Excellent old PALO CORTADO.

Gutiérrez de la Vega Alic ★→★★★ Remarkable BODEGA specializing in sweet wine. In ALIC, but no longer in DO, after disagreement over regulations. Expert in MOSCATEL, FONDILLÓN. Daughter Violeta now leading business alongside own project Curii, which she runs with partner Alberto Redrado (focuses on Giró r).

Harvey's Sherry ★→★★★ Once-great Sherry name, famed for Bristol Cream. Now owned by Emperador, owners of FUNDADOR PEDRO DOMECQ. V.gd VORS Sherries.

Hidalgo, Emilio Sherry ★★★→★★★★ Outstanding family BODEGA. All wines (except PX) start by spending time under FLOR. Excellent unfiltered 15-yr-old La Panesa FINO, thrilling 50-yr-old AMONTILLADO Tresillo 1874, rare Santa Ana PX 1861.

Hidalgo-La Gitana Man ★★→★★★★ Historic (1792) SANLÚCAR firm. MANZANILLA La Gitana a classic. Finest Manzanilla is single-vyd Pastrana Pasada, verging on AMONTILLADO. Outstanding VORS, incl Napoleon Amontillado, Triana PX, Wellington PALO CORTADO.

Jerez de la Frontera Sherry Capital of Sherry region, between Cádiz and Seville. "Sherry" is corruption of C8 "Sherish", Moorish name of city. Pronounced "hereth". In French, Xérès. Hence DO is Jerez-Xérès-Sherry. MANZANILLA has own DO: Manzanilla-SANLÚCAR DE BARRAMEDA.

Joven Young, unoaked wine.

Juan Gil Family Estates Jum ★→★★★ Family BODEGA; has helped transform reputation of JUM. Gd young MONASTRELLS (eg. 4 Meses); long-lived top Clio, El Nido. Other wineries incl Ateca (Calatayud), Can Blau (MONT), Shaya (RUE).

Jules, Alexander Sherry ★★→★★★ US-based négociant bottling selected BUTTS of distinctive Sherries.

Jumilla Mur ★→★★★ Arid vyds in mtns n of Mur with heritage of old MONASTRELL vines. Top: CASA CASTILLO, JUAN GIL.

Juvé y Camps Pen, Cava ★★→★★★ Consistently gd CAVA. RES de la Familia is stalwart, La Capella is CAVA DE PARAJE CALIFICADO.

La Mancha C-La M ★→★★ Don Quixote country; Spain's least impressive (except for its size) wine region, s of Madrid. Key source of grapes for distillation to brandy, particularly neutral AIRÉN. Too much bulk wine, yet excellence still possible: MARTÍNEZ BUJANDA's Finca Antigua, PESQUERA's El Vínculo and newbie VERUM.

Landi, Daniel Gomez Jiménez Mén Leader in new generation of GARNACHA producers, making wines at higher altitude across GREDOS (CEBREROS, MÉN, around).

López de Heredia R Alt ★★→★★★★ Haro's oldest (1877), a family business in the BARRIO DE LA ESTACIÓN with wines that have become a cult. Take a look at its "Txoritoki" tower and Zaha Hadid designed shop. See how RIO was made (as it still is, here). Cubillo is younger range with GARNACHA; darker Bosconia; delicate, ripe *Tondonia*. Whites have seriously long barrel-and-bottle-age; GRAN RES ROSADO is like no other. No short cuts here.

Loxarel Pen ★★ Josep Mitjans is passionately committed to his terroir and XAREL·LO (Loxarel is anagram). Range incl skin-contact and amphora wines. Cora is fun, fresh (w). Cent Nou 109 Brut Nature RES is quirky treat: traditional fizz, never disgorged. Complex, cloudy, unsulphured, youthful after 109 mths. Bio.

Lupier, Doms Nav ★★★ Rescued scattered vyds of old GARNACHA to create two exceptional wines: floral La Dama, bold El Terroir. Bio. Put NAV back on map.

Lustau Sherry ★★★→★★★★ Launched original ALMACENISTA collection. Benchmark Sherries from JEREZ, SANLÚCAR, EL PUERTO. Only BODEGA to produce EN RAMA from three Sherry towns. Emilín is superb MOSCATEL, VORS PX is outstanding, carrying age and sweetness lightly. Try Sherry-based Vermouth.

Maestro Sierra, El Sherry ★★★ Discover how a JEREZ cellar used to be. Run by Mari-Carmen Borrego, following on from her mother, the redoubtable Pilar Plá. Fine AMONTILLADO 1830 VORS, FINO, OLOROSO 1/14 VORS. Brilliant quality wines.

Málaga ★→★★★ MOSCATEL-lovers should explore hills of Mál. TELMO RODRÍGUEZ began process reviving ancient glories with subtle, sweet *Molino Real*. Barrel-aged No 3 Old Vines Moscatel from Jorge Ordóñez is gloriously succulent. BENTOMIZ has impressive portfolio at different categories of sweetness. Sierras de Málaga DO for dry table wines; Ordóñez' Botani is delicately aromatic dry Moscatel.

Mallorca ★→★★★ Uneven quality, some v.gd, some simply prestige projects. Can be high-priced and hard to find off island. Incl 4 Kilos, Ánima Negra, Bàrbara Mesquida, Biniagual, Binigrau, Can Ribas, Miquel Gelabert (with a wide array), Son Bordils, Toni Gelabert, Tramuntana. Reds blend traditional varieties (Callet, Fogoneu, Mantonegro) plus CAB, SYRAH, MERLOT. Whites (esp CHARD) improving fast. DOS: Binissalem, Pla i Llevant.

Manchuela ★→★★★ Traditional region for bulk wine, finally showing promise with BOBAL, MALBEC, PETIT VERDOT. Leaders: Alto Landón, FINCA SANDOVAL, PONCE.

Marqués de Cáceres R Alt ★→★★★ Fresh white, rosé. Gaudium is modern top wine; GRAN RES traditional classic. Owns Deusa Nai in R BAI.

Tempranillo Blanco, a recent genetic mutation, spotted in Rio's red vines in 1988.

Marqués de Murrieta R Alt ★★★→★★★★ Between them, the marqueses of RISCAL and Murrieta launched RIO. At Murrieta, step change in quality continues with new BODEGA on estate. Two styles, classic and modern: Castillo Ygay GRAN RES is one of Rio's traditional greats. Latest release of Gran Res Blanco is 86, and Gran Res Tinto 75. Dalmau is impressive contrast, glossy modern Rio, v. well made. *Capellania* is fresh, taut, complex white, one of Rio's v. best; ROSADO, v. pale, unusual Primer Rosé from Mazuelo; v.gd Pazo de Barrantes ALBARIÑO (R BAI).

Marqués de Riscal R Ala, C y L, Rue ★★→★★★★ Riscal is living history of RIO, able to put on a tasting of every vintage going back to its 1st in 1862. Take your pick of styles: reliable RES, modern Finca Torrea, balanced GRAN RES. Powerful *Barón de Chirel Res*. The Marqués discovered and launched RUE (1972) and makes vibrant DYA SAUV BL, VERDEJO and v.gd Barón de Chirel Verdejo, though prefers to put wines in C Y L not Rue. Eye-popping Frank Gehry hotel attached to Rio BODEGA.

Mas de la Rosa Pri ★★★ Exceptional CARIÑENA vyd part-owned by Vall-Llach/TORRES.

Mas Doix Pri ★★→★★★★ Elegant BODEGA in Poboleda, PRI, enables Mas Doix to expand, funded by new joint owners Lede Family Winery (California). Doix's treasures are superb CARIÑENA (grape), all blueberry and velvet, astonishingly pure, named after yr vyd was planted: *1902*; old-vine GARNACHA (*1903*). Now makes white too: Murmuri, DYA GARNACHA BLANCA.

Mas Martinet Pri ★★→★★★ Sara Pérez is daughter of one of original PRI quintet. Venus La Universal is MONT project with partner René Barbier Jnr of Clos Mogador. Also consults on projects across Spain.

Mendoza, Abel R Ala ★★→★★★ For knowledge of RIO villages and varieties Abel and Maite Mendoza have few equals. Discover no fewer than five varietal whites. Grano a Grano are only-the-best-berry-selected TEMPRANILLO and GRACIANO.

Méntrida C-La M ★→★★★ Former co-op country s of Madrid, now being put on map by ARRAYÁN, Canopy, DANIEL GOMEZ JIMÉNEZ-LANDI with Albillo, GARNACHA.

Monasterio, Hacienda Rib del D ★★★ PETER SISSECK co-owns, consults here, where he 1st started in RIB DEL D. More accessible in price, palate than his DOMINIO DE PINGUS.

Montecillo Rio ★→★★ Long est BODEGA (1870), passed to OSBORNE in 1973. Beginning to return to former glories with classic releases.

Monterrei Gal ★→★★★ Small DO on Portuguese border, with traces of Roman winemaking. Still to reveal full potential. Best: Quinta da Muradella.

Nav's Pacharán is sloes macerated in anis, 25–30% abv. Serve cold.

Montilla-Moriles ★→★★★ Andalucian DO nr Córdoba. Hidden treasure, unfairly regarded as JEREZ's poor relation. Makes dry to sweetest wines, all with PX. Shop nr top end for superbly rich treats, some with long ageing in SOLERA. Top: ALVEAR, PÉREZ BARQUERO, TORO ALBALÁ. Important source of PX for use in Jerez DO.

Montsant Cat ★→★★★ Tucked in around PRI, plenty to discover. Fine GARNACHA BLANCA, esp Acústic, characterful reds: Can Blau, Capçanes, Domènech, Espectacle, Joan d'Anguera, Mas Perinet, Masroig, Venus la Universal.

Muga R Alt ★★→★★★★ Muga brothers and cousin are friendly giants of BARRIO DE LA ESTACIÓN, making some of RIO's finest reds. Pale ROSADO; lively traditional-method sparkling; classic reds delicately crafted. Best: classical GRAN RES **Prado Enea;** modern, powerful **Torre Muga;** expressive, complex Aro. Gets better and better.

Mustiguillo V'cia ★★→★★★ Toni Sarrión led renaissance of unloved BOBAL grape, also reviving Merseguera (w) and creating VINO DE PAGO Finca El Terrerazo with top Quincha Corral. New: Hacienda Solana (RIB DEL D). *See also* GRANDES PAGOS.

Navarra ★→★★★ Next door to RIO and always in shadow. Early focus on international varieties confused its identity. Best: old-vine GARNACHA (DOMS LUPIER). Also CHIVITE, Nekeas, OCHOA, Tandem, VIÑA ZORZAL. Also sweet MOSCATELS.

Numanthia Toro ★★→★★★★ One of TORO's heavyweights. Founded by Egurens of SIERRA CANTABRIA who sold to LVMH. Exceptional, powerful wines. Top Termanthia comes round with 10 yrs of age.

Ochoa Nav ★→★★ Ochoa *padre* led modern growth of NAV. Winemaker daughter Adriana calls her range 8a, incl Mil Gracias GRACIANO, fun, sweet, Asti-like sparkling MdO, classic MOSCATEL.

Osborne Sherry ★★→★★★★ Historic BODEGA, treasure trove of richer styles, incl AOS AMONTILLADO, PDP PALO CORTADO. Owns former Domecq VORS incl 51–1a Amontillado. Based in EL PUERTO; its Fino Quinta and mature Coquinero Fino typical of town. Wineries in RIO (MONTECILLO), RUE, RIB DEL D.

Pago de Carraovejas Rib del D Strikingly situated on slopes below Peñafiel's romantic castle. Major improvements here with a focus on single vyds. Further investment in v. fine properties, EMILIO ROJO (RIBEIRO) and Ossian, top-quality VERDEJO producer in C Y L. V.gd Ambivium restaurant.

Pago de los Capellanes Rib del D ★★→★★★ V. fine estate, once belonging to church as name suggests, founded 1996. All TEMPRANILLO. El Nogal has plenty of yrs ahead; top El Picón reveals best of RIB DEL D.

Palacio de Fefiñanes Gal ★★★→★★★★ Standard DYA R BAI one of finest ALBARIÑOS. Two superior styles: barrel-fermented 1583 (yr winery was founded, oldest of DO); super-fragrant, lees-aged III. Visit palace/winery at Cambados.

Palacios, Álvaro Bier, Pri, Rio ★★★→★★★★ Eloquent ambassador who has built global reputation of Spanish wine by obsession with quality. One of quintet who revived PRI. Finca Dofí mainly GARNACHA, superbly aromatic; Les Aubaguetes, from Bellmunt, boosted by 20% CARIÑENA. L'Ermita is powerful, from low-yielding Garnacha. Also at PALACIOS REMONDO in RIO, restoring reputation of R OR and its Garnachas, and with nephew Ricardo at DESCENDIENTES DE J PALACIOS in BIER.

Palacios, Descendientes de J Bier ★★★→★★★★ MENCÍA at its best. Ricardo Pérez P, Álvaro's nephew, grows old vines on steep slate. Sadly not all BIER lives up to this. Gd-value, floral Pétalos and Villa de Corullón; Las Lamas and Moncerbal are different soil expressions, one clay, the other rocky. Exceptional single-vyd *La Faraona* (only one barrel), grows on tectonic fault. BIO.

Palacios, Rafael Gal ★★★→★★★★ Rafael P can't put a foot wrong in VALDEORRAS. Singular focus on GODELLO across many tiny vyds over decade+. Lovely Louro do Bolo; As Sortes, a step up; *Sorte O Soro*, surely Spain's best white. Sorte Antiga (old vines), v. delicate orange wine, Sorte Souto (tiny production late harvest).

Palacios Remondo R Baj ★★→★★★ ÁLVARO PALACIOS has put deserved spotlight on R OR and its GARNACHAS. Complex Plácet (w) originally created by brother RAFAEL PALACIOS. Top is Quiñón de Valmira from slopes of Monte Yerga.

Pariente, José Rue ★★→★★★ Victoria P makes VERDEJOS of shining clarity. Cuvée Especial is fermented in concrete eggs; silky late-harvest Apasionado. Daughter Martina runs Prieto Pariente with brother Ignacio, and works in C Y L and GREDOS.

Pazo Señorans Gal ★★★ Consistently excellent ALBARIÑOS from glorious R BAI estate. Outstanding Selección de Añada, proof v. best Albariños age beautifully.

Penedès Cat ★→★★★★ Region w of Barcelona, most significant and diverse of CAT. Best: Agustí Torelló Mata, Alemany i Corrio, Can Rafols dels Caus, GRAMONA, Jean León, Parés Baltà, TORRES.

Peninsula Vinicultores Rio, C y L ★★ Youthful project working across central and n Spain, committed to sustainability, authenticity. Badiola (RIO) promising; Vinos de Montana (CEBREROS, SIERRA DE GREDOS): fresh, altitude wines; also fine TXAKOLÍ.

Pepe Mendoza Casa Agrícola Alic ★→★★★ After a long career in the family wine business (Enrique Mendoza), Pepe launched his personal project in 2016 focusing on elegant MONASTRELL, Giró (r), MOSCATEL. Blends, varietals, experimental wines, amphora aged wines. Worth a visit.

Pérez, Raúl Bier ★★→★★★ A star, but avoids celebrity. Renowned for finesse, non-intervention. Provides generous house-room for new winemakers in cellar in BIER. Magnet for visiting (eg. Spanish, Argentine) winemakers. Outstanding Vizcaina Mencías; *El Rapolao* exceptionally pure.

Pérez, Willy Jer, Sherry Leader with colleague Ramiro Ibáñez of COTA 45 of return to old ways in JEREZ, researching and reviving practices, traditions, terroirs – and jointly writing a book. Family purchased former estate with old *lagares*. Rare varieties. Interest in unfortified PALOMINO. Projects incl DE LA RIVA, La Barajuela.

Pérez Barquero Mont-M ★→★★★ Part of revival of MONT-M PX. GD Gran Barquero FINO, AMONTILLADO, OLOROSO; La Cañada PX. Supplier to EQUIPO NAVAZOS.

Pesquera, Tinto Rib del D ★★ Alejandro Fernández put RIB DEL D on map with simply named but majestic Tinto Pesquera. Family divisions mean business is now under different management as Familia Fernández Rivera.

Pie franco Ungrafted vine, on own roots. Typically on sandy soils where phylloxera could not penetrate. Some are well over a century old.

Pingus, Dominio de Rib del D ★★★★ One of RIB DEL D's greats. Tiny bio winery of Pingus (PETER SISSECK's childhood name), made with old-vine TINTO FINO, shows refinement of variety in extreme climate. Flor de Pingus from younger vines; Amelia is single barrel named after his wife. PSI uses grapes from growers, long-term social project to encourage them to stay on land. *See also* VIÑA CORRALES.

Spain has the most organic vyds in Europe – 100,000 ha+.

Ponce Man ★★ Juan Antonio P has single-mindedly transformed family business into pre-eminent producer in DO. One of those building reputation of BOBAL grape, and has a PIE FRANCO bottling in range: P.F. from pre-phylloxera vines. Bio.

Priorat ★★→★★★★ Some of Spain's finest wines. Named after former monastery tucked under craggy cliffs. Key is the slate soil – known as *llicorella*. Best show remarkable purity, finesse, sense of place. Pri has pioneered classification pyramid rising from village wines through Vi de Finca to Gran Vi de Vinya. After a period when CAB SAUV, SYRAH were thought best, producers now returning to traditional GARNACHA, CARIÑENA vines, and have toned down new oak.

Raventós i Blanc Cat ★→★★★ Pepe R led historic family business out of Cava in 2012. Created Conca del Riu Anoia origin for high-quality sparklings with strict controls. Wines: De Nit ROSADO, Mas del Serral, ringingly pure Textures de Pedra. In 2017, began Can Sumoi estate natural wine project. Incl XAREL·LO, pét-nats.

Recaredo Pen ★★→★★★★ Outstanding producer of traditional-method sparkling, small family concern. Few wines, all outstanding. Hand-disgorges all bottles. Tops are characterful, mineral *Turó d'en Mota*, from vines planted 1940, ages brilliantly, and RES Particular. Bio. Member of CORPINNAT.

Remelluri, La Granja Nuestra Señora R Ala ★★→★★★ TELMO RODRÍGUEZ's family property. Focus on exceptional old GARNACHA single vyds, ethereal wines.

Reserva (Res) Has actual meaning in RIO. Reds: aged min 3 yrs, of which min 1 yr in oak of 225 litres and min 6 mths bottle. Whites and ROSADOS: min 2 yrs age, of which min 6 mths barrel. Many now follow own rules. *See* GENÉRICOS.

Rías Baixas Gal ★★→★★★ Atlantic DO, split in five subzones, mostly DYA. Best: Forjas del Salnés, Gerardo Méndez, Martín Códax, PALACIO DE FEFIÑANES, Pazo de Barrantes (MARQUÉS DE MURRIETA), *Pazo de Señorans*, Terras Gauda, ZÁRATE. Land of *minifundia*, tiny landholdings: many small producers to discover. Until recently Spain's premier DO for whites, now at risk of overproduction. Influential new generation of consultants, eg. Dominique Roujou de Boubée, RAÚL PÉREZ. ALBARIÑO is the variety here; v. best can age, reaching burgundian elegance.

Ribeira Sacra Gal ★★→★★★ Magical DO with vyds running dizzyingly down to River Sil. Some impressive, original fresh, light reds from MENCIA. Top: Adegas Moure, ALGUEIRA, Dominio do Bibei, Guímaro.

Ribeiro Gal ★→★★★ Historic region, famed in Middle Ages for Tostado (sw). Deserving rediscovery, with textured whites made from GODELLO, LOUREIRO, Treixadura. Top: Casal de Armán, Coto de Gomariz, EMILIO ROJO, Finca Viñoa.

Ribera del Duero ★→★★★★ Ambitious DO with great appeal in Spain, created 1982. Anything that incl AALTO, HACIENDA MONASTERIO, PESQUERA, PINGUS, VEGA SICILIA has to be serious. Domestic demand for oaky concentration. At last, elegance breaking through. Wineries in Soria (to e) provide most delicate wines (Dominio de Atauta, Dominio de Es). Try ALONSO DEL YERRO, PAGO DE CARRAOVEJAS, PAGO DE LOS CAPELLANES. Also: Arzuaga, Bohórquez, Cillar de Silos, Garmón, Hacienda Solano, Tomás Postigo, Valduero. *See* C Y L neighbour ABADÍA RETUERTA.

Rioja ★→★★★★ Spain's most famous wine region. Three subregions: R Ala, R Alt and R OR. Two key provinces are La Rioja and Álava, or the Basque country. Growing political differences between them reflected in movement by Alavesa producers to separate from the DO.

Rioja Alta, La R Ala, R Alt ★★→★★★★ For lovers of classic RIO, a favourite choice. *Gran Res 904* and GRAN RES 890 are stars. But rest of range from *Ardanza*, down to Arana, Alberdi each carry classic house style; all of them qualify as Gran Res. Also owns R Ala modern-style Torre de Oña, R BAI Lagar de Cervera, RIB DEL D Àster. Hard to fault.

Rioja Oriental Nothing new here except the name: this was Rioja Baja. Renamed to remove any pejorative sense of "baja" as "low", and to identify fact it is e-most or oriental (and largest) subregion of RIO. Was poor relation, rapidly gaining attention for its GARNACHA, led by PALACIOS REMONDO.

Riva, De La Jer ★★→★★★ Young project from WILLY PÉREZ and Ramiro Ibáñez of COTA 45 based on the old De La Riva BODEGA. Reviving old methods of winemaking, buying SOLERAS from ALMACENISTAS. Releases small in quantity, v. fine.

Roda Rib del D, R Alt ★★→★★★ At the far tip of the BARRIO DE LA ESTACIÓN. TEMPRANILLO specialist: Roda, Roda I, Cirsión, approachable Sela. Also RIB DEL D BODEGAS La Horra, Corimbo (w), Corimbo I. Polished, intense. Fine contrast to neighbours MUGA, LÓPEZ DE HEREDIA, and all three at top of game.

Rojo, Emilio Gal ★★★ Rojo's single, eponymous wine is Treixadura/LOUREIRO/ALBARIÑO/Lado/TORRONTÉS/GODELLO. Superb, thrilling freshness. Star of RIBEIRO. Bought by RIB DEL D PAGO DE CARROVEJAS (2019); Rojo still involved in winemaking.

Rosado Rosé. NAV dark rosados were defeated by Provence pinks. Spain has fought back with pale hues, esp: SCALA DEI's Pla dels Àngels (PRI), MARQUÉS DE MURRIETA's Primer Rosé (RIO), Dominio del Águila Pícaro Clarete (RIB DEL D).

Rueda C y L ★ →★★★ Spain's response to SAUV BL: zesty VERDEJO. Mostly DYA. Too much poor quality. Best: **Belondrade**, JOSÉ PARIENTE. Pálido is FLOR-aged Verdejo, with 3 yrs in oak. Exceptional SOLERA-aged BODEGAS DE ALBERTO.

Saca A withdrawal of Sherry from the SOLERA (oldest stage of ageing) for bottling. For EN RAMA wines most common *sacas* are in *primavera* (spring) and *otoño* (autumn), when FLOR is richest, most protective.

Sancha, Juan Carlos Rio ★★ Professor of oenology turned winemaker, understands soils, traditions of RIO. Works with lesser-known varieties (Tempranillo Blanco, Maturana Tinta, Maturana Blanca, Monastel) as well as with GARNACHA.

Sánchez Romate Sherry ★★ →★★★ Old (1781) BODEGA with wide range, also sourcing and bottling rare BUTTS for négociants and retailers. 8-yr-old *Fino Perdido*, nutty AMONTILLADO NPU, PALO CORTADO Regente, excellent VORS AMONTILLADO and OLOROSO La Sacristía de Romate, unctuous Sacristía PX.

Sandoval, Finca Man ★ →★★ Founded by Victor de la Serna, wine critic. New investors and consultant winemaker Javi Revert indicate renewed energy, direction.

Sanlúcar de Barrameda Sherry-triangle town (with JEREZ, EL PUERTO) on River Guadalquivír. Port where Magellan, Columbus, admiral of Armada set sail. Humidity in low-lying cellars encourages FLOR. Sea air said to encourage "saltiness". Wines aged here qualify for DO MANZANILLA-Sanlúcar de Barrameda.

Scala Dei Pri ★★ →★★★ Tiny vyds of "stairway to heaven" cling to craggy slopes. Managed by part-owner CODORNÍU. Winemaker Ricard Rofes has returned to the old ways, eg. fermenting in stone *lagares*. Focus on local varieties, esp GARNACHA and now CARIÑENA. Single-vyds Sant'Antoni and *Mas Deu* show terroir. Also rare GARNACHA BLANCA/CHENIN BL blend.

Sierra Cantabria R Ala, Toro ★★★ Elegant, single vyd, low-intervention wines.

Rioja on a roll?

RIOJA has liked to present itself as a consistent, unified source of supple, cherry-fruited, creamy, vanilla, US-oaked reds. Of course with 14,800 growers, 567 BODEGAS and 28 co-ops it's nothing of the sort. Wineries themselves are taking on a different look, with amphorae and concrete eggs appearing amid the concrete, stainless steel and oak. There's French, and a little Spanish and Caucasian oak, and the occasional acacia-wood barrel. While ageing in a 225-litre barrel is the regulation size to qualify as a CRIANZA, RESERVA or GRAN RESERVA, many producers prefer 300, 500, 2000 litre. There are the centenarian bodegas, with extensive landholdings, and cross-regional blending, mixing R Alt TEMPRANILLO with R OR GARNACHA. In contrast there are new arrivals or next-generation producers, purchasing or renting small vyds, starting in a new direction. They bring experience from other countries, and are keen to experiment. There are plenty to look out for, incl Artuke, Bárbara Palacios with Barbarot, BODEGAS BHILAR, JAVIER ARIZCUREN, Sandra Bravo at Sierra de Toloño, Tom Puyaubert. There are also new projects from famous names, such as Villota, former partner of CONTINO. Time to be surprised.

Organza (w). Reds, all TEMPRANILLO. At Viñedos de Paganos, superb El Puntido; structured La Nieta. Other properties: Señorio de San Vicente in RIO and Teso la Monja in TORO, where Alabaster is the star.

Sierra de Gredos C y L ★→★★ Gredos is mtn region nw of Madrid, has built reputation on GARNACHA. Best are pale, ethereal. DOS are gradually appearing: CEBREROS, Madrid, MÉNTRIDA. Producers: 4 Monos, Bernabeleva, Canopy, Comando G, DANIEL GOMEZ JIMÉNEZ-LANDI, Marañones, TELMO RODRÍGUEZ.

Sisseck, Peter Sherry, Rib del D Dane who attracted world interest to RIB DEL D with DOMINIO DE PINGUS. With release of FINO VIÑA CORRALES and purchase of vyd in Pago Balbaina, he should work same magic for Sherry. Also at Ch Rocheyron (B'x).

Solera Sherry System for blending Sherry and, less commonly, Madeira (*see* Portugal). Consists of topping up progressively more mature BUTTS with younger wines of same sort from previous stage, or *criadera*. With FINOS, MANZANILLAS it maintains vigour of FLOR. For all wines gives consistency, refreshes mature wines.

Somontano ★→★★ DO in Pyrénéan foothills still searching for an identity, growing international varieties. Opt for GEWURZ – rare for Spain. Try Enate, Viñas del Vero (GONZÁLEZ BYASS) – high-altitude Secastilla GARNACHA, GARNACHA BLANCA.

Suertes del Marqués Can ★→★★ Rising star in TENERIFE. Works with LISTÁN Blanco, Listán Negro, Vijariego, Tintilla, making vibrant village and single-vyd wines. Exceptional vyds, with unique local *trenzado* – plaited – vines. Worth a visit.

Telmo Rodríguez, Compañía de Vinos Rio, Mál, Toro ★★→★★★ Groundbreaking winemaker Rodríguez returned to REMELLURI in RIO but continues his business across Spain with Pablo Eguzkiza: in MÁL (*Molino Real* MOSCATEL), ALIC (Al-Murvedre), RUE (Basa), TORO (Dehesa Gago), Cigales (Pegaso), Valdeorras (DYA Gaba do Xil GODELLO). Return to Rio and BODEGA Lanzaga has led to work on recuperating old vyds, esp exceptionally pure La Estrada, Las Beatas, Tabuérniga.

Tenerife Can Rising star of CAN. Top: Borja Pérez, ENVINATE, SUERTES DEL MARQUÉS.

Terra Alta Cat Up-and-coming inland DO neighbouring PRI. GARNACHA territory, esp Bárbara Forés, Celler Piñol, Edetària, Lafou. 90% of Catalan GARNACHA BLANCA vyds, 75% of Spain's.

Tinaja Aka amphora. Clay pots of all sizes used in revival of traditional winemaking. Found across Spain, incl ALVEAR, CELLER DEL ROURE, LOXAREL, MAS MARTINET.

Toro ★→★★★★ Small DO w of Valladolid famed for rustic reds from Tinta del Toro (TEMPRANILLO). Today best more restrained, but still firm tannic grip. Dense old-vine San Román. Glamour from VEGA SICILIA-owned Pintia, and LVMH property NUMANTHIA. Also: Las Tierras de Javier Rodríguez, Paydos, Teso la Monja.

Toro Albalá Mont-M ★→★★★★ From young dry FINOS to glorious sweet wines, a triumph for MONT-M. Among them lively AMONTILLADO Viejísimo. Don PX Convento Selección 31 is sumptuous, but GRAN RES 90 and Cosecha 18 v.gd.

Torres Cat, Pri, Rio ★★→★★★★ Celebrated 150 yrs in 2020. Miguel Jnr runs business, sister Mireia is technical director and runs Jean León, Miguel Snr is busy on many fronts incl leadership in sustainability. Top wines in Familia Torres collection: outstanding, B'x-blend **Res Real**, top PEN CAB **Mas la Plana**; CONCA DE BARBERÀ duo (burgundy-like **Milmanda**, one of Spain's finest CHARDS, **Grans Muralles** blend of local varieties) oustanding. Newest launch in PRI is single-vyd **Mas de la Rosa**. Newer, improving wineries in RIB DEL D (Celeste), Pri (Perpetual) and RIO (Ibéricos). Also famous, consistent, gd-value portfolio eg. Viña Sol. Pioneer in Chile. Marimar T a star in Sonoma (US).

Tradición Sherry ★★→★★★★ BODEGA assembled by the great José Ignacio Domecq from exceptional selection of SOLERAS. Based on oldest-known Sherry house (1650). Glorious VOS, VORS Sherries, also a 12-yr-old FINO. Outstanding art collection, and archives of Sherry history. Worth a visit.

Txakolí / Chacolí P Vas ★→★★ Wines from Basque country DOS in Getaria, Bizkaya and Álava. Many vyds face Atlantic winds and soaking rain, hence acidity of pétillant whites, esp in Getaria where DYA Txakolí is poured into tumblers from a height to add to spritz. Bizkaya wines, with less exposed vyds, have depth and need not be DYA. Top: Ameztoi, ASTOBIZA, Doniene Gorrondona, Txomín Etxaníz. Also Gorka Izagirre, with Michelin three-star restaurant Azurmendi.

Valdeorras Gal ★→★★★★ Warmest, most inland of GAL'S DOS, named after gold Romans found in valleys. Exceptional GODELLO, potentially more interesting than ALBARIÑO. Best: RAFAEL PALACIOS, also Godeval, TELMO RODRÍGUEZ, Valdesil.

Valdepeñas C-La M ★→★★ Large DO s of LA MANCHA. Historic favourite for cheap reds. ARA reds now offer best quality/value.

Valdespino Sherry ★★→★★★★ Winemaker Eduardo Ojeda oversees Inocente FINO from top Macharnudo single vyd, rare oak-fermented Sherry (EN RAMA bottled by EQUIPO NAVAZOS). Plus terrific dry AMONTILLADO Tío Diego; outstanding 80-yr-old *Toneles* MOSCATEL, JEREZ's v. best. Owned by Grupo Estévez (owns LA GUITA).

Valencia ★→★★★ Known for bulk wine, cheap MOSCATEL. Slowly on move with higher-altitude old vines and min-intervention winemaking: eg. Aranleon, Baldovar 923, CELLER DEL ROURE, El Angosto, Javier Revert, Los Frailes, Rafael Cambra.

VDT (Vino de la Tierra) Table wine usually of superior quality made in a demarcated region without DO. Covers immense geographical possibilities; category incl many prestigious producers, non-DO by choice to be freer of inflexible regulation and use varieties they want. (*See* Super Tuscan, Italy).

For tiptop tapas: dry, intense, solera-aged, Sherry Consejo-regulated Sherry vinegar.

Vega Sicilia Rib del D ★★★★ A venerable institution, while its DO – RIB DE D – is a baby. Wines have age too, and will benefit with more. Único has 6 yrs in oak; *Valbuena* outstanding. Flagship: RES Especial, a NV blend of three vintages, with up to 10 yrs in barrel. Neighbouring Alión (modern take on Rib del D) is coming into its own. Pintia (TORO) much transformed in last decade. Also joint-venture project Macán (RIO) with Rothschild, plus Oremus in Tokaj (Hungary).

Verum C-La M ★ Elias López started with most unpromising beginnings and is having success. He is in LA MANCHA, in Tomelloso, heart of Spain's AIRÉN-growing, brandy distilling industry. Making waves with still wines. One to watch.

Viña Literally, a vyd.

Vinos de Pago Officially, top category of DOP; actually, not always. Currently fewer than 20, typically in less famous zones. Obvious regions RIO, PRI, RIB DEL D absent.

Williams & Humbert Sherry ★→★★★★ Winemaker Paola Medina transforming historic BODEGA. Initially famed for eg. Dry Sack, Winter's Tale AMONTILLADO, As You Like It sweet OLOROSO. Now pioneering specialities such as organic Sherry, vintage Sherries, incl FINO. One of Sherry's new leaders.

Yecla Mur Traditional bulk wine country, but changing. Drivers are Castaño family with MONASTRELLS (eg. Hécula), blends (GSM). Castaño Dulce a modern classic.

Ysios Rio ★→★★ Famous winery for its Calatrava architecture and undulating roof. Wines now growing to match building's reputation.

Yuste Sherry, Man ★★→★★★ BODEGA with a growing collection of SOLERAS. Home to MANZANILLAS Aurora, La Kika. Acquired Herederos de Argüeso, bringing with it v.gd San León, dense, salty San León RES and youthful Las Medallas. Conde de Aldama label has AMONTILLADO, PALO CORTADO both over 100 yrs old.

Zárate Gal ★★→★★★ BODEGA in R BAI. Elegant ALBARIÑOS with long lees-ageing. El Palomar is from centenarian vyd, one of DO's oldest, on own rootstock, aged in *foudre*. Ethereal. Owner/winemaker Eulogio Pomares one of key figures in GAL.

Zorzal, Viña Nav, Rio ★→★★★ Family business. Entrepreneurial new generation – young, gd-value, eg. GRACIANO. Restoring old-vine NAV GARNACHA eg. Malayeto; v. promising projects with old vines; consultant is Jorge Navascués of CONTINO.

Sherry styles

Manzanilla: lightest of Sherries, v. dry, matured by the sea at SANLÚCAR where FLOR grows thickly and wine grows salty. Usually a mere 15% alc. Serve cool with almost any food, esp crustaceans. eg. I Think (EQUIPO NAVAZOS), Deliciosa (VALDESPINO), LA GUITA, La Gitana.

Manzanilla Pasada: with 8 yrs+, where flor is dying, turning into AMONTILLADO; v. dry, complex. Eg. LUSTAU'S ALMACENISTA Cueva Jurado.

Fino: dry, biologically aged in JEREZ or EL PUERTO; weightier than MANZANILLA; min age is 2 yrs (as Manzanilla) but don't drink so young. Trend for mature FINOS aged 8 yrs+, eg. FERNANDO DE CASTILLA Antique, GONZÁLEZ BYASS Palmas range. New trend to cellar and age Finos and Manzanillas in bottle.

Amontillado: Fino in which layer of protective flor has died. Oxygen gives more complexity. Naturally dry. Eg. LUSTAU Los Arcos. Many brands are sweetened, indicated by "medium" on label.

Oloroso: not aged under flor. Naturally ultra-dry, superbly savoury, even fierce. May be sweetened and sold as CREAM. Eg. EMILIO HIDALGO Gobernador (dr), Old East India (sw). Keeps well.

Palo Cortado: a cult. Traditionally wine that had lost flor – between Amontillado and v. delicate OLOROSO. Difficult to identify with certainty. Always refined, complex. Eg. BARBADILLO Reliquía, Fernando de Castilla Antique. Drink with meat or cheese.

Cream: blend sweetened with grape must, PX and/or MOSCATEL for a commercial medium-sweet style. Can be gd with ice cream.

En Rama: another cult. Bottled from BUTT with v. low filtration and no cold stabilization to reveal full character of wine. Typically Manzanilla or Fino. More flavoursome, said to be less stable. *Saca* or withdrawal is typically when flor is most abundant, in spring.

Pedro Ximénez (PX): raisined sweet, dark, from partly sun-dried PX grapes (grapes mainly from MONT-M; wine matured in Jerez DO). Unctuous, decadent, bargain. Sip with ice cream. Tokaji Essencia apart, world's sweetest wine. Eg. Emilio Hidalgo Santa Ana 1861, Lustau VORS.

Moscatel: aromatic appeal, around half sugar of PX. Eg. Lustau Emilín, Valdespino Toneles.

VOS / VORS: age-dated Sherries, some of treasures of Jerez BODEGAS; v. necessary move to raise perceived value of Sherry. Wines assessed by carbon dating to be 20 yrs old+ are called VOS (Very Old Sherry/Vinum Optimum Signatum); 30 yrs old+ are VORS (Very Old Rare Sherry/Vinum Optimum Rare Signatum). Also 12-yr-old, 15-yr-old examples. Applies only to Amontillado, Oloroso, PALO CORTADO, PX. Eg. VOS Hidalgo Jerez Cortado Wellington. Some VORS wines are softened with PX: sadly producers can overdo the PX. VORS with more than 5g/l residual sugar are labelled Medium.

Añada "Vintage": Sherry with declared vintage. Runs counter to tradition of vintage blended SOLERA. Formerly private bottlings now winning public accolades. Eg. WILLIAMS & HUMBERT series, Lustau Sweet Oloroso Añada 1997.

Unfortified Palomino: not (yet) strictly Sherry, rule changes wait on European Commission. Meantime, making still white wines is a strong trend among new producers. Some of uneven quality but will improve with experience. Eg. EQUIPO NAVAZOS, Forlong, Muchada-Leclapart.

Portugal

Fortified powerhouses Port and Madeira have taken Portugal around the world for centuries. The modern history of Portuguese table wine, however, stems from the wine revolution of the last 30 years. From the Douro to the Alentejo to the islands, skillful viticulture and educated winemaking have blended tradition and modernity. With 14 official wine regions, 31 DOCs and 200+ native varieties, Portugal's diversity is a weapon in fighting climate change: field blends, high-altitude vineyards and Atlantic-influenced regions are part of the future. Behind these changes is a maturing, well-travelled generation that is making happen ideas and projects that would have been impossible just a few years ago: putting old regions on the map (Bairrada, Beira Interior, Dão, Lisboa, Portalegre); launching large sustainability plans (Esporão, Symington); making early drinking but age-worthy Vintage Port (most of the Port industry); growing a fine-wine range (*see* p.202). All signs of a promising future for Portuguese wine. Sit back with a glass of Baga and enjoy.

Recent Port vintages

A vintage is "declared" when a wine is outstanding by shippers' highest standards. In gd but not quite classic yrs (increasingly in top yrs too by single-estate producers) shippers use the names of their estates for single-quinta wines of real character (and value) but needing less ageing in bottle. Growing number of limited-production, often single-vyd, Vintage Ports. The vintages to drink now are 63 66 70 77 80 83 85 87 92 94 00 03 04 05 07 though v. young Vintage Port is a modern hedonistic delight.

2020 Challenging yr: weather (v. low yields due to heat), pandemic (some avoided foot-treading, used robots). Pockets of quality.

2019 Balance, freshness but less structure.

2018 Gd quality, declaration for some, esp Dou Superior. Stars: Ferreira, Noval, Sandeman, Taylor, Vesúvio.

2017 Superlative yr, widely declared. V. hot, dry yr, compared to historic 1945.

2016 Classic yr, widely declared. Great structure, finesse.

2015 V. dry, hot. Controversial yr. Declared by many (top-quality Niepoort, Noval), but not Fladgate, Symingtons or Sogrape.

2014 Excellent from vyds that ducked September's rain; production low.

2013 Single-quinta yr; mid harvest rain. Stars: Vesuvio, Fonseca Guimaraens.

2012 Single-quinta yr. Stars: Noval, Malvedos. Elegant, drink now.

2011 Classic yr, widely declared. Considered by most on par with iconic 1963. Inky, outstanding concentration, structure. Stars: Dow, Noval Nacional, Vargellas Vinha Velha, Fonseca. You can even start on them now.

2010 Single-quinta yr. Hot, dry. Stars: Vesuvio, Senhora da Ribeira.

2009 Controversial yr. Declared by Fladgate, but not Symingtons or Sogrape. Stars: Taylor, Niepoort, Fonseca, Warre.

Fine vintages: 07 03 00 97 94 92 91 87 83 80 77 70 66 63 45 35 31 27.

Recent table wine vintages

2020 Gd quantity overall. V.gd whites. Pick your red producer.

2019 No rain, cool summer. V.gd quality all around. Keep.

2018 Heavy rains. V. low yields. Aromatic whites, concentrated reds.

2017 3rd consecutive fine vintage. V.gd quality all around. Keep for yrs.

2016 V.gd quality for those who had patience. Keep for yrs.

See Portugal map p.174.

2015 Fine yr. Aromatic, balanced reds drinking v. well. Keep.
2014 Fresh whites, bright reds (picked before rain). Drink now.
2013 Great whites, balanced reds (picked before rain). Keep/drink.

Açores / Azores ★→★★★ Mid-Atlantic archipelago of nine volcanic islands with DOCS Pico, Biscoitos and Graciosa for whites and traditional *licoroso* (late-harvest/fortified). Pico landscape, incl vine-protecting *currais* (pebble walls), is UNESCO World Heritage Site. Dynamic winemakers, thrilling volcanic soil, sea-threatened whites from indigenous varieties Arinto dos Açores, Terrantez do Pico, VERDELHO. Watch: Azores Wine Company, Magma, PICO WINES.

Adega A cellar or winery.

AdegaMãe Lis ★→★★★ Ambitious estate run by codfish group Riberalves. Bright, age-worthy Atlantic-influenced range incl gd-value Dory label, single-variety range, esp Viosinho, ARINTO. Top-notch Terroir label is classy, fresh, oak-aged blend (Viosinho/ALVARINHO/Arinto). Visit: tasting room, restaurant.

Alentejo ★→★★★ Diverse yet reliably warm region. Subregional DOCS Borba, Évora, Granja-Amareleja, Moura, PORTALEGRE (fresh high altitude vyds), Redondo, Reguengos, Vidigueira (unusual fresh w). Up-and-coming Costa Vicentina (watch: CORTES DE CIMA, VICENTINO) makes Atlantic-influenced fresh wines (r/w). Ancient clay amphora technique Vinho de Talha (also DOC) trendy (watch: Mestre Daniel, Rocim). More liberal VR Alentejano preferred by many top estates. Rich reds, esp from ALICANTE BOUSCHET, SYRAH, TRINCADEIRA, TOURIGA N. New classics incl CARTUXA, ESPORÃO, JOÃO PORTUGAL RAMOS, JOSÉ DE SOUSA, Malhadinha Nova, MOUCHÃO. Watch: Coelheiros, do Peso, Fita Preta, Fonte Souto (SYMINGTON-owned), MONTE DA RAVASQUEIRA, SUSANA ESTEBAN, Terrenus.

Algarve ★ On s coast producing mostly VR, national and international varieties. Wines progressing but still fall short of famous beaches, Michelin-starred gastronomy. Home to indigenous Negra Mole variety. AVELEDA's Villa Alvor, Barranco Longo, João Clara, honourable mentions.

Aliança Bair ★→★★★ Large firm with reliable gd reds and *sparkling*. Art and wines at Aliança Underground Museum. Interests in ALEN (Alabastro, da Terrugem), DÃO (da Garrida), DOU (dos Quatro Ventos). Owner of popular Casal Mendes brand.

Ameal, Quinta do Vin ★★★ Superior VIN. Age-worthy, racy, organic LOUREIRO incl oaked Escolha and top-yrs-only, low-yield, low-intervention Solo Único. Charming hotel. ESPORÃO-owned.

Andresen Port ★★→★★★★ Portuguese-owned house with excellent wood-aged Ports, esp 20-yr-old TAWNY. Outstanding *Colheitas* 1900' 1910' (bottled on demand) 68' 80' 91' 03'. Pioneered age-dated WHITE PORTS 10-, 20-, v.gd 40-yr-old.

Aveleda, Quinta da Vin ★→★★ DYA Home of Casal García, biggest VIN seller (since 1939). Regular range of estate grown wines. Now owns DOU'S QUINTA DO VALE DONA MARIA and new ALGARVE project Villa Alvor. Visitor centre 30 mins from Porto.

Bacalhôa Vinhos Alen, Lis, Set ★★→★★★ Principal brand and HQ of billionaire art-lover José Berardo's group. Also owns National Monument QUINTA da Bacalhôa (v.gd B'X blend incl CAB SAUV 1st planted 1974, also used in iconic red Palácio da Bacalhôa), sparkling estate Quinta dos Loridos. Top MOSCATEL DE SETÚBAL barrels,

---

Wine and dine

These are some of the best wine lists with fine Portuguese food to match. ALG: Bon Bon, Ocean, Vila Joya; LIS or nr: Alma, Belcanto, Feitoria, Fifty Seconds, Midori, Solar dos Presuntos, Veneza; BAIR: Rei dos Leitões; Porto or nr: Antiqvvm, Casa da Chá da Boa Nova, DOC, DOP, *Euskalduna*, *Gaveto*, Largo do Paço, Paparico, Pedro Lemos The Yeatman; MAD: Il Gallo d'Oro.

incl rare Roxo. Owner of historic Quinta do Carmo ALEN brand making v.gd reds, and a botanic garden in Funchal. Modern, well-made brands: Catarina, Cova da Ursa, Serras de Azeitão (SET), TINTO da Ânfora (Alen).

Bairrada ★★→★★★★ Atlantic-influenced DOC and Beira Atlântico VR also famous for roast suckling pig. Age-worthy, structured yet increasingly approachable, young BAGA reds (many from old vines). V.gd sparklings ("Baga Bair" for best). Top: Bágeiras, Casa de Saima, CAVES SÃO JOÃO, FILIPA PATO, FOZ DE AROUCE, LUÍS PATO, São Domingos, Sidónio de Sousa, Vadio. Watch: NIEPOORT'S QUINTA de Baixo, V PUTO.

Barbeito Mad ★★→★★★★ Leading MAD producer with striking labels. Unique, single-vyd, single-cask COLHEITAS. Outstanding 20-, 30-, 40-yr-old MALVASIAS. Excellent Ribeiro Real range with 20-yr-old BOAL, Malvasia, SERCIAL, VERDELHO, with dash of 50s TINTA NEGRA. Historic Series: MAD most coveted wine in US in C18 and C19. V.gd, salty new table wines.

Barca Velha Dou ★★★★ Portugal's iconic red; 1st bottled in 1952, decades ahead of DOU's world-class table-wine revolution. Aged several yrs pre-release, launched only in exceptional yrs incl 91' 95' 99 00 04 08' 11'. V.gd 2nd label in v.gd yrs not declared BV, from CASA FERREIRINHA's best barrels, *Res Especial* 89' 94' 97' 01' 07 09. Both last decades. Arguably 89' 94' 97' 01' 09 could have been BV.

Barros Port ★★→★★★ Founded 1913, Sogevinus-owned since 2006, maintains substantial stocks of aged TAWNY, COLHEITA. V.gd Colheitas from the 30s on, and 63 66' 74' 78 80' 97'. V.gd 20-, 30-, 40-yr-old Tawny. VINTAGE PORT: 87 95 05 07 11 16 17 18.

Beira Interior ★→★★★ High-potential hidden-gem DOC. High mtn region between DÃO and Spanish border. V.old, high (up to 750m/2461ft) vyds gd for white Fonte Cal, Siria. Rufete is red variety star. Best: ANSELMO MENDES, BEYRA, do Cardo, dos Currais, dos Termos.

Blandy Mad ★★→★★★★ Historic MAD family firm. Charming, historic *Funchal lodges* hold vast library of FRASQUEIRA (BUAL 1920' 1957' 1966', MALMSEY 1988' 1977' 1981', SERCIAL 1968' 1975' 1980' 1988', Terrantez 1975' 1980', VERDELHO 1976 1979'). V.gd 20-yr-old Terrantez and COLHEITAS (Bual 1996 2008, Malmsey 1999 2004, Sercial 2002, Verdelho 2000 2008). Superb 50-yr-old Malmsey; Expensive, rare MCDXIX blends 11 yrs between 1863 and 2004, celebrates Mad's 600 yr history. Also RAINWATER, and Atlantis table wine.

Branco White.

Bual (or Boal) Mad Classic MAD grape: medium-rich (sweet), tangy, smoky wines; less rich than MALVASIA. Perfect with harder cheeses and lighter desserts. Old vintages can be stunning.

Buçaco Bei At ★★ ★★★ Manueline-Gothic monument *Bussaco Palace hotel* lists its classic, austere, age-worthy wines back to 40s. Blends of two regions. R: BAGA (BAIR), TOURIGA N (DÃO). W: ENCRUZADO (Dão), MARIA GOMES, Bical (Bair). Barriques, new oak since 2000 have slightly modernized style (esp w).

Bucelas Lis ★★ Tiny LIS DOC set for comeback. Makes gd-value dry, racy, Atlantic-influenced, ARINTO-based whites, fizz. Watch: PANCAS, ROMEIRA (bought by SOGRAPE). Indigenous Vital is back in spotlight.

Burmester Port ★→★★★ SOGEVINUS-owned Port house making elegant, wood-aged, gd-value Ports, esp 20-, 40-yr-old TAWNY, 1890 1900' 37' 52' 55' 57' COLHEITAS. Age-dated WHITE PORTS, incl fine 30-, 40-yr-old. Gd VINTAGE PORT, DOU wines.

Cálem Port ★→★★★ SOGEVINUS-owned Port house; lodge in Gaia with over 300,000 visitors/yr. Popular entry-level Velhotes. Best: COLHEITAS 61', 10-, 40-yr-old TAWNY.

Canteiro Mad Natural cask-ageing method for finest MAD (now also TINTA NEGRA). Slow warming in humid lodges for greater complexity than ESTUFAGEM.

Carcavelos Lis ★★★ Unique, mouthwatering, gripping, off-dry fortified. Villa Oeiras breathed life into v.old, tiny, ailing 12.5-ha seaside DOC.

Cartuxa, Adega da Alen ★★→★★★★ Historic ALEN estate with old cellars, new restaurant, modern art centre. Flagship Pêra Manca (r) draws connoisseurs. Consistent best-buy Cartuxa RES. Scala Coeli is single variety, different each yr.

Carvalhais, Quinta dos Dão ★→★★★ SOGRAPE-owned DAO estate. V.gd, consistent, age-worthy range, esp oak-aged ENCRUZADO, RES (r/w), TINTA RORIZ, TOURIGA N, top red Único. Unusual BRANCO Especial blends Encruzado yrs. V.gd Alfrocheiro from plot since destroyed by fire. Popular brands Duque de Viseu, Grão Vasco.

Aromatic Dão's Jaen travelled to Spain to become Mencía.

Cello, Casa de Dão, Vin ★★ Family-run, two-region project. Unique QUINTA de San Joanne (VIN) age-worthy whites: top Superior. V.gd Escolha, gd-value Terroir Mineral. Distinctive classic Quinta da Vegia (DÃO) range (r), esp RES, Superior.

Chocapalha, Quinta de Lis ★★★ Family-run estate blending mostly native, with some international varieties. Winemaker Sandra Tavares da Silva (WINE & SOUL). *Among Lisboa's best.* V.gd, age-worthy QUINTA, CASTELÃO. V.gd flagship Vinha Mãe and TOURIGA N CH. Vibrant, fresh whites, esp v.gd RES, old-vine Arinto CH.

Chryseia Dou ★★★★ Bruno Prats (B'x) and SYMINGTON FAMILY ESTATES DOU partnership. Polished, structured TOURIGA-driven. V.gd-value second label *Post Scriptum.*

Churchill Dou, Port ★★★ Family-run Port house, est 1981 by John Graham. V.gd DRY WHITE PORT (10 yrs old), 20-, 30-yr-old, unfiltered LBV, VINTAGE PORT 82 85 91 94 97 00 03 07' 11' 16' 17' 18'. V.gd QUINTA da Gricha DOU reds esp Churchill's Estates label and single-vyd TOURIGA N.

Cockburn's Port ★★→★★★ SYMINGTON-owned house, back on form. Gaia visitor centre incl cooperage tour. Drier, fresher style of VINTAGE PORT in 11' 15' 16' 17' 18'. Extraordinary 08' 27' 34 63 67 70'. Consistently gd Special RES aged longer in wood than others. Vibrant LBV aged 1 yr less. V.gd single-QUINTA dos Canais.

Colares Lis ★★★ Unique, historic, coastal DOC (1908). Windswept, ungrafted vines on sandy soil make tannic Ramisco reds and fresh, salty MALVASIA whites. Watch: modern Casal Santa Maria, classic ADEGA Regional de Colares, Viúva Gomes. Old vintages still available in shops.

Colheita Port, Mad Crowd-pleasing single-yr TAWNY Port or MAD. Cask-aged: min 7 yrs for Port (often 50 yrs+, some superb 100 yrs+); min 5 yrs for Mad. Bottling date printed on label. Serve chilled.

Cortes de Cima Alen ★★★ ALEN SYRAH and sustainability pioneer. V.gd, now more elegant, top red Incógnito. Consistent range, esp (r/w) Cortes de Cima, RES, varietals (ARAGONEZ, PINOT N, Syrah, TRINCADEIRA). V.gd whites from coastal vyds incl ALVARINHO, SAUV BL. Gd-value Dois Terroirs (r/w) blends coastal, inland vyds. New organic red added to amphora/talha range.

Cossart Gordon Mad ★★★ MADEIRA WINE COMPANY owned brand. V.gd single-yr bottlings. Drier style than BLANDY.

Covela, Quinta de Vin ★★ Impressive VIN/DOU border property making v.gd age-worthy whites incl single-variety Edição Nacional (Avesso, ARINTO), Res (Avesso), Escolha (Avesso/CHARD), RES (Avesso/Chard/Arinto oak-aged). Gd rosé.

Crasto, Quinta do Dou, Port ★★★→★★★★ Reputed DOU's family-run estate; striking hilltop location. Jewels in crown are v.old, field-blend, single-vyd reds Vinha da Ponte and Vinha Maria Teresa. Honore, a "super-blend" of both. Also name of exquisite 100-yr-old+ TAWNY. Gd-value old-vyd RES. Superb varietal TINTA RORIZ. Great TOURIGA N. Dou Superior: attractive red, innovative acacia-aged white, SYRAH with VIOGNIER dash. Gd VINTAGE PORT and unfiltered LBV. Member of DOURO BOYS.

Croft Port ★★→★★★ FLADGATE-owned shipper, with visitor centre in glorious vyds at Pinhão. Sweet, fleshy VINTAGE PORT 75 77 82 85 91 94 00 03' 07 09' 11' 16' 17'. V.gd-value **Quinta da Roêda** VINTAGE PORT 07 08' 09 12' 15' 18'. Superlative old-vine Sērikos 17'. Popular: Indulgence, Triple Crown, Distinction, Pink ROSÉ PORT.

Crusted (Port) Port's affordable hidden gem. Fine, rare, traditional NV Port style. Blend of two or more vintage-quality yrs, aged up to 4 yrs in casks and 3 yrs in bottle. Unfiltered, forms deposit ("crust") so decant. Look for DOW, FONSECA, GRAHAM'S, NIEPOORT, NOVAL.

Dão ★★→★★★★ Historic DOC undergoing revival. Elegant, age-worthy reds and tasty, ENCRUZADO-based whites. Newcomers CASA DA PASSARELLA, TABOADELLA add prestige. Quality classics incl Cabriz, CARVALHAIS, Casa de Santar, Falorca, Lusovini, Ribeiro Santo. To watch: Boas Quintas, CASA DE MOURAZ, Conciso (NIEPOORT-owned), (outstanding) Druida, MOB. Dão Nobre ("noble") is top designation. Superb, v.gd-value GARRAFEIRAS. Often called Portugal's Burgundy.

DOC / DOP (Denominação de Origem Controlada / Protegida) Quality-oriented, label-printed designation of a protected origin. Similar to France's AOC. *See* VR.

Doce (vinho) Sweet: late harvests and fortifieds (MAD, MOSCATEL DE SETÚBAL, PORT).

Douro ★→★★★★ World's 1st demarcated and regulated wine region (1756), high up the eponymous river. Dramatic UNESCO World Heritage Site. Once inaccessible, now wine-tourism ready. Famous for Port, now also for quality table wine (Dou DOC). Three subregions (cooler Baixo Corgo, Cima Corgo and warmer, fast-expanding Dou Superior). Over 100 native varieties incl 80 yrs+ field blends) in terraces of unforgiving schist. Powerful, structured reds; fine, attractive, high-altitude whites. Best: ALVES DE SOUSA, *Barca Velha*, Boavista, Carvalhas, *Casa Ferreirinha*, *Chryseia*, CHURCHILL, CRASTO, *Maria Izabel*, *Muxagat*, *Niepoort*, POÇAS, Poeira, Quanta Terra, QUINTA NOVA, RAMOS PINTO, VALE D. MARIA, Vale Meão, Vallado, VESÚVIO, *Wine & Soul*. To watch: Esmero, Ferradosa, KRANEMANN, Lavradores de Feitoria, Maçanita, MÁRCIO LOPES, Murças (ESPORÃO-owned), NOVAL, Pôpa, REAL COMPANHIA CELHA, RUI ROBOREDO MADEIRA, VR is Duriense.

Douro Boys Dou Group of friends with different winemaking styles: CRASTO, NIEPOORT, VALE D. MARIA, VALE MEÃO, VALLADO.

Dow Port ★★★★ Historic, reputed SYMINGTON-owned house. Drier-style VINTAGE PORT 85' 94' 00' 07' 11' 16' 17'. Single-QUINTAS do Bomfim and *Senhora da Ribeira* (v.gd 15 18) in non-declared vintage yrs. *Bomfim visitor centre* in Pinhão.

Duorum Dou, Port ★★→★★★ Consistent DOU Superior project of JOÃO PORTUGAL RAMOS and ex-FERREIRA/BARCA VELHA José Maria Soares Franco. Top-notch, undervalued O. Leucura, fine RES, gd-value fruity, entry-level *Tons*, COLHEITA. V.gd dense, pure-fruited VINTAGE PORT from 100-yr-old vines. Fine second label Vinha de Castelo Melhor and gd-value LBV.

Esporão Alen ★★→★★★ Dynamic eco-conscious group with organic landmark ALEN estate. Attractive visitor centre. High-quality, fruit-focused, modern; v.gd, reputed RES (r/w). Sophisticated GARRAFEIRA-like wood-aged Private Selection and rare Torre do Esporão. New talhas (clay amphorae), native varieties (r/w). Auspicious DOU project (QUINTA dos Murças) makes elegant single-vyd reds. VIN project AMEAL makes v gd LOUREIRO-focused whites. Leading olive oil producer.

Espumante Sparkling. Best come from BAIR (watch for ALIANÇA, Marquês de Marialva, Poço do Lobo, São Domingos). Look out for BAGA Bair quality designation. Gd-value Távora-Varosa (esp MURGANHEIRA). DOU's Vértice is reputed icon.

Dou's Tinta Roriz is same as Alen's Aragonez, same as Spain's Tempranillo.

Esteban, Susana Alen ★★→★★★ ALEN rising star. Flagship Procura (r/w), from PORTALEGRE's v. old low-yield vyds (red adds ALICANTE BOUSCHET from Évora). Value second label: Aventura. Innovative: Sidecar (invites other winemakers), Sem Vergonha (elegant, fresh, single-variety CASTELÃO made with Dirk NIEPOORT).

Estufagem Mad "Stove" process of heating MAD for min 3 mths for faster ageing, characteristic scorched-earth tang. Used mostly on entry-level wines. Finer results with external heating jackets and lower max temperature (45°C/113°F).

Falua Tej ★→★★ French-owned estate undergoing revival. Well-made export-focused Tagus Creek. Gd-value entry-level Conde de Vimioso (RES a step up). Gd Falua Res (r/w) range. New v.gd single-vyd, stony-soil Vinha do Convento.

Ferreira Port ★★★→★★★★ Historic SOGRAPE-owned Port house. Stand out 11' 16' 18' vintages, v.gd-value single-QUINTA do Porto 17'. Winemaker Luis Sottomayor (BARCA VELHA) reckons *LBV* now as gd as last decade's VINTAGE PORT; both on the up here. V.gd-value spicy TAWNY incl Dona Antonia RES, 10-, 20-yr-old Tawny (Quinta do Porto, *Duque de Bragança*).

Ferreirinha, Casa Dou ★★→★★★★ Large, reputed SOGRAPE-owned DOU brand. Gd-value entry-level range, v.gd, age-worthy QUINTA da Lêda and single-variety Tinta Francisca, rare Touriga Fêmea. V.gd *Antónia Adelaide Ferreira* (r/w). Rarely released *Res Especial* and (iconic) BARCA VELHA.

Fladgate Port Important independent family-owned partnership. Owns leading Port houses (CROFT, FONSECA, KROHN, TAYLOR), hotels and restaurants in Lisbon, Pinhão, Porto and VILA NOVA DE GAIA. Restaurant/hotel The Yeatman and new, ambitious, six-museum World of Wine (WOW) visitor centre are highlights.

Fonseca Port ★★★→★★★★★ FLADGATE-owned Port house, founded 1815. Gd-value Bin 27; v.gd 20-,40-yr-old TAWNY. Excellent VINTAGE PORT 63' 70' 85' 94' 00' 03' 11' 16' 17'. Superb Fonseca Guimaraens 13' 15' 18'. Single-QUINTA Panascal.

Fonseca, José Maria da Alen, Set ★→★★★★ 200-yr-old, 7th-generation producer, visitor centre in Azeitão, attractive Lisbon wine bar. LANCERS, CASTELÃO-based PERIQUITA incl RES are value brands. Jewel in crown is fortified *Moscatel de Setúbal*, which mines aged stock to great effect esp great-value *20-yr-old Alambre*. Superior *55' 66 71* and limited-release Roxo Superior 18'. Owner of historic, amphora-based, great-value ALEN *José de Sousa* estate.

Foz de Arouce Bei At ★★★ Historic, family-run estate, JOÃO PORTUGAL RAMOS Beira Atlântico outpost. V.gd, age-worthy range: characterful Cercial, TOURIGA N/BAGA blend. Superb, dense, old-BAGA-vines VINHAS VELHAS.

Frasqueira Mad Highly respected, sought-after MAD category. Also called Vintage. Single-yr, single-noble-variety aged min 20 yrs in wood, usually much longer. Date of bottling required. Best: BARBEITO, MADEIRA WINE COMPANY.

Garrafeira Often a hint for v.gd value. Must be aged for min 2 yrs in cask and 1 yr in bottle (often much longer). Whites need 6 mths in cask, 6 mths in bottle.

Global Wines Bair, Dão ★★→★★★ Also known as DÃO Sul. One of Portugal's biggest producers, Dão-based, with estates in many other regions. Great-value popular brands Cabriz (esp RES) and Casa de Santar (esp Res, superb Nobre). Classy Paço dos Cunhas single-vyd Vinha do Contador. Modern wines, striking architecture, visitor centre at BAIR'S QUINTA do Encontro. Other brands: Encostas do Douro, Grilos (DOU), Monte da Cal (ALEN), Quinta de Lourosa (VIN).

Young guns

A new generation of winemakers incl some veterans are raising the stakes with native varieties, min intervention wines. To watch. AZORES: ADEGA do Vulcão; ALG: Monte da Casteleja; ALEN: Argilla Wines, Cabeças de Reguengo. BAIR: COZs, FILIPA PATO, Tiago Teles. BEI INT: Biaia, Casas Altas. COLARES: Viúva Gomes. DÃO: CASA de MOURAZ, João Tavares de Pina. DOU: Bago de Touriga, Carolina, Costa do Pinhão, Esmero, Folias de Baco, Infantado, Mafarrico, Pormenor, Romeu. LIS: Baías e Enseadas, Ermegeira, Espera Wines, Hugo Mendes, Humus, Marinho, Montalto, Olival da Murta, Serradinha, Vale da Capucha, Várzea da Pedra. TEJO: Areias Gordas. TRÁS-OS-MONTES: Arribas Wine Company, Casa do Jôa, Menina d'Uva. VIN: A&D, Aphros, Palmirinha, Santiago, Sem Igual. Multi-region: ANTÓNIO MAÇANITA, LUÍS SEABRA, NIEPOORT Projects.

Graham's Port ★★★ →★★★★ Highly reputed SYMINGTON-owned Port house. Top-notch, age-worthy VINTAGE PORT 85' 91' 94' 97 00' 03' 07′ 11' 16' 17', now enjoyable when released. Superlative Stone Terraces 11' 15' 16' 17'. Gd-value RES RUBY Six Grapes. V.gd-value single-QUINTA dos Malvedos 12 15 18', attractive 20-, 30-, 40-yr-old TAWNY, LBV. Fine Single-Harvest (COLHEITAS), esp 40' 52' 61' 63' 69' 72' 82 94' 03. Top-notch Ne Oublie V. Old Tawny, one of three 1882 casks, is a stunner.

Gran Cruz Port ★→★★★ Port's largest brand (Porto Cruz) owned by French group La Martiniquaise, focused on volume and cocktails. VILA NOVA DE GAIA museum, popular rooftop terrace bar, new Porto hotel. Dalva brand has outstanding TAWNY stocks incl COLHEITAS and *stunning golden white* 52' 63' 71'. Gd Pinhão-based QUINTA de Ventozelo wines, *charming hotel.*

Grous, Herdade de Alen, Dou ★★ →★★★ Prestigious estate and hotel owned by the Pohl family (of ALG's luxury resort Vila Vita). Consistently gd range, incl RES (rich, oak-aged w; fine r). Moon Harvested and best-barrels 23 Barricas labels are plush ALEN reds. Outpost QUINTA de Valbom makes v.gd, old-vines DOU reds.

Henriques & Henriques Mad ★★→★★★ MAD shipper owned by rum giant La Martiniquaise. Best are *20-yr-old Malvasia and Terrantez*, Single Harvest (aged in old bourbon barrels, 1997' 1998', BUAL 2000'), Vintage (VERDELHO 1957, Terrantez 1954', SERCIAL 1971'). V.gd TINTA NEGRA 50-yr-old.

Justino Mad ★→★★★★ Largest MAD shipper, owned by rum giant La Martiniquaise, makes Broadbent label. Stars: Terrantez Old Res (NV, probably around 50 yrs old), *Terrantez* 1978' (oldest in cask), MALVASIA 1964' 1968' 1988'.

Kopke Port ★→★★★★ Sogevinus-owned. Oldest Port house, est 1638. Known for outstanding spicy, structured COLHEITAS 35' 40', 41' 57' 64' 65' 66' 78 80' 84 87 00 02 05 07 09, remarkable WHITE PORT range, esp now-rare 35' 40' and 30-, 40-yr-olds. V.gd Winemaker's Collection range, old-vines DOU red.

Kranemann Wine Estates Dou ★★→★★★ Historic, C12 estate revival by German surgeon. Consultant Diogo Lopes (of ADEGAMAE) makes DOU and PORT. V.gd, high-altitude QUINTA do Convento, 10-, *20-yr-old* TAWNY. V.gd-value Hasso (r/w) label.

Krohn Port ★→★★★ Now FLADGATE-owned. Exceptional stocks of aged TAWNY, now source of TAYLOR's yearly released 50-yr-old Single Harvest. V.gd, rich COLHEITAS, 10-, 20-yr-old. Gd, elegant VINTAGE PORT 16' 17'.

Lancers ★ JOSÉ MARIA DA FONSECA's newly rebranded semi-sweet, semi-sparkling, ROSADO, now white, fizzy (w/rosé) and alc-free versions.

Lavradores de Feitoria Dou ★★→★★★ Innovative collaboration of 15 DOU producers. Gd-value whites, esp SAUV BL, Meruge (100% oak-aged old-vines Viosinho). Great value reds incl Três Bagos RES. V.gd Grande Escolha incl cellar-release Estágio Prolongado, QUINTA da Costa das Aguaneiras, elegant Meruge.

LBV (Late Bottled Vintage) Port Splendid, accessible, affordable alternative to VINTAGE PORT. A single-yr wine, aged 4–6 yrs in cask (twice as long as Vintage Port) for early drinking. V.gd, age-worthy, unfiltered versions eg. FERREIRA, NIEPOORT, NOVAL, RAMOS PINTO, SANDEMAN, TAYLOR, WARRE. A delicious dessert on its own.

Lisboa ★→★★★ Seaside region. Large generic companies contrast with dynamic, boutique, often organic producers. Great-value, age-worthy reds: CHOCAPALHA, SYRAH pioneer MONTE D'OIRO. Unique COLARES microclimate. Historic, crisp BUCELAS (w) popular again. Watch: ADEGAMAE (superb w), QUINTA de SANT'ANA, Pinto (value blends), (PINOT N, RIES, new Ramisco). Natural: Serradinha, Vale da Capucha. Newcomers: Boa Esperança, Espera Wines, Hugo Mendes, Olival da Murta.

Lopes, Márcio Dou, Vin ★★→★★★ Ambitious rising-star winemaker with diverse interests: VIN (gd-value ALVARINHO/LOUREIRO-focused Pequenos Rebentos brand), DOU (Proibido Clarete, clairet-style – *see* France), single-vyds (Vinha do Pombal, Dou Superior – Anel), RIBEIRA SACRA (70-yr-old vine Telegrafo).

Maçanita, António Alen, Dou ★★ →★★★ Unstoppable winemaker/consultant, interests in many regions. ALEN (fashionable Sexy, characterful Fita Preta, esp v.gd Palpite, AZORES (started revival of volcanic Pico island wines incl superb *Terrantez do Pico*, v.gd ARINTO do Açores) and DOU (gd-value r/w with sister Joana, incl Arinto, As Olgas, Cima Corgo, Gouveio, TOURIGA N).

Madeira ★→★★★★ Island and DOC, famous for thrilling fortifieds. Growing VERDELHO-focused table-wine range: Atlantis, Barbeito, Primeira Paixão, Terras do Avô. Unusual TINTA NEGRA based Ilha.

Riveting red grapes to try: Alfrocheiro, Rufete, Moreto.

Madeira, Rui Roboredo Bei Int, Dou ★★→★★★ Dynamic, high-altitude pioneer winemaker with interest in DOU Superior (gd-value, popular Castello d'Alba, reputed QUINTA da Pedra Escrita) and BEI INT (v.gd-value, fresh, up-to-750m/2461ft vyds Beyra range incl v.gd Grande RES TINTA RORIZ/TOURIGA N/Jaen and elegant *100% Jaen*). Top-notch, high-altitude, old-vines eponymous label.

Madeira Wine Company Mad Family-run company owns renowned brand BLANDY, COSSART GORDON, Leacock, Miles and accounts for over 50% of bottled MAD exports.

Malvasia (Malmsey) Mad Sweetest and richest of traditional MAD noble grape varieties, yet with Mad's unique sharp tang. Delightful with rich fruit, chocolate puddings or just dreams.

Maria Izabel, Quinta Dou ★★★ New-wave DOU rising star. Consistent range made with Dirk NIEPOORT's overlook, esp QUINTA, old-vine Vinhas da Princesa. Unique, elegant, limited-edition Sublime and rare, expensive Bastardo.

Mateus Rosé ★ Medium-dry, lightly carbonated rosé and wider range.

Mendes, Anselmo Vin ★★★→★★★★ VIN's star winemaker. Several benchmark, age-worthy ALVARINHOS, incl v.gd-value (aged on lees) *Contacto*, excellent skin-contact, voluptous *Curtimenta*, superb single-vyd Parcela Única, classy Muros de Melgaço and vibrant Expressões. Gd LOUREIRO, silky, modern red Vin (Pardusco), surprising orange Tempo. Watch: BEI INT range.

Minho Vin River (and province) between n Portugal and Spain, also VR covering same region as VIN. Popular white varieties: ALVARINHO, Avesso, LOUREIRO, Pedernã (ARINTO), Trajadura.

Monte de Ravasqueira Alen ★★→★★★ Family-owned estate, v.gd terroir (high amphitheatre, clay-limestone, granite). V.gd Premium range, esp ALICANTE BOUSCHET. Gd-value, single-vyd (ex-pomegranate orchard) Vinhas das Romãs.

Monte d'Oiro, Quinta do Lis ★★→★★★ Family estate started with Hermitage vines from Chapoutier. Now organic. Savoury red (SYRAH), fine RES (Syrah/VIOGNIER), age-worthy TINTA RORIZ; crisp white (Viognier/MARSANNE/ARINTO), Res (Viognier). V.gd Ex-Aequo, Bento & Chapoutier Syrah/TOURIGA N.

Moscatel de Setúbal Set ★★→★★★★ One of Portugal's fortified treasures. Exotic sweet MOSCATEL incl exquisite Roxo and *Superior*. Best: BACALHÔA VINHOS, Horácio Simões, JOSÉ MARIA DA FONSECA (holds 100-yr-old+ stocks). Value: ADEGA DE PEGÕES, Casa Ermelinda Freitas, do Piloto, SIVIPA.

Moscatel do Douro Dou High Favaios region produces surprisingly fresh, fortified MOSCATEL Galego Branco (Petits Grains). Look for: ADEGA de Favaios, POÇAS, Portal.

Mouchão, Herdade de Alen ★★★ Historic family-run ALICANTE BOUSCHET pioneer estate. New, dynamic winemaker. V.gd estate red (1st bottled 1949), COLHEITAS Antigas (cellar releases) 02' 03', iconic *Tonel 3–4* 05' 08 11' 13', fortified *licoroso*. V.gd-value Ponte (TOURIGA N/TOURIGA FRANCA/SYRAH). Gd old-vine Dom Rafael.

Mouraz, Casa de Dão ★★ Organic pioneer run by winemaker couple Antonio Lopes Ribeiro, Sara Dionísio. Characterful wines from family-owned vyds at 140–400m (459–1312ft). Rebuilding after cellar, some vyds lost in forest fires. Organic AIR label from bought-in ALEN, DOU, VIN. Nina is new Clairet.

Murganheira, Caves ★★★ Gd ESPUMANTE producer; owns popular Raposeira. Blends and varietal (native, French grapes) fizz: Vintage, Grande RES, Czar rosé and rare, expensive Esprit de la Maison PINOT (N/BL/M).

Muxagat Dou ★★★ DOU Superior (Mêda) estate with distinct, fresh, elegant wines (consultant LUIS SEABRA). Benchmark, complex, high-altitude Rabigato-based *Xistos Altos*. V.gd varietal reds (Tinta Barroca/Tinta Francisca), unique Cisne (blend r/w, Tinto Cão/Rabigato).

Niepoort Bair, Dão, Dou ★★★→★★★★ Estate owned by pioneer, larger-than-life Dirk Niepoort. Gd-value, globetrotter Diálogo/Fabelhaft. Fine Dou range, esp *Redoma*, Batuta, top-notch *Coche* (w), iconic *Charme*. Cross-region/winemaker projects: Nat'cool natural range, Projectos (BUÇACO, Gonçalves Faria); Spanish partnerships Ladredo (Ribeira Sacra), Navazos (Jerez). Dirk's vision incl BAIR's QUINTA de Baixo (esp GARRAFEIRA, Poeirinho, VV), DÃO (esp Conciso), VIN. Port highlights: VINTAGE PORT 15' 17', CRUSTED, demijohn-aged Garrafeira and single-vyd, organic Bioma. V.gd TAWNY, esp bottle-aged COLHEITAS.

Noval, Quinta do Dou, Port ★★★→★★★★ Historic estate owned by AXA since 1993. Consistent, fine VINTAGE PORT 97' 00' 03' 07' 08' 11' 12' 13' 15' 16' 17'. Superlative *Nacional* 63' 66' 94' 96' 97' 00' 01' 03' 04' 11' 16' 17' from 2.5 ha ungrafted vines is pricey jewel in crown. V.gd unfiltered LBV. Superb COLHEITAS, 20-, 40-yr-olds. Gd-value Cedro (native/SYRAH r, Viosinho/Gouveio w), v.gd RES, single-variety PETIT VERDOT, TOURIGA N. Now also runs Passadouro.

Offley Port ★→★★ Old house now owned by SOGRAPE. Gd recent fruit-driven VINTAGE PORT, unfiltered LBV, TAWNY. New cocktail-ready Clink WHITE PORT and ROSÉ PORT.

Palmela Set ★→★★★ CASTELÃO-focused DOC. Popular: Casa Ermelinda Freitas. Best: Horácio Simões, Pegos Claros, Piloto.

Pancas, Quinta de Lis ★★ Historic C15 LIS estate known for native/international blends. Atlantic-influenced vyds make bright white and complex red. Gd single-variety range, age-worthy CAB SAUV/MERLOT/SYRAH. Gd, decade-old cellar releases.

Passarella, Casa da Dão ★★→★★★★ Historic estate run by star winemaker Paulo Nunes. Flagship Villa Oliveira, single-vyd Pedras Altas (r), Vinha do Provincio (w), 2ª Edição (five vintages ENCRUZADO blend), 125 Anos (r). V.gd-value boutique Fugitivo range esp Enólogo, Vinhas Centenárias (100-yr-old field blend). Cellar-release *Vindima* 09' (80-yr-old field blend) sets new regional benchmark.

Pato, Filipa Bair ★★→★★★★ Star bio winemaker, daughter of LUIS P. Stands for "wines with no make-up". Superb pre-phylloxera, 130-yr-vine Nossa Missão, 90-yr-vine Nossa Calcario. Silky, perfumed BAGA, complex Bical/ARINTO blend and boundary-testing amphora-aged Post Quer**s range. Racy old-vine, oak-*lagares* fermented Territorio Vivo.

Pato, Luís Bair ★★→★★★★ Nonconformist star, father of FILIPA P; *seriously age-worthy, single-vyd Baga* (Vinhas Barrio, Barrosa, Pan) and two Pé Franco (ungrafted) wines (superb sandy-soil *Ribeirinho*, chalky-clay Valadas). Ready to drink VINHAS VELHAS (r/w), BAGA Rebel. Age-worthy whites: Vinhas Velhas (single-vyd Vinha Formal), fizzy MARIA GOMES Método Antigo, early picked (Informal).

Cercial synonym Esgana Cão ("dog strangler") grape known for its harsh acidity.

Península de Setúbal Set Atlantic-influenced region s of Lisbon. Home to MOSCATEL DE SETÚBAL. Value-driven VR wines mostly from chalky or sandy banks of Sado and Tagus Rivers. Popular: ADEGA de Pegões, BACALHÔA VINHOS, Casa Ermelinda Freitas, JOSÉ MARIA FONSECA. Watch: Brejinho da Costa, Piloto.

Pereira d'Oliveira Mad ★★→★★★★ Family-run producer with vast stocks (1.6 million litres) of bottled-on-demand old FRASQUEIRA, many available to taste at travel-back-in-time 1619 cellar door. Best incl stunning C19 vintages (MOSCATEL 1875, SERCIAL 1875, Terrantez 1880) and rare *Bastardo 1927*.

Periquita Grape, aka CASTELÃO. Trademark of JOSÉ MARIA DA FONSECA's successful brand.

Pico Wines Azores ★★ Largest, oldest AZORES co-op, rising in quality with winemaker Bernardo Cabral (also VICENTINO). Gd-value Terras de Lava label; v.gd, salty, varietal VERDELHO, ARINTO, exquisite Terrantez do Pico; gd Frei Gigant blends all. Delicious 10-yr-old Licoroso.

Poças Dou, Port ★★→★★★ 100-yr-old family-owned firm with growing, gd table wine range. V.gd Símbolo (with Hubert de Boüard of B'x), oak-aged Branco da Ribeira (w). Gd RES (r), v.gd-value Vale de Cavalos (r/w). New unusual Fora da Série range incl orange, amphora, elegant *Roga*. Old stocks allow for fabulous 90-yr-old+ 1918 Very Old TAWNY, outstanding 20-, 30-, 40-yr-old Tawny, remarkable COLHEITAS. V.gd VINTAGE PORT 15′ 16′ 17′ 18′.

Portalegre Alen ★→★★★ Most n subregion of ALEN undergoing a revival. SYMINGTON and SOGRAPE's acquisition of cooler, high-altitude (often v. old field-blend) vyds bodes well. Revival pioneers incl ESPORÃO, Fonte Souto (SYMINGTONS), Cabeças do Reguengo, RUI REGUINGA (Terrenus), SUSANA ESTEBAN, Tapada do Chaves. To watch.

Quinta Portuguese for "estate". "Herdade" in ALEN. "Single-quinta" denotes single-estate VINTAGE PORTS (often v.gd value) made in non-declared yrs (increasingly made in top yrs too).

Quinta Nova Dou ★★→★★★★ Hilltop, historic 250-yr-old DOU estate revamped by Amorim family (of cork fame). Charming hotel. Auspicious new DÃO project TABOADELLA. Top-notch oak-aged Mirabilis (r/w), *Referência* (TINTA RORIZ), Grande RES (TOURIGA N), homage Aeternus (100-yr vines). Gd-value (r/w) Grainha, Pomares. ALEN's Aldeia de Cima is Luisa Amorim's new personal project.

Bastardo, used in Port and table wines, same as Jura's Trousseau.

Rainwater Mad Lighter, drier, Tinta Negra-based style of MAD. Popular in US. Pleasing apéritif, with food.

Ramos, João Portugal Alen ★→★★★ ALEN's pioneer winemaker now also in VIN, DOU (DUORUM), Beira Atlântico (FOZ DE AROUCE). Success due to gd-value, true-to-region wines with commercial appeal incl Marquês de Borba (r, RES r), VINHAS VELHAS (r/w), Vila Santa. V.gd single-vyds Estremus, Jeremias, São Lázaro, Viçosa.

Ramos Pinto Dou, Port ★★★ Owned by Champagne Roederer. Gd, consistent range esp Duas Quintas RES (r), Res Especial (mainly TOURIGA N). V.gd age-worthy VINTAGE PORT incl single-QUINTAS Ervamoira, Bom Retiro. Complex single-quinta TAWNY 10-yr-old (Ervamoira) and best-in-class *20-yr-old* (Bom Retiro). Gd 30-yr-old incl a dash of centenarian Tawny.

Raposeira Dou ★★ MURGANHEIRA-owned. Classic-method fizz. Flagship Velha RES, CHARD/PINOT N lees-aged 4 yrs.

Real Companhia Velha Dou, Port ★→★★★ Family-run, historic (1756) company with new Port museum and wine bar in Gaia. Silva Reis family renewing Port (incl Royal Oporto and Delaforce) and DOU portfolio with precision viticulture (540 ha) and winemaking. Grandjó is best late-harvest in Portugal. V.gd old-vine flagship Carvalhas (r/w), VINTAGE PORT, 20-yr-old TAWNY, Cidrô. Value brands incl Aciprestes, Evel. V.gd whites from Síbio esp ARINTO.

Reguinga, Rui Alen, Tej ★★★ Consultant winemaker with own projects. ALEN: old-vines Terrenus range, incl single-vyd, 100-yr-old vines Vinha da Serra (w). TEJO: Rhône-inspired SYRAH/GRENACHE/VIOGNIER Tributo. Also in Argentina.

Reserve / Reserva (Res) Port Higher quality than basic, or aged before being sold. Grande Reserva one step up, approved by a regional tasting board. Rules vary between regions, apply pinch of salt. In Port, bottled without age indication (used in RUBY, TAWNY).

Romeira, Quinta da ★→★★ SOGRAPE-owned, historic BUCELAS estate. ARINTO-focused vyds. V.gd-value, oaked Morgado Sta Catherina RES. Gd-value Prova Regia, RES.

Rosa, Quinta de la Dou, Port ★★★ Family-run Pinhão estate with Port and DOU

PORTUGAL | Pic–Tab | 201

range ever better under winemaker Jorge Moreira. V.gd VINTAGE PORT, LBV, 30-yr-old TAWNY. Rich but elegant wines, esp RES (r/w). V.gd, age-worthy white TIM. Generous gd-value Passagem label.

Rosado Rosé. Growing category. Best incl COVELA, QUINTA NOVA, NIEPOORT, VÉRTICE (sp).

Rosé Port Port Pioneered by CROFT'S Pink (2005) now made by other shippers (OFFLEY, POÇAS). Quality variable. Serve chilled, on ice, or, if you must, in a cocktail.

Rozès Dou, Port ★★★ Owned by Vranken-Pommery. VINTAGE PORT, incl LBV, sourced from DOU Superior QUINTAS (Anibal, Canameira, Grifo). Gd Terras do Grifo table wines incl RES, Grande Res.

Ruby Port Most simple, young, cheap sweet Port style. Can still be delicious. RES a worthy step up.

Sandeman Port Port ★★→★★★ Historic house, SOGRAPE-owned, famous for caped man (the don) image. V.gd-value 20-, 30-, 40-yr-old TAWNY, unfiltered LBV. Great VINTAGE PORT 07' 11' 16' 18' brings back quality. Superb Very Old Tawny Cask 33.

Sant'Ana, Quinta de Lis ★★→★★★ Historic idyllic family-run estate making Atlantic-influenced wines. Consultant ANTONIO MAÇANITA works native, international varieties. V.gd whites: ALVARINHO, ARINTO, RIES, VERDELHO. Age-worthy reds: PINOT N, RES, Homenagem (Merlot/Touriga N). Exquisite new NV *Ramisco*.

São João, Caves Bair ★★→★★★ Established firm known for gd old-fashioned wines, esp BAIR (*Frei João*, Poço do Lobo), DÃO (Porta dos Cavaleiros). Rare gd-value cellar releases from vast stock. Gd ARINTO/CHARD white, sparkling blends.

Seabra, Luis Dou, Vin ★★★ New-wave, min intervention winemaker. V.gd, fresh, elegant single-vyd DOU and VIN from indigenous varieties. Consultant at MUXAGAT, Pormenor. To watch.

Sercial Mad White grape. Makes driest MAD. *Supreme apéritif;* Racy, perfect with gravadlax, sushi or seared tuna. *See* Grapes chapter.

Smith Woodhouse Port ★★★ SYMINGTON-owned small Port firm est 1784. Gd unfiltered LBV; some v.gd drier VINTAGE PORT 83 85 91 94 97 00' 03 07 11' 16. Single-QUINTA da Madelena.

Soalheiro, Quinta de Vin ★★→★★★ Leading Monção e Melgaço (VIN subregion) ALVARINHO specialist. V.gd, age-worthy range incl mineral Granit, subtly barrel-fermented old-vine *Primeiras Vinhas*, oak-aged RES, natural Terramatter, unfiltered Pur Nature. Oppaco (1st red) is unique PINOT N/Vinhão/Alvarinho blend. V.gd Pinot N/Alvarinho blend rosé. Great fizz (w/rosé).

Sogrape Alen, Dou, Vin ★→★★★★ Portugal's most successful firm, global interests (Portugal, Argentina, Chile, NZ, Spain). Makes MATEUS ROSÉ. Port brands: FERREIRA, OFFLEY, SANDEMAN. By region: ALEN (gd-value Herdade do Peso), DÃO (boutique CARVALHAIS), DOU (popular CASA FERREIRINHA, prestigious BARCA VELHA), LIS (ARINTO-focused QUINTA DA ROMEIRA), VIN (gd-value Azevedo). Fine-wine range: *Antónia Adelaide Ferreira*, Legado, Série Ímpar, Touriga-Fêmea.

Sousa, Alves de Dou, Port ★★→★★★ Family-run DOU pioneer located in cooler Baixo Corgo area. Gd, age-worthy *Quinta da Gaivosa*, unique late-released RES Pessoal. V.gd old-vine field-blends Abandonado, Vinha de Lordelo. Expanding Port range incl elegant VINTAGE PORT, 20-yr-old TAWNY.

Sousa, José de Alen ★→★★★ Owned by JOSÉ MARIA DA FONSECA. Historic estate keeping tradition alive with 114 (Portugal's largest collection) amphorae/*talhas*. Superb J de José de Sousa. Great-value Mayor, classic José de Sousa, new RES.

Symington Family Estates Dou, Port ★★→★★★★ DOU's biggest landowner now exploring ALEN. Family-run, owns clutch of top Port houses incl COCKBURN, DOW, GRAHAM, VESUVIO, WARRE. Classy Dou range (incl top-notch CHRYSEIA, VESÚVIO) and gd-value Altano range incl RES. High-altitude-vyds Fonte Souto Alen range incl v.gd Vinha do Souto ALICANTE BOUCHET/SYRAH.

Taboadella Dão ★★→★★★ Amorim ambitious new DÃO project. Winemaking/

viticulture by QUINTA NOVA's Jorge Alves/Ana Mota. Promising range: gd-value Villae; varietal *Alfrocheiro*, ENCRUZADO, Jaen, TOURIGA N; top-level Grande Villae (r/w). Striking, cork-coated cellar.

Tawny Port Wood-aged Port. RES, age-dated (10-, 20-, 30-, 40-yr-old) wines go up in complexity, price. *20-yr-old* best balance between ages. Single-year COLHEITAS cask-aged up to 100 yrs, can cost gd deal more than VINTAGE PORT. Luscious *Very Old Tawny* Ports (min 40-yrs-old, often much older) are time-travelling experience. Stars: 1900 1910 (ANDRESEN) 1918 (POÇAS), 5G (WINE & SOUL), CNK (KOPKE), Ne Oublie (GRAHAM'S), Scion, new Kingsman Edition (TAYLOR), VV (NIEPOORT).

Taylor's Port ★★→★★★★ Historic Port shipper, FLADGATE's jewel in the crown. Imposing VINTAGE PORTS 63' 66' 83 70' 77' 92' 94 97 00' 03' 07' 09' 11' 16' 17' 18', incl single-QUINTAS (Terra Feita, Vargellas), rare Vargellas VINHA VELHA from 70-yr-old+ vines. Market leader for TAWNY incl v.gd 50-yr-old COLHEITAS 68' 69' 70' and Very Old Tawny 1863' Scion, new Kingsman Edition (average 90 yrs old).

Tejo ★→★★★ Region surrounding River Tagus (Tejo) n of Lisbon. Shifting from quantity to quality. Solid: Alorna, Lagoalva de Cima, Lapa. More ambitious: Casal Branco, RUI REGUINGA and FALUA show potential of v.gd terroir. Old vines produce gd results with stalwart CASTELÃO, FERNÃO PIRES. Watch: Casal das Aires.

Tinto Red.

Trás-os-Montes Tras ★★ Mountainous inland DOC just n of DOU; promising high-altitude terroir. Valle Pradinhos is reference. Watch: Arcossó, Casa do Joa, Sobreiró de Cima.

Vale Dona Maria, Quinta do Dou, Port ★★→★★★ DOU table wine pioneer, owned by AVELEDA. V.gd, lush reds incl estate label, single-vyd Vinha do Rio, Vinha da Francisca. Gd, smoky, oaky but brisk whites incl VVV, single-vyd Vinha do Martim. New, gd-value Dou Superior range. Gd VINTAGE PORT 15' 16' 17, LBV. Member of DOURO BOYS.

Vale Meão, Quinta do Dou ★★★ Family-run DOU Superior estate. Fine, age-worthy, elegant top red. Gd-value second label Meandro (r/w). Gd single-QUINTA VINTAGE PORT. V.gd varietal TOURIGA N, TINTA RORIZ Monte Meão range. Member of DOURO BOYS.

Vallado, Quinta do Dou ★★→★★★ Family-owned Baixo Corgo estate, modern hotel/winery. V.gd-value DOU Superior organic (QUINTA do Orgal incl charming hotel Casa do Rio). V.gd RES field blend, varietal TINTA RORIZ, TOURIGA N, Sousão range. Gd 10-, 20-, 30-, 40-yr-old TAWNY. Top, 80-yr-old vine Adelaide red. Thrilling, rare, pre-phylloxera Very Old Tawny (1866 1888). Member of DOURO BOYS.

Vasques de Carvalho Dou, Port ★★★ New producer (rare in Port), est 2012 by António Vasques de Carvalho (inherited family cellars, stock, vyd) and business

---

Top of the table

Top-notch Portuguese table wines, often from v. old vines, are growing in number and price (get them while still affordable). Here are the best. Reds: Aldeia de Cima Alyantiju; CASA DA PASSARELLA Vindima 09; CASA FERREIRINHA Antónia Adelaide Ferreira/BARCA VELHA; CHRYSEIA; DUORUM O.Leucura; FILIPA PATO Nossa Missão; JOSÉ DE SOUSA J; Legado; LUIS PATO Ribeirinho; MOUCHÃO Tonel 3-4; NIEPOORT Charme; QUINTA DO CRASTO Maria Teresa/Vinha da Ponte; Quinta do Gradil Ganita; QUINTA DO VESUVIO; QUINTA MARIA IZABEL Sublime; QUINTA NOVA Aeternus/Mirabilis; VALE D. MARIA Vinha do Rio; WINE & SOUL Pintas/Manoella VINHAS VELHAS. Whites: ADEGAMÃE Terroir; ANSELMO MENDES Parcela Única; AZORES Wine Company Terrantez do Pico; Casa da Passarella Villa Oliveira; ESPORÃO Private Selection; Niepoort Coche; SOGRAPE Série Ímpar Sercialinho; Vinhos Imperfeitos; Wine & Soul Guru.

partner Luís Vale (capital). Top-notch, expensive, stylish 10-, 20-, 30- and 40-yr-old TAWNY. New boutique in Gaia.

Verdelho Mad Grape of medium-dry MAD; pungent but without spine of SERCIAL. Gd apéritif with hard cheeses.

Vértice Dou ★★★→★★★★ DOU-fizz producer, often considered Portugal's best. V.gd-value Gouveio, Millésime. Remarkable, high-altitude, 84-mth-aged PINOT N.

Sousão, Vinhão: grapes of Vin increasingly popular for making fresher Ports.

Vesuvio, Quinta do Dou, Port ★★★→★★★★ Magnificent, historic riverside QUINTA making v.gd, age-worthy, old-vine, high-altitude estate red. V.gd-value second label *Pombal do Vesuvio* and Port on par with best: 07' 08' 11' 13' 15' 16' 17' 18'. Still foot-trodden by people.

Vicentino Alen ★★ Modern seaside pioneer. Fresh, Atlantic-influenced range blends native/international varieties: gd-value COLHEITAS, racy, varietal ALVARINHO, ARINTO, PINOT N, SAUV BL, SYRAH. To watch.

Vilacetinho, Casa de Vin ★★ C18 VIN estate on border with DOU. Gd value Escolha, Avesso-based range incl blends with ALVARINHO/ARINTO/Azal/LOUREIRO; V.gd Superior, RES.

Vila Nova de Gaia Dou, Port Historic home of major Port shippers, arguably Oporto's best viewpoint. Best tourist attractions incl cable car, double-deck bridge, boat tours, hotels (The Yeatman, Michelin-starred fine dining), restaurants/bars (Vinum, Enoteca 17•56), classy cellars (CÁLEM, COCKBURN'S, FERREIRA, GRAHAM'S, POÇAS, SANDEMAN, TAYLOR'S), new FLADGATE's ambitious World of Wine museum.

Vinhas Velhas Old vines; frequently found on labels but meaning changes by region: n (60–120 yrs) to s (30–40 yrs). Regulation under review.

Vinho Verde ★→★★★ Portugal's biggest region in rainy, verdant nw. Signs of a renaissance with gd-value, fresh, elegant whites. Best: high-end ALVARINHO from Monção e Melgaço (ANSELMO MENDES, Regueiro, SOALHEIRO), LOUREIRO from Lima (eg. AMEAL, Aphros), Avesso from Baião (A&D, Covela). Large brands (ADEGA de Monção, Aveleda, Azevedo) often slightly fizzy (Casal Garcia, Gazela, Muralhas); DYA. Watch: AVELEDA's new range, bio Aphros, Camaleão, CASA DE VILACETINHO, LUIS SEABRA, San Joanne, Santiago, Vale dos Ares.

Vintage Port Port Classic vintages are best wines declared in exceptional yrs by shippers. Increasingly back-to-back 15 16 17 18 due to precision viticulture/winemaking. Bottled without filtration after 2 yrs in wood, mature v. slowly in bottle, throwing a deposit – always decant. Modern vintages broachable earlier (and hedonistic young) but best will last more than 50 yrs. Single-QUINTA Vintage Ports also drinking earlier; best can last 30 yrs+.

VR / IGP (Vinho Regional / Indicação Geográfica Protegida) Same status as French IGP. More leeway for experimentation than DOC/DOP.

Warre's Port ★★★→★★★★ 1st and oldest of British Port shippers (1670), now owned by SYMINGTON FAMILY ESTATES. Rich, long-aging VINTAGE 83 85 91 94 97 00' 03 07' 09' 11' 16' 17' and unfiltered LBV. Elegant Single-QUINTA and 10-, 20-yr-old TAWNY Otima reflect Quinta da Cavadinha's cool elevation.

White Port From white grapes. Mostly off-dry. Growing, high-quality, niche: age-dated 10-, 20-, 30-, or 40-yr-old eg. ANDRESEN, KOPKE; rare COLHEITAS eg. *Dalva*, *Kopke*. Lágrima is affordable, v. sweet. Port and Tonic is refreshing apéritif.

Wine & Soul Dou, Port ★★★→★★★★ Family-owned DOU boutique estate run by winemaking couple Sandra Tavares and Jorge Serôdio Borges. Superb, oak-aged Guru (w), old-vine QUINTA da Manoella VINHAS VELHAS (r) and age-worthy, complex, dense (80-yr vine) Pintas (r). Great value, field blend Pintas Character and second-label Manoella (r w). V.gd Pintas VINTAGE PORT. Oustanding 120-yr-old, Very Old TAWNY 5G.

Switzerland

Abbreviations used in the text:

Aar	Aargau
Ber	Bern
Gris	Grisons
Luc	Lucerne
Neu	Neuchâtel
Schaff	Schaffhausen
Thur	Thurgau
Tic	Ticino
Val	Valais
Vd	Vaud
Zür	Zürich

The Swiss are a thirsty lot: they drink 2.5 million hl wine/year, or 30 litres/head. Given that the country's own production is only one million hl, you would think that consumers would drink all of it. But no: the volume of unsold domestic wines in stock came to 1.6 million hl by the end of 2019. But, luckily, some of the best Swiss growers, like Gantenbein, Donatsch or Bovard, are fighting back: they're going abroad and promoting their top wines to educated consumers worldwide. Other estates should follow their example. Currently, wine-lovers in Paris, Rome and Berlin have little, or – even worse – the wrong idea about Swiss wines. They don't know that the most burgundian Pinots outside Burgundy grow in Switzerland; they haven't discovered the intriguing terroir expression of Swiss Chasselas; they know nothing about the stand-alone character of Merlot del Ticino. Maybe it needs foreign drinkers to go crazy about Swiss wine before those in Zurich, Geneva and Lugano do the same.

Recent vintages

2020 Early, small harvest, 20–40% less: uneven flowering, drought, v.gd quality.

2019 Rain at harvest time, esp E Switzerland; Vaud and Valais better.

2018 Powerful, round wines all over the country.

2017 Frost; some cantons have only 20% of a normal crop. V.gd quality.

2016 Frost in April, rainy summer then sun: mostly mid-weight wines.

2015 Great vintage, ripe fruit, perfectly balanced acidity.

Fine vintages: 13 10 (Pinot N) 09 05 (all) 99 (Dézaley) 97 (Dézaley) 90 (all).

Aigle Vd ★→★★★ CHASSELAS AOC, famous (and easy to pronounce for non-native speakers of French), but be selective. BADOUX, Terroir du Crosex Grillé.

AOC Equivalent of France's Appellation Contrôlée, 62 AOCs countrywide.

Auvernier, Ch d' Neu ★★→★★★ Important estate (60 ha) with reliable, typical NEU CHASSELAS, plus CHARD, OEIL-DE-PERDRIX, PINOT N (best: single-vyd Les Argiles).

Bachtobel, Schlossgut Thur ★★★ Since 1784 owned by Kesselring family, known for refined PINOT N from slopes nr Weinfelden. Estate's own clonal selection, in early C20 dismissed because of high acidity, now rediscovered.

Bad Osterfingen Schaff ★★★ Restaurant and wine estate in historical baths (est 1472). Michael Meyer is a PINOT specialist with a famous line in Spätzle (noodles). Co-producer of ZWAA.

Badoux, Henri Vd ★★ AIGLE les Murailles (classic lizard label) is most popular Swiss brand. Ambitious Lettres de Noblesse series has gd barrel-aged YVORNE.

Baumann, Ruedi Schaff ★★★ Perfectionist family estate at Oberhallau. Beatrice, Ruedi, son Peter best known for delicately fruity PINOT N (eg. Ann Mee, R, ZWAA).

Bern Capital and canton. Villages Ligerz, Schafis, TWANN (Lake Biel) and Spiez (Lake Thun). Mainly CHASSELAS, PINOT N. Top growers: Andrey, Johanniterkeller, Keller am See, KREBS & STEINER, Schlössli.

Besse, Gérald et Patricia Val ★★★ Leading VAL family estate; Gérard and Patricia B, daughter Sarah. Mostly steep terraces up to 600m (1969ft); intense old-vines *Ermitage Les Serpentines* 10' 13' 15 16 17 (MARSANNE on granite soils, planted 1945).

Bonvin Val ★★→★★★★ Old name of VAL, intriguing local grapes: *Nobles Cépages* series (eg. HEIDA, PETITE ARVINE, SYRAH).

Bovard, Louis Vd ★★→★★★★★ Top estate at Cully (ten generations), classic, age-worthy; La Médinette 99' 05' 12' 15 16 17' 18' 19 is paradigmatic DÉZALEY, wines from other LAVAUX AOCs equally reliable, old vintages available from dom.

Percentage of organically grown vines in Switzerland: 10%.

Bündner Herrschaft Gris ★★→★★★★ 13' 15' 16 17 18' 19 PINOT N with structure, fruit, great capacity to age. Only four villages: FLÄSCH, JENINS, MAIENFELD, MAIANS. Climate balanced between mild s winds and coolness from nearby mtns.

Calamin Vd ★★★ GRAND CRU of LAVAUX, 16 ha of deep calcareous soils on a landslide, tarter CHASSELAS than neighbour DÉZALEY, growers incl BOVARD, Dizerens, DUBOUX.

Chablais Vd ★★→★★★ Wine region at upper end of Lake Geneva around AIGLE and YVORNE. Name is from Latin *caput lacis*, head of the lake.

Chanton Val ★★★ Family estate and Noah's Ark for old VAL varieties (Eyholzer Roter, Gwäss, HEIDA, Himbertscha, Lafnetscha, Resi), vyds up to 800m (2625ft).

Chappaz, Marie-Thérèse Val ★★★→★★★★★ Small bio estate, arguably Switzerland's best sweet from Petite ARVINE and Ermitage (MARSANNE), tiny quantities.

Colombe, Dom La Vd ★★→★★★★ Family estate of FÉCHY, LA CÔTE, 15 ha, bio. Best-known for range of ageable CHASSELAS, eg. La Brez.

Cortaillod Neu Village on shores of Lake Neuchâtel renowned for refined PINOT N. Eponymous, low-yielding local clone.

Côte, La Vd ★→★★★ 2000 ha w of Lausanne on Lake Geneva, mainly CHASSELAS of v. light, commercial style. Villages incl FÉCHY, Mont-sur-Rolle, Morges.

Cruchon Vd ★★★ Bio producer of LA CÔTE, now led by young Catherine C, lots of SPÉCIALITÉS (eg. outstanding Altesse). Top growth: PINOT N Raissennaz. Sublime Coeur de Cuvée Sparkling (5 yrs on lees).

Dézaley Vd ★★★ LAVAUX GRAND CRU on steep slopes of Lake Geneva, 54 ha; planted in C12 by Cistercian monks. Potent CHASSELAS develops with age (7 yrs+). Best: DUBOUX, *Fonjallaz*, LEYVRAZ, *Louis Bovard*, Monachon, VILLE DE LAUSANNE.

Dôle Val ★→★★★ VAL'S answer to Burgundy's Passetoutgrains: PINOT N plus GAMAY for light, quaffable red. Dôle Blanche: fashionable pale Blanc de Noirs, rarely exciting.

Donatsch, Thomas Gris ★★★ Barrique pioneer (1974) at MALANS. Now son Martin in charge: 13' PINOT N Res Privée fetched 1075 CHF/bottle at auction.

Duboux, Blaise Vd ★★★ Family estate, 5-ha, in LAVAUX. Outstanding DÉZALEY vieilles vignes Haut de Pierre (v. rich, mineral), CALAMIN Cuvée Vincent.

Einsiedeln, Kloster Schw ★★ Benedictine abbey, founded 934, famous for its black Madonna; 8 ha of vines at Lake Zürich (ZÜRICHSEE), eg. Konvent PINOT N.

Epesses Vd ★→★★★ Well-known LAVAUX AOC, sturdy, full-bodied whites. Growers incl BOVARD, DUBOUX, Fonjallaz, Massy.

Féchy Vd ★→★★★ Famous though unreliable AOC of LA CÔTE, mainly CHASSELAS.

15 yrs ago, Switzerland was 50:50 white/red. Today: 43:57.

Federweisser / Weissherbst German-Swiss pale rosé or even Blanc de Noirs made from BLAUBURGUNDER.

Fendant Val ★→★★★ Full-bodied VAL CHASSELAS, ideal for fondue or raclette. Try BESSE, Cornulus, GERMANIER, PROVINS, SIMON MAYE.

Fläsch Gris ★★★→★★★★ Village of BÜNDNER HERRSCHAFT known for PINOT N from schist and limestone. Lots of gd estates, esp members of Adank, Hermann, Marugg families. *Gantenbein* is outstanding.

Flétri / Mi-flétri Late-harvested grapes for sweet/slightly sweet wine.

Fribourg On shores of Lake Murten (Mt Vully), 115 ha; round CHASSELAS, elegant TRAMINER. Best: Chervet, Cru de l'Hôpital.

Fromm, Georg Gris ★★★ 05' 13' 15' 16 17 18 19 Top grower in MALANS, known for subtle single-vyd PINOT N (Fidler, Selfi/Selvenen, Schöpfi, Spielmann). Now bio.

Gantenbein, Daniel & Martha Gris ★★★★ 10' 13' 15' 16 17 18 19 Star growers, based in FLÄSCH. PINOT N is famous, but CHARD (v. small quantity) even more intriguing.

Geneva 1400 ha of vines remote from the lake (vyds there belong mainly to VD canton). Growers: Balisiers, Grand'Cour, Les Hutins, Novelle.

Germanier, Jean-René Val ★★→★★★ Big estate (150 ha), reliable FENDANT Les Terrasses, SYRAH Cayas, nobly sweet AMIGNE Mitis from schist at Vétroz.

Glacier, Vin du (Gletscherwein) Val ★★★ A sort of Alpine "Sherry" from rare Rèze grape of Val d'Anniviers, aged in larch casks. Taste at the Town Hall of Grimentz.

Grain Noble ConfidenCiel Val Quality label for authentic sweet wines, eg. CHAPPAZ, DOM DU MONT D'OR, Dorsaz (both estates), GERMANIER, Philippe Darioli, PROVINS.

Grand Cru Val, Vd Inconsistent term, in use in VAL (commune Salgesch for PINOT N) and VD (as "Premier Grand Cru" for a range of single-estate wines). Only two Grands Crus in the sense of a classification of vyd sites: CALAMIN, DÉZALEY.

Grisons (Graubünden) Mtn canton, German- and Rhaeto-Romanic-speaking. PINOT N king. *See* BÜNDNER HERRSCHAFT. Best (other areas): Manfred Meier, VON TSCHARNER.

Huber, Daniel ★★→★★★ Pioneer who reclaimed historical sites from fallow in 1981. Partly bio. Son Jonas taken over. Top: Montagna Magica (MERLOT/CAB FR).

Johannisberg Val VAL name for SILVANER, often off-dry or sweet; great with fondue. Excellent: *Domaine du Mont d'Or*.

Joris, Didier Val ★★★→★★★★ Oenological consultant and organic mini-estate (3 ha, dozen varieties). Outstanding MARSANNE. Reviving nearly extinct local Diolle (w).

Krebs & Steiner Ber ★★★ Merger of two Lake Bienne familiy estates. Best: Clos au Comte CHARD under Steiner label.

Lavaux Vd ★★→★★★★ 30 km (19 miles) of steep s-facing terraces e of Lausanne; UNESCO World Heritage site. Uniquely rich, mineral CHASSELAS. GRANDS CRUS DÉZALEY, CALAMIN, several village AOCs.

Leyvraz, Pierre-Luc Vd ★★★→★★★★ Perfectionist grower at Chexbres; intensely terroir-driven ST-SAPHORIN and DÉZALEY.

Litwan, Tom Aar ★★★ Passionate bio grower at Schinznach. 3 ha. Delicate, fine-grained PINOT N Auf der Mauer ("On Top of the Wall") and Chalofe ("Lime Kiln").

Maison Carrée, La Neu ★★★ Family estate, 10-ha, est 1827, v. traditional winemaking incl use of old wooden press, esp PINOT N (Auvernier, Hauterive).

Malans Gris ★★→★★★★ Village in BÜNDNER HERRSCHAFT. Top PINOT N producers incl DONATSCH, FROMM, Liesch, Studach, Wegelin. Late-ripening local grape Completer gives a long-lasting phenolic white. Adolf Boner 01′ 05′ is keeper of the grail.

Maye, Simon et Fils Val ★★★ Family estate, 11 ha. Dense SYRAH Vieilles Vignes perhaps best in Switzerland; spicy, powerful Païen (HEIDA).

Mémoire des Vins Suisses Union of 57 leading growers in effort to create stock of Swiss icon wines, to prove their ageing capacities. Oldest wines from 1999.

Mercier Val ★★★→★★★★ SIERRE family estate, now young Madeleine M in charge, meticulous vyd management produces dense, aromatic reds, eg. rare CORNALIN 05′ 09′ 10′ 11 15 16 17 18 and SYRAH.

Mont d'Or, Dom du Val ★★→★★★★ Emblematic VAL estate for nobly sweet wines, esp JOHANNISBERG Saint-Martin. Recently, more emphasis on dry wines.

Neuchâtel ★→★★★ 600 ha around city and lake on calcareous soil. Slightly sparkling CHASSELAS, exquisite PINOT N from local clone (CORTAILLOD). Best: CH D'AUVERNIER, Dom de Chambleau, LA MAISON CARRÉE, PORRET, TATASCIORE.

Oeil de Perdrix "Partridge's eye": PINOT N rosé, originally from NEU, now elsewhere.

Pircher, Urs Zür ★★★→★★★★ Urs P produces top wines with admirable consistency from a steep s-facing slope overlooking the Rhine at Eglisau. Crystal-clear whites, complex PINOT N Stadtberger Barrique 15′ 16 17 18 from old Swiss clones.

Porret Neu ★★→★★★★ Leading family estate at CORTAILLOD with burgundian approach to CHARD and PINOT N (best: Cuvée Elisa, made to age for decades). Also vyds in Aloxe-Corton (*see* France).

Provins Val ★→★★★ Co-op with 4000+ members, Switzerland's biggest producer, 1500 ha, 34 varieties. Sound entry level, v.gd oak-aged Maître de Chais range.

R3 Zür ★★★ 08′ 09 12′ 17′ 18 19 Räuschling (local grape) collaboration of three leading ZÜRICHSEE growers: Luthi, Rütihof, SCHWARZENBACH.

Rouvinez Vins Val ★→★★★ VAL giant at Sierre, est 1947; cuvées La Trémaille (w) and Le Tourmentin (r) founded reputation. Strong expansion through takeover of BONVIN (2009), Caves Orsat (1998), Imesch (2003).

Ruch, Markus Schaff ★★★ Excellent PINOT N from Hallau (Chölle from 60-yr-old vines, Haalde from steep slope), Gächlingen (Schlemmweg on limestone); 3 ha.

St. Jodern Kellerei Val ★★→★★★ VISPERTERMINEN co-op famous for *Heida Veritas* from ungrafted old vines.

St-Saphorin Vd ★→★★★ Neighbour AOC of DÉZALEY, lighter, but equally delicate. Best: LEYVRAZ, Monachon.

Schaffhausen ★→★★★ Deemed "BLAUBURGUNDERLAND", but a flood of cheap supermarket wines has damaged reputation. Top growers (eg. BAD OSTERFINGEN, BAUMANN, RUCH, Stamm, Strasser) among Switzerland's best.

Schenk SA Vd ★→★★★ Wine giant with worldwide activities, based in Rolle, founded 1893. Classic wines (esp VD, VAL); substantial exports.

Chasselas the unknown

Nowhere else has CHASSELAS the importance that it has in Switzerland. Glance at the wine quickly and it looks, well, harmless. Only gradually do you realize its nuances. And it is genetically v. variable: VD growers BOVARD and Paccot (DOM LA COLOMBE) have set up – together with the research station at Pully – two collections containing almost 400 different Chasselas. There is one with reddish shoots, one with violet-coloured berries, another that smells of musk. The berries of the Giclet-type splash if pressed between the fingertips, while the Fendant-type bursts open without releasing juice. This is by no means a simple grape.

Schwarzenbach, Hermann Zür ★★★ Alain S is 5th generation at family estate on Lake Zürich that saved (in the 50s/60s) local grape Räuschling (Seehalden 15' 17 18' 19 20) from exctinction. Many other SPECIALITIES (eg. Completer, Freisamer) too.

Spécialités / Spezialitäten Quantitatively minor grapes producing some of best Swiss wines, eg. Räuschling, GEWURZ or PINOT GR in German Switzerland, or local varieties (and grapes like JOHANNISBERG, MARSANNE, SYRAH) in VAL.

Sprecher von Bernegg Gris ★★★ Historic estate at Jenins, BÜNDNER HERRSCHAFT, esp PINOT N: Lindenwingert, vom Pfaffen/Calander.

Stucky-Hügin Tic ★★★ MERLOT pioneer Werner Stucky and son Simon plus Jürg Hügin. Best: Conte di Luna (MERLOT/CAB SAUV), Soma (Merlot/CAB FR), Temenos (Completer/SAUV BL).

Tatasciore, Jacques Neu ★★★★ Refined (and rare) NEU PINOT N.

Ticino ★→★★★★ Italian-speaking. MERLOT (leading grape since 1948) in a taut style. Best: Agriloro, Castello di Morcote, Gialdi, HUBER, Klausener, Kopp von der Crone Visini, STUCKY, Tamborini, Valsangiacomo, Vinattieri, ZÜNDEL.

Tscharner, von ★★★ Family estate, 6 ha, led by father Gian-Battista and son Johann-Baptista, at Reichenau castle at confluence of Vorder-Rhine and Hinter-Rhein. Epic, tannin-laden PINOT N (Churer Gian-Battista, Jeninser Alte Reben), worthy its position as 1st wine estate along River Rhine's 1230 km (764 mile) length.

Twann Ber ★→★★★ Village of Bielersee, famous for GUTEDEL (CHASSELAS), PINOT N, but variable in quality. Gd: Johanniterkeller, Klötzli, KREBS & STEINER, Schott (bio).

Valais (Wallis) Largest wine canton, in dry, sunny upper Rhône Valley, best MARSANNE, SYRAH rival French legends. Many exquisite local varieties. Plenty of gd family estates. Youngsters incl Mathilde Roux, Cave de l'Orlaya (Fully); Romain Cipolla (Raron); Sandrine Caloz (Miège).

Vaud (Waadt) The 2nd largest wine canton, on shores of Lake Geneva. Family estates known for conservative spirit. Big houses incl Bolle, Hammel, Obrist, SCHENK. *See* CHABLAIS, LA CÔTE, LAVAUX.

Ville de Lausanne Vd ★★→★★★ Five important estates (together 36 ha) owned by commune of Lausanne. Most famous: Clos des Moines and Clos des Abbayes in DÉZALEY. In conversion to bio.

Visperterminen Val ★→★★★ Upper VAL vyds, esp for HEIDA. One of highest vyds in Europe (at 1000m/3281ft+; called Riben). Try CHANTON, ST. JODERN KELLEREI.

Yvorne Vd ★★→★★★ CHABLAIS village with vyds on detritus of 1584 avalanche, eg. BADOUX, Ch Maison Blanche, Commune d'Yvorne, Dom de l'Ovaille.

Zündel, Christian Tic ★★★→★★★★ Bio estate, 4 ha, at Beride. Perfectionist Christian Z now joined by daughter Myra. Wines of purity and finesse, esp MERLOT/CAB SAUV Orizzonte and CHARDS Velabona, Dosso.

Zürich Biggest city, and largest wine-growing canton in German Switzerland, 610 ha. Mainly BLAUBURGUNDER. Best: Besson-Strasser, E Meier, Gehring, Lüthi, PIRCHER, SCHWARZENBACH, Staatskellerei, Zahner. Even the city has several vyds: the Bürgli-Enge site (Landolt) is only 1.5 km (1 mile) away from central Paradeplatz.

Zürichsee Zür, Schw Dynamic AOC uniting vyds of cantons ZÜRICH and Schwyz on shores of Lake Zürich. Best: Bachmann, Diederik, E Meier, Höcklistein, KLOSTER EINSIEDELN, Lüthi, Rütihof, Schipf, Schnorf, SCHWARZENBACH. Räuschling (autochthonous), MÜLLER-T, PINOT N and SPEZIALITÄTEN.

Zwaa Schaff ★★★ Collaboration: BAUMANN (calcareous, deep soil) and BAD OSTERFINGEN (light, gravelly). PINOT N 94' 09' 13' 15' 16 17 18; PINOT BL/CHARD equally long-lasting.

Wine regions
Switzerland has six major wine regions: VAL, VD, GENEVA, TIC, Trois Lacs (NEU, Bienne/BER, Vully/FRIBOURG) and German Switzerland (Aar, GRIS, SCHAFF, St Gallen, Thur, ZÜR and some smaller wine cantons).

Austria

Abbreviations used in the text:

Burgen	Burgenland
Carn	Carnuntum
Kamp	Kamptal
Krems	Kremstal
Nied	Niederösterreich
Stei	Steiermark
S Stei	Südsteiermark
Therm	Thermenregion
Trais	Traisental
V Stei	Vulkanland Steiermark
Wach	Wachau
Wag	Wagram
Wein	Weinviertel
W Stei	Weststeiermark

Spurred by global success and a series of good vintages, Austria's pristine, clear-cut wines are winning more and more friends; not least because even entry-level wines share that taut purity of style. Wine producers are mostly family-owned and artisanal, and use a unique mix of indigenous and international varieties: it's a winning formula, and allows for some lively experiments in vineyard and cellar. Are there regional styles? Yes, definitely. What might at first look like fragmentation (all those small growers doing their own thing) has been organized into a legal framework that helps define regional identities. What started in 2002 with one DAC, or Districtus Austriae Controllatus, is now a steadily growing list of 16 regional appellations, all linked to provenance and grape variety. A recent addition is the historic sweet wine from the town of Rust, known as Ausbruch; *see* the entries below for others.

Recent vintages

2020 Some disease pressure and some hail. Balanced and classic.
2019 Dream vintage boasting both ripeness and freshness.
2018 The heatwave yr: ripe wines. Gd and plentiful.
2017 Gd juicy, rounded wines.
2016 Lovely fruit expression, fine freshness, but choose growers carefully.
2015 V.gd quality. Full-bodied, ripe, with the stuffing to age.
2014 Difficult, cooler yr. Tread carefully.
Don't hesitate to try more mature vintages from known producers.

Allram Kamp ★★★ 16 17 19 Exquisitely expressive GRÜNER V (esp Renner, Gaisberg), RIES Heiligenstein.

Alzinger Wach ★★★★ 10 13 15 16 17 Most clear-cut, crystalline, long-lived style of RIES; spicy GRÜNER V.

Ambrositsch, Jutta Vienna ★★ VIENNA's only *garagiste;* delicious field blends.

Artner Carn ★★★ 15 16 17 Wonderfully silky, sumptuous reds, varietals and blends.

Atzberg Wach ★★★ Impressive high-altitude re-cultivation project of abandoned vyds under the auspices of GRITSCH family and a Viennese property investor.

Ausbruch Quality/style designation for Prädikat wine; restricted to RUST and botrytized, dried grapes. Min must weight 27°KMW or 138.6°Oechsle. DAC 2020.

Ausg'steckt ("Hung out") Greenery and branches hung prominently outside traditionally signal that a HEURIGE or Buschenschank is open.

Bauer, Anton Wag ★★★★ Master of profound, spicy GRÜNER V: single-vyds Rosenberg, Spiegel. Bold reds but purist PINOT N.

Braunstein, Birgit Burgen ★★★ 15 16 17 19 Individualistic bio star of LEITHABERG. Wonderful BLAUFRÄNKISCH. Try amphora-aged series Magna Mater.

Bründlmayer, Willi Kamp ★★★★ 10 13 15 17 19 Iconic KAMP producer of pristine entry-level to world-class GRÜNER V, RIES, esp Heiligenstein Lyra, Alte Reben. Also fine Sekt, francophile PINOT N.

Burgenland Federal state and wine region bordering Hungary. Warmer than NIED, hence reds like BLAUFRÄNKISCH, ST-LAURENT, ZWEIGELT prevalent. Shallow NEUSIEDLERSEE, eg. at RUST, creates ideal botrytis conditions.

Carnuntum Nied Previously unsung region se of VIENNA now blossoming with accomplished fresh reds, esp ZWEIGELT marketed as Rubin Carnuntum. Look out for BLAUFRÄNKISCH from Spitzerberg. Best: G Markowitsch, MUHR, NETZL, TRAPL.

Christ Vienna ★★★ Leading light of VIENNA and favourite HEURIGE. Exquisite GEMISCHTER SATZ and unusual red blends.

DAC (Districtus Austriae Controllatus) Provenance- and quality-based appellation system denoting regionally typical wines and styles. Creation of 1st DAC 2002, WEIN, prompted regional quality turnaround. Currently 16 DACs: EISENBERG, KAMP, KREMS, LEITHABERG, MITTELBURGENLAND, NEUSIEDLERSEE, Rosalia, S STEI, TRAIS, V STEI, Wein, Wiener GEMISCHTER SATZ, W STEI. Latest: CARN, WACH, RUSTer AUSBRUCH.

Domäne Wachau Wach ★★★ World-leading co-op with enviable vyds. Clean-cut and expressive, purist style. Whistle-clean GRÜNER V, RIES, esp Achleiten, Kellerberg. Always great value. Try experimental marble-aged Grüner V Steinwerk.

Ebner-Ebenauer Wein ★★★ More expressive each yr. Driving force in WEIN. Single-vyd GRÜNER V, old-vine ST-LAURENT, elegant PINOT N. Fine Blanc de Blancs Brut Nature.

Eichinger, Birgit Kamp ★★★ Consistently outstanding RIES, esp Heiligenstein, unusually spicy and sleek GRÜNER V, esp Hasel.

Eisenberg Burgen Small DAC (since 2009) restricted to BLAUFRÄNKISCH from local slate soil. Powerful but elegant.

Erste Lage Single-vyd quality designation in CARN, KAMP, KREMS, TRAIS, VIENNA, WAG: 62 member estates with 81 sites classified as Erste Lage, ongoing process. *See* ÖTW.

Brilliant blends

Austria has always had a fine line in blends. First and foremost GEMISCHTER SÄTZE, or field blends. Most are white but try juicy, vivid red Querfeldein by **Gebeshuber**. The historic marriage of SPÄTROT/ ROTGIPFLER in THERM made GUMPOLDSKIRCHEN *the* wine village of Austria. Try **Christian Fischer**'s concentrated, aromatic version. The 80s and 90s saw powerful BURGEN reds come to the fore: indigenous BLAUFRÄNKISCH and ZWEIGELT blended with international varieties. **Andreas Gsellmann**'s structured, plummy **Gabarinza** uses MERLOT to great effect. From this followed the PANNOBILE idea of blending indigenous reds only. **Paul Achs'** Lust&Leben is a great example.

Federspiel Wach VINEA WACHAU middle category of ripeness, min 11.5%, max 12.5% alc. Understated, gastronomic wines as age-worthy as SMARAGD.

Feiler-Artinger Burgen ★★★★ Intuitive bio-winemaker of fine-boned reds and stellar AUSBRUCH in historic Baroque house in town centre of RUST.

Gemischter Satz Vienna Revived historic concept of co-planted and co-fermented field-blend of white varieties. Complex, "winey" wines. Prevalent in WEIN and VIENNA: determined producers achieved DAC status in 2013 for Vienna. No variety to exceed 50%. Look for AMBROSITSCH, CHRIST, GROISS, WIENINGER.

V. little Ruster Ausbruch 2019: flocks of starlings ate the lot. Gd yr for starling stew?

Geyerhof Krems ★★★ World-class estate with super-bio credentials. Wonderful GRÜNER V, RIES, notable entry-level Stockwerk.

Gritsch Mauritiushof Wach ★★★ Always vividly fruit-driven, concentrated RIES, esp 1000-Eimerberg vyd. Peppery GRÜNER V in quaint town of Spitz. Winemaker for ATZBERG project.

Groiss, Ingrid Wein ★★★ Known for reviving old vyds, this WEIN youngster specialises in GEMISCHTER SATZ and peppery GRÜNER V. Lovely rosé Hasenhaide.

Grosse Lage Stei Highest vyd classification in STEI; work still in progress along Danube (*see* ERSTE LAGE).

Gruber-Röschitz Wein ★★★ Unusually for WEIN this sibling-run bio-estate also makes racy RIES from granite soils, fine GRÜNER V.

Gumpoldskirchen Therm Once famed, still popular HEURIGEN village s of VIENNA. Home to white rarities ZIERFANDLER, ROTGIPFLER.

Gut Oggau Burgen ★★★★ Not only the labels are eye-catching at this bio estate.

Hager, Matthias Kamp ★★★ Longstanding bio icon. Try GRÜNER V Mollands, exquisite TBA and Eiswein, and unsulphured Urgestein.

Harkamp S Stei ★★★ STEI's best traditional method Sekt, try long-aged Große Res.

Hartl, Heinrich Therm ★★★ Rising THERM star specializing in sinuous PINOT N and champion of indigenous whites ZIERFANDLER, ROTGIPFLER.

Heinrich, Gernot Burgen ★★★★ PANNOBILE member, made his name with powerful BLAUFRÄNKISCH; new focus on compelling, skin-fermented whites.

Heinrich, J Burgen ★★★ 10 15 19 Wonderful BLAUFRÄNKISCH at every level. Juicy, bright entry-level; smooth, brooding single vyds, esp Goldberg.

Heuriger Wine of most recent harvest. **Heurige**: homely tavern where growers serve own wines with rustic, local food often in the open air – integral to Austrian culture. Called Buschenschank outside Vienna. *See* AUSG'STECKT.

Hiedler Kamp ★★★ Beautifully crafted, spicy GRÜNER V, esp Thal and Kittmannsberg.

Hirsch Kamp ★★★ 15 17 19 Consistently overdelivering RIES, GRÜNER V from Heiligenstein, Lamm. Fun entry-level GRÜNER V Hirschvergnügen.

Hirtzberger, Franz Wach ★★★★ 08 10 13 14 15 19 Iconic producer in Spitz, instrumental in defining WACH style. Known for opulence; dialling into elegance now. Outstanding single-vyd RIES, GRÜNER V, esp Honivogl, Singerriedel.

Huber, Markus Trais ★★★ Emblematic of the fine-boned TRAIS style from limestone soils with RIES, GRÜNER V. Citrus brilliance, radiance, slenderness.

Illmitz Burgen A SE SEEWINKEL town on NEUSIEDLERSEE, famous for BA, TBA (*see* Germany). Best from KRACHER.

Jalits Burgen ★★★ An est EISENBERG estate; concentrated, complex BLAUFRÄNKISCH, single-vyds Szapary and Diabas long-lived.

Jamek, Josef Wach ★★★★ Stalwart and WACH institution, once again in top tier, esp RIES, GRÜNER V from single-vyds Achleiten, Klaus.

Johanneshof Reinisch Therm ★★★ Three Reinisch brothers embody THERM by championing local specialities ROTGIPFLER, ZIERFANDLER. Deservedly famous for long-lived PINOT N, world-class for ST-LAURENT.

Jurtschitsch Kamp ★★★★ Young German-Austrian couple pushing boundaries in bio farming and invigorating KAMP with stellar site interpretations of single-vyds Heiligenstein, Käferberg, Loiserberg.

Kamptal Nied Wine region along Danube tributary Kamp n of WACH; rounder style, lower hills. Top vyds: Heiligenstein, Lamm. Best: BRÜNDLMAYER, EICHINGER, HIEDLER, HIRSCH, JURTSCHITSCH, LOIMER, SCHLOSS GOBELSBURG. DAC for GRÜNER V, RIES.

Klosterneuburg Wag Wine town in WAG, seat of 1860-founded viticultural college and research institute. *See* next entry.

KMW Abbreviation for KLOSTERNEUBURGER Mostwaage ("must level"), Austrian unit denoting must weight, ie. sugar content of grape juice. 1°KMW = 4.86°Oe (*see* Germany). 20°Bx = 83°Oe.

Knoll, Emmerich Wach ★★★★ 05 06 07 08 10 15 19 WACH icon perpetuating a tradition of cool, expressive purity in *Ries*, GRÜNER V. Single-vyd Ried Schütt emblematic of crystalline style. Look out for long-lived Vinothekfüllung bottlings.

Kracher Burgen ★★★★ 05 07 08 10 15 16 Towering genius of botrytized wines. Unoaked range is Zwischen den Seen, oak-matured range is Nouvelle Vague. Dazzling array of super complex, deliriously sweet wines across varieties.

Kremstal Wine region and DAC for GRÜNER V, RIES. Top: MALAT, MOSER, NIGL, SALOMON-UNDHOF, STIFT GÖTTWEIG, WEINGUT STADT KREMS.

Krutzler Burgen ★★★ 11 13 15 16 Local icon for highly concentrated, bold, big BLAUFRÄNKISCH, esp cult wine Perwolff.

Lagler Wach ★★★ Under-the-radar, elegant RIES, GRÜNER V, rare NEUBURGER SMARAGD.

Leithaberg Burgen Important DAC on n shore of NEUSIEDLERSEE, limestone and schist soils. Red restricted to BLAUFRÄNKISCH, some of Austria's best, whites can be GRÜNER V, PINOT BL, CHARD or NEUBURGER.

Lesehof Stagård Krems ★★★ Austro-Swedish winemaker on a mission for pure, bold, electric single-vyd RIES.

Loimer, Fred Kamp ★★★★ 10 13 15 19 Individualistic bio producer of long standing. Famed for RIES, GRÜNER V, esp single-vyds Heiligenstein, Steinmassl. Increasingly elegant PINOT N and *lovely sparkling*, both NV and vintage.

Malat Krems ★★★→★★★★ Clean-cut, concentrated RIES, GRÜNER V, esp single-vyds Gottschelle, Silberbichl. Pioneering PINOT N producer.

Mantlerhof Krems ★★★ Sumptuous, rounded GRÜNER V from bio-farmed loess soils.

Mayer am Pfarrplatz Vienna ★★ Heiligenstadt institution. HEURIGE where Beethoven wrote his 3rd symphony, now tourist heaven. Try single-vyd RIES Alsegg.

Mittelburgenland Burgen DAC (since 2005) on Hungarian border: structured, age-worthy BLAUFRÄNKISCH. Producers: GESELLMANN, J HEINRICH, Kerschbaum, WENINGER.

Moric Burgen ★★★★ 10 11 13 15 19 Cult producer, unrelenting focus, deservedly famed for BLAUFRÄNKISCH; note old-vine single-vyds Neckenmarkt, Lutzmannsburg.

Moser, Lenz Krems ★→★★ Austria's largest producer and négociant.

Muhr Carn ★★★ PR-cum-winemaker reviving limestone slopes of Spitzerberg. Unforced yet profound BLAUFRÄNKISCH of rare, scented beauty.

Netzl, Franz & Christine Carn ★★★ Ambitious father-daughter team, sumptuous reds, both varietal ZWEIGELT, esp Haidacker, and blends.

Neumeister V Stei ★★★★ 12 15 18 19 World-class address for aromatic whites. Outstanding SAUV BL, esp single-vyds Klausen, Moarfeitl. Look for Stradener Alte Reben. Also notable GEWÜRZ.

Neusiedlersee (Lake Neusiedl) Burgen Largest European steppe-lake and nature reserve on Hungarian border. Lake mesoclimate and humidity key to botrytis. Eponymous DAC limited to ZWEIGELT and sweet wines, botrytized or not.

Niederösterreich (Lower Austria) A ne region comprising three parts: Danube (KAMP, KREM, TRAIS, WACH, WAG), WEIN (ne) and CARN, THERM (s); 59% Austria's vyds.

Nigl Krems ★★★★ Vivid, expressive, flavour-laden RIES, GRÜNER V, esp Privat bottlings.

Nikolaihof Wach ★★★★ 08 10 13 15 17 19 One of world's first bio wine estates. Influential and groundbreaking. Exemplary, pure, textured RIES, GRÜNER V; look out for late-release Vinothek series.

Nittnaus, Anita & Hans Burgen ★★★★ PANNOBILE member and bio-pioneer with ever increasing precision in single-vyd BLAUFRÄNKISCH from Jungenberg, Lange Ohn, Tannenberg. Enticing entry-level Kalk & Schiefer. Famous for MERLOT blends.

Nittnaus, Hans & Christine Burgen ★★★ Estate famed for reds and sweet. Esp ZWEIGELT Heideboden, BLAUFRÄNKISCH Edelgrund; red blend Nit'ana; otherworldly TBA and thrilling Eiswein.

Ott, Bernhard Wag ★★★★ Iconic bio producer, salty, savoury GRÜNER V of increasingly fine-boned elegance, esp Rosenberg, Spiegel, Stein vyds. Fass 4 has cult status.

ÖTW (Österreichische Traditionsweingüter) Kamp, Krems, Trais, Wag Private association working on vyd classification. Currently 62 member estates and 81 classified sites. *See* ERSTE LAGE, GROSSE LAGE; excludes WACH.

Pannobile Burgen Association of nine progressive NEUSIEDLERSEE quality growers centred on Gols. Pannobile bottlings may only use indigenous reds (ZWEIGELT, BLAUFRÄNKISCH, ST-LAURENT), whites only PINOTS BL, GR, CHARD. Members: Achs, Beck, HEINRICH, NITTNAUS, PITTNAUER, PREISINGER.

Pfaffl Wein ★★→★★★ 15 16 19 Large, enterprising négociant/grower. Gd RES and opulent single vyds but famed for ultra-successful brand The Dot Austrian Pepper, Austrian Cherry, etc.

Wachau terraced vyds need c.1200 hrs work/ha/yr; flat vyds need just 200.

Pichler, Franz X Wach ★★★★ 08 10 13 15 19 Storied estate, long-lived RIES, GRÜNER V, from top WACH sites. Cult Ries Unendlich. Ultra-rare Gelber MUSKATELLER.

Pichler, Rudi Wach ★★★★ 10 13 15 17 19 Magnificent, clear-cut RIES, GRÜNER V from top sites Achleiten, Steinriegl.

Pichler-Krutzler Wach ★★★ Reliably energetic and thrilling *Ries* from WACH single vyds, esp In der Wand, Kellerberg.

Pittnauer, Gerhard Burgen ★★★★ Continuous evolution at this thoughtful wunderkind of reinvention. Rare talent for long-lived, elegant ST-LAURENT, fun bottlings of skin-fermented MashPitt, refreshing pét-nat.

Prager, Franz Wach ★★★★ 10 13 14 15 Toni Bodenstein is erudite éminence grise of WACH; philosopher/winemaker with spellbinding RIES, GRÜNER V, esp Stockkultur.

Preisinger, Claus Burgen ★★★ Hip but grounded bio-winemaker with both serious and fun offerings like crown-capped Puszta Libre.

Prieler Burgen ★★★★ Leading light of quality revolution in 80s. Famed for muscular BLAUFRÄNKISCH requiring bottle age, esp Goldberg, Marienthal; lesser known for compelling age-worthy, profound PINOT BL.

Proidl, A&F Krems ★★★ Reliably brilliant RIES, GRÜNER V, both from Ehrenfels. Look out for library Ries releases.

Rebenhof S Stei ★★★ Exciting, vivid skin-fermented whites from bio luminary Hartmut Aubell.

Reserve (Res) Attribute for min 13% alc and prolonged (cask) ageing.

Ried Vyd. As of 2016 compulsory term for single-vyd bottlings.

Rust Burgen Fortified C17 town on NEUSIEDLERSEE. Watch for noisy nesting storks. Famous for Ruster AUSBRUCH. Top: FEILER-ARTINGER, SCHRÖCK, TRIEBAUMER.

Sabathi, Hannes S Stei ★★★ Leading estate, esp single-vyd SAUV BL Kranachberg.

Salomon-Undhof Krems ★★★→★★★★ Consistently sleek, elegant, slender GRÜNER V, RIES, single-vyds Kögl, Pfaffenberg, Wachtberg. Fun pét-nat, summery pink fizz.

Sattlerhof S Stei ★★★★ 12 15 18 19 Effortlessly brilliant, world-class, creamy, age-worthy SAUV BL, MORILLON, esp single-vyds Kranachberg, Sernauberg.

Sax Kamp ★★★ Winemaking twins producing uncommonly savoury GRÜNER V.

Schauer S Stei ★★★ Utterly light-bodied but consistently profound whites. RIES, SAUV BL and esp notable PINOT BL Höchtemmel.

Schiefer & Doms Kilger Burgen ★★★ Savoury, unusual, individualistic BLAUFRÄNKISCH in EISENBERG; expressive, transparent WELSCHRIESLING.

Schilcher W St Racy, peppery rosé of local importance from indigenous Blauer Wildbacher grape, speciality of w STEI. Also try sparkling version.

Schilfwein (Strohwein) Sweet wine made from grapes dried on reeds from NEUSIEDLERSEE. *Schilf* = reed, *Stroh* = straw.

Schloss Gobelsburg Kamp ★★★★ 13 14 15 16 Cistercian-founded mansion and estate making exquisite RIES, GRÜNER V under quality-champion Michael Moosbrugger. Notable Tradition series and single-vyds Gaisberg, Heiligenstein, Lamm, Renner. Fine sparkling. Also elegant ZWEIGELT, PINOT N.

Schlumberger C19 Sekt pioneer. Today high-volume, value producer of traditional method fizz. Try sparkling GRÜNER V.

Schmelz Wach ★★★ Exquisite, authentic wines strangely below the radar.

Schödl Loidesthal Wein ★★ Three ambitious siblings with vivacious WEIN offering. Super-savoury GRÜNER V In den Kreuthern.

Schröck, Heidi Burgen ★★★★ Doyenne of RUST speciality AUSBRUCH on mission to broaden its food-pairing appeal, also notable dry FURMINT.

Seewinkel Burgen ("Lake corner") nature reserve and region e of NEUSIEDLERSEE; ideal conditions for botrytis.

Smaragd Wach Ripest category of VINEA WACHAU, min 12.5% alc but can exceed 14%, dry, potent, age-worthy. Often botrytis-influenced but dry. Named after emerald (=Smaragd) lizard.

Spätrot-Rotgipfler Therm Blend of ROTGIPFLER/Spätrot (ZIERFANDLER). Aromatic, weighty, textured. Typical for GUMPOLDSKIRCHEN. *See* Grapes chapter.

Spitz an der Donau Wach Bijou town at cool w end of WACH on Danube. Famous vyds Singerriedel, 1000-Eimerberg. GRITSCH MAURITIUSHOF, HIRTZBERGER, LAGLER.

Stadlmann Therm ★★★ Exemplary, clear-cut ZIERFANDLER/ROTGIPFLER, esp single-vyds Tagelsteiner, Mandelhöh. Subtle, poetic PINOT N.

Steiermark (Styria) Most s region of Austria, known for aromatic, expressive dry whites, esp SAUV BL. *See* S STEI, V STEI, W STEI.

Steinfeder Wach Lightest VINEA WACHAU category for dry wines of max 11.5% alc. Named after fragrant Steinfeder grass. Increasingly difficult/impossible to produce in warming conditions, barely exported.

Stift Göttweig ★★→★★★ Prominent hilltop Benedictine abbey surrounded by vyds; quality ethos, crystalline RIES, GRÜNER V from single-vyds Gottschelle, Silberbichl.

Strobl, Clemens Wag ★★ Ex-marketer Strobl has been an impressive newcomer on WAG loess and gravel. Expressive PINOT N.

Südsteiermark (South Styria) STEI region close to Slovenian border, famed for light but highly aromatic MORILLON, MUSKATELLER, SAUV BL from breathtakingly steep slopes. DAC (2018). Best growers: SABATHI, SATTLERHOF, TEMENT, WOHLMUTH.

Tement, Manfred S Stei ★★★★ 12 13 15 17 18 19 Incredible subtlety and age-worthiness. Esp SAUV BL, MORILLON. Top sites: Grassnitzberg, Zieregg. Look out for Zieregg RES Sauv Bl made only in exceptional yrs.

Thermenregion Nied Spa region e of VIENNA centred on GUMPOLDSKIRCHEN, home to

---

Essence of Mitteleuropa

BLAUFRÄNKISCH is Mitteleuropa's noble grape, of real structure and ageability. It's deeply ingrained in all Central European wine cultures. For Austria's winemakers, it's the red grape that speaks most eloquently of place. Try these growers for size: HANS & ANITA NITTNAUS, KRUTZLER, MORIC, MUHR, TRAPL, WACHTER-WIESLER, WAGENTRISTL.

indigenous ZIERFANDLER, ROTGIPFLER; historic PINOT N hotspot. Producers: Alphart, HARTL, JOHANNESHOF REINISCH, STADLMANN.

Tinhof, Erwin Burgen ★★★ Below-the-radar but exquisite bio LEITHABERG estate. BLAUFRÄNKISCH Gloriette from old vines and ST-LAURENT Feuersteig. Also specialist for PINOT BL, NEUBURGER from Golden Erd vyd.

Traisental Nied Tiny district s of KREMS. Notable for limestone soils lending finesse. Top: HUBER, Neumayer.

Until the 80s Sauv Bl was known as Muskat-Sylvaner in Austria.

Trapl, Johannes Carn ★★★ Brilliant wunderkind with a flair for poetic, expressive, site-specific reds. Floral BLAUFRÄNKISCH, esp Sitzerberg and PINOT-esque ZWEIGELT.

Triebaumer, Ernst Burgen ★★★★ 08 09 10 12 15 17 Iconic RUST producer, now led by his progressive children. Try skin-fermented Urwerk series.

Tschida Burgen Cult star in natural wine circles. Notable ZWEIGELT/CAB SAUV Himmel auf Erden.

Umathum, Josef Burgen ★★★★ 13 15 16 17 Bio pioneer, now legend. Exceptionally elegant reds. Probably Austria's best ZWEIGELT: single-vyd Hallebühl. Also BLAUFRÄNKISCH Kirschgarten.

Velich ★★★ Publicity-shy SEEWINKEL producer with cult following for CHARD Tiglat.

Veyder-Malberg Wach ★★★ Boutique WACH producer specializing in old vines from 4 ha of tiny parcels. RIES, GRÜNER V.

Vienna (Wien) Capital boasting 637 ha vyds within city limits. Ancient tradition, reignited quality focus. Local field-blend tradition enshrined as DAC GEMISCHTER SATZ (2013). *Heurigen among vines; must visit.* Try: CHRIST, Lenikus, WIENINGER, Zahel.

Vinea Wachau Wach Pioneering quality WACH growers' association est 1983. Strict charter with three-tier ripeness scale for dry wine: FEDERSPIEL, SMARAGD, STEINFEDER.

Vulkanland Steiermark (Southeast Styria) Formerly Süd-Oststeiermark, DAC (2018), famous for GEWURZ. Best: NEUMEISTER, Winkler-Hermaden.

Wachau Nied Danube region of world repute for age-worthy RIES, GRÜNER V. Top: ALZINGER, DOMÄNE WACHAU, F PICHLER, HIRTZBERGER, JAMEK, KNOLL, NIKOLAIHOF, PICHLER-KRUTZLER, PRAGER, R PICHLER, Tegernseerhof, VEYDER-MALBERG.

Wachter-Wiesler, Weingut Burgen ★★★ Defining producer of sinuous, concentrated but elegant EISENBERG BLAUFRÄNKISCH, also WELSCHRIESLING.

Wagentristl Burgen ★★→★★★ Rising star, esp PINOT N, BLAUFRÄNKISCH.

Wagram Nied Region just w of VIENNA, incl KLOSTERNEUBURG. Deep loess soils ideal for GRÜNER V and increasingly also PINOT N. Best: BAUER, Leth, OTT, STROBL.

Weingut Stadt Krems Krems ★★→★★★ Brilliant municipal wine estate with 31 ha vyds within city limits. Same exacting winemaker as STIFT GÖTTWEIG.

Weinviertel ("Wine Quarter") Austria's largest wine region, 13,858 ha between Danube and Czech border, eponymous DAC for GRÜNER V. Region once slaked VIENNA's thirst, now quality counts. Try: EBNER-EBENAUER, GROISS, GRUBER-RÖSCHITZ, PFAFFL, SCHÖDL, LOIDESTHAL.

Weninger, Franz Burgen ★★★★ 10 13 15 16 17 Brilliant, brooding BLAUFRÄNKISCH, esp single-vyds Hochäcker, Kirchholz.

Werlitsch S Stei ★★★ Ewald Tscheppe one of s STEI's natural wine stars. Try SAUV BL/ CHARD blend Ex Vero.

Weststeiermark (West Styria) Small region specializing in SCHILCHER. New DAC 2018.

Weszeli Kamp ★★★ Quiet star of concentrated RIES, GRÜNER V, esp Schenkenbichl.

Wieninger, Fritz Vienna ★★★★ 13 14 15 16 18 Driving force behind VIENNA renaissance and bio pioneer. Exemplary GEMISCHTER SATZ from Nussberg, Rosengartl. Great PINOT N. Viennese HEURIGE among Nussberg vines an institution.

Wohlmuth S Stei ★★★★ Stellar, subtle but dazzling CHARD, RIES, SAUV BL, esp single-vyds Edelschuh, Gola, Hochsteinriegl; recultivating steep Dr Wunsch vyd.

England

The number of good, recommendable sparklers continues to rise, with a top layer of serious quality. Still is improving, but fizz is the star. The best English fizz shouldn't be drunk too young, and benefits from bottle-age; it's worth buying some and tucking it away for a year or so. Alternatively try and find something from 15 or earlier, which will be drinking beautifully. Warmer summers help temper the English acidity, and while there is a local style of apples and flowers, Champagne is the model; and need not be ashamed of its English followers. My new favourite drink? English fizz with a dash of S African vermouth (specifically, Caperitif from AA Badenhorst). It's heaven. Abbreviations: Berkshire (Berks), Buckinghamshire (Bucks), Cornwall (Corn), East/West Sussex (E/W S'x), Hampshire (Hants), Herefordshire (Heref).

Gusbourne has a vyd called Heartbreak. Ideal for Valentine's Day?

Black Chalk Hants ★★★ Combines delicacy, accuracy; complex, v. elegant. Clever, evocative names too.

Breaky Bottom E S'x ★★★★ Wines named after artists, musicians loved by owners. Beautiful wines, all precision, depth, from tiny vyd.

Bride Valley Dorset ★★ Super-freshness is aim, not time on lees. Appley Brut, gd Bella rosé and Crémant. Gd still CHARD.

Busi Jacobsohn E S'x Chunky, flavoursome rather than graceful; gd rosé.

Camel Valley Corn ★★→★★★ Interesting rosé PINOT N Brut, vibrant Cornwall Brut; plenty of flavour, gd balance, gd value.

Chapel Down Kent Agreeable, commercial wines made in quantity. ★★ Kit's Coty range (still, sp).

Coates & Seely Hants ★★★ Weight plus finesse; lovely depth. Blanc de Noirs Perfide 14, a beauty; will age well.

Cottonworth Hants Gd length and depth here. Classic Cuvée is best.

Court Garden E S'x Rich style with bit of power. Subtle, taut Blanc de Blancs; elegant, biscuity Classic Cuvée; rich Blanc de Noirs. Rosé is red-fruited, crunchy.

Denbies Surrey Large and commercial, marked toastiness. Well-organized tourism: new vyd hotel.

Digby Hants, Kent, W S'x ★★★ Always delicious, made by Dermot SUGRUE under contract at WISTON, so gd pedigree. Res Brut crisp and taut; vintage Rosé ripe, red-fruit flavours.

Exton Park Hants ★★★ Brilliant new RB (Res Blend) wines with in-built maturity. Fine, precise, savoury.

Grange, The Hants ★★★ Impressive Brut, savoury and salty, from new winery in progress. Great opera too.

Greyfriars Surrey ★★ Best are balanced Classic Cuvée 13 and Blanc de Blancs 13. NV from CHARD/PINOTS N/M also worth a look.

Gusbourne Kent, W S'x ★★★ Gets better and better: ripeness, poise, precision, finesse. Savoury Blanc de Blancs 14, nicely aged.

Hambledon Vineyard Hants ★★★ Deep, sleek wines, gd complexity, poise. Rosé has weight, power. Meonhill is cheaper label.

Harrow & Hope Bucks ★★ Subtle, flavoursome Brut Res, sleek, poised Blanc de Blancs, stylish Brut Rosé.

Hart of Gold Her ★★ Rounded and biscuity; v. appealing Brut.

Hattingley Valley Hants ★★★ Gd balanced style; Classic Cuvée crisp, hedgerow fruit; gd still rosé too.

Henners E S'x ★★ Nice biscuity, reliable Brut and cherry-spice Rosé. Always elegant, delicate, structured. Pretty Native Grace still.

Herbert Hall Kent ★★→★★★ Lovely precision, tension, ripeness, v.gd length. A treat.

Hoffmann & Rathbone ★★ Using bought-in fruit, S'x-based. Sleek 12 Rosé (sp), and light, savoury Pinot N (still).

Hush Heath Estate Kent ★★★ Flagship Balfour Brut Rosé as gd as ever; Skye Blanc de Blancs superb. Noteworthy Winemaker's wines, incl light, pretty still reds. Well-organized tourism, with gd restaurant.

Jenkyn Place Hants ★★ Dermot SUGRUE makes these, so they're going to be gd. Grown-up, poised.

Langham Wine Estate Dorset Culver Classic Cuvée is young, fruity, balanced; gd savoury Corallian. On the up.

Leckford Estate Hants ★ Waitrose's own estate, vinified by RIDGEVIEW. Nicely mature, gd fruit, straightforward.

Litmus Made at DENBIES, outpaces host. Graceful orange BACCHUS, saline Element.

Nyetimber W S'x ★★★★ 1086 is the millionaire's choice; rest of us v. happy with depth, complexity of NV, excellent Classic Cuvée, Rosé with flesh and bones.

Plumpton College E S'x ★★ UK's only wine college; makes pretty wines with fruit. Gd still too.

Pommery England Hants Crisp, poised wines made at HATTINGLEY VALLEY until own vines come on stream.

Raimes Hants ★★ Gd fruit, tense, fresh style. Made at HATTINGLEY VALLEY. Blanc de Noirs has gd weight.

Rathfinny E S'x ★★★ Elegant, refined, precise wines; Blanc de Blancs esp gd. New light Classic Cuvée. Cradle Valley still is sappy, v. pretty. Look for gin and vermouth too.

Ridgeview E S'x ★★ Flavoursome, slightly more solid style; reliable. Various cuvées: tops are Blanc de Blancs, Blanc de Noirs, Rosé de Noirs. Contract maker of several brands.

Roebuck W S'x Newcomer; v.gd, well aged wines. Savoury, salty Classic Cuvée 14; food-friendly Blanc de Noirs 15.

Simpsons Kent ★★ Lovely Chalklands fizz and well-judged Blanc de Noirs, plus gd still wines. Heading upwards.

Stopham Estate W S'x Still better than sparkling. BACCHUS, PINOT GR competent and agreeable.

Sugrue E S'x ★★★★ England's best. Dermot S is winemaker at WISTON. His own The Trouble with Dreams now has a ripe zero dosage version, and Blanc de Blancs. Cuvée Dr Brendan O'Regan gives any de luxe cuvée you can think of a run for its money.

Trotton W S'x Spectacular Sparkling (that's the brand, not a description) elegant, fine, well made; gd still BACCHUS/PINOT GR.

Westwell Kent ★★★ Pure, taut, fine Pelegrim fizz; v.gd red Field PINOT N/CHARD with indigenous yeasts. Amphora Ortega pleasant.

Wiston W S'x ★★★★ Cleverly made by Dermot SUGRUE, superb elegance, finesse. Steely, tense style that shouldn't be opened too young. Blanc de Noirs a treat.

But still...

Where is English still wine going? The answer is, it depends on the weather. The last few summers have produced lovely PINOT NS – light, to be sure, but properly spicy and cherry-fruited. Seek them out. For whites, there's a lot of BACCHUS, but be cautious, unless you enjoy that strident note. An exception is Yotes Court, newly released. Other new to look for: Ashling Park Rosé; Heppington Vyd PINOT GR; Wayfarer CHARD.

ENGLAND

Central & Southeast Europe

More heavily shaded areas are the wine-growing regions.

Abbreviations used in the text:

Bal	Balaton	(U) Pann	(Upper) Pannonia
Cri & Mar	Crişana & Maramureş	Pod	Podravje
Cro Up	Croatian Uplands	Pos	Posavje
Dalm	Dalmatia	Prim	Primorje
Dan P	Danubian Plain	Sl & CD	Slavonia & Croatian Danube
Dob	Dobrogea	Thr L	Thracian Lowlands
Is & Kv	Istria & Kvarner	Tok	Tokaj
Mold	Moldovan Hills	Trnsyl	Transylvania
Mun	Muntenia & Oltenia Hills	U Hun	Upper Hungary

HUNGARY

Tokaji continues to be the motor driving Hungary's reputation in everything from fine fizz to gorgeous Aszú, but Hungary is not just Tokaji. It's a dynamic place of young winemakers and engaged consumers, along with a buzzing food culture. Rosé is being joined by orange wines, pét-nat and amphorae. Reds are moving on from extraction and oak, becoming increasingly refined. Hungary is, more and more, the place to go for quality in the region.

Aszú Tok Botrytis-shrivelled grapes and the resulting sweet wine from TOK. Legal min for Aszú is 120g/l residual sugar, equivalent to 5 PUTTONYOS (similar to Château d'Yquem). 6 Puttonyos category is even richer. Gd Aszú in 99' 05 06 07 08 09 13' 16 17 19. Late rains destroyed much of Aszú crop in 20.

Aszú Essencia / Eszencia Tok Term for 2nd-sweetest TOK level (7 PUTTONYOS+), not permitted since 2010. Do not confuse with ESSENCIA/ESZENCIA.

Badacsony Bal Volcanic slopes n of Lake Balaton; full, rich whites, esp rare and age-worthy KÉKNYELŰ. Look for Borbély, Gilvesy, Laposa, Sabar, Szászi, SZEREMLEY, ValiBor, Villa Sandahl.

Balassa Tok ★★★ Excellent FURMINT vyd selections, esp Mézes-Mály, Szent Tamás. Gorgeous Villő ASZÚ, SZAMORODNI.

Balatonboglár Bal Wine district s of Lake Balaton, also major winery of TÖRLEY. Gd: Budjosó, GARAMVÁRI, IKON, KONYÁRI, (bio) Kristinus, Légli Géza, Légli Otto, Pócz.

Barta Tok ★★★ Highest vyd in TOK, HQ in MÁD's historic Rákóczi mansion. Excellent dry whites, esp Öreg Király FURMINT. Gorgeous SZAMORODNI, ASZÚ (esp 16).

Béres Tok ★★→★★★ Past winner of most beautiful vyd in Hungary. (There's an award I bet you never knew existed.) V.gd ASZÚ and dry wines, esp Lőcse FURMINT.

Bikavér ★→★★★ Means "Bull's Blood". PDO only for EGER and SZEKSZÁRD. Always a blend, min four varieties. In Szekszárd, at least 5% KADARKA is compulsory, with min 45% KÉKFRANKOS, specified oak ageing. Look for: Eszterbauer (esp Tüke), HEIMANN, Meszáros, Sebestyén, TAKLER, Vestergombi, VIDA. Egri Bikavér is majority Kékfrankos and no grape more than 50%, oak-aged for min 6 mths. Superior and Grand Superior restricted yield, 12 mths in barrel. Best for Egri Bikavér: BOLYKI, Csutorás, DEMETER, GÁL TIBOR, Grof Buttler, ST ANDREA, Thummerer.

Bock, József Pann ★★→★★★ In VILLÁNY, making rich, full-bodied, oaked reds. Try: Bock CAB FR Fekete-Hegy, Bock & Roll, Ermitage.

Bolyki U Hun ★★ Dramatic winery in a quarry in EGER, great labels. V.gd Egri Csillag, Meta Tema, rosé and BIKAVÉR, esp Bolyki & Bolyki.

Csányi Pann ★→★★ Largest winery in VILLÁNY. Much improved entry-level varietals plus premium Ch Teleki, gd Kővilla CAB FR.

Csopak Bal Protected status for top vyd OLASZRIZLING; n of Lake Balaton. Béla És Bandi, Dobosi, Figula, Homola, Jasdi (esp single vyds), St Donát (Magma KÉKFRANKOS).

Cellar mould *Zusmidium cellare*, common in Tok, metabolizes ethanol from air.

Degenfeld, Grót Tok ★★→★★★ Hungary's most beautiful wine estate winner 2019. Sweet is best: Andante botrytis FURMINT, Fortissimo, 6 PUTTONYOS ASZÚ.

Demeter, Zoltán Tok ★★★★ Benchmark cellar for elegant, intense dry wines, esp Boda, Veres FURMINTS; excellent Szerelmi HÁRSLEVELŰ, lovely Őszhegy MUSCAT. V.gd PEZSGŐ (sp). Eszter late-harvest cuvée, superb ASZÚ.

Dereszla, Ch Tok ★★→★★★ Excellent ASZÚ. Gd dry FURMINT, Kabar. Also reliable PEZSGŐ. Rare flor-aged dry SZAMORODNI Experience.

DHC (Districtus Hungaricus Controllatus) Sub-category of Protected Designation of Origin (PDO): Oltalom alatt álló Eredetmegjelölés (OEM) in Hungary.

Disznókő Tok ★★★→★★★★ Dramatic estate with gd restaurant and consistently top-quality sweet, esp ASZÚ, superb *Kapi* cru in top yrs. V.gd 1413 SZAMORODNI. Inspiration dry white also recommended.

Dobogó Tok ★★★ Pretty family winery in TOKAJ town. Benchmark ASZÚ 6 PUTTONYOS and late-harvest Mylitta, excellent long-lived dry FURMINT and unusual but gd PINOT N Izabella Utca.

Dúló Named single vyd or cru. Top *dúló* in TOKAJ, incl Betsek, Bomboly, Király, Mézes-Mály, Nyúlászó, Szent Tamás, Úrágya.

Duna Duna Great Plain. Districts: Hajós-Baja (try Sümegi, Koch – also owns VinArt in VILLÁNY), Csongrád, Kunság (Frittmann, Font).

Eger U Hun Region for burgundian-style reds and elegant fresh whites, esp noted for Egri BIKAVÉR and Egri Csillag "Star of Eger", dry white blend of Carpathian grapes. Wineries worth trying: Csutorás, Gróf Buttler, Kaló Imre (natural), Pók Tamás, Thummerer, Tóth Ferenc.

Essencia / Eszencia Tok ★★★★ Legendary, luscious free-run juice from ASZÚ grapes, alc usually well below 5%, sugar (and price) off charts. Reputed to raise the dead.

Etyek-Buda U Pann Dynamic region, expressive, crisp whites, gd sparklers and promising PINOT N. Leading producers: ETYEKI KÚRIA, György-Villa, HARASZTHY, Kertész, Nyakas, Rókusfalvy.

Etyeki Kúria U Pann ★★ Leading winery in ETYEK-BUDA, producing v.gd SAUV BL, elegant reds. Winemaker Meresz Sandor also has natural project – gd Zenit.

Figula Bal ★★→★★★ Family winery nr CSOPAK, notable vyd selections of OLASZRIZLING, esp Öreghegy, Sáfránkert, Szákas. Excellent Köves (w blend).

Gál Tibor U Hun ★★ Try appealing Egri Csillag, fine KADARKA and vibrant, modern TiTi BIKAVÉR. Hugely improved with new cellar.

Hungarian oak forests are managed according to laws of King Zsigmond in 1456.

Garamvári Bal ★→★★★ Leading bottle-fermented fizz (previously Ch Vincent). Try Optimum Brut, FURMINT Brut Natur, PINOT N Evolution Rosé. Gd Garamvári range, esp SAUV BL, IRSAI OLIVÉR. Lellei label is consistent, great-value varietals.

Gere, Attila Pann ★★★→★★★★ Standard-setting family winery in VILLÁNY, some of country's best reds: Solus MERLOT, Kopar Cuvée, VILLÁNYI FRANC (CAB FR), Attila barrel selection. V.gd Fekete-Járdovány from rare historic grape. Reliable Cuvée Phoenix under Weninger-Gere label (joint venture with WENINGER Snr).

Gizella Tok ★★★ Superb small winery. Impeccable dry FURMINT, Barát HÁRSLEVELŰ, delicious SZAMORODNI.

Grand Tokaj ★→★★★ Biggest producer in TOK. New winery and innovative viticulture improved top wines, esp Arany Késői Late-Harvest, Dry FURMINT Kővágó DŰLŐ, v.gd ASZÚ. Winemaker Karoly Áts won Winemakers' Winemaker title in 2019.

Haraszthy U Hun ★★ Beautiful estate at ETYEK-BUDA, v.gd SAUV BL, zesty Sir Irsai (w).

Heimann Pann ★★→★★★ Impressive family winery in SZEKSZÁRD, esp intense Barbár, Franciscus. Fine KADARKA, Alte Reben KÉKFRANKOS.

Hétszőlő Tok ★★★ Historic cellar and stunning organic vyd, owned by Michel Reybier of Cos d'Estournel (B'x). Try elegant Kis-Garai Furmint, fine ASZÚ.

Heumann Pann ★★★ German/Swiss-owned estate in Siklós making great KÉKFRANKOS Res, CAB FR Trinitás, delicious rosé, classy SYRAH.

Hilltop Winery U Pann ★★ In Neszmély. Meticulous, value DYA varietals, Hilltop, Moonriver export labels. V.gd Kamocsay Premium range (CHARD, Ihlet Cuvée).

Holdvölgy Tok ★★→★★★ Super-modern winery in MÁD, noted for complex dry wines (esp Vision, Expression), plus v.gd Eloquence SZAMORODNI.

Ikon Bal ★★ Well-made wines from KONYÁRI and former Tihany abbey vyds. Try Evanglista CAB FR.

Juliet Victor Tok ★★★ Ambitious investment by founder of Wizzair. Already impressing with estate and vyd selection dry FURMINTS (notable **Bomboly** and Király) and superb rich SZAMORODNI.

Kikelet ★★★ Beautifully balanced wines from small family estate in Tarcal owned by French winemaker and her Hungarian husband.

Királyudvar Tok ★★★ Bio producer in old royal cellars at Tarcal. Top FURMINT Sec, Henye PEZSGŐ, Cuvée Ilona (late-harvest), flagship 6 PUTTONYOS Lapis ASZÚ.

Konyári Bal ★★→★★★ Gd family estate nr BAL. Try DYA rosé; Loliense (r/w). V.gd Jánoshegy KÉKFRANKOS, Páva.

Kovács Nimród Winery U Hun ★★→★★★ EGER producer, jazz-inspired labels. Try Battonage CHARD, Blues KÉKFRANKOS, Monopole Rhapsody, 777 PINOT N, NJK.

Kreinbacher Somió, Bal ★★→★★★ Hungary's best PEZSGŐ, always FURMINT blend. V.gd Classic Brut, superb Prestige Brut. Also gd still: Juhfark, Öreg Tőkék (old vines).

Mád Tok Historic wine-trading town with superb vyds, cellars. Mád Circle of leading producers: Árvay, Áts, BARTA, Budaházy, Demetervin (gd Mád FURMINT, Úrágya DŰLŐ), HOLDVÖLGY, JULIET VICTOR, Lenkey (unique long-aged and age-worthy wines), Mád Hill, MAD WINE, Orosz Gabor, Pelle, ROYAL TOKAJI, SZEPSY, Tokaji Classic.

MAD Wine Tok ★★ Sizeable winery (with handy café) named for village of MÁD. Refocused ranges under MAD label. Gd Dry FURMINT, late harvest, v.gd single-vyd Furmints and SZAMORODNI. MAD One for flagship wines.

Malatinszky Pann ★★★ Certified organic VILLÁNY cellar. Top long-lived Kúria *Cab Fr*, Kövesföld (r). Gd: Noblesse labels.

Mátra U Hun ★→★★ Region for decent-value, fresh whites, rosé and lighter reds. Better producers: Balint, Benedek, Gábor Karner, NAG, Nagygombos (rosé), NAGYRÉDE, Szöke Mátyás.

Mór U Pann Small region, famous for fiery local *Ezerjó*. Try ★★ Czetvei Winery.

Nagyréde U Hun ★ Gd-value, commercial DYA varietals under Nagyréde and MÁTRA Hill labels.

Oremus Tok ★★★→★★★★ Perfectionist Tolcsva winery, owned by Spain's Vega Sicilia, makes top ASZÚ; plus v.gd late harvest, SZAMORODNI and notable dry FURMINT Mandolás.

Pajzos-Megyer Tok ★★→★★★ French-owned, two estates under one management. Megyer for gd-value, bright, dry and late-harvest varietals and v.gd dry SZAMORODNI. Pajzos for premium dry and age-worthy ASZÚ.

Pannonhalma U Pann ★★→★★★ 800-yr-old Abbey winery. Tricollis range is gd value, consistent, fruity. V.gd RIES (esp Prior), SAUV BL, lovely Hemina (w).

Patricius Tok ★★→★★★ Beautiful estate. Consistent dry FURMINT, esp Selection, gd late-harvest Katinka, ASZÚ. Appealing PEZSGŐ.

Pendits Winery Tok ★★ Demeter-certified bio estate. Luscious long-ageing ASZÚ, pretty, dry DYA MUSCAT.

Pezsgő Hungarian for sparkling – a growing trend. Since 2017 must be bottle-fermented if PDO TOK.

Puttonyos (putts) Traditional indication of sweetness in TOK ASZÚ. Based on number of 25 kg buckets or hods (*puttony*) of ASZÚ grapes added to a 136-litre barrel (*gönci*) of base must or wine.

Royal Tokaji Wine Co Tok ★★★→★★★★ MÁD winery that led renaissance of TOK in 1990 (Hugh Johnson was co-founder). Excellent 6-PUTTONYOS single-vyd bottlings: esp Betsek, *Mézes-Mály*, Nyulászó, *Szent Tamás*. Blue and Red Labels are benchmark 5-puttonyos blends. Also appealing gd-value Late Harvest.

St Andrea U Hun ★★★→★★★★ Leading name in EGER for modern, high-quality BIKAVÉR (Áldás, Hangács, Merengő, Igazán). Gd white blends: Napbor, Örökké and delicious Szeretettel rosé. Flagships: Mária (w) and Nagy-Eged-Hegy (r). New Axios Bikavér made by son.

Sauska Pann, Tok ★★→★★★★ Immaculate wineries in VILLÁNY, TOK. V.gd KADARKA, KÉKFRANKOS, CAB FR and impressive red blends, esp Cuvée 7 and Cuvée 5. Also Sauska-Tok with focus on excellent dry whites, esp Medve and Birsalmás FURMINTS. V.gd PEZSGŐ Extra Brut (w/rosé).

Somló Bal Dramatic extinct volcano famous for long-lived, austere whites esp Juhfark (sheep's tail). Region of small producers, esp Fekete, Györgykovács, Kolonics, Royal Somló, Somlói Apátsági, Somlói Vándor, Spiegelberg. Bigger TORNAI, *Kreinbacher* also v.gd.

Sopron U Pann On Austrian border overlooking Lake Fertő. KÉKFRANKOS most important. Bio WENINGER is excellent, maverick Ráspi for natural wines. Also Luka, Pfneiszl, Taschner.

Budapest Metro is oldest underground electrified railway in Europe.

Szamorodni Tok Name of Polish origin for TOK made from whole bunches, with botrytis or not. Gaining popularity since 3 and 4 PUTTONYOS ASZÚ stopped – seen as more authentically Tok than late harvest. *Édes* or sweet style is min 45g/l sugar (usually sweeter), 6 mths oak ageing. Try BALASSA, BARTA, Bott, GIZELLA, HOLDVÖLGY, JULIET VICTOR, KIKELET, MAD WINE, OREMUS, Pelle, SZEPSY. Best dry (*szaraz*) versions are flor-aged like Sherry; try CH DERESZLA, Karádi-Berger, *Tinon*.

Szekszárd Pann Famous rich reds. Increasing focus on BIKAVÉR, KÉKFRANKOS, reviving lighter KADARKA. Dúzsi (rosé), Eszterbauer (Nagyapám Kadarka, Tüke Bikavér), HEIMANN, Lajver, Remete-Bor (Kadarka), Sebestyén (Ivan-Volgyi Bikavér), Szent Gaál, TAKLER, Tüske, Vesztergombi (Csaba's Cuvée, Turul), VIDA.

Szepsy, István Tok ★★★★ Brilliant, soil-obsessed, no-compromise 17th-/18th-generation producer in MÁD. Focus: dry FURMINT (Urbán, Bányász, Percze, Szent Tamás DŰLŐ), excellent sweet SZAMORODNI. Superb ASZÚ incl new single-vyd releases.

Should Tok Aszú be classified as orange wine? White grapes, extended skin contact.

Szeremley Bal ★★ Pioneer in BADACSONY. Intense, fine RIES, Szürkebarát (aka PINOT GR), age-worthy rare KÉKNYELŰ.

Takler Pann ★★ Super-ripe, supple SZEKSZÁRD reds. Decent, gd-value, entry-point red, rosé. Best: Res selections of CAB FR, KÉKFRANKOS.

Tinon, Samuel Tok ★★★ Bordelais in TOK since 1991. Wonderful dry flor-aged *Szamorodni* and sweet (*édes*) version. Distinctive complex ASZÚ with long maceration and ageing. Fine range of vyd selection FURMINT.

Tokaj Nobilis Tok ★★★ Fine small bio producer run by Sarolta Bárdos, one of TOK's inspirational women. Excellent dry Rány & Barakonyi FURMINT, v.gd SZAMORODNI, rare Kövérszőlő Édes (sw).

Tokaj / Tokaji Tokaj is the town and wine region; Tokaji the wine. Recommended producers without individual entries: Árvay, Áts, Bardon, Basilicus, Bodrog Bormúhely, Bott Pince, Budahazy, Carpinus, Demetervin, Erzsébet, Espák, Füleky, Harsányi, Hommona Atilla, Karádi-Berger, Kvaszinger, Lenkey, Orosz Gábor, Pelle, Peter, Sanzon, Szarka, Szóló, Zombory, Zsadányi, Zsirai.

Törley ★→★★ Chapel Hill is major export brand. Well-made, gd-value DYA international and local varieties. Major fizz producer (esp Törley, Gala, Hungaria labels), v.gd classic method, esp *François President Rosé Brut*, CHARD Brut. György-Villa for top selections.

Tornai Bal ★★ Second-largest SOMLÓ estate. Gd-value entry-level varietals, excellent Top Selection range FURMINT, Juhfark.

Túzkő Pann ★★ Antinori-owned estate. Gd CAB FR, KÉKFRANKOS, MERLOT, TRAMINI.

Vida Pann ★★ Next-generation family winery in SZEKSZÁRD. Appealing entry-point Tündértánc. V.gd Bonsai (old vine) KADARKA, Hidaspetre KÉKFRANKOS, La Vida.

Villány Pann Most s wine region. Noted for serious ripe B'x varieties, esp CAB FR (labelled VILLÁNYI FRANC). Juicy examples of KÉKFRANKOS, PORTUGIESER. High-quality without own entry: Gere Tamás & Zsolt (Aureus Cuvée), Günzer Tamás (Mátyás Cuvée, Bocor), Hummel, Jackfall, Janus, Kiss Gabor, Lelovits (CAB FR), Maul Zsolt (Creátor Kékfrankos, Dávid), Polgar, Riczu (Symbol Cuvée), Stier (MERLOT, Villányi Cuvée), Ruppert, Tiffán, Wassmann.

Villányi Franc Pann New classification for CAB FR from VILLÁNY. Premium version has restricted yield, 1 yr in oak. Super-premium from 2015 is max 35 hl/ha.

Vylyan Pann ★★→★★★ Red specialist making v.gd vyd selections, esp Gombás PINOT N, Mandolás CAB FR, Montenuovo, Pillangó MERLOT. *Duennium Cuvée* is flagship red. Also delicious rare Csoka.

Weninger U Hun ★★★ Standard-setting bio winery in SOPRON run by Austrian Franz Weninger Jr. Single-vyd *Steiner Kékfrankos* is superb. SYRAH, CAB FR and red Frettner blend also impressive. Intriguing Orange Zenit.

BULGARIA

There are so many great women working in wine in Bulgaria, and they're part of its dynamism. Local grapes are being revived, and there are more new wineries. Local taste for quality wine grows, but exports are still largely of value varietals. Twin scourges of drought and coronavirus made 2020 difficult, but Bulgaria is worth another look.

Alexandra Estate Thr L ★★ Svetlana Slavova's personal vision. V.gd VERMENTINO in acacia, elegant rosé, impressive Res.

Angel's Estate Thr L ★★ Best for ripe, polished reds esp Stallion Classic, Stallion and impressive Deneb labels.

Bessa Valley Thr L ★★★ Pioneering estate nr Pazardjik. Increasingly refined, ripe reds. Try Enira, v.gd SYRAH and Enira Res, excellent *Grande Cuvée*.

Better Half Thr L ★★★ Proper garage winery. V.gd Res red, CHARD, Qvevri MARSANNE/ ROUSSANNE, VERMENTINO.

Black Sea Gold Thr L ★ Major Black Sea coast winery. Better labels: Pentagram, Salty Hills, Vera Terra.

Bononia Dan P ★★ Historic brewery-turned-winery, with highly regarded winemaker. V.gd *Gomotartzi Gamza*, SAUV BL, VIOGNIER.

Borovitsa Dan P ★★★ Handcrafted terroir wines in far nw. Dux is long-lived flagship. V.gd Great Terroirs series, Cuvée Bella Rada (RKATSITELI), GAMZA (Black Pack), Sensum, rare local grape Bouquet.

Skip red roses: Feb 14 is St Trifon Zarezan's day, local patron saint of wine-growers.

Boyar, Dom Thr L ★→★★★ Large commercial winery. Sound entry-level labels like Bolgare, Deer Point, via mid-range Elements, Platinum, Quantum, to top single-vyd Solitaire (MERLOT). Boutique Korten cellar: v.gd Natura, Grand Vintage.

Bratanov Thr L ★★ Low-intervention family estate in Sakar. V.gd Tamianka, CHARD, SYRAH and red blends.

Burgozone Dan P ★★ Family estate overlooking Danube. Gd whites, fine reds, esp Tamianka, SAUV BL, Eva, Esperanto (r).

Damianitza Thr L ★★→★★ Holistic producer in STRUMA VALLEY. Try Redark, Dzindzifkite CAB FR, Uniqato and flagship Kometa.

Dragomir Thr L ★★→★★★ Intense long-lived reds, esp Pitos, flagship RUBIN Res, CAB FR, plus lovely Sarva (p). New DIMIAT orange.

Eolis Thr L ★★→★★★ Tiny bio-run estate. V.gd VIOGNIER, SYRAH, Inspiration (r blend).

Katarzyna Thr L ★→★★ Large modern winery in s for clean supple wines. Try MAVRUD, Chopin and flagship Res.

Logodaj Thr L ★★ Weighty wines from STRUMA V; fine bottle-fermented *Satin, esp rosé*.

Maryan Dan P ★→★★ Family winery; v.gd Res (r), Ivan Alexander (r), orange DIMIAT.

Medi Valley Thr L ★★→★★★ Highest commercial vyd in Bulgaria, plus plot nr Vidin. Try Great Bulgarian, Incanto Black, MELNIK 55, VIOGNIER.

Menada, Dom Thr L ★ Large producer, cheerful Tcherga blends.

Midalidare Estate Thr L ★★→★★★ Immaculate boutique winery. Precise whites, v.gd reds, country's best sparkling.

Minkov Brothers Thr L ★→★★ Boutique arm of large Bulgarian producer. Try value Cycle range, Le Photografie PINOT N, SYRAH, Enoteca Rubin.

Miroglio, Edoardo Thr L ★★→★★★ Italian-owned estate noted for v.gd bottle-fermented sparkling. Exciting PINOT N in all styles, incl age-worthy Heritage, v.gd flagship Soli Invicto, also Elenovo CAB FR, MAVRUD.

Neragora Thr L ★★ Organic estate, gd MAVRUD plus Cherno and Ares blends.

Oldest, richest gold treasure ever found was in a Varna necropolis, 4600 BC.

Orbelia Thr L ★★ Family winery in STRUMA VALLEY. Bright Sandanski MISKET, gd Via Aristotelis range, fine CAB FR.

Orbelus Thr L ★★ Organic STRUMA winery. Vibrant Orelek whites, gd MELNIK 55.

Rossidi Thr L ★★→★★★ Pioneering winery nr Sliven. Fine, part concrete egg-fermented CHARD. V.gd RUBIN, excellent SYRAH. Intriguing orange GEWURZ.

Rumelia Thr L ★★ V.gd MAVRUD specialist. Try Rumelia Res, Erelia, unoaked Merul.

Salla Estate Dan P ★★ Precise whites, esp Vrachanski MISKET, RIES. Elegant CAB FR.

Santa Sarah Thr L ★★★ Quality pioneer, now with own estate. Bin reds are v.gd; long-lived Privat is flagship. Appealing No Saints rosé.

Stefan Pirev Wines ★★ Personal project of respected winemaker. V.gd Eager (r), Top Blend (w), CHARD Kosara.

Orange wines on rise: Dragomir, Libera, Maryan, Rossidi, Via Vinera, Villa Melnik.

Struma Valley Thr L Lovely scenery in Bulgaria's warmest region, dynamic wineries and well organized for tourism. Focus on local grapes: MELNIK 55, Sandanski MISKET, Shiroka Melnik. Names (without own entries) to watch: Abdyika, Augeo, Kapatovo, Libera, Rupel, Seewines, Via Verde, Zlaten Rozhen.

Svishtov Dan P ★→★★ Much-improved large producer close to Danube with Italian consultancy. Try Gorchivka, Imperium.

Terra Tangra Thr L ★★ Large estate in Sakar, certified organic red vyds. Gd MAVRUD (r/rosé), MALBEC, serious Roto.

Tohun Dan P ★★ Bright refreshing whites and rosé, esp Greus CHARD, Tohun rosé, promising Tohun CAB SAUV/MERLOT.

Tsarev Brod Dan P ★★ Innovative estate in n. Try pét-nat RIES, rare local Gergana, Amber CHARD, Evmolpia Rosé, complex SAUV BL Res. V.gd Ries Icewine.

Villa Melnik Thr L ★★ Family winery, focus on local grapes esp MELNIK, MAVRUD. Gd orange SAUV BL, impressive Res and Hailstorm labels.

Villa Yambol Thr L ★ Fair value, varietal wines/blends in Kabile range.

Vinex Slavyantsi Thr L ★→★★ "Fair for Life" certified for work with local Roma. Reliable budget varietals and blends, esp Leva brand.

Yamantiev's Thr L ★→★★ Sound, commercial, plus excellent top *Marble Land (r)* and Yamantiev's Grand Res CAB SAUV.

Zagreus Thr L ★★ Organic vyd, MAVRUD in all styles: white via rosé to complex Amarone-style Vinica from semi-dried grapes. Gd-value St Dimitar label.

Zelanos Thr L ★★ Pristine new winery. Try fresh Red MISKET, PINOT GR, elegant Z series PINOT N and CAB FR.

SLOVENIA

Slovenia's green, hilly, forested landscape is home to some of the best wines of the Balkan Peninsula, often not cheap, but still fantastic value. It's still more a white country than red (especially in east), and also increasingly noted for skin-contact, orange, natural wines in addition to classic styles from local and international grapes. Refined sparklers based on local Rebula and Šipon (aka Furmint) have been a strong recent trend.

Albiana Pos ★★ Family with beautiful vyds in DOLENJSKA. Try: Modra Frankinja Alto, Zeleni Silvanec, Rosé.

Batič Prim ★★ Bio/natural wines in VIPAVA. Top-selling rosé, also PINELA, REBULA, Angel blends, Valentino (sw).

Bjana Prim ★★★ Refined traditional-method PENINA from BRDA, esp Cuvée Prestige, Blanc de Noir, Brut Rosé.

New names, new addresses

Bulgaria's wine laws allow lots of room for experimentation: by new estates and personal projects, with wines progressing every yr – keep watching this space. Look for: Abdyika, Augeo, Bendida, Ch Copsa, Four Friends, Georgiev/Milkov, Glushnik, Haralambievi, Ivo Varbanov, Kapatovo, Levent Wine House, Libera Estate, Pink Pelican, Seewines, Staro Oryahovo, Stratsin, Uva Nestum, Varna Winery, Via Verde, Via Vinera Karabunar, Villa Yustina, Yalovo.

Blažič Prim ★★→★★★ Long-ageing, complex REBULA, esp Selekcija. Blaž in top yrs.

Brda Prim Top-quality district. Recommended wineries: Benedetič, Dobuje (Malvazija), Emeran Reya, Klinec (orange), Medot (v.gd PENINA), Moro (v.gd Margherita r/w), Mulit, Zanut (Rebula, vyd-selections Jama, Brjač).

Burja Prim ★★★★ Exciting organic VIPAVA estate. Excellent Burja Bela, Burja Noir (PINOT N), Burja Reddo based on SCHIOPPETTINO.

Čotar Prim ★★ Intriguing organic/natural wines from KRAS, esp Vitovska (w), MALVAZIJA, SAUV BL, TERAN, Terra Rossa (r).

Dolenjska Pos Region focusing on better quality as sales of traditional sharp, light red Cviček decline. Promising sparkling from local Žametovka (Dom Slapšak, FRELIH), Rumeni Plavec, Kraljevina. Watch: ALBIANA, Dular, FRELIH, KOBAL (esp superb Luna MODRA FRANKINJA), Kozinc.

Dolfo Prim ★★→★★★ Family winery in BRDA: Spirito PENINA, REBULA, MERLOT Res.

Slovenia celebrated its 30th birthday on 25 June 2021.

Dveri-Pax Pod ★★→★★★ Historic Benedictine-owned estate nr Maribor (name means Gate of Peace). Crisp, bright, gd-value whites. V.gd old-vine selections, esp FURMINT Ilovci, also excellent *Furmint Penina*.

Erzetič Prim ★★ Young winemaker, v.gd amphora wines: Amfora Belo (w), PINOT GR.

Ferdinand Prim ★★★ Small estate, fine Sinefinis sp with Gradis'ciutta (Italy), v.gd Brutus (r/w), Epoca REBULA.

Frelih Pos ★★ Improved family winery for gd PENINA, SIVI PINOT, Echo (w).

Gašper Prim ★★★ Brand of Slovenia's top sommelier with KLET BRDA. V.gd MALVAZIJA, PINOT GR, REBULA Selekcija, refined CAB FR.

Gross Pod ★★★→★★★★ Amazing terroir wines. Superb Gorca and Iglič FURMINTS, Colles SAUV BL, RIES. Furmint Brut Natur impresses.

Guerila Prim ★★ Bio; in VIPAVA. V.gd PINELA, Retro (w), BARBERA, Amphora REBULA.

Istenič Pos ★★ Gd fizz specialist. Try Prestige Extra Brut, Gourmet Rosé, N°1 Brut, Barbara Sec.

Istria (Slovenska Istra) Coastal zone partly in Croatia; main grapes: MALVAZIJA, REFOŠK. Best: Bordon, Brič, Korenika & Moškon (bio), MonteMoro, Polič, Pucer z Vrha, Rodica (organic), Rojac, SANTOMAS, Steras, VINAKOPER, Zaro.

Jakončič Prim ★★★ V.gd BRDA producer: Bela (w), Carolina REBULA, Traditional Red.

Joannes Pod ★★ RIES specialist nr Maribor. Also fresh light SAUV BL, PINOT N.

Kabaj Prim ★★★ French-directed. Long-aged Amfora, also skin-contact REBULA, Ravan (FRIULANO), Corpus, serious MERLOT.

Klet Brda Prim ★★→★★★ Slovenia's largest co-op, surprisingly gd, forward-thinking. Try Bagueri vyd selections. Also v.gd Quercus varietal whites, unoaked Krasno, Colliano for US. Excellent flagship A+ (r/w), Motnik REBULA (orange).

Kobal Pod ★★ Personal vision of Bojan K. V.gd FURMINT, Black label SAUV BL.

Kogl Pod ★★ Historic estate nr Ormož, from 1542. Vibrant, precise whites, esp Mea Culpa AUXERROIS, Ranina (aka BOUVIER).

Krapež, Vina Prim ★★→★★★ VIPAVA family producer. Lapor Belo, Rdece always v.gd, *stunning new Malvazija*.

Kras Prim District on Terra Rossa soil in PRIM. Best-known for controversial TERAN denomination. Try Vinakras (esp Prestige).

Kristančič Prim ★★ Family producer in BRDA. Try Pavó from old vines.

Kupljen Pod ★★ Dry pioneer nr Jeruzalem: ŠIPON, Aldebaran RIES, Loona, White Star.

Marof Pod ★★→★★★ Pioneering estate in Prekmurje. Marof classic (oak-aged), Marof Breg (barrel-fermented) and cru range from best vyds.

Movia Prim ★★★ High-profile bio winery. Excellent v. long-lived *Veliko Belo (w)*, Rdeče (r), showstopping *Puro Rosé* (sp). V.gd MODRI PINOT. Orange Lunar spends eight full moons on skins.

Pasji Rep Prim ★★ Next-generation organic VIPAVA estate. Much improved, refined, esp MALVAZIJA, Jebatschin blends, PINOT N.

Penina Name for quality sparkling wine (Charmat or traditional method). Trendy.

Podravje Largest region (43% of production) covering Štajerska Slovenija and Prekmurje in e. Best for crisp dry whites, gd sweet, reds typically lighter from MODRA FRANKINJA, PINOT N.

Slovenia is one of the top ten tallest countries: men average 1.8m (5.9ft) tall.

Posavje Region in se. V.gd sweet, esp Mavretič, Prus, Šturm. Improving PENINA (Dom Slapšak, FRELIH, ISTENIČ) and dry, esp in subregions of DOLENJSKA, Bizeljsko-Sremič (look for Klet Krško, esp MODRA FRANKINJA, Izbor sweet SAUV BL).

PRA-VinO Pod 70s pioneer of private production. Best for sweet, incl Icewine (*ledeno vino*), botrytis.

Primorje Region in w covering Slovenian ISTRIA, BRDA, VIPAVA, KRAS. Aka Primorska.

Puklavec Family Wines Pod ★★→★★★ Large family winery, consistent crisp aromatic whites in Puklavec & Friends and Jeruzalem Ormož ranges. V.gd Seven Numbers label. Also in N Macedonia for reds.

Pullus (Ptujska Klet) Pod ★★ Fresh, crisp whites, light-hearted pinks. G range and sweet wines impress.

Radgonske Gorice Pod ★→★★ Makes bestselling Slovenian sparkler Srebrna (silver) PENINA, classic-method Zlata (golden) Penina. New, fine Untouched by Light made in dark to avoid light-strike.

Santomas Prim ★★→★★★ V.gd for REFOŠK and Refošk/CAB SAUV, esp Antonius from 60-yr-old vines. Also gd MALVAZIJA, SYRAH.

Ščurek Prim ★★★ Family estate in BRDA, five sons. Gd varietal entry-point wines. Superb *Rebula Up* and attractive Stara Brajda (r/w).

Simčič, Edi Prim ★★★★ Standard-setter in BRDA. Superb reds: Duet Lex, barrel-selection Kolos. Classy whites: REBULA, SAUV BL; Triton Lex; lovely Kozana CHARD, MERLOT. Excellent new Fojana vyd selections.

Simčič, Marjan Prim ★★★★ Single-vyd Opoka range is world class. Also gd Selekcija range. Teodor blends always v.gd. Leonardo (sw) consistently great.

Štajerska Slovenija Pod Major region in e incl important districts of Haloze, Ljutomer-Ormož, Maribor. Crisp, vibrant whites and top sweet. Recommended (without individual entries): Conrad Furst & Sohne, Dom Ciringa, Doppler,

---

Balkans go orange

Slovenia may be the centre of the revival of skin-contact in white winemaking, but orange wines are now everywhere. Skin contact may be just a few days or several mths, in barrels, concrete eggs or amphorae. Local grapes like REBULA and MALVAZIJA are exciting, though there are v.gd versions from international grapes too. Some personal favourites from **Slovenia** incl FERDINAND's salty, complex Brutus Rebula; MARJAN SIMČIČ's wonderfully classy Opoka Rebula; KLET BRDA's herby, sleek Motnik; ERZETIČ's ginger-and-peach scented Amfora; beautiful BURJA Belo. Over the border in **Croatia** favourites incl: AHEARNE Wild Skins with its saline, tangerine notes; salted-lemon sapidity of VINA LAGUNA Riserva 240 Duga Maceracija Malvazija; TOMAC's exotic, exciting Amfora TRAMINEC; silky-textured KRAJANČIČ POŠIP Macerirano; zesty, honeyed BENVENUTI AD Malvazija. Also check out orange Žilavka from **Bosnia & Herzegovina**: Vina Škegro's inviting Krš Orange and Brkić's fascinating Mjesečar (Moonwalker). Other names to try: BATIČ, BLAŽIĆ, ČOTAR, GUERILA, JNK, KABAJ, Klinec, Lepa Vida, Mlečnik, MOVIA in **Slovenia** plus CLAI, KABOLA, KOZLOVIĆ, ROXANICH in **Croatia** and Bikicki, Kovačević in **Serbia**.

Frešer, Gaube, Heaps Good Wine, Krainz, M-vina (esp ExtremM SAUV BL), Oskar, Roka, Sanctum, Šumenjak, Valdhuber, Zlati Grič.

Steyer Pod ★★ TRAMINER specialist in ŠTAJERSKA.

Sutor Prim ★★★ Excellent small producer from VIPAVA. Try Primus REBULA/MALVAZIJA, Sutor White, also v.gd Malvazija, fine CHARD, elegant red.

Tilia Prim ★★→★★★ "House of Pinots" in VIPAVA (co-owner has PhD in PINOT N). Pinot N in all forms, esp Merljaki. Also Benchmark PINOT GR, appetizing SAUV BL.

Verus Pod ★★★ Fine, focused, vibrant whites, esp v.gd FURMINT, flavoursome PINOT GR, refined RIES, crisp SAUV BL.

Vinakoper Prim ★★ Improved large winery nr coast. Look for Capo D'Istria and young MALVAZIJA, REFOŠK under Rex Fuscus, Capris labels.

Vipava Prim Valley noted for cool breezes in PRIM. Recommended without own entry: Benčina (PINOT N), Fedora (Goli Breg, Zelen), Guštin (MALVAZIJA Premium), JNK (orange), Lepa Vida (Malvazija, 0Oo orange), Marc (excellent PINELA), Miška (PINELA), Mlečnik (orange/natural), Štokelj (Pinela), Vina Ušaj Ussai (MERLOT).

Vipava 1894 Prim ★→★★ Much improved large winery, new management. Esp Lanthieri range, Terase MALVAZIJA.

CROATIA

Record numbers of tourists (21 million) visited Croatia in 2019. Top destination was Istria, then Dalmatia: Split, Dubrovnik, Zadar. At the same time, food culture is building with multiple Michelin stars and Istria winning the title of world's best olive oil region for the 6th year in a row (also great truffles). Most local wines are drunk in Croatia – an excuse to go and explore.

Ahearne Dalm ★★ British Master of Wine Jo Ahearne makes elegant PLAVAC MALI, deep Rosina Darnekuša rosé, Wild Skins (w) on HVAR.

Antunović Sl & CD ★★ Mother and son winery on Danube. Lovely GRAŠEVINA, Jubilea Grand Res, refined Tango with Life (r).

Arman, Franc Is & Kv ★★ Family winery, 6th generation. V.gd reds, DYA MALVAZIJA, skin-contact Malvazija Classic.

Arman, Marijan Is & Kv ★★ Excellent MALVAZIJA, esp G Cru and Res. Gd TERAN.

Badel 1862 ★→★★ Drinks group with three wineries. Try: smooth reds under Korlat label. Also sound PLAVAC MALI, DINGAČ 50°.

Benvenuti Is & Kv ★★★ Leading family winery at Motovun. V.gd reds, esp Caldierosso, TERAN esp Santa Elisabetta. Consistent fresh MALVAZIJA, complex Anno Domini (w), gorgeous San Salvatore MUŠKAT (sw).

BIBICh Dalm ★★→★★★ Family winery, 500 yr history. Focus on local grapes, esp Debit (w), plus SYRAH, blends. Try Lučica single-vyd and sweet Ambra.

Bire Dalm ★★ Specialist in v.gd Grk in multiple styles on Korcula.

Boškinac Dalm ★★→★★★ Michelin-starred restaurant on Pag island plus impressive long-lived reds, esp Cuvée.

Bura-Mrgudić Dalm ★★ Family winery renowned for weighty, traditional Bura PLAVAC MALI. Also modern Benmosche DINGAČ, ZIN.

Cattunar Is & Kv ★★ Specializes in MALVAZIJA from different soils. Excellent Nono 4 Terre, Collina.

Clai Is & Kv ★★ Admired skin-contact orange: Sveti Jakov MALVAZIJA, Ottocento blends.

Coronica Is & Kv ★★ Standard-setting producer, esp barrel-aged Gran MALVAZIJA and benchmark Gran TERAN.

Dalmatia Rocky coastline, lovely islands, many exciting wineries.

Damjanić Is & Kv ★★→★★★ Increasingly impressive family winery. V.gd Borgonja (aka BLAUFRÄNKISCH), MALVAZIJA, Clemente (r/w).

Dingač Dalm PDO for serious reds from PLAVAC MALI, on Pelješac peninsula. Try:

> **Istria & Kvarner**
> The N Adriatic peninsula and nearby islands. MALVAZIJA main grape. Gd
> CAB SAUV, MERLOT, TERAN. Gd producers (without own entry): Banko Mario,
> Capo, Cossetto, Degrassi (VIOGNIER, CAB FR), Deklić, Dom Koquelicot
> (Belaigra Grand Cru, Nomad), Dubrovac, Franković, Medea, Misal
> Peršurić (sp), Novacco, Piquentum, Radovan (REFOŠK, Merlot), Rossi
> (Malvazija, Templara), Sirotić, Tercolo, Trapan, Veralda, Zigante.

Benmosche, BURA-MRGUDIĆ, KIRIDŽIJA, Lučić, Madirazza, Matuško, Miličić, SAINTS HILLS, SKARAMUČA, Vinarija Dingač.

Enjingi, Ivan Sl & CD ★★ Legendary natural winemaker in SLAVONIJA. Noted for GRAŠEVINA and long-lived Venje.

Fakin Is & Kv ★★★ Exciting young *garagiste* impressing with MALVAZIJA, esp La Prima, Il Primo TERAN.

Feravino Sl & CD ★→★★ Large winery improving under new young team and Slovenian consultancy.

Galić Sl & CD ★★★ Stunning winery, immaculate wines: v.gd sparkling, Bijelo 9, Crno 9, GRAŠEVINA, SAUV BL, PINOT N.

Geržinić Is & Kv ★★ Brothers making v.gd TERAN (r/rosé), MALVAZIJA, SYRAH, MUŠKAT Zuti (aka Yellow Muscat).

Gracin Dalm ★★→★★★ Prof. Leo Gracin pioneered revival of BABIĆ from Primošten's UNESCO-listed rocky vyds.

Grgić Dalm ★★→★★★ Napa Valley legend Mike Grgich, ex-Ch Montelena (*see* California), returned to Croatian roots to make PLAVAC MALI, rich POŠIP on Pelješac peninsula with daughter and nephew.

Hvar Dalm Beautiful island, UNESCO protection for world's oldest continuously cultivated vyd. Noted for PLAVAC MALI. Gd: AHEARNE, Carić, Duboković, PZ Svirče, TOMIĆ, ZLATAN OTOK.

Iločki Podrumi Sl & CD ★→★★ Oldest winery in Europe with continuous production, cellar from 1450, plus historic royal palace. Try: Premium GRAŠEVINA, TRAMINAC, Principovac range.

Kabola Is & Kv ★★→★★★ Immaculate organic estate. V.gd MALVAZIJA as fizz, young wine, cask-aged Unica, Amfora. Tasty DYA rosé; v.gd TERAN.

Katunar Is & Kv ★★ Leading producer of Žlahtina found only on island of Krk. Try Sv. Lucija. Also gd PLAVAC MALI.

Kiridžija Dalm ★★ Gd PLAVAC MALI and v.gd weighty but fruity DINGAČ.

Korta Katarina Dalm ★★ US-owned luxury hotel resort and winery on Korcula. Gd POŠIP, PLAVAC MALI.

Kozlović Is & Kv ★★★→★★★★ Beautiful winery, gorgeous wines, esp exciting, complex Santa Lucia (r/w), superb Selekcija, pretty MUŠKAT Momjanski.

Krajančić Dalm ★★→★★★ Specialist in POŠIP: Intrada, Sur Lie, Statut, orange.

Krauthaker Sl & CD ★★★ Pioneering producer from Kutjevo, esp GRAŠEVINA Mitrovac, Zelenac Rosenberg and TBA, decent PINOT N.

Kutjevo Cellars Sl & CD ★★ Historic cellar from 1232. GRAŠEVINA specialist: gd-value entry-level plus complex, honeyed De Gotho, lovely Icewine.

Laguna, Vina Is & Kv ★★→★★★ Large but v.gd consistent winery on *terra rossa*. Look for Festigia and Riserva ranges (notable MALVAZIJA, esp Vižinada, orange 240 Duga). Increasingly classy reds: Castello, Festigia Riserva LV.

Matošević Is & Kv ★★★ Benchmark MALVAZIJA, esp Alba, Alba Antiqua, Alba Robinia (in acacia). Also v.gd Grimalda (r/w) and SAUV BL.

Međimurje Cro Up Coolest wine county in n with focus on Pušipel (aka FURMINT) and fresh SAUV BL. Try: Cmrečnjak, Dvanajščak-Kozol, Jakopić, Kocijan, Štampar.

Meneghetti Is & Kv ★★ Luxury hotel, winery: Sleek, well-made blends (r/w).

Miloš, Frano Dalm ★★ Admired for traditional structured Stagnum, also easier PLAVAC MALI and rosé.

Pilato Is & Kv ★★ Consistent family winery; v.gd MALVAZIJA, PINOT BL, MERLOT, TERAN.

Postup Dalm The 2nd-oldest vyd designation nw of DINGAČ. Full-bodied, rich PLAVAC MALI. Try: Madirazza, Miličić, Mrgudić Marija, Vinarija Dingač.

Prošek Dalm Historic sweet made from sun-dried local grapes in DALM; 1st mention 1556. Gd: GRACIN, STINA, TOMIĆ Hectorovich.

Roxanich Is & Kv ★★→★★★ Wine hotel, natural producer noted for long-macerated whites (Antica, Milva, Ines); complex reds, esp TERAN Ré, Superistrian Cuvée.

Saints Hills Dalm, Is & Kv ★★→★★★ Two wineries, consultant Michel Rolland. V.gd Nevina (w), Frenchie (w), Posh (Pošip), richly fruity PLAVAC MALI St Roko, structured DINGAČ.

Skaramuča Dalm ★★ Family winery making gd POŠIP, modern PLAVAC MALI, DINGAČ under Elegance label.

Slovenia-Croatia row over Teran may be over: Croatians can use "Hrvatska Istra – Teran".

Slavonija / Slavonia Region in ne, famous for oak. Most noted for whites, esp GRAŠEVINA. Also gd reds now. Look for Adzić, *Antunović*, Bartolović, Belje, ENJINGI, FERAVINO, GALIĆ, KRAUTHAKER, KUTJEVO, Mihalj, Orahovica, Sontacchi, Zdjelarević.

Stina Dalm ★★→★★★ Dramatic steep vyds on Brač island; v.gd POŠIP, Vugava, PLAVAC MALI, esp Majstor label, top Remek Djelo. Gd Tribidrag (aka ZIN).

Testament Dalm ★★→★★★ Organic Swedish-owned winery for v.gd POŠIP and BABIĆ, esp Opolo (rosé), Dalmatian Dog (r).

Tomac Cro Up ★★→★★★ Amphora pioneer nr Zagreb working towards bio. Notable sparkling and orange TRAMINEC.

Tomaz Is & Kv ★★★ Family winery at Motovun. Seriously impressive Barbarossa TERAN, complex MALVAZIJA Sesto Senso.

Tomić Dalm ★★ Outspoken personality, bold wines on HVAR; organic PLAVAC MALI. Gd reds, esp Plavac Barrique, PROŠEK Hectorovich.

Volarević Dalm ★★★ From new organic region of Komarna. V.gd PLAVAC MALI as rosé, Syrhis, Limited Edition. Fine POŠIP.

Zlatan Otok Dalm ★★ Family winery from HVAR with vyds also at Makarska, Šibenik. Famous for ripe reds, gd DYA POŠIP.

BOSNIA & HERZEGOVINA, KOSOVO, NORTH MACEDONIA, SERBIA, MONTENEGRO

Blatina, Prokupac, Trnjak, Vranac, Žilavka and many more: local grapes – often workhorse grapes in the past – are leading the new wave. A new generation wants to drink differently to their parents, and quality is rising. There are still few exports, though growing.

Bosnia & Herzegovina White Žilavka is the calling card, esp from sunny rocky vyds of Herzegovina. Also juicy supple red Blatina, more structured Trnjak and some v.gd Vranac in s. Look out for: Andrija (Žilavka Barrique, Vranac), Begić (PLAVAC MALI rosé), *Brkić (Mjesečar)*, Carska Vina (David, Fine Edition), Hercegovina Produkt (Zlatna Dolina, Charisma labels), Jungić (Premium CAB SAUV, Šikar), Keža (Ž range), Marjanović (Blatina Barrique), Nuić (Žilavka, Blatina), Rubis (Veteribus Blatina), *Škegro (Zilavka, Krš Orange, Trnjak, Blatina)*, Tolj (Trnjak, Blatina Ivanis), Tvrdos Monastery (HUM Cab Sauv, Vranac), Vilinka (Žilavka, X-Line), Vinarija Čitluk (Teuta range), Vino Milas (Blatina Res), *Vukoje (Carsko-Vino, Selekcija, Vranac)*.

Kosovo is recognized as independent by 101 countries but still has two wine laws – its own and Serbia's. Approx 2460 ha of wine grapes, Rahovec the largest region; 27 licensed wineries; Stonecastle and Old Cellar (Bodrum i Vjeter) biggest. Smaller names like Kosova, Sefa getting better. Most planted grapes incl GAMAY, Prokupac, Smederevka, Vranac, WELSCHRIESLING.

North Macedonia focuses on bottled wine in on-going moves away from cheap bulk. Vranec (local spelling) is flagship, covering c.11,000 of total 25,000 ha. Largest wineries are driving quality. Giant *Tikveš* has French-trained winemaker, research programme; impresses with *Barovo, Bela Voda* single vyds; gd Special Selection and rich, oaked Dom Lepovo. Dalvina much improved, esp Armageddon, Dionis, Hermes, Synthesis labels. *Stobi v.gd Vranec Veritas*, also gd Vranec classic, Aminta (r), RKATSITELI, Žilavka. Ch Kamnik is leading boutique winery, with gd 10 Barrels, Winemaker's selection (organic) Cuvée Prestige, Vranec Terroir. Also gd: Bovin (try unoaked Alexandar, super-rich A'gupka, Imperator, Dissan), Ezimit (gd-value varietals), Imako (Black Diamond, Montovo River), Lazar (Kratošija, Erigon r), Puklavec Family Vyds Instinct range (also Slovenia).

Montenegro Vranac dominates (over 90% plantings) as does 13 Jul Plantaže with 2310 ha in single site, one of Europe's largest. Wines are pretty gd (esp Vranac in many forms). Small wineries getting better. Bogojevic, Lipovac (gd Amfora, Vranac Concept), Rupice, Sjekloča, Vukicevic. Recent research shows Montenegro as origin of ZIN (local name Kratošija).

Serbia has 25,000 ha of registered vyds, c.400 wineries, many new and tiny. Focus on reinventing former workhorse grapes like Prokupac, obscurities like Bagrina, Seduša and trying newer local grapes like Morava, Neoplanta, Probus. Try: Aleksandrović (Trijumf range, Regent Res, Vizija), Aleksić (Amanet), Bikicki (S/O, Orange TRAMINER), Botunjac (Sveti Grai), Budimir (Triada, Svb Rosa, Boje Lila), Chichateau (CHARD, Fabula Mala, Fabula Lagum), Cilić, Čokot (Experiment), Despotika (Morava, Dokaz, Trag), Deurić (Probus, Talas, PINOT N), *Doja* (*Breg Prokupac*), *Dukay-Sagmeister (Kadarka, esp cru selections)*, Erdevik (*Omnibus Lector Chard*, SHIRAZ), Grabak (Vivat Prokupac), Ivanović (Prokupac, No.1/2), Janko (Vrtlog, Zavet Stari, Zapis), Kovačević (Chard, Orange, Aurelius), Lastar (Triangl Pinot N, Chard, Tamjanika), Matalj (*Kremen Kamen*, Kremen Chard), *Maurer (Kadarka, Fodor)*, Pusula (CAB FR), Radovanović (Cab Res, Saga), Rubin (Rubinov Prokupac), Šijački (Seduša), Temet (Ergo, Tri Morave), Tonković (Rapsodija, Fantazija KADARKA), Virtus (733 Prokupac, MARSELAN), Zvonko Bogdan (Icon Campana Albus, Cuvée No.1).

CZECHIA

Wine has become the fashionable beverage for the new elites, and the huge investments of recent years have led to plenty of wines whose quality rivals that of better-known nations. Production is concentrated in the larger of two regions, Moravia (Mor), accounting for 96% of the total, from a multitude of grapes, and 25-times smaller Bohemia (Boh) near Prague. Here you'll find Germanic-style Riesling as well as Pinot Noir, the latter brought here from Burgundy in the 14th century by Emperor Charles IV.

Cibulka, Vino Mor ★★★ Prize-winning CAB SAUV/MERLOT and intriguing Blauer Silvaner Sekt, all organic.

Dobrá Vinice Mor ★★★ Impressive SAUV BL, RIES, PINOT N and WELSCHRIESLING in *qvevri* from Georgia. Top blends: Quatre, Cuvée Kambrium and long-lived VDB, VDČ, also Crème de Vin Brut Nature.

Dva Duby Mor ★★★ Focus on BLAUFRÄNKISCH/ST-LAURENT grown on granodiorite subsoil typical of Dolní Kounice. Also MALVASIA. Bio principles. Flagship labels: Rosa Inferni, Ex Opere Operato, Vox Silentium.

Lobkowicz, Bettina Boh ★★→★★★ V.gd PINOT N Barrique Selection, classic-method RIES sekt, also Saphira and v.gd-value entry-level Lady Lobkowicz (r/w/rosé).

Ludwig Mor ★→★★ Ultra-modern winery making 1.5 million bottles, approachable wines, reasonable prices. China-oriented. Aromatic Solaris a curiosity.

Mádl Mor ★★ Nicknamed "Malý vinař" (small vintner), family run; top reds Mlask, Cuvée 1+1, also v.gd PINOT GR, SAUV BL.

Porta Bohemica Boh ★★ Est 2010, vyds on marlstone bedrock n of Prague. MÜLLER-T, RIES, PINOT N. Outstanding Frühroter Veltliner. Also blends Charpin, MüVé.

Stapleton & Springer Mor ★★★ Remarkable PINOT N, also Roučí blend (under Jaroslav Springer label), single-vyd Čtvrtě (Tomáš Springer), Ben's Res (Benjamin F. Stapleton).

Stávek, Richard Mor ★★→★★★ Dedicated terroirist, best vyd sites incl: Kolberg, Špigle-Bočky, Veselý.

Vican Mor ★★★ Est 2015 by film producer Tomáš Vican. Accent on distinctive WELSCHRIESLING from Pálava Hills nr Mikulov (Nikolsburg) where it excels. V.gd Quevri House range.

Znovín-Znojmo Mor ★→★★ Important centre in s, nr Austrian border, emphasis on SAUV BL, RIES, esp Robinia, aged in acacia wood.

SLOVAKIA

Central European vines dominate, alongside international favourites. Slovakia's 12,000 ha of vineyards are divided into six wine regions: Lesser Carpathians (L Car), Nitra (Nit), Central Slovakia (C Slo), Southern Slovakia (S Slo), Eastern Slovakia (E Slo) and Tokaj (Tok). Château Topoľčianky (Nit), Víno Matyšák (L Car) and Sekt JE Hubert Sereď (Nit) largest producers. Exports are negligible.

Slovakian fizz Ch Palugyay was served on the *Titanic*. More ice, waiter!

Belá, Ch S Slo ★★★ Fine RIES by Egon Müller (*see* Germany) and Miroslav Petrech joint venture.

Elesko L Car ★★ Large super-modern facility unrivalled in Central Europe with art gallery featuring Warhol originals.

Fedor Malík Jr L Car ★★ Son of professor of oenology planted 15 ha, makes still and Modragne classic sparkling.

J&J Ostrožovič Tok ★★★ V.gd Slovak Tok, traditional and modern products.

Karpatská Perla L Car ★★ V.gd wines from immaculately maintained vyds.

Movino C Slo ★★ Most important Central Slovakia producer, est 1973 in Veľký Krtíš.

Pivnica Brhlovce Nit ★★★ Est 2011 by photographer Ján Záborský. Artisanal production of "volcanic" wines in troglodyte dwellings.

Rúbaň, Ch S Slo ★★ Ambitious enterprise, top-quality, gastronomic aspirations. Interesting Cuvée d'Balance, CAB SAUV Blanc and Noria Sekt.

Villa Víno Rača L Car ★★ Emphasis on BLAUFRÄNKISCH. Recent relaunch Ch Palugyay.

ROMANIA

Diversity is Romania's strength: climates range from cool Transylvania to the warm Black Sea coast. A huge and increasing range of good examples of local varieties play their part in this fascinating mosaic, from Alutus to Zghihara. For many export markets, Romania is about Pinot Noir, but it's hard to sell at home where heftier reds are preferred.

Avereşti, Domeniile Mold ★→★★ Much improved large winery, esp Nativus label for local Busuioaca, FETEASCĂ NEAGRĂ, Zghihara.

Avincis Mun ★★ Dramatic state-of-art winery in DRĂGĂŞANI. Try v.gd varietal Negru de Drăgăşani, Cuvée Grandiflora blend. Crâmposie Selecţionată impresses.

Balla Géza Cri & Mar ★★→★★★ V.gd Miniş estate run by professor of horticulture. Excellent Stone Wine range is flagship, plus v.gd Cadarca, FETEASCĂ NEAGRĂ.

Banat Dynamic region in w. Recommended: Agape, Crama Aramic, Pivniţele Birăuaş, Thesaurus.

Bauer Winery Mun ★★→★★★ Excellent experimental family winery of Oliver and Raluca Bauer (also at PRINCE ŞTIRBEY). Small batches from old vines, unusual grapes, eg. Sauvignonasse, PETIT VERDOT, sweet Crâmposie. Orange wine pioneer.

Budureasca Mun ★→★★ DEALU MARE estate with longstanding British winemaker. Noble 5 is gd, plus Vine-in-Flames export range.

Catleya Mun ★★ Personal project of French winemaker Laurent Pfeffer; gd Freamăt, excellent Epopée selection.

Corcova Roy & Dâmboviceanu Mun ★★ Exceptional vyds and C19 royal cellar. Try FETEASCĂ NEAGRĂ, SYRAH, appealing SAUV BL, rosé. Res PINOT N gd with age.

Cotnari, Casa de Vinuri Mold ★→★★ Next generation in Cotnari, 350 ha. Colocviu label best (esp GRASĂ de Cotnari, Busuioacă de Bohotin), new focus on sparkling.

Cotnari Winery Mold ★ Privatized former state winery, same name as DOC. Mostly dry and semi-dry whites from local grapes. Aged sweet Collection can impress.

Transfăgărăşan road has been voted Europe's most beautiful. Don't drink and drive.

Crişana & Maramureş Region in nw. Look for Carastelec (v.gd Carassia bottle-fermented sp and RIES) and organic producer Nachbil (BLAUFRĂNKISCH, RIES, Grandpa), Weingut Edgar Brutler (roşu).

Dagon Clan Mun ★★→★★★ Small, increasingly impressive vyd guided by Mark Haisma, esp Sandridge and Clearstone.

Davino Winery Mun ★★★→★★★★ Excellent, consistent producer in DEALU MARE. Focus on blends for v.gd, age-worthy Dom Ceptura, Flamboyant, Rezerva, Revelatio (w). V.gd FETEASCĂ NEAGRĂ under Purpura Valahica label.

Dealu Mare / Dealul Mare Mun Regarded widely as Romania's top region. Means "Big Hill". Plans for Romania's 1st DOCG (DOC Garantat) by 2021 are progressing. Location of several leading producers.

Dobrogea Nr Black Sea. Incl DOC regions of Murfatlar, Badabag and Sarica Niculiţel.

DOC Romanian term for PDO. Sub-categories incl DOC-CMD: harvest at full maturity, DOC-CT: late-harvest and DOC-CIB: noble-harvest. PGI is Vin cu indicatie geografică or simply IG.

Domeniul Coroanei Segarcea Mun ★→★★ Historic royal estate. Famous for TĂMÂIOASĂ Roze. Also try Minima Moralia CAB SAUV, Principesa Margareta MARSELAN, Simfonia red blend.

Drăgăşani Mun Dynamic region with long history and unique grapes incl Novac, Crâmposie Selecţionată, Negru de Drăgăşani. Leading producers: AVINCIS, BAUER, PRINCE ŞTIRBEY.

Gîrboiu, Crama Mold ★→★★ 200 ha in earthquake-prone Vrancea, hence Tectonic label (try Şarba) and Epicentrum. Constantin and Petite Helena new and gd.

Iconic Estate Mun ★→★★ Consistent gd-value commercial La Umbra range, Colina Pietra blends. Try Theia CHARD, Kronos PINOT N and top Hyperion label: try FETEASCĂ NEAGRĂ.

Jidvei Trnsyl ★→★★ Romania's largest single vyd with over 2500 ha. Best for Owner's Choice (with Marc Dworkin of Bulgaria's Bessa Valley), also Eiswein and Extra Brut (sp).

LacertA Mun ★★ Quality estate in DEALU MARE. Cuvée IX (r), Cuvée X (w), SHIRAZ.

Licorna Wine House Mun ★★ In DEALU MARE, opened 2013; impressing with Serafim for local grapes and Bon Viveur for international blends.

Liliac Trnsyl ★★★ Impeccable Austrian-owned estate. Crisp fine whites, delicious sweet Nectar, Icewine with Kracher (Austria). V.gd super-premium Titan.

Go rowing on a lake at bottom of stunning C17 Turda salt mine: 113m/370ft down.

Metamorfosis, Viile Mun ★★★ Part-Antinori-owned (*see* Italy) estate in DEALU MARE. Top: Cantvs Primvs, esp FETEASCĂ NEAGRĂ. V.gd Coltul Pietrei SAUV BL, Via Marchizului Negru de Drăgăşani, PINOT N), fruit-driven Metamorfosis range.

Moldovan Hills Largest wine region in ne – don't confuse with Republic of Moldova. Crisp fresh whites and rosé incl Gramma, Hermeziu, newcomer Strunga.

Muntenia & Oltenia Hills Major region in s covering DOC areas of DEALU MARE, Dealurile Olteniei, DRĂGĂŞANI, Pietroasa, Sâmbureşti, Stefaneşti, Vanju Mare.

Oprişor, Crama Mun ★★→★★★ Consistent German-owned winery. Gd La Cetate range; Jiana Rosé, Rusalca Alba, Crama Oprişor CAB SAUV, excellent Smerenie (r).

Petro Vaselo Ban ★★ Organic vyd in BANAT. Gd Bendis (sp), Melgris FETEASCĂ NEAGRĂ, Ovas (r). Appealing fruit-driven entry-level range, PV label for top wines.

Prince Ştirbey Mun ★★★ Pioneering estate in DRĂGĂŞANI. Fine, vibrant dry whites, esp Crâmpoşie Selecţionată (still and sparkling), FETEASCĂ REGALĂ, TĂMÂIOASĂ, Genius Loci SAUV BL and local reds (Novac, Negru de Drăgăşani).

Recaş, Cramele Ban ★★→★★★ Romania's most successful exporter thanks to progressive, consistent wines with longstanding Australian and Spanish winemakers. V.gd-value, bright varietals sold under multiple labels incl Calusari, Wildflower, Paparuda, Schwaben Wein. Mid-range: Regno Recas, Sole. Excellent premium wines, esp Cuvée Uberland, La Stejari, Selene.

Sarica Niculiţel, Via Viticola Dob ★→★★ Raising standards in overlooked region. Gd ALIGOTĔ, FETEASCĂ NEAGRĂ, rosé. Also owns Domeniile Prince Matei in DEALU MARE: MERLOT Rezerva impresses.

S.E.R.V.E. Mun ★★→★★★ First private winery in Romania, founded by late Count Guy de Poix. V.gd Terra Romana, esp PINOT N, Cuvée Sissi rosé, Cuvée Amaury (w), impressive Guy de Poix FETEASCĂ NEAGRĂ. *Cuvée Charlotte* quality red benchmark.

Transylvania Cool mtn plateau encircled by Carpathians. Noted for crisp whites. New producers in Lechinţa zone incl organic Lechberg, Jelna.

Valahorum Mun ★★→★★★ Premium joint-venture in DEALU MARE from Tohani and Mennini. Look for FETEASCĂ ALBĂ, Apogeum FETEASCĂ NEAGRĂ.

Villa Vinèa Trnsyl ★★ Italian-owned Târnave estate. Gd whites, esp Diamant, GEWURZ, KERNER and red blend Rubin.

Vişineşcu, Aurelia Mun ★★ DEALU MARE estate. Try Artizan (w) using local grapes, TĂMÂIOASĂ Dulce. Anima is top label, esp CHARD, Fete Negre.

Carpathian Mtns are home to 60% of Europe's brown bears.

MALTA

There are local grapes for the adventurous, and international grapes for the rest: Cabernet Sauvignon and Merlot, Syrah and Grenache make some beefy styles in this hot, humid climate. International whites include Sauvignon Blanc, Chenin Blanc, Viognier, Chardonnay. The local vines are red Gellewza, relatively light in style, and white Girgentina, soft and delicate. If you come across a grape called Sirakusan, it's Nero d'Avola. Meridiana is regarded as the best producer and is certainly the biggest. Mar Casar makes an interesting amphora Chardonnay. On Gozo, try Ta'Mena. Whatever you choose, beware of overoaking.

Greece

The modern age of high-quality Greek wine started in the 80s, during what is usually called "the revolution of small producers". Now we're seeing "the revolution of youth". Young people, usually in their 20s, either the offspring of established producers or just passionate about wine, are crafting some ambitious, but most of all delicious wines. We list some on p.236. Abbreviations: Aegean Islands (Aeg), Central Greece (C Gr), Ionian Islands (Ion), Macedonia (Mac), Peloponnese (Pelop), Thessaloniki (Thess).

Alpha Estate Mac ★★★ Acclaimed KTIMA in AMYNTEO with largest vyd investment in Greece. Ktima Alpha (r/w) are classics. Ecosystem range a terroir study, Barba Yiannis XINOMAVRO from century-old vines.

Amynteo Mac (POP) Captivating XINOMAVRO reds, excellent rosés (and sp) from coolest Greek POP. Becoming trendy.

Argyros Aeg ★★★★ Top SANTORINI producer; VINSANTOS (the older the better). Evdemon, Monsigniori and Nyhteri cuvées are dazzling.

Avantis C Gr ★★★ Boutique winery in Evia and SANTORINI. Exquisite Collection SYRAH and Afoura Santorini.

Biblia Chora Mac ★★★ A popular KTIMA and justifiably so. Classic SAUV BL/ASSYRTIKO. Ovilos range (r/w) could rival B'x at triple the price. Sister estate of GEROVASSILIOU. New wineries in Pelop (Dyo Ipsi), SANTORINI (Mikra Thira) and GOUMENISSA.

Boutari, J & Son ★→★★★ Historic brand. Excellent value, esp *Grande Res Naoussa* to age 40 yrs+. Top: 1879 Legacy NAOUSSA, from v. old vyd.

Carras, Dom Mac ★★ Historic estate at Halkidiki, recently changed hands. Ch Carras a timeless classic.

Cephalonia Ion Important island with three POPs: mineral and floral ROBOLA (w), rare MUSCAT (w sw) and MAVRODAPHNE (r sw). Dry Mavrodaphne is a must-try but cannot be POP.

Dalamaras ★★★→★★★★ Prodigious producer in NAOUSSA. Delectable range of great purity; Palaiokalias is world class. Try to find Vieilles Vignes.

Dougos C Gr ★★★ On the foothills of Mt Olympus, an ambassador for RAPSANI. Expressive reds esp Old Vines.

Economou Ktima Crete ★★★★ One of great artisans of Greece; in Sitia. V. rare.

Gaia Aeg, Pelop ★★★ Exquisite Thalassitis SANTORINI (rare Submerged aged, well, submerged), orange Clay ASSYRTIKO might be best of genre. From NEMEA: ever-evolving *Gaia Estate.*

Gentilini Ion ★★★ Historic CEPHALONIA winery, incl *steely Robola*. Wild Paths redefines ROBOLA. Dry MAVRODAPHNE Eclipse (r) is benchmark.

Gerovassiliou Mac ★★★ Possibly the leader in Greece. Captivating ASSYRTIKO/MALAGOUSIA and top Malagousia (he's the specialist). Top red: Evangelo SYRAH/VIOGNIER. Linked with BIBLIA CHORA.

Goumenissa Mac ★→★★★ (POP) Excellent XINOMAVRO/Negoska (r), finally getting away from the shadow of NAOUSSA. Try Aidarinis, Chatzyvaritis, TATSIS.

Volcanic wines

Sommeliers across the globe increasingly see volcanic wines as an entity on their own with the obvious contender from Greece being SANTORINI. Yet Greece has a wealth of volcanos, about 40, most of which engulf vine-growing. like Lemnos, Ikaria, Lesvos and even Methana, Nisiros and Chios.

The Greeks are coming
With increasing plantings in Australia (Jim Barry), Italy (Alois Lageder), S Africa (Sadie, Jordan), Turkey (Chamlija) and California, Bulgaria and others in pipeline, ASSYRTIKO is the 1st Greek variety going international. But XINOMAVRO, AGIORGITIKO will, for sure, soon follow.

Hatzidakis Aeg ★★★ Top-class producer of SANTORINI; children of late Haridimos now in charge, less adventurous but v. fine. Try Skytali.

Karydas Mac ★★★ Tiny family KTIMA and amazing vyd in NAOUSSA, crafting refined, age-worthy XINOMAVRO.

Katogi Averoff Pelop, Epir ★★→★★★ Historic name and v. popular red. Top: Vlahiko from Rossiu di Munte range from plots at 1000m (3281ft)+.

Katsaros Thess ★★★ Tiny winery on Mt Olympus. KTIMA (CAB SAUV/MERLOT) is a Greek classic. Also try XINOMAVRO Valos.

Kechris ★★→★★★ Oak-aged, ASSYRTIKO-based The Tear of the Pine, possibly *world's best Retsina*: fantastic wine. No kidding.

Kir-Yianni Mac ★★→★★★ Initially vyds in NAOUSSA but AMYNTEO too (and new winery there). Age-worthy, XINOMAVRO-based reds delectable.

Ktima Estate. Should be used on export labels instead of "estate". Not that difficult.

Lazaridi, Ktima Costa Att, Mac ★★★ KTIMA in Drama and Att (Oenotria Land label). Crisp, aromatic Amethystos redefined Greek white in 90s. Top: Cava Amethystos CAB FR, then opulent Oenotria Land CAB SAUV/AGIORGITIKO. New plantings in upper Drama v. promising: try MALAGOUSIA.

Ancient Greece had specific amphora shapes for umpteen demarcated ACs. Simpler now.

Lazaridi, Nico Mac ★→★★★ Originally from Drama. Several large-volume, gd-value ranges, like Dama Koupa. Top: Magiko Vouno (r/w).

Ligas Mac ★★ Full-blown natural producer in Pella. For hard-core fans of the style but could convert others too.

Lyrarakis Crete ★★→★★★ Heraklio-based, reviving old, almost extinct Cretan varieties like Plyto and Dafni. *Single-vyd versions* extraordinary. Karnari Kotsifali is Cretan tradition re-imagined.

Malvasia Group of POPS recreating famous Medieval "Malmsey". Not from MALVASIA, but all local varieties. Four POPs: Monemvassia-M. in Laconia, M. of Paros, M. Chandakas-Candia and M. of Sitia, both from Crete.

Manoussakis (Nostos) Crete ★★★ Great KTIMA, initially Rhône-inspired, but Greek varieties here to stay: ASSYRTIKO, full Muscat of Spinas, Vidiano and even Romeiko (r).

Mantinia Pelop (POP) High-altitude, cool region. Floral, crisp, almost Germanic styles from MUSCAT-like *Moschofilero*. Excellent sparklers from TSELEPOS. Bosinakis, Troupis rising stars.

Mercouri Pelop ★★★ Beautiful KTIMA on w coast. V.gd dry MAVRODAPHNE/REFOSCO, delicious Foloi RODITIS (w).

Naoussa Mac ★★★ (POP) Top-quality region for sophisticated, structured XINOMAVRO. Best on par in quality, style (but not price) with Barolo. Top: DALAMARAS, KARYDAS, KIR-YIANNI, THIMIOPOULOS. Even standard bottlings age for 10 yrs++.

Nemea Pelop ★★→★★★ (POP) AGIORGITIKO reds. Can be stunning but always charming; styles from fresh to classic to exotic. Try Driopi from TSELEPOS, Aivalis (oak), GAIA, Ieropoulos, Mitravelas, PALYVOS, PAPAÏOANNOU, SKOURAS.

Palyvos Pelop ★★→★★★ Fine Ktima in NEMEA making big-framed reds with AGIORGITIKO and French varieties.

Papaioannou Ktima Pelop ★★★ If NEMEA were Burgundy, Thanassis P would have been Jayer. Now in able hands of son Giorgos. Excellent value KTIMA, Palea Klimata (old vines), Microclima (micro-vyd), top-end Terroir. Age everything.

Pavlidis Mac ★★★ Premium KTIMA based in Drama. Trendy Thema (w) ASSYRTIKO/ SAUV BL, (r) AGIORGITIKO/SYRAH. Emphasis: expressive varietals incl Agiorgitiko, Assyrtiko and TEMPRANILLO.

Probably less than 50% native Greek varieties commericaly available. Get planting!

PGE / PGI Regional wines; used to be labelled TO. *See* POP.

POP Greek equivalent of AOP. Many amazing wines not incl. *See also* PGE.

Rapsani Thess POP on Mt Olympus. Made famous in 90s by TSANTALIS (try Grande Res); now DOUGOS and others add excitement. XINOMAVRO based blends.

Retsina New Age Retsinas (eg. GAIA, KECHRIS, natural style Kamara) have freshness, character – great alternative to Fino Sherry. A revolution in making, and one you mustn't miss.

Samos Aeg ★★→★★★ (POP) Island famed for sweet MUSCAT BL. Esp fortified Anthemis, sun-dried Nectar. Rare old bottlings are steals, eg. hard-to-find Nectar 75 or 80. New producers emerging, like Nopera.

Santorini Aeg ★★★→★★★★ Dramatic volcanic island with POP white (dr/sw) wines to match. Luscious VINSANTO, salty, **bone-dry Assyrtiko**. Top: ARGYROS, GAIA, HATZIDAKIS, SANTO, SIGALAS. Although getting expensive, still cheapest ★★★★ whites around, age 20 yrs. MAVROTRAGANO reds (not incl in POP) can be sublime. Image leader for Greek wine.

Santo Wines Aeg ★★→★★★ Successful SANTORINI co-op. Try rich Grande Res, dry Irini (aged in VINSANTO barrels) and complex Vinsantos. Great value by Santorinian standards.

Semeli C Gr, Pelop ★★ Vast range, gd value. Main focus on NEMEA, MANTINIA but expanding in other regions.

Sigalas Aeg ★★★★ Leading light of SANTORINI. Kavalieros, Nychteri, Roptro out of this world; Seven Villages micro-cuvées a thesis on local terroir. Frequently gives Grand Cru Chablis run for its money.

Skouras Pelop ★★★ Innovative. Lean, wild-yeast Salto MOSCHOFILERO. Top reds: high-altitude Grande Cuvée NEMEA, Megas Oenos. Solera-aged Labyrinth is beautiful, Peplo rosé is thought-provoking. *Recioto*-like Titanas a new breath-taking addition.

Tatsis Mac ★★★ Natural producer in GOUMENISSA but has pure, clean, beautiful style.

Thimiopoulos Mac ★★★★ Superstar producer in NAOUSSA, RAPSANI (Terra Petra). Aftorizo Naoussa (own-rooted vines) best but Earth and Sky conquers markets.

Tsantalis Mac ★→★★★ Long est producer. Huge range. Gd RAPSANI Res, Grande Res, gd value from Thrace. Monastery wines from **Mount Athos** noteworthy.

Tselepos Pelop ★★★ Leader in MANTINIA, NEMEA (as Driopi) and SANTORINI (Canava Chrysou). Greece's best MERLOT (★★★★ Kokkinomylos). Avlotopi CAB SAUV not far behind. Great Driopi Res and amphora Laoudia Santorini.

Vinsanto Aeg ★★★★ Sun-dried, cask-aged luscious ASSYRTIKO and Aidani from SANTORINI that can age forever. Insanely low yields.

The young generation

Here are some names to watch for among the new generation of producers. At existing estates: Argiris GEROVASSILIOU, Aris TSELEPOS, Chloe Chatzyvaritis, Dimitris SKOURAS, Evripidis KATSAROS, Federica LAZARIDIS, PALYVOS sisters, Theodora Rouvalis and many more. New entries: Foivos Papastratis (Foivos), Girlemis brothers (Girlemis), Iliana Mahilin (Mahilin Chryssos), Konstantinos Psaroulis (Psaroulis), Lefteris Digenakis (Digenakis), Michalis Kanakaris (Kanakaris).

Eastern Mediterranean and North Africa

EASTERN MEDITERRANEAN

This wine region, part of the Ancient World, has become very dynamic. To most it is a paradox. A wine-lover from 2000 years ago would have had no problem with the idea of fine wine from here; but a lot has happened since then. Nowadays there is much innovation and rising quality.

CYPRUS

Heroic viticulture defines Cyprus – on drought-prone land, high in the mtns to avoid baking summer temperatures. Next-generation winemakers are experimenting and exploring terroir, with many now releasing single-vyd wines. Local varieties like Promara, Yiannoudi, Morokanella continue their rise, joined by another rediscovered variety named Vasilissa. Genuinely old vines are another feature of Cyprus (phylloxera never made it here) while producers hope the trend for Cypriots to support and visit their local wineries continues.

Wine residues from clay jars on Cyprus date back 5500 yrs.

Aes Ambelis ★★ V.gd modern COMMANDARIA. Also gd Morokanella, Promara, rosé.

Anama Concept ★★ Husband and wife handcrafting amazing rich COMMANDARIA from old-vine MAVRO only.

Argyrides Vineyards ★★ Stunningly beautiful family winery in picturesque village of Vasa. Excellent MARATHEFTIKO, MOURVÈDRE. V.gd VIOGNIER.

Commandaria Rich, sweet PDO wine from sun-dried XYNISTERI and MAVRO grapes. Probably most ancient named wine still in production – since 800 BC. Survived Ottomans by exporting to Christian churches. New-generation producers: AES AMBELIS, ANAMA CONCEPT, Gerolemo, KYPEROUNDA, TSIAKKAS. Traditional styles: Alasia (Loel), Centurion (ETKO), St Barnabas (KAMANTERENA), St John (KEO).

Constantinou ★→★★ Lemesos region. Gd CAB SAUV, SHIRAZ.

ETKO & Olympus ★ Oldest Cyprus winery (1844). Traditional-style COMMANDARIA, Haggipavlou label for better dry wines.

Gerolemo ★ Modern family winery at 900m (2953ft), noted for expressive aromatic whites and improving reds.

Kamanterena (SODAP) ★→★★ Largest producer in Pafos hills, grower-owned. Gd-value DYA whites, esp XYNISTERI, and rosé MARATHEFTIKO.

KEO ★ Winemaking at Mallia Estate. Ktima Keo range best. St John ★★ COMMANDARIA.

Kyperounda ★★→★★★ Some of Europe's highest vyds at 1450m (4757ft). *Petritis* remains standard-setting XYNISTERI. Flagship Epos CHARD and red from own vyd. V.gd: Skopos SHIRAZ, Andessitis blend. Excellent modern COMMANDARIA.

Makkas ★→★★ Pafos region. Garage winery. Gd MARATHEFTIKO, SYRAH, XYNISTERI.

Tsiakkas ★★→★★★ Dynamic mtn winery, expressive whites: SAUV BL, Promara, XYNISTERI. Also v.gd COMMANDARIA, Vamvakada (aka MARATHEFTIKO), Yiannoudi, organic Rodinos rosé.

Keep an eye on newcomers: Ekfraseis Winery and Makarounas.

Vasilikon, K&K Winery ★★ Only female winemaker on Cyprus. V.gd whites: XYNISTERI, Vasilissa. Appealing reds: Ayios Onoufrios, MARATHEFTIKO, Mcthy.

Vlassides ★★→★★★ UC Davis-trained Vlassides makes superb SHIRAZ, gd DYA Grifos, promising Yiannoudi, excellent long-ageing Opus Artis from best sites.

Vouni Panayia ★★→★★★ The 1st ever private regional winery in 1987, local grape focus. Try Alina XYNISTERI, MARATHEFTIKO, Promara, Spourtiko, Yiannoudi.

Zambartas ★★→★★★ Australia-trained winemaker making v.gd single-vyd range incl Margelina from centenarian vines, XYNISTERI. V.gd Zambartas range esp MARATHEFTIKO, SHIRAZ/Lefkada, fruity Koukouvagia range.

ISRAEL

Encouraging changes are taking place, with more blends appearing instead of a reliance on varietals; some v.gd new whites. The Israelis are strong on technology and R&D, and it's an excellent place to study ways of dealing with climate change. Best regions: high-elevation Upper Galilee (Up Gal), Golan Heights (Gol) and Judean Hills (Jud). Other abbreviations: Gailiee (Gal), Negev (Neg), Samson (Sam), Shomron (Shom).

1848 Gal, Jud ★→★★ Best of Shor family, winemakers since 1848. Classic CAB FR, new single-vyd Argaman, monster PETITE SIRAH.

Abaya Shom ★→★★ Terroirist who rehabilitates forgotten vyds. Focused, tannic Shuni CARIGNAN. White and orange COLOMBARD.

Ashkar Gal ★→★★ Israeli-Arab family, spotless domestic winery. Gd SAUV BL.

Barkan-Segal Jud, Sam ★→★★★ Largest winery; winemaker new MW. Barkan: cherry-berry Argaman, zesty COLOMBARD; Segal: charming whole-cluster PINOT N, SYRAH, new CARIGNAN. Savoury Marawi, Dabouki. Cypriot project with SODAP.

Bar-Maor Shom ★→★★ Min-intervention winemaking. Crisp, fresh rosé.

Carmel Gal, Shom ★→★★ Historic winery, est 1882. Focus on basic wines.

Castel, Dom du Jud ★★★★ Jud pioneer, setting standards for style and quality. Beautiful, advanced winery. Grand Vin is rich, deep, complex. Plush Petit Castel, great-value second label. Refreshing rosé. Well-balanced "C" Blanc du Castel (CHARD). La Vie entry-level.

Clos de Gat Jud ★★★ Estate with style, individuality. Powerful Sycra SYRAH, rare, rich MERLOT, gd CHARD. Great-value Harel Syrah, entry-level Chanson (w).

Cremisan ★→★★ Central Mtns. Palestinian wine in a monastery. Indigenous grapes pioneers: Baladi, Dabouki, Hamdani, Jandali. Hamdani/Jandali (w) best.

Dalton Up Gal ★★ Family winery, with creative winemaker. Lively Levantina (r), refreshing CARIGNAN, full Wild One CHENIN BL.

Feldstein Jud, Gal ★★ Individualist. Specialist in Dabouki, dried-grape Argaman. Characterful SEM/SAUV BL. Tends to be expensive.

Flam Jud, Gal ★★★→★★★★ Brothers run this Jud family winery. Elegant B'x-blend Noble, fruit-forward SYRAH, deep MERLOT. Classico always great value. Fresh, fragrant SAUV BL/CHARD, crisp rosé. Prestige Chard Camellia: silky, elegant.

Galil Mountain Up Gal ★ Prestige blend Yiron gd value. Refreshing GRENACHE.

Golan, Ch Gol ★★★ Innovative, expressive winemaker. V.gd Geshem (r/w) Med blends. Excellent SYRAH, bold Eliad.

Gvaot Shom ★★→★★★ Winemaker researching local varieties. Deep CAB, expressive PINOT N, hefty PETIT VERDOT, fruity Bittuni, Hamdani/Jandali (w).

Jezreel Valley Shom ★→★★ Voluptuous CARIGNAN and Argaman. Prestige Icon.

Kosher Necessary for religious Jews; irrelevant to quality. Wines can be v.gd; 90%+ Israeli wine is kosher. Largest wineries only make kosher.

Lahat Gal ★★→★★★ Rhône specialist. Enchanting GSM; white, ageing ability.

Lewinsohn Gal ★★★ Quality *garagiste*. V.gd CHARD, chunky, spicy SYRAH, whole-cluster PETITE SIRAH.

Maia Shom ★→★★ Med-style with Greek consultants. Refreshing, drinkable wines.

Margalit Gal, Shom ★★★ Father and son making Israel's 1st cult wine. B'x-blend Enigma; rich, complex CAB FR. Gd cellaring potential.

Mia Luce Gal ★★→★★★ *Garagiste*. Rhôney SYRAH, superb MARSELAN, fine COLOMBARD.

Nana Neg ★→★★ Neg pioneer. V.gd CHENIN BL, robust SYRAH.

Pelter-Matar Gol ★★ A v. popular brand. Gd CHARD, SAUV BL. Matar kosher label.

Psagot Jud ★→★★★ Central Mtn vyds. Peak is big, succulent Med blend.

Raziel Jud ★★ New from Ben Zaken family (CASTEL). Characterful rosé; tight, fine-textured SYRAH/CARIGNAN. Fizz coming.

Climate change and plague ended the Neg's thriving wine industry 1500 yrs ago.

Recanati Gal ★★ Rich, wild CARIGNAN, bold Special Res. Building new winery.

Sea Horse Jud ★★→★★★ Idiosyncratic, with intense Châteauneuf-style Antoine. Varietal Counoise. Intriguing Oz, mainly CINSAULT/ GRENACHE.

Shiloh Jud ★★ Award-winning. Cab Sauv: robust, rich, oaky. Central Mtns.

Shvo Up Gal ★★★ Non-interventionist winemaker, a true vigneron. Super-rustic chewy red, rare Gershon SAUV BL, great value Cheninchik, characterful rosé.

Somek Shom ★→★★ Characterful CARIGNAN, from Hanadiv Valley; 5th generation.

Sphera Jud ★★★→★★★★ White only; fizz is planned. Crisp White Concept varietals, racy RIES. Harmonious First Page (SEM/ROUSSANNE/CHENIN BL). Complex, rare White Signature (Sem/Chard). Cool-climate style from Judean Hills.

Tabor Gal ★→★★ V.gd whites, esp SAUV BL. Ecological vyds. Flavourful Eco.

Teperberg Jud, Sam ★→★★ Israel's largest family winery. Five generations, 150th anniversary. Full-bodied CAB FR; fruit driven MALBEC/MARSELAN.

Tulip Gal ★★ →★★★ Innovative, progressive. Opulent Black Tulip, deep SHIRAZ, bracing SAUV BL. Works with adults with special needs.

Tura Shom ★→★★ Central Mtns. MERLOT with structure and mouthfilling flavour.

Tzora Jud ★★★★ Terroir-led, precision winemaking. Beautiful Shoresh vyd in Jud. Talented winemaker (Israel's 1st MW). Wines show intensity, balance, elegance. Crisp, complex Shoresh Blanc; Judean Hills (r/w) always superb value. Graceful Misty Hills with finesse (CAB SAUV/SYRAH).

Vitkin Jud ★★→★★★ ABC icebreaker, and quality CARIGNAN pioneer. Excellent old-vine Carignan, PETITE SIRAH. Complex GRENACHE BL, new MACABEO.

Vortman Shom ★→★★ V.gd whites: COLOMBARD, FUMÉ BL. New SEM.

Yaacov Oryah Sam ★★→★★★ Creative artisan. Silent Hunter (w). Ten orange wines.

Yarden Gol ★★→★★★★ The pioneering winery of Israel. Rare, prestige Katzrin. New single-vyd wines. Kings of CAB s at every price point. Refreshing PINOT GR, superb Blanc de Blancs (sp). Second label: Gamla. SANGIOVESE of interest. Mt Hermon (r) big-selling brand.

Yatir Jud ★★→★★★ Desert winery, forest vyds. Velvety, elegant Yatir Forest, intense PETIT VERDOT, gd value Mt Amasa.

LEBANON

Despite a gruesome year, small-volume producers continue to shine, especially with off-piste styles made with indigenous whites Merwah and Obeideh. Watch out for more red Aswad Karesh. Heritage varieties CINSAULT, GRENACHE, CARIGNAN and MOURVÈDRE still challenging the B'x/Rhône classics, but CAB FR making a name as a varietal. High-altitude (1000m/3281ft+) CHARD, SAUV BL, VIOGNIER jockeying for equal billing with the reds. Ditto grown-up, darker rosés.

Aurora ★★ Small Batroun winery, hitting right notes with serious gravelly, plush CAB FR; also PINOT N, CHARD.

Baal, Dom de ★★ Serious, crisp CHARD/SAUV BL, organic heady estate red.

Belle-Vue, Ch ★★★ Le Chateau and Le Renaissance, plush blends of B'x grapes/ SYRAH. Also Petit Geste (SAUV BL/VIOGNIER).

Clos St. Thomas ★→★★★ The Toumas are a famous Bekaa wine family. Fruity, elegant CINSAULT-based Les Gourmets, also in white and rosé. Aromatic Obaidy (sic) and muscular, high altitude PINOT N.

Coteaux du Liban ★★ CINSAULT blend, Obeideh, CHARD/VIOGNIER. One to watch.

IXSIR ★★→★★★ Stony SYRAH-based blends, floral whites and prestige El. Altitudes range and Grande Res Rosé excellent.

Kefraya, Ch ★★→★★★★ Fine, ripe, rich, complex **Comte de M.** Full, fragrant, oaky Comtesse de M (CHARD/VIOGNIER). Les Breteches is fruity, CINSAULT-based red. Aswad Karesh and SAPARAVI varietals, latter made in amphorae.

Ksara, Ch ★★★ Founded 1857. Res du Couvent is fruity, easy-drinking, full of flavour. Blanc de Blancs (CHARD/SAUV BL/SEM) and Chard outstanding whites. New CARIGNAN and Merwah varietals show willingness to innovate.

Marsyas, Ch ★★ Powerful CAB/SYRAH; B-Qa de Marsyas more Rhône-y. Owner of complex ★★★ Bargylus (Syria), miracle wine made in impossible conditions.

Massaya ★★ Terraces de Baalbeck: refined GSM. Entry-level Les Colombiers v.gd value. Also Cap Est (r) from E Bekaa vyds on Anti-Lebanon Mtns. Punchy rosé.

Musar, Ch ★★★→★★★★★ Icon wine of E Med, CAB SAUV/CINSAULT/CARIGNAN 02 03 05' 07' 08 09 10 11 12. **Unique recognizable style.** Best after 15–20 yrs in bottle. Indigenous Obaideh, Merweh age indefinitely. Second label: Hochar (r) now higher profile. Musar Jeune is softer, easy-drinking.

Najm, Dom ★★★ Tiny winery in Batroun. One red: seriously earthy, red fruit, MUSAR-esque CAB SAUV/GRENACHE/MOURVÈDRE. Lebanon's unicorn wine.

Sept ★★★ *Garagiste enfant terrible.* Skin-contact Obeideh; other min-contact varietals.

Terre Joie ★★ Small W Bekaa winery. Only reds and a crunchy rosé. CINSAULT, CAB FR and rare (in Lebanon) high-quality MERLOT.

Tourelles, Dom des ★★→★★★★ Blockbuster SYRAH, gd Marquis des Beys. Outstanding old-vine CINSAULT, CARIGNAN; equally gd classic red. Classy rosé.

Vertical 33 ★→★★★ Organic CINSAULT, CARIGNAN, Obeideh, PINOT N. Neo-MUSAR!

Hyper-inflation has pushed whisky drinkers to switch to arak, 55% abv (aniseed).

TURKEY

It does not get easier for Turkish winemakers. Despite this, many are investing in quality and their indigenous grapes are always fascinating for the curious.

Buzbag ★ Still being made (KAYRA.) Rustic ÖKÜZGÖZÜ/BOĞAZKERE is better these days.

Chamlija ★★→★★★ Django is 1st £100 Turkish wine. Praiseworthy PINOT N too.

Corvus ★★ Bozcaada island. Intense, oaky style.

Doluca ★→★★ Three generations of same family. Kav is from local varieties.

Kalpak ★ One to watch. Gd single-vyd B'x varieties.

Kavaklidere ★→★★★ Oldest and largest winery; modern wines. Pendore estate best, esp ÖKÜZGÖZÜ, SYRAH. Easy-drinking Yakut.

Kayra ★→★★★ SHIRAZ, NARINCE, ÖKÜZGÖZÜ. Benefit of E Anatolia vyds, winery.

Pasaeli ★→★★★ Fresh, vibrant B'x-style blends from single vyd.

Sevilen ★→★★★ International variety specialist. Spicy SYRAH, aromatic SAUV BL.

Shiluh Unique from SE Anatolia. Wines made in buried clay jars, no filtration or fining. Owned by members of ancient Syriac community.

Suvla ★→★★★ Full-bodied B'x blend Sur, and fruity SYRAH backed by oak.

Urla ★★→★★★★ Tempus (r) has complexity. NERO D'AVOLA Karasi is firm, spicy.

Notable names in North Africa

In **Morocco**: Baccari (Première de Baccari), Castel Frères (Boulaouane Vin Gris), Celliers de Meknès (Ch Roslane), Ouled Thaleb (Tandem/ Syrocco ★★), Val d'Argan (Orian; organic), Volubilia (gd Vin Gris, Epicuria label). In **Tunisia**: Neferis (Selian Carignan).

Asia & Black Sea & Caucasus

ASIA

China For all the attention lavished on CAB, China's foremost red is MARSELAN. Of the c.120,000 ha producing wine, Marselan has just 3% (but continues to grow) against 60% Cab Sauv and 8% Cabernet Gernischt. The consistently best Marselan is Xinjiang's Ch Zhongfei. Look out also for Zhongfei SYRAH. Other successful Marselans incl Grace Vyds and Tiansai Skyline. The Cab crown goes to Jia Bei Lan of Ningxia, but Lafite's Dom de Long Dai in Shandong's Qiu Shan Valley sets a record in eye-watering prices. LVMH-owned Ao Yun completes the Cab triumvirate in quality and pricing. Look out for Silver Heights, Legacy Peak, Ch Rongzi, Ch Chanson's CAB FR, Ch Silk Road Six Star Dry Red (90% Cab Gernischt (CARMENÈRE), 10% PETIT VERDOT), and Sha Po Tou's 100% Cab Gernischt from 25-yr-old vines too. Arguably Dom du 1er Juin produces the most consistent PINOT N, and has gd RIES, as does Guofei. China's best white is Taila Winery's rich, sweet, fresh Petit MANSENG. Wine giant Changyu also produces award-winning Icewine from VIDAL. The sparkling crown goes to Dom Chandon, a Moët Hennessy outpost. MUSCAT has promise and Puchang Vyds offers a rich, dry version. CHARD – as with Cab Sauv, even Marselan – tends to be too oaky. Almost always, the mid-range shows more fruit while the top tier – invariably designated "Reserve" – means more new oak, higher toast and northerly prices. Commendable Chards are made by Pernod Ricard's Dom Helan Mountain, Tiansai Skyline of Gobi, Legacy Peak and Helan Qingxue. Ch Changyu Moser XV Cab Sauv Blanc de Noir is Provencal-inspired rosé in collaboration with winemaker and consultant Laurenz Maria Moser V of Austria.

Indian wine "enjoys" two harvests/yr, but quality-minded producers only pick once; c.2000 ha dedicated to wine, mainly in Maharashtra, Karnataka and Andhra Pradesh states. Moët Hennessy's Chandon and homegrown York are best sparkling. Most consistent SAUV BL is Sula; also gd: Vallonne VIOGNIER, CHENIN BL; Charosa CAB SAUV, TEMPRANILLO, Fratelli (r/w); KRSMA Sauv Bl, CHARD, Cab Sauv. RIES vines are young but to watch out for. Word of caution for winelovers of fruit: many Indian reds are overwhelmed by oak.

Japan is now making more Koshu than all its reds put together.

Japan Delicate, subtle KOSHU is Japan's indigenous grape, and is sometimes oak-aged, though oaking Koshu is like cooking sashimi. Top is Grace Wine, esp Cuvée Misawa Akeno. Koshu arrived in Japan with a returning traveller: it contains DNA from wild Chinese vines. Between 630 and 838, the Japanese court sent 19 missions to Tang China, and a Buddhist monk called Gyoki is believed to have planted the 1st vines in the grounds of Daizenji Temple in Katsunuma, Yamanashi, in 718. Also gd Koshu from Aruga Branca, Ch Mercian, Dom Hide, Haramo, L'Orient, Lumiere, Marquis, Soryu and Suntory, esp single-vyd Tomi No Oka. Look for orange versions. Muscat Bailey A is most widely planted red: candy floss/bubble-gum aroma, flavour, which serious winemakers try to suppress. Try Dom Hide, Chanter Wine (also known as Diamond Shuzo) Carre Cuvée K. Chitose Winery (owned by Grace Wine) makes gd PINOT N, also try Grace's Blanc de Blanc (sp CHARD); Suntory Tomi Noble d'Or is v.gd noble-rot RIES. Yamanashi Prefecture is heart of industry; Nagano for natural wines.

BLACK SEA & CAUCASUS

Georgia is a model and a source of inspiration for macerated, amphorae-fermented wines, which are now super-popular among wine geeks and adepts of natural winemaking. If Georgia has millennia of wine tradition and original first-class local grapes, so does Armenia, its neighbour, which also boasts mountainous phylloxera-free vineyards. In Russia and Ukraine, locally produced quality wines in dry styles are on the rise. Moldova is taking the world by surprise with its new outstanding wines. Off the beaten track is a significant production in Kazakhstan, where an eclectic mix of varieties is cultivated above 1000m (3281ft).

Armenia's winemaking is as old as Georgia's (the most ancient winery dates back 6100 yrs), with a shared use of amphorae, known here as *karas*. Indigenous grapes (w) Voskeat, Garandamak, (r) Areni, Hindogny, Kakhet give gd quality. Try larger Armenia Wines and Hin Areni or boutique ArmAs, Old Bridge, Van Ardi, Voskeni, Voskevaz, v.gd Zorah.

Georgia's affinity for ancient winemaking methods, using buried *qvevris* for skin-macerated fermentation, resounds well today with the idea of natural wines, but they've been practised in this country for 8000 yrs as its unbroken viticultural history attests. Equally fascinating are indigenous varieties (over 500, though less than 10% used for commercial production). Signature red is SAPERAVI, made in many styles from light semi-sweet to powerful, dry, tannic and age-worthy. Vibrant white Rkatsiteli lends itself well to skin-contact fermentation, known as Kakheti method in Georgia and orange wine elsewhere. White Mtsvane and Kisi gain recognition. Est producers incl Badagoni, Ch Mukhrani, Dakishvili, GWS, Jakeli Khashmi, Kindzmarauli Marani, Marani (TWC), Pheasant's Tears, Schuchmann, Tbilvino, Tsinandali.

Moldova, in the se of Europe, has more vyds than S Africa, and boasts the highest density of plantings and largest cellars in the world. Backed by ancient history and fame in tsarist Russia, its modern production is export-oriented, offering value. International grapes dominate, but worth seeking local: (w) FETEASCĂ ALBĂ, FETEASCĂ REGALĂ, Viorica, (r) FETEASCĂ NEAGRĂ, Rară Neagră. Try unusual red blend Negru de Purcari (Cab Sauv/SAPERAVI/Rară Neagră) and Icewine. Leading producers incl Cricova (sp), Milestii Mici, Vinăria Purcari. Gd-to-excellent quality at Asconi, Castel Mimi, Ch Vartely, Et Cetera, Lion Gri, Vinăria Bostavan.

Russian wines are becoming mainstream in the home market; international recognition is yet low. Young winemakers who studied and worked abroad shape the future. Natural conditions for production best by Black Sea and River Kuban, but some vyds planted as far as Caspian Sea. Harsh climate in Don Valley, known for indigenous grapes (r Krasnostop, Tsimliansky), requires vines to be buried in winter. Elsewhere winemaking is centred around international grapes. Acclaimed quality by Lefkadia. Est large producers: Abrau Durso (sp), Fanagoria, Kuban Vino (Ch Tamagne). Exciting smaller wineries incl Burnier, Gai-Kodzor, Golubitskoe Estate, Sikory, Usadba Divnomorskoe.

Ukraine's wine production stretches from temperate conditions of Black Sea to continental climate of Carpathian Mtns. Grapes mainly international. Crimea continues to be hotspot for premium wines (Uppa Winery, Oleg Repin). Wines modelled on Champagne an important/popular heritage: try ArtWinery, Novy Svet, Odessavinprom, Zolotaya Balka. Ch Chizay, Koktebel, Massandra, Solnechnaya Dolina known for traditional fortified styles, now niche production. Est producers for dry still wines incl Beykush Winery, Guliev Wines, Inkerman, Kolonist, Prince Trubetskoy Winery, Satera, Shabo, Veles.

United States

Abbreviations used in the text (*see also* Principal Viticultural Areas pp.245, 263, 269):

Arroyo GV	Arroyo Grande Valley, CA
Clark	Clarksburg, CA
Coomb	Coombsville, CA
Mad	Madera, CA
Oak Knoll	Oak K, CA
PNW	Pacific Northwest
San LO	San Luis Obispo, CA
Santa Cz Mts	Santa Cruz Mountains, CA
Son	Sonoma, CA

The US, to most outsiders, doesn't extend far beyond California; and California is probably just one place, with that place probably being Napa, and the wine probably being Cabernet. Blame the likes of Robert Mondavi: doing such a brilliant job of promoting your home region means that the rest of this (rather large) country is overshadowed. But take a pin and stick it in a map: chances are the state you've pinned makes wine. (One of my favourite stories of the year was an illicit winery discovered in a waste-water plant in Alabama, although that's not quite what I mean.) We list 24 states here; everywhere is experimenting, and some have established classic styles: how about Amador County's old-vine Zinfandels? Or Sonoma Coast's pure, tense Pinot Noir? Go north, and there's more outstanding Pinot in Oregon; Viognier in Virginia; Riesling in New York State; Rhône varieties in Texas. A new generation, even in Napa, is making styles far from the points-focused wines that used to rule. So much is new in the US. Time to look around.

American Viticultural Areas

With no production rules or traditions to protect, AVAs are only loosely comparable to appellations contrôlées. Administered by the US government's TTB, they are instead guides to location – and climate, soil, market – and are a wine-minded alternative to state or county labels. Whether a region within a state or a traits-based overlap such as high-toned Columbia Gorge shared by WA and OR, or NY, PA, OH's cool, water-tempered Lake Erie, there are 251 est AVAs – and a steady queue of applied and pending. Most (140) are in CA, which boasts a wealth of nested AVA subregions, some hyperfocused, like Napa V's Stag's Leap District. While an AVA label indicates a min higher standard at the federal level (state and county labels mean 75% provenance, AVA promises 85%) some states have stricter rules: OR famously demands 100% for the former, 95% for the latter. AVA approval standards are rigorous: petitions must show distinguishing features verifiable on US Geological Survey maps, and how they affect viticulture inside vs. outside the petitioned zone – whose proposed name must be one historically applied to the area, as shown by "newspapers, magazines, historical or modern books". As wine-growing quality and know-how rise across the US, the TTB says AVAs allow "producers to better describe the origin of their wines and... consumers to better identify wines." Some even translate to higher prices.

Arizona (AZ)

Tremendous growth driven by hip vibe, high-profile names and commitment to quality transcending state lines. Three regions (two AVAs) of high-desert terroir: volcanic rock and limestone, gd ripening weather. Wineries incl **Alcantara Vyds** elegant, earthy reds, esp Confluence IV and Grand Rouge. **Arizona Stronghold** ★★★ flagship Rhône blend Nachise (r) and excellent Tazi (w blend) and VIDAL Bl dessert. **Bodega Pierce** estate-grown SAUV BL. **Burning Tree Cellars** artisanal, small-batch, intense red blends. **Caduceus Cellars** ★★★ owned by Alt-rocker Maynard James Keenan, once a disruptor, now est; excellent Dos Ladrones (w blend), top Sancha (r), Nagual del Marzo. **Callaghan Vyds** ★★→★★★ pioneering winery making compelling AGLIANICO, TANNAT, quality red blends; Lisa's aromatic field blend (w). **Ch Tumbleweed** relative newcomer: Gen-X owners, focused wines, heritage plots. **Dos Cabezas WineWorks** blends across AVAs; El Signature El Campo (r/w). **Javelina Leap Vyd & Winery** awarded ZIN. **Page Springs Cellars** GSM, Rhône white, notable fresh UGNI BL. **Pillsbury Wine Company ★★** Filmmaker Sam Pillsbury's estate-grown Rhône varieties. Guns & Kisses SHIRAZ, PETITE SIRAH Special Res, and Roan Red. Try WildChild aromatic blend (w).

California (CA)

Whatever you could possibly want exists here in CA. You can have buttery or racy CHARD, even within the same county. Massive CABS or elegant; you can have both right in the NAPA V. Rhône and Iberian varieties are staking a claim inland, and ZIN craftsmanship is still a CA art form. Cloudy pét-nats and orange wines aged in clay amphorae are trendy. Cool, elevated areas nr the Pacific continue to impress, and innovative winemakers and growers farther inland continue to pursue freshness with heat-tolerant grapes, emphasizing simplicity and drinking pleasure. Global warming looms large, though. For the 4th yr running wildfires ripped through many counties. Smoke blanketed the entire state in late Sept and early Oct 2020. Numerous Napa, SON, Lake County wineries did not make reds in 2020, a promising vintage foiled by those fires and that heavy smoke. Earlier-harvested white wines may be outstanding, so all is not lost. AND V, PASO R, SANTA B avoided worst damage and should make terrific wines. Wines from s parts of Napa may be fine, time will tell.

Recent vintages

CA is too diverse for simple summaries. There can certainly be differences between the N, Central and S thirds of the state, but no "bad" vintages in over a decade. Wildfires and smoke have proved challenging in recent yrs, but only for latest-picked grapes.

2020 Small crop: great whites. N Coast reds: smoke issues.
2019 Solid harvest. Minor late losses in Alex V to fires, smoke taint.
2018 Bumper crop of great quality, but smoke issues in Lake County.
2017 Wildfires in Napa, Son after most grapes picked; quality mostly v.gd.
2016 Gd quality: reds/whites show great freshness, charm.
2015 Dry yr, low yields, but quality surprisingly gd, concentrated.
2014 Despite 3rd year of drought, quality high.
2013 Another large harvest with excellent quality prospects.
2012 Cab Sauv oustanding. V. promising for most varieties.

Principal viticultural areas

There are well over 100 AVAs in CA. Below are the key players.
Alexander Valley (Alex V) Son. Warm region in upper Son. Best-known for gd Zin, Cab Sauv on hillsides.
Amador County (Am Co) Warm Sierra County with wealth of old-vine Zin; Rhône grapes also flourish.
Anderson Valley (And V) Mend. Pacific fog and winds follow Navarro River inland. Superb Pinot N, Chard, sparkling, v.gd Ries, Gewurz, some stellar Syrah.
Atlas Peak E Napa. Exceptional Cab Sauv, Merlot.
Calistoga (Cal) Warmer n end of Napa V. Red wine territory esp Cab Sauv.
Carneros (Car) Napa, Son. Cool AVA at n tip of SF Bay. Gd Pinot N, Chard; Merlot, Syrah, Cab Sauv on warmer sites. V.gd sparkling.
Coombsville (Coomb) Napa. Cool region nr SF Bay; top Cab Sauv in B'x pattern.
Diamond Mountain Napa. High-elevation vines, outstanding Cab Sauv.
Dry Creek Valley (Dry CV) Son. Top Zin, gd Sauv Bl; gd hillside Cab Sauv, Zin.
Edna Valley (Edna V) San LO. Cool Pacific winds; v.gd Chard.

El Dorado County (El Dor Co) High-altitude inland area surrounding Placerville. Some real talent emerging with Rhône grapes, Zin, Cab and more.

Howell Mountain Napa. Briary Napa Cab Sauv from steep, volcanic hillsides.

Livermore Valley (Liv V) Suburban, gravelly, warm region e of SF, gd potential.

Mendocino Ridge (Mend Rdg). Emerging region in Mend, dictated by elevation over 365m (1198ft). Cool, above fog, lean soils.

Mendocino County (Mend) Large county n of Son County, incl warm Red V and cool And V.

Monterey County (Mont) Big ranches in Salinas V provide affordable Chard and Pinot N in cool, windy conditions. Carmel V bit warmer, Arroyo Seco moderate.

Mount Veeder Napa. High mtn vyds for gd Chard, Cab Sauv.

Napa Valley (Napa V) Cab Sauv, Merlot, Cab Fr. Look to sub-AVAs for meaningful terroir-based wines, and mtn areas for most complex, age-worthy.

Oakville (Oak) Napa. Prime Cab Sauv territory on gravelly bench.

Paso Robles (P Rob) San LO. Popular with visitors. Reds: Rhône, B'x varieties.

Pritchard Hill (P Hill) E Napa. Elevated, woody, prime terrritory for Cab Sauv.

Red Hills of Lake County (R Hills) N extension of Mayacama range, great Cab Sauv country.

Redwood Valley (Red V) Mend. Warmer inland region; gd Zin, Cab Sauv, Sauv Bl.

Russian River Valley (RRV) Son. Pacific fog lingers; Pinot N, Chard, gd Zin on benchland.

Rutherford (Ruth) Napa. Outstanding Cab Sauv, esp hillside vyds.

Saint Helena (St H) Napa. Lovely balanced Cab Sauv.

Santa Barbara County (Santa B) County n of LA; transverse valleys, several notable subzones, cool and warm.

Santa Lucia Highlands (Santa LH) Mont. Higher elevation, s-facing hillsides, great Pinot N, Syrah, Rhônes.

Santa Maria Valley (Santa MV) Santa B. Coastal cool; gd Pinot N, Chard, Viognier.

Sta Rita Hills (Sta RH) Santa B. Excellent Pinot N.

Santa Ynez (Santa Ynz) Santa B. Rhônes (r/w), Chard, Sauv Bl best bet.

Sierra Foothills (Sierra F'hills) El Dor Co, Am Co, Calaveras County. All improving.

Sonoma Coast (Son Coast) V. cool climate; edgy Pinot N, Chard, Syrah.

Sonoma Valley (Son V) Gd Chard, v.gd Zin; excellent Cab Sauv from Son Mtn sub-AVA. Note Son V is area within Son County.

Spring Mountain Napa. Elevated Cab Sauv, complex soil mixes and exposures.

Stags Leap (Stags L) Napa. Classic red, black fruited Cab Sauv; v.gd Merlot.

Acorn RRV ★★→★★★ Preserving CA heritage making lively co-fermented field blends from historic Alegria vyd featuring ZIN plus 17 other mixed black grapes.

Alban Vineyards Edna V ★★★ John A, a SYRAH frontiersman, specialist and original Rhône Ranger, still making great wine in EDNA V climate sweet spot. Top VIOGNIER, GRENACHE too. His vision has paid off.

Albatross Ridge Mont ★★★ Bowlus family rules high-elevation roost 11 km (7 miles) from Pacific nr Carmel. Early CHARDS, PINOT NS fresh and lively, warrant watching.

Alma Rosa Sta RH ★★★ Pioneer Dick Sanford's 2nd act after selling namesake winery. Continuing tradition of refined PINOT N, CHARD, also v.gd rosé.

Andrew Murray Vineyards Santa B ★★★ Rhônes around the clock, hits keep coming. SYRAH leads pack, but white VIOGNIER, ROUSSANNE, fresh GRENACHE BL hits too.

Anthill Farms Son Coast ★★★ Here three hard-working WILLIAMS-SELYEM alumni produce consistently lively, ethereal cool-climate PINOT N, SYRAH, old-vine, head-trained CHARD from coastal SON COAST and AND V. And V Pinot N is great value, worth seeking out. Serious up-and-comer.

Antica Napa Valley Napa V ★★★ Piero Antinori's ATLAS PEAK project initially flopped, subsequent lessees improved vyds, proving potential for fine CHARD, CAB SAUV. Antinori wisely reclaimed property.

Artesa Car ★★→★★★ Spanish-owned property back on track. Inspired architecture of winery, tasting room attracted visitors even as vision floundered between sparkling, CAR PINOT N and CHARD and Spanish varieties. These days wines generally strong across board, so enjoy the views and taste them all.

Au Bon Climat Santa B ★★★ Jim Clendenen made PINOT N, crisp CHARD before it was hip, and advocated elegant style now trending. Relevant as ever.

Baileyana Edna V ★★★ Cool, certified sustainable Paragon vyd planted by Jack Niven in 1973 delivers reliably superb, balanced PINOT N and peppery, lively SYRAH. Sister brands Tangent and Zocker bang out zesty whites sealed with screwcaps. ALBARIÑO, SAUV BL from Tangent; GRÜNER V, RIES from Zocker rock solid.

Banshee Wines Son Coast ★★★ Growing, scrappy PINOT N-driven brand with no vyds, but gd connections. Well-made single-vyd wines.

Barnett Spring Mtn ★★★ Under-the-radar mtn-top gem managed by David Tate, who also makes CHARD, PINOT N from SON V. Screaming gd wines across board, towering views, plus 1st rate NAPA V CAB SAUV – all well worth drive up mtn.

Baxter And V ★★★ Phil B, 2nd-generation winemaker makes subtly earthy, burgundian PINOT N (Oppenlander or Valenti vyds), exudes passion, confidence, competence. Small, but influential.

Beaulieu Vineyard ("BV") Napa V ★★→★★★ Iconic Georges de Latour Private Res CAB SAUV was NAPA V icon, but lost its lustre. Coastal Estate brand great in a pinch, lots of middling wines offering gd value.

Beckmen Vineyards Santa B ★★★ Steve Beckmen's bio Purisma Mtn estate produces formidable SYRAH, GRENACHE, GRENACHE BL. Affordable, excellent Cuvée le Bec red blend rightly popular nationwide.

Bedrock Wine Co. Son V ★★★ Morgan Peterson's label is a paean to historic ZIN vyds, techniques. Wisdom of ages seen through clear young eyes.

Beringer Napa ★★→★★★★ (Private Res) Big producer of average to high-level wines. Private Res CAB SAUV, single-vyd Cabs serious, age-worthy. HOWELL MTN Cab Sauv strong, CHARDS now fresher, better. Grand historic estate well worth a visit.

Berryessa Gap Vineyards Central V ★★ Upstart Yolo County project nr Sacramento making fresh, lightly oaked, Iberian inspired wines. TEMPRANILLO dazzling, VERDEJO and DURIF also delicious. Popular locally, beyond.

Bevan Cellars Napa V, Son ★★★→★★★★ Outsized personality with great taste, Russell B sources from prime single vyds making superb B'x varieties; CABS SAUV, FR most desirable. Bit of PINOT N and heavenly Dry Stack vyd SAUV BL from Bennett V also superb. Not cheap, but highly recommended.

Boeger Sierra F'hills ★★ Stalwart gold-country winery since 70s known for BARBERA, CHARBONO, ZIN. Surprising CHARD among best from SIERRA FOOTHILLS.

Bogle Central V, Lodi ★★ Dependable under-$15 grocery store family-owned brand delivers ever-reliable varietal wines from LODI, Clarksburg and now more coastal zones, all aged in real barrels. Respect.

Bokisch Vineyards Lodi ★★→★★★ Emergent Lodi star promoting Spanish varieties. V.gd TEMPRANILLO heads list backed by superb GRACIANO, ALBARIÑO, flirty Rosado.

Bonny Doon Mont ★★★ Randall Grahm's marketing is whimsical, but his wines

---

Aprill with his shours soote

Consider a pilgrimage to CA wine country in March or April. It's wondrous! Imagine intermittent showers, green hillsides, luminous yellow-mustard cover-crops, and naked old vines making for a colourful, ebullient setting. Tasting rooms are relaxed and less crowded, and no worries about fires scuttling your vacation.

CALIFORNIA

are serious, more terroir-driven than ever. *Vin gris* is superb, juicy Clos de Gilroy GRENACHE, Le Cigare Volant blend a CA Rhône classic. Sold 2020, Grahm stays on for now.

Brewer-Clifton Santa B ★★★ Estate STA RH PINOT N, CHARD producer now owned by JACKSON FAMILY WINES, OG Pinot N brand still in fine form, zesty Chards matured in neutral oak.

Bronco Wine Company ★→★★ Provocateur, populist Fred Franzia's company, famous for Two-Buck Chuck and scores of other commercial labels.

Buena Vista Son V ★★→★★★ Historic winery est 1857, now bedazzled by owner Jean Charles Boisset (DE LOACH, Raymond) with period costume tours, coloured lights and animatronics straight outta Disneyland. BYO mushrooms.

CADE Napa V ★★★ Superb wines: CAB SAUV, SAUV BL, ultra-modern winery on HOWELL MTN. Partnership: Getty family, CA Governor Newsom, GM John Conover.

Cakebread Napa V ★★★ CAB SAUV still has massive cachet with baby boomers. SAUV BL popular, CHARD v.gd. Diverse direct-to-consumer offerings.

Calera ★★★→★★★★ Central Coast. Mt Harlan pioneer Josh Jensen sought limestone and altitude for PINOT N, CHARD and struck gold. Sold to DUCKHORN (2017), brand in gd hands. Jensen, Selleck vyds always stylish.

Carlisle Son V ★★★ The best way to save historic vyds is to make extraordinary wines from them. Mike Officer crafts brilliant ZIN-based field blends from N CA, preserving history with updated growing tech. Rhône reds also notable.

Olé, Olé, Olé, Olé! Cheer on Spanish and Portuguese varieties in CA.

Carneros, Dom Car ★★★→★★★★ Taittinger outpost in CAR offering consistently gd bubbly, esp Vintage Blanc de Blancs Le Rêve. V.gd NV Rosé. Vintage Brut impressive. The Famous Gate PINOT N formidable.

Caymus Napa V ★★★ One of NAPA's foremost international status brands. Special Selection CAB SAUVS esp iconic, but on rich, sappy end of style spectrum.

Cedarville Sierra F'hills ★★★ Bootstrappers Jonathan Lachs and Susan Marks built a powerhouse in the granite-rich Fairplay District of EL DOR CO. Superb wines across board, mostly red. GRENACHE, SYRAH, fine CAB SAUVS, ZIN.

Chandon, Dom Napa V ★★→★★★ Moët outpost in Yountville, top bubbly is v.gd. NV Res Étoile Blanc, Rosé. Great pairings, experience at outdoor restaurant.

Chappellet Napa V ★★★★ Pritchard Hill original, great since 60s. Rugged terrain gives v. durable, exotic Cabs. Signature series CAB SAUV superb, dry CHENIN BL a rare treat. Still family owned, also owns PINOT N, CHARD themed SONOMA-LOEB.

Chimney Rock Stags L ★★★→★★★★ Underrated Terlato-owned brand making best wines ever under steady hand of winemaker Elizabeth Vianna. Tomahawk Vyd CAB SAUV top-notch.

Cliff Lede Stags L ★★★ Excellent CAB SAUVS, big but balanced with tannin, gd acid. Small production Cabs from NAPA V hillsides, leesy SAUV BL notable. Owns Fel brand in AND V, SON V.

Clos du Val Napa V ★★★ STAGS L classic. New owners slashed production, moved to upscale, estate-based model. Can estate vyds make cut? CAB SAUV can improve, CAR PINOT N solid, jury still out.

Cobb Wines Son Coast ★★★ Ross C makes restrained, natural SON COAST PINOT N, CHARD. Pinots improve with few yrs. Emaline Ann, Coastlands top sites.

Constellation ★→★★★ Publicly traded major wine/beer/spirits company owns famed ROBERT MONDAVI brand, Meiomi, The Prisoner, Woodbridge. Lately re-focusing on beer and cannabis products.

Continuum St H, Napa V ★★★★ Scion Tim Mondavi's P HILL estate spares no expense making one of NAPA's greatest, most complex B'x blends. Second label Novicium from younger vines.

Copain Cellars And V ★★★ Old World-influenced, classically proportioned wines; recently sold to JACKSON FAMILY. PINOT N is strong suit, esp bright, spicy Kiser vyd versions. Tous Ensemble line easy-going, friendly.

Corison Napa V ★★★ While many in NAPA V follow $iren call of bloated wines for big scores, diminishing pleasure, Cathy C consistently makes elegant, fresh Cabs, esp focused age-worthy Kronos vyd CAB SAUV.

Côte, Dom de la Sta RH ★★★ Raj Parr and Sashi Moorman make critically acclaimed, elegant PINOT N and CHARD. Burgundy-inspired, but with differences in latitude, soils, making for distinctly CA wines steered by great taste.

Cuvaison Car ★★★ Quiet historic property, making great wine yr after yr. Top marks to PINOT N, CHARD from CAR estate; gd SYRAH, CAB SAUV from MT VEEDER. Single Block bottlings incl lovely rosé, SAUV BL.

Dalla Valle Oak ★★★★ A 1st-rate hillside estate transitioning to 2nd generation. Maya CAB SAUV is legendary, eponymous Cab Sauv a cult wine, Collina label best affordable introduction to luxury NAPA Cab.

Daou P Rob ★★★ Elevated estate in Adelaida District is driving CAB SAUV in P ROB to new heights in altitude and price.

Dashe Cellars Dry CV, N Coast ★★★ RIDGE veteran Mike D makes tasteful, affordable and balanced DRY CV and ALEX V ZIN from urban winery in Oakland. Terrific old-vine CARIGNANE, zesty GRENACHE rosé.

Dehlinger RRV ★★★ PINOT N specialist still on par after more than four decades. Also v.gd CHARD, SYRAH, balanced CAB SAUV.

DeLoach Winery Son ★★★ Flamboyant maestro JC Boisset saw gd value in this progressive organic, bio-oriented winery making great PINOT N, CHARD. Solid down-to-earth investment, if not his sexiest.

Diamond Creek Napa V ★★★★ Napa Mtn jewel known for site-driven, minerally, age-worthy CAB SAUV from hillside vyds on DIAMOND MTN. Patience is rewarded.

Dominus Estate Napa V ★★★★ Moueix-owned (*see* France). Winery is dazzling but not open to public. Wines from gravelly bench soils consistently elegant, impressive. Second label: Napanook, v.gd. Important vision of s NAPA V.

Donum Estate N Coast ★★★→★★★★ Anne Moller-Racke has passionately worked CAR soils since 1981. PINOT N from four sites is focused, generous, complex. Adding vyds in AND V, SON COAST.

Drew Family And V, Mend ★★★→★★★★ MEND RDG visionary making minimalist, savage PINOT N from AND V and higher up hills. Look for estate Field Selections Pinot N from Mend Rdg, SYRAH from coastal Valenti Vyd. Hunt these down.

Dry Creek Vineyard Dry CV ★★★ Standard bearer on its A-game. Trustworthy, Loire-inspired, grassy FUMÉ BL and other SAUV BL always delicious, CHENIN BL and all reds better than ever, great stop nr Healdsburg. What's not to love? ZIN/B'x-blend Mariner also better than ever.

Duckhorn Vineyards Napa V ★★★→★★★★ Crowd-pleasing, super-consistent CAB SAUV, MERLOT, esp Three Palms vyd, gd SAUV BL. Second label Decoy wines exceptional values. Parent company owns Migration brand, Goldeneye in AND V, CALERA and Kosta Browne.

Dunn Vineyards Howell Mtn ★★★ Randy Dunn, a mtn man, stubbornly resisted stampede to jammy, lush CAB SAUV styles, favouring restraint, ageability. Wines aren't always spotless, but when great can last decades.

Dutton-Goldfield RRV ★★★ Steady-handed, classical cool-climate CA PINOT N, CHARD from RRV-based powerhouse grower, not super-edgy or risky, maybe a gd thing.

E&J Gallo Winery ★→★★★ Privately held, secretive company, titan in under-$20 sector. Major CA brands incl Apothic, Barefoot, Louis Martini. Recent buys: Black Box, Clos du Bois, RAVENSWOOD, Jayson. *See also* GALLO OF SONOMA.

Edwards, Merry RRV ★★★ PINOT N pioneer just retired, but quality should stay high.

Single vyds from SON always wildly popular. Ripe, rounded, reds sometimes a tad sweet by today's standards. Slightly sweet musqué SAUV BL also popular.

Emeritus RRV ★★★→★★★★ Emergent estate, three home dry-farmed (!) vyds making focused, structured PINOT N under supervision of talented winemaker Dave Lattin. Hallberg Ranch bottlings are exquisite and singular in style.

Etude Car ★★★ Ever-trustworthy brand that always succeeded at making great CAB SAUV, PINOT N under same roof, using same attentive techniques. Now owned by Treasury Wine Estates, but legacy stays true. PINOT rosé to die for.

Failla Napa V ★★★ Adept Ehren Jordan crafts superb PINOT N, SYRAH, CHARD from scattered prime vyds in N CA, even OR. SON COAST Pinot N shows great blending.

Far Niente Napa V ★★★→★★★★ Pioneer of CAB SAUV, CHARD in big, generous, NAPA style. Hedonism with soul. Dolce: celebrated dessert wine. Also makes Nickel & Nickel single vyd Cabs.

Farrell, Gary RRV ★★★ Namesake founder long gone, but wines still terrific despite a few ownership changes. Much credit to winemaker Theresa Heredia, Farrell's handpicked successor. Basic RRV CHARD beams brightly, Hallberg and Fort Ross single-vyd PINOT N among top offerings.

Fetzer Vineyards N Coast ★★ Early champion of organic/bio viticulture in MEND, still gd, best under Bonterra brand. Owned by Concha y Toro (Chile).

Field Recordings P Rob ★★★ Impressively subtle, perceptive wines from P ROB's Andrew Jones. Best are blends Neverland and Barter & Trade, but don't miss Alloy and Fiction, delicious in 500ml *cans*.

Flowers Vineyard & Winery Son Coast ★★★→★★★★ Extreme SON COAST pioneer 3 km (2 miles) from Pacific. PINOT N, CHARD remain great illustrations of that climate, elevation.

Foppiano Son ★★→★★★ Honest RRV wines loaded with sunny fruit and little pretence. PETITE SIRAH, SAUV BL notable.

Fort Ross Vineyard Son Coast ★★★ Dazzling high-elevation estate a stone's-throw from Pacific; terrific, savoury PINOT N, zesty CHARD, surprisingly gd PINOTAGE (!).

Freeman RRV, Son Coast ★★★→★★★★ Restrained terroir-driven PINOT N, CHARD from cool-climate SON COAST and RRV, with nod to Burgundy. The Ryo-fu Chard ("cool breeze" in Japanese) is amazing, as is Akiko's Cuvée Pinot N.

Freemark Abbey Napa V ★★★ Classic name claimed by JACKSON FAMILY WINES in 2006, improved. Great values: classic single-vyd Sycamore, Bosché CAB SAUV bottlings.

Frog's Leap Ruth ★★★ John Williams, pioneer champion of organic, bio viticulture, coaxes best out of NAPA V floor. Supple CAB SAUV, MERLOT, elegant CHARD, popular SAUV BL, great ZIN.

Gallo of Sonoma Son ★★★ Formidable wines from great SON sources and broader lands, unfussy as founders would have wanted. Fruit quality speaks loudly.

Gloria Ferrer Car ★★★ Exceptional CA bubbly. Toast to decades-long team of owners, growers, winemakers that made this Freixenet-owned venture extraordinary. All wines v.gd, Vintage Royal Cuvée best of all.

Graziano Family Redwood V ★★→★★★★ Flavourful, reliably delicious, mostly Italian-inspired, with deep roots in MEND. Brands incl Enotria, Graziano, Monte Volpe, Saint Gregory. MONTEPULCIANO, PINOT GR, SANGIOVESE delish.

Sauvignon Blanc sets a style

At last a coherent style of elite CA SAUV BL is emerging in NAPA V, DRY CV, Bennet V and elsewhere, and consumers are buying it. The common thread is concentrated flavour and mouthfeel, some creamy neutral oak influence, zesty grapefruit and passion-fruit flavours laced with mint, clover, or grass herbal notes. BEVAN CELLARS Dry Stack, DRY CREEK VINEYARD, Gamble's Heart Block and ST-SUPÉRY Dollarhide Ranch are fine examples.

Gundlach Bundschu Son V ★★★ Terrific wines, welcoming vibe, popular tasting destination with adventurous cool Huichica Fest music concerts for hipster set. Best bets MERLOT, CAB SAUV, GEWURZ.

Hahn Santa LH ★★★ Always overdelivers for $; B'x varieties combine MONT/P ROB fruit to great effect, Meritage often killer. Lucienne PINOT N releases fantastic.

Can we please see more top CA reds sealed with screwcaps?

Hall Napa V ★★★→★★★★ Glitzy ST H winery makes great NAPA CAB SAUV, but bewildering variety of selections. Signature offering best, velvety SAUV BL v.gd, MERLOT among best in CA. Also owns WALT coastal PINOT N, CHARD brand.

Halter Ranch P Rob ★★→★★★ Boasting 200 acres+ of sustainably farmed vyds on P ROB's west side, Halter reckons large as a premium grower and winery in the AVA. Solid CAB SAUV, SYRAH. PICPOUL a sprightly surprise.

Hanzell Son V ★★★ Pinot pioneer of 50s still making CHARD, PINOT N from estate vines. Both reward cellar time, and Chard still eye-opening. Sebella Chard, from young vines is all bright, crisp fruit.

Harlan Estate Napa V ★★★★ Concentrated, robust CAB SAUV – one of original cult wines only available via mailing list at luxury prices. Still all those things today. Son Will makes The Mascot from younger vines and now Promontory, at OAK.

Harney Lane Lodi ★★ Family owned with century of grape-growing under its belt. Old-vine ZIN (Home Ranch and Lizzy James vyds) are stars, but ALBARIÑO, TEMPRANILLO also impress as Iberian grapes blossom in warm parts of CA.

HdV Wines Car ★★★ CAR gem makes fine complex CHARD with a honed edge and v.gd PINOT N, from grower Larry Hyde in conjunction with Aubert de Villaine of DRC (*see France*). V.gd CAB SAUV, SYRAH.

Heitz Cellar Napa V ★★→★★★ Once iconic, now steady source of gd CAB SAUV at fair price, sold in 2018. Gd SAUV BL, even GRIGNOLINO.

Hendry Oak K ★★★ Classic, soulful, minimalist wines est 1939. Of note: brambly, distinctive CAB SAUV, ZIN (try Block 28) from cool pocket of valley nr Napa town. Never disappointing.

Hess Collection, The Napa V ★★★ Great mtn-top visit with world-class art gallery, also makes gd wine. CAB SAUV from MT VEEDER speciality, esp exceptional 19 Block Cuvée, blockbuster with gd manners.

Hirsch Son Coast ★★★ Pioneer of SON COAST, David H's vyd won acclaim growing premium grapes; now family label gets cream of crop from towering Pacific ridge. Lithe PINOT N, breathtaking CHARD.

Honig Napa V ★★★ Sustainably grown NAPA V CAB SAUV, SAUV BL nationwide benchmarks thanks to consistent quality, hard-working family and team. Top Cab from Bartolucci vyd in ST H.

Hope Family P Rob ★★→★★★★ Veteran winemaker Austin H steadily delivers quality reds, excellent Austin Hope CAB SAUV, SYRAH at fair prices. Also makes Treana; solid Liberty School is value label.

Inglenook Oak ★★★ FF Coppola's Rubicon reclaims original brand with classic central NAPA V CAB SAUV – balanced, elegant, historic. Also v.gd CHARD, MERLOT. Victorian showpiece.

Iron Horse Vineyards Son ★★★ Amazing selection of 12 vintage bubblies, all wonderfully made. Ocean Res Blanc de Blancs is v.gd, Wedding Cuvée a winner. V.gd CHARD, PINOT N.

Jackson Family Wines ★★→★★★★ Visionary, massive vyd owner in CA with prime elevated sites, owns popular Kendall-Jackson brand, and high achievers like COPAIN, FREEMARK ABBEY, Hartford Family. Lokoya, MATANZAS CREEK, Verité. Jackson Estate series great for mtn CAB SAUV.

Jessie's Grove Lodi ★★→★★★★ Est. 1868 with deep roots in Lodi, Royal Tee vyd is among CA's oldest ZIN plantings. Boss Greg Burns knows Zin inside-out, and shows in fine, generous wines. Try *Westwind bottling*, or ALBARIÑO, VERMENTINO if you're in mood for white.

Jordan Alex V ★★★ Adjustments in grape sourcing led to brilliant revival of balanced, elegant wines from showcase ALEX V estate. CAB SAUV homage to B'x: and it lasts. Zesty, delicious CHARD.

Small wineries dependent on restaurant sales/visitors, may not survive pandemic.

Joseph Swan Vineyards Son ★★★ Longtime RRV producer of intense old-vine ZIN and single-vyd PINOT N. Sleeper for overlooked Rhône varieties also v.gd, esp SYRAH, ROUSSANNE/MARSANNE blend.

Josh N Coast ★★ Shooting star from Joseph Carr. Solid varietal bulk brand successfully competing with GALLO and CONSTELLATION offerings.

Keller Estate Son Coast ★★★ One more example of balanced, elegant CA wine coming off the cool coastal regions. PINOT N, CHARD thrilling.

Kistler Vineyards RRV ★★★ Style of PINOT N, CHARD adapted over yrs, wines only improved. Still from a dozen designated vyds in any given yr. Highly sought.

Korbel ★★ Cheap fizz sold in grocery stores, but all traditional-method and remarkably decent for price. And a fun visit by Russian River.

Krug, Charles Napa V ★★→★★★ Historically important winery made recent comeback, demanding recognition for role in modern NAPA V. Late owner Peter Mondavi was Robert's estranged brother. Supple CAB SAUV, crisp, pure SAUV BL.

Ladera Napa V ★★★→★★★★ The Stotesbery clan sold their HOWELL MTN winery and set up shop in ST H. Hillside CAB SAUVS, MALBEC great; don't miss superb SAUV BL from NZ winemaker.

Lang & Reed Mend, Napa ★★★ No-one in CA has flown CAB FR banner more passionately than L&R's John Skupny. Wines capture perfume, litheness with NAPA generosity. Also delicious MEND CHENIN BL.

Larkmead Napa V ★★★★ Historic gravel-laced NAPA V estate revived; *outstanding Cab Sauv*, supple, balanced; bright, delicious SAUV BL. Rare Tocai FRIULANO a delight.

Lindquist Family – Verdad Arroyo Seco ★★★ Rhône Ranger Bob Lindquist's 2nd act(s) after trailblazing QUPÉ. More outstanding Rhône varieties under Lindquist brand; Verdad label is reserved for Spanish varieties, incl *auténtico* ALBARIÑO, TEMPRANILLO from nearby bio Sawyer L estate vyd in nearby EDNA V.

Lioco N Coast ★★★ Influential minimalist brand champions elegant, subtle PINOT N, CHARD, CARIGNAN. Wines are dependable, restrained, satisfying.

Littorai Son Coast ★★★ Burgundy-trained Ted Lemon's N Coast PINOT NS, CHARDS are pure, inspiring wines with sense of place. Breathtaking, modern, worth seeking.

Lohr, J ★★→★★★ Prolific producer of Central Coast makes CAB SAUV, PINOT N, CHARD for balance and gd value. Cuvée Pau and Cuvée St E pay homage to B'x. Don't miss seductive, floral Beaujolais-like Wildflower Valdiguié.

Long Meadow Ranch Napa V ★★★→★★★★ Smart, holistic vision incl destination winery with restaurant, cattle on organic farm. Supple, age-worthy, fresh CAB SAUV has reached ★★★★ status; lively Graves-style SAUV BL.

Louis M Martini Napa V ★★→★★★ Since buying the Martini brand and epic Monte Rosso vyd, GALLO has restored latter to greatness. Martini brand is solid for prosaic CABS, ZINS.

Macchia Lodi ★★★ One of Lodi's most accomplished winemakers, Tim Holdener vacuums up medals like a supermagnet in blind tastings yr after yr. Speciality is balanced old vine ZIN, but also interesting TEROLDEGO, SANGIOVESE, v.gd PETITE SIRAH.

MacPhail Son Coast ★★★ Now owned by HESS COLLECTION, making mostly PINOT N from cool sites in Son and Mend, highlights are Gap's Crown, Sundawg Ridge and Toulouse vyd bottlings.

MacRostie Son Coast ★★★ New tasting room is a modern beauty; screwcapped wines steadily improving. Lovely PINOT N, SYRAH; SON COAST CHARD absolute delight. Excellent consistency, value. Buy these wines!

Marston Spring Mtn ★★★★ Not-quite-cultish small production mtn CAB SAUV from fascinating estate with a history of Hollywood escapism and grape-growing, arguably among best Cabs of NAPA V, wines currently made by Sierra-Leone-born Marbue Marke. Gd stories collide with great wine.

Masút Mend ★★★ Newish elevated Eagle Peak property run by Ben and Jake FETZER shines brightly. Estate PINOT NS lithe, ethereal. Will inspire others to explore area.

Matanzas Creek Son ★★★ Exceptional JACKSON FAMILY WINES property in cool Bennett V focuses on excellent MERLOT, SAUV BL from lavender-perfumed estate.

Matthiasson Napa V ★★★ Experimental wines have become cult hits. Racy CHARD, elegant CAB SAUV, epic white blend, plus esoterica like RIBOLLA GIALLA, SCHIOPPETTINO.

Mauritson Dry CV ★★★ Clay M, 6th-generation grower, captains extraordinary holdings in elevated Rockpile district; wines only got better under his two decades. ZIN is flagship; as with many DRY CV wineries, SAUV BL, CAB SAUV excellent.

Mayacamas Vineyards Mt Veeder ★★★ Now owned by Charles Banks, former partner in SCREAMING EAGLE. CA classic has not changed classic big-boned style, only improved. Age-worthy CAB SAUV, CHARD recall great bottles of 70s, 80s.

Miraflores Sierra F'hills ★★★ Marco Cappelli left NAPA V to set up in Sierra Mtns, vinifies subtle, sublime, broad array from estate, region he rightly believes in.

Montelena, Ch Napa V ★★★ Tons of history, great continuity of ownership, style. Serious, if slightly funky CAB SAUV is cellar-worthy; CHARD holds up well too. Castle-like winery, heavenly setting.

Mount Eden Vineyards Santa Cz Mts ★★★→★★★★ Gorgeous vistas from high vyd, one of CA's 1st boutique wineries with Burgundian clones dating back to Martin Ray days. Taut, mineral CAB SAUV, PINOT N, stunning CHARD since 1945. Inspired by Burg, but pure rugged CA character.

Mount Veeder Winery Mt Veeder ★★★ Classic CA mtn CAB SAUV, CAB FR grown at 500m (1640ft) on rugged, steep hillsides. Dense wines: ripe, integrated tannins.

Mumm Napa Valley Napa V ★★★ At Ruth since 1970. Quality bubbly, notably Blanc de Noirs and pricier, complex DVX single vyd left on lees for a few yrs.

Nalle Dry CV ★★★ Refined craftsmanship level ZIN, impeccable, elegant claret-style reds. Great family owned stop nr Healdsburg.

Newton Vineyards Spring Mtn ★★→★★★★ Beautiful estate at base of SPRING MTN, now LMVH-owned; wines have improved recently. Look for CAB SAUV and opulent unfiltered CHARD.

Niner Edna V, P Rob ★★→★★★★ Young, ambitious family estate with excellent CAB SAUV from P ROB, great EDNA V ALBARIÑO, CHARD; CA cuisine restaurant gd for lunch in P Rob countryside.

Obsidian Ridge Lake ★★★ Star of Lake County extension of Mayacamas mtn range. Super CAB SAUV, SYRAH from hillside vyds, volcanic soils scattered with glassy obsidian. Half Mile Cab 1st rate. Also owns Poseidon brand from CAR.

Ojai Santa B ★★★ In a change of style from big, super-ripe to leaner, finer, former AU BON CLIMAT partner Adam Tolmach making best wines of his career. V.gd PINOT N, CHARD, Rhône styles. SYRAH-based rosé is delicious.

Your amphora wine experiment was cute, but may we move on now?

Opus One Oak ★★★★ Mouton Rothschild family controlled standard bearer for fine Napa CAB SAUV; popular luxury export. Wines designed to cellar 10 yrs+.

Pahlmeyer Napa V ★★★ Jammy, pricey, well-made NAPA V wines, B'x blend, MERLOT, lavish CHARD most notable. Popular volume label Jayson. Now in GALLO portfolio.

Patz & Hall N Coast ★★★★ James Hall is one of CA's most thoughtful winemakers;

culls fruit from top vyds from Central Coast to Mend. Style is generous, tasteful, super-reliable. Zio Tony **Chard** v. special, lemony, electric, opulent.

Paul Hobbs Wines N Coast ★★★→★★★★ Globe-trotting winemaker Paul H still a local hotshot. Bottlings of single-vyd CAB SAUV, CHARD, PINOT N, SYRAH are top. V.gd-value second label: Crossbarn.

Peay Vineyards Son Coast ★★★→★★★★ Standout brand from one of coast's coldest zones. Finesse-driven CHARD, PINOT N, SYRAH superb. Second label, Cep, also v.gd, esp rosé. Weightless, impeccably made wines.

Pedroncelli Son ★★ Old-school DRY CV winery updated vyds, winery; still makes bright, elbow-bending CAB SAUV, ZIN, solid CHARD. Refreshingly unpretentious.

Peter Michael Winery Mont, Son ★★★★ *Sir* Peter Michael to you. Brit in Knight's Valley, NAPA V, SON COAST sells mostly to restaurants, mailing list. Quality outstanding: rich, dense CHARD, B'x blend Les Pavots, hedonist's PINOT N.

Phelps, Joseph Napa V ★★★→★★★★ Expensive NAPA "First Growth" Insignia, one of CA's 1st ambitious B'x blends, still dependably great, as is Napa CAB SAUV. Most offerings excellent quality, esp SYRAH. *See also* SON brand FREESTONE.

Philip Togni Vineyards Spring Mtn ★★★★ 10 12 14 15 Legendarily age-worthy SPRING MTN CAB SAUV. Stiff mtn terroir generally needs time, rewards patience. All class.

Pine Ridge Napa V ★★★ Outstanding CAB SAUV from several NAPA V vyds. Estate STAGS L bottling, silky, graceful. Lively CHENIN BL/VIOGNIER innovative classic.

Pisoni Vineyards Santa LH ★★★ Family winery in SANTA LH became synonymous with PINOT N explosion and big, jammy wines. Still, Pinot N is and always was well-made and remains popular.

Presqu'ile Santa MV ★★★ New Central Coast winery, elegantly styled PINOT N, SYRAH. Concrete egg-fermented SAUV BL of note, as is estate Pinot N.

Pride Mountain Napa V, Spring Mtn ★★★→★★★★ Epic Mayacamas mtn-top estate straddles NAPA V and SON border; superb, bold CAB SAUV; amazing MERLOT.

Quintessa Ruth ★★★★ Magnificent estate at heart of NAPA V owned by Chilean international player Augustin Huneeus makes single wine: superb, refined B'x blend justifies triple-digit price.

Qupé Santa B ★★★ One of original SYRAH champions, brilliant range of Rhônes, esp X Block, from one of CA's oldest vyds. Hillside Estate also epic; don't miss impeccable MARSANNE, ROUSSANNE. Central Coast SYRAH unbeatable for $.

Radio-Coteau Son Coast ★★★ Notable new-wave SON COAST PINOT N, serious coastal SYRAH and old-vine, dry-farmed ZIN. CHARD and Zin are bulletproof, but Pinot N steals show. Veg gardens, cider orchard, goats, chickens, honeybees and cats too.

Rancho Sisquoc Santa MV ★★→★★★ Rustic tasting room and historic chapel deliver satisfying spectrum of B'x-style wines incl standout CAB FR, CHARD, PINOT N.

Ravenswood ★★★ Owned by CONSTELLATION, but single-vyd ZINS still from remarkable sites like Bedrock, Old Hill, Teldeschi. "No wimpy wines" motto still applies.

Red Car Son Coast ★★★ Hip, artsy estate-based label making precise CHARD, lacy, fruit-forward PINOT N and killer rosé.

Renwood Sierra F'hills ★★→★★★ Historic Sierra-Nevada brand on rebound after purchase by international New Frontier Wine Co. Joe Shebl assembles lovely, robust ZIN from ancient, head-pruned, dry-farmed vyds.

Drinking stars

When it comes to fizz, CA can give Champagne a run for its money, taking price into account. Among v. best: ROEDERER ESTATE's outstanding, affordable AND V Brut and longer-aged, superb L'Ermitage. SCHRAMSBERG's precise Blanc de Blancs and sublime J. Schram Brut warrant massive praise, as do GLORIA FERRER's plush Royal Cuvée, DOM CARNEROS' creamy, dreamy Le Rêve and IRON HORSE's complex, seasoned Brut LD.

Ridge N Coast, Santa Cz Mts ★★★★ Saintly founder Paul Draper semi-retired, but his spirit lives on. Majestic, legendary, age-worthy estate Montebello CAB SAUV is always superb. Keep 10 yrs. Outstanding single-vyd field-blend ZINS are special. Don't overlook top-rank, minerally CHARD.

Robert Mondavi Winery ★★→★★★ Owned by CONSTELLATION since 2004, many wines could be better; changing of winemaking guard appears at hand. Home To Kalon vyd, still a great site; potential there.

Robert Sinskey Vineyards Car ★★★ Great, idiosyncratic NAPA estate favouring balance, restraint. Impressive CAB SAUV and CAR PINOT N. Racy Abraxas white blend and Pinot rosé excellent.

Rodney Strong Vineyards Son ★★★ Strong indeed, across board, from 14 significant vyds. Sinewy coastal PINOT N, CHARD, super ALEX V CAB SAUV from Alexander's Crown, Rockaway vyds. Also owns Davis Bynum.

Roederer Estate And V ★★★★ Adventurous Champagne Roederer venture brought glamour to And V. Finesse, class off the charts, esp luxury cuvée L'Ermitage. Also makes Scharffenberger fizz. Dom Anderson PINOT NS also excellent.

Rombauer Napa V ★★★ Buttery CHARD is the calling card; boomers adore this prestige brand. Solid CAB SAUV, MERLOT, ZIN also sunny, flavourful.

St Jean, Ch Son V ★★★ Rock of SON V, solid wines on all fronts, but consensus flagship wine for decades has been Cinq Cépages blend of five B'x varieties, reliable and age-worthy CA classic.

Saintsbury Car ★★★ Regional pioneer and benchmark still making v.gd, highly relevant PINOT N, CHARD, yummy Vincent Vin Gris rosé.

St-Supéry Napa ★★★ Bought by owners of Chanel (and Ch Rausan-Ségla, B'x), but some continuity of talent. Tasteful, balanced Virtú (w) and Élu (r) B'x blends and SAUV BL, esp *Dollarhide Ranch*, thrilling.

Sandhi Sta RH ★★★ *See* DOM DE LA CÔTE. Same winemaking team, grapes bought from top local vyds. Must for lovers of white burgundy: racy CHARD. Gd PINOT N.

Sanford Santa B, Sta RH ★★★ Now owned by Terlato family, wines still exceptional, esp La Rinconada, Sanford & Benedict PINOT N, SANTA B CHARD.

Schramsberg Napa V ★★★★ Best bubbles in CA? Exacting quality in every bottling, esp luxurious J Schram and Blanc de Noirs kept pace with French competition. Memorable tours of historic caves by reservation.

Screaming Eagle Napa V, Oak ★★★★ Original "cult" CAB SAUV, famously ripe, rare, and four-figures *cher* from primo Oakville terroir. Also limited production SAUV BL. Sister winery is Jonata.

Scribe Son ★★★ Hipster gentleman-farmer aesthetic a hit with younger set. Tasting room pours well-made esoterica like SYLVANER, ST-LAURENT and PINOT N rosé all day.

Sea Smoke Sta RH ★★★ Cultish, high-end, opulent PINOT N, CHARD, sparkling estate-driven model. Great wines, but drink while young (them, and you).

Seghesio Son ★★★ Cassic ZIN from ALEX V, DRY CV. Rich, strong, but graceful. Old Vine bottling benchmark for price. Rockpile Zin dynamite.

Shafer Vineyards Napa V, Stags L ★★★→★★★★ Solid brand, widely respected by critics, sommeliers alike. Hillside Select CAB SAUV a lavish CA classic; Relentless SYRAH/PETITE SIRAH blend powerful, artful. One Point Five, absolute beauty for money. Fine MERLOT, CHARD from nearby CAR.

Shannon Ridge Lake ★★→★★★ Ambitious large estate situated in impressive high-elevation Lake County site. V.gd wines, great values. Fast-growing brand, incl second label Vigilance.

Silverado Vineyards Stags L ★★★ Walt Disney descendants owned vyds since 1976; kept up with times. Single-vyd Solo CAB SAUV, powerful, smooth; new release of Geo B'x blend from COOMB, dark, dense. CAB FR excellent.

Silver Oak Alex V, Napa V ★★★ Juicy, plush CABS in consistent, fruit-driven style.

CALIFORNIA

Sonoma-Cutrer Vineyards Son ★★★ Flagship CHARD, classic, by-the-glass pour at restaurants all over country, rich but zesty, bright. Owsley PINOT N from RRV lush.

Sonoma-Loeb Car, RRV ★★★ CHAPPELLET'S Son PINOT N, CHARD label. Sangiacomo vyd Chard stands out.

Spottswoode St H ★★★★ Crown jewel of ST H, sublime estate always chasing perfection. CAB SAUV pricey, not bulky; worth it. Value Lyndenhurst Cab Sauv 2nd wine, Spottswoode SAUV BL delightful.

P Rob Cab warrants a hard look; may be a gd option for fire-ravaged vintage 2020.

Spring Mountain Vineyard Spring Mtn ★★★★ Top-notch estate delivers site-driven, age-worthy mtn wines. Signature Elivette B'x blend layered and sturdy, Estate CAB SAUV v.gd, estate SAUV BL is Rubenesque treat.

Staglin Family Vineyard Ruth ★★★★ Perennial 1st-class, potent CAB SAUV from family-owned estate. Also formidable, complex Salus CHARD.

Stag's Leap Wine Cellars Stags L ★★★ Gd to see quality maintained since founder sold to large corp. Flagship silky, seductive CABS (top-of-line Cask 23, Fay, SLV).

Stags' Leap Winery Napa V, Stags L ★★★→★★★★ Important, beautiful estate recently restored by corporate owners, exceptional spot to visit (by appt only), wines great now. CAB SAUV leads, but PETITE SIRAH and field-blend Ne Cede Malis have always been special.

Sterling Napa V ★★ A great spot to visit; take aerial tram to tasting room with 90m (295ft)-high view of valley.

Stony Hill Vineyard Spring Mtn ★★★ Revered NAPA V estate mostly famous for whites, esp mineral, ageable CHARD, plus GEWURZ, RIES. Sold to LONG MEADOW RANCH (2018). Expect to hold steady.

Tablas Creek P Rob ★★★→★★★★ Figures huge among CA's most outstanding wineries, esp those focused on Rhône varieties. Bulletproof line-up of crafty blends and varietals. They make a lot of stuff and never disappoint. Buy these!

Terra Valentine Napa V, Spring Mtn ★★★ Wurtele family lovingly rehabbed this winery in early 2000s, then handed off to winemaker Sam Baxter; mtn CAB SAUV is focus, romanticizes SANGIOVESE with some success. Don't underestimate.

Terre Rouge / Easton Sierra F'hills ★★★ Single company with two sides: traditional old-vine ZIN (Easton) and Rhône varieties (Terre Rouge). Mostly reds. Affordable Tête-à-tête red blend a steal, Ascent SYRAH reliably special.

Tongue Dancer And V, Son Coast ★★★ James MacPhail's solo venture after exiting his eponymous brand follows similar plan: robust PINOT N, CHARD from stellar N Coast vyds. Bacigalupi vyd Chard can wow.

Trefethen Family Vineyards Oak K ★★★ Underappreciated winery in cool OAK K deserves more credit, elegant CAB SAUV, MERLOT, CHARD and delicious dry RIES.

Tribute to Grace, A N Coast ★★★ Kiwi Angela Osborne's homage to GRENACHE. Fruit from exceptional vyds, diverse terroirs all over state, none more exciting than 975m (3199ft), mtn-ringed SANTA B Highlands.

Trinchero Family Estates Napa V ★→★★★ Bewildering slew of labels, incl mass-market Sutter Home. Esp pleasing CAB SAUV under Napa Wine Company label.

Truchard Car ★★★ Estate est 1974, planted to pastiche of B'x, Rhône, Burg; lovely MERLOT, CHARD, ROUSSANNE.

Turley Wine Cellars P Rob ★★★★ Sells mostly to mailing list. Brilliant brambly old-vine ZINS from vyds scattered across state. True CA treasures.

Unti Dry CV ★★★ Wines start in vyds; grower delivers soulful, luscious, tasty BARBERA, GRENACHE, SYRAH, ZIN.

Viader Estate Howell Mtn ★★★★ Ripe, powerful expression still turns heads. "V" is marvellous B'x blend based on PETIT VERDOT, CAB FR.

Villa Creek P Rob ★★★ Former restaurateur Chris Cherry sees P ROB's climate through a Spanish lens; makes brilliant, focused GARNACHA from 60-acre bio MAHA estate, plus solid CAB SAUV, Rhône-style blends.

Vineyard 29 Napa V ★★★→★★★★ Top winemaker Philippe Melka's fingerprints all over gorgeous CAB SAUVs at maturing estate venture. Gd but oaky SAUV BL.

Vino Noceto Sierra F'hills ★★ Down-to-earth, classic Cal-Ital winery in Plymouth loved for BARBERA, SANGIOVESE, reasonable prices.

Volker Eisele Family Estate Napa V ★★★ Special site tucked way back in Chiles Valley continues to overdeliver with CAB SAUV and more. Looking for an adventure? Try a twisty Chiles V road trip.

Wente Vineyards ★★ Oldest continuing family winery in CA, decent whites/reds. Outstanding gravel-grown SAUV BL leads. Murietta's Well: some gd blends (r/w).

Wilkes, J. Santa B ★★→★★★ Work in progress with passionate, brainiac oenologist Wes Hagen (formerly of Clos Pepe) at reins. Can't fail if tireless Wes is on board. SANTA B, P ROB reds, whites.

Williams-Selyem RRV ★★★ SON PINOT N benchmark since 70s, inspired by Burgundy; put RRV on map as international Pinot centre. Rochioli Riverblock Pinot N legendary, priced accordingly. Wines are minimally processed; you might encounter a funky bottle here and there.

Wind Gap Son Coast ★★★ Pax Mahle one of CA's most talented winemakers, esp in cool climates. PINOT N, CHARD excellent, in best vintages. SON COAST SYRAH displays relevatory new wave terroir.

Wine Group, The Central V ★ By volume, world's 2nd-largest wine producer; budget brands like Almaden, Big House, Concannon, Cupcake, Glen Ellen.

Colorado (CO)

High desert, wide diurnal temperature ranges, some of highest-altitude vyds in US; 140 wineries. Climate similar to Rhône, Central Coast and Mendoza. Both B'x and cool-climate varieties thrive. AVAs incl Grand Valley and West Elks. **Bookcliff** ★★ excellent MALBEC, SYRAH, Res CAB FR, CAB SAUV, VIOGNIER. **Carlson** ★ family run, GEWURZ, RIES, LEMBERGER (r) and other fruit wines. **Colterris** premium, B'x style. Coral White Cab Sauv; stylish signature wine. **Grande River Vyds** traditional B'x, Rhône styles; noted SAUV BL, Lavande Vin Blanc, Viognier blend infused with lavender. **Jack Rabbit Hill Farm** ★ only certified bio winery in state. Eye-catching orange wine, Lone Eagle Proprietary Blend of RIES and Hungarian Bianca; trendy grower ciders. **Snowy Peaks (Grande Valley)** v.-high-altitude vines, 100% CO grapes, Rhône varieties; Oso (r) blend uses hybrid grapes. **Stone Cottage Cellars** organic, cold-climate grapes. Pretty GEWURZ; seductive MERLOT. **Sutcliffe Vyds** v.gd Cab Fr, CINSAULT, CHARD, from Welsh winemaker/ex-restaurateur. **The Storm Cellar** up-and-coming, high-elevation, white-focused project from two sommeliers. V.gd PINOT GR extended skin-contact rosé. **Two Rivers** excellent Cab Sauv, v.gd Chard, Ries and Port-style.

Georgia (GA)

Shares Upper Hiwassee Highlands AVA with NC; 1st all-GA AVA Dahlonega Plateau, rocky hills; B'x, CHARD, PINOT N, PETIT MANSENG. Best: **Crane Creek**; **Engelheim** (PINOT GR); **Frogtown** (SANGIOVESE); **Habersham**; **Sharp Mtn** (Sangiovese, GEWURZ); **Stonewall Creek** (NORTON); **Three Sisters** (oldest on plateau; PINOT BL, AVA CAB FR); **Tiger Mtn**; **Wolf Mtn** (traditional sp); **Yonah Mtn**.

Idaho (ID)

Though 1st grapes planted 1860, ID is still a young region with only 60 wineries. Growers, winemakers determining what to plant where and how to farm it, but SYRAH looking to be a star.

Cinder Wines Snake RV ★★ Melanie Krause (ex-Ch Ste Michelle, WA) makes SYRAH, RIES in Snake River Valley AVA. VIOGNIER also v.gd.

Coiled Snake RV ★★ One of state's top producers, making tasty dry RIES, SYRAH.

Colter's Creek L-CV ★★ Husband-and-wife team located in nascent Lewis-Clark Valley AVA. Produces estate offerings and others. SYRAH the standout. Rocinante red blend also tops. NEGROAMARO rosé lovely.

Ste Chapelle Snake RV ★ ID's 1st and largest, owned by WA-based Precept Wines. Focus on dry and off-dry style reds, whites, incl quaffable RIES, SAUV BL.

Maryland (MD)

East Shore sandy soils, hills of Garrett and Allegheny mtns, blue-crab-rich Chesapeake Bay checks freezing winters, stifling summers; B'x grapes incl reliable ripener PETIT VERDOT, SAUV BL; MERLOT, ALBARIÑO. For MD-terroirs tastes: **Big Cork**; **Black Ankle** (1st post-Prohibition winery); **Boordy** (founded 1945 by hybrid-minded *Sun*-journalist; today PINOT GR to CAB FR); **Bordeleau** (B'x); **Catoctin Breeze** (barrel-ferment CAB SAUV); **Crow** (BARBERA, r/rosé); **Dodon**; **Elk Run** (PINOT N); **Linganore** (Merlot, Albariño on old dairy farm); **Old Westminster** (bio, GAMAY, MOSCATO, SYRAH; 90 new hybrids on unfarmed hillside); **Sugarloaf Mtn** (Cab Fr, VIOGNIER; Albariño planted).

Naturally high-acid grapes + wild herbs = gd new vermouths from eastern US.

Massachusetts (MA)

Only AVA: Martha's Vyd, within SE New England, shared with CT and RI. Cool Atlantic climate moderated by Gulf Stream. Like rest of New England, many fruit wines, occasionally v.gd. CHARD, GEWURZ, PINOTS N/BL/GR, RIES, some Cayuga; Concord developed here 1849; 25+ small producers: estate incl **Truro Vyds** (MERLOT, CAB FR in sea-breezed vyd); **Turtle Creek** (1–6 barrels of single-varietal, incl Cab Fr); **Westport** (PINOT M: traditional-method, still).

Michigan (MI)

The "Third Coast," on huge Lake Michigan. Five AVAs, two downstate, three up incl n-most Tip of the Mitt. Production up, nouveau wines trend; 140 wineries+. Three Pinots do well, also CHARD, RIES, CAB FR, MERLOT, occasional TEROLDEGO. Terroir, quality: **2 Lads**, **Bel Lago** (incl AUXERROIS); **Amoritas** (PINOTS BL/GR, RIES lineup; white field-blend); **Big Little** (still Blanc de Noirs, sparkling GEWURZ blends; traditional-method PINOTS N/M); **Black Star Farms** (GAMAY); **Left Foot Charley** (in cherry-rich Traverse City; KERNER, single-vyd sparkling Pinot Bl); **Mari**, **Mawby** (all-sparkling, incl traditional-method Chard, spontaneous-fermentation blends); **Nathaniel Rose** (MI-wide single-vyd focus); **Rove Estate** (fresh whites); **Shady Cellars** (MUSCAT); **Verterra** (strong Ries); **Wyncroft** (single-vyd Pinot N, Chard, BLAUFRÄNKISCH).

Missouri (MO)

New ambitious plan by Hoffman Family of Cos: $100 million, 700 acres, to create Napa-style destination, golf course, hotel, etc. Until then, try: Chambourcin, SEYVAL BL, VIDAL, Vignoles (dr/sw). **Hermannhof** notable for Chardonel, Norton, Vignoles; **Stone Hill** in Hermann produces v.gd Chardonel (frost-hardy hybrid, Seyval Bl x CHARD), Norton and gd Seyval Bl, Vidal. Also: **Adam Puchta** for fortifieds and Norton, Vidal, Vignoles; **Augusta Winery** for Chambourcin, Chardonel, Icewine; **Les Bourgeois** for Chardonel, Montelle, Norton, SYRAH, v.gd Chambourcin, Cynthiana; **Mount Pleasant** in Augusta for rich fortified and Norton; **St James** for Norton, Seyval, Vignoles.

Nevada (NV)

Few commercial wineries. **Churchill Vyds** in high desert region producing gd SEM/CHARD, all NV-grown grapes. **Pahrump Valley** oldest winery here, three lines with irreverant names of which award-winning Nevada Ridge is most serious.

New Jersey (NJ)

Some of 60 wineries+ among best in E US; 150 growers, need more, across three AVAs: B'x varieties in S NJ's flat gravelly Outer Coast Plain (incl Cape May); limestone, granite hills in Warren Hills in n for elegant BLAUFRÄNKISCH, GEWURZ, GRÜNER V, PINOT N, RIES, SYRAH; plus Central Delaware Valley shared with PA. Yearly symposium by Rutgers U Cooperative Extension hones skills for canopy management, traditional-method, fighting spotted lantern fly. Quality NJ cheese and meats at some wineries.

San Marco: new vine crossing, Teroldego x Lagrein. Taste at Bellview Winery.

Alba ★★★ Limestone, granite in Warren Hills AVA. One of largest PINOT N plantings on E Coast. Burgundy aspiration, incl earthy 30-mths Grand Res; excellent CHARD, gd GEWURZ, RIES, 30-days-macerated CAB FR.

Beneduce Vineyards ★★★ Family estate; serious BLAUFRÄNKISCH, CHARD, PINOT N for ageing, Alto-Adige-style GEWURZ, also made as orange wine and pét-nat.

Mount Salem ★★★ Austrian varieties to match terroir. Wild ferment, min sulphur: no-temp-control RIES; barrel-ferm whites. Outside-fermented reds, incl BLAUFRÄNKISCH, CAB FR, ST-LAURENT, ZWEIGELT.

Unionville ★★★ Nutty concentrated Rhône (w), v.gd SYRAH, aromatic CAB SAUV. Counoise rosé; PINOT N, CAB FR (no oak), MOURVÈDRE, fresh PINOT GR. GEWURZ planted.

William Heritage ★★★ In Cape May since 1999. Top sparkling (CHARD/PINOT N co-fermented). Rosés in meaty MERLOT-led or linear SYRAH. Attention-getting Syrah/VIOGNIER. Own-rooted Chard. Experimental side incl pét-nats (CHENIN BL), piquette (Syrah), carbonic Chambourcin.

Working Dog ★★★ Barrel-fermented CHARD, VIOGNER (ripeness, lift). MERLOT, SYRAH; several oak-aged CAB FR, incl flagship Retriever (creamy, rustic, lasting).

New Mexico (NM)

The 1st state to have planted *Vitis vinifera* (1629), high-altitude, three AVAs. Diurnal variations give crispness, lower alc. Historic sparkling production; success with both warm- and cold-climate varieties. **Black Mesa** ★★ reds, local grapes, award-winning MERLOT, PETITE SIRAH; **D.H. Lescombes Family Vyds** Burgundy heritage in pioneering winery; **Gruet** ★★★ longtime regional benchmark for sparkling; **La Chiripada** ★ oldest winery in state, 20 varieties+, top-notch Res CAB SAUV, new DOLCETTO, late-harvest RIES; **Luna Rossa Winery** Italian-focused pioneer, Old-World heritage, v.gd Res ALGIANICO, NEGROAMARO; **Noisy Water** ★★ breathing life in old region with gd Res CAB, Wild Ferment old-vine PINOT N; unfiltered Dirty; **Vivác** ★★ excellent red blends Divino (Italian grapes), Diavolo (French), v.gd Port-style Amante.

New York (NY)

US's 3rd-largest producer. 470 wineries, several on old dairy farms in once cattle-focused state. Knowledge, experimentation keep quality high and rising. Ten AVAs, plus Lake Erie (CHARD, sea of grape-juice-bound Concord) shared with OH, PA. Climate like N Europe's: winter freeze; lakes, rivers, ocean influence give vinifera (BLAUFRÄNKISCH, CAB FR, GEWURZ, RIES, B'x and GAs) crucial relief for some of nation's most compelling, lower-alc wines; hybrids, increasingly made seriously, dry; 113 km (70 miles) from NYC – maritime

Long Island (Long I) and colder Hudson Valley (Hudson V; most complex soils). Largest is remote Finger Lakes (Finger L; sunlight hours same as Napa's over fewer days; 140 wineries). Farther n and w: Champlain Valley (sparkling, Icewine), Niagara Escarpment (up-and-coming, NY-rare limestone).

Serious fizz: old-vine Blanc de Noirs, long-lees Blanc de Blancs, hybrids, pét-nats.

21 Brix ★★ Estate on Lake Erie with 1st-rate CHARD, GEWURZ, GRÜNER V, RIES; aromatic BLAUFRÄNKISCH, CAB SAUV; v.gd PINOT N. Serious NOIRET. VIDAL BL Icewine.

Arrowhead Spring Vineyards ★★★ Estate est 2006 on Niagara Escarpment, 1 hr n of Finger L, starring PINOT N. B'x blends, CAB FR, SYRAH manage richness, spice, grippy tannins via 13% alc and cool-climate acidity. Focused CHARD, 12% alc.

Bedell Long I ★★★ Leading, stalwart estate since 1980. Winemaker leads LISW (*see* box). Native-yeasts *pied de cuve*, maritime climate shows in powerful, saline wines: Musée (MERLOT/PETIT VERDOT/MALBEC) is top label; varietal bottlings of same, also v.gd CAB FR, SYRAH. CHARD, SAUV BL, VIOGNIER (blended, varietal). Artist labels, eg. April Gornik, Chuck Close.

Bloomer Creek Finger L ★★★ Grapes of two sites, min-intervention winemaking, separate bottlings. PINOT N (r/rosè; some ungrafted), CAB FR (with some GAMAY). Tanzen Dame RIES in vintage-variance, late-harvest, or EDELZWICKER styles; GEWURZ, GRÜNER V. CHENIN BL coming soon. White Horse is clever Cab Fr/MERLOT blend.

Boundary Breaks Finger L ★★★ Top-notch dry to dessert RIES, all lush, acid-driven. Serious GEWURZ. Gd cool-climate CAB FR, MERLOT.

Channing Daughters Long I ★★★ Deliciously experimental wines from S Fork, incl BLAUFRÄNKISCH, DORNFELDER, LAGREIN, MALVASIA, RIBOLLA GIALLA, single-vyd FRIULANO, SAUV BL, a range of *pétillants*, plus CAB FR, MERLOT, SYRAH. CHARD, made masterfully and playfully, from strong oak influence to hands-off, skin-macerated. VerVino line of seasonal vermouths 1st in current E Coast aromatized-wines rush.

Element Winery Finger L ★★★ Christopher Bates MS explores terroir-driven CHARD, RIES, CAB FR, LEMBERGER, PINOT N, SYRAH. Small production, cult status. Latest focus incl MERLOT (ripe, herbal) and belief in GAMAY (still too little grown in Finger L).

Fjord Hudson V ★★★ Floral ALBARIÑO v.gd. Excellent, vintage-reflecting CAB FR (spontaneous fermentation) setting high standards in Hudson V AVA. Gd CHARD. Estate GAMAY, MERLOT planted 2020. Owner/winemaker also 2nd-generation of BENMARL WINERY: pioneer (NY Farm Winery license no.1) overlooking river. Elegant estate BACO NOIR (rosé too), MUSCAT OTTONEL, SEYVAL BL. Gd Cab Fr (incl pétillant). SAPERAVI on way.

Floral Terranes Long I ★★★ Small-scale, innovative "suburban terroir" garage wines (CAB SAUV, MERLOT, CHARD), ciders spontaneously fermented. Local fruit sources: in forgotten vyds, MACARI vyds, apples foraged in untended orchards.

Fox Run Finger L ★★★ RIES line v.gd, incl single vyd and barrel fermented; rare Res CAB FR 19, LEMBERGER; herbal CAB SAUV; ageable MERLOT. Winemaker Peter Bell mentored many of Finger L's greatest. Sustainable: solar panel powered.

Frank, Dr. Konstantin Finger L ★★★ Founder est vinifera in Finger L, then advised the E Coast; winery on Keuka Lake. Top RIES producer. Also v.gd GRÜNER V, PINOT GR, RKATSITELI, SAPERAVI; gd GEWURZ, old-vine PINOT N; impeccable Blancs de Blancs/ de Noirs (PINOT M), RIES nature.

Heart & Hands Finger L ★★★ Small production, excellent, and just three grapes: CHARD, RIES, PINOT N for exploring limestone (Devonian, and rare in Finger L) vyd on shores of Cayuga Lake. Classic cool-climate white, rosé; delicate red.

Hermann J Wiemer Vineyard Finger L ★★★ Among top US RIES producers; incl original bio vyds now expanded to 16 ha, some single bottlings. Fine CHARD (also bio), GEWURZ (vines among NY's oldest), CAB FR, PINOT N and superlative fizz. Owns fantastic Standing Stone (SAPERAVI; new Blanc de Blancs from 1974 vyd).

Hosmer Finger L ★★★ On w side of Cayuga Lake, vyd est 1972. Awarded RIES, incl limited bottlings; also CAB FR, CHARD. 80s PINOT N vines, some for Blanc de Noirs.

Hudson-Chatham Winery Hudson V ★★★ As serious about (dry) hybrids as vinifera: Baco Noir in old-vine and plot-specific bottlings; rare maker of Leon Millot; Chelois; hybrid field blends; CAB FR, PINOT N, CHARD. Res styles age 5 yrs+.

Keuka Lake Vineyards Finger L ★★★ Vivacious RIES, incl Falling Man from steep slopes on Keuka Lake; v.gd CAB FR. Hybrids incl Vignoles and old-vine Alsatian Leon Millot (cult bottles).

Keuka Spring Vineyards Finger L ★★★ On scenic Keuka Lake. World-class GEWURZ line-up incl site blends, single sites; Alto-Adige-style; 19 esp age-worthy. CAB FR, LEMBERGER, MERLOT.

Lakewood Vineyards Finger L ★★★ A 3rd-generation estate. High-quality Res CAB FR; everyday bottle too. Impressive GEWURZ, PINOTS GR/N, multiple RIES.

Lamoreaux Landing Finger L ★★★ Wildly varied sites lead to excellent RIES (many bottlings, norm in Ries-happy, varied-terrain Finger L), *Chard*, GEWURZ, Icewine, plus CAB FR, MERLOT, PINOT N. Creamy, classic Blanc de Blancs, 4 yrs lees. Library wines incl no-oak Cab Fr. Greek Revival building, views of Lake Seneca.

Liten Buffel ★★★ Niagara Escarpment estate, two PINOT NS (c.12% abv), PINOT GR Ramato, RIES (vinified whole-cluster; also skin-contact) planted on long slope from escarpment to ancient lake ridge. Co-ferment BLAUFRÄNKISCH/SAUV BL. Wild yeasts in neutral oak, no filtering, no sulphur. Noble rot some yrs.

Macari Long I, North F ★★★ Clifftop estate on Long I Sound. Bio-minded. Top-notch SAUV BL. Premium reds: Bergen Road (B'x blend, library wines too), CAB FR. MERLOT, B'x-blend Alexandra in best vintages. Popular Horses is bottle-fermented CAB FR rosé. Austrian Jungwein inspired Early Wine, out each Nov.

Reds to lay down: Long I Merlot, B'x blends; Finger L Pinot N, Lemberger.

McCall Long I, North F ★★★ Known for top PINOT N, incl single-vyd, Res, rosé. Gd CAB FR, SAUV BL. Red B'x blends. Also home to French-origin Charolais cattle.

Millbrook Hudson V ★★★ Was 1st to grow vinifera in Hudson V; estate RIES, CHARD, PINOT N. Single-vyd Tocai (FRIULANO), CAB FR. Acidity lets reds age a few yrs.

Paumanok Long I ★★★ Racy, ageable CHENIN BL, excellent B'x blends, CAB SAUV, RIES. Fine CHARD, single-vyd MERLOT, CAB FR; occasional Grand Vintage for all three. Spontaneous ferments, low sulphur. Heads 1983-founded Palmer: saline PINOT BL, longlasting, elegant MERLOT, excited about ALBARIÑO.

Ravines Finger L ★★★ Inspired RIES, GEWURZ, CAB FR, PINOT N (a focus), plus traditional sparkling CHARD/Pinot N. Since 15 Le Petit Capora is Res Cab Fr/CAB SAUV/MERLOT, from limestone Argetsinger vyd on Seneca Lake. Sophisticated bistro.

Sustaining New York's wines

With waves of weird weather, climate change is taken seriously throughout NY. Winemakers, who wield economic influence in rural communities, are fighting back through sustainability programmes. In 2012 Long I built the E Coast's 1st certification (and educational) programme: Long Island Sustainable Winegrowing (LISW). Buoyed by consumer interest, as of 2021, a statewide programme incl certification is to begin with 2022 vintage. Unifying techniques incl canopy management, reducing chemicals, new varieties whether vinifera or hybrid. In this state of smaller producers who compete on quality over price, *sustainable* means people too: above-min wage for workers, fundraisers for neighbours in need, healthy vyds and cellars and realistic economic models. "Growing sustainably and for quality are one and the same goal," notes one leading producer.

Red Newt Finger L ★★★ Terroir- and RIES-focused, incl Seneca Lake crus, top US quality. Elegant GEWURZ, Pinot Gr; gd CAB FR, MERLOT, PINOT N. Tierce Ries is collaboration with Anthony Road, ARROWHEAD SPRING. Bistro, local produce.

Red Tail Ridge Finger L ★★★ Seneca. Super CHARD, RIES (one-block, wild-ferment), PINOT N, BLAUFRÄNKISCH. Lean, fruity TEROLDEGO, sells out. Sparkling incl Blanc de Noirs, pét-nats, Sekt.

Shaw Vineyard Finger L ★★★ On Seneca Lake, quieter w side. Once trellised, vines grow "wild" with min interference, multiple trunks allowed. Output is full-body, acidity-lifted reds like CAB SAUV, MERLOT, PINOT N; focused GEWURZ, RIES. Orange wine PINOT GR/SAUV BL.

Sheldrake Point Finger L ★★ Cayuga Lake. Exuberant cool-climate GAMAY, fresh earthy B'x blends, multiple RIES, single-plot PINOT GR, MUSCAT Ottonel. No-barrel whites. Experiments incl vyd pine staves for fuller-bodied CHARD.

Silver Thread Finger L ★★★ V.gd bio CHARD, RIES, CAB FR, PINOT N. Terroir-convinced: regenerating vyd soil to match surrounding forest's; solar-powered.

Sparkling Pointe Long I ★★★ Convincing *fizz*; French winemaker, Champagne grapes, loam soil. Traditional method. Cuvée Carnaval line (r/w/rosé) lets MERLOT into mix. PINOT M is star of 2020 vintage.

Suhru Long I ★★★ Founded 2008 by Australian. Maritime, glacial-soil SHIRAZ. V.gd B'x blend, age-worthy. SAUV BL, TEROLDEGO. Provence-style rosé (MERLOT/CAB FR).

Hybrid Traminette instead of disease-prone Chard? With climate change, why not?

Whitecliff Hudson V ★★ Site-, soils-driven, incl ex-cherry orchard, quartz-rich historic Olana slope for v.gd barrel-aged GAMAY, CAB FR. PINOT N on limestone ridge. Peachy, stony CHARD; robust Res RIES.

Wölffer Estate Long I ★★★ Premier S Fork estate and destination; classical approach. Quality CAB SAUV, MERLOT, PINOT N. Premium whites incl CHARD made burgundy-style; new maritime-minded SAUV BL. Gd rosé set off Hamptons vacationers' craze for the stuff.

North Carolina (NC)

Long hot summers; dry or rainy yrs. Winters can turn frigid. Four AVAs incl Yadkin Valley. Blue Ridge Mtns offer High Country elevation or Piedmont hills for best quality; unremarkable vyds clustered on old tobacco fields. Plenty of native Scuppernong grape: traditional SE US wine. Gd CAB FR, MERLOT, CHARD, VERMENTINO, VIOGNIER. Best: **Jones Von Drehle** (TEMPRANILLO; MALBEC Res); **Junius Lindsay** (SYRAH); **McRitchie** (dry MUSCAT); **Raffaldini** (MONTEPULCIANO, SAGRANTINO; PETIT MANSENG, TREBBIANO planted); **RayLen; Sanctuary Vyds** (Outer Banks, Viognier on skins, bold PETIT VERDOT/TANNAT); **Shelton**.

Ohio (OH)

Lake Erie moderates winters. Five AVAs. CHARD, MÜLLER-T, RIES, PINOT GR, B'x varieties, DOLCETTO, PINOT N. **Debonné** since 70s; family-run **Ferrante** (GEWURZ, GRÜNER V); **Firelands**; **Harpersfield** (KERNER/RIES/MUSCAT Ottonel); **Laurentia** (concrete tank whites); **Markko** (Lake Erie CAB SAUV, Chard, Pinot N; learned from NY's Dr. Frank to plant Ohioan vinifera in 1968); **M Cellars** (RKATSITELI); **St Joseph Vyd** (experiments with CORVINA, SANGIOVESE).

Oklahoma (OK)

Two AVAs: Ozark Mtn and Texoma, c.40 wineries. Mostly reds, esp CAB SAUV. **Clauren Ridge** gd Meritage. For better or worse, finding success with canned wine trend: **Stable Ridge** v.gd Bedlam CHARD; **The Range Winery** 13 varieties; gd white blend Jackwagon.

Oregon (OR)

Oregon viticulture is as diverse as CA and WA, but maintains a strong focus on WILL V CHARD, PINOT GR, PINOT N. In the s, Rhône and Iberian grapes dominate; simple, fruity Pinot N also grown. Cooler Columbia Gorge puts an elegant spin on lower-alc wines, while in the far ne the Rocks District produces top-tier SYRAH of distinct character. After fine 15 16 18, smoke from forest fires made 2020 challenging. Gd young yrs are listed in entries, but for drinking Will V Pinots at peak choose 2011–14 and 17.

Principal viticultural areas

Southern Oregon (S OR) encompasses much of w OR, s of Will V, incl sub-AVAs Applegate (App V), Elkton OR, Rogue (Rog V), Umpqua (Um V) Valleys. Plenty of experimentation: Albariño, Grüner V, Viognier, Cab Fr, Grenache, Syrah, Tempranillo standouts.

Willamette Valley (Will V) heart of the industry, with sub-AVAs Chehalem Mts, Dundee Hills (Dun H), Eola-Amity Hills (E-A Hills), McMinnville (McM), Ribbon Ridge (Rib R), Van Duzer Corridor, Yamhill-Carlton (Y-Car) and recently added Laurelwood District in n face of Chehalem Mtns AVA and Tualatin Hills w of Portland. Coming next: Mt Pisgah, Polk County AVA, with Freedom Hill vyd notable, and Lower Long Tom at far s end of valley. Chard, Pinots Bl/Gr, Ries excel throughout, but Pinot N remains the star with c.60% of total plantings.

Rocks District of Milton-Freewater (Walla Walla Valley [Walla]) entirely in OR produces cult wines from Cayuse and dense Syrah from others. Important new projects are Willamette Valley Vyds (Pambrun, Maison Bleue), Force Majeure.

Pinots Bl/Gr/M/N all mutations of same vine. Can even mutate in same bunch.

00 (Double Zero) Will V ★★★→★★★★ 17' 18' Exciting new CHARD, PINOT N specialist. Best are Hermann cuvées.

Abacela Um V ★★→★★★★ 15' 16' 17 (18) Planted 1st TEMPRANILLO in US; Barrel Select v.gd, Fiesta, NV Vintner's Blend for value. Deep Res MALBEC, SYRAH, ALBARIÑO.

Adelsheim Will V ★★★ 15' 16' 17 (18) Founders retired, new owners still making reliable PINOT N, CHARD, esp single-vyd Pinot N and Bryan Creek PINOT BL. Staking Claim Chard, Breaking Ground Pinot N v.gd value.

Alexana Dun H ★★→★★★★ 15' 16' 17 18' (19) Estate Revana PINOT NS, clone, block and res selections. Gd CHARD, RIES.

Alloro Chehalem Mts ★★★ 15' 16' 17' (18) Beautiful site with elegant CHARD, PINOT N, RIES. Estate Riservata, Justina age v. well.

Antiquum Farm Will V ★★★ 15' 16 17 18' 19' Consistent excellence, esp Daisy PINOT GR, Luxuria and Passiflora PINOT N.

Archery Summit Dun H ★★★→★★★★ 15' 16 17 18' New winemaker Ian Burch firmly in control. Summit, Looney, Arcus vyds excel; also Whole Cluster Cuvée and exotic Ab Ovo PINOT GR fermented in concrete egg.

Argyle Will V ★★ 15 16 17 18 Decent Vintage bubbly, esp Brut Rosé; Nuthouse, Spirithouse CHARD, RIES better than spotty PINOT NS.

A to Z Wineworks S OR ★★ 16 17 18' 19 Value-priced, soundly made, widely available. CHARD, PINOT GR, RIES, rosé best.

Authentique E-A Hills ★★★ 15 16' 17' (18') Numerous block selections, fermentations in amphorae and oak. Keeler estate PINOT N, Fond Marin CHARD best.

Ayoub Dun H ★★★→★★★★ 15' 16' 17 18' Brilliant handling of oak, superb vyd sources for long-lived, cult-quality CHARD, PINOT N.

Bergström Rib R ★★★★ 15' 16' 17' 18' Elegant, powerful PINOT N, CHARD. Sigrid Chard ethereal, Old Stones Chard v.gd value. Bergström, Shea, Silice, Temperance Hill, Winery Block best Pinot N.

Bethel Heights E-A Hills ★★★★ 15' 16' 17' (18') Brilliant old-vine High Wire, Justice, Casteel CHARD; Res Casteel PINOT N, muscular. Mid-priced Aeolian v.gd value.

Big Table Farm Will V ★★★→★★★★ 15' 16' 17 18' (19') Hand-drawn, letterpress labels; quirky, complex wines, esp Elusive Queen CHARD, Laughing Pig rosé and all single-vyd PINOT N.

Brick House Rib R ★★★→★★★★ 15' 16' 17' (18') All bio; owned by ex-newsman Doug Tunnell. Fine Cascadia CHARD; Evelyn's, Les Dijonnais and Cuvée du Tonnelier PINOT N show gamey, earthy, textural strengths. Rare GAMAY Noir v.gd.

Brittan Vineyards McM ★★★★ 15' 16' 17' (18') Veteran Robert B makes superb, estate-driven portfolio of austere, age-worthy PINOT N; full CHARD. Cygnus block is tops.

Broadley Will V ★★★ 15' 16 17' 18' Estate (esp Jessica) and purchased (Zenith, Shea) grapes yield spicy, polished PINOT N.

Brooks E-A Hills ★★★ 15' 16' 17' 18' 19 Exceptional RIES (up to 20 cuvées, incl fizz; look for Ara, Bois Joli). Also v.gd PINOT BL, PINOT N, Amycas (w blend).

Cowhorn App V ★★★→★★★ 16' 17 18' 19 Bio, best for dense, age-worthy GRENACHE, SYRAH, VIOGNIER; v.gd Rhône blends (r/w).

Cristom Will V ★★★ 15' 16' 17 18' Highly regarded producer of earthy, long-lived PINOT N from estate vyds. V.gd PINOT GR, VIOGNIER, herbal SYRAH.

Divio, Dom Rib R, Dun H ★★★★ 15' 16' 17' 18' French-born/-trained Bruno Corneaux's estate already among OR best. Aromatic, sleek, polished PINOT N, CHARD; lovely Pinot-based rosé and rare OR Passetoutgrain.

Drouhin Oregon, Dom Dun H ★★★★ 15' 16' 17' 18' Burgundy-inspired, not surprisingly. Édition Limitée, Louise PINOT N, CHARD best. Sister label Drouhin Oregon Roserock in E-A HILLS making equally fine wines, esp Zéphirine Pinot N.

Some marketing smoke-flavoured wines (from fires) as a USP. Will they catch on?

Elizabeth Chambers Cellar Will V ★★→★★★ 15 16 17 18' Original owner deceased, current releases return to previous excellence. Durant vyd selections lead pack.

Elk Cove Will V ★★★ 15 16' 17' 18' 19 V.-fine single-vyd PINOT N, esp Clay Court, Mt Richmond; also v.gd PINOT BL, RIES. Sister label Pike Road from purchased grapes.

Evesham Wood ★★★ 17' 18' (19) Restrained, evocative PINOT N from multiple vyds. Cuvée J best of all-star lineup.

Eyrie Vineyards, The Dun H ★★★★ 14' 15' 16' 17' 18' Jason Lett, 2nd-generation, continues pioneering tradition with elegant, age-worthy, low alc wines. Original Vines CHARD, PINOT GR, PINOT N textural wonders; rare Trousseau, PINOT M.

Failla E-A Hills ★★★ 16' 17 18' (19) CA superstar Ehren Jordan builds OR portfolio with stunning GAMAY, PINOT N, esp Björnson, Chehalem Mtn, Eola Springs, Seven Springs vyd selections.

Foris App V, S OR ★★ 15' 16' 17 18' 19 Estate-grown GEWURZ, PINOT BL, RIES mirror Alsace with acid-driven, low alc, refreshing dry style. Well-balanced Cedar Ranch PINOT N, Rogue V TEMPRANILLO.

Geodesy Will V ★★★★ 17' 18' Judy Jordan's project shines with superb CHARD from Eola Springs and Chehalem Mtn vyds. Supple, seductive PINOT NS in CA style.

Haden Fig Will V ★★★→★★★★ 17' 18' (19) Sister brand to EVESHAM WOOD; single-vyd PINOT NS and Juliette CHARD: aromatic, intriguing, gd value.

Hyland McM ★★→★★★★ 15' 16 17' 18 19' 50-yr-old vyd with estate PINOT N, dry GEWURZ and RIES. Age-worthy, impressively dense. Also decent CHARD, fine new bubbly.

Ken Wright Cellars Will V ★★★★ 15' 16' 17' Superb vyd knowledge informs deeply fruited PINOT N. Overall quality v. high, esp Abbott Claim, Bryce, McCrone, Shea and res Auric. Less-expensive WILL V cuvée overdelivers.

King Estate Will V ★★★ 16' 17 18' 19 Estate now 100% bio. PINOT GR (esp Backbone, Domaine, Johnson School, Steiner) core of portfolio with a dozen PINOT NS plus CHARD, GEWURZ, SAUV BL and new bubbly.

Lange Estate Will V, Dun H ★★★ 15' 16' 17' 18' 19 Fine PINOT GR and Assemblage, estate, Freedom Hill PINOT N; CHARD still tops here. Classiqué line v.gd value.

Lavinea Will V ★★★→★★★★ 15' 16' 17' (18') Brilliant portfolio with sub-AVA specific, single-vyd CHARD, PINOT NS. Lazy River, Nysa, Temperance vyds best.

Lingua Franca E-A Hills ★★★ 15' 16 17' 18' Sommelier Larry Stone co-founded and manages: focus on dense, stylish CHARD (Avni, Sisters), PINOT N (Mimi's Mind, Ryan's Plow). French-trained Thomas Savre oversees winemaking.

Ovum OR ★★★ 15' 16 17' 18' 19' Artisanal, quirky, ethereal RIES, GEWURZ from both N/S OR. Big Salt (w) blend fine value.

Panther Creek Will V ★★→★★★ 15 16 17' 18 19 Revitalized single-vyd PINOT N lineup. Lazy River, Carter, Kalita selects best.

Patricia Green Cellars Will V ★★★★ 15' 16' 17' 18' (19') Cult-calibre lineup of single-vyd PINOT NS. Founder deceased; value and quality remain intact. Etzel Block, Bonshaw Block, Mysterious, Notorious superb. Rare OR SAUV BL.

Ponzi Will V ★★★→★★★★ 15' 16 17 (18') Luisa P, 2nd-generation, outstanding across all price points. Abetina, Aurora PINOT N knockout; Aurora, Avellana CHARD also. Tavola, Classico Pinot N v.gd value.

Purple Hands Will V, Dun H ★★→★★★ 16' 17' 18' Cody Wright (son of Ken) offers juicy, well-balanced, single-vyd PINOT N. Holstein, Latchkey, Shea standouts.

Quady North App V, S OR, Rog V ★★→★★★ 16 17 18' (19) Herb Quady excels with VIOGNIER and fascinating lineup of three rosés. GRENACHE/SYRAH/MOURVÈDRE blend, varietals, Pistoleta (w blend) noteworthy.

Résonance Will V ★★★ 15' 16' 17 (18) Jadot's OR project; age-worthy CHARD, PINOT N from winemaker Guillaume Large. Estate wines tops; WILL V cuvée best value.

Rex Hill Will V ★★→★★★ 15' 16' 17 (18) Jacob-Hart PINOT N and fine, toasty barrel-fermented CHARD standouts.

Rich, Andrew Will V ★★→★★★ 15 16' 17' (18) Fine value Volcanic, Marine Sedimentary PINOT N, v.gd Croft vyd *Sauv Bl.*

Roco Will V ★★→★★★ 15' 16' 17 (18) Crafts superb vintage RMS Brut bubbly and layered, age-worthy PINOT N, CHARD. Private Stash is Res, Gravel Rd for value.

Serene, Dom Dun H ★★★★ 15' 16' 17' 18' Superb single-vyd CHARD (Clos de Lune, Récolte), PINOT N (Grace and Mark Bradford). Coeur Blanc (w Pinot N); Grand Cheval Pinot N/SYRAH blend; 1st sparklings v.gd.

Shea Wine Cellars Will V, Y-Car ★★★★ 15' 16' 17' (18') Top-tier winemakers clamour for Shea fruit; in-house wines just as gd. Block selections, Homer PINOT N tops; excellent CHARD also.

Sokol Blosser Will V, Dun H ★★ 16' 17 18 Value Evolution series v.gd. PINOT NS Peach Tree and Orchard tops; the rest ordinary.

Soter Will V ★★★→★★★★ 15' 16 17 18' 18' CA legend Tony Soter shines with CHARD, PINOT N, bubbly (all styles). Three labels: estate-grown Mineral Springs Ranch, mid-priced North Valley, Planet Oregon for value.

Stoller Family Estate Dun H ★★→★★★ 15' 16' 17 18' Steadily improving PINOT N, CHARD (Elsie's Res). Stoller Wine Group now incl Canned Oregon, Chehalem, History and Chemistry brands.

Trisaetum Will V, Rib R ★★★★ 15' 16' 17' 18' Meticulous estate wines; all styles of RIES, v.gd CHARD, PINOT N, impressive sparkling under Pashey label.

Walter Scott Will V ★★★★ 16' 17' (18') Dense, detailed, buzz-worthy CHARD, GAMAY, PINOT N. X-Novo, Seven Springs and Sojourner vyds top list.

Willamette Valley Vineyards Will V ★★→★★★ 15 16 17 18 Hundreds of shareholder/owners; extensive vyds, principally CHARD, PINOT N. ROCKS DISTRICT now home to Maison Bleue, Pambrun brands.

Winderlea Will V ★★★→★★★★ 15' 16' 17' 18' Top bio producer, vibrant single-vyd PINOT N: Crawford Beck, Shea, Weber, Winderlea Legacy. V.gd, age-worthy CHARD.

Pennsylvania (PA)

280 wineries+. Three AVAs, continental climate. Lake Erie-softened nw; gentler temperatures in se, rainy growing season fixed by rocky soils, cover crops. ALBARIÑO, GRÜNER V new stars; v. flexible reds: PINOT N, B'x varieties, native Carmine. Many Italians, BARBERA to FIANO. **Allegro**, reliable since 70s; **Armstrong Valley** (CAB FR, MERLOT); **Fero Vyds** (celebrated SAPERAVI); v.gd Albariño at **Galen Glen**, **Galer**, **Maple Springs**; **Karamoor**; **Mazza** (Lake Erie TEROLDEGO); **Pennswoods** (lasting Merlot); **Presque Isle**; **Va La** (cult Avondale field blends incl CORVINA and nine NEBBIOLO clones); **Vox Vineti** (*garagiste* N Piedmont-style Nebbiolo, barrel-fermented rosé); **Vynecrest** (luscious lifted LEMBERGER blend, limestone); **Waltz** (SAUV BL); **Wayvine** (gd barrique-aged Carmine).

PA largest US target of spotted lantern fly, sap-sucking super-pest. See it, squash it.

Rhode Island (RI)

Smallest US state, just e of NY's North Fork across cold-tempering Sound; B'x reds, PINOT N, CHARD. **Diamond Hill** (chemical-free farming, barrel-aged PINOT N); **Greenvale** (minimal CHARD, MALBEC, CAB FR); **Mulberry Vyds** (PINOT GR, SYRAH); **Newport** (GEWURZ); **Sakonnet** (Gewurz, red blends); **Verde** (biology prof. turned small farmer; BLAUFRÄNKISCH; St Croix, other hybrids).

Texas (TX)

Texas Fine Wine, group of gd producers, leads movement for state appellation wines; as a result, state now boasts some serious wineries, with horticulturists now bonafide winemakers. About 400 wineries mostly in two enormous AVAs – Hill County and High Plains best known, but producers now leverage regionality to distinguish styles, with a movement toward single vyds. TANNAT is exploding in popularity. Portuguese and Med varieties star: MARSANNE, ROUSSANNE, VIOGNIER; GARNACHA/GRENACHE, MONTEPULCIANO, MOURVÈDRE, PICPOUL, SOUZÃO. Pét-nat a favourite too. Vintage 17 one of recent best.

Becker Vineyards ★★★ Big, ripe B'x and Rhône styles. Prairie Rotie is signature wine; V.gd TEMPRANILLO Res, CAB FR Res, MALBEC/PETIT VERDOT blend Raven, Res Newsom Vyd CAB SAUV, refined VIOGNIER Res.

Bending Branch Winery ★★★ Pioneer of PICPOUL, TANNAT, focus on bold reds. V.gd ROUSSANNE, Souzão, Newsom Vyds CAB SAUV, PETITE SIRAH.

Brennan Vineyards ★★★ Signature dry VIOGNIER, white Rhône blend Lily; Res TEMPRANILLO; v.gd NERO D'AVOLA Super Nero. Deeper style of MOURVÈDRE dry rosé. Austin St off-dry red is popular.

Burklee Hill High Plains growers-turned-winemakers. Worth trying SANGIOVESE- and MONTEPULCIANO-driven blends, fresh rosé.

Calais Winery Frenchman Ben C makes B'x styles here and Rhône varieties for French Connection Wines. High-elevation vyds for complexity, concentration. Cuvée L'Exposition CAB SAUV a standout.

Crowson Wines Single-varietal, low-intervention natural wines from new producer. Known for dry MALVASIA Bianca; rich, intense rosé.

Duchman Family Winery **★★★★** Reliable producer specializing in Italian varieties. Award-winning AGLIANICO, TEMPRANILLO, plus flagship dry VERMENTINO and Progression 2 red blend. Grapes sourced from prestigious Bingham Family, Oswald, Reddy Vyds.

Fall Creek Vineyards **★★★** Legacy Hill Country winery. Early pioneer of CHENIN BL. Excellent B'x blend Meritus, high-altitude Terroir Reflection line. Premium ExTerra focused on MOURVÈDRE, SYRAH, TEMPRANILLO from Salt Lick vyds.

Kuhlman Cellars Young winery, Burgundy-trained winemaker, proprietary Rhône and B'x red blends. Signature is TEMPRANILLO/CAB SAUV Ignis. Estate MARSANNE/ROUSSANNE blends.

Lewis Wines ★★★ Focus on single-vyd Portuguese varieties, esp ALICANTE BOUSCHET, Tinta Cão, TOURIGA NACIONAL. Impressive estate rosé and CHENIN BL.

1st anti-phylloxera, limestone-friendly rootstocks (saved Champagne) found in TX.

Llano Estacado ★★★ Historic winery. Excellent MALBEC, 1836 (r/w). V.gd Viviana (w), Viviano (r) mimics Super Tuscan. Outstanding THP TEMPRANILLO from all-TX fruit. Affordable signature rosé is powerful, exotic.

McPherson Cellars ★★★ One of TX's fathers of wine; 1st to plant SANGIOVESE, but now more Rhône-focused. Affordable line incl solid Les Copains blends (r/w/rosé), excellent Res ROUSSANNE.

Messina Hof Winery ★★★ Big range. Bonarrigo dry white blend taps family's Sicilian roots. SAGRANTINO pioneer. Range of desserts, Papa Paulo Port style.

Pedernales Cellars ★★★ Known for VIOGNIER Res, four versions of signature TEMPRANILLO. New Signature Series of single varietal reds, esp MALBEC.

Perissos Vineyard and Winery ★★ Family run winery; ripe, concentrated reds, esp AGLIANICO-driven Racker's Blend. Excellent TEMPRANILLO. Strong in Italian blends.

Ron Yates ★★→★★★ Ambitious TEMPRANILLO specialist, sister winery to SPICEWOOD. Focus on Rhône, Spanish, Italian styles. V.gd GSM blend, VIOGNIER, award-winning CAB SAUV from Friesen vyd.

Southold Farm and Cellar ★★★ Cult-in-the-making Hill Country winery. Winemakers Regan and Carey Meador, moved to TX after successful run on Long Island. Proprietary names like Foregone Conclusion change yearly. Low-intervention styles, with organic Robert Clay vyds and neutral ageing vessels.

Spicewood Vineyards ★★★ Estate-grown; outstanding Sancerre-like SAUV BL. TEMPRANILLO-driven Good Guy red blend is top, award-winning CAB Claret; v.gd estate SYRAH, dry GRENACHE rosé.

William Chris Vineyards ★★→★★★ Low-intervention, vyd-focused; look for MOURVÈDRE range, incl crisp rosé. flagship blend Enchante (r). Now added small-batch winery Lost Draw Cellars to portfolio.

Vermont (VT)

With mtns, harsh winters, brief, sunny summers, frost, hail, humidity: a few hardy souls plant vyds anyway, rely on own-rooted hybrids like Frontenac Noir, La Crescent plus BLAUFRÄNKISCH, RIES in extreme n terroirs. **Lincoln Peak** (incl nouveau Marquette). Bio-farmed, natural-thinking **La Garagista** (new Brianna plantings); same-minded, fizz-focused **Shelburne Vyds** and **ZAFA Wines** pioneers to look for. **Iapetus** is experimental bio side of Shelburne winemaker, 72-day-maceration Marquette.

Virginia (VA)

Continental climate, weather tied to E Coast. Ten AVAs; challenge is to beat humidity, winter freeze, harvest-time hurricanes; heights of Shenandoah Valley offer mtn quality for still and sparkling; more being planted here. Some elegant outcomes in classical (lots of rain on well-drained clay for CAB FR, PETIT VERDOT) and experimental (hardy, high-acid PETIT MANSENG sings; noteworthy high-altitude PINOT N). VIOGNIER, TANNAT favoured too. Plenty of CAB SAUV, MERLOT. The vyd is 79% vinifera (about half is CHARD and CAB FR), 15% hybrids, <1% American incl Norton, US's oldest wine grape.

Cab Fr makes top reds across E Coast, VA adding Petit Verdot, maybe Tannat.

Ankida Ridge ★★★ Top, low-alc, ageable PINOT N poss best in VA, for a lucky few: <1000 cases. Steep granite slopes, 518m (1700ft) up in Blue Ridge Mtns. CHARD, gd Blanc de Blancs. GAMAY promising.

Barboursville ★★★ In Monticello where phylloxera-thwarted Jefferson tried a century earlier. BARBERA, FIANO, VERMENTINO. Elegant B'x-style reds (more CAB FR planted 2020), led by Octagon, plus fine CAB SAUV, NEBBIOLO, PETIT VERDOT. VIOGNIER Res is steady award-winner. Paxxito is luscious VIDAL/MUSCAT Ottonel. On-site inn and restaurant set tone for VA country elegance.

Boxwood ★★ Founder of Middleburg AVA. Blends based on CAB FR, MERLOT, plus CAB SAUV, PETIT VERDOT in both classic B'x style and drink now; rosé of same grapes; SAUV BL. New: Sauvignon Gr. Short drive from Washington DC.

Chrysalis ★★ In protected agricultural district, producer is advocate for Norton, VA's native grape. Among 1st to grow VIOGNIER; also ALBARIÑO, PETIT VERDOT, TEMPRANILLO.

Early Mountain ★★★ Quality B'x blends (heft, e-coast acidity): luxury-bottling Rise and flagship Eluvium; poised PETIT MANSENG; terroir-driven lineup of four CAB FR; single-vyd TANNAT; pét-nats of SYRAH, MERLOT; Loire-ish fresh Chamborcin and Cab Fr/SAUV blends. Tasting room pours several VA producers.

Glen Manor Vineyards ★★ Historic farm, 5th-generation. Vines on steep rocky slopes in Blue Ridge Mtns 305m (1000ft)+ up. Began with planting SAUV BL in 1995, now joined by rich CAB FR from 20–30-yr-old vines, off-dry PETIT MANSENG, PETIT VERDOT.

King Family Vineyards ★★★ French winemaker, age-worthy Meritage; top tiny-production *vin de paille*-style PETIT MANSENG; experimental Small Batch Series (member of state's Winemaker Research Exchange), in recent yrs lively no-sulphur CHARD, whole-cluster CAB FR, skin-contact VIOGNER. SAVAGNIN planted 2020.

Lightwell Survey ★★★ EARLY MTN winemaker's Shenandoah Valley project for less-known mtn vyds, fruit from small, top-quality, pioneer growers. Curiosity (ambient yeasts) and skill (partial whole-cluster) then guide wild wines: CAB FR co-fermented with PETIT MANSENG; rosé (PINOT GR/BLAUFRÄNKISCH), red (RIES/ Blaufränkisch) blends; site-focused Ries alone or plus Petit Manseng. Midland Construction is winemaker siblings' project on family's multi-generation farm – so far CHARD, Blaufränkisch, co-fermented Ries/Petit Manseng.

Linden ★★★ Estate founded in n VA in 80s by early believer in site over fruit; VA-wine mentor ever since. Notable high-altitude wines from three sites: rich, mineral CHARD, vivacious SAUV BL, savoury PETIT VERDOT, elegant, complex B'x-style reds often require ageing. Some library wines; vertical pours in tasting room.

Michael Shaps Wineworks ★★ Longtime VA producer with solid CHARD, VIOGNIER, luscious PETIT MANSENG; tasty TANNAT, PETIT VERDOT, Raisin d'Être (w Petit Manseng and r blend) from grapes dried in old tobacco barns. Custom crusher too.

Pollak ★★ Estate since 2003, wines on international side: heftier CABS FR/SAUV, MERLOT, Meritage; creamy PINOT GR; lush, spicy VIOGNIER.

Ramiiisol ★★★ New, no-expense-spared CAB FR from Blue Ridge Mtns, iron-rich granite gneiss; v. elegant, concentrated. Bio. NEBBIOLO planted too.

Rausse, Gabriele ★★★ Small, quality estate nr Monticello, owned Italian viticulturalist who planted BARBOURSVILLLE with Gianni Zonin. Varietal CHARD, PINOT GR; MALBEC, NEBBIOLO; PINOT N as *vin gris*.

RdV Vineyards ★★★★ Red blends (B'x-inspired), from granite soil hillside. Elegance, complexity, power: MERLOT-led Rendevous; CAB SAUV-driven Lost Mountain (released 4 yrs after vintage; 1st, 2010) was VA's 1st $100 wine.

Veritas ★★★ Solid estate, founded 1995, incl steep 20-yr-old forest vyds. Concentrated, floral CAB FR can age 10 yrs+. Paul Schaffer PETIT VERDOT is flagship, for tannin lovers. Restrained SAUV BL, richer VIOGNIER. Gd CHARD, MERLOT. Traditional-method sparkling to come.

Washington (WA)

The secret of WA is the Cascade Mtns, or rather Col V's position to the e of the Cascades, in arid and semi-arid desert. Summer days are warm, giving ripeness, but nights are cool, esp as harvest approaches, helping preserve acidity. The wines have one foot in New World plushness and another in Old World structure. The state's rising-star status means land and therefore grapes are relatively inexpensive, so that many wines offer v.gd value – for now.

Principal viticultural areas

Columbia Valley (Col V) Huge AVA in central and e WA with a touch in OR. High-quality Cab Sauv, Merlot, Ries, Chard, Syrah. Key sub-divisions incl Yakima Valley (Yak V), Red Mtn, Walla AVAs.

Red Mountain (Red Mtn) Sub-AVA of Col V and Yak V. Hot region known for Cabs and B'x blends.

Walla Walla Valley (Walla) Sub-AVA of Col V with own identity and vines in WA and OR. Home of important boutique brands and prestige labels. Syrah, Cab Sauv and Merlot.

Yakima Valley (Yak V) Sub-AVA of Col V. Focus on Merlot, Syrah, Ries.

Col V only has 15–20cm (6–8in) rain p.a. No work for umbrella-makers.

Abeja Col V, Walla ★★★ Production now in hands of Dan Wampfler (ex-Dunham Cellars) and wife Amy Alvarez-Wampfler. High-quality COL V CAB SAUV, CHARD.

Andrew Will Col V, Red Mtn ★★★★ 10' 12' 14' Will Camarda, 2nd-generation winemaker, now in place, continuing to craft some of state's best, most age-worthy B'x blends; reserved style. Involuntary Commitment, v.gd value.

Avennia Yak V, Col V ★★★ 10 12' 14' 16' 18' Few 10-yr-old wineries have made such an impact. Distinctive, classy; old vines, top vyds. Sestina B'x blend and Arnaut SYRAH tops. SAUV BL v.gd. Lydian value label.

Betz Family Winery Col V ★★★→★★★★ 10 12' 14' 16' 18' Woodinville stalwart has been making high-quality B'x, Rhône styles for 20 yrs+. Père de Famille CAB SAUV flagship. La Côte Patriarche SYRAH consistent standout. Untold Story gd value.

Cadence Red Mtn ★★★ 10' 12' 14 16' 17' Winemaker Ben Smith has unique take: all single-vyd, B'x blends, reserved, structured style. Patience required. Bel Canto and Cara Mia tops. Coda from declassified barrels exceptional value.

Cayuse Walla ★★★★ 10 11 12' 14 16' Not only some of best SYRAH in US; some of best on planet. All estate vyd. Stratospheric scores, but mailing list only, with yrs-long wait. Steep prices on secondary market but worth it. Sister wineries Hors Categorie, Horsepower, No Girls also top quality.

Charles Smith Wines Col V ★★ Eponymous winemaker spun off this brand to wine giant Constellation. Focus remains on value CAB SAUV, MERLOT, RIES.

Col Solare Red Mtn ★★★→★★★★ 10 12' 14 CH STE MICHELLE and Tuscany's Antinori partner to create CAB SAUV with complexity, longevity.

Columbia Crest Col V ★★→★★★ By far WA's largest producer; v.gd, well-priced Grand Estates label. Res wines cut above but still v.gd value, esp CAB SAUV, Walter Clore.

Columbia Winery Col V ★★ One of WA's founding wineries; value; higher end.

Corliss Estates Col V ★★★ 08' 10 12' Cult WALLA producer; extended time in barrel/ bottle before release. Sister winery Tranche focuses on Blue Mtn fruit, v.gd value

Côte Bonneville Yak V ★★★ 09' 10 12' All estate wines from DuBrul, highly regarded vyds. Extended bottle-age before release. *Carriage House* v.gd value.

DeLille Cellars Col V, Red Mtn ★★★ 10' 12' 14' 16 One of Woodinville's founders, known for high-end B'x, Rhône styles. Chaleur Bl one of state's best whites. Chaleur Estate, Harrison Hill top reds. No misses in lineup.

Doubleback Walla ★★★ 10' 12 16 Ex-footballer Drew Bledsoe's winery isn't a vanity project; classy, elegant CAB SAUV. Bledsoe Family sister winery. Bledsoe-McDaniels new OR PINOT and WA SYRAH project.

Dunham Cellars Walla ★★ Longtime producer of v.gd CAB SAUV, Syrah. Three Legged Red gd value.

Dusted Valley Vintners Walla ★★ Brothers-in-law Chad Johnson and Corey Braunel focus on COL V, WALLA, from value Boomtown to high-end single-vyd offerings.

Fielding Hills Col V ★★ Producer of estate vyd wines from Wahluke Slope made in rich, ripe style. V.gd value.

Most of WA vines are ungrafted: not so much pre-phylloxera as non-phylloxera.

Figgins Walla ★★★ 10 12 14 16 18 Founded by 2nd-generation winemaker Chris F (LEONETTI); focus on single vyd in Upper Mill Creek. Structured B'x blends. Patience/decanting required.

Force Majeure Red Mtn ★★★ All estate wines from RED MTN, WALLA: big, bold style.

Gorman Red Mtn ★★★ Hedonism the driver: rich, ripe wines. Evil Twin CAB SAUV/SYRAH blend calling card. Ashan CHARD project.

Gramercy Cellars Walla ★★★ 10 12' 13 16 While new WA wineries zigged in 2000s making big reds, master sommelier Greg Harrington zagged, producing lower-alc/oak, higher-acid, food-focused wines. Speciality earthy SYRAHS, herby CAB SAUV. Lower East value label.

H3 Col V ★ Recent spin-off from COLUMBIA CREST. Value CAB, MERLOT, Red Blend.

Hedges Family Estate Red Mtn ★★ In appellation known for ripe reds, this long-time RED MTN bio producer focuses on more reserved, savoury offerings. CMS blend gd value.

Januik Col V ★★★ 10 12' Mike J cut his teeth at CH STE MICHELLE before launching this Woodinville luminary 20 yrs ago. V.gd-value B'x styles, some of state's best CHARD. Novelty Hill sister winery. Son Andrew has eponymous label.

Kevin White Winery Yak V ★★★ Micro-producer of high quality, outrageous value. The trick? Getting them before they're gone.

Kiona Red Mtn ★★ Founding RED MTN winery; v.gd estate wines, old-vine LEMBERGER.

K Vintners Col V, Walla ★★★ Outsized personality, former rock band manager CHARLES SMITH makes single-vyd SYRAH, Syrah/CAB SAUV blends with iconic, black-and-white cattle brand label. Sixto CHARD-focused sister winery. Other brands CasaSmith, Substance, ViNo.

Latta Wines Col V ★★★ Ex-K VINTNERS winemaker Andrew L; stunning GRENACHE, MALBEC, MOURVÈDRE, SYRAH. Latta Latta v.gd value. Disruption side project, value.

L'Ecole No 41 Walla ★★★ 10 12' 14 16 One of valley's founding wineries makes range of WALLA, COL V wines, offering quality, superb value. Ferguson flagship B'x blend. CHENIN BL, SEM v.gd value.

Leonetti Cellar Walla ★★★★ 08 10' 12' 14 WALLA's founding winery with well-deserved cult status, steep prices for cellar-worthy CAB SAUV, MERLOT, SANGIOVESE. Res B'x blend flagship. Single-vyd wines v. limited but knee-buckling.

Liminal Red Mtn ★★★→★★★★ New cult producer of high-elevation reds and whites that demand attention.

Long Shadows Walla ★★★→★★★★ Brings globally famous winemakers to WA to make one wine each. Pedestal Michel Rolland MERLOT. Poet's Leap RIES one of best in state. All high quality, worth seeking.

Luke Col V ★★ Producer of well-priced Wahluke reds that way overdeliver.

Mark Ryan Winery Yak V, Red Mtn ★★★ Founder Mark McNeilly original member of Woodinville's "grape killers" known for big bold style. But there's refinement too. MERLOT-based Long Haul and Dead Horse CAB SAUV stand out. Board Track Racer second label gd value.

Maryhill Col V ★ Variety prices/styles: quaffable Winemaker's Select to single-vyd.

Milbrandt Vineyards Col V ★★ Wahluke Slope winery focusing on value plus smaller production single-vyd offerings. Look for PINOT GR, RIES.

Northstar Walla ★★★ When MERLOT was WA's guiding star, this producer helped lead way. Decades later, it still does.

Owen Roe Yak V ★★★ Longtime producer of SYRAH, CAB SAUV and B'x blends emphasizing restraint. Recently purchased by CA giant Vintage Wine Estates.

Pacific Rim Col V ★★ Founded by Randall Graham, RIES specialist now owned by Banfi. Oceans of tasty, inexpensive, eloquent Dry to Sweet and Organic. For more depth, single-vyd releases.

Passing Time Col V ★★★→★★★★ Former pro quarterbacks Dan Marino, Damon Huard focus on appellation-specific CAB SAUV. Winemaker Chris Peterson (AVENNIA). Horse Heaven Hills tops. Quickly earning cult status.

Pepper Bridge Walla ★★★ Estate wines, B'x style, from top sites Pepper Bridge, Seven Hills. Structured, classy. Time in cellar required.

Quilceda Creek Col V ★★★★ 04' 07 10 12' 14' 16' 18' Flagship producer of WA, cult CAB SAUV known for richness, layering, ageing potential. One of most lauded in world. Sold by allocation. Buy it if you can find it – and if you can afford to.

Reynvaan Family Vineyards Walla ★★★ 10' 11 12' 14 16 Wait-list winery focusing on estate vyds in Rocks District, Blue Mtn foothills. Reds get raves – deservedly so – but don't miss whites.

Rôtie Cellars Walla ★★★ Rhône-style specialist once best known for reds but now increasingly for whites too. Northern Blend consistent standout.

Ste. Michelle, Ch Col V ★★→★★★ State's founding winery offers gd-value (r/w), plus estate offerings and higher end res. World's largest RIES producer, dry and off-dry COL V exceptional value.

Saviah Cellars Walla ★★★ Always under-the-radar, always high quality-to-value ratio. Res Funk Vyd and Stones Speak SYRAH tops. Une Vallée flagship B'x blend. The Jack label gd value.

Seven Hills Winery Walla ★★★ 10 12' 14 16 18 One of WALLA's founding wineries. Age-worthy B'x reds made in restrained, sophisticated style. MERLOT v.gd value.

Sleight of Hand Walla ★★★ Audiophile Trey Busch makes dazzling B'x blends and Rhône styles. Seek Funkadelic SYRAH from Rocks District. Renegade value label.

Sparkman Cellars Yak V, Red Mtn ★★★ Woodinville "grape killer" producer focuses on power, diversity, making two dozen-plus wines. Stella Mae, Ruby Leigh B'x blends consistent standouts.

Spring Valley Vineyard Walla ★★★ CH STE MICHELLE property focusing on estate reds. Uriah MERLOT B'x blend the headliner.

Syncline Cellars Col V ★★★ Rhône-dedicated, Columbia Gorge producer with distinct, fresh style. Subduction Red v.gd value. Sparkling GRÜNER V insider wine. PICPOUL consistent standout.

Tamarack Cellars Col V ★★ Longtime WALLA producer, CAB SAUV, MERLOT and CAB FR. Firehouse Red gd value.

Waterbrook Walla ★→★★ One of state's oldest wineries, now owned by wine giant Precept, focuses on value.

Woodward Canyon Walla ★★★★ 07 10 12' 14 16 Founding WALLA producer, focus on B'x styles: Old Vines CAB SAUV. CHARD always best in state. Nelms Road value label.

W.T. Vintners Yak V ★★★ Sommelier-winemaker Jeff Lindsay-Thorsen picks earlier, pulls back the oak on his single-vyd GRENACHE, SYRAH and GRÜNER V

Wisconsin (WI)

Wollersheim Winery (est 1840s) is one of best estates in midwest, with hybrid and Wisconsin-native American hybrid grapes. Look for Prairie Fumé (SEYVAL BL), Prairie Blush (Marechal Foch).

Mexico

Valle de Guadalupe, along the Baja Peninsula, has grown up. In the past five years, new wine resorts have sprung up, including some 150 wineries on the Ruta del Vino, where the valley's "godfather", Hugo d'Acosta, has trained some 300 winemakers in his school, with alumni starting their own endeavours. The region produces 90% of Mexico's wine, and attracts winemakers and, now, food entrepreneurs, from across the border. Many say this is reminiscent of Napa Valley 50 years ago. Most are small-scale, most vines are Mediterranean, and benefit from high-altitude, cool-climate sites. The better wines are produced on hillsides where water comes from mountain springs. Flavours are ripe, bold and often with a touch of rusticity to keep it real.

Chihuahua region has vyds at 1585m (5200ft). That's a long way for a small dog.

Adobe Guadalupe ★★★★ Hugo d'Acosta helped est this showcase winery. Wines incl B'x and Med blends, named after archangels or gardens. Serafiel blend of CAB SAUV/SYRAH is top. Unoaked Jardín Romántico CHARD is fresh, tropical; Uriel rosé blends TEMPRANILLO/SYRAH.

Bichi ★★ Called the "new visionary" of Mexican natural wine, ex-lawyer Noel Téllez and chef brother run this Tecate winery, focus on terroir, old vines. Look for trendy pét-nat Pét-Mex and Listan made from heritage Mission grapes (r).

Bruma Valle de Guadalupe Chic winery attached to eco-luxury hotel; young B'x-trained winemaker Lulu Martinez Ojeda (top chef in kitchen). Invested in rosé.

Camou, Château ★★★ Pioneering, French-inspired, serious B'x credentials. Award-winning Gran Vinos, complex, elegant CAB SAUV-driven, worthy of ageing.

Carrodilla, Finca La First certified organic winery in Valle de Guadalupe. CAB SAUV, SHIRAZ among best; gd Canto de Luna blend (r).

Casa de Piedra ★★★ Modern winery in historic stone house; 1st project of Hugo d'Acosta. CAB SAUV/TEMPRANILLO v.gd; invested in sparkling.

Casa Vieja, La ★ Natural-style wines, ungrafted vines, some 120 yrs+. Handcrafted PALOMINO, Mission grapes.

Henri Lurton, Bodegas ★★ Venture of B'x's Lurton family, proponent of local CHENIN BL. Centenario is signature; promising SAUV BL, NEBBIOLO.

Monte Xanic ★★★ First modern premium winery with excellent CAB SAUV, v.gd MERLOT. Awarded whites; look for SAUV BL, unoaked CHARD, fresh CHENIN BL. Calixa blend (r) and NEBBIOLO Limitada are top. High-elevation PINOT N breaks new ground.

Nubes, La ★ Sustainable winery, experiments with Med grapes. Gd Res red blends named for clouds. NEBBIOLO, Kuiiy fresh SAUV BL-driven blend.

Paralelo ★★ Early pioneering eco-constructed winery by Hugo d'Acosta, ultra-modern. Small production. Intense Emblema SAUV BL, B'x-style Ensamble (r).

Pijoan, Viños Honest *garagista*-style wines named for winemaker's family. Mostly French varieties. Flagship B'x blend Leonora. New blends, showy artistic labels.

Tres Mujeres ★★★ Bucolic, female-owned co-op with casual garden-to-table dining. Top TEMPRANILLO; v.gd GRENACHE/CAB SAUV, La Mezcla del Rancho; Isme MERLOT.

Tres Valles ★★ Est 1999, powerful reds from Guadalupe, San Antonio, San Vicente Valleys. V.gd Kuwal blend driven by TEMPRANILLO. Top-rated single varieties: Maat (GRENACHE), Kojaa (PETITE SIRAH) and new CHARD/CHENIN BL.

Vena Cava ★★★ Lauded as Mexico's hippest winery, est by husband/wife former music-industry execs and sailors; built from reclaimed fishing boats; farm-to-table dining. Well-priced, modern, organic. Ten house labels and ten rotating experiments. Top CAB SAUV, SAUV BL, TEMPRANILLO.

Canada

Canadians are knowledgeable wine drinkers, and they're in love with their local wines. Climate change, technology and a generation of environmentally conscious growers have done much: pure, savoury, electric wines that reflect their origins have so supercharged Canadian wine that it can barely keep up with local demand. And it's not small: Canadian vineyards are spread across 9300 kilometres (5779 miles) from west to east. Icewine started the rush but is now behind unlikely favourites like Gamay, sparkling, Albariño, Grüner Veltliner and reimagined versions of Chardonnay, Cabernet Franc, Pinot Noir, Riesling and red blends as exciting as anything in the wine world.

Ontario

Prime appellations of origin: Niagara Peninsula (Niag), Lake Erie North Shore (LENS) and Prince Edward County. Within the Niagara Peninsula: two regional appellations – Niagara Escarpment and Niagara-on-the-Lake – and ten sub-appellations. New LENS sub-appellation South Islands.

At around 43°N, Niag is at roughly same latitude as n Italy.

Bachelder Niag ★★★★ 18 19 20' Thomas B is the passionate conscience of Niag; pure, precise, elegant, age-worthy CHARD, PINOT N. New online sales.

Cave Spring Niag ★★★★ 18 19 20' Regional pioneer with impressive old-vine vyds. Elegant CSV wines age effortlessly: RIES, late-harvest, Icewine.

Henry of Pelham Niag ★★★ 18 19 20' Sustainable practices from 6th generation, soil to shelf. Top label Speck Family Res, Cuvée Catherine Brut, RIES Icewine.

Hidden Bench Niag ★★★★ 17 18 19 20' Reference producer of RIES, PINOT N, CHARD; certified organic vyds: Felseck, Locust Lane, Rosomel; top picks Nuit Blanche, Tête de Cuvée Chard, Felseck Ries.

Inniskillin Niag ★★★ 18' 19 20' Icon Icewine pioneer since 1984. Classic RIES leads with VIDAL, CAB FR and Cab Fr/Vidal (sp).

Leaning Post Niag ★★★ 18 19 20' Focused on subregion nuances; V.gd CHARD, GAMAY, PINOT N, eclectic Freaks & Geek series.

Malivoire Niag ★★★★ 18 19 20' Certified ON Sustainable Winemaking Program; Members at Large Oregon LIVE. V.gd CHARD, GAMAY, PINOT N, a trio of rosés.

Megalomaniac Niag ★★★ 18' 19 20' Sébastien Jacquey offers French awareness crafting terroir-sensitive CHARD, CAB FR, GAMAY, PINOT N on Twenty Mile Bench.

Organized Crime, The Niag ★★★ 18' 19 20' Family-owned, 2nd-generation, s-facing Beamsville Bench vyds. Quality CHARD, RIES and aromatics; gd CAB FR, PINOT N.

Prince Edward County Home to some 40 producers at e end of Lake Ontario on limestone-rich soils. High-quality CHARD, PINOT N. Closson Chase, Hinterland, Huff, Rosehall Run, Trail Estate, Stanners.

Ravine Vineyard Niag ★★★ 18' 19 20' Organic 14-ha St David's Bench vyd. Top Res CAB FR, CHARD; drink-now: Sand and Gravel. Delicious farm dining.

Stratus Niag ★★★ 17 18' 19 20' JL Groux and Dean Stoiko embrace reductive style. V.gd CAB FR/GAMAY blends; Charles Baker age-worthy RIES speak to origin, terroir.

Tawse Niag ★★★ 18' 19 20' Certified organic/bio producer; v.gd CHARD, RIES; gd CAB FR, MERLOT, PINOT N.

Thirty Bench Niag ★★★ 17 18' 19 20' Small lot, low-temperature ferments. Top single-block old-vine RIES. Steel Post, Triangle, Wood Post on Beamsville Bench.

Two Sisters Niag ★★★ 17 18' 19 20' Top estate reds CAB FR, CAB SAUV, MERLOT; flagship Stone Eagle blend. Cult traditional-method Cab Fr sparkler Blanc de Franc.

British Columbia

Geographical Indications for BC wines of distinction and BCVQA are BC, Fraser Valley, Gulf Islands, Kootenays, Lillooet, Okanagan Valley (Ok V) – Golden Mile Bench, Naramata Bench, Okanagan Falls, Skaha Bench (subregions of Ok V) – Shuswap, Similkameen Valley (Sim V), Thompson Valley, Vancouver Island (Van I) and its newest subregion: Cowichan Valley.

99%+ of wine is carbon, oxygen, hydrogen. It's how they combine that's interesting.

Blue Mountain Ok V ★★★ 18 19 20' Traditional-method fizz legacy and complex RD versions; age-worthy PINOT N, CHARD; new single-block Pinot N trio.

CedarCreek Ok V ★★★★ 18 19 20' Serious, organic, N Ok V aromatic RIES, GEWURZ; Platinum single-vyd blocks PINOT N, CHARD. Must-visit restaurant, visitor centre.

Checkmate Ok V ★★★★ 16' 17 18 19 Next World CHARD (six) and MERLOT (five) from S Ok V vyds micro-blocks. Top: (w) Attack, Queen Taken; (r) End Game, Silent Bishop. Breathtaking visitor centre.

Clos du Soleil Sim V ★★★ 18 19 20' Old-World-inspired blends grown organically in windswept stone-laden Similkameen Valley. Top: Signature (r), Capella (w).

Cowichan Valley Van I PINOTS N/GR hotbed, ancient volcanic soils on Van I. Top: Averill Creek, Blue Grouse, Emandare, Rathjen, Unsworth, Venturi Schulze.

Haywire Ok V ★★★ 18 19 20' Innovative organic growers: natural, pét-nat, concrete ferments, amphorae, for precision, grace. CHARD, PINOTS GR/N, GAMAY, sparkling.

Martin's Lane Ok V ★★★★ 16' 17 18 19 Detail-obsessed, gravity-only PINOT N, RIES from n single vyds in Naramata and Kelowna.

Mission Hill Ok V ★★★★ 17 18 19 20' Regional leader with 500 ha certified organic vyds. Top (r/w): Legacy, Terroir series. Reimagined visitor experience, acclaimed al fresco dining.

Nk'Mip Ok V ★★★ 16' 17 18 19 20' Bright RIES, top-end Qwam Qwmt CHARD, SYRAH, Mer'r'iym White. Part of $25-million aboriginal resort, Desert Cultural Centre.

Osoyoos Larose Ok V ★★★ 17 18 19' 20' B'x-based Groupe Taillan owns this 33-ha 25-yr-old single vyd. Track record of age-worthy Le Grand Vin echoes B'x.

Painted Rock Ok V ★★★ 18 19 20' Skaha Bench, steep, 24-ha, 15-yr-old estate vyd below 500-yr-old native pictographs; SYRAH, CAB FR, CHARD, signature red Icon.

Phantom Creek Ok V ★★★★ 17 18 19 20' Stunning $100-million facility, organic vyds on Black Sage Bench, Golden Mile Bench, Similkameen Valley. Impressive SYRAH, CAB SAUV, PINOT GR, red blends.

Quails' Gate Ok V ★★★ 18 19 20' Inspired style. Fresh, aromatic RIES, CHENIN BL; continued refinement of core PINOT N, CHARD, new 200-acre, E Kelowna vyd.

Road 13 Ok V ★★★ 18 19 20' Exciting Rhône-style VIOGNIER, SYRAH and treasured old-vine (1968) CHENIN BL (w/sp); premium Golden Mile Bench and Similkameen Valley Jackpot series.

Tantalus Ok V ★★★★ 18 19 20' Electric producer of lauded old-vine (1968) RIES, silky PINOT N, quality CHARD farmed sustainably.

Nova Scotia

Benjamin Bridge Gaspereau V ★★★ 15 16' 20' Traditional-method fizz. Excellent age-worthy Vintage and NV Brut from CHARD/PINOTS N/M blends.

Partridges and clouds

Canada's other speciality is fruit wine, and it's getting better, just as grape wine is improving. Alberta, Saskatchewan, Manitoba and Newfoundland specialize in fruit-based wines with pure fruit flavours: try wines from blueberries, partridge berries, cloudberries and lingonberries.

South America

Abbreviations
used in the text:
CHILE

Aco	Aconcagua
Bío	Bío-Bío
Cach	Cachapoal
Casa	Casablanca
Cho	Choapa
Col	Colchagua
Coq	Coquimbo
Cur	Curicó
Elq	Elqui
Ita	Itata
Ley	Leyda
Lim	Limarí
Mai	Maipo
Mal	Malleco
Mau	Maule
Rap	Rapel
San A	San Antonio

ARGENTINA

Cata	Catamarca
La R	La Rioja
Luján	Luján de Cuyo
Men	Mendoza
Neu	Neuquén
Pat	Patagonia
Río N	Río Negro
Sal	Salta
San J	San Juan
Uco V	Uco Valley

CHILE

Chile has coast (lots of it), mountains (plenty), vines in the Atacama Desert and vines on the slopes of Patagonian volcanoes. The ever-expanding wine map has moved far beyond the Central Valley and its Merlots and Sauvignon Blancs, and now ranges from Syrah blends from granite hills in Elqui to laser-sharp Pinot Noir from volcanic soils in Malleco and chiselled Chardonnay from Limarí's coastal limestone terraces. For ten years Chile has been moving away towards tautness and freshness, and seeking out more marginal mountainous and coastal sites. Coastal vineyards are cool because the ocean is cold. Dip a toe in if you don't believe me.

Recent vintages

Vintages are still relatively consistent in Central Valley, but wine map is bigger and more varied than it was. Most vintage variation comes from El Niño/ La Niña. 2020 excellent; 19 drought yr, v.gd; 18 cool, dry, v.gd; 17 v. hot and dry.

Abolengo Cach ★★ Promising CARMENÈRE/SYRAH and CHARD.

Aconcagua Major region covering CASA and SAN A, although Aco proper is in n from Los Andes to Zapallar. Bold mtn reds and fresh coastal CHARD, PINOT N, SYRAH.

Almaviva Mai ★★★★ Top MAI wine and 1st non-B'x to be sold by B'x négociants alongside top ch. A child of Mouton Rothschild (B'x) and CONCHA Y TORO. Opulent blend from rocky soils of Puente Alto.

Altaïr Wines Rap ★★★ SAN PEDRO's finest. Complex B'x blend from Cach Andes with impressive Sideral as second label.

Antiyal Mai ★★★ Classy reds by top bio winemaker Alvaro Espinoza. Elegant, age-worthy wines from MAI.

Least likely patch of vines: crater of Rano Kau volcano, Easter Island. Self-seeded.

Apaltagua ★★ Diverse portfolio from all over Chile, often gd value. Based in Col.

Aquitania, Viña Mai ★★★ Pioneer of Mal and making top CHARD, PINOT N, SAUV BL there. Richer reds from MAI, incl v.gd Lazuli CAB SAUV.

Arboleda, Viña Aco ★★ Refreshing ACO Costa wines by ERRÁZURIZ team. Gd for SYRAH, SAUV BL, CHARD, PINOT N.

Aristos Cach ★★★→★★★★ Burgundy's L-M Liger-Belair's boutique brand with Pedro Parra and François Massoc. Complex, layered CAB SAUV, CHARD from Cach Andes.

Bío-Bío Cool s region now stepping into limelight for vibrant RIES, SAUV BL, PINOT N. Old vines (PAÍS, MUSCAT) also exciting.

Bouchon Mau ★★→★★★ MAU family winery with energetic new generation in charge. Stellar SEM, juicy reds. Putting PAÍS on map.

Caliboro Mau ★★→★★★ Count Cinzano (Italy) makes organic, boutique wines in MAU. Juicy reds and delicious old-vine, late-harvest Torontel.

Calyptra Cach ★★→★★★ V.gd family winery: vibrant mtn reds, top barrel-aged SAUV BL.

Carmen, Viña Casa, Col, Mai ★★→★★★ Big MAI winery with 170-yr history and exciting future under winemaker Emily Faulconer. Fantastic DO range and Gold Res CAB SAUV.

Casablanca Leading coastal region in Chile. Renowned for fresh CHARD, SAUV BL, PINOT N but increasingly SYRAH and CAB FR too.

Casa Marín San A ★★★ Excellent boutique family producer with own DO in Lo Abarca, just 4 km (2.5 miles) from sea. Top: racy RIES, SAUV BL, Sauvignon Gr.

Casas del Bosque Casa, Mai ★★ CASA wines with cool, coastal character. Try Pequeñas Producciones, esp SAUV BL, CHARD.

Casa Silva Col, S Regions ★★→★★★ Traditional Col family with wines from Lolol to Los Lingues. Often v.gd value, esp CARMENÈRE. Lago Ranco PINOT N, SAUV BL in Pat is thrilling stuff.

Clos des Fous Cach, Casa, S Regions ★★→★★★ Terroir buffs Pedro Parra and François Massoc make an eclectic collection around Chile, incl. v.gd Mal RIES, CHARD.

Concha y Toro Cent V ★→★★★★ S America's biggest player, in most Chilean categories and regions from LIM to BÍO. Casillero del Diablo is gd-value, everyday, but it gets exciting from Marquis and *Terruño* up. MAYCAS DEL LIMARÍ is a highlight of Lim, Gravas SYRAH is one of Chile's best, and top CAB SAUV Don Melchor is classier by the vintage. *See also* ALMAVIVA, TRIVENTO (Argentina).

Cono Sur Casa, Col, Bío ★★→★★★ Top-value wines from all over Chile, but based in Col. Biggest *Pinot N* producer in S America, but CAB SAUV, RIES also worth trying.

Cousiño Macul Mai ★★→★★★ Historic family winery, founded 1856, making MAI wines incl top Lota CAB SAUV.

De Martino Cach, Casa, Elq, Mai, Mau, Ita ★★→★★★★ Family winery in MAI, but making wines all over Chile; special focus on old vines with v.gd CINSAULT and MOSCATEL from ITA. Understated wines, moved right away from richness and oak.

Elqui Known for stargazing, Pisco and now distinctive SYRAH. Wines typically white and fresh by coast, powerful and meaty in mtns.

Emiliana Casa, Rap, Bío ★★ Large organic producer with gd-value wines from around Chile. Álvaro Espinoza (*see* ANTIYAL) leads the charge. Top of line G and Coyam particularly complex.

Errázuriz Aco, Casa ★★→★★★★ Biggest winery in ACO exploring all its coastal and mtn terroirs. Pizzaras CHARD, PINOT N from coast and Don Maximiliano CAB SAUV blend from mtns are highlights. *See also* SEÑA, VIÑA ARBOLEDA, VIÑEDO CHADWICK.

Falernia, Viña Elq ★★ Pioneer of fine wine in ELQ with plots from mtns to sea. Fresh SAUV BL, meaty SYRAH, sun-dried CARMENÈRE memorable. Mayu is sister winery.

Garcés Silva, Viña San A ★★ →★★★ Important grower with one of few wineries in LEY. Cool, coastal wines: Amayna label more complex, Boya more taut.

Haras de Pirque Mai ★★→★★★ Polished, stylish portfolio of Alto MAI reds owned by Italy's Antinori.

Itata Dry-farmed old CINSAULT, PAÍS, MUSCAT in heritage region in s: distinctive artisanal wines.

Koyle Col, Ita ★★→★★★ Family winery with bio estate in COL and old vines in ITA. Cerro Basalto from hills is top Med blend.

Lapostolle Cach, Casa, Col ★★→★★★★ Grand Marnier family making fine bio wines in Apalta. Clos Apalta B'x blend is icon, exclusive Collection line is thrilling.

Leyda, Viña Col, Mai, San A ★★→★★★ Leader in Ley with impressive portfolio of coastal whites/reds. SAUV BL, SYRAH, PINOT N particularly worth trying.

Limarí Limestone terraces by cool coast in desert. Some of Chile's best CHARD, SAUV BL, PINOT N.

Luis Felipe Edwards ★★ Family winery based in COL but with vyds all over. Often excellent value and gd varietal definition.

Maipo World-class CAB SAUV region, esp Alto Mai in foothills of Andes. River gravels and high altitude offer ideal combo for defined B'x style reds.

Malleco Exciting s region: cool-climate PINOT N, CHARD, SAUV BL on volcanic soils.

Matetic Casa, San A ★★★ Bio leader in New World; classy SYRAH, *Sauv Bl* and other coastal wines on CASA/SAN A border. V.gd value too.

Maule Chile's breadbasket but long overlooked for being big but boring. Now stepping into light for distinctive old-vine CARIGNAN (*see* VIGNO) and PAÍS. Diverse region, but best for reds.

Maycas del Limarí Lim ★★→★★★ CONCHA Y TORO side-hustle making excellent coastal wines from limestone-rich LIM region. V.gd SAUV BL, CHARD.

Montes ★★→★★★★ Stunning Apalta estate and feng shui winery now with vyds in Zapallar to Chiloe. COL wines are typically opulent, *Folly Syrah* is worthy icon.

MontGras Col, Ley, Mai ★★ COL-based producer with vyds in MAI (rich reds under Intriga label) and LEY (zippy SAUV BL under Amaral).

Montsecano Casa ★★★ Cult following for this boutique bio producer. V.gd PINOT N.

Morandé Casa, Mai, Mau ★★→★★★ This large company has grown since it was founded (and later sold) by Pablo Morandé in 1996. Gd-value varietals from all over Chile, v.gd MAU reds, Brut Nature NV bubbly is top pick.

Neyen Col ★★★ 130-yr-old CAB SAUV blended with 90-yr-old CARMENÈRE in Apalta; just one wine. Owned by VERAMONTE.

Odfjell Cur, Mai, Mau ★→★★★ Organic and bio, owned by Norwegian shipping merchant who also breeds beautiful blond Fjord horses. CARIGNAN is top stuff.

Pérez Cruz, Viña Mai ★★→★★★ Polished portfolio of mainly B'x reds from MAI; Med blends proving exciting too. Chaski among Chile's best PETIT VERDOTS.

CHILE

Andes to Costa

As well as regional appellations, Chile has a climate appellation system, dividing regions from the mtn influence in e (Andes) to maritime influence in w (Costa). Entre Valles, the warmer valley floor, falls in the middle.

Pisco Brandy made in Chile and Peru. Drink neat, with Coke, or with whipped egg whites, lime and sugar for a "sour".

Polkura Col ★★→★★★ Coastal producer Sven Bruchfeld makes v.gd meaty SYRAH.

Quebrada de Macul, Viña Mai ★★→★★★ Seductive CAB SAUV and B'x blends from Alto MAI, just outside of Santiago. Domus Aurea is worth the hunt.

Rapel Umbrella term for Col and Cach in Central Valley. Used on big-brand blends.

RE, Bodegas Casa ★★★ Offbeat, exciting natural wines by Pablo Morandé Snr and Jnr. CASA and MAU but not as you know it: orange, unfiltered, amphorae, flor.

San Antonio Smaller but cooler than CASA next door. Renowned for SAUV BL, CHARD, SYRAH, PINOT N, esp in subregion Ley.

San Pedro Cur ★→★★★ Enormous stable of brands: 2nd-biggest group in Chile, based in CUR. 1865 line offers top-value single vyds, Cabo de Hornos CAB SAUV is Cach at its best; 35 Sur, Castillo de Molina are everyday value. New PINOT N project with Mapuche farmers in MAL is exciting. (*See* ALTAÏR, TARAPACÁ).

Santa Carolina, Viña Mai ★★→★★★★ MAI-based but working all over, this historic producer has reinvented itself with quirky varieties and limited releases. Herencia CARMENÈRE and Luis Pereira CAB SAUV are cream of the crop.

Santa Rita Mai ★★→★★★★ Large, old winery with new vision. Floresta is excellent single-vyd line, *Casa Real Cab Sauv* is an icon from MAI; CAB SAUV, CARMENÈRE consistent across board. Tres Medallas, 120, Medalla Real everyday labels.

Seña Aco ★★★★ Fine, ACO B'x blend from Chadwick/ERRÁZURIZ clan. Bold and age-worthy but with finesse.

Tabalí Lim ★★→★★★★ One of Chile's top coastal producers, from limestone soils of LIM. Stellar Talinay CHARD, SAUV BL, PINOT N are highlights; also v.gd bubbles.

Tarapacá, Viña Casa, Ley, Mai ★★ VSPT-owned mega-winery with 600-ha estate in Isla de Mai. V.gd CAB SAUV, esp Etiqueta Negra.

Torres, Miguel Cur ★★→★★★★ A leader in Chile with innovation aplenty, now under exciting winemaker Eduardo Jordan. Champion of fairtrade, pioneer of sparkling PAÍS, guardian of complex CAB SAUV from Cur. Old-vine CINSAULT, MUSCAT from ITA v.gd. Escaleras de Empedrado PINOT N on MAU schist and SAUV BL from Osorno thrilling.

Undurraga Casa, Ley, Lim, Mai ★→★★★ Large, diverse producer. TH range is v.gd-value single vyds with precise, on-point wines.

Valdivieso Cur, San A ★→★★★ Leader in fizz, since 1879. Mainly everyday bubbles, but still wines too. Gd CAB FR, MALBEC, esp. Caballo Loco top pour.

Vascos, Los Rap ★★ Rich B'x blends from Lafite-Rothschild in COL, including 70-yr-old vines in Le Dix. More "Fifth Growth" than "First".

Ventisquero, Viña Casa, Col, Mai ★→★★★ Large producer, mainly everyday wines, some gems: *Tara* natural wines from Atacama Desert, Grey SAUV BL from Huasco, and opulent Enclave CAB SAUV, Pangea SYRAH. Kalfu is fresh Costa brand.

Veramonte Casa, Col ★★→★★★ On warmer side of CASA, making fruit-driven whites/reds. V.gd Ritual line. Owned by González Byass (*see* Spain).

Vigno Mau Project promoting sustainable, old-vine, dry-farmed CARIGNAN in MAU. Range of producers, each with own style, one common cause.

A decade of a megadrought in Central Valley is pushing viticulture further s: to Osorno, 40.57°S.

VIK Cach ★★→★★★ Extraordinary investment in CACH by Norwegian billionaire. 400 ha vines in 4000 ha estate and less than 10% of grapes make cut for top VIK wine: a rich, B'x blend.

Villard Casa, Mai ★★ Est 1989. Family winery with fresh whites, perfumed reds.

Viñedo Chadwick Mai ★★★★ Elegant, exclusive CAB SAUV from Puente Alto, owned by Chadwick/ERRÁZURIZ.

Viu Manent Casa, Col ★★ Family winery, champions MALBEC and hearty Col reds. Coastal SAUV BL also gd.

Von Siebenthal, Viña Aco ★★→★★★ Full-bodied reds from Mauro von S and family in ACO. Parcela 7 blend v.gd value; try Toknar PETIT VERDOT.

Distance from most n vyds in Chile to most s is distance from London to Senegal.

ARGENTINA

With 500 years of wine history, Argentina has got its mountain reds down to a fine art. Malbec is king, accounting for 20% of vines, and Mendoza is its main kingdom, with 70% of production. But make sure to delve into high-altitude Cabernets Sauvignon and Franc, Petit Verdot and Tannat. Mountain whites lead with Chardonnay, Sauvignon Blanc and Semillon. Old-vine Bonarda, Criolla and Torrontés are well worth a look, from the heights of the Calchaquí Valleys down to the Andean corridors of San Juan. But Argentina isn't only about mountains and the Andes. Vineyards are popping up along the coast and on the steppes of Patagonia, with promising Pinot Noir, Chardonnay and Gewürztraminer. The ink isn't dry on Argentina's wine story.

Achaval Ferrer Men ★★→★★★ Helped bring MALBEC to fame and continues to make polished wines. Owned by Stolichnaya.

Aleanna Men ★★→★★★★ Stellar wines from CATENA ZAPATA winemaker Alejandro Vigil, best known for its El Enemigo brand. Gorgeous CAB FR, MALBEC, CHARD, BONARDA, mainly from Uco V.

Alicia, Viña Men ★★★ Arizu family (LUIGI BOSCA) making small quantities from old vines in Luján. Rich reds, full-bodied whites.

Alta Vista Mcn ★→★★★ Pioneer of single-vyd MALBEC, still making fine job of it. French twist on MEN terroir.

Altocedro Men ★★→★★★ Bio wines from Uco V. V.gd TEMPRANILLO, old-vine MALBEC.

Altos las Hormigas Men ★★★→★★★★ Thrilling Appellation line of MALBEC from Uco V, and top value in other lines. Alberto Antonini and Attilio Pagli's vision, incl BONARDA under Colonia Las Liebres label.

Anita, Finca La Men ★★ Boutique producer with appealing CAB SAUV, SYRAH, PETIT VERDOT and old vines in Luján.

Atamisque Men ★→★★★ Modern estate in Tupungato; top value from peppery Serbal blend to luscious Catalpa MERLOT.

Benegas Men ★★→★★★ Wine dynasty now focused on bold reds mainly from Luján. V.gd CAB FR.

Bianchi, Bodegas Men ★→★★ Leader in San Rafael with gd-quality bubbles and still; now v.gd reds from new estate in Los Chacayes, Uco V. Enzo Bianchi is top stuff.

Bosca, Luigi Men ★★→★★★ Large, historic producer in Luján specializing in concentrated reds. Las Nobles is age-worthy, La Linda entry-level.

Bressia Men ★★→★★★ Renowned winemaker now working with his children: complex red blends, bright Sylvestra varietals. Ultima Hoja worth cellaring.

Callia San J ★→★★ Value wines from SAN J, gd everyday SYRAH.

Canale, Bodegas Humberto Río N ★→★★★ Leading producer in RÍO N, 110-yr history. V.gd old-vine RIES, MALBEC, PINOT N.

Caro Men ★★★ CATENA ZAPATA and (Lafite) Rothschild joined forces to make opulent, seductive B'x blends in MEN.

Casarena Men ★★→★★★ Focus on single lots in Luján. Best is CAB SAUV but try MALBEC too. Ramanegra, 505 everyday lines.

Catena Zapata, Bodega Men ★★→★★★★ Pioneer and leader in MEN, esp Uco V.

Excellent Adrianna vyd in Gualtallary (MALBEC, CHARD, CAB FR), but range is diverse, from bubbles to orange. Alamos is entry-level. (*See also* CARO.)

Chacra Río N ★★★→★★★★ Bio artisanal wines by Piero Incisa della Rocchetta of Sassicaia (*see* Italy) making classy old-vine **Pinot N**, and now CHARD.

Clos de los Siete Men ★★ B'x producers (*see* BODEGA ROLLAND, CUVELIER LOS ANDES, DIAMANDES, MONTEVIEJO) living and working together in one 850-ha clos in Uco V, making a village red, blended by Michel Rolland.

Cobos, Viña Men ★★★→★★★★ Top-notch single-vyd MALBEC, CAB SAUV, CHARD from Uco V and Luján by international winemaker Paul Hobbs.

Colomé, Bodega Sal ★★→★★★ Seriously high-altitude (up to 3100m/10,171ft) wines. Inky reds, perfumed TORRONTÉS, delicate SAUV BL.

Cuvelier Los Andes Men ★★→★★★ Classy B'x blends from Léoville-Poyferré family in Uco V.

Decero, Finca Men ★★→★★★ Precise, modern, from Luján. V.gd PETIT VERDOT and Owl and The Dust Devil blend.

DiamAndes Men ★★ Polished portfolio of B'x varieties plus VIOGNIER, CHARD from Bonnie family (B'x's Malartic-Lagravière). Look for steel diamond in the cellar.

Doña Paula Men ★★→★★★★ From Chile's SANTA RITA stable, large producer leading in Luján, and Uco V too. Parcel series is excellent, Los Cardos is v.gd value.

Durigutti Men ★★→★★★ Durigutti bros make classic portfolio; Las Compuertas is step up, 5 Suelos MALBEC one of Luján's best.

Esteco, El Sal ★★→★★★ Making some of best in Calchaquí with old-vine definition, character. CAB SAUV, TORRONTES, MALBEC highlights. Don David, Ciclos value.

Etchart Sal ★→★★ One of Cafayate's most important wineries, founded 1850. Smart reds, top for TORRONTÉS.

Fabre Montmayou Men, Río N ★★→★★★ Red blends best from this B'x family in MEN and RÍO N, also one of Argentina's top MERLOTS.

Fin del Mundo, Bodega Del Neu ★→★★ Largest player in NEU, helped put this new region on the map. Ripe, concentrated reds (v.gd CAB FR). Postales, Ventus, Newen are everyday lines.

Flichman, Finca Men ★★ Consistent, gd value, esp Caballero de la Cepa range. Maipú-based but vyds in Uco V too. Dedicado top pour. Owned by Sogrape (*see* Portugal).

Kaikén Men ★★→★★★ Rich reds, perfumed whites from Chilean MONTES family, based in Luján.

Manos Negras / Tinto Negro / TeHo / ZaHa Men ★★→★★★ Soil specialist Alejandro Sejanovich makes vibrant MALBEC, CAB FR, PINOT N from around Argentina.

Masi Tupungato Men ★★→★★★ Italians in Uco V. *Ripasso*-style MALBEC/CORVINA blend.

Mendel Men ★★★ One of Argentina's finest winemakers, Roberto de la Motta's own Mendel is consistent, classy. Plush Finca Remota MALBEC, Lunta blend superb value, solid SEM.

Mendoza Capital of Argentine wine with 75% of production: E MEN is the engine room, Maipú is historic, Luján is the MALBEC heartland, cooler Uco V is top for fresh whites.

Moët-Hennessy Argentina Men ★→★★ Best known as Chandon, this LVMH outpost has been making everyday wines and bubbly in MEN for 70 yrs. Baron B is traditional method fizz. *See* TERRAZAS DE LOS ANDES.

Monteviejo Men ★★→★★★★ V.gd Vista Flores producer: top-value B'x varieties from

---

Franc-ophiles

CAB FR is more than just a trend in Argentina, it's become a bonafide classic. Peppery, herbal, light-bodied – it's the yin to the yang of Malbec and an ideal blending partner too.

everyday Festivo line, mid-range Petite Fleur and top-end Lindaflor. La Violeta is superb. B'x family behind Ch Le Gay.

Moras, Finca Las San J ★→★★ Leader in gd-value and quality reds, and some tiptop SYRAH. Owned by TRAPICHE.

Neuquén Pat Pioneered two decades ago, and next door to RÍO N. Sunnier exposure means richness, concentration. Best for hearty MALBEC, CAB FR, fruity PINOT N.

Bequignol vine, nearly extinct in France, 500 ha in Argentina. 30+ synonyms.

Nieto Senetiner, Bodegas Men ★→★★★ Historic but growing. Now one of MEN's biggest players, lines range from everyday value (Benjamin, Emilia) to Don Nicanor and Cadus. Gd MALBEC, fresh SEM. Big in bubbles.

Noemia Pat ★★★→★★★★ Old-vine red B'x blends (RÍO N), by Hans Vinding-Diers.

Norton, Bodega Men ★→★★★ English rail engineer got Norton on track in 1895; today one of MEN's biggest wineries, owned by Swarovski. Gd value across board, esp bubbles. Lot MALBEC is excellent.

Passionate Wine Men ★★→★★★ Uco V consultant Matias Michelini's own wines take a wilder approach: native ferments, skin contact and always gripping acidity. Agua de Roca SAUV BL ages like a dream.

Pelleriti, Marcelo Men ★★→★★★ Musician by night, winemaker by day (also MONTEVIEJO), Pelleriti makes classy reds often with Argentine rock stars.

Peñaflor Men ★→★★★ Argentina's biggest group with EL ESTECO, FINCA LAS MORAS, Mascota, Navarro Correas, Santa Ana, Suter, TRAPICHE in its fold.

Piatelli Sal ★★ Smart wines from Cafayate and Luján showing two sides of the coin. V.gd CAB SAUV, MALBEC.

Piedra Negra Men ★→★★★ Rich, intense reds and complex, fresh whites from Los Chacayes at François Lurton's Argentine outpost.

Porvenir de Cafayate, El Sal ★★→★★★ One of n Argentina's finest. Delicate TORRONTÉS, vibrant reds incl Amauta blends. Excellent value.

Pulenta Estate Men ★★→★★★ Pulenta dynasty now focused on complex reds (excellent CAB FR, MALBEC), perfumed whites. La Flor gd-value, everyday line.

Renacer Men ★★ Chilean-owned, energetic Luján winery. Bright portfolio: Amarone-style blend, fresh SAUV BL from CASA in Chile.

Riccitelli, Matias Men ★★→★★★ Excellent range from Riccitelli Jnr, from everyday Apple to single vyds. Top SEM too.

Riglos Men ★★→★★★ Gualtallary estate making modern reds (v.gd CAB FR), CHARD.

Riojana, La La R ★→★★ Over 500 families involved in this co-op in n. Gd-value everyday wines.

Río Negro Río N Region in s with milder temperatures, old vines and lots of cool wind. Fresh, distinguished MALBEC, PINOT N, SEM.

Rolland, Bodega Men ★★★ Michel Rolland's outpost in CLOS DE LOS 7: polished B'x-style reds, intense PINOT N, extrovert SAUV BL.

Salentein, Bodegas Men ★★→★★★ One of most stunning wineries in New World; pretty striking wines too. Single-vyd line from cool San Pablo is mouthwatering (v.gd PINOT N, SAUV BL); El Portillo range top value.

Salta Province in n with vyds in high-altitude Calchaquí mtn range. Fresh, perfumed TORRONTÉS, intense reds (TANNAT, MALBEC) with concentration, freshness. Cafayate is main region.

San Juan The 2nd-largest region in Argentina to n of MEN. Best for gd-value BONARDA, SYRAH and TORRONTÉS.

San Pedro de Yacochuya Sal ★★★ High-altitude, intense reds and TORRONTÉS by ETCHART family and Michel Rolland in Cafayate.

Schroeder, Familia Neu ★★ NEU producer with PINOT N and dinosaur fossils in cellar. Gd-value bubbles too.

Sophenia, Finca Men ★★→★★★ Powerful wines from Gualtallary. V.gd SAUV BL in top Synthesis range. Altosur (esp BONARDA) is excellent value.

Susana Balbo Wines Men ★★→★★★★ Argentina's 1st female winemaker and leading pack now. Splendid range from complex reds (Nosotros, Ben Marco) and vibrant whites (White Blend is superb) to top-value everyday Crios line.

Malbec so called after M. Malbeck, propagated it in B'x in C18. Called Cot until then.

Tapiz Men ★★→★★★ Large winery with vyds in Uco V, Luján and coastal RÍO N. MALBEC Black Tears and Notas MERLOT top pours from San Pablo.

Terrazas de los Andes Men ★★→★★★★ Polished wines from LVMH. Best: old-vine MALBEC, superb *Cheval des Andes* blend, in collaboration with Cheval Blanc (B'x).

Tikal / Alma Negra / Animal Men ★★→★★★ Ernesto CATENA's (mainly natural) adventures in Uco V and Luján. From bold reds to funky orange and fizz, refreshingly offbeat.

Toso, Pascual Men ★★→★★★ Traditional winery, old vines, concentrated, polished wines. Magdalena Toso top of pyramid.

Trapiche Men ★→★★★★ Historic winery with big role. Vyds from coastal project Costa y Pampa (try ALBARIÑO) to old vines in Uco V. *Medalla* is renowned, but Iscay MALBEC/CAB FR and SYRAH/VIOGNIER blends are also top picks. Part of enormous PEÑAFLOR group.

Trivento Men ★→★★★ Gd-value, mainly everyday wines from Chile's CONCHA Y TORO in MEN. Top Eolo comes from centenarian vines in Luján.

Vines of Mendoza / Winemaker's Village Men ★★ Over 100 micro-brands in this real estate project. Best of all is Winemaker's Village where Abremundos (*see* MARCELO PELLERITI), Corazon del Sol, Gimenez Riili, Super Uco live.

Zorzal Men ★★→★★★ Fresh, bright, juicy, from Gualtallary. Eggo line (v.gd CAB FR, SAUV BL) made in concrete eggs.

Zuccardi Men ★★→★★★★ Seba Z in charge, 3rd-generation winemaker. Modern wines with single-vyd Uco V focus at top end. Excellent Alluvional MALBEC, Concreto, Emma BONARDA, Fossil CHARD. Santa Julia in Maipú is weekday brand.

BRAZIL

The tough climate of the sub-tropics of Brazil means this country has had a 500-year stop-start wine history. Now, however, it is coming on nicely. Vineyards are in the cooler, drier southern regions of Rio Grande do Sul but also increasingly in high-altitude sites around São Paulo and Minas Gerais where winter harvests or rain nets are common. Bahia also sounds an unlikely candidate for viticulture, with two harvests/year, but it is thriving and makes tropical-scented wines. Hybrids still dominate by quantity, but the quality is found in fizz and Med-style reds.

Aurora ★→★★ Over 1000 families send grapes to crush at Brazil's largest co-op in Serra Gaucha.

Casa Valduga ★→★★★ Top for fizz but also for serious B'x-style reds and CHARD. Fab family producer in Serra Gaucha.

Cave Geisse ★★★ Sublime traditional-method sparkling from top Brazilian bubble terroir, Pinto Bandeira.

Lidio Carraro ★★ V.gd family producer with vyds in Vale dos Vinhedos and Serra do Sudeste ranging from B'x varieties to NEBBIOLO.

Miolo ★→★★★ Leading premium market, Miolo's diverse portfolio incl v.gd TOURIGA N blend, lively varietals and some top bubbles.

Pizzato ★→★★★ Flavio P puts his heart into his wines, and result is some of Bento's best. V.gd CHARD, MERLOT. Fausto is young range.

Salton ★→★★ Top party fizz and v.gd-value everyday wines from one of Serra Gaucha's leaders and pioneers, founded in 1878. Gerações blend more complex.

URUGUAY

With an Atlantic climate more akin to Galicia or Bordeaux, Uruguay is a world apart from its neighbours. This is perhaps why its star varieties of Tannat and Albariño are rarely found elsewhere in Latin America. The clay-limestone soils of Canelones and Montevideo host the lion's share of vines and producers, while the granite outcrops in coastal Maldonado are witnessing a growth spurt with a handful of new vineyards and wineries, and the riverbanks of Colonia continue to draw in investors.

Alto de la Ballena ★→★★ Juicy SYRAH, peppery CAB FR, spicy TANNAT from pioneer of cooler, coastal Maldonado. Cetus is excellent.

Bouza ★★→★★★ One of Uruguay's finest, consistent in quality and innovation. Superb ALBARIÑO and top RIES, MERLOT, TANNAT.

Deicas, Familia ★→★★★ Historic estate with strong local presence (Establecimiento Juanicó) and own premium lines with innovation aplenty from Santi Deicas. Single-vyd TANNAT series v.gd, esp Mahoma and Maldonado.

Garzón, Bodega ★→★★★★ World-class winery and estate nr Punta del Este with Alberto Antonini as consultant. Fresh, focused, energetic. Balasto blend tops.

Marichal ★→★★ Third generation now making wines. Gd TANNAT, PINOT N (and blend of both).

Pablo Fallabrino Wines ★★→★★★ Lo-fi, natural wines from wild child of Canelones. ARNEIS, NEBBIOLO, TANNAT, of course.

Pisano ★→★★★ One of Uruguay's most successful in exports, Pisano bros make consistent, exciting wines. V.gd PINOT N, TANNAT, TORRONTÉS, VIOGNIER.

OTHER SOUTH AMERICAN WINES

Bolivia You can't get much higher in altitude than Bolivia. If 3000m (9843ft) doesn't make your head spin, maybe the 300-year-old MUSCAT vines will. A diamond in the rough but increasingly polished, with reds of intense colour, vibrant acidity and full body (esp CAB SAUV, SYRAH, MALBEC, TANNAT) and fragrant, bone-dry Muscat. Biggest wineries: Campos de Solana, Kohlberg, Kuhlmann, La Concepción.

Peru More than just Pisco, Peru was the first wine country in S America (since 1500s). It's been slow to catch up in quality but a revival is gradually underway. Look for Intipalka, Mimo, Tacama, Vista Alegre.

Cruzat Men ★★★ Top-quality fizz from Luján and Uco V. Finca La Dama is precise, Millésime (10 yrs on lees) is luxurious.

Laberinto Mau ★★★ Thrilling MAU wines from high-altitude slopes of Lake Colbun. Rafael Tirado makes racy SAUV BL and mouthwatering mtn reds.

South America shrinks the oak

South America's finest reds are increasingly ditching the oak. Heavy vanilla and toast flavours are fading, with winemakers turning to concrete, large *foudres* or old barrels to keep the fruit at the fore. Modern "naked" icons in the making incl herbal, wild **Bouchon Granito**; linear, perfumed **Errazuriz Pizzaras**; peppery, spicy **Maquis Franco**; mineral, chiselled **Tabalí Talinay** (Chile). Mouthwatering, crunchy **Aleana El Enemigo El Cepillo**; floral, grippy **Michelini i Mufatto La Cautiva**; chalky, taut **Zuccardi Supercal** (Argentina). Energetic, dark **Garzón Balasto** (Uruguay).

Australia

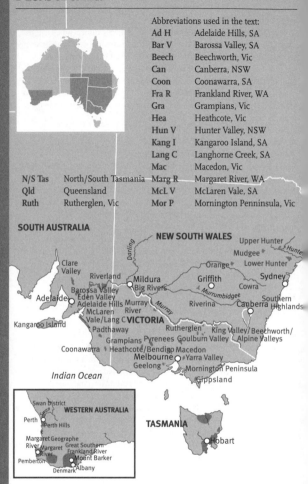

Abbreviations used in the text:

Ad H	Adelaide Hills, SA
Bar V	Barossa Valley, SA
Beech	Beechworth, Vic
Can	Canberra, NSW
Coon	Coonawarra, SA
Fra R	Frankland River, WA
Gra	Grampians, Vic
Hea	Heathcote, Vic
Hun V	Hunter Valley, NSW
Kang I	Kangaroo Island, SA
Lang C	Langhorne Creek, SA
Mac	Macedon, Vic
N/S Tas	North/South Tasmania
Marg R	Margaret River, WA
Qld	Queensland
McL V	McLaren Vale, SA
Ruth	Rutherglen, Vic
Mor P	Mornington Penninsula, Vic

A ustralian wine has become the broadest of churches, as likely to be found on the fine dining tables of the world as it is in the supermarket. Let's hope that the theories are right and that there really is strength in diversity, because Australia had one hell of a year in 2020. What happens when you build an industry around exports to China and then have the tap turned off overnight? We're in the process of finding out. And that's in addition to a 2020 vintage of poor fruit set, drought and bushfires. Over the past decade Australia had become the number one wine exporter to China; in November 2020 China imposed dramatic tariffs on essentially all Australian wine, in effect making the trade unworkable. The result is that there is a lot of Australian wine in need of a new home. As is always the case when supply and demand channels fall out of whack, there will be wine offers and bargains aplenty. The coming few years will be hard on Australian wineries but a boon for drinkers. The technical term for this is "silver lining". So what should we be looking for? The grand and important wines, of course. But also the wines that have evolved so dramatically in the last few years: delicate, aromatic Grenache; Chardonnay in more styles than you can shake a stick at; Shiraz from vines older than any in the Rhône; natural wines, orange wines, pét-nats. You can be as traditional or as trendy as you want.

Recent vintages

New South Wales (NSW)

2020 Hot, fire-affected yr with all manner of challenges.
2019 Hot, with just enough rain for generous whites/reds.
2018 Big ripe reds for long haul. Hot/tough yr for whites.
2017 Hot summer followed a wet spring; whites/reds lapped it up; in general.
2016 Drink early Hun V reds, but gd mid-term ageing red/white elsewhere.
2015 Difficult in most parts, but Orange and Can excellent; Hilltops v.gd.

Victoria (Vic)

2020 Fire-affected in the ne and generally challenging. Yields down.
2019 Compressed season but wines (r/w) look vibrant.
2018 Overshadowed by yr before. Slow-evolving.
2017 Excellent yr. Reds/whites looked gd young and will stay.
2016 Warm, dry season produced many overripe reds. Tread carefully.
2015 Strong yr across board.

South Australia (SA)

2020 Hard/tragic yr, but Ries and reds look promising. Seriously low yields.
2019 Exceptionally low yields should produce concentrated wines.
2018 Gutsy reds with yrs up their sleeve. Whites gd but not in same class.
2017 High yield, high quality, highly drinkable young.
2016 Hopes are high for a special vintage for red/white.
2015 Warm regions coped well with summer of wild temperature swings.

Western Australia (WA)

2020 Early, low yield, high concentration yr.
2019 Cool vintage, the kind to sort the wheat from the chaff.
2018 Reds will outlive most of us; whites will do medium-term in a canter.
2017 Tricky vintage. Medium-term wines.
2016 Humid, sultry vintage. Nothing wrong with wines; mid-termers.
2015 Challenging, mixed results; be selective.

Accolade Wines Name of once-mighty Constellation, HARDYS groups. BAY OF FIRES, Hardys, HOUSE OF ARRAS, PETALUMA, ST HALLETT.

Adams, Tim Clare V, SA ★★ Ever-reliable (in gd way) RIES, CAB SAUV/MALBEC blend, SHIRAZ and (full bodied) TEMPRANILLO. FIANO to watch.

Adelaide Hills SA Cool 450m (1476ft) sites in Mt Lofty ranges. CHARD, SAUV BL, SHIRAZ outgun PINOT N. ASHTON HILLS, BASKET RANGE, HAHNDORF HILL, HENSCHKE, JERICHO, MIKE PRESS, SHAW & SMITH, TAPANAPPA all in excellent form.

Adelina Clare V, SA ★★★ SHIRAZ, GRENACHE, MATARO, NEBBIOLO stars here. Imposing, intense, polished. Label designs of note too. One of best of "new Australia".

AUSTRALIA

A, Dom S Tas ★ V.gd oak-matured SAUV BL. Polarizing cool-climate CAB SAUV. Charismatic, let's call it. Owned by MOORILLA.

Alkoomi Mt Barker, WA (RIES) 10' **17' 18' 19** (CAB SAUV) 10' **12'** 16 Veteran maker of fine Ries; rustic reds; more accessible young than they were.

All Saints Estate Ruth, Vic ★★★ Rating for fortifieds. Serviceable table wines, led by B'x blend.

Alpine Valleys Vic In valleys of Victorian Alps. BILLY BUTTON, MAYFORD, Ringer Reef. TEMPRANILLO, SHIRAZ the headliners; aromatic whites for the "in the know".

Angove's SA ★ MURRAY V family business. Cheapies (r/w) often standouts of a broad range. Mainstream face of organic grape-growing, both value and premium ends. Single-vyd MCL V GRENACHE, SHIRAZ can be excellent.

Arenberg, d' McL V, SA ★★ Wine names pretty whacky (eg. The Cenosilicaphobic Cat SAGRANTINO) but the styles are no-nonsense and the quality is generally high, incl sumptuous SHIRAZ, GRENACHE.

Ashton Hills Ad H, SA ★★ (PINOT N) 15' 17' 18' 19 Compelling Pinot N from 30-yr-old+ vyds. Bought in 2015 by WIRRA WIRRA.

Bailey's NE Vic, Glenrowan, Vic ★ Rich SHIRAZ, magnificent dessert MUSCAT (★★★) and TOPAQUE. Vyds all organic. Sold by TWE to CASELLA 2017.

Balgownie Estate Vic ★★ Capable of medium-bodied, well-balanced, minty CAB, SHIRAZ of finesse, character from its BENDIGO heartland. Separate YARRA V arm.

Balnaves of Coonawarra SA ★★ Family-owned COON champion. Lusty CHARD; v.gd spicy, SHIRAZ, full-bodied Tally CAB SAUV flagship. "Joven-style" Cab gd.

Bannockburn Vic ★★ (CHARD) 15' 17' 18' 19 (PINOT N) 12' 17 Intense, complex CHARD, sappy PINOT N. Put GEELONG region on map, but not as reliable as it once was.

Barossa Valley SA Ground zero of Aussie red. V.-old-vine SHIRAZ, MOURVÈDRE, CAB SAUV, GRENACHE. Can produce bold, black, beautiful reds with its eyes closed, and has done for just about ever. ELDERTON, GRANT BURGE, HENTLEY FARM, JOHN DUVAL, LANGMEIL, OCHOTA BARRELS, PETER LEHMANN, ROCKFORD, RUGGABELLUS, ST HALLETT, SALTRAM, SEPPELTSFIELD, SPINIFEX, TEUSNER, WOLF BLASS, YALUMBA.

Barry, Jim Clare V, SA ★★★ Great vyds provide v.gd RIES, McCrae Wood SHIRAZ and richly robed, pricey, oaked-to-the-devil The Armagh Shiraz.

Basket Range Ad H, SA ★★ Lead player in new/avant garde of AD H producers. Pét-nat, CAB SAUV, PINOT N.

Bass Phillip Gippsland, Vic ★★★★ (PINOT N) 14' 15' 16' 17 Tiny amounts of variable but mostly exceptional Pinot N. Sold in 2020 to, among others, Jean-Marie Fourrier.

Bay of Fires N Tas ★★★ PINOT N shouldn't be passed over but HOUSE OF ARRAS *super-cuvée sparklings* rightly dominate.

Beechworth Vic The rock-strewn highlands of ne Vic. Tough country. CHARD, SHIRAZ best-performing varieties, but NEBBIOLO fast rising from (winter) fog. A. RODDA, CASTAGNA, DOMENICA, FIGHTING GULLY ROAD, GIACONDA, SAVATERRE, SCHMÖLZER & BROWN, SORRENBERG, TRAVIARTI essential producers.

Bendigo Vic Hot central Vic region. BALGOWNIE ESTATE, PASSING CLOUDS, SUTTON GRANGE. Home of rich CAB SAUV, SHIRAZ.

Best's Great Western Gra, Vic ★★★ (SHIRAZ) 10' 15' 17' 18 Shiraz master; *v.gd mid-weight reds*. Thomson Family Shiraz from 120-yr-old vines superb. Wines generally on plush side of elegant. Old-vine PINOT M pinpoint's tip.

Billy Button Vic ★★ So many wines, such small quantities. Everything from SHIRAZ and CHARD to Verduzzo, VERMENTINO, SAPERAVI, SCHIOPPETTINO and more. Low oak in general; fruit-fresh wines.

Bindi Mac, Vic ★★★ (PINOT N) 10' 15' 17' 18' 19 Ultra-fastidious maker of long-lived Pinot N (esp), CHARD. Tiny production.

Bise, La Ad H, SA ★★ Small range, consistently gd (r/w), CHARD usually best.

Bortoli, De Griffith, NSW, Yarra V, Vic ★★★ (Noble SEM) Both irrigation-area winery and leading producer. Excellent cool-climate PINOT N, SHIRAZ, CHARD, gd sweet, botrytized, Sauternes-style Noble Sem. YARRA V arm where quality is.

Brash Higgins McL V, SA ★★ Brad Hickey is a smart cookie. He has degrees in English and botany, but has also worked as a brewer, baker, sommelier and now makes radical expressions of MCL V (r/w).

Brave New Wine Marg R, WA ★★ Natural wine producer capable of v. high highs, so to speak. SHIRAZ, CHARD, GEWURZ can all be excellent.

Bremerton Lang C, SA ★★ Silken CAB, SHIRAZ with mounds of flavour. Never mean, always generous. MALBEC can be v.gd too. All about the reds.

Brokenwood Hun V, NSW ★★★ (ILR Res SEM) 11' 14 (Graveyard SHIRAZ) 09' 13' 14' 19 HUN V classic. *Cricket Pitch* Sem/SAUV BL gd value. Quality generally v.gd.

Brown Brothers King V, Vic ★ Wide range of crowd-pleasing styles, varieties. General emphasis on sweetness. Innocent Bystander (YARRA V) and Devil's Corner/Tamar Ridge (TAS) savvy acquisitions.

Burge, Grant Bar V, SA ★★ Smooth red/white from best grapes of Burge's large vyd holdings. Owned by ACCOLADE.

By Farr / Farr Rising Vic ★★★★ (PINOT N) 15' 17' 18' 19 Best-in-region producer. CHARD, Pinot N can be minor masterpieces.

Campbells Ruth, Vic ★ Smooth ripe reds (esp Bobbie Burns SHIRAZ); extraordinary Merchant Prince Rare *Muscat*, Isabella Rare TOPAQUE (★★★★).

Canberra District NSW One of the most significant cool-climate regions in Oz, for quality at least. CLONAKILLA the leader but Collector, GUNDOG ESTATE, MOUNT MAJURA, Nick O'Leary, RAVENSWORTH all v.gd.

Cape Mentelle Marg R, WA ★★★ (CAB SAUV) 10' 14' 15' 16' MR pioneer on great form. Robust Cab has become more elegant (with lower alc), CHARD v.gd; old-vine ZIN has been tamed; v. popular SAUV BL/SEM. LVMH Veuve Clicquot-owned.

Casella Riverina, NSW ★ Casella's Yellow Tail range of budget reds/whites has developed into an Australian wine empire. Now owner of heritage brands BAILEY'S, Brand's of Coonawarra, MORRIS, PETER LEHMANN.

Castagna Beech, Vic ★★★ (SYRAH) 10' 12' 14' 15' 16 Julian C leads Oz bio brigade. Estate-grown SHIRAZ/VIOGNIER, SANGIOVESE/Shiraz excellent. Non-estate Adam's Rib range worth investigating.

Chambers Rosewood NE Vic Viewed with MORRIS as greatest maker of sticky TOPAQUE (★★★★), *Muscat*.

Chandon, Dom Yarra V, Vic ★★ Cool-climate sparkling and table wine. Owned by Moët & Chandon. Known in UK as Green Point. NV cuvées in best ever shape.

Fortify me

The fortified wines of Australia are the world's greatest wine bargain. Sure, the odd one is (rightly) expensive but all the main producers of MUSCAT, in particular, put out fantastic examples at ridiculously low prices. If you're new to this arena then you pretty much just have to look for one word: RUTHERGLEN. The Rutherglen region is the home of most of Australia's best fortified producers; it is to Australian fortified what Champagne is to sparkling. All Muscat is NV because it incl varying amounts of aged material. To make it easier, Rutherglen Muscat is classified as: Rutherglen Muscat: 3–5 yrs average age. Classic Rutherglen Muscat: 6–10 yrs average age. Grand Rutherglen Muscat: 11–19 yrs average age. Rare Rutherglen Muscat: min 20 yrs average age. You don't need tasting notes or vintage recommendations. Simply look for the best of Rutherglen's fortified producers: ALL SAINTS, CAMPBELLS, CHAMBERS, Jones Winery, MORRIS. The older the average age of the wine, the more intense it will taste. Thank us later.

Chapel Hill McL V, SA ★★ High-profile MCL V producer. SHIRAZ, CAB the bread and butter, but TEMPRANILLO and esp GRENACHE on rise. Changed hands 2019.

Chatto Tas ★★★★ Young vyd, but already among Australia's best PINOT N producers. Fruit, spice and all things nice. Smoky savouriness abounds.

Clarendon Hills McL V, SA ★★ Full-Monty reds (high alc, intense fruit) from grapes grown on hills above MCL V. Cigar wines.

Clare Valley SA Small, pretty, high-quality area 160 km (100 miles) n of Adelaide. Best toured by bike, some say. Australia's most prominent RIES region. Gumleaf-scented SHIRAZ; earthen, tannic CAB SAUV. ADELINA, GROSSET, KILIKANOON, KIRRIHILL, MOUNT HORROCKS, TIM ADAMS, WENDOUREE (esp) lead way.

Ricky Ponting joins growing band of ex-cricketers with eponymous wine brand. Decent wines too.

Clonakilla Can, NSW ★★★★ (SHIRAZ) 07' 09' 10' 14' 15' 17' 18' 19 CAN region superstar. RIES, VIOGNIER excellent, Shiraz/Viognier famous, SYRAH a rare treat.

Clos du Tertre Fra R, WA ★★ Stunning RIES. Textural, intense, long. Made by and for Ries fanatics.

Clyde Park Vic ★★ Broody single-vyd CHARD, PINOT N v.gd form. SHIRAZ turning heads.

Coldstream Hills Yarra V, Vic ★★★★ (CHARD) 15' 17' 18' 19 (PINOT N) 10' 15' 17' 19 Est 1985 by critic James Halliday. Delicious Pinot N to drink young, *Res and single-vyd to age*. Excellent Chard (esp Res). Part of TWE.

Coonawarra SA Home to some of Australia's best CAB SAUV, and certainly to its richest red soil (on limestone). WYNNS COONAWARRA ESTATE is the champion resident. BALNAVES, KATNOOK, LINDEMANS, MAJELLA, PARKER COONAWARRA ESTATE, YALUMBA too are all key. Cachet of region dimmed in recent decades.

Coriole McL V, SA ★★ (Lloyd Res SHIRAZ) 10' 14' 16' Renowned producer of SANGIOVESE and old-vine SHIRAZ Lloyd Res. Interesting Italians: FIANO, NERO D'AVOLA.

Corymbia Marg R, WA, Swan V, WA ★★★ Producer of beautifully pitched CAB SAUV, CHENIN BL, among others. Star in making, if not already.

Craiglee Mac, Vic ★★★ (SHIRAZ) 14' 15' 16' Salt-of-the-earth producer. N Rhône inspired. Fragrant, peppery Shiraz, age-worthy CHARD. New Res Shiraz is terrific.

Crawford River Henty, Vic ★★★ Outstanding RIES producer. Cool, cold, scintillatingly dry but intense style, great for seafood. Highly age-worthy.

Cullen Wines Marg R, WA ★★★★ (CHARD) 13' 15' 16' 17' 18 (CAB SAUV/MERLOT) 09' 12' 13' 14' 15' 16' 17' 18 Vanya Cullen makes substantial but subtle SEM/SAUV BL, outstanding Chard, elegant, sinewy Cab/Merlot. Bio in all she does. Best of Oz.

Curly Flat Mac, Vic ★★★ (PINOT N) 13' 14' 15' 16' 17' 18 Robust but perfumed Pinot N on two price/quality levels. Full-flavoured CHARD. Both age-worthy. Gradual turn towards elegance. New winemaker has introduced single-vyd offerings of note.

Dalwhinnie Pyrenees, Vic ★ Now owned by the FOGARTY GROUP. Ultra quiet in recent yrs but SHIRAZ can be excellent.

Dal Zotto King V, Vic ★★ "Prosecco" specialist across a range of styles, the drier and funkier of which are v.gd. Col Fondo NEBBIOLO bit of a treat too.

Dappled Yarra V, Vic ★★★ Top-flight/value, elegant-but-complex PINOT N, CHARD.

Deep Woods Estate Marg R, WA ★★★ Compelling CHARD, CAB SAUV. Powerhouse wines, built to impress/last.

Devil's Lair Marg R, WA ★★ Opulent CHARD, CAB SAUV/MERLOT is this estate at its best. At cool s-end of MARG R. Owned and therefore largely hidden by TWE.

Domenica Beech, Vic ★★★ Exciting BEECH producer with est vyds. Exuberant, spicy SHIRAZ. Textural MARSANNE. But NEBBIOLO is "the one".

Dr Edge Tas ★★★ Peter Dredge makes wine for various TAS wineries; his own brand CHARD and (esp) PINOT N have more personality than clients would likely allow.

Eden Valley SA Closest neighbour of BAR. Hilly region to e, home to Chris Ringland,

HENSCHKE, PEWSEY VALE, Radford, TORZI MATTHEWS and others; racy RIES, (perfumed, bright) SHIRAZ, CAB SAUV of top quality.

Elderton Bar V, SA ★★★ Old vines; rich, oaked CAB SAUV, SHIRAZ. All bases covered. Some organics/bio. Rich reds in excellent form.

Eldorado Road Ruth, Vic ★★ Pet project of winemaker Paul Dahlenburg. DURIF, SHIRAZ, NERO D'AVOLA all show elegance and power not mutually exclusive.

Eldridge Estate Mor P, Vic ★★★ Winemaker David Lloyd is a fastidious experimenter. PINOT N, CHARD worth the fuss. Varietal GAMAY can be quite special.

Epis Mac, Vic ★★★ (PINOT N) Long-lived Pinot N; elegant CHARD. Cold climate. Powerful at release; complexity takes time. Pinot N 19 of particular note.

Evans & Tate WA ★ Large-scale producer of gd value (r/w).

Faber Vineyards Swan V, WA ★★ (Res SHIRAZ) 14' 15' 17 John Griffiths is a guru of WA winemaking. Home estate redefines what's possible for SWAN VALLEY Shiraz. Polished power.

Fighting Gully Road Beech, Vic ★★★ Touchstone producer of BEECH region. CHARD, AGLIANICO, TEMPRANILLO kicking goals but SANGIOVESE is king.

Flametree Marg R, WA ★★ Exceptional CAB SAUV; spicy, seductive SHIRAZ and CHARD often compelling.

Fogarty Group Increasingly important stable of wineries, among them DALWHINNIE, DEEP WOODS ESTATE, EVANS & TATE, LAKE'S FOLLY, Smithbrook and Tasmanian Vintners.

Fraser Gallop Estate Marg R, WA ★★ Concentrated CAB SAUV, CHARD, (wooded) SEM/SAUV BL. Cab has been particularly strong in recent yrs.

Freycinet Tas ★★★ (PINOT N) 13' 18 Pioneer family winery on TAS's e coast producing dense Pinot N, gd CHARD, excellent Radenti sparkling.

Garagiste Mor P, Vic ★★★ CHARD, PINOT N of intensity, finesse. Quality always seems to be high or higher. Multi-vyd blends really take value cake.

Geelong Vic Region w of Melbourne. Cool, dry climate. Best names: BANNOCKBURN, BY FARR, CLYDE PARK, LETHBRIDGE, PROVENANCE.

Gembrook Hill Yarra V, Vic ★★★ Cool site on upper reaches of Yarra River: fine-boned PINOT N, CHARD par excellence.

Gemtree Vineyards McL V, SA ★★ Warm-hearted SHIRAZ alongside TEMPRANILLO and other exotica, linked by quality. Largely bio.

Giaconda Beech, Vic ★★★★ (CHARD) 15' 16' 17' 18 (SHIRAZ) 15' 17 In mid-80s Rick Kinzbrunner kickstarted BEECH region. Australian Chard royalty. Tiny production of powerhouse wines.

Giant Steps Yarra V, Vic ★★★ Top single-vyd CHARD, PINOT N, SHIRAZ. Vintages 15' 17' 18' 19 exciting for three main varieties. Sold to Jackson Family Wines (US) 2020.

Glaetzer-Dixon Tas ★★★ Nick Glaetzer turned his family history on its head by setting up camp in cool TAS. Euro-style RIES, Rhôney SHIRAZ, autumnal PINOT N.

Goulburn Valley Vic Temperate region in mid-Vic. Full-bodied, earthy table wines. MARSANNE, CAB SAUV, SHIRAZ the pick, MITCHELTON, TAHBILK perpetual flagbearers. Aka Nagambie Lakes.

Grampians Vic Temperate region in nw Vic previously known as Great Western. Spicy SHIRAZ, sparkling Shiraz, limey RIES. Home to SEPPELT (for now), BEST'S, Montara, MOUNT LANGI, The Story.

As a winery name, Ch Acid from Central Ranges, NSW, takes some beating.

Granite Belt Qld High-altitude, (relatively) cool, improbable region just n of the Qld-NSW border. Spicy SHIRAZ and rich SEM, eg. Boireann, Golden Grove, Ridgemill Estate.

Great Southern WA Remote cool area at bottom left corner of Oz; Albany, Denmark, Frankland River, Mount Barker, Porongurup are official subregions; 1st-class RIES, SHIRAZ, CAB SAUV. *Style, quality, value here.*

Grosset Clare V, SA ★★★ (RIES) 15' 17' 18' 19' 20 (Gaia) 12' 13' 14' 15' 16 Fastidious winemaker. A leader of Oz Ries, elegant CHARD, v.gd *Gaia* CAB SAUV/MERLOT. PINOT N can surprise.

Gundog Estate Can, NSW ★★★ Highly aspirational SEM SHIRAZ from CAN, HUN V. Shiraz starting to turn heads.

Hahndorf Hill Ad H, SA ★★★ Made GRÜNER V its own in Oz, consistently producing richly spiced, textured examples; interest and experimentation across range.

Hardys SA ★★ (Eileen CHARD) 15' 16' 17 (Eileen SHIRAZ) 12' 15 Historic company now part of ACCOLADE. Both Chard, Shiraz can be excellent in richer/fuller mode.

Heathcote Vic Region's 500-million-yr-old Cambrian soil has great potential for high-quality reds, esp SHIRAZ, with ample body and spice. JASPER HILL, PAUL OSICKA, TAR & ROSES, Whistling Eagle, WILD DUCK CREEK.

Henschke Eden V, SA ★★★★ (SHIRAZ) 04' 06' 12' 14' 15 (CAB SAUV) 04' 06' 10' 15' 16 Pre-eminent 150-yr-old family business; delectable Hill of Grace (Shiraz), v.gd Cab Sauv, red blends, gd whites, scary prices. Wonder of modern world.

Hentley Farm Bar V, SA ★★★ Consistently produces SHIRAZ of immense power, concentration – wall-of-flavour territory – though importantly in a (generally) fresh, almost frisky, context.

Hewitson SE Aus ★★ (*Old Garden Mourvèdre*) 12' 14' 16 Dean Hewitson sources some of the "oldest Mourvèdre vines on the planet". V.gd SHIRAZ, various prices.

Hoddles Creek Estate Yarra V, Vic ★★★ Made name as value producer of CHARD, PINOT N, but it's more than just value; quality is outstanding, full stop.

Houghton Swan V, WA ★★ (Jack Mann) 11' 12' 13' 14' 15' Once-legendary winery of SWAN VALLEY nr Perth. Part of ACCOLADE. Inexpensive white blend was long *a national classic*. V.gd CAB SAUV, SHIRAZ, etc. sourced from GREAT SOUTHERN, MARG R.

House of Arras Tas ★★★ Best-performing and most prestigious sparkling house in Oz. Part of ACCOLADE.

Howard Park WA ★★ (RIES) 16' 17' 18 (CAB SAUV) 10' 11' 12' 13' 16 CHARD 15' 18 Scented Ries, Chard; earthy Cab. Second label *MadFish* can be gd value.

Hunter Valley NSW Sub-tropical coal-mining area 160 km (100 miles) n of Sydney. Mid-weight, earthy SHIRAZ, gentle SEM can live for 30 yrs. Arguably most terroir-driven styles of Oz. ANDREW THOMAS, BROKENWOOD, MOUNT PLEASANT, *Tyrrell's* (esp).

Hutton Wines Marg R, WA ★★ V.gd CAB SAUV, SHIRAZ, but CHARD is where things tip into outstanding territory. Powerful palate, powerhouse finish.

Inkwell McL V, SA ★★ High polish, high opinion, high character. Full house of intriguing wines, mostly SHIRAZ-based.

Jacob's Creek Bar V, SA ★ Owned by Pernod Ricard. Almost totally focused on various tiers of uninspiring-but-reliable JC wines, covering all varieties, prices.

Jasper Hill Hea, Vic ★★ (SHIRAZ) 10' 17' 19 Emily's Paddock Shiraz/CAB FR blend, Georgia's Paddock Shiraz from dry-land estate are intense, burly, long-lived. NEBBIOLO to watch. Bio.

Jericho Ad H, McL V, SA ★★ Excellent fruit selection and skilled winemaking produce a suite of modern, tasty, well-presented wines, esp FIANO, GRENACHE, SHIRAZ, TEMPRANILLO.

Award for best name for a new wine brand goes to fledgling NSW outfit Frankly, Bob Made This.

John Duval Wines Bar V, SA ★★★ John D – former maker of PENFOLDS Grange – makes *delicious Rhôney reds* of great intensity, character.

Kalleske ★★ Old family farm at Greenock, nw corner of BAR V, makes rather special single-vyd SHIRAZ among many other intensely flavoured things. Bio/organic.

Katnook Estate Coon, SA ★★ (Odyssey CAB SAUV) 13' 14' 15 Pricey icons Odyssey, Prodigy SHIRAZ. Concentrated fruit, slathered in oak.

> **Blockchain open for business**
> Winemaker Jeffrey GROSSET and grape-grower David Travers have launched an ambitious new "blockchain" trial in an effort to increase wine and label integrity. We don't pretend to know how it works but given Grosset's starring role in Australia's nr-total adoption of screwcap seals, if it can be done it will be done.

Kilikanoon Clare V, SA ★★ RIES, SHIRAZ excellent performers. Luscious, generous, beautifully made. Sold to Chinese investment group (2017).

King Valley Vic Altitude range 155–860m (509–2821ft) has massive impact on varieties, styles. Over 20 brands, headed quality-wise by BROWN BROTHERS, Chrismont, DAL ZOTTO, PIZZINI (esp).

Kirrihill Clare V, SA ★★ V.gd CAB SAUV, SHIRAZ, RIES at, often, excellent prices.

Knappstein Wines Clare V, SA ★ Reliable RIES, SHIRAZ, CAB SAUV. Sold by Lion Nathan to ACCOLADE (2016). Gd value.

Kooyong Mor P, Vic ★★★ PINOT N, excellent CHARD of harmony, structure. PINOT GR of charm. High-quality single-vyd wines.

Lake Breeze Lang C, SA ★★★ Succulently smooth, gutsy, value SHIRAZ, CAB SAUV; few producers do mid-level wines so consistently well.

Lake's Folly Hun V, NSW ★★ (CHARD) 17' 18 (CAB SAUV) 14' 17 Founded by surgeon Max Lake, pioneer of HUN V Cab Sauv. Chard is often better than the Cab blend. Idiosyncratic.

Lambert, Luke Yarra V, Vic ★ Off-beat producer of variable but at times v.gd (cool-climate, mostly) SHIRAZ, PINOT N, NEBBIOLO.

Langmeil Bar V, SA ★★ Holder of some of world's oldest SHIRAZ vines (planted mid-1800s), plus other old vyds, for full-throttle CAB SAUV, GRENACHE, Shiraz.

Larry Cherubino Wines Fra R, WA ★★★ Intense SAUV BL, RIES, *spicy Shiraz*, polished CAB SAUV. Ambitious label and justifiably so.

L.A.S. Vino Marg R, WA ★★★ Highly individual producer of exceptional CHARD, CHENIN BL, CAB SAUV. Groundbreaker.

Leeuwin Estate Marg R, WA ★★★★ (CHARD) 13' 14' 15' 16' 17 Iconic producer. All about the full-bodied, age-worthy Art Series Chard. SAUV BL, RIES less brilliant. *Cab Sauv* occasionally v.gd.

Leo Buring Bar V, SA ★★ 14' 18 Part of TWE. Exclusively RIES; Leonay top label, *ages superbly*. Doesn't get much love but nothing wrong with wine quality.

Lethbridge Vic ★★★ Small, stylish producer of CHARD, SHIRAZ, PINOT N, RIES. Forever experimenting. Cool climate but wines are meaty, substantial.

Limestone Coast Zone SA Important zone, incl Bordertown, COON, Mt Benson, Mt Gambier, PADTHAWAY, Robe, WRATTONBULLY.

Lindemans Owned by TWE. Low-price Bin range now focus, far cry from glory days.

Macedon and Sunbury Vic Adjacent regions: Macedon higher elevation, Sunbury nr Melbourne airport. Quality from BINDI, CRAIGLEE, CURLY FLAT, EPIS, Hanging Rock, PLACE OF CHANGING WINDS.

Mac Forbes Yarra V, Vic ★★★ Mover and shaker of YARRA V. Myriad (in both number, styles) single-vyd releases, mainly PINOT N, CHARD, RIES. Wines more about structure than brightness; unusual in Oz.

McHenry Hohnen Marg R, WA ★★ Among best producers of MARG R CHARD. Tends to focus more on breadth of flavour than mere depth.

McLaren Vale SA Beloved maritime region on s outskirts of Adelaide. Big-flavoured reds in general but BRASH HIGGINS, CHAPEL HILL, CLARENDON HILLS, CORIOLE, D'ARENBERG, GEMTREE, INKWELL, JERICHO, MARIUS, PAXTON, SAMUEL'S GORGE, SC PANNELL, WIRRA WIRRA, YANGARRA can show elegance too. SHIRAZ the hero but old-vine, dry-grown GRENACHE often outshines it.

AUSTRALIA

McWilliam's SE Aus ★★★ Family-owned until 2020. Hanwood for value, *Mount Pleasant* for quality.

Main Ridge Estate Mor P, Vic ★★★ Rich, age-worthy CHARD, PINOT N. Founder Nat White is legend of MOR P wine, but new owners (2015) have the place singing.

Majella Coon, SA ★★ As reliable as the day is long. Opulent SHIRAZ, CAB SAUV. Essence of modern COON.

Margaret River WA Temperate coastal area s of Perth. Powerful CHARD, structured CAB SAUV. CAPE MENTELLE, CORYMBIA, CULLEN, DEEP WOODS ESTATE, DEVIL'S LAIR, FLAMETREE, FRASER GALLOP, HUTTON WINES, L.A.S VINO, LEEUWIN ESTATE, MCHENRY HOHNEN, MOSS WOOD, PIERRO, STELLA BELLA, TRIPE.ISCARIOT, VASSE FELIX, VOYAGER ESTATE, WOODLANDS and others. Great touring (and surfing) region.

Marius McL V, SA ★★★ Varietal SHIRAZ and blends of dramatic concentration. Quality in inverse proportion to fuss; latter kept to a min.

Mayford NE Vic, Vic ★★★ Tiny vyd in hidden valley. Put ALPINE VALLEYS region on map. SHIRAZ, CHARD, silken TEMPRANILLO.

Meerea Park Hun V, NSW ★★ Brothers Garth and Rhys Eather create age-worthy SEM, SHIRAZ often as single-vyd expressions.

Mike Press Wines Ad H, SA ★★ Tiny production, tiny pricing. CAB SAUV, SHIRAZ. Crowd favourite of bargain hunters.

Mitchelton Goulburn V, Vic ★★ Stalwart producer of CAB SAUV, SHIRAZ, RIES, plus speciality of *Marsanne*, ROUSSANNE. Top spot to visit; fancy new hotel set among those fab river red gums.

Montalto Mor P, Vic ★★★ A "must try" of MOR P. Single-vyd PINOT N, CHARD releases can be eyebrow-raisingly gd.

Moorilla Estate Tas ★★ Pioneer nr Hobart on Derwent River. Gd CHARD, RIES; PINOT N. V.gd restaurant, extraordinary art gallery. Owner also of nearby DOM A.

Moorooduc Estate Mor P, Vic ★★★ Long-term producer of complex CHARD, PINOT N.

Moppity Vineyards Hilltops, NSW ★ Affable SHIRAZ, CAB SAUV (Hilltops). Elegant CHARD (TUMBARUMBA). Best known for its value offerings.

Mornington Peninsula Vic Coastal area 40 km (25 miles) se of Melbourne. Cool climate. PINOT N, CHARD, PINOT GR. Wine/surf/beach/food playground. ELDRIDGE ESTATE, GARAGISTE, KOOYONG, MAIN RIDGE ESTATE, MONTALTO, MOOROODUC ESTATE, PARINGA ESTATE, STONIER, TEN MINUTES BY TRACTOR, WILLOW CREEK, YABBY LAKE and more.

Morris NE Vic ★★★ RUTH producer of Oz's (the world's?) greatest dessert *Muscats*, TOPAQUES. Owned by CASELLA.

Moss Wood Marg R, WA ★★★ (CAB SAUV) 05' 12' 14' 15' 16' 17 MARG R's most opulent (red) wines. SEM, CHARD, super-smooth *Cab Sauv*. Oak- and fruit-rich.

Mount Horrocks Clare V, SA ★★★ Fine dry RIES, celebrated sweet Cordon Cut Ries. SHIRAZ, CAB SAUV, SEM in fine form.

Mount Langi Ghiran Gra, Vic ★★★ (SHIRAZ) 13' 14' 15' 17' 18 Rich, peppery, *Rhône-like Shiraz*. Excellent Cliff Edge Shiraz. Estate-grown on a pretty special patch of dirt.

Mount Majura Can, NSW ★★ Leading TEMPRANILLO producer. RIES, SHIRAZ, CHARD all gd. Reds sturdy, spicy.

Mount Mary Yarra V, Vic ★★★★ (PINOT N) 14' 15' 16' 17' 18 (Quintet) 10' 14' 15' 16' 17' 18 Late Dr. Middleton made tiny amounts of suave CHARD, complex Pinot N,

---

Taras Ochota, texture like sun

Of all the natural and new-wave producers in Australia there was none who cut through, and affected so many, quite like Taras Ochota of OCHOTA BARRELS. He was a rare human being with a rare touch for wine, and this combination built an aura of respect and affection far greater than the volume production of his wines. He lost his battle to illness in 2020; Oz wine is much the less.

elegant CAB SAUV blend. All age impeccably. Post-Dr. era has brought, quite remarkably, improvement.

Mount Pleasant Hun V, NSW ★★★★ Owned by MCWILLIAM'S. NB single-vyd SEMS (esp *Lovedale*), SHIRAZ; 18 reds quite incredible. Oz terroir at its finest.

Mudgee NSW Region nw of Sydney. Earthy reds, fine SEM, full CHARD. Gd quality but needs a hero.

Ngeringa Ad H, SA ★★ Perfumed PINOT N, NEBBIOLO. Rhôney SHIRAZ. Savoury rosé. Bio.

After 140 yrs+ of family ownership, McWilliam's went into receivership in 2020.

Oakridge Yarra V, Vic ★★★★ Leading producer of CHARD in Oz, and more recently a noteworthy producer of PINOT N. Multiple single-vyd releases.

Ochota Barrels Bar V, SA ★★★ Brilliant producer of old-vine GRENACHE, SHIRAZ from MCL V, BAR V. Oz wine world saddened by premature passing of winemaker Taras Ochota in 2020.

O'Leary Walker Clare V, SA ★★ Low profile but excellent quality. CLARE V RIES, CAB SAUV standout. MCL V SHIRAZ oak-heavy but gd.

Orange NSW Cool-climate, high-elevation region. Lively SHIRAZ (when ripe), but best suited to (intense) aromatic whites and CHARD.

Osicka, Paul Hea, Vic ★★★ Vines dating back to 50s. Both character/flavour writ large. Small-scale, low-profile, high-impact and quality SHIRAZ, CAB SAUV.

Padthaway SA V.gd SHIRAZ, CAB SAUV. Rarely mentioned but important region. Soil salinity ongoing issue.

Pannell, SC McL V, SA ★★★ Excellent (spicy, whole-bunch-fermented) SHIRAZ (often labelled SYRAH) and (esp) GRENACHE-based wines. Watch NEBBIOLO. Every egg a bird.

Paringa Estate Mor P, Vic ★★★ Maker of irresistible PINOT N, SHIRAZ. Fleshy, fruity, flashy styles. Seductive is the word.

Parker Coonawarra Estate Coon, SA ★★ First vintage 1988. In gd yrs it produces full-bodied, age-worthy, tannic CAB SAUV of authority, distinction.

Passing Clouds Bendigo, Vic ★★★ Pioneer of modern Vic wine. Off radar for many yrs but burst back in 2016 with a gloriously elegant, textured signature CAB blend. Gd form since.

Paxton McL V, SA ★ Prominent organic/bio grower/producer: ripe SHIRAZ, GRENACHE.

Pemberton WA Region between MARG R and GREAT SOUTHERN; initial enthusiasm for PINOT N replaced by RIES, CHARD, SHIRAZ.

Penfolds ★★★★ (Grange) 90' 96' 04' 06' 08' 10' 12' 14' 15' 16 (CAB SAUV Bin 707) 02' 05' 06' 10' 12' 15' 16' 18 and of course *St Henri*, "simple" SHIRAZ. Originally Adelaide, now SA, Champagne and California. Oz's best warm-climate red-wine company. Superb *Yattarna* CHARD, Bin Chard now right up there with reds.

Petaluma Ad H, SA ★★ (RIES) 17' 18 (CHARD) 16' 17' 19 (CAB SAUV COON) 05' 08' 12' 13' 15 Has its moments but never quite been same since ex-owner/creator Brian Croser left the building.

Peter Lehmann Wines Bar V, SA ★ Well-priced wines incl easy RIES. Luxurious/ sexy Stonewell SHIRAZ among many others (r/w). Heroic Peter L died 2013; company sold 2014 to CASELLA (Yellow Tail).

Pewsey Vale Eden V, SA ★ V.gd RIES, standard and (aged-release) The Contours, grown on lovely tiered vyd.

Pierro Marg R, WA ★★★ (CHARD) 16' 17' 18' 19 Producer of expensive, tangy SEM/ SAUV BL and full-throttle, utterly convincing Chard.

Pipers Brook Tas ★★ (RIES) 13' 17' 19 (CHARD) 16' 18 Cool-area pioneer; gd Ries, *restrained Chard and sparkling* from Tamar Valley. Second label: Ninth Island. Owned by Belgian Kreglinger family.

Pizzini King V, Vic ★★ (SANGIOVESE) 16' 17 A leader of Italian varieties in Oz, esp NEBBIOLO, SANGIOVESE (recently stepped up a gear). Dominant KING VALLEY producer.

Place of Changing Winds Mac, Vic ★★★ CHARD, PINOT N of great power, complexity, grown on high-density vyds. Most exciting new Oz winery of recent yrs.

Pooley Tas ★★★ Est 1985 in Coal River Valley. Age-worthy PINOT N, CHARD. Family-run across generations. Among TAS's best.

Primo Estate SA ★★ Joe Grilli's many successes incl rich MCL V SHIRAZ, tangy COLOMBARD, potent Joseph CAB/MERLOT, (exceptionally) complex sparkling Shiraz.

Provenance Geelong, Vic ★★★ Exciting CHARD from GEELONG and surrounding regions. PINOT N less reliable but can be super.

Punch Yarra V, Vic ★★★ Lance family ran Diamond Valley for decades. Retained close-planted PINOT N vyd when they sold: can grow decisive, age-worthy wines.

Pyrenees Vic Central Vic region making rich, often minty reds. Blue Pyrenees, DALWHINNIE, Dog Rock, Mount Avoca, Summerfield, TALTARNI leading players, though it's also a happy hunting ground for assorted small producers.

Ravensworth Can, NSW ★★ Suddenly in hot demand for various wine experiments. SANGIOVESE best-known, but buzz over skin-contact whites and GAMAY Noir.

Riverina NSW Large-volume irrigated zone centred on Griffith.

Robert Oatley Wines Mudgee, NSW ★★ Ambitious venture of ROSEMOUNT ESTATE creator Robert Oatley. Quality/price ratio usually well aligned.

Rochford Yarra V, Vic ★★ Main outdoor entertainment venue in YARRA VALLEY now makes complex CHARD, PINOT N of note.

Rockford Bar V, SA ★★★ Sourced from various old, low-yielding vyds; reds best; iconic Basket Press SHIRAZ and noted *sparkling Black Shiraz*.

Rodda, A. Beech, Vic ★★ Bright CHARD from est vyds; *Tempranillo* grown at high altitude can be a beauty.

Rosemount Estate ★ Once the pacesetter. Periodically loses way, reds can be gd.

Ruggabellus Bar V, SA ★★★ Causing a stir. Funkier, more savoury version of BAR V. Old oak, min sulphur, wild yeast, whole bunches/stems. Blends of CINSAULT, GRENACHE, MATARO, SHIRAZ.

Rutherglen & Glenrowan Vic Two of four regions in warm ne Vic zone, justly famous for sturdy reds, magnificent fortified dessert wines. ALL SAINTS, CAMPBELLS, ELDORADO ROAD, SCION, SIMAO & CO, STANTON & KILLEEN, TAMINICK CELLARS.

St Hallett Bar V, SA ★★ (Old Block) 12' 13' 14' 15' 16 Old Block SHIRAZ the star; rest of range is smooth, sound, stylish. ACCOLADE-owned.

Saltram Bar V, SA ★★ Value Mamre Brook (SHIRAZ, CAB SAUV) and (rarely sighted) No.1 Shiraz are leaders. Main claim to fame is ubiquitous Pepperjack Shiraz.

Samuel's Gorge McL V, SA ★★ Justin McNamee makes (at times) stunning GRENACHE, SHIRAZ, TEMPRANILLO of character and place.

Savaterre Beech, Vic ★★★ (CHARD) 16' 17' 18 (PINOT N) 13' 16 Excellent producer of full-bodied Chard, meaty Pinot N, close-planted SHIRAZ, SAGRANTINO.

Schmolzer & Brown Beech, Vic ★★ CHARD, PINOT N and rosé of intense, spice-drenched interest. Textural RIES of note. One of highest vyds in BEECH.

Scion Ruth, Vic ★★ Fresh, vibrant approach to region's stalwart SHIRAZ, Durif.

Sentio Beech, Vic ★★★ Picks eyes out of various cool-climate regions to produce compelling CHARD, PINOT N, SHIRAZ.

Seppelt Gra, Vic ★★★ (St Peter's SHIRAZ) 12' 13' 14' 16' 17' Historic name owned by TWE. Impressive CHARD, RIES, (esp) peppery Shiraz.

Seppeltsfield Bar V, SA ★★ National Trust Heritage Winery bought by Warren Randall (2013). Fortified wine stocks back to 1878.

Serrat Yarra V, Vic ★★★ Micro-vyd of noted winemaker Tom Carson (YABBY LAKE) and wife Nadege. Complex, powerful, precise SHIRAZ/VIOGNIER, PINOT N, CHARD.

Seville Estate Yarra V, Vic ★★★ (SHIRAZ) 14' 15' 17' 18 Excellent CHARD, spicy Shiraz, structured PINOT N. YARRA V pioneer with a fresh lease on life.

Shaw & Smith Ad H, SA ★★★ Savvy outfit. Crisp *harmonious* SAUV BL, complex

CHARD and, surpassing them both, *Shiraz*. PINOT N slowly improving. Worthy of serious investigation.

Shy Susan Tas ★★★ New range by winemaker Glenn James, former maker of top-end HARDYS and PENFOLDS whites. CHARD, RIES, PINOT N particularly strong.

Simao & Co Ruth, Vic ★★ Young Simon Killeen, of STANTON & KILLEEN family, makes scrumptious TEMPRANILLO, UGNI BL, SHIRAZ and more. Personality+.

Sorrenberg Beech, Vic ★★★★ No fuss but highest quality. SAUV BL/SEM, CHARD, (Australia's best) GAMAY, B'x blend. Ultimate "in the know" winery of Oz.

Southern NSW Zone NSW Incl CAN, Gundagai, Hilltops, TUMBARUMBA. Savoury SHIRAZ; lengthy CHARD.

Spencer, Nick Can, NSW ★★★ Former Eden Road winemaker. CHARD and red blend (SHIRAZ/TEMPRANILLO/TOURIGA/CAB SAUV) of particular interest.

Spinifex Bar V, SA ★★★ Bespoke BAR V producer. Complex SHIRAZ, GRENACHE blends. Rich reds with a savoury turn.

Stanton & Killeen Ruth, Vic ★★ Fortified vintage is dominant attraction.

Stefano Lubiana S Tas ★★★ Beautiful vyds on banks of Derwent River, 20 mins from Hobart. Excellent PINOT N, sparkling, MERLOT, CHARD and more recently, SHIRAZ. As homely as it is ambitious. Bio.

Stella Bella Marg R, WA ★★★ Humdinger wines. CAB SAUV, SEM/SAUV BL, CHARD, SHIRAZ, SANGIOVESE/Cab Sauv. Sturdy, characterful.

Stoney Rise Tas ★★ Joe Holyman used to be a world-class wicketkeeper; he's an even better winemaker/grower, particularly with PINOT N, CHARD.

Stonier Wines Mor P, Vic ★★★ (CHARD) 17' 18' 19 (PINOT N) 15' 17' 18' 19 Consistently gd; Res notable for elegance. *Pinot N* in particularly fine form, tense, resonant. Excellent single-vyd releases now.

Sunbury Vic *See* MACEDON AND SUNBURY.

Sutton Grange Bendigo, Vic ★★★ (AGLIANICO) 17' 18 (SHIRAZ) 16' 17' 18 Organic: intense-but-savoury Shiraz; impeccably crafted whites, FIANO the leader.

Swan Valley WA Birthplace of wine in the w, 20 mins n of Perth. Hot climate makes strong, low-acid wines. FABER VYDS leads way.

Swinney Fra R, WA ★★★ A grape-grower for decades; initial releases under own steam are outstanding. GRENACHE, SHIRAZ, RIES all shine.

Tahbilk Goulburn V, Vic ★★★ (MARSANNE) 16' 17' 18' 19' 20 (SHIRAZ) 12' 16' Historic Purbrick family estate: long-ageing reds, also some of Oz's best old-vine *Marsanne*. Res CAB SAUV can be v.gd. Rare 1860 Vines Shiraz. Rustic styles.

Taltarni Pyrenees, Vic ★★ SHIRAZ, CAB SAUV in gd shape. Long-haul wines but jackhammer no longer required to remove tannin from your gums.

Taminick Cellars Glenrowan, Vic ★★ Booth family been farming this tough, dry patch since 1914. A fair amount of character accumulated along the way.

Tapanappa SA ★★★ WRATTONBULLY collaboration between Brian Croser, Bollinger, J-M Cazes of Pauillac. Splendid CAB SAUV blend, SHIRAZ, MERLOT, CHARD. Surprising *Pinot N* from Fleurieu Peninsula.

Tar & Roses Hea, Vic ★★ SHIRAZ, TEMPRANILLO, SANGIOVESE of impeccable polish, presentation. Modern success story; 2017 death of co-founder Don Lewis a great loss but quality remains strong.

Kylie in dastardly locomotion

It was pretty bad, from an Aussie perspective, when our own beloved Kylie Minogue launched a wine, and then a range of wines, that weren't grown and made in her homeland. It got worse when Aussie-maker De Bortoli started distributing Kylie's French-made Signature Rosé down under. If the wines had been from NZ, Australia's *Neighbours*, maybe it wouldn't have seemed so bad.

Tarrawarra Estate Yarra V, Vic ★★ (Res CHARD) 13' 17' (Res PINOT N) 13' 17' Moved from hefty, idiosyncratic to elegant, long. Res generally a big step up on standard.

Tasmania Tas Cold island region with hot reputation. Outstanding sparkling, PINOT N, RIES. V.gd CHARD, PINOT GR, SAUV BL.

Taylors Wines Clare V, SA ★ Large-scale production led by RIES, SHIRAZ, CAB SAUV. Exports under Wakefield Wines brand.

Ten Minutes by Tractor Mor P, Vic ★★★ Wacky name, smart packaging, even better wines. *Chard, Pinot N both excellent* and will age. Style meets substance.

Pepperjack Shiraz goes cut-specific: "Porterhouse Graded", "Scotch Fillet Graded".

Teusner Bar V, SA ★★ Old vines, clever winemaking, pure fruit flavours. Leads a BAR v trend towards "more wood, no good".

Thomas, Andrew Hun V, NSW ★★ Old-vine SEM; silken SHIRAZ. Reds particularly gutsy in HUN V context.

Thousand Candles Yarra V, Vic ★★ Beautiful site producing beautiful wines. Delicate PINOT N, spicy SHIRAZ, lively field blend. Quality on steady march forward.

Tolpuddle Tas ★★★ SHAW & SMITH bought this outstanding 1988-planted vyd in TAS's Coal River Valley in 2011. Scintillating PINOT N, CHARD in lean, lengthy style.

Topaque Vic Replacement name for iconic RUTH sticky "Tokay", thanks to EU; a decade later it's still hard to find anyone who likes the name.

Torbreck Bar V, SA ★★★ Dedicated to (often old-vine) Rhône varieties led by SHIRAZ, GRENACHE. Ultimate expression of rich, sweet, high-alc style.

Torzi Matthews Eden V, SA ★★★ Aromatic, stylish, big-hearted SHIRAZ. Value RIES, SANGIOVESE. Incredible consistency yr-on-yr.

Traviarti Beech, Vic ★★ Made name with TEMPRANILLO, but NEBBIOLO is fast becoming a force to be reckoned with.

tripe.Iscariot Marg R, WA ★★ Hard to spell, easy to drink. Complex whites/reds by its own design. Natural wine specialist.

Tumbarumba NSW Cool-climate NSW region tucked into Australian Alps. Sites 500–800m (1640–2625ft). CHARD the out-and-out star. PINOT N generally to avoid.

Turkey Flat Bar V, SA ★★★ Top producer of complex rosé, GRENACHE, SHIRAZ from core of 150-yr-old vyd. Controlled alc/oak. New single-vyd wines. Old but modern.

TWE (Treasury Wine Estates) Aussie wine behemoth. COLDSTREAM HILLS, DEVIL'S LAIR, LINDEMANS, PENFOLDS, ROSEMOUNT, SALTRAM, WOLF BLASS, WYNNS COONAWARRA ESTATE among them.

Two Hands Bar V, SA ★★★ Big reds and many of them. They've turned volume down a fraction lately; glory of fruit seems all the clearer.

Tyrrell's Hun V, NSW ★★★★ (SEM) 15' 16' 17' 18' 19' (Vat 47 CHARD) 15' 16' 17' 18' 19 Oz's greatest maker of Sem, Vat 1 now joined with series of individual vyd or subregional wines. *Vat 47*, Oz's 1st Chard, continues to defy climatic odds. Outstanding old-vine 4 Acres SHIRAZ, Vat 9 Shiraz. One of the true greats.

Vasse Felix Marg R, WA ★★★★ (CHARD) 15' 17' 18 (CAB SAUV) 12' 14' 15' 16 With CULLEN, pioneer of MARG R. Elegant Cab Sauv for mid-weight balance. Complex/funkified Chard. Estate grown-only now.

Voyager Estate Marg R, WA ★★★ Big volume of (mostly) estate-grown, rich, powerful SEM, SAUV BL, (esp) CHARD, CAB SAUV/MERLOT.

Wanderer, The Yarra V, Vic ★★★ Upper YARRA VALLEY producer of exceptionally fine-boned PINOT N.

Wantirna Estate Yarra V, Vic ★★★ Regional pioneer showing no sign of slowing down. CHARD, PINOT N, B'x blend all in excellent form. Small on quantity, big on quality, low on fuss.

Wendouree Clare V, SA ★★★★ Treasured maker (tiny quantities) of powerful, tannic, concentrated reds, based on CAB SAUV, MALBEC, MATARO, SHIRAZ. Recently moved to screwcap; the word "longevity" best defined with a picture of a Wendouree red. Beg, borrow or steal.

West Cape Howe Denmark, WA ★ Affordable, flavoursome reds the speciality.

Westend Estate Riverina, NSW ★★ Thriving family producer of *tasty bargains*, esp Private Bin SHIRAZ/Durif. Recent cool-climate additions gd value.

Wild Duck Creek Hea, Vic ★★ Super-concentrated, high-octane reds using SHIRAZ (mostly), CAB SAUV, MALBEC. Vigour, freshness somehow kept intact.

Willow Creek Mor P, Vic ★★ Gd gear. Impressive producer of CHARD, PINOT N in particular. Power, poise.

Wirra Wirra McL V, SA ★★ (RSW SHIRAZ) 10' 15' 17 (The Angelus CAB SAUV) 12' 13' 15' 17 High-quality, concentrated wines in flashy livery. The Angelus Cab Sauv named Dead Ringer outside Australia.

Wolf Blass Bar V, SA ★★ (Black Label CAB SAUV blend) 12' 13' 14' 17 Owned by TWE. Not the shouty player it once was, but still churns through an enormous volume of clean, inoffensive wines.

Woodlands Marg R, WA ★★★ 7 ha of 40-yr-old+ CAB SAUV among top vyds in region, plus younger but v.gd plantings of other B'x reds. Brooding impact.

Wrattonbully SA Important grape-growing region in LIMESTONE COAST ZONE; profile lifted by activity of TAPANAPPA, Terre à Terre, Peppertree.

Wynns Coonawarra Estate Coon, SA ★★★★ (SHIRAZ) 14'16'17' (CAB SAUV) 12'13'14' 15 16' 17' 18 TWE-owned COON classic. RIES, CHARD; Shiraz all v.gd; Cab Sauv outstanding, esp Black Label, *John Riddoch*. Single-vyd releases are the icing.

Yabby Lake Mor P, Vic ★★★ Made its name with estate CHARD, PINOT N, boosted with single-site releases, now spice-shot SHIRAZ adds yet more to reputation.

Yalumba Bar V, SA ★★★ 170-yrs+, family-owned. *Full spectrum of high-quality wines*, from budget to elite single vyd (eg. *The Caley*). Entry-level Y Series v.gd value.

Yangarra Estate McL V, SA ★★★★ Conventional in part, inventive in others. Whatever it takes to make great wine. Full box and dice here, across most price points. Varietal GRENACHE, SHIRAZ emphatically gd.

Yarraloch Yarra V, Vic ★★ CHARD can be terrific. PINOT N can be exceptional too.

Yarra Valley Vic Thriving area, ne of Melbourne. Emphasis on CHARD, PINOT N, SHIRAZ, sparkling. Understated, elegant CAB SAUV. Formidable lineup: COLDSTREAM HILLS, DE BORTOLI, DOM CHANDON, GEMBROOK HILL, GIANT STEPS, HODDLES CREEK ESTATE, LUKE LAMBERT, MAC FORBES, PUNCH, ROCHFORD, SERRAT, SEVILLE ESTATE, TARRAWARRA, THOUSAND CANDLES, WANTIRNA ESTATE, YARRALOCH, YARRA YERING, YERINGBERG, YERING STATION.

Yarra Yering Yarra V, Vic ★★★★ (Dry Reds) 06' 15' 17' 18' 19 One-of-a-kind YARRA V pioneer. Powerful PINOT N; deep, herby CAB SAUV (Dry Red No.1); SHIRAZ (Dry Red No.2) and more. Absolute upper echelon (r/w).

Yellow Tail NSW *See* CASELLA.

Yeringberg Yarra V, Vic ★★★★ (MARSANNE/ROUSSANNE) 14' 15' 16' 17 (CAB SAUV) 10' 12' 13' 14' 15' 16' 17 Historic estate still in hands of founding (1862) Swiss family, the de Purys. Extremely small quantities of v.high-quality CHARD, Marsanne, Roussanne, Cab Sauv, PINOT N.

Yering Station / Yarrabank Yarra V, Vic ★★ On site of Vic's 1st vyd; replanted after 80 yr gap. Snazzy table wines (Res CHARD, PINOT N, SHIRAZ, VIOGNIER); Yarrabank (sparkling in joint venture with Champagne Devaux).

Where there's smoke ...
Bushfire is now such an issue for Australian wine that the Australian Wine Research Institute has developed smoke-taint kits to help grape growers monitor risk on the run. Smoke taint affects reds more than whites because it sits on the skins and gives a stale-ashtray note to wines; the more smoke, the more risk.

New Zealand

Abbreviations used
in the text:

Auck	Auckland
B of P	Bay of Plenty
Cant	Canterbury
Gis	Gisborne
Hawk	Hawke's Bay
Hend	Henderson
Marl	Marlborough
Mart	Martinborough
Nel	Nelson
N/C Ot	North/Central Otago
Waih	Waiheke Island
Waip	Waipara Valley
Wair	Wairarapa

Almost two-thirds of NZ's total harvest in 2020 was of a single variety from a single region – Marlborough Sauvignon Blanc. The "leap out of the glass", aromatic, zesty, green-edged style that has wowed wine-lovers around the world since the 80s is still mainstream, but many of the top-ranked wines now exhibit riper, tropical-fruit flavours, while retaining their appetizing acidity, and use a small portion of barrel fermentation to add complexity. It's extraordinary to have a country's output so dominated by a single grape, but Sauvignon Blanc refuseniks could take refuge in NZ's reds. They may be more of a minority production, but Bordeaux grapes, Syrah and Pinot N all have centres of excellence here. The smart money, too, is on top Chardonnay: watch out for this. There is also more and more rosé: a new breed of dry rosés has emerged in the last five years, in the North Island principally made from Merlot and in the South Island from Pinot Noir.

Recent vintages

2020 Bumper vintage in spite of drought, Marl: crisp, intense flavours; warm but not hot in Hawk: prospects for outstanding reds, Chard.

2019 Weighty, textured Marl Sauv Bl. Hawk Chard and reds esp promising.

2018 Hottest-ever summer. Ripe, less herbaceous Marl Sauv Bl.

2017 Challenging vintage, with rain before harvest. C Ot more successful.

Akarua C Ot ★★★ PINOT NS: classy, complex Bannockburn, matures well for a decade; drink young Rua. Lively fizz, incl Brut NV. Full-bodied, dry PINOT GR.

Allan Scott Family Winemakers Marl ★★ Fresh, easy-drinking wines: ripely herbal SAUV BL; vibrant CHARD; off-dry PINOT GR, fragrant, savoury (Black Label) PINOT N.

Alpha Domus Hawk ★★ Family winery in Bridge Pa Triangle. B'x-style reds, esp v.

classy, rich AD CAB SAUV The Aviator. Vivacious, intense CHARD-based bubbly, Cumulus. AD is top range (generous, savoury Chard).

Amisfield C Ot ★★★ Intense, fully dry sparkling. Classy RIES (dr/medium-sweet). Savoury PINOT N (RKV Res is Rolls-Royce model). Lake Hayes to drink young.

Astrolabe Marl ★★→★★★ Impressive range: ripely herbal SAUV BL, crisp ALBARIÑO, CHENIN BL. Scented, supple PINOT N. Durvillea is 2nd tier: v.gd value.

Ata Rangi Mart ★★★→★★★★ Much-respected family affair. PINOT N **14' 15'** 16' 17, a NZ classic; perfumed, savoury (1st vines 1980). Rich Craighall CHARD (planted 1983); dry Lismore PINOT GR; lush Kahu Botrytis RIES.

C Ot has 5% of NZ's vyd area; nearly 20% of its wineries.

Auckland Largest city (n, warm, cloudy) in NZ; 1% vyd area but 14% of producers (incl head offices of big firms.) Nearby wine districts: W Auckland, incl Henderson, Kumeu, Huapai, Waimauku (long est); newer (since 80s): Matakana, Clevedon, WAIH (island vyds, popular with tourists). Savoury B'x blends in dry seasons **13' 14'** 19' 20', bold SYRAH **13' 14'** 19' 20' is fast-expanding and rivals HAWK for quality; underrated CHARD.

Auntsfield Marl ★★→★★★ Classy, characterful wines from site of region's 1st (1873) vyd (replanted 1999). Weighty, sweet-fruited SAUV BL; tight CHARD (esp single-block Cob Cottage), powerful, dense PINOT N.

Awatere Valley Marl Key subregion (pronounced "Awa-terry"), with v. few wineries, but huge vyd area (more than HAWK), pioneered in 1986 by VAVASOUR. Major component in many regional blends of MARL SAUV BL. YEALANDS is key producer. Slightly cooler, drier, windier, less fertile than WAIRAU VALLEY, with racy ("tomato stalk") SAUV BL (rated higher by UK than US critics); vibrant RIES, PINOT GR; often slightly herbal PINOT N.

Babich Hend ★★→★★★ NZ's oldest family-owned winery (1916). Croatian origin. HAWK, MARL vyds; wineries in AUCK, MARL. Age-worthy Irongate (single vyd) from GIMBLETT GRAVELS: weighty CHARD and B'x-like Irongate CAB/MERLOT/CAB FR **13' 14'** 15' 16. Biggest seller: tropical Marl SAUV BL. Graceful Winemakers' Res Marl PINOT N. Top red: powerful The Patriarch (B'x-style, MALBEC-influenced) **13' 14'** 15' 16.

Blackenbrook Nel ★★ Small winery, impressive aromatic whites, esp Alsace-style GEWURZ; PINOT GR, off-dry PINOT BL; vivacious rosé; bold Res PINOT N.

Black Estate Cant ★★ Small organic WAIP producer with mature (1994) vines. Powerful Home CHARD; refined CAB FR; fragrant Home PINOT N.

Blank Canvas Marl ★★ Matt Thomson (ex-SAINT CLAIR) and Sophie Parker-T own. Refined, incisive SAUV BL; distinctive Reed CHARD; hedonistic, botrytized Meta RIES.

Borthwick Wair ★★ Gladstone vyd, with Paddy Borthwick brand. Pungent SAUV BL; peachy CHARD; charming, dry Pinot Rosé. Cherryish, slightly nutty PINOT N.

Brancott Estate Marl ★→★★★ Major brand of PERNOD RICARD NZ that replaced Montana worldwide (except in NZ). Top wines: Letter Series. Huge-selling Sauv Bl, gd value. Identity range: subregional focus. Living Land: organic. Flight: plain, low alc. Top-value bottle-fermented Brut Cuvée.

Brightwater Nel ★★ Impressive whites, high-flavoured, low-alcohol Natural Light RIES. Rich PINOT N. Top: Lord Rutherford (incl ripe Sauv Bl); refined Chard.

Brookfields Hawk ★★→★★★ Smallish, long-est winery, typically great value. Full-flavoured Bergman CHARD; sturdy VIOGNIER. Firm Ohiti CAB SAUV, dense Sun-Dried MALBEC; deep Back Block SYRAH. Top wines: Marshall Bank Chard; Hillside Syrah.

Burn Cottage C Ot ★★→★★★ Organic, vyds at Pisa and Bannockburn, owned by Nevada-based Sauvage family. Moonlight Race PINOT N, delicious young. Refined, notably rich Burn Cottage Vyd Pinot N. Also dryish RIES/GRÜNER V.

Canterbury NZ's 4th-largest wine region (ahead of GISBORNE), with 70+ producers; most vyds in relatively warm n WAIP district (increasingly called N Cant). Greatest success with aromatic RIES and savoury PINOT N. Emerging strength in Alsace-style PINOT GR. SAUV BL heavily planted, but mostly sold as minor component in other regions' wines.

Carrick C Ot ★★★ Bannockburn winery with organic focus. Classy RIES (Josephine); elegant CHARD, esp EBM. Attractive Unravelled Pinot N. Placed in receivership early Nov 20 and owner Elizabeth Zhong murdered late Nov 20.

Catalina Sounds Marl ★★→★★★ Export-focused, Australian-owned producer, with estate-grown wines from large Sound of White vyd in upper Waihopai Valley. Also regional blends. Gently oaked SAUV BL; full-bodied PINOT GR; creamy CHARD.

C Ot Pinot N casks now used to finish Irish whiskey. Better than other way round.

Central Otago High-altitude, dry inland region (now NZ's 3rd largest) in s of S Island, with many tiny, "weekend" producers. Sunny, hot days, v. cold nights. Most vines in Cromwell Basin (incl Bannockburn, Bendigo). Crisp RIES, PINOT GR; growing interest in vibrant, tight-knit CHARD; famous PINOT N (78%+ vyd area) has drink-young charm; older vines now more savoury, complex. Excellent Pinot N rosé and traditional-method fizz.

Chard Farm C Ot ★★ Pioneer in striking gorge setting. Fleshy, dry PINOT GR. Typically mid-weight PINOT N (fruity River Run; single-vyd The Tiger and elegant, savoury The Viper more complex). Mata-Au Pinot N is sweet-fruited, signature red. Rabbit Ranch Pinot N: drink young charm.

Church Road Hawk ★★→★★★ PERNOD RICARD NZ winery with historic HAWK roots. Buttery CHARD; partly oak-aged SAUV BL; Alsace-style PINOT GR; dark MERLOT/CAB SAUV; drink young SYRAH. V. impressive Grand Res wines. McDonald Series, between standard and Grand Res, offers top quality, value. Prestige (NZ$150–220) TOM selection: lush Merlot/Cab Sauv, powerful Chard, refined Syrah. Elegant, intense new "1" range: single vyd.

Churton Marl ★★ Elevated Waihopai Valley site with bone-dry SAUV BL; savoury PINOT N (esp The Abyss: oldest vines, greater depth). Honey-sweet PETIT MANSENG.

Clearview Hawk ★★→★★★ Coastal vyd at Te Awanga (also grapes from inland). Hedonistic Res CHARD (Beachhead Chard is jnr version); rich Enigma (MERLOT-based); savoury Old Olive Block (CAB SAUV/MALBEC/CAB FR blend).

Clos Henri Marl ★★→★★★ Organic, founded 2001 by Henri Bourgeois of Sancerre. Weighty, tropical SAUV BL from stony soils, one of NZ's best; savoury PINOT N 16' (on clay). Second label: Bel Echo (reverses variety/soil match). Third label: Petit Clos, from young vines. Distinctive, satisfying wines, priced right.

Cloudy Bay Marl ★★★ Large-volume, still-classy SAUV BL is NZ's most famous wine. Also complex CHARD, savoury, supple PINOT N. Stylish Pelorus NV (sp), esp Rosé. Te Koko (barrel-fermented Sauv Bl) has strong personality. More involvement in C OT for Te Wahi Pinot N (fleshy 14' 15' 16 17'). Owned by LVMH.

Constellation New Zealand Auck ★→★★ Largest producer, previously Nobilo Wine Group, now owned by Constellation Brands (New York-based). Strong in US market (KIM CRAWFORD MARL SAUV BL is no.1-selling NZ wine). Strength mainly in solid, moderately priced (esp Sauv Bl) Kim Crawford, Monkey Bay and SELAKS brands. Sold NOBILO brand to GALLO 2020.

Cooper's Creek Auck ★★→★★★ Innovative, gd value. Res is top range (incl rich Swamp Res HAWK CHARD; fragrant, dense Res Hawk SYRAH); SV (Select Vyd) range is mid-tier. NZ's 1st: ALBARIÑO, ARNEIS, GRÜNER V, MARSANNE.

Craggy Range Hawk ★★★→★★★★ High-profile, top restaurant, large vyds in HAWK, MART. Stylish CHARD, PINOT N; excellent mid-range MERLOT, SYRAH, Te Kahu (B'x red blend) from GIMBLETT GRAVELS. Les Beaux Cailloux: elegant, age-worthy Chard ($NZ150). Dense Sophia (Merlot); show-stopping Syrah Le Sol 14' 15' 16'; sturdy The Quarry (CAB SAUV); refined Aroha (Pinot N) 14' 15' 16' 17'.

Delegat Auck ★★ Large listed family company. Hugely successful OYSTER BAY brand. Vibrant CHARD; light PINOT GR; instantly likeable Merlot under Delegat brand. Also owns Barossa Valley Estates.

Delta Marl ★★→★★★ Owned by SAINT CLAIR. V.gd-value, full-flavoured PINOT N, aromatic SAUV BL; generous CHARD. Hatters Hill range: greater complexity.

Destiny Bay Waih ★★→★★★ Expat Americans make high-priced (but cheaper to Patron Club members), brambly B'x-style reds. Flagship is savoury Magna Praemia. Mystae is mid-tier: lush. Destinae: softly textured, earlier drinking. Two top labels not made in 17 18, but back from 19.

Deutz Auck ★★★ Champagne house gives name to great-value fizz from MARL by PERNOD RICARD NZ. Popular Brut NV has min 2 yrs on lees. Much-awarded Blanc de Blancs. Easy-drinking Rosé NV; outstanding Prestige (disgorged after 3 yrs).

Dog Point Marl ★★★ Organic range from Ivan Sutherland and James Healy (both ex-CLOUDY BAY). Incisive, oak-aged SAUV BL (Section 94); CHARD (elegant); harmonious PINOT N, all among region's finest. Larger volume, but v.gd unoaked Sauv Bl.

Dom-Thomson C Ot ★★→★★★ Small, organic, PINOT N vyds in two hemispheres: Gevrey-Chambertin and Lowburn, overlooking Cromwell Basin. Explorer: savoury, v. approachable; Surveyor Thomson: fragrant.

Dry River Mart ★★★ Small pioneer winery, now US-owned. Reputation for long-lived whites: PINOT GR (NZ's 1st outstanding example). Dense TEMPRANILLO.

Elephant Hill Hawk ★★→★★★ Stylish winery on coast at Te Awanga, also grapes from inland. Outstanding Res range, incl Chard, MERLOT blend, Syrah. Top pair: Airavata Syrah (notably complex 17); Hieronymus (powerful blended red).

Escarpment Mart ★★★ Australian-owned, (ex MARTINBOROUGH VYD) winemaker Larry McKenna. Known for savoury PINOT N. Top label: Kupe. Single-vyd, old-vine reds esp gd. MART Pinot N is regional blend. Lower tier: The Edge.

Esk Valley Hawk ★★→★★★ Owned by VILLA MARIA. Impressive quality, value. Acclaimed MERLOT-based blends; barrel-fermented CHARD (classy Winemakers Res); full-bodied VERDELHO. Striking flagship red Heipipi The Terraces: MALBEC/Merlot/CAB FR.

Felton Road C Ot ★★★★ Celebrated winery at Bannockburn, best-known for PINOT N, but RIES, CHARD notably classy too. Bold yet graceful Pinot N Block 3 15' 17' 18' 19', more powerful Block 5 15' 17' 18' 19' from The Elms Vyd; intense Ries (dr, s/sw); refined Chard (esp Block 2, Block 6). Key label is poised Bannockburn Pinot N, four-vyd blend. Other fine single-vyd Pinot N: Calvert, Cornish Point.

Forrest Marl ★★ Big success with The Doctors' MARL SAUV BL, low alc (9.5%), lively, green-edged. Wide range of value Marl whites, esp Sauv Bl. Tatty Bogler label; reserved for WAITAKI VALLEY (intense PINOT GR). Top range: John Forrest Collection.

Framingham Marl ★★→★★★ Owned by Sogrape (*see* Portugal). Aromatic whites: intense RIES, esp zesty, organic Classic from mature vines. Perfumed PINOT GR. Creamy CHARD. Subtle SAUV BL; lush Noble Ries; silky PINOT N.

Fromm Marl ★★★ Swiss-owned. Distinguished PINOT N, esp hill-grown Clayvin Vyd 15' 16' 17'. Fromm Vyd sturdier. Cuvee H Pinot N: savoury, multi-site blend. Vibrant SYRAH, powerful Fromm Vyd Syrah. Racy RIES Spätlese. Refined Clayvin CHARD. Earlier-drinking La Strada range, incl tangy SAUV BL; excellent Rosé.

Cabernet – the comeback kid

A new breed of CAB SAUV has emerged since 2013, esp in HAWK: dark, full-bodied and dense, but not heavy, with a B'x-like fragrance and finesse. It has been grown commercially in NZ since the 60s, but typically produced light, leafy reds. What happened? Selection of warm, free-draining sites and major advances in vyd management, incl slashing grape yields, has vastly improved quality.

Gibbston Valley C Ot ★★→★★★ Strong name for PINOT N, esp fragrant, rich GV Collection. Silky Le Maitre, mostly from 1st vines planted in 80s. Racy GV RIES; intense Red Shed Ries. Full-bodied GV PINOT GR (esp organic School House); classy CHARD (esp Chablis-like China Terrace). Memorable Rosé **13'** (sp).

Giesen Cant ★★ Large winery, family-owned (ex-Neustadt, in Germany's Rheinpfalz) making huge-volume, crisp MARL SAUV BL. The August Sauv Bl: barrel-fermented, complex. Popular RIES, intensity and value; characterful single-vyd Gemstone Ries, partly fermented in granite tanks. Memorable Clayvin SYRAH.

Gimblett Gravels is on same latitude as Ibiza. Less nightlife, though.

Gimblett Gravels Hawk Defined area (800 ha planted, mostly since early 80s) of old riverbed, so arid that rabbits rarely venture onto it without taking a cut lunch. Noted for rich B'x-style reds (mostly MERLOT-led, but stony soils also suit CAB SAUV – recent renewed interest). Super SYRAH. Best reds world-class (look for **19' 20'**). Also age-worthy CHARD from siltier soils.

Gisborne NZ's 5th-largest region, on e coast of N Island. Declining in planted area and producer numbers. Abundant sunshine but often rainy; fertile soils. Key is CHARD (ripe, soft). Excellent GEWURZ, CHENIN BL, VIOGNIER; MERLOT, PINOT GR more variable. Interest in ALBARIÑO (rain-resistant). Top wines from MILLTON.

Gladstone Vineyard Wair ★★ Largest producer in n WAIR, bought by Asian investment company (2018). Fruit-packed PINOT N (18 single-vyd reds finest yet). 12,000 Miles lower-priced, early drinking range.

Grasshopper Rock C Ot ★★→★★★ Estate-grown by PINOT N specialist. Subregion's finest red: cherry, spice, dried-herb flavours. Age-worthy, great value.

Greenhough Nel ★★→★★★ One of region's best boutiques; intense Apple Valley RIES, punchy, ripe River Garden SAUV BL, consistently gd CHARD, PINOT N. Top label: Hope Vyd (organic Chard; old-vine PINOT BL is NZ's finest; mushroomy Pinot N).

Greystone Waip ★★★ Star producer (also owns Muddy Water), partly organic, with aromatic whites (dr RIES, Alsace-style PINOT GR; GEWURZ; lush CHARD, oak-aged SAUV BL; PINOT N (complex). Thomas Brothers is top, notably savoury Pinot N. Delicious dry Rosé.

Greywacke Marl ★★★ Distinguished wines from Kevin Judd, ex-CLOUDY BAY. Fleshy SAUV BL; weighty CHARD; rich PINOT GR; gently sweet RIES; fragrant, savoury PINOT N. Wild Sauv: barrel-fermented, full of personality.

Grove Mill Marl ★★ Attractive, gd-value whites with WAIRAU VALLEY subregional focus: tropical SAUV BL; generous CHARD; easy-drinking PINOT GR; slightly sweet RIES. Full PINOT N. Owned by Foley Family Wines.

Haha Hawk, Marl ★★ Fast-growing producer, v.gd value. Generous Hawk MERLOT; gd drink-young Hawk SYRAH, excellent Brut Cuvée NV.

Hans Herzog Marl ★★★ Warm, stony, organic vyd, many varieties. Classy MERLOT/CAB; delicious PINOT N Duc. Fleshy CHARD; apricot-coloured PINOT GR; oak-aged SAUV BL; deep VIOGNIER. Classy TEMPRANILLO, MONTEPULCIANO. Dark LAGREIN. Sold under Hans brand in EU, US.

Hawke's Bay NZ's 2nd-largest region (12.4% vyd area). Founded 1850s; sunny, dryish climate. Classy, B'x-like MERLOT and CAB SAUV-based reds in favourable yrs; SYRAH (perfumed) fast-rising star; weighty, ripe CHARD; SAUV BL (tropical, suits oak) is now most widely planted variety; NZ's best VIOGNIER. Promising PINOT N from cooler, elevated, inland districts. *See also* GIMBLETT GRAVELS.

Hunter's Marl ★★→★★★ Strength in whites and fizz. Crisp, vigorous SAUV BL, Home Block Sauv Bl: mature, low-cropped vines. Vibrant CHARD. Excellent fizz Miru Miru NV (esp late-disgorged Res). RIES (off-dry), GEWURZ, fleshy PINOT GR, all rewarding, value. PINOT N: powerful **19'** is best yet.

Invivo Auck ★★ Young producer, aromatic MARL SAUV BL. Focus on celebrity labels, incl "chief winemaker" Graham Norton's Own Sauv Bl, Sarah Jessica Parker Sauv Bl aimed at US.

Johanneshof Marl ★★ Small winery; exotic GEWURZ (one of NZ's finest). Excellent fizz; v.gd RIES, powerful PINOT GR.

Jules Taylor Wines Marl ★★ Stylish, gd value. Refined MARL CHARD, incisive Marl SAUV BL; scented PINOT GR; generous PINOT N. Classy, complex OTQ ("On The Quiet").

Kim Crawford Wines Hawk ★→★★ Owned by CONSTELLATION NEW ZEALAND. High-impact MARL SAUV BL is biggest-selling NZ wine in US, available in bottles and cans (many Americans assume wrongly that co-founder, Kim Crawford, no longer involved, is a woman.) Easy-drinking. Top range: Small Parcels.

Kumeu River Auck ★★★★ Complex Estate CHARD is multi-site blend; value. Top, single-vyd Mate's Vyd Chard (planted 1990); single-vyd Hunting Hill Chard rising star. Lower-tier Village Chard great value. New Rays Road range from recently acquired vyd in HAWK: tight SAUV BL, Chablis-like Chard, savoury PINOT N.

Lawson's Dry Hills Marl ★★→★★★ Best-known for incisive SAUV BL, exotic GEWURZ. Vibrant CHARD; off-dry PINOT GR. Top range: The Pioneer (gorgeous old-vine Gewurz). Mid-tier Res range (incl delicious Chard).

Lindauer Auck ★→★★ Hugely popular (in NZ), low-priced fizz, esp bottle-fermented Lindauer Brut Cuvée NV. Latest batches easy-drinking. Ever-expanding range: low-alc; single-variety; "strawberry-infused"; frothy, sweetish Moscato "perfect for lunching with the girls". Special Res range: more complexity, top value.

Mahi Marl ★★ Weighty SAUV BL, peachy CHARD (csp Twin Valleys Vyd), scented PINOT GR, savoury, supple PINOT N.

Man O' War Auck ★★ Largest vyd on WAIH. Powerful Valhalla CHARD; fresh PINOT GR; complex Gravestone SAUV BL/SEM. Reds: supple SYRAH, sturdy Ironclad (B'x-style).

Marisco Marl ★★ Large Waihopai Valley producer (owned by Brent Marris, ex-WITHER HILLS). Several brands: The Ned, The Kings Series, The Craft Series, Leefield Station. Best known for lively The Ned SAUV BL; more concentrated The King's Favour Sauv Bl.

Marlborough NZ's dominant region (69% plantings) at top of S Island (land ideal for planting now in short supply); 1st modern vines 1973, SAUV BL 1975. Hot, sunny days, cold nights give aromatic, crisp whites and PINOT N-based rosés. Intense Sauv Bl, from green capsicum to ripe tropical fruit; some top wines oak influenced. Fresh RIES (recent wave of sweet, low-alc); some of NZ's best PINOT GR, GEWURZ; CHARD slightly leaner than HAWK, more vibrant, can age well. High-quality, gd-value fizz and classy botrytized Ries. Pinot N (almost 60% of NZ's total in 2020) underrated, top examples (from n-facing clay hillsides) among NZ's finest. Interest stirring in ALBARIÑO, GRÜNER V.

Martinborough Wair Small, prestigious but not expanding district in s WAIR (foot of N Island). Cold s winds reduce yields, warm summers, usually dry autumns, free-draining soils (esp on Martinborough Terrace). Success with several whites (SAUV BL, PINOT GR, CHARD, RIES, GEWURZ), but renowned for sturdy PINOT N (higher % of mature vines than other regions).

Original name of Ngaruroro River, Hawk: *Ngaruroro moko tuararo ki rangatira*.

Martinborough Vineyard Mart ★★★ Famous PINOT N since 1984 (perfumed Home Block). Classy Home Block CHARD; intense Manu RIES. Gd-value Te Tera range (PINOT GR, SAUV BL, Pinot N). Owned by American Bill Foley (2014).

Matawhero Gis ★★ Former star GEWURZ producer of 80s, now different ownership. Perfumed Gewurz; scented, off-dry PINOT GR; buoyant MERLOT.

Matua Auck ★→★★ Producer of NZ's 1st SAUV BL in 1974 (from AUCK grapes) long known as Matua Valley. Formerly an industry leader, but currently low profile in NZ. Owned by TWE. Most wines offer pleasant, easy-drinking.

Maude C Ot ★★ Scented, rich, dry PINOT GR; citrus CHARD; outstanding RIES (dr, medium) from mature vines at Mt Maude Vyd, at Wanaka. Generous PINOT N, esp age-worthy Mt Maude Vyd.

Mills Reef B of P ★★→★★★ Purchased by The Wine Portfolio (owner of Leveret Estate brand) 2020. Easy-drinking Estate range from HAWK and MARL grapes. Top Elspeth range from Hawk. Mid-tier Res range gd value. Two prestige reds, Arthur Edmund, $350 each: fragrant Syrah 13' and dark CAB/MERLOT 13'.

Millton Gis ★★→★★★★ Region's top wines from NZ's 1st organic producer, despite warm, moist climate. Hill-grown, single-vyd Clos de Ste Anne range in favourable seasons. Long-lived Chenin Bl (honeyed in wetter vintages), fleshy Chard, fragrant VIOGNIER. Drink-young Crazy by Nature (gd value).

Misha's Vineyard C Ot ★★ Large vyd at Bendigo. Scented PINOT GR; vivacious RIES (Limelight, Lyric). PINOT N: graceful High Note, drink young Impromptu.

Mission Hawk ★★ NZ's oldest producer, 1st vines 1851; still owned by Catholic Society of Mary. Wide range of gd-value regional varietals. Large vyd in AWATERE VALLEY. Owns Ngatarawa (Stables Res SYRAH).

Mondillo C Ot ★★ Rising star with lively off-dry RIES. Lovely, late-harvest Nina Ries. Powerful PINOT N, dense Bella Res Pinot N.

Mount Edward C Ot ★★ Small, respected, organic. Fleshy CHARD; racy RIES; fragrant, complex PINOT N; delicious GAMAY. Ted by Mount Edward: drink young.

Mount Riley Marl ★★ Medium-sized family firm, great value (esp GEWURZ, Limited Rel SAUV BL, PINOT N). Top range is Seventeen Valley.

Mt Beautiful Cant ★★ Large vyd at Cheviot, n of WAIP. Fragrant, esp weighty SAUV BL, characterful Rosé, harmonious PINOT N.

Mt Difficulty C Ot ★★★ Producer with extensive vyds at Bannockburn, owned by US billionaire Bill Foley. Powerful PINOT N. Roaring Meg popular blend, early drinking. Expanding range of single vyds, incl Chablis-like Packspur CHARD, elegant Packspur Pinot N. Classy whites esp Dry RIES.

Mud House Cant ★★→★★★ Large, Australian-owned, MARL-based (also vyds in WAIP, C OT). Brands: Mud House, Waipara Hills, Hay Maker (lower tier). Gd-value regional blends (Waip RIES). Excellent Single Vyd collection (Home Block Waipara PINOT GR) and gd Estate range (lively C OT PINOT N).

Nautilus Marl ★★→★★★ Medium-sized, owned by S Smith & Sons (*see* Yalumba, Australia). Yeasty NV sparkler one of NZ's best. Excellent ALBARIÑO, CHARD, GRÜNER V, PINOT N.

Nelson Small region w of MARL; climate wetter but equally sunny. Clay soils of Upper Moutere hills (suits CHARD, PINOT N), and silty WAIMEA plains (strength in aromatic whites). SAUV BL most extensively planted, but also v.gd GEWURZ, PINOT GR, RIES.

Neudorf Nel ★★★→★★★★ Smallish, 1st vintage 1981, big reputation. Refined Moutere CHARD one of NZ's greatest; stylish Rosie's Block Chard. Savoury Moutere PINOT N (Tom's Block: gd 2nd-tier Pinot N); lightly oaked SAUV BL; off-dry PINOT GR.

No. 1 Family Estate Marl ★★ Family-owned company of regional pioneer Daniel Le Brun, ex-Champagne. No longer controls Daniel Le Brun brand (owned by Lion). Specialist in v.gd fizz. Best known for CHARD-based NV, 2 yrs on lees.

Fancy some age? Hans Herzog, Pegasus Bay, Puriri Hills sell wines up to 10 yrs old.

Nobilo Marl *See* CONSTELLATION NEW ZEALAND.

Oyster Bay Marl ★★ From DELEGAT. A marketing triumph: huge sales in UK, US, Australia. Easy-drinking, mid-priced wines with touch of class from MARL, HAWK. Marl SAUV BL is biggest seller. Marl CHARD, Hawk MERLOT.

Palliser Mart ★★→★★★ One of district's largest; multiple shareholders. Classy CHARD; Alsace-style PINOT GR; passion-fruit SAUV BL; rich PINOT N; incisive sparkling. Lower tier: Pencarrow (gd value, majority of output).

Pegasus Bay Waip ★★★ Family firm, superb range. Powerful CHARD; lush RIES; perfumed PINOT N. Second label: Main Divide, top value.

Peregrine C Ot ★★ Vibrant organic whites: sturdy PINOT GR; lively SAUV BL. Rich PINOT N; 2nd tier: Saddleback, gd value.

Pernod Ricard NZ Auck ★→★★★ Paris based, one of NZ's largest, originally Montana. Wineries in HAWK, MARL. Extensive co-owned vyds for Marl whites: huge-selling BRANCOTT ESTATE SAUV BL. Major strength in fizz, esp DEUTZ Marl Cuvée. Top-value CHURCH ROAD reds and CHARD. Other key brands: STONELEIGH.

Size of bubbles in fizz shows pressure, not quality. Less pressure, smaller bubbles.

Prophet's Rock C Ot ★★→★★★ Small, top producer with Alsace-style PINOT GR, Dry RIES. Top-tier: Cuvée Aux Antipodes PINOT N, 3rd-tier Rocky Point Pinot N.

Puriri Hills Auck ★★★→★★★★ Distinguished, B'x-like MERLOT-based blended reds from Clevedon 10' 13' 14'. Harmonie Du Soir (formerly Res) impressive, more new oak. Top label dense, silky Pope.

Pyramid Valley Cant ★★→★★★ Elevated limestone vyd at Waikari, owned by US investor Brian Sheth and viticulturist Steve Smith (ex-CRAGGY RANGE). Estate-grown: steely CHARD, savoury PINOT N. New regional range: deep MARL CHARD; rich N CANT SAUV BL, savoury C OT Pinot N.

Quartz Reef C Ot ★★★ Small, bio. Classy PINOT GR, intense GRÜNER V. Graceful PINOT N. Stylish fizz, esp Vintage Blanc de Blancs 13'.

Rapaura Springs Marl ★★ Skilfully crafted, gd value, esp Res whites (SAUV BL). Impressive single vyds: Bouldevines CHARD; Bull Paddock Sauv Bl.

Rippon Vineyard C Ot ★★★→★★★★ Pioneer vyd on shores of Lake Wanaka; arresting view and wines. Fragrant, savoury style. Mature Vine PINOT N, from vines planted 1985–91, is "the farm voice". Majestic Tinker's Field Pinot N: oldest vines, age-worthy. Striking GAMAY. Drink young: Wanaka Village.

Rockburn C Ot ★★ Gd PINOT GR, RIES, perfumed, silky PINOT N from Cromwell Basin (mostly) and GIBBSTON grapes. Eleven Barrels Pinot N: ripe, dense. Devil's Staircase Pinot N: drink-young charmer.

Sacred Hill Hawk ★★→★★★ Acclaimed Riflemans CHARD from mature vines, inland, elevated site. Wine Thief Chard from same vyd, more toasty. Long-lived Brokenstone MERLOT, Helmsman CAB/Merlot and Deerstalkers SYRAH from GIMBLETT GRAVELS. Halo and Res (oak-aged SAUV BL): mid-tier.

Saint Clair Marl ★★→★★★ Largest family-owned company in region. SAUV BL from coolish sites at Dillons Point, lower WAIRAU VALLEY – esp punchy Wairau Res. Res is top selection; then impressive, 2nd-tier Pioneer Block (single vyds), incl several classy PINOT N; James Sinclair (subregional focus); Origin (large-volume regional blends); Vicar's Choice (everyday). Now owns Delta, Lake Chalice.

Seifried Estate Nel ★★ Region's biggest winery, family owned. Best-known for medium-dry RIES, perfumed GEWURZ. PINOT N 19' best yet. Top wines: Winemakers Collection (Sweet Agnes Ries). Old Coach Road: 3rd tier, gd value.

Selaks Marl ★→★★ Old producer of Croatian origin, now a brand of CONSTELLATION NEW ZEALAND. Solid, easy-drinking. The Taste Collection: Luscious HAWK PINOT GR (not really luscious); Silky Smooth Hawk MERLOT (actually fairly firm).

Seresin Marl ★★→★★★ Quality organic producer. Winery and adjacent vyd (but not brand or other vyds) sold 2018. Sophisticated SAUV BL one of NZ's finest; generous CHARD. Res: top range; 3rd-tier Momo (v.gd quality/value).

Sileni Hawk ★★ Large, owned by investment company. Strong Grand Res range, incl complex Lodge CHARD; generous Triangle MERLOT; fleshy Pacemaker CAB FR, Peak SYRAH. Cellar Selection: fresh, easy-drinking (Chard, Merlot).

Smith & Sheth Cru Hawk ★★→★★★ Partnership of Steve Smith (ex-CRAGGY RANGE) and US billionaire Brian Sheth. Classy single-vyd range.

Spy Valley Marl ★★→★★★ High achievers, extensive vyds. Flavoury whites superb value. Classy Envoy top selection. Satellite: lower-tier.

Starborough Family Estates Marl ★★ Family-owned vyds in AWATERE, WAIRAU VALLEYS. Punchy SAUV BL; generous PINOT N.

Stonecroft Hawk, Marl ★★ Small organic winery. Excellent CHARD, GEWURZ, VIOGNIER. NZ's 1st serious SYRAH (1989), still v.gd (Res).

Stoneleigh Marl ★★ Owned by PERNOD RICARD NZ. Based on relatively warm Rapaura vyds. Popular MARL whites. Top: Rapaura Series. Latitude range: top-value SAUV BL.

Stonyridge Waih ★★★→★★★★ Boutique winery known since mid-80s for exceptional CAB SAUV-based blend, Larose, one of NZ's greatest. Airfield, little brother of Larose. Dense, Rhône-style, SYRAH-based blend, Pilgrim. Super-charged Luna Negra MALBEC. Lower profile than decade ago.

Te Awa Hawk ★★→★★★ GIMBLETT GRAVELS vyd and site of key new VILLA MARIA winery. Smoky CHARD; classy CAB FR Rosé; refined MERLOT/CAB; supple SYRAH. Fruity TEMPRANILLO. Left Field range: easy-drinking, gd value.

Te Kairanga Mart ★★→★★★ One of district's oldest, largest wineries, recently rejuvenated. Refined PINOT GR. Charming PINOT N. Mid-tier Runholder (Pinot N). Top tier John Martin: complex CHARD; savoury, age-worthy Pinot N.

Te Mata Hawk ★★★→★★★★ Winery of high repute (1st vintage 1895) run by Buck family since 1974. Coleraine (CAB SAUV/MERLOT/CAB FR) 13' 14' 15' 16 17 18 19' is B'x-like, great longevity). Much lower-priced Awatea Cabs/Merlot also classy, more forward. Bullnose SYRAH among NZ's finest. New powerful Alma HAWK PINOT N. Elegant Elston CHARD. Estate Vyds range for early drinking.

Terra Sancta C Ot ★★ Bannockburn's 1st vyd, founded 1991 as Olssens. Drink-young Mysterious Diggings PINOT N; mid-tier Bannockburn Pinot N; Slapjack Block Pinot N from district's oldest vines. Pinot N Rosé arguably NZ's finest.

Te Whare Ra Marl ★★ Label: TWR. Small WAIRAU VALLEY producer, some of region's oldest vines, planted 1979. Estate-grown wines organic. Known for perfumed off-dry GEWURZ; vibrant SAUV BL, RIES (dr D, medium M).

Tiki Marl ★★ McKean family own extensive vyds in MARL, WAIP. Top tier: Koro (HAWK CHARD; C OT Pinot N). Mid-range: single vyd. Second label: Maui.

Tohu Marl, Nel ★★ Maori-owned venture, extensive vyds in MARL, NEL. V.gd Blanc de Blancs (sp). Top: Res Pinot N; intense Single Vyd Whenua Awa CHARD.

Trinity Hill Hawk ★★→★★★ Highly regarded. Refined B'x-style blend The Gimblett. Stylish GIMBLETT GRAVELS CHARD. Outstanding single-vyd 125 Gimblett Chard. Prestigious Homage SYRAH 14' 15' 16 17 18'. Impressive TEMPRANILLO. Lower-tier "white label" range gd value, esp drink young MERLOT.

Two Paddocks C Ot ★★ Actor Sam Neill makes several PINOT NS. Main label is estate-grown, multi-site. Single-vyd Prop Res range: First Paddock (more herbal, from cool Gibbston district), Last Chance (riper, from warmer Alexandra). Latest is earthy The Fusilier, grown at Bannockburn. Picnic: drink young. Lively dry Rosé.

Two Rivers Marl ★★→★★★ Intense SAUV BL, vibrant CHARD; vivacious Rosé; supple PINOT N. Second label: Black Cottage (v.gd value).

Kunekune pigs used by Yealands to munch weeds between rows. Old Maori breed.

Valli C Ot ★★→★★★ Superb range of single-vyd PINOT N (esp refined Bannockburn, powerful Bendigo).

Vavasour Marl ★★→★★★ Owned by Foley Family Wines. Rich CHARD, esp lovely Anna's Vyd, intense SAUV BL. Also classy dry Rosé; generous PINOT N.

Vidal Hawk ★★→★★★ Owned by VILLA MARIA, *see* next. Top Legacy and 2nd-tier Soler ranges now being phased out, leaving the standard Res ranges. Fine-value Res: generous HAWK CHARD; refined Hawk MERLOT/CAB SAUV; vibrant plum/pepper Hawk SYRAH.

Can't get much rarer than that
What are NZ's rarest wines? If you are prepared to hunt around and are
a fan of grapes like Breidecker, FIANO, GRENACHE, Marzemino, ST-LAURENT,
Wurzer, ZIN or ZWEIGELT, you can find a single example of each variety.
Which makes Chambourcin, LAGREIN, MARSANNE, MUSCAT, NEBBIOLO and
SANGIOVESE look common – two of each.

Villa Maria Auck ★★→★★★ NZ's largest fully family-owned winery, est 1961 by
Sir George Fistonich; daughter Karen chairs board. Change underway to fund
growth, incl sale of vyd land at Auck HQ, new shareholders. Also owns ESK
VALLEY, TE AWA, VIDAL. Wine-show focus, with glowing success. Distinguished top
ranges: Res (regional character) and Single Vyd (individual sites). New Platinum
Selection (some organic, much lees-ageing). Cellar Selection: 3rd tier (less oak),
excellent, superb value (esp HAWK MERLOT). Huge-volume Private Bin (4th tier)
can also be v.gd (MARL SAUV BL). Small volumes of v.gd ALBARIÑO, GRENACHE, MALBEC.
New icon red, Ngakirikiri The Gravels 14': CAB SAUV-based, powerful, lush.

Waiheke Island Lovely, sprawling island in AUCK's Hauraki Gulf (temperatures
moderated by sea). Acclaim since 80s for stylish CAB SAUV/MERLOT blends, esp
from warm Onetangi district; more recently for dark, bold SYRAH. Sturdy, ripe
CHARD. Popular tourist destination; many helipads.

Waimea Nel ★★ One of region's largest, best-value, owned by investment fund.
Punchy SAUV BL, spicy PINOT GR, generous GEWURZ; lively Rosé. Full-bodied PINOT N.
Spinyback is 2nd tier.

Waipara Valley CANT's dominant subregion, n of Christchurch (89% plantings).
High profile for full, savoury PINOT N, richly scented RIES (also heavy plantings of
SAUV BL). Increasingly calling itself "North Canterbury", after Waipara met name
confusion in overseas markets.

Wairarapa NZ's 7th-largest wine region (not to be confused with WAIP). *See* MART.
Also incl Gladstone subregion in n (slightly higher, cooler, wetter). Driest,
coolest region in N Island, but exposed to cold s winds (causing small crops);
little expansion in past 5 yrs. Strength in whites; SAUV BL esp widely planted,
CHARD, GEWURZ, PINOT GR, RIES. Famous for Pinot N from relatively mature vines.
Starting to promote itself as "Wellington Wine Country".

Wairau River Marl ★★ Whites gd. Res top: single-vyd CHARD; VIOGNIER; RIES (botrytis).

Wairau Valley Marl MARL's largest subregion (1st vyd planted 1873; modern era since
1973). Vast majority of region's 30+ cellar doors. Three important side valleys to
s: Brancott, Omaka, Waihopai (known collectively as Southern Valleys), SAUV BL
thrives on stony, silty plains (shingly soils speed ripening, giving riper, more
tropical fruit notes); PINOT N on clay-based, n-facing slopes. Much recent planting
in wetter, more frost-prone upper Wairau Valley.

Waitaki Valley Small subregion in N Ot (59 ha), with cool, frost-prone climate,
0.02% NZ harvest in 2020. Handful of producers. V. promising PINOT N, can be
leafy; racy PINOT GR, RIES superb in top vintages.

Whitehaven Marl ★★ Medium-sized family producer, part-owned by Gallo. Flavour-
packed SAUV BL big seller in US. Rich, creamy CHARD; excellent Rosé. Top range:
Greg (intense Sauv Bl).

Wither Hills Marl ★★ Big producer, owned by Lion brewery. Popular, gd-value
SAUV BL; peachy CHARD; full-bodied PINOT GR. Top label: The Honourable PINOT N.

Yealands Marl ★★ NZ's biggest "single v'yd", at lower AWATERE VALLEY site, owned
by utility firm, Marlborough Lines. Financial problems in 2020: sale of 187 ha.
Partly estate grown, mostly MARL. Past high profile for sustainability, but most
not certified organic. Weighty, high-impact Res Awatere Sauv Bl is top value.
Other key brands: Babydoll, Crossroads, The Crossings.

South Africa

Abbreviations used in the text:

Bre	Breedekloof	**Kl K**	Klein Karoo
C'dorp	Calitzdorp	**Oli R**	Olifants River
Cape SC	Cape South Coast	**Pie**	Piekenierskloof
Ced	Cederberg	**Rob**	Robertson
Coast	Coastal Region	**Sla**	Slanghoek
Const	Constantia	**Stell**	Stellenbosch
Ela	Elandskloof	**Swa**	Swartland
Elg	Elgin	**Tul**	Tulbagh
Fran	Franschhoek	**V Pa**	Voor Paardeberg
Hem	Hemel-en-Aarde	**Wlk B**	Walker Bay
Rdg/Up/V	Ridge/Upper/Valley	**Well**	Wellington

Wine-growers were still celebrating the end of four parched years when the coronavirus crisis started unfolding. The immediate impact was nationwide lock-down and a total ban, initially, on local sales and exports of wine. It has been a challenge. But the wines themselves have never been better, or more varied and exciting, with new and rediscovered varieties, areas and approaches in the mix. Fresher, livelier styles with lower alcohol are a focus, aided by vineyard/cellar techniques like earlier picking and bunch-pressing, and less (or no) wood. Minimal intervention are words increasingly on winemakers' lips, along with no (or near-zero) additions, gentle handling, eschewed fining/filtering, organic and biodynamic practices – all intended to express region, site, variety or clone as fluently and memorably as possible. The finest wines of SA knock the rest of the world sideways for value, and blends from Swartland, Pinot N from cool maritime spots and classic flavours from Stellenbosch should be on every shopping list.

Recent vintages

2020 Post-drought vintage a humdinger: exceptional structure, intensity, verve with moderate alcohol.

2019 Yet another arid yr, but milder temps balance concentrated fruit/freshness.

2018 Intense, flavourful wines though probably not for long cellaring.
2017 Quality, character comparable to great 15. Accessible young, possibly peaking earlier too.
2016 Extreme conditions favoured later-ripening varieties, cooler areas. Drink while waiting for 15.

AA Badenhorst Family Wines Coast, Swa ★★→★★★★ "Renovator's dream" when bought by new-wave grower Adi Badenhorst and cousin Hein in 2008; Paardeberg Mtn farm Kalmoesfontein now locus of widely hailed portfolio reflecting every trend: focus on site, heirloom grapes, old vines, wild yeasts, orange wine. Centrepiece is suite of single-vyd CHENIN BL. Gd-value range Secateurs is fun but serious. Brilliant Caperitif vermouth.

Alheit Vineyards W Cape ★★★★ Husband and wife Chris and Suzaan epitomize pinnacle of modern SA wine with fine, pure expressions of mostly old-vine CHENIN BL: multi-region Cartology, and site-specific bottlings eg. Broom Ridge from recently acquired SWA property. Also SEM La Colline ex-FRAN and Vine Garden field blend from HEM home farm Hemelrand. Now-solo assistant Franco Lourens' own label, Lourens Family Wines, right up there.

Anthonij Rupert Wyne W Cape ★→★★★★ Extensive, impressive portfolio honours owner Johann R's late brother. From own vyds in DARLING, SWA, Overberg, elegant home farm L'Ormarins nr FRAN. Best ranges: flagship Anthonij Rupert, site-specific Cape of Gd Hope, premium Jean Roi (p).

Aristea Wines Coast ★★★ Recent UK/France/SA venture fronted by Matthew Krone, scion of famed local wine family. Mostly varietal bottlings of classic B'x/Burgundy grapes ex-STELL, ELG and HEM. Also MCC sparkling, a Krone speciality: his own bubblies named for daughters and released only in leap yrs.

Bartinney Private Cellar Stell ★★→★★★ Rising star on steep Banhoek Valley sides, family-owned; original CAB SAUV, CHARD since joined by Res versions. "Lifestyle" brand Noble Savage and newer upscale sibling Montegray, featuring own SHIRAZ vyd and parcels that catch consultant winemaker's eye.

Beaumont Family Wines Cape SC, Bot R ★★→★★★★ Excellence from C18 estate in Bot River. Rare solo-bottled MOURVÈDRE, CAPE BLEND Vitruvian, elegant, always superlative Hope Marguerite CHENIN BL 12' 15' 16' 17' 18' 19' 20. Matriarch Jayne Beaumont's own PINOT N, CHARD Electrique worth a try.

Beck, Graham W Cape ★★★ Front-rank MCC house nr ROB. Seven labels (vintage/NV; Brut, Brut Nature, Demi-Sec) led by CHARD Cuvée Clive. Long-time cellarmaster Pieter "Bubbles" Ferreira's own-brand Chard Blanc de Blancs and new PINOT N Rosé arguably even finer.

BEE (Black Economic Empowerment) Initiative aimed at increasing wine-industry ownership and participation by previously disadvantaged groups.

Beeslaar Wines Stell ★★★★ KANONKOP winemaker's personal take on PINOTAGE 13' 14' 16' 17' 19 20. Refined, rather special.

Bellevue Estate Stellenbosch Stell ★→★★★ Morkel family in Bottelary WARD, local pioneers of PINOTAGE. Standout Res and single-vyd versions, latter from estate's original vines planted in 1953.

Bellingham Coast, W Cape ★★→★★★ Enduring DGB brand with low-volume, high-quality The Bernard Series, incl scarce monovarietal ROUSSANNE. Also gd-value Homestead Series.

Benguela Cove Lagoon Wine Estate Wlk B ★→★★★ Cellar, vyds, tourist destination on Bot River mouth, latterly owned by Penny Streeter OBE. SEM Catalina and Vinography experimental wines. Winemaker Johann Fourie also responsible for Streeter's UK wines (Mannings Heath, Leonardslee) and SA brand Brew Cru, owned by Fourie and friends, showcasing parcels (r w) in cool S Cape.

Beyerskloof W Cape ★→★★★★ SA's PINOTAGE champion: ten versions (11, incl spirit to fortify Lagare Cape Vintage "Port"). Powerful varietal Diesel **13'** 16' 17' 18' 19, clutch of CAPE BLENDS. Even Pinotage burgers. Also classic CAB SAUV/MERLOT field blend.

Boekenhoutskloof Winery Coast, W Cape ★→★★★★ Top FRAN winery, exemplary quality, consistency with SWA SYRAH 09' 10 12' 13 15' 16 17' 18 19 20; Fran CAB SAUV 10 11' **13** 15' 16 17' 18' 19 20 (also newer STELL version); old-vines SEM; newer Patina CHENIN BL; simpler Porcupine Ridge, Wolftrap and Vinologist lines. Major development, Cap Maritime, underway in HEM; PINOT N, CHARD. *See* PORSELEINBERG.

Bon Courage Estate Rob, W Cape ★→★★★ Bruwer family with broad range. Stylish Brut MCC trio, aromatic desserts (RIES, MUSCAT), delightful COLOMBARD (DYA).

Boplaas Family Vineyards W Cape ★→★★★ Growers Carel Nel and daughter Margaux at C'DORP, known for Port styles, esp Cape Vintage Res 09' **12'** 15' 16 17' 18' 19 20 and Tawny (mostly NV). Now table wines of Portuguese grapes (r/w).

Boschendal Wines W Cape ★→★★★ Popular DGB brand on lovely C17 estate nr FRAN. Notable SHIRAZ, SAUV BL, CHARD, MCC in various tiers, some ex-ELG. B'x/Rhône (r/w) blends (Black Angus, Nicolas, new Suzanne) designed to impress.

Boschkloof Wines Stell, W Cape ★★→★★★★ Young-gun Reenen Borman in STELL with eg. stellar SYRAH (varietals, blends), CHENIN BL under Boschkloof (home farm's name) and Kottabos labels. With partners, standout Syrah, Chenin Bl, new varietal COLOMBARD Doortjie in Patatsfontein range.

Botanica Wines W Cape ★★→★★★★ American Ginny Povall on flower- and wine-farm Protea Heights nr STELL. Superlative CHENIN BL Mary Delany Collection from old w-coast bush vines; PINOT N partly ex-HEM; new ALBARIÑO among 1st local solo bottlings of Iberian variety.

Bouchard Finlayson Cape SC ★★→★★★★ HEM pioneer with fine versions of area specialities PINOT N (Galpin Peak, occasional barrel-selected Tête de Cuvée **13'** 17' 19') and CHARD (Missionvale, Sans Barrique; also Crocodile's Lair ex-Ela).

Breedekloof Large (c.12,600 ha) inland area known for bulk- and entry-level wine. Fine winemaking in small/family cellars eg. Bergsig, Deetlefs, Le Belle Rebelle, OLIFANTSBERG, OPSTAL. But recent initiative, Breede Makers, prompts large/co-op ventures too, to step up by vinifying special/old parcels of mostly CHENIN BL. Some thrilling results.

Bruce Jack Wines W Cape ★★→★★★ Never a dull bottle at FLAGSTONE founder Bruce Jack's solo venture in cool S Cape. Endlessly creative blends, varietals, rosé and bubbly. New Res Collection (r/w). Delightful labels by artist wife, Penny.

Buitenverwachting W Cape ★★→★★★ Classy family winery in CONST. Standout CHARD, Husseys Vlei SAUV BL, B'x red Christine 09' 10 11 13 **14** 15 16. Labelled Bayten for export.

Calitzdorp KLEIN KAROO DISTRICT (290 ha) climatically similar to the Douro, known for Port styles and latterly unfortified Port-grape blends (r/w), varietals.

Cape Blend Usually red with significant PINOTAGE component; occasionally CHENIN BL blend, or simply wine with "Cape character".

Cape Chamonix Wine Farm Fran ★★→★★★ Excellent winemaker-run mtn property. Distinctive PINOT N, *ripasso*-style PINOTAGE, CHARD, SAUV BL, B'x blends (r/w), CAB FR, new venerable-vine CHENIN BL, all worth keeping.

Lite, lighter, (almost) zero

In a win for livers, SA's wine regulator has revisited the reduced-alc category and now recognizes four classes for use on bottle labels: Lower in Alcohol (4.5%–10%), Low Alcohol (0.5%–4.5%), De-Alcoholised (aka "Non-Alcoholic" and "Alcohol Removed", 0.5%) and Alcohol Free (less than 0.05%).

Cape Coast Umbrella appellation ("OVERARCHING REGION" in officialese) for COAST (w and central) and CAPE SC regions.

Capensis W Cape ★★★ SA/US venture, GRAHAM BECK's Antony Beck and Jackson Family's Barbara Banke, specializing in CHARD. Multi-region Capensis, dual-site Silene and single-vyd Fijnbosch. *See* JACKSON WINE ESTATES (SA).

Cape Point Vineyards Cape T ★→★★★★ Family winery nr tip of CAPE TOWN peninsula. Complex, age-worthy SAUV BL/SEM Isliedh, CHARD, Sauv Bl. Sibling venture Cape Town Wine Co.

Is Bastardo do Castello snappier than Trousseau? Local name for Jura grape, now on sale.

Cape Rock Wines W Cape ★★→★★★ OLI R's leading boutique grower. Characterful, strikingly packaged Rhône- and Port-grape blends (r/w).

Cape South Coast Cool-climate REGION (c.2650 ha) comprising DISTRICTS of Cape Agulhas, ELG, Lower Duivenhoks River, Overberg, Plettenberg Bay, Swellendam, WLK B, plus standalone WARDS Herbertsdale, Napier, Stilbaai East. *See* CAPE COAST.

Cape Town Maritime DISTRICT (c.2700 ha) covering Cape Town city, its peninsula WARDS, CONST and Hout Bay, plus neighbour WARDS DUR and Philadelphia.

Cape West Coast New/1st subregion; incl Darling and Lutzville Valley DISTRICTS, and St Helena Bay, Bamboes Bay and Lamberts Bay WARDS.

Cape Winemakers Guild (CWG) Independent, invitation-only association of 43 top growers. Stages benchmarking annual auction of limited premium bottlings.

Catherine Marshall Wines W Cape ★★★ Cool-climate (chiefly ELG) specialist Cathy M focuses mostly on PINOT N, SAUV BL, CHENIN BL; delightful dry, mineral RIES.

Cederberg Tiny (c.100 ha) high-altitude standalone WARD in Cederberg mtns. Mostly SHIRAZ, CHENIN BL. Driehoek and CEDERBERG PRIVATE CELLAR main producers.

Cederberg Private Cellar Ced, Elim ★★→★★★★ Nieuwoudt family cellar, among SA's highest (CED), most s (ELIM) vyds. Elegant intensity in CAB SAUV, PINOT N, rare Bukettraube, CHENIN BL, SAUV BL, SEM, MCC, SHIRAZ (exceptional CWG Teen die Hoog).

Central Orange River Previously an oversized WARD (c.8600 ha, more than half is Sultana for dried/table grape market), now a DISTRICT in N CAPE GU. Hot, dry, irrigated; traditionally white and fortified but major producer ORANGE RIVER CELLARS pushing boundaries.

Certified Heritage Vineyard *See* OLD VINE PROJECT.

Charles Fox Cap Classique Wines Elg ★★★ Traditional-method bubbly house with French consultant. Six classic, delicious Bruts incl pair of NV Res (w/rosé).

Coastal Largest REGION (c.45,100 ha). Incl sea-influenced DISTRICTS of CAPE TOWN, DARLING, Lutzville Valley, STELL and SWA, plus WARDS Bamboes Bay, Lamberts Bay and St Helena Bay. Confusingly, Coastal also incl non-maritime FRAN, PAARL, TUL, WELL DISTRICTS.

Colmant Cap Classique & Champagne W Cape ★★★→★★★★ Exceptional *méthode traditionnelle* house at FRAN, Belgian family-owned. Brut and Sec Res, Rosé, CHARD, Absolu Zero Dosage; all MCC, NV and excellent.

Constantia Scenic CAPE TOWN WARD (c.430 ha) on cool Constantiaberg slopes, SA's 1st and most historically famous area, revitalized in recent yrs by GROOT CONST, KLEIN CONST et al.

Constantia Glen Const ★★★ Waibel family-owned gem on upper reaches of Constantiaberg. Superb B'x blends (r/w), varietal SAUV BL.

Constantia Uitsig Const ★★★ Premium vyds and imposing glass-walled cellar producing mostly MCC and still white. Consistent, striking, individual SEM.

Creation Wines Cape SC ★★→★★★ Family-owned range of B'x, Rhône, Burgundy and newer Loire varietals/blends. Winemaker Gerhard Smith's newer project, Die Kat se Snor ("The Cat's Whiskers") more than a joke.

Crystallum W Cape ★★★→★★★★ Star winemaker Peter-Allan Finlayson with brother Andrew and Eben van Wyk, specializing in cool-climate PINOT N, CHARD. Eight bottlings, some single vyd, all superb but original Pinot N from HEM, Cuvée Cinéma, and more recent Ela sibling Mabalel probably edge it.

Darling DISTRICT (c.2750 ha) around this w-coast town. Best vyds in hilly Groenekloof WARD. Cloof, Darling Cellars, Groote Post/Aurelia, Mount Pleasant, Ormonde, Withington bottle under own labels; most other fruit goes into 3rd-party brands, some spectacular.

Modish winemaker wish list: fewer barrels, more amphorae, concrete tanks, demijohns, *foudres*.

David & Nadia Swa ★★★★ Sadie husband and wife follow natural-wine principles of SWA Independent Producers. Exquisite Rhône red Elpidios, GRENACHE Noir, CHENIN BL (varietals incl arresting, identically vinified single-vyd trio), PINOTAGE. Some from old vines. Assistant André Bruyns' own collection City on a Hill, recently expanded, also v. fine.

De Grendel Wines W Cape ★★→★★★ Sir De Villiers Graaff's Table-Mtn-facing venture in DUR draws on own and contracted vyds in far-flung areas, incl snowy Ceres Plateau for Op Die Berg PINOT N, CHARD, and tip-of-Africa ELIM for brilliant newer SHIRAZ.

De Krans Wines W Cape ★→★★★ Nel family at C'DORP noted for Port styles (esp Vintage Res 10' 11' 12' 13' 16' 17' 18 19 20) and fortified MUSCAT. Latterly success with unfortified Port grapes.

Delaire Graff Estate W Cape ★★→★★★★ UK diamond merchant Laurence Graff's eyrie vyds, winery and visitor venue nr STELL. Glittering portfolio headed by age-worthy CAB SAUV Laurence Graff Res 09' 11 12' 13' 14 15 17' 18.

Delheim Wines Coast ★→★★★ Eco-minded family winery nr STELL. Vera Cruz SHIRAZ, PINOTAGE; cellar-worthy, best-yrs CAB SAUV-driven Grand Res, scintillating botrytis RIES Edelspatz.

DeMorgenzon Stell ★→★★★★ Appelbaums' manicured property hits high notes with B'x, Rhône varietals/blends (r/w), CHARD, CHENIN BL. Occasional Chenin Bl The Divas is spectacular. Classical music played in vyds/cellar 24x7.

De Toren Private Cellar Stell ★★★ Majority Swiss-owned, on ocean-facing Polkadraai Hills. Consistently flavourful B'x Fusion V, earlier maturing MERLOT-based Z; light-styled Délicate (DYI).

De Trafford Wines Stell ★★★→★★★★ Boutique-grower David Trafford with track record for bold yet harmonious wines. B'x/SHIRAZ Elevation 393, CAB SAUV, SYRAH Blueprint, CHENIN BL (dry, incl new Skin Contact, and *vin de paille*). *See* SIJNN.

DGB W Cape Long-est, WELL/FRAN-based producer/wholesaler, owner of high-end brands The Bernard Series, BOSCHENDAL and, via subsidiary, newer Old Road Wine Company; easy-drinking BELLINGHAM, Brampton, Douglas Green and others.

Diemersdal Estate W Cape ★→★★★ DUR family farm excelling with various site-/row-specific SAUV BL (incl recent collaboration with Marlborough's Glover family), red blends, PINOTAGE, CHARD, SA's 1st/only commercial GRÜNER V.

Distell W Cape SA's biggest drinks company, in STELL. Owns or has interests in many brands, spanning styles/quality scales. *See* DURBANVILLE HILLS, FLEUR DU CAP, JC LE ROUX, NEDERBURG WINES.

District *See* GU.

Dorrance Wines W Cape ★→★★★★ French family-owned, with cellar in Cape Town city heritage building (more reason to visit). Fine-boned, consistently excellent SYRAH, esp, also CHARD, CHENIN BL.

Durbanville Cool, hilly WARD (c.1420 ha) in CAPE TOWN DISTRICT, best-known for pungent SAUV BL; also MERLOT, white blends. Corporate co-owned DURBANVILLE HILLS and many family ventures.

Durbanville Hills Dur ★→★★★ Owned by DISTELL, local growers and staff trust, with awarded PINOTAGE, CHARD, SAUV BL. V.gd B'x blend Tangram (r/w).

Eagles' Nest Coast, Const ★→★★★ CONST family winery with reliably superior MERLOT, SHIRAZ, VIOGNIER. Also vibrant SAUV BL, cellar-door-only Little Eagle.

Edgebaston W Cape ★★→★★★ Owned by David Finlayson, of esteemed Cape wine family; vyds/cellar nr STELL. V.gd CAB SAUV GS, old-vine Camino Africana series, classy early drinkers. Stand-alone exploratory label, Van der Merwe & Finlayson (r/w), with resident winemaker, fine new PINOTAGE, GRENACHE BL.

Eikendal Vineyards W Cape ★★★ Swiss-owned high performer nr STELL. B'x red Classique, MERLOT, vintage-blend Charisma (r). Excellent wooded CHARD trio: multi-site, bush-vine, single-clone; unoaked version no slouch.

Elgin Cool-climate DISTRICT (c.720 ha) recognized for SAUV BL, CHARD, PINOT N; also exciting SHIRAZ, RIES, CHENIN BL, MCC. Mostly family boutiques, incl one of only two certified-bio wineries in SA, Elg Ridge (other is REYNEKE in STELL).

Elim Windswept WARD (c.150 ha) in most s DISTRICT, Cape Agulhas, producing aromatic SAUV BL, white blends, SHIRAZ. Grape source for majors like CEDERBERG and boutiques eg. TRIZANNE.

Ernie Els Wines W Cape ★→★★★★ Star golfer's wine venture with Baron Hans von Staff-Reitzenstein nr STELL; long-lived varietal/blended CAB SAUV under Signature, CWG, Major Series and Proprietor's labels; ready earlier Big Easy range. See STELLENZICHT.

Estate Wine Grown, made and bottled on "units registered for the production of estate wine". Not a quality designation.

Fable Mountain Vineyards W Cape ★→★★★ US-owned TUL grower with v.gd SYRAH (varietal/blend) and rare MOURVÈDRE rosé, special-site/-vintage Small Batch Series, easy-drinking Raptor Post range. Winemaker Tremayne Smith moonlights with star viticulturist and college mate Jaco Engelbrecht as The Horsemen for special parcels; solo as The Blacksmith.

Fairview W Cape ★→★★★ Charles Back's imagination creates a smorgasbord of varietal, blended and single-vyd bottlings under Goats do Roam, La Capra and Fairview labels, latter now with GRENACHE BL from variety's oldest SA vines, in Pie. SWA-based Spice Route features qvevri-vinified Obscura (r/w).

FirstCape Vineyards W Cape ★→★★ DYA Huge export joint venture of four local co-ops and UK's Brand Phoenix. Mostly entry-level wines in over a dozen ranges, some sourced outside SA.

Flagstone Winery W Cape ★→★★★ Accolade Wines' high-end venture in former dynamite factory at Somerset W. Sources widely for impressive eg. PINOTAGE, SAUV BL, B'x white. Mid-tier Fish Hoek, entry-level KUMALA are siblings.

Certified wine in (aluminium) tins permitted in 2019; now even fizz is in tins.

Fleur du Cap W Cape ★→★★★ DISTELL premium label, incl v.gd Series Privée Unfiltered, always-stellar botrytis dessert and B'x red Laszlo.

Foundry, The Stell, V Pa ★★★→★★★★ Winemaker Chris Williams and partner James Reid among 1st to focus on (varietally bottled) Rhône grapes in 2000. Recently moved cellar to PAARL's Voor Paardeberg; sensational GRENACHE BL sourced from there, rare solo ROUSSANNE et al from STELL.

Franschhoek Huguenot-founded DISTRICT (c.1230 ha) known for CAB SAUV, CHARD, SEM, MCC. Home to some of SA's oldest farms and vines, eg. SEM planted in 1902 by great-grandfather of Eikehof owner-winemaker Francois Malherbe.

Free State Province and GU. Mile High Vyds sole producer (under The Bald Ibis label) in viticulturally challenging e highlands.

Gabriëlskloof W Cape ★→★★★ Recent CWG inductee Peter-Allan Finlayson produces this expanding and improving lineup in family cellar nr Bot River. Headline Landscape Series vies for attention/quality with Special Collection, now featuring whole-bunch, semi-carbonic SYRAH and amphora-vinified SAUV BL. *See also* CRYSTALLUM.

Glenelly Estate ★★★→★★★★ Former Pichon-Lalande (*see* B'x) owner May-Eliane de Lencquesaing's "retirement" venture in STELL. Impressive flagships Lady May (B'x red) and Estate Res duo (B'x/SHIRAZ, CHARD). Superior-value Glass Collection.

Groot Constantia Estate Const ★★→★★★ Historic property and tourist mecca in SA's original fine-wine area. Suitably distinguished wines, esp MUSCAT de Frontignan Grand Constance 12 13 14' 15' 16 17 18 helping restore CONST dessert to C18 glory.

GU (Geographical Unit) Largest of the WO demarcations: FREE STATE, KWAZULU-NATAL and LIMPOPO, plus E, N, W Cape – last three constitute the recently declared OVERARCHING GU known as Greater Cape. The other WO appellations, recently tweaked, are (in descending size) overarching region, REGION, subregion, DISTRICT and WARD.

Hamilton Russell Vineyards Swa, Wlk B ★★→★★★★ First to succeed with Burgundy grapes in cool S Cape in 1979 at Hermanus. Elegant PINOT N, long-lived CHARD under HRV label. Same varieties in newer, stand-alone offshoot brand Tesselaarsdal, by long-time employee Berene Sauls. Super SAUV BL, PINOTAGE (varietal and blend), Sauv Bl/Chard Sandstone in Southern Right and Ashbourne ranges. Promising HRV venture in Oregon recently released 1st Pinot N vintage, with Chard in prospect.

Hartenberg Estate Stell, W Cape ★★→★★★★ Welcoming STELL family farm never disappoints with SHIRAZ (top-line Gravel Hill, several other varietals and blend); B'x red, CHARD, RIES (dr/s-sw/botrytis).

Hemel-en-Aarde Trio of cool-climate WARDS (Hem V, Up Hem, Hem Rdg) in WLK B DISTRICT, producing outstanding PINOT N, CHARD, SAUV BL.

Iona Vineyards Elg, Cape SC ★★→★★★ Family winery co-owned by staff excels with ELG's signature grapes, CHARD, SAUV BL, PINOT N, some single vyd, from mostly exposed, high-lying sites. Also excellent SYRAH (blended One Man Band, varietal Brocha Solace). Cut-above lifestyle brand, Sophie & Mr P, portion wider sourced.

Jackson Wine Estates (South Africa) ★★★ California's Jackson Family Wines' newest SA venture is CHENIN BL from vines on Kalmoesfontein, SWA home farm of AA BADENHORST. *See* CAPENSIS.

JC le Roux, The House of W Cape ★→★★★ SA's largest specialist bubbly producer nr STELL, DISTELL-owned. Best label is Scintilla MCC. Now offers on-trend canned and de-alcoholised fizz.

Joostenberg Wines Paarl, W Cape ★★→★★★★ Owners and brothers Tyrell and Philip Myburgh with back-to-basics ethos in Joostenberg organic label from PAARL for SYRAH, CHENIN BL (incl botrytis dessert). Honour forebears via newer Myburgh Bros, also partner with STARK-CONDÉ in revitalized STELL estate Lievland, and in volume value brand MAN Family Wines.

Jordan Wine Estate W Cape ★→★★★★ Admired family venture nr STELL, consistency,

---

Spotlight on Semillon

The name may not be a marketer's dream, but the wine labelled "GD1" is piquing interest. The grape is SEM, colloquially known as Groendruif and once SA's most-planted variety. It's associated historically with FRAN, and a dozen local growers are collaborating on a new bottling of the original clone, GD1, whose oldest surviving pockets are a remarkable 100 yrs old+. Those growers vinify their own version, and they're blended together. Sold at individual cellar doors and online.

quality, value from entry Chameleon to immaculate CWG bottlings. Flagship CHARD Nine Yards, B'x reds Sophia and Cobblers Hill. Success with newer Chard MCC augurs well for foray into bubbly production in UK.

Kaapzicht Wine Estate Stell ★→★★★ Family winery in STELL; widely praised top range Steytler (best-yrs CAPE BLEND Vision, PINOTAGE, B'x-red Pentagon, old-vines CHENIN BL The 1947). Newer CINSAULT Skuinsberg.

Locals love their "Château Cardboard": fully 40% of wine sold domestically is in bag-in-box.

Kanonkop Estate Coast ★★→★★★★ Decades-long undisputed "First Growth" status, mainly with PINOTAGE ("regular", and old-vine Black Label), B'x red Paul Sauer and CAB SAUV. Insatiable demand for 2nd-tier Kadette.

Keermont Vineyards Stell ★★★ Low-key but high-performing family estate, neighbour and a grape-supplier to top-ranked DE TRAFFORD, on steep Stell Mtn slopes. SHIRAZ (incl single-vyd pair) and CHENIN BL (varietal/blend).

Keet Wines Stell ★★★ Owner-winemaker Chris K with a single wine, First Verse, beautfully crafted, classic B'x blend.

Ken Forrester Wines W Cape ★→★★★ With international wine specialist AdVini as partner, STELL vintner/restaurateur Ken F concentrates on Med varieties and CHENIN BL (dry, off-dry, botrytis). Unputdownable budget lineup, Petit.

Klein Constantia Estate W Cape ★★→★★★★ Iconic property focused on SAUV BL, with nine different varietal bottlings, and on luscious, cellar-worthy non-botrytis MUSCAT de Frontignan *Vin de Constance* 12' 13' **14'** 15' 16' 18, convincing re-creation of legendary C18 CONST. Sibling winery Anwilka (r) in STELL with SYRAH/CAB SAUV.

Kleine Zalze Wines W Cape ★→★★★★ STELL-based star with brilliant CAB SAUV, SHIRAZ, CHENIN BL, SAUV BL in Family Res and Vyd Selection lines. Exceptional value in Cellar Selection series.

Klein Karoo REGION (c.2100 ha), mostly semi-arid, known for fortified, esp Port style in C'DORP. Revived old vines beginning to feature in young-buck bottlings eg. COLOMBARD Patatsfontein (*see* BOSCHKLOOF).

Krone W Cape ★→★★★ Krone lineup now 100% MCC bubbly, vintage-dated, refined and classic, with avant-garde touches eg. some 1st ferments in amphorae. Made at revitalized Twee Jonge Gezellen estate in TUL. The TJG label, dormant for some yrs, back in action with savoury GRENACHE Noir from Pie.

Kumala W Cape ★ DYA Major entry-level export label, and sibling to premium FLAGSTONE and mid-tier Fish Hoek. All owned by Accolade Wines.

KwaZulu-Natal Province and GU on e coast; summer rain; sub-tropical/tropical climate nr ocean; cooler in central Midlands plateau, home to Abingdon, Highgate wineries, and, further n, Cathedral Peak Estate in central Drakensberg mtn area.

KWV W Cape ★→★★★ Formerly national wine co-op and controlling body, today one of SA's biggest producers and exporters, based in PAARL. More than a dozen labels, headed by serially decorated The Mentors, with newer, rarely seen varietal CARMENÈRE.

Leeu Passant *See* MULLINEUX.

Le Lude Cap Classique W Cape ★★★→★★★★ Celebrated MCC sparkling house in FRAN, family-owned. Innovative offering incl CHARD/PINOT N Agrafe, 1st locally to undergo 2nd ferment under cork.

Le Riche Wines Stell ★★★→★★★★ Fine, modern-classic boutique CAB SAUV (varietal, "heritage" blend with CINSAULT Richesse) by Christo le Riche and family.

Limpopo Most n province and GU in WO system. Currently single grower, Camel Thorn Estate.

Lowerland N Cape ★★→★★★ Literally "Verdant Land", part of extensive family agribusiness in Prieska WARD beside Orange River; area's most exciting winery. Just 9 ha, vinified in W Cape by top names. Heirloom COLOMBARD re-imagined, TANNAT tamed.

MCC (Méthode Cap Classique) EU-friendly name for bottle-fermented sparkling, one of SA's major success stories; c.370 labels and counting.

Meerlust Estate Stell ★★★→★★★★ Myburgh-family-owned vyds, cellar since 1756. Elegance, restraint in flagship Rubicon 09' 10' 15' 16 17' 18, was among SA's 1st B'x reds; excellent MERLOT, CAB SAUV, CHARD, PINOT N.

Quest for brighter, fresher styles: carbonic maceration à la Beaujolais now modish.

Miles Mossop Wines Coast ★★★→★★★★ CWG member Miles M's elegant, excellent wines. Red and white blend, botrytized CHENIN BL, all named for children; after 20 yrs, wife Sam name-checked at last in beautiful CAB SAUV. Mostly STELL, recently more labels, wider sourcing.

Morgenster Wine & Olive Estate W Cape ★→★★★ Prime Italian-owned farm nr Somerset W, advised by Pierre Lurton of B'x (Cheval Blanc). Elegant Morgenster Res and second label Lourens River Valley (both B'x r). Old-country varieties incl one of only two SA VERMENTINOS.

Motte, La W Cape ★★→★★★ Graceful estate, winery and cellar door at FRAN owned by Koegelenberg-Rupert family. Old-World-styled B'x/Rhône varietals, blends, CHARD, SAUV BL, MCC, VIOGNIER *vin de paille*. Neighbour and sibling Leopard's Leap emphasizes food side of wine match.

Mulderbosch Vineyards Coast, W Cape ★★→★★★ Highly regarded, US-owned STELL winery, sibling to FABLE MTN VYDS, with single-block CHENIN BL, B'x-red Faithful Hound, huge-selling CAB SAUV rosé.

Mullineux & Leeu Passant Fran, Kl K, Stell, Swa, Well, W Cape ★★★→★★★★ Chris M and US-born wife Andrea with star viticulturist Rosa Kruger transform SWA SHIRAZ, CHENIN BL and handful of compatible varieties into ambrosial mono-varietals and blends based on soil type (granite, quartz, schist), CWG bottlings and *vin de paille*. Wider-sourced Leeu Passant portfolio – incl old-vine CINSAULT pair – as sublime.

Mvemve Raats Stell ★★★★ Mzokhona Mvemve, SA's 1st qualified black winemaker, and Bruwer Raats (RAATS FAMILY): best-of-vintage B'x blend, MR de Compostella.

Nederburg Wines W Cape ★→★★★★ Among SA's biggest (two million cases) and best-known brands, PAARL-based, DISTELL-owned. Excellent flag-bearer CAB SAUV Two Centuries; Heritage Heroes, Manor House ranges. Delicious, long-lived desserts CHENIN BL botrytis Edelkeur, MUSCAT Eminence. Many value quaffers.

Neil Ellis Wines W Cape ★★→★★★★ Pioneer STELL-based négociant sourcing mostly cooler-climate parcels for site expression. Masterly Terrain Specific range, esp *Jonkershoek Valley Cab Sauv* and Pie GRENACHE. Newer No Added Sulphite lineup (r/w/rosé).

Newton Johnson Vineyards Wlk B, Cape SC ★→★★★★ Acclaimed family winery in UP HEM. Top Family Vyds PINOT N, CHARD, SYRAH/MOURVÈDRE Granum. SA's 1st commercial ALBARIÑO. Some fruit from partner vyds. Entry-level brand Felicité.

Northern Cape (N Cape) Largest province and GU in WO scheme. Semi-arid to arid, with temperature extremes. Handful of producers incl giant ORANGE RIVER CELLARS and exciting boutique LOWERLAND in recent Prieska WARD. *See* SUTHERLAND-KAROO.

Oak Valley Estate Cape SC ★★★→★★★★ Extensive Rawbone-Viljoen family agribusiness in ELG with stellar PINOT N, CHARD, RIES, SAUV BL from mtn vyds. New "deconstructed" range, Tabula Rasa, featuring single-clone bottlings of Chard.

Old Vine Project Recent groundbreaking initiative aided by businessman and vintner Johann Rupert (ANTHONIJ RUPERT) to locate, catalogue and preserve

SA's old vyd blocks (35 yrs+). Certified Heritage Vyd seal on bottle shows planting date.

Olifantsberg Family Vineyards Bre ★★→★★★ Dutch-owned rising star, focused on Rhône grapes, new-wave PINOTAGE, CHENIN BL on mtn slopes. SHIRAZ-based Silhouette, sophisticated Blanc from mostly ROUSSANNE/GRENACHE BL.

Olifants River REGION on w coast (c.6350 ha). Warm valley floors, conducive to organics; and cooler, fine-wine-favouring sites in vaunted Citrusdal Mtn DISTRICT and its WARD, Pie.

Opstal Estate Bre, Sla ★ ›★★★ One of area's quality leaders, family-owned, in mtn amphitheatre. V. fine CAPE BLEND (r/w), old-vines CHENIN BL, SEM.

Orange River Cellars N Cape ★→★★★ Vast operation with 620 grower-owners, 2300 ha under vine and five cellars on Orange River banks. Increasingly impressive and interesting Res portfolio incl new SAUV BL Lyra Altair.

Overarching GU/Region *See* GU.

Paarl DISTRICT (c.8630 ha) around historic namesake town with WARDS Agter Paarl, Simonsberg-Paarl, Voor Paardeberg. Diverse styles, approaches; best results from Med vines (r/w), CAB SAUV, PINOTAGE, CHENIN BL.

Paul Cluver Estate Wines Elg ★★→★★★ Area's pioneer, Cluver family-owned/run; convincing PINOT N (incl nr-gluggable Village bottling), elegant CHARD, knockout RIES (botrytis and partly *foudre*-fermented semi-dry).

Porseleinberg Swa ★★★★ BOEKENHOUTSKLOOF's organically farmed vyds and cellar with expressive SYRAH. Handcrafted, incl ethereal front label printed on-site by winemaker.

Raats Family Wines Stell ★★★→★★★★ Pure-fruited CAB FR and CHENIN BL (oaked and unwooded) esp Eden single-vyd bottlings. Bruwer Raats and cousin Gavin Bruwer Slabbert are also partners in B Vintners, unearthing vinous gems. *See also* MVEMVE RAATS.

Radford Dale W Cape ★★→★★★ STELL venture with Australian-French-SA-UK owners. Creative and compatible blend of styles, influences, varieties and terroirs. Winemaker Jacques de Klerk's Reverie CHENIN BL and newer PINOTAGE subtle beauties.

Rall Wines Coast ★★★→★★★★ Owner/winemaker and consultant Donovan R has phenomenal track record since debut 08. Original SWA blends (r/w) since joined by eg. Ava pair (SYRAH, CHENIN BL) showing house's flavour-filled understatement. Now also vinifies Callender Peak boutique wines from vines (some ungrafted, v. rare) on high/cold Ceres Plateau – watch this space.

Region *See* GU.

Reyneke Wines W Cape ★ ›★★★ Leading certified-bio producer nr STELL; apt Twitter handle "Vine Hugger". Luminous SHIRAZ, CHENIN BL, SAUV BL, newer barrel-selected CAB SAUV.

Richard Kershaw Wines W Cape ★★★→★★★★ UK-born MW Richard Kershaw's refined PINOT N, SYRAH, CHARD from ELG; consituent sites showcased in separate Deconstructed bottlings. Newer GPS and Smuggler's Boot ranges spotlight other areas and new techniques, respectively.

Possible new WO appellation: Koo – also SA's favourite tinned-food brand name.

Robertson Valley Low-rainfall inland DISTRICT with record 14 WARDS; c.12,730 ha; lime soils; historically gd CHARD, desserts; more recently SAUV BL, SHIRAZ, CAB SAUV. Major cellars, eg. GRAHAM BECK, ROBERTSON WINERY, and many family boutiques, incl single-vyd specialist Arendsig.

Robertson Winery Rob ★→★★★ (Mostly DYA) Consistency, value throughout extended portfolio. Best: Constitution Rd (SHIRAZ, CHARD).

Rupert & Rothschild Vignerons W Cape ★★★ Top vyds and cellar nr PAARL owned by Rupert and Rothschild families. Red blends Baron Edmond and Classique, CHARD Baroness Nadine.

Rustenberg Wines W Cape ★→★★★★ Barlow family cellar and vyds nr STELL. Beautiful site. Flagship CAB SAUV Peter Barlow, outstanding red blend John X Merriman, savoury SYRAH, distinctive single-vyd CHARD Five Soldiers.

Rust en Vrede Wine Estate Stell, W Cape ★→★★★★ Historic STELL property with acclaimed fine-dining restaurant, red-only line of powerful but polished varietals/blends. Also in Jean Engelbrecht's portfolio: Stellenbosch Res (mostly single-variety wines, all WO STELL); Donkiesbaai (mostly from Pie, incl v.gd CHENIN BL, dry and *vin de paille*); new label, Afrikaans, with a trendy "heritage" blend (CAB SAUV/CINSAULT); and Guardian Peak range, vyds and cellar, where all non-estate wines are made.

Sadie Family Wines Stell, Swa, Oli R ★★★★ Revered SWA-based Eben Sadie's traditionally made portfolio. Signature Series with SYRAH blend Columella and multivariety Palladius (w), both Cape benchmarks. Magnificent Old Vine Series a celebration of heritage, esp Mev. Kirsten from SA's oldest CHENIN BL. Similar linear styling for co-winemaker Paul Jordaan and partner Pauline's CHENIN BL Bosberaad, under brand name Paulus.

Saronsberg Cellar Coast, W Cape ★→★★★ Art-adorned TUL family estate; awarded B'x/Rhône blends/varieties, esp SHIRAZ, new ROUSSANNE, bracing CHARD MCC.

Savage Wines W Cape ★★★→★★★★ Duncan S ranges far and wide from Cape Town city base for thrilling, understated wines from mostly Med varieties and CHENIN BL. Talent for catchy names (Never Been Asked To Dance, Are We There Yet?). Consults to promising UK-owned Brookdale in PAARL.

Shannon Vineyards Elg ★★★→★★★★ Arguably SA's top MERLOT, also cracking PINOT N, SAUV BL, SEM, newer B'x white Capall Bán, grown by Downes brothers, James and Stuart, vinified at/by NEWTON JOHNSON.

Sijnn Cape SC ★★★ DE TRAFFORD co-owner David Trafford and partners' pioneer venture on CAPE SC. Pronounced "Sane". Stony soils, maritime climate, distinctive varietals and blends. Winemaker Charla Haasbroek's eponymous brand also compelling.

Silverthorn Wines W Cape ★★★→★★★★ Specialist MCC sparkling boutique in ROB owned/run by ex-STEENBERG John Loubser and wife Karen. Handcrafted trio of Brut mostly CHARD, some PINOT N, rosé ex-SHIRAZ. New River Dragon from COLOMBARD, heritage variety long associated with the area. For v. special occasions.

Simonsig Wine Estate W Cape ★→★★★ Malan family venture nr STELL admired for consistency and lofty standards. Pinnacle wine is powerful mtn CAB SAUV The Garland; SA's original MCC, Kaapse Vonkel, still a delicious celebrator. Newer Rhône-inspired white blends under The Grapesmith label.

Spice Route *See* FAIRVIEW.

Spier W Cape ★→★★★★ Large, multi-awarded winery and tourist magnet nr STELL. Highlights incl Frans K Smit flagship, Creative Block, 21 Gables and Seaward ranges, all certified vegan.

Old flames rekindled

CAB SAUV and CINSAULT were partners for half a century, until uprooting reduced the latter, traditionally known as "Hermitage", from 27% of the national vyd in 1960 to less than 2%. Now, along with renewed interest in heirloom varieties generally, the pair are making a comeback in what are sometimes referred to as Cape Heritage Blends. Examples worth seeking out incl Naudé Wines Oupa Willem, Spider Pig The Black Pig, Strydom Family Retro, The Ahrens Family Bottelary Seventy and Kumusha Cab Sauv/Cinsault.

Spioenkop Wines Elg, Stell ★★★ Belgian Koen Roose and family on ELG estate with Second Boer War-themed ranges ("1900", Spioenkop, Tugela R). V.gd and individual PINOTAGE, CHENIN BL, RIES.

Stark-Condé Wines Stell ★★★→★★★★ US-born boutique vigneron José Conde in STELL's Jonkershoek. Exceptional CAB SAUV, SYRAH and Field Blend (w) in High Altitude, Stark-Condé ranges. Kara-Tara, winemaker Rüdger van Wyk's fledgling brand (PINOT N and new CHARD), looking gd too. Also vinifies neighbours' Syrah blend, Lingen, dubbed "BBQ wine for billionaires".

Steenberg Vineyards W Cape ★★→★★★ Top CONST winery, vyds and chic cellar door, GRAHAM BECK-owned; SAUV BL/SEM blend, Sauv Bl, MCC, polished reds incl rare varietal NEBBIOLO.

Stellenbosch University town, demarcated wine DISTRICT (c.12,350 ha) and heart of wine industry – the Napa of SA. Many top estates, esp for reds, tucked into postcard mtn valleys and foothills. All tourist facilities.

Stellenbosch Vineyards Coast, Stell ★→★★★ Big-volume winery with impressive Flagship range. Limited Release lineup has only solo bottling of locally developed white grape Therona. Budget range Welmoed.

Stellenrust Coast ★→★★★★ Family winery with extensive portfolio from three prime STELL terroirs. Headliner is magnificent *Barrel Fermented Chenin Bl* from 50-yr-old+ vines. Newer, wider-sourced ArtiSons line-up also has top-flight *Chenin Bl The Mothership* plus surprises eg. White CINSAULT.

Stellenzicht Wines Coast ★★★ Famous name back in bottle after 4-yr rejuvenation of Helderberg Mtn cellar and vyds under Baron Hans von Staff-Reitzenstein (also now owner of neighbour Alto Estate, formerly in DISTELL portfolio, and longtime partner in nearby ERNIE ELS). CAB SAUV, SYRAH (solo/blended), powerful but not blockbusting.

Storm Wines U Hem, Hem V, Hem Rdg ★★★→★★★★ PINOT N, CHARD specialist Hannes Storm expresses favoured HEM sites with precision and sensitivity. Side project is textured SAUV BL Wild Air.

Sutherland-Karoo DISTRICT in challenging N CAPE, not to be confused with separate, distant KLEIN KAROO. Only 5 ha under vine, chiefly PINOT N, SHIRAZ, CHARD nr SA's coldest town, Sutherland. Scintillating SYRAH by Super Single Vyds, vinified offsite in STELL. NEBBIOLO, TEMPRANILLO also v. fine.

Swartland Coastal DISTRICT with many fans abroad; c.9650 ha of mostly shy-bearing, unirrigated bush vines produce concentrated, distinctive, fresh wines. Home to heavies like SADIE FAMILY, MULLINEUX, RALL, source for lengthening list of others.

Testalonga Swa ★★→★★★ Range name El Bandito says it all: Craig Hawkins' natural vinifications of organic/bio-grown Med/heritage varieties and fizz defy convention; much-respected, loved and Instagrammed nonetheless. Earlier/easier approachable Baby Bandito label for iconoclasts-in-training.

Thelema Mountain Vineyards W Cape ★→★★★★ STELL pioneer of SA's modern wine revival, still beacon of quality, consistency; CAB SAUV, MERLOT Res, B'x red Rabelais, new/1st Rhône blend (r) The Abbey. Extensive Sutherland vyds in ELG broaden repertoire/interest.

Thorne & Daughters Wines W Cape ★★★→★★★★ John Thorne Seccombe and wife Tasha's wines, some from v. old vines, marvels of purity and refinement. White blend (with eg. CLAIRETTE Blanche) Rocking Horse epitomizes Bot River vintners' cerebral-yet-sensual style and love of heirloom varieties.

Tokara W Cape ★★→★★★★ Wine, food, art showcase nr STELL. Vyds also in ELG. Gorgeous Director's Res blends (r/w); elegant CHARD, SAUV BL. Newer CAB SAUV Res, Chard MCC.

Trizanne Signature Wines W Cape ★★★ Number of women in SA's cellar teams rising rapidly, but female soloists like Trizanne Barnard still v. unusual.

Avid surfer sources from mostly COAST vyds for seriously gd boutique SYRAH, varietal/blended SAUV BL, local rarity BARBERA. Sister lone rangers: Christa von La Chevallerie (Huis van Chevallerie), Lucinda Heyns (Illimis Wines), Jocelyn Hogan Wilson (Hogan Wines), Marelise Niemann (Momento Wines), newcomer Alexandra McFarlane (McFarlane Wines).

Tulbagh Inland DISTRICT (c.1000 ha) historically associated with MCC and still white, latterly also red (esp PINOTAGE, SHIRAZ), some sweet styles.

Uva Mira Mountain Vineyards Stell ★★★ Helderberg Mtn eyrie vyds and cellar owned by Toby Venter, CEO of Porsche, Bentley, Lamborghini SA. Brilliant lineup incl newer SYRAH plus longtime performers CHARD, SAUV BL.

Van Loggerenberg Wines W Cape ★★★→★★★★ PAARL-based Lukas VL recent entrant (2016), but already star of light-styled, new-wave scene. Half-dozen wines, all brilliant; standouts are CAB FR Breton, pair of CHENIN BLS, serious, savoury pink from CINSAULT Break a Leg. Vinifies also excellent Carinus Family portfolio of mostly CHENIN BL.

Vergelegen Wines Stell ★★★→★★★★ Historic mansion and gardens (incl c.1700 camphor trees) owned by Anglo-American plc mining company. Immaculate vyds and wines, stylish cellar door at Somerset W. Powerful CAB SAUV V, sumptuous and perfumed B'x blends (r/w) named GVB.

Vilafonté Paarl ★★★ California's Zelma Long (ex-Simi) and Phil Freese (ex-Mondavi viticulturist) partnering ex-WARWICK Mike Ratcliffe. Trio of deep-flavoured B'x blends given distinctiveness by CAB SAUV, MERLOT or MALBEC predominance.

SA has 3300 ha of vines 35 yrs and older, maybe more than any other country.

Villiera Wines Elg, Stell, Hem Rdg ★★→★★★ Grier family nr STELL with exceptional quality/value ratio, esp brut MCC bubbly quintet incl low-alc Starlight.

Vondeling V Pa ★→★★★ UK-owned, sustainability focused estate in PAARL's Voor Paardeberg. Eclectic offering incl SA's 1st certified *méthode ancestrale* bubbly.

Walker Bay Highly regarded maritime DISTRICT (c.1000 ha); WARDS HEM, Bot River, Sunday's Glen, Stanford Foothills, newer Springfontein Rim. PINOT N, SHIRAZ, CHARD, SAUV BL standout.

Ward *See* GU.

Warwick Estate W Cape ★→★★★★ Tourist drawcard on STELL outskirts, prime vyds extended and redeveloped under recent US owners. V-fine full-flavoured CAB SAUV, CAB FR, CHARD, new B'x-blend Pitch Black and old-vine CHENIN BL.

Waterford Estate W Cape ★→★★★ Ord and Arnold families' winery nr STELL with savoury Kevin SHIRAZ, elegant CAB SAUV, intricate Cab Sauv-based flagship The Jem, latter now with its own tasting lounge at classy quadrangular cellar door.

Waterkloof W Cape ★→★★★ British wine merchant Paul Boutinot's organic/ bio-farmed vyds, winery and glass-curtained cellar door nr Somerset W. Top tiers: Waterkloof, Circle of Life, Seriously Cool and Astraeus MCC. Quality easy-drinkers False Bay, Peacock Wild Ferment.

Wellington Warm-climate DISTRICT (c.3840 ha) bordering PAARL and SWA. Growing reputation for PINOTAGE, SHIRAZ, red blends, CHENIN BL.

Western Cape (W Cape) Most s province and most important GU in WO system, with 116 of 135 official appellations.

Worcester Sibling DISTRICT (c.6480 ha) to ROB, BRE in Breede River basin. Mostly bulk produce for export but bottled wines of Alvi's Drift, Arendskloof, Conradie, Leipzig, Stettyn, Survivor (by Overhex) and Tanzanite are taste-worthy, mostly family made exceptions.

WO (Wine of Origin) SA's "AOC" but without French restrictions. Certifies vintage, variety, area of origin. Opt-in sustainability certification additionally aims to guarantee eco-sensitive production. *See* GU.

The ten best things about wine right now

Wine is in a sweet spot. The pendulum has swung away from the excesses of overripeness and overextraction back to balance and freshness: tasting notes like "chocolatey" and "massive" are no longer complimentary. Climate change has brought most European wine regions back into their comfort zones, though with extra unpredictability, and the threat of too much heat in the future. Wine will change again.

But for the moment, good news abounds. In this year's Supplement we're celebrating ten of the best things about wine right now. And the first of them is:

There are hardly any bad wines. It is possible to find poor wine if you look hard, it's true. Climate change and technology have combined to help us: grapes are routinely ripe these days, and winemaking is routinely clean and correct. And the advent of screwcaps forced the cork manufacturers to pull their socks up: "corky", TCA-affected wines are rarer and rarer.

There are beautifully elegant wines from Croatia and Slovenia, parts of Italy, parts of Spain; even some classic regions of France. Austria is making some of the best, most consistently brilliant wines in the world right now. Germany is superb too, with top reds as well as Rieslings. Portugal has banished overripeness and embraced the natural acidity of its native grapes, and there are plenty of them. Chile is making wines from further and further south; and, perhaps most importantly of all for the future, the technology that brought us clean, fresh wines in the first place is now being tempered. Natural yeasts might replace laboratory ones; white grapes might be fermented on their skins. Every winemaker worth their salt has a concrete egg or two, and a brace of amphorae.

In the vineyards, sustainability might involve natural solutions to pests, rather than sprays; wildlife corridors and biodiversity promote a more natural balance. Biodynamism is restoring health to soils. At the same time "natural" wines, originally an extreme reaction to what had become extreme use of technology, are influencing the mainstream, to the mainstream's benefit.

We'll be looking at these ideas and more in greater detail in the pages that follow. We're not saying that everything is perfect in the world of wine; just that there are reasons to be cheerful.

Most wines can be drunk young

Most "serious" wines, that is – we always drank everyday wines young. But anything decent was for tucking away for some years: it was a promise for the future.

That was because of the way wine used to be: tannins were hard. Only a long sojourn in a cellar would soften red wines. Now, with warmer summers, getting tannins ripe is no longer a problem. Red wines start off more supple. And now that they are no longer overloaded with oak (*see* p.324) and massive extraction, they don't need time to shake all that weight into some sort of balance. They're good to go early, although they might have a sullen adolescence between drinkability and more drinkability.

This is heresy, you should realize, to many producers; and consumers too. Take burgundy, for example. Over the years red burgundy evolves into something wonderfully silky and perfumed, with notes of mushrooms and undergrowth rather than cherries and incense. I am not trying to decry the benefits of ageing. It's a mark of a serious wine, that it will not only endure, but improve with age. It's just that they're so delicious when they're young... so vibrant, so juicy, so full of life. I will age Grand Cru burgundies, no question. They are (or should be) like tightly wound springs in youth; what you see is only a fraction of what you will get. But village wines? I would drink them straight from the barrel if I could.

You have to judge wine by wine, of course. Sometimes it's obviously better to wait a bit. But Vintage Port, now. It has a window of a year or two from bottling when it will be glorious: intensely perfumed and compelling. Then it shuts down, and you need to leave it for a decade or more. That's a long time. How much more fun is it, in our impatient world, to open a bottle or two immediately? You could call it getting two wines for the price of one.

Cabernet Sauvignon? Winemakers across the world take a lot of trouble to ensure that their wines can be drunk early, simply because newcomers to wine often want that. Why should newcomers have all the fun? Yes, Cabernet will improve for years, of course. Again, there's nothing to stop us putting some aside and drinking some now: some 2018 Bordeaux, even quite grand ones, especially on the Right Bank, were lush and exuberant straight after bottling. A waste to open them so early? Yes – but the thing is that you could. That's a massive turnaround. And on p.104, James Lawther gives some less extreme examples of wines that you really don't need to lay down for long.

You still can, of course. And much of it might outlive you. Depends on how much you like your heirs.

Rosé is all-year-round

It was always rosé's weak point, that it was seen as something you only drank on holiday. It meant that people didn't really take it seriously, even while the producers were taking it more and more seriously.

What does this mean? It means not regarding rosé as a by-product of red. That's what *saignée* rosés are: pale wine run off the red vats a short while into fermentation, when the colour is still light. But much better rosé is made if you do everything with pink wine as the end in itself: if you select your vineyards and your vines for rosé, cultivate and pick them for rosé and vinify them for rosé. You'll get more delicacy and far better balance, not to mention more controllable tannins.

Provence led the way in this, putting a lot of research into the matter and focusing on ever paler colours as the ideal. That model has now conquered the world: dark rosés, with more flesh and richness, are a rarity now. Everything is pale.

Some grapes seem naturally suited to making rosé: Syrah, Carignan, Cinsault, Pinot Noir, Tempranillo are all good. Cabernet can be a bit too strict. Blends are often the most interesting. Some producers have tried some oak influence, but you tend to lose in fresh vibrancy more than you gain.

Some super de-luxe brands have emerged, charging remarkable prices. Are they worth it? If you want people to recognize the label, then yes. But for actual drinking? I would avoid the cheapest wines: it's worth paying more for poise and texture. But for the supposed snob value of a particular label, no. As always with wine, the best value is to be had a notch or two down from the show-off wines.

Any colour is fashionable as long as it's pale.

The taste of oak is old hat

Some of us are old enough to remember when the flavour of new oak barrels first arrived. How we loved it! All that vanilla and toast and coconut; it was so exotic.

But exoticism, it turns out, palls as much as anything else. Now what we want is stones and salt and tension. The word "minerality" is bandied about: it's the most popular tasting note now, and even though there's little agreement what it actually means, it undoubtedly signifies a complete turnaround in consumer taste. Oak is out.

You see it all over the world. Everywhere winemakers will say that they're using less new oak, more old barrels, bigger barrels, barrels designed to impart less oak flavour. In Chile, for example, all the money was on big, rich, extracted wines; and then in 2010–11, everything changed. Now it's about elegance and a sense of place. Amanda Barnes lists a few gems on p.283.

But no oak flavour doesn't have to mean no oak. In the past, paying an arm and a leg for oak that gave you no taste of oak would have seemed madness. But oak ageing imparts more important things to wine than mere vanillin. The gentle oxidation of slow ageing in a big barrel gives a subtle rounding that emphasizes the tension of the wine. It can add complexity and aromas without drawing attention to itself. Other containers for wine boast neutrality; oak is the only one with as much complexity as grapes themselves. Winemakers are not about to give it up; they just use it more cleverly.

All oak barrels are not alike. At Stockinger, an Austrian cooperage dedicated to barrels that will impart no oak flavour, each barrel you buy will be made by the same craftsman, and the numbers made are limited by the number of craftsmen. Each barrel is tailored to the wine in question: they are some of the most expensive barrels you can buy. Coopers have got better, just as winemakers have. Winemakers will invite coopers to taste their wines in order to understand them. Winemakers will use this cooper for this wine, that cooper for that; coopers have a house style, and choosing your cooper is as crucial as choosing your wood. The difference between coopers can be far greater than the difference between different forests.

Forests are enormous, and a tree will grow more slowly in one spot than in another – and will therefore have a tighter grain, which in turn tends to give more aromas and slower ageing to a wine. Such a tree might be better for a lush, ebullient wine that needs toning down than for a tight one that needs loosening up: oak is a winemaking tool, and no longer a disguise.

And of course the older the barrel, the less oak flavour it imparts to a wine. Switching from new barrels to old is one option for growers

Concrete eggs lined up in Argentina.

as they move away from oak flavours. Switching to *foudres*, to be used again and again, from an annual supply of new barriques is another. One Chilean winemaker jokes that doing that gave him a problem with his coopers: "they wanted to kill me".

Or they can move away from wood altogether. Stainless-steel vats have been with us for decades: wine won't age or develop in them, so if you want the ultra-crispness of youth, steel is the way. Or concrete: once despised as terminally dowdy, concrete is fashionable again as being the most neutral of all containers. Concrete eggs – quite big, up to 2m (6.5ft) high – are lauded because they keep the lees in constant, gentle movement; clay amphorae, either buried or above ground, are beloved of every experimental winemaker. The idea is that you throw in the grapes, usually crushed but not necessarily so, put on the lid and go away. Six months later you run off the clear wine, and hope it is wonderful rather than spoiled. It can go either way, in truth – this is the riskiest of all winemaking techniques.

All these materials can be combined with oak in different permutations: winemakers like to play with materials. It's all about emphasizing difference – differences of grape, climate, approach. When the oak fashion was at its peak, and in league with overripeness and overextraction, differences disappeared. It became difficult to tell if a wine came from the Barossa, Napa or Duero. As oak retreats, those differences are revealed again. Except, of course, for those who aren't interested in differences, and just want reassurance. They constitute the last market for obvious oak flavours. For them, oak is simply what wine tastes like. What a lot they're missing.

Winemakers love blends

Most of the classic wines of the world are as they are because of factors that have nothing to do with winemaking.

Ease of transport to a city or a royal court meant demand for finer wine; conversely, purely local demand was more price-conscious. Wines that were exported were expected to satisfy the demands of foreign tastes: that was how Port evolved, and indeed claret.

If there was one grape that was clearly better than all others that was what ambitious growers planted – that's how Riesling took over swathes of German hillside. But in the absence of one obviously superior grape you'd probably plant as many different vines as was feasible, because they flowered and ripened at different times; a late frost, a summer storm would, you would hope, not wipe out the entire crop. All the vines were picked and fermented together: the art of making a harmonious blend lay partly in selecting compatible varieties, and partly in luck. The Gemischer Satz of Vienna is an example of this sort of field blend.

More precise blending became possible when varieties were planted separately, but the reason was the same: hedging your bets against bad weather. However, there was another reason too: most grapes do not make wine that is complete in itself. Cabernet Sauvignon, solo, can be a little hollow; it needs filling out with something softer and rounder – which is where Merlot (or the equivalent) comes in.

54 different varieties grow in Quinta do Crasto's Maria Theresa vineyard, Douro Valley.

Varietal wines took all the attention from the 1980s onwards and are still easier for novices to buy. But winemakers usually prefer the challenge and the subtlety of blends, the fun of making something that is more than the sum of its parts. And often the fun of making something that is not completely predictable too. Most varietal Shiraz, however faithfully it reflects its site, is easily recognizable as varietal Shiraz. A Shiraz blended with Grenache, Mourvèdre, Carignan and one or two others – the sort of thing that makes S Africa's Swartland so fascinating – can taste like nothing else.

Blending is to my mind the most extraordinary aspect of making wine. You are putting together something that has to be delicious straight away, but which also needs to be able to age and improve for years – perhaps many years. You have to be able to look into the future and see how your particular blend of flavours and acidity and tannin and weight will develop. Champagne blenders have an even more difficult task: their blends will be bottled and re-fermented in bottle before being aged on the lees: that's several more fences that the blender has to see past. I once asked one Champagne chef de cave how on earth he did it. "It's my job," he shrugged.

Most grapes are better blended, most of the time: a cautious statement because the list of exceptions is as long as your arm. Let's start with the obvious ones: Pinot Noir and Riesling, both of which are hardly ever improved by blending; Pinot possibly never, Riesling only in rare cases, like one of those Viennese field blends. Gamay mostly loses more than it gains in blends. Assyrtiko, ditto. Nebbiolo, probably ditto, Garganega, mostly ditto. Then there's a raft of grapes that can go either way: the ever-obliging Chardonnay, Marsanne and Roussanne, Sémillon, Cabernet Franc, Garnacha, Viognier, Syrah/Shiraz.

A glance at grapes that are seldom allowed out on their own includes some lesser known names: Rotgipfler, Zierfandler, Corvinone, Donzelinho, Erbamat, Juan García, Petit Verdot, Manseng Noir... they may be localized, they may be rare, but they add something to a blend. Two of them, Rotgipfler and Zierfandler, are the Tweedledum and Tweedledee of Austria's Thermenregion, combining to make honeyed, exotically aromatic Gumpoldskirchner. On p.210 Anne Krebiehl lists some more Austrian blends.

In the New World blends had to be invented all over again, often determined by what was available. There wasn't enough Cabernet in Australia to make much varietal Cabernet, so it was blended with Shiraz, of which there was lots. And lo, a classic was born. Is a great Shiraz/Cab better than the varietal equivalents? Very often, yes.

Remember, too, that labelling laws allow a bit of leeway. EU rules allow 15% of other varieties into what is ostensibly a varietal wine. For winemakers, it's called having your cake and eating it.

Sparkling doesn't have to be Champagne

Not that there's anything wrong with Champagne, you understand – I'm a most enthusiastic consumer.

And it can take a bit of mental adjustment to taste a fizz made somewhere else from totally different grapes and assess it as not-Champagne; something that isn't meant to taste like that but works on its own terms.

Obviously, there's Prosecco. It's too easy to dismiss this as tasting of soapy water, although the cheapest stuff usually does; not always very clean soapy water, either. But if you go to single-estate, single-vineyard wines ("Rive" is the term to look for; and "Cartizze" indicates the top level of Prosecco) you will find some very different flavours. Honeysuckle, wisteria, jasmine notes; a touch of steel, extra depth; Prosecco is never as complex as good Champagne, so don't expect it. But the top wines have a lot to offer.

Then there's Sekt. This is seriously serious stuff, when made from Riesling by a top grower: tense, ripe, compelling. Again, don't bother with the cheap stuff. On p.156 Ulrich Sautter lists some glorious Sekts. "The joy of Sekts" is a really old joke, but you're welcome to use it when you serve these wines. There's always someone who hasn't heard it.

And Cava: forget about the stuff on permanent discount, and look higher, to the top wines, sold at Champagne prices, made by the likes of Gramona and Recaredo. Freixenet has a top range too. The local grapes, Xarel·lo, Parellada and Macabeo are a threesome every bit as interesting as Pinot, Chardonnay and Meunier, with Xarel·lo bringing grip to the fruit and perfume of the others. Really good Cava has notes of lemon zest and coriander and handles food with ease.

I'm not avoiding the Champagne lookalikes of the world; it's just that there are so many of them. Have any of them evolved a genuinely native style of fizz, or are they more about imitating Champagne? Mostly the latter, if one's honest. Let's start with the New World. California was one of the first places to demonstrate that stylish blends of Chardonnay, Pinot Noir and Pinot Meunier were not confined to the rolling hills east of Paris, not least because several Champagne houses moved in with the intention of producing something as close to their house style as possible. They had to seek out the cooler spots – Roederer settled in the Anderson Valley, for example – because the limiting factor is always reproducing the coolness of Champagne in places that are generally warmer. You can make fizz in warmer spots, but it won't have the same tension, the same finesse – but if you go for somewhere too cold the wines will be green and raw. It's a difficult spot to hit. Carneros can do it too; that's where Taittinger's Domaine Carneros is, as well as Freixenet-owned

England's South Downs, here planted for fizz by Rathfinny.

Gloria Ferrer. Tim Teichgraber gives his pick of these and homegrown fizz on p.254. Australia has its share of Champagne investment too, as well as brilliant native innovators: Moët-owned Domaine Chandon (Green Point in the UK), Freycinet, House of Arras, Croser; Campbell Mattinson covers his favourites on pp.284–297. Tasmania is a hotspot (coolspot?) for sparkling; interestingly, it seemed almost too cold and windy when the first people set up there. Genuinely marginal climates need managing, and that takes time and experience. South Africa is fizz heaven, with hundreds of labels of Méthode Cap Classique, the local term for traditional-method fizz. (Producers outside Champagne can't call their wines "Champagne method", incidentally: "traditional method" is the best they're allowed.) It's hard to fault Graham Beck wines, and I love Silverthorn.

Which brings us, or could bring us, back to Europe. Italy has Franciacorta, which is correct and sometimes better than that, and Trentodoc can be very good, particularly from independent producers. And, of course, Prosecco, which we looked at earlier. France? Lots of Loire and Alsace fizz, some from Burgundy, mostly okay and some good. Pick your grower. But don't assume that just because it comes from France it will rival Champagne. For that you have to look further afield. As far afield as England, even. Am I biased? It's not all great, by any means, and some is frankly disappointing. On pp.216–7 we sort out the best from the rest, and the best is very good indeed. If I had to pick one English fizz to drink for the rest of my life it would be Sugrue, made by Dermot of that name. The man's a genius.

Everybody wants old varieties

Old varieties of vine, that is. What ho! I hear you exclaim. Aren't all varieties of vine pretty ancient? Don't they all date back to the Ark, at least?

Well, not quite. Pinot and Muscat are probably the oldest we have – Pinot is very close to wild grapevines, and could be just one generation away; it is probably 1000 years old or more. (Wild vines are male and female; cultivated ones are hermaphrodite.) Muscat is certainly as old and could be older, but there is no sure evidence. To put that in perspective, vines were first domesticated from wild vines 8000-ish years ago.

The truth is that unless somebody wrote down what they were growing, and unless the names used then can be definitely correlated with a vine we know, we haven't the faintest idea what anybody was growing, anywhere. The further back you go the vaguer it gets. Vines were given local names until very recently. Mostly nothing was documented; why would it have been? The only reason we can be sure that Pinot was being grown on the Côte d'Or in the Middle Ages was because there were so many royal decrees insisting on it and forbidding the planting of Gamay.

What did happen, however, is that what was being grown changed over the centuries. The climate changed: suddenly vine X wouldn't ripen, but vine Y would. Trade patterns changed: if you are selling your wine to a rich city, a royal court, or a demanding foreign market, rather than selling it at the cheapest price locally, that will affect what you grow. If you were in a backwater that nobody visited you probably kept your own indigenous vines; but if travellers were constantly to-ing and fro-ing you probably encountered vines from elsewhere – and planted them to see what would happen. The vast range of vines in deepest SW France, for example, probably comes from the constant traffic across the Pyrénées to Santiago de Compostela.

Vine varieties, left to themselves, will proliferate like rabbits. If they seed themselves, what comes up will be an altogether new vine, juggling the genes into a brand-new pattern. That's why, if you want to propagate a vine, you have to take cuttings. Most of the vine varieties we have now are the result of chance crossings over the years, which is another reason we don't know where or when they first appeared. Only when people started doing it deliberately, as with Scheurebe in 1916, do we know.

Today, with the challenge of climate change, growers are having to consider if what they are growing now will survive more frequent droughts, less availability of water and the wish for moderate alcohol and not excessive ripeness. Often, the grapes we know were selected because they ripened easily: the challenge 50 years ago was getting grapes ripe. Now the challenge is overripeness. Old varieties, grown perhaps in warmer periods or at times when high alcohol was not a requirement, can fit the bill. In SW France, the brilliant Producteurs de Plaimont are planting Manseng Noir, a vine that was much admired locally for 300 years, but which almost died out with phylloxera. It is aromatic, seldom goes over 13% and has fine tannins. Bingo, you might say.

Everywhere in Europe has old vine varieties that have been forgotten, often because when phylloxera hit they turned out not to graft well, or didn't ripen well enough, or yielded too little to be profitable. Bordeaux grew dozens of varieties before phylloxera. Where old vineyards have survived amazing discoveries have been made, and almost extinct vines propagated. When Torres in Spain wanted to investigate old indigenous varieties it put an ad in the local paper and found hundreds, sometimes growing in a hedge or against someone's house. Portugal is full of them. So is Italy, and on p.147 Ian D'Agata and Michele Longo list a few of them. Georgia is said to have hundreds, but seldom plants them.

For anyone wanting a point of difference, rescued varieties are gold dust. The world has enough Cabernet and Chardonnay. The pendulum has swung – now we want authenticity, typicity, local produce. Why buy yet another international variety when you can buy Forcada or Querol? There is an Ark of grape varieties, after all, and it's providing us with a constant stream of new discoveries.

Test-tube babies: old vine varieties in the Torres lab.

Fortifieds are still undiscovered

We all know they exist. But when did you last open a bottle of aged Fino Sherry, pungent, silky and on the edge of Amontillado? When did you last open a bottle of 20-Year-Old Tawny Port with your Lincolnshire Poacher or Vacherin de Mont d'Or? When did you last even think about the splendid fortifieds of Australia?

I don't know why these wines are so neglected. Yes, they have plenty of alcohol, but nobody's suggesting you drink the whole bottle in one go. Is it because we're frightened of sugar? Not if the huge slice of red velvet cake my neighbour brought round while I was writing this is anything to go by. (Very good it was too.)

Besides, fortifieds are not just about sweetness. Sherry, for a start, is not sweet. There is PX, which is super-sweet, with a savoury, grassy edge, and is the best thing to drink with vanilla ice cream – the Jerezanos embed PX-fattened raisins in the ice cream, and then pour more over. But Oloroso, Palo Cortado and Amontillado are now, by law, dry. (These styles are explained on p.190.) They are the perfect pre-lunch apéritif on a winter Sunday when you've got friends coming round and there's something roasting in the oven. Or even when nobody's coming round, work has been hell and it's raining. If what is for lunch is a tagine, keep drinking the Amontillado. It's a perfect match. No, I didn't believe it either, until I tried it. We give a few more

A marriage of equals: Fino and Manchego.

ideas for matching Sherry with food in the Wine & Food section on p.25, and they all work. Sometimes there is just nothing better. And the good news is that Sherry is cheap as chips, for the quality. You can buy a very good Fino aged for seven or eight years, and bottled in limited quantities, for little more than a big-brand everyday Aussie Shiraz. You can pay a lot more for a VSOP Oloroso, but the equivalent in Bordeaux or Burgundy would cost an eye-watering figure. Fine Sherry is incomparable value. And if anyone suggests that Sherry is for grandmothers and vicars, then take their glass away and give them hot milk instead. Sometimes you have to be cruel to be kind.

Madeira? Even more obscure or relegated to cooking. Here I would go for the oldest I can afford, because only time will give that pungent *rancio* that is so compelling. Sometimes you see very old bottles for sale at auction, and it's worth considering them, because it's so oxidized in the cellar that it's more or less bullet-proof in bottle. I've tasted bottles from the 18th century, and they've been wonderful.

Other fortifieds get those *rancio* flavours too; they come with age and oxidation. Penfolds Australian Great-Grandfather Tawny is aged in solera, like a Sherry, but since it is made from Mourvèdre, Shiraz, Cabernet and Grenache, and maybe some others, there the resemblance ends. It has all the fig, raisin, orange peel, mocha and spice that you'll find in a great aged Tawny Port, but with dryness too. It's a fascinating example of what Australia can do. On p.287 Campbell Mattinson gives a few more.

Vintage Port itself has been getting a bit drier in recent years. It is also finer than ever, with the silkiest tannins, the most vibrant violet fruit and the most precise detailing. We're seeing a proliferation of small bottlings alongside classic vintages: the obsession with individual sites has invaded the Douro too. There are old-vine bottlings, like Taylor's Vinha Velha; Croft has Serikos, a bottling of old vines from Quinta da Roeda; Graham's has The Stone Terraces, from the coolest spots at Quinta dos Malvedos. Dow has a special bottling of Capela de Vesuvio, from three plots at its wonderful Quinta do Vesuvio.

And that's before we get on to special bottlings of very old Tawnies, usually presented in the most elaborate packaging and at enormous prices. These are trophy wines, released in tiny quantities for collectors. To describe these as "undiscovered" when you'd have to shell out four figures for them is not quite accurate. Really, they're market-makers, designed to attract attention. Whether anyone drinks them I don't know. The ones I've tasted have been tremendously good, but were they ten times better than a Vintage or a 20-Year-Old Tawny? Or 20 times better? Of course not. Let them mop up the plutocrat money. For the rest of us, fortifieds of all sorts offer remarkable drinking and remarkable value. Even if it's not raining.

Natural yeasts aren't weird any more

Not that they were, for most of the history of wine. Yeasts were always natural – wild, indigenous, autochthonous, whichever word you prefer. There was nothing else.

Yeasts were present on the skins of the grapes when they came into the cellar. There were other yeasts running around in the cellar itself. Between them they got the fermentation started. It might start quickly in some years, slowly in others, but in the end it produced wine. If it went a bit wrong, well, there were ways of cleaning it up, some more drastic than others.

But then laboratory yeasts came along, and the appeal was instant: guaranteed results, no delays, no problems. That meant cleaner wine, without any of the side effects of using what nature gave you. Laboratory yeasts were a weapon in the battle to make wine clean and reliable; and that, remember, was a huge advance. We've all benefited from that.

But just as we hit peak technology in the winery, the pendulum began to swing. Spontaneous fermentation (yet another term for the same thing) had not disappeared in the technological years, but it was a rarity. Those who used it maintained that it gave a truer terroir expression to their wines, and as it was only used by skilful and meticulous winemakers who really cared about such things, it produced exceptional results. The difference is that with natural yeasts, you have a varied population of different yeasts in your winery and your vineyards, and that particular mix is unique to you. Each vineyard seems to have its own mix, as well: the yeast strains in each vineyard are being seen as a marker for terroir. The mix will vary every year. A hot, dry year will encourage some yeasts to flourish; a wet one will encourage others. Since climate is a part of terroir, along with soil and aspect, you can see that letting each vineyard ferment with its own yeasts is impeccably logical, if terroir expression is more important to you than brand consistency.

Some of these yeasts will be *Saccharomyces cerevisae*, or wine yeast; others may be non-*Saccharomyces* yeasts. Some will start the fermentation, others will take over, and perhaps others again may finish it. You can analyze the yeasts in your vineyards and in your cellar, but keeping track of what's actually going on in your vats is another matter. There are risks. Not all yeasts are friendly, and some may produce off-flavours. Or you might get a stuck fermentation, which can be a real pain to get started again. But the use of natural yeasts has spread widely and continues to do so.

The alternative, a laboratory-produced yeast, will do the job from start to finish, with predictable results. You knock out everything else

Wild yeasts ferment less predictably, but their popularity is growing.

first with a dose of sulphur, then you can use neutral yeasts, which will add as few flavours as possible. Or you can get aromatic yeasts, which encourage different aromas and flavours in the wine; the effects of these can be alarmingly flashy. Most lab yeasts are more efficient than wild yeasts, which means they produce more alcohol from the same amount of sugar. As you might guess, less efficient yeasts are sought by many producers these days.

Can you taste the difference? Yes. Lab yeasts seem to emphasize fruit flavours; wild yeasts less so. So, wines made by spontaneous fermentation have less fruit flavour, and often less varietal expression and more sense of terroir, more subtlety, more of that saline quality known vaguely as minerality and often more precision and detail. The texture is different too: spontaneous fermentations tend to go on longer (another reason why risk-averse winemakers avoid them), and longer fermentations give more texture to the wine. You can recognize wild ferments blind, by that subtlety, that privileging of terroir over grape variety. To me, they are compelling.

But winemakers don't want and can't afford mistakes. Apart from stuck fermentations, wild yeasts can give you high levels of volatile acidity and high levels of free sulphur, neither of which do you want. Some wineries find that these problems escalate the longer you use wild yeasts. One solution is to get a lab to analyze your yeasts so that you can choose one; the lab will then produce it for you and ship it to you in neat packets. It's a compromise: it won't give you the same results as a mixed population of yeasts, but at least it's a taste of home.

Wine can be orange too

Three colours never seemed enough, did it? So, hooray for a fourth. Especially when it gives us so much to explore.

Orange wines are white wines fermented on the skins, in the manner of red. They may be fermented in steel, but amphorae or other suchlike vessels are popular, and in keeping with the whole antique-revival spirit of the wine: this is an age-old method. There are many variations on the technique, but basically you put grapes into an amphora, either crushed or uncrushed, and leave them to it. Natural yeasts (*see* p.334) are the order of the day; the mix in the amphora just gets on with it.

The colour, when the wine is run off, is not clementine-bright, but it is certainly tawny, from the skins. And the wine will be tannic. White grapes don't have as much tannin as red, but they have enough to give a grippy edge to a wine. The varietal character, perhaps counter-intuitively, is less obvious, or perhaps just different to what we're used to: the differences between varieties seems less, and a skinsy savouriness dominates. You can get a lovely note of fresh plums or orange peel, along with sourdough.

They are, or are mostly, delicious. They're not just a different colour; everything about them is different, and can be shocking at first. You can decant them – they often benefit from a bit of air – and they go with all sorts of food (fish, chicken, spice, even red meat). But they vary a lot in weight and power, so it's difficult to generalize. Each wine will suit different foods, so it's time to engage your wine merchant in conversation – or just experiment yourself.

They come from all over the world these days, even England, but the first ones we saw came from Slovenia, and you'll find some of the most accomplished examples from here and from neighbouring countries. Caroline Gilby lists some on p.226.

Amphorae can be updated to modern methods: these are in Tuscany.

A little learning...

A few technical words

Winemaking terms inevitably creep into any discussion of wine styles and changing fashions: here are the ones we use most in the book.

Acidity is both fixed and volatile. Fixed is mostly tartaric, malic and citric, all from the grape, and lactic and succinic, from fermentation. Acidity may be natural or (in warm climates) added. Volatile (VA), or acetic acid, is formed by bacteria in the presence of oxygen. A touch of VA is inevitable, and can add complexity. Too much = vinegar. Total acidity is fixed + VA combined.

Alcohol content (mainly ethyl alcohol) is expressed as per cent (%) by volume of the total liquid. (Also known as "degrees".) Table wines are usually 12.5–14.5%; controlling alcohol levels is big challenge of modern viticulture.

Amphora the fermentation vessel of the moment, and the last 7000 years. Remove lid, throw in grapes, replace lid, return in six months. Risky.

Barriques small (225-litre) oak barrels, for fermentation and/or ageing. The newer the barrel, the stronger the smell and taste of oak; French oak is more subtle than American. Oak use is now far more restrained across most of the globe.

Bio (Biodynamic) viticulture uses herbal, mineral and organic preparations in homeopathic quantities, in accordance with the phases of the moon and the movements of the planets. Now mainstream. NB: "bio" in French means organic as well, but in this book it means biodynamic.

Carbonic maceration whole (red) berries go into closed vat; fermentation starts within each berry. Gives juicy, light style.

Concrete eggs fashionable: the shape keeps lees moving. Concrete generally has returned to fashion as part of move away from oak.

Field blend different varieties planted together, picked and fermented together. Ultra trendy.

Malolactic fermentation occurs after the alcoholic fermentation, and changes tart malic acid into softer lactic acid. Can add complexity to red and white alike. Often avoided in hot climates where natural acidity is low and precious.

Micro-oxygenation is a widely used bubbling technique; it allows controlled contact with oxygen during maturation. Softens flavours and helps to stabilize wine.

Minerality a tasting term to be used with caution: fine as a descriptor of chalky/stony flavours; often wrongly used to imply transference of minerals from soil to wine, which is impossible.

Natural wines are undefined, but start by being organic or bio, involve minimal intervention in the winery and minimal sulphur or none. At best, wonderful; shouldn't be an excuse for faults. Often made in amphorae or concrete eggs.

Old vines give deeper flavours. No legal definition: some "vieilles vignes" turn out to be c.30 years. Should be 50+ to be taken seriously.

Orange wines are tannic whites fermented on skins, perhaps in amphorae. Like natural wines, some good, some not. Excellent with food.

Organic viticulture prohibits most chemical products in the vineyard; organic wine prohibits added sulphur and must be made from organically grown grapes.

Pét-nat (pétillant naturel) bottled before end of fermentation, which continues in bottle. Slight residual sugar, quite low alcohol. Dead trendy.

pH is indication of acidity: lower pH indicates more acidity. Wine is normally 2.8–3.8. High pH can be a problem in hot climates. Lower pH gives better colour, helps stop bacterial spoilage and allows more of the SO_2 to be free and active as a preservative. So low is good in general.

Residual sugar is that which is left after fermentation has ended or been stopped, measured in grams per litre (g/l). A dry wine has almost none.

Sulphur dioxide (SO_2) added to prevent oxidation and other accidents in winemaking. Some combines with sugars, etc. and is "bound". Only "free" SO_2 is effective as a preservative. Trend worldwide is to use less. To use none is brave.